EDITION
5

EXCEPTIONAL CHILDREN AND YOUTH

Nancy Hunt

California State University, Los Angeles

Kathleen Marshall

University of South Carolina

WADSWORTH
CENGAGE Learning

Australia • Brazil • Japan • Korea • Mexico • Singapore • Spain • United Kingdom • United States

Exceptional Children and Youth, **Fifth Edition**
Nancy Hunt and Kathleen Marshall

Publisher: Linda Ganster

Executive Editor: Mark Kerr

Developmental Editor: Beth Kaufman

Assistant Editor: Joshua Taylor

Editorial Assistant: Greta Lindquist

Senior Media Editor: Ashley Cronin

Marketing Manager: Kara Kindstrom

Senior Marketing Communications Manager: Heather Baxley

Content Project Manager: Samen Iqbal

Senior Art Director: Jennifer Wahi

Manufacturing Planner: Rebecca Cross

Rights Acquisitions Specialist: Thomas McDonough

Production Service: Teresa Christie, MPS

Photo Researcher: Stacey Dong

Text Researcher: Isabel Saravia

Copy Editor: Kelly McNees

Text Designer: Diane Beasley

Cover Designer: Jeff Bane

Cover Image: Jeff Bane

Compositor: MPS Limited, a Macmillan Company

For product information and technology assistance, contact us at
Cengage Learning Customer & Sales Support, 1-800-354-9706

For permission to use material from this text or product,
submit all requests online **at www.cengage.com/permissions**
Further permissions questions can be e-mailed to
permissionrequest@cengage.com

Library of Congress Control Number: 2012930176

Student Edition:
ISBN-13: 978-1-111-83342-8

ISBN-10: 1-111-83342-7

Loose-leaf Edition:
ISBN-13: 978-1-133-59159-7

ISBN-10: 1-133-59159-0

Wadsworth
20 Davis Drive
Belmont, CA 94002-3098
USA

Cengage Learning is a leading provider of customized learning solutions with office locations around the globe, including Singapore, the United Kingdom, Australia, Mexico, Brazil, and Japan. Locate your local office at **www.cengage.com/global**

Cengage Learning products are represented in Canada by Nelson Education, Ltd.

To learn more about Wadsworth, visit **www.cengage.com/wadsworth**
Purchase any of our products at your local college store or at our preferred online store **www.CengageBrain.com**

Printed in the United States of America
4 5 6 7   19 18 17 16 15

To our students and their students

About the Authors

Nancy Hunt graduated from Canisius College in Buffalo, New York, her hometown. She then received her M.A. from Teachers College, Columbia University, where she was a beneficiary of early federal policies that provided funding to universities for the preparation of teachers of children with disabilities. She taught children who were deaf for nine years in New York and California, and those early experiences formed the foundation and inspiration for all that followed. Dr. Hunt received her Ph.D. from the University of Southern California and has taught at California State University, Los Angeles, since then, preparing teachers first in education of the deaf and now in early childhood special education. Her current scholarly interests are in the long-term development of infants at risk and early literacy experiences for young children with disabilities.

Kathleen J. Marshall grew up in Virginia Beach, Virginia, and graduated with both an undergraduate and master's degree in special education from Old Dominion University. She taught children with intellectual disabilities for four years and children with learning disabilities for three years, at both the elementary and middle-school level. Dr. Marshall received her Ph.D. in special education, with an emphasis on Learning Disabilities, from the University of Virginia. She teaches at the University of South Carolina in Columbia, South Carolina. Her focus is on preparing teachers in the area of learning disabilities and on directing the Ph.D. programs in special education. Dr. Marshall's current interests include early literacy preparation for children at risk for learning difficulties, reading strategies for adolescents with learning disabilities, and post-secondary programs for individuals with intellectual disabilities.

Brief Contents

Contents

Preface

A Look Inside Our Book

Our commitment to this book, *Exceptional Children and Youth*, arises from our deep love of our work as teacher educators. We both teach the course that this book is designed for (Introduction to Special Education) and find it a powerful means for introducing our college students to children with disabilities and their families. Time and time again, we have watched as our students—potential elementary, secondary, and special education teachers; future speech pathologists, counselors, school nurses, school psychologists and other school professionals—become "hooked"—fascinated by the issues that arise from thinking about how we can best educate students with disabilities. Stereotypes fall to the side, attitudes open up, understanding develops, and willingness emerges. The information presented in this book and students' reactions to it are powerful tools for the ultimate improvement of services to students with disabilities.

Our Student-Oriented Approach and Voice

Our book has always been based on the idea that students learn best through *a warm and respectful authorial voice* which recognizes their experiences and challenges. We firmly believe that complex content can be presented in a comprehensible manner without resorting to a stiff and formal professional tone. We dedicate this book to our college and university students, and we mean it. They are the ones who have taught us the importance of making this material meaningful by relating it personally to the reader and by telling stories about real people that illustrate our points. We consider ourselves lucky to be involved in this meaningful and important work.

Text Organization and Resulting Benefits

Our book is divided into two major sections, or parts. Part I of the text, entitled "Building Blocks for Working with Exceptional Children and Youth," covers the foundations of special education and contains Chapters 1 through 4. In Chapters 1 and 2, we provide a historical context for the book's content and introduce the reader to the "culture" of special education—the language, values, artifacts, and traditions that form our field. We emphasize the laws that dictate our practices; the litigation that preceded and followed the passage of IDEA in 1975; individualized education; the early teachers who set the stage for the rest of us; and some of the major issues in the field—such as the disproportionate representation of ethnically and racially diverse students within special education. Chapter 2 ends with a description of the major concepts that organize and inform the instruction of students with disabilities—evidence-based practices, Universal Design for Learning (UDL), assistive technology, accommodations and modifications, differentiated instruction, three-tiered models like Response to Intervention (RtI), and teacher- and peer-directed practices. We will discuss all these important topics in greater detail throughout the rest of the book.

Chapter 3, "Risk Factors and Early Intervention," is unique to our book. Through a study of the factors that can cause or be associated with the development of disability, we hope our readers will become knowledgeable about the causes and, more importantly, the prevention of disability—in the United States and throughout the world. Early intervention is linked naturally with risk factors because early intervention can prevent the worsening of disabilities and allow young children at risk to develop well. Part I ends with a chapter on families (Chapter 4). Our hope is that our readers will come to recognize the experiences of families, some like their own and some not, and the need to form strong and respectful partnerships with families to ensure student success.

Part II of the text, entitled "Learning About the Potential of Exceptional Children" (Chapters 5 through 14), addresses the traditional categories of special education eligibility. For better or worse, these sometimes arbitrary boundaries are described in federal law, and we must try to fit exceptional students into these "boxes" to qualify them for services. We also try to communicate to our readers the idea that each individual has his or her own characteristics, strengths, and needs, and that the content of each categorical chapter may not be reflective of every child with that label. The book ends with our chapter on students who are gifted and talented (Chapter 14). Although this group of students does not qualify for services under federal law the way that students with disabilities do, they are often served by special education programs in schools, and many believe that their education should be "special." In addition, there is plenty of crossover between this chapter and the other categorical chapters. Many students with disabilities also qualify as gifted or talented, but they are not always considered for these services.

New to the Fifth Edition

In this new fifth edition, we spend a great deal of time discussing what may be the most important issue within special education today (and perhaps all of education)—*the increasing cultural and linguistic diversity of our students.* Our revised Chapter 4, "Families of Students with Disabilities," retains a strong focus on culture, but our views on diversity have evolved over time. We believe that diversity is so central to our concerns that it should not be "segregated" in its own chapter. *Instead, you will find issues related to the diversity of our students and their families infused throughout this book*—in examples, case studies, and throughout the narrative and features within each chapter. Through our experiences in New York, Los Angeles, Virginia, and South Carolina over the past 40 years, we have come to see this "diversity" as a welcome and important part of everyday life. Our shared experiences form the foundation for our belief that infusing these topics through the book is the best avenue for teaching the reader about their centrality.

New Content and Coverage within Each Chapter

Chapter 1: An Introduction to Special Education.
Here we aim to draw the reader into the "culture" of special education—its language, history, and values—with an introduction to the basic tenets of the field and stories of people who make the content come alive. We are excited about our expanded presentation of the foundations of special education—the history, laws, services, and issues that are the building blocks of the field.

Chapter 2: Making Special Education Work for All Children.
In this all-new chapter, we describe the students who receive special education services and the challenges and benefits of inclusion for teachers and students. The last section of the chapter reviews the range of instructional models and supports that students with IEPs may require in the general education classroom, including accommodations and modifications, Universal Design for Learning (UDL), Response to Intervention (RTI), and School-Wide Positive Behavior Interventions and Supports (SWPBIS).

Chapter 3: Risk Factors and Early Intervention.

Our signature chapter continues our ongoing emphasis on causes and prevention of disability. It has been updated and has acquired a more international focus. The section on early intervention describes its goals and importance as a way to prevent the effects of disability from escalating. The focus on partnerships with families paves the way for the next chapter.

Chapter 4: Families of Children with Disabilities.

We have refocused and strengthened our focus on families of diverse students. Although we still insist on the importance of recognizing and respecting differing cultural perspectives on disability, that content and emphasis is now better integrated into the narrative. We have added more "parent voices" to the chapter and an expanded emphasis on family concerns for the future.

Chapter 5: Children with Learning Disabilities.

Students with learning disabilities are the largest group of students receiving special education services. This chapter has been substantially revised to reflect the many changes in the ways we identify and work with students with LD. New information includes a focus on the processes and perspectives related to Response to Intervention (RTI). In addition, we've increased the depth and breadth of our focus on evidence-based academic interventions.

Chapter 6: Children with Intellectual Disabilities.

This chapter focuses on intellectual disabilities. Our revisions reflect the many social and educational changes in this field that have occurred in recent years. These updates include changes in terminology and a focus on transition and post-secondary opportunities for individuals with intellectual disabilities. We also look closely at the continuing issue of overrepresentation.

Chapter 7: Children with Severe Disabilities.

Our chapter on severe disabilities takes a close look at interventions and opportunities that emphasize maximizing independence and quality of life for individuals with severe and multiple disabilities. We've also updated information on technology and communication. In this chapter, we acknowledge the critically important role of the family, and highlight educational strategies that honor self-determination and emphasize transition to adult life.

Chapter 8: Children with Behavior Disorders.

This chapter highlights educational and behavioral supports for students with emotional and behavior disorders. In addition to updating information on the role of Schoolwide Positive Behavior Interventions and Supports and the effects of this process on students with behavior disorders in the schools, we also discuss the current critical issue of bullying. We've expanded coverage on academic interventions for students with behavior disorders to reflect recent research in this area, and we also take a closer look at transition and student outcomes.

Chapter 9: Children with Autism Spectrum Disorders.

The area of autism and autism spectrum disorders (ASD) has had a dominant presence in the field of special education in recent years. The rapid increase in the number of individuals identified with autism and ASD has resulted in much attention and research in all areas of identification and intervention. Consequently, we've updated much of the content in this chapter, including the proposed diagnostic criteria in the upcoming DSM V, causes of autism, characteristics of individuals with autism, the importance and nature of early intervention, the role of families, and behavioral interventions. We also highlight effective instructional strategies based on new and emerging technology.

Chapter 10: Children with Communication Disorders.

Students with communication disorders are the second-largest group receiving special education services, and their needs surpass what a speech pathologist alone can provide. We emphasize the importance of professional partnering and encourage teachers to think of themselves as teachers of language for all their students.

Chapter 11: Children Who Are Deaf and Hard of Hearing.

In this chapter, we provide an introduction and overview of the characteristics and needs of this complex group—especially for those who will work with them in schools. We also describe the recent movement of many students who are deaf or hard of hearing from special schools and classes to inclusive classrooms and the implications of that change.

Chapter 12: Children Who Are Blind or Have Low Vision.

As a group, students who are blind or have low vision are increasingly difficult to characterize because they range from the gifted (see our First Person in this chapter) to those with multiple disabilities. New content on the Expanded Core Curriculum gives the reader a handle on how individualization should occur with these students.

Chapter 13: Children with Physical Disabilities and Health Impairments.

Individuals with physical disabilities and health impairments are among the strongest and most effective advocates for all individuals with disabilities. In this chapter, we've updated descriptive information and medical advances related to the various conditions experienced by many of the students receiving services in this area of special education. Whenever medical advances are involved, the role of technology takes center stage, so we highlight some of the ways technology is affecting outcomes and quality of life for individuals with physical disabilities. We also highlight the role of families and pay particular attention to individual voices.

Chapter 14: Children Who Are Gifted and Talented.

Although federal focus on students who are gifted and talented may have waned, our schools still serve many very competent and talented students, and teachers must find a way to challenge and teach them. We emphasize the need to identify and serve students who are underrepresented in this category: students of color and those with disabilities.

Special Text Features That Enhance Student Learning

- *New! Marginal Video Case* boxes—All chapters in the fifth edition contain marginal TeachSource Video Case boxes that bring text content to life. The marginal Video Case boxes direct students to the accompanying Education CourseMate website where they can view a variety of video clips about exceptional children and youth. Students can then connect what they have watched to important content within each chapter. Students can access the Education CourseMate website through **CengageBrain.com**.

- *First Person* boxes—In each chapter, we allow the reader to experience the main topic of the chapter through the voice of someone who "has been there." Most of the First Person boxes have been updated and replaced for the fifth edition. We have included the most insightful and engaging pieces available.

- *An Emphasis on Teaching Strategies and Accommodations*—Although an introductory course in special education does not usually cover teaching methodology in great detail, we want our text to lay the groundwork for current models of instruction and effective teaching strategies. *In this fifth edition, we therefore emphasize specific teaching strategies that our readers can use in their work with individuals with disabilities. The majority of these strategies are evidence-based practices.* They are infused into the narrative of the textbook and also presented in the multiple *Teaching Strategies & Accommodations* boxes that you will see throughout the text. This edition also further develops the topic of Universal Design for Learning (UDL). Although UDL was discussed in our last edition, the research and scholarly activity on this topic has blossomed over the last several years, and we have increased our coverage. UDL is introduced and developed in Chapter 2 and included in several of the Assistive Technology Focus features (described below). References to it are integrated throughout the book

- *Assistive Technology Focus* boxes—This thoroughly updated feature appears in each chapter and spotlights the most current and important assistive technologies for each disability category. We have also tried to include visuals or photographs for many of these new technology tools.

- *A Closer Look* boxes—This key feature examines subjects of special interest to the chapter topic at hand, such as relevant news clips, model programs, treatments, or professionals who work with specific groups of children. We have listened to our students about what they found interesting and revised or refined most of these boxes to make them as useful as possible.

- *Portfolio Activities*—Readers will find these at the end of each chapter. Linked to the Council for Exceptional Children (CEC) Initial Content Standards, these student activities provide ideas for learning more about a topic, volunteering with a group, or putting new learning into action through a hands-on activity. These Portfolio Activities may also be completed on our accompanying Education CourseMate website, accessible through **CengageBrain.com**.

Student Learning and Study Features

In addition to the features described above, *Exceptional Children and Youth* now contains an expanded set of student-oriented learning tools in each chapter, including the following:

- **Chapter-opening outlines,** which provide an advance organizer for the reader.

- **Chapter-opening learning objectives,** listed at the front of each chapter.

- *Pause & Reflect* boxes, interspersed throughout the chapters, usually at the end of each major chapter section. These breaks in the text allow the reader to pause and think about the information that has just been presented, usually in the context of a personal point of view.

- **New! Marginal web icons** point readers to relevant web-based resources that contain more detailed information on the topic being addressed.

- **Marginal notes** pull out main ideas and definitions for easy reference.

- **Chapter summaries** provide a detailed recap of each chapter's major points for review.

- **Key terms with text page numbers** are included for review at the end of each chapter. These terms are defined in the glossary at the end of the book.

- **New!** *Useful Resources* lists at the end of each chapter include descriptions of organizations, books, journal articles, and websites related to each chapter topic that are relevant to the reader's personal interest and professional development.

Student and Instructor Support Materials for the Fifth Edition

Exceptional Children and Youth, fifth edition, is accompanied by a robust teaching and learning package. Please ask your local Cengage Learning sales representative for further information about the following supplements: You can locate your local sales representative at www.Cengage.com.

Instructor's Manual

An online Instructor's Manual accompanies this book. The Instructor's Manual contains information to assist the instructor in designing the course, including a sample syllabus, learning objectives, teaching and learning activities, and additional print and online resources.

Test Bank

For assessment support, the updated test bank includes true/false, multiple-choice, matching, short answer, and essay questions for each chapter.

Online ExamView

Available for download from the instructor website, ExamView® testing software includes all the test items from the printed Test Bank in electronic format, enabling you to create customized tests in print or online.

Presentation Slides

Microsoft PowerPoint lecture slides for each chapter, prepared by the authors, incorporate text, art, and figures to offer a comprehensive presentation tool.

Education CourseMate for Instructors and Students

Cengage Learning's Education CourseMate brings course concepts to life for both students and instructors with interactive learning, study, and exam preparation tools that support the printed textbook. CourseMate includes an integrated eBook, quizzes, flashcards, TeachSource Videos, portfolio resources, and more, along with EngagementTracker, a first-of-its-kind tool that monitors student engagement in the course. The accompanying instructor website offers access to password-protected resources such as an electronic version of the instructor's manual, test bank, and PowerPoint® slides. *The instructor URL is login. cengage.com, and students can access Education CourseMate through CengageBrain .com.*

WebTutor

Jumpstart your course with customizable, rich, text-specific content within your Course Management System. Whether you want to web-enable your class or put an entire course online, WebTutor™ delivers. WebTutor™ offers a wide array of resources including access to the eBook, quizzes, TeachSource Videos, web links, exercises, and more.

Acknowledgments

First and foremost, we greatly thank our colleagues nationwide who reviewed this text and made important suggestions for improvement:

James Chapple, Ashland University

Nicole Hamilton, Kaplan University

Juliet Hart, Arizona State University

Thienhuong Hoang, California State Polytechnic University, Pomona

Jack Hourcade, Boise State University

Jennifer Johnson, Vance-Granville Community College

Jacqueline Mongeau, Community College of Rhode Island

Brenda Naimy, California State University, Los Angeles

Roberta Wiener, Pace University

Barbara Wilson, Bloomsburg University of Pennsylvania

We will always be grateful to our first editor at Houghton Mifflin, Loretta Wolozin, whose spirit and enthusiasm in the early life of this book continues to inspire us and give us confidence in what we do. At Cengage Learning, Mark Kerr had the vision required to move us to a fifth edition, and he has been an excellent colleague with a sense of humor that we appreciate. Our developmental editor, Beth Kaufman, once again brought her heart and her smarts to our work, and we are grateful to her for her keen eye and her commitment to this book. Teresa Christie ably and cordially coordinated the "putting everything together" final stage of the work, and Isabel Saraiva and Stacey Dong graciously solicited text and photo permissions.

We would like to acknowledge once more the contributions of the authors who contributed either complete or partial chapters in the first edition: Dr. Phillip Chinn, Dr. Elaine Silliman, Janet Stack, Dr. Cay Holbrook, Dr. Mary Scott Healy, Dr. Emma Guilarte, and Dr. James Delisle.

At Cal State, Los Angeles, Nancy would like to thank Brenda Naimy, a trusted resource on all things visual impairment, my companion in teaching the course for which this book is used, and the model for what a "real professional" should be; my friend and "office mate" Holly Menzies, my consultant about every big and little thing, whose industriousness I disturb regularly; and "the Dianes"—Fazzi, Haager, and Klein, resident experts, without whom I would be considerably less "expert" myself. Our Dean Mary Falvey, consummate special educator, has always set the standard for commitment to children with disabilities. In the Department of Communication Disorders at the university, Cari Flint reviewed Chapter 10 and helped me make it real. My husband, Dewey Gram, continued to extend his patient support for my work. Without our darling daughters, Maggie, Lucy, and Nell, there would be little joy in this work and in my life. They're the best.

We dedicate this edition of our book to our students, so Kathleen would like to acknowledge students, both past and present; you not only challenged me to become a better teacher, you became my teachers as well. I would also like to acknowledge my colleagues at the University of South Carolina for their support, great breadth of knowledge, and sense of humor. I would also like to thank my parents, Harold and Vivian Marshall, for always supporting me; my husband, Richard, for his patience and unique perspectives; and my sister, Cynthia, whose newly found love of teaching has been the source of inspiration for me this year. Finally, I would like to thank my co-author, Nancy Hunt for a 20-year partnership. Thanks for your inspiration, your friendship, and your acerbic wit. I cannot imagine doing this with anyone else.

—Nancy Hunt and Kathleen Marshall

BUILDING BLOCKS FOR WORKING WITH EXCEPTIONAL CHILDREN AND YOUTH

Part 1 introduces you to the major topics in the field of special education. You'll learn how special education has evolved during the past four decades and its implications for your future career. You'll learn about the factors that may affect individual students' educational experiences: their individual strengths, their families, their cultural backgrounds, and their exposure to risk. In your role as a teacher, you will need to take all of these factors into account. As you will see, the building blocks we discuss here are a vital foundation for your work with exceptional individuals.

Part Outline

CHAPTER

An Introduction to Special Education

Learning Objectives

After reading this chapter, the reader will:

- Define and use the basic terms of special education appropriately.

- Understand the foundations and history of special education in the United States.

- Describe how legislation and litigation have opened doors for individuals with disabilities.

- Describe the concept of individualized education, and the Individualized Education Plan (IEP).

- Identify ways in which general and special educators work together to improve educational outcomes for *all* children.

Most people enter teaching, or service to children in schools, with the hope that they can make things better for their students, and for their communities. Even the cynical among us enter our classrooms with a spark of hope that we can do good. But the realities of schools often make it hard to keep that spark alive. We must face working conditions that are often far from ideal; mountains of paperwork; demands from administrators and families; students who don't seem to want to learn; and tremendous pressure from school boards and state education agencies to improve student achievement and meet state standards in the subject areas.

What keeps us going? Our students, of course—the connections we make with them, and the successes, small and large, that come about as a result of our hard work (and theirs). But even the students in U.S. schools are becoming more complex. American schools are places of great student diversity. We are not always sure that our "tried and true" methods of teaching will work with students who are not fluent in English, for example, or for those with complex disabilities like autism. Yet each teacher is expected to teach all students, every day. It is not easy work.

We are about to embark on the study of some of those children—those who present special challenges to their teachers because of their disabilities and their special gifts and talents. With so much expected of teachers, so much responsibility resting on your shoulders, will you be able to teach and see progress in each of your students? In this book, we hope to show you that the differences among children are simply variations on a theme of *commonalities*. You can reach and teach every one of them—and you will.

Terms and Definitions

What *is* special education, you may wonder, and what is so special about it? **Special education** is the educational program designed to meet the unique learning and developmental needs of a student who is exceptional. What is special about special education is the recognition of the unique nature of each individual, and the accompanying design of an educational program specifically planned to meet that person's needs. Special education is not limited to a particular "special" place. Most special educators believe that special education should take place in the most normal, natural environment possible. It is a set of services that can be provided almost anywhere for a student with a disability. That may be in a baby's home, in a general education classroom, or in the Pizza Hut in the student's community; sometimes it may be in a hospital or a special school designed for a particular group of students, such as a school for students who are deaf. This book is designed to help you learn more about special education; we hope that it will help you find your own role in serving students who are exceptional.

Like other fields of study, special education has its own terminology. We use several terms to describe the group of students we work with. Among them is **exceptional,** used in the title of this book. We use this word to describe the range of students—those who are called blind, gifted, deaf—who receive special education services in the schools. It does not simply refer to students who are gifted, but to any student who may be an "exception" to the rule. Some of these students have a **disability** (students who are gifted do not usually fall into this category). A disability is a limitation, such as a difficulty in learning to read or an inability to hear, walk, or see. A **handicap** is not the same as a disability; a handicap results from the limitations imposed by the environment and by attitudes toward a person with disabilities. The American Psychological Association puts it this way:

> It is recommended that the word *disability* be used to refer to an attribute of a person, and *handicap* to the *source* of limitations. Sometimes a disability itself may handicap a person, as when a person with one arm is handicapped

Special education is the set of services designed to meet the unique needs of exceptional children.

Exceptional students are all those who receive special education services in the school.

A disability is a limitation; a handicap results from the limitations imposed by the environment and by people's attitudes.

in playing the violin. However, when the limitation is environmental, as in the case of attitudinal, legal, and architectural barriers, the disability is *not* handicapping—the environmental factor is. This distinction is important because the environment is frequently overlooked as a major source of limitation, even when it is far more limiting than the disability. Thus, prejudice handicaps people by denying access to opportunities; inaccessible buildings surrounded by steps and curbs handicap people who require the use of a ramp. (Committee on Disability Issues in Psychology, 2003; Source: **http:// www.apastyle.org/manual/related/nonhandicapping-language.aspx**)

Some examples will help here. Some adults who are deaf, for example, admit that they are disabled—they hear very little. But they do not consider themselves handicapped. Their disability does not limit them in ways that they consider significant. They associate with a community of other deaf people with whom they can communicate freely; they do not often encounter people who manifest prejudice against them. Most are satisfied with their lives, their abilities, and limitations. The deaf schoolchild, however, may be considered handicapped; she may not yet have learned how to communicate efficiently or to read English well, which considerably limits her ability to communicate with others and to achieve in school.

A young person who has experienced a spinal cord injury may emerge from the hospital unable to walk—a serious disability and perhaps a handicap. Through physical therapy and rehabilitation, however, that person can often learn strategies to cope with the handicap associated with the disability. Use of a wheelchair and adaptive devices in the car will enable him to become mobile again; modifications of workspace and the home may make those places accessible to him using a wheelchair. Nowadays, a physical limitation does not prevent a person from participating in sports, from wheelchair racing to mountain climbing.

Overcoming the attitudes of others toward a disability may be a more difficult fight. Will the behavior of friends and family change? Will job opportunities exist? Will new acquaintances think of him as a disabled person, or as a person who happens to have a disability?

Present-day concepts of disability are a reflection of the values and beliefs of contemporary culture, which emphasizes verbal and intellectual achievement, speed and mobility, and flawlessness in personal appearance. In addition to the terms we use to group all students receiving special education services together, there are 14 specific disability categories listed in the federal law governing the education of students with disabilities (IDEA). They are listed in Table 1.1. In order to be eligible for special education services, a student must be labeled as having one (or more) of those disabilities. (You will see later in this chapter that students who are gifted or talented are not included under federal disability law.) These disability "labels" carry a lot of weight in schools, and some have stigma attached to them. Do you think they are necessary? Harry and Klingner (2007) ask:

> Many students have special learning needs, and many experience challenges learning school material. But does this mean they have *disabilities*? Can we help students without undermining their self-confidence and stigmatizing them with a label? Does it matter whether we use the word *disability* instead of *need* and *challenge*? (p.16)

> One of the "handicaps" that some people with disabilities experience is the negative attitudes of others.

Is Labeling and Defining Appropriate?

We use terms that we call "labels" to describe groups of exceptional children. In this book, you will read about students with intellectual disabilities, learning disabilities, physical and health impairments, speech and language impairments,

Table 1.1 The 14 Categories of Disability Under IDEA

Autism	Multiple disabilities
Deaf-blindness	Orthopedic impairment
Deafness	Other health impairment
Developmental delay	Specific learning disability
Emotional disturbance	Speech or language impairment
Hearing impairment	Traumatic brain injury
Intellectual disability	Visual impairment, including blindness

The nation's special education law is called the **Individuals with Disabilities Education Act,** or IDEA. As part of making special education and related services available to children with disabilities in the public schools, IDEA defines the term "child with a disability." That definition includes specific disability terms, which are also defined by IDEA.

The IDEA's disability terms and the federal definitions you will read throughout this book guide how individual states define disability and who is eligible for a free, appropriate public education under special education law. Note that in order to fully meet the definition (and eligibility for special education and related services) as a "child with a disability," a child's educational performance must be adversely affected by the disability.

Source: Adapted from National Dissemination Center on Children with Disabilities (2009). http://nichcy.org/disability/categories

and emotional disturbance, as well as students who are deaf and hard of hearing, visually impaired, or gifted and talented.

Think of the labels that could be applied to you. Are you a Caucasian female? A Latino male? A Catholic, Protestant, Jew, or Muslim? Would you want those labels to be the first piece of information other people learn about you? People with disabilities and their families and advocates have worked very hard to erase the "disability-first" perception of people who are disabled.

Why use labels at all? Many people feel that we should not. But labels do serve some useful purposes. First, they help us count individuals with exceptionalities. Just as the U.S. government wants to know your sex, race, and age in order to provide representation and services to your community, the federal government and the states count the number of students with disabilities in order to plan for and provide educational and supportive services.

Labels also help professionals differentiate methods of instruction and support services to different groups. Children who have visual impairments may learn to read with materials that are quite different from those used by children who have learning disabilities. Children who are deaf or hard of hearing need the support services of an audiologist and possibly a speech-language specialist. Gifted and talented students may learn more from a differentiated curriculum tailored to their learning strengths and needs (Clark, 2007). Many special educators would argue, however, that instructional methods do not vary significantly for students who are identified as having learning disabilities, mild intellectual disabilities, or emotional disturbance, although the emphasis of instruction might vary from student to student, depending on individual student learning needs.

Labels enable professionals to communicate efficiently about children and their needs. But these labels are frequently misused and can carry an enormous stigma. Words like *hyperactive, autistic,* and *dyslexic* are often used freely to describe children who are having academic or behavioral difficulties in school. Using

Sometimes labels stigmatize, and sometimes they are helpful.

such terms may make a professional sound knowledgeable, but labels like these may alter the perceptions of others about the learning potential of such children. Moreover, labels often obscure individual differences among children (Ferri & Connor, 2006; Hobbs, 1975); we assume, for example, that all children identified as "learning-disabled" are somehow the same. Table 1.2 shows how labels have changed over time.

Many professionals within special education see categorical labels as a necessary evil and would like to replace current labels with terminology that is directly related to instruction and that minimizes negative connotations (Adelman, 1996; Harry & Klingner, 2007). For example, students with learning disabilities could be described as *students with intensive reading instruction needs*!

Labels have long been defended in special education because they enable schools to count the number of students with learning difficulties whom they serve, and therefore apply for state and federal funds to pay for their education.

> Some special education professionals would like to replace current labels with terminology directly related to instruction.

Table 1.2 Terms Reflecting Social Changes

Areas of Disability	Past	Present
Intellectual and developmental disabilities	Idiots, feebleminded, cretin, mentally deficient, mentally retarded, educably retarded or trainably retarded, morons, high level or low level	Mild, moderate, severe intellectual and/or developmental disabilities
Learning disabilities	Dyslexia, minimal cerebral dysfunction, specific learning disabilities, learning disabilities	Learning disabilities
Emotional disturbance	Unsocialized, severely or seriously emotionally disturbed, acting out, withdrawn	Emotional/behavioral disorders (E/BD)
Attention deficit disorder (with or without hyperactivity)	Hyperactivity, specific learning disabilities	ADD (attention deficit disorder without hyperactivity) or ADHD (with hyperactivity) and combined
Head injuries	Strephosymbolia, brain-crippled children, brain-injured, closed head injury	Traumatic brain injury
Deafness	Deaf and dumb, deaf-mute	Deaf or hard of hearing
Persons with orthopedic disabilities	Crippled children, physically handicapped	Physical disabilities
Learning disability in reading	Dyslexia, minimal cerebral dysfunction, specific learning disabilities	Dyslexia
Autism	Childhood schizophrenia, children with refrigerator parents, Kanner's syndrome, autoid	Autism; autism spectrum disorders; Asperger's syndrome
Placements for individuals with more severe disabilities	Asylums, institutions, residential schools, group homes	Community living, assistive living, supportive employment
Placements for individuals with disabilities	Normalization, mainstreaming, regular education initiative, integration	Inclusion
Assessment	Testing, measurement	High-stakes assessment, alternative assessment, progress monitoring
Preassessment	Diagnosis, child study teacher assistance teams	Prereferral teams, student support teams, student success teams

Source: Adapted and updated from G. Vergason and M. L. Anderegg (1996). The ins and outs of special education terminology, *Teaching Exceptional Children, 29*(5) (May/June 1997), p.36.

But using labels implies a number of assumptions: that disability is the defining characteristic of that student; that all students with that label are more similar than different; that there are specific methods for teaching labeled students that the average teacher may not be familiar with (so he or she can give up!). According to Harry and Klingner (2007): "Language in itself is not the problem. What *is* problematic is the belief system that this language represents" (p. 16). And labels tend to lead to the belief that there is an intrinsic deficit in the student. You will see in Chapter 3 and throughout this book that there are many other explanations for learning and behavioral differences in children.

You will notice that we try to use **people-first language** in this book; first we describe the person and then the disability (see the nearby Closer Look box, "Eliminating Stereotypes: Words Matter!"). For example, rather than say *an autistic child*, we suggest saying *a child with autism.* This is so that we can think about individuals who have disabilities, such as the young person just described, as *people* who happen to have a disability.

One last note about labels. The field of special education is in the midst of a transition in describing students formerly labeled as having mental retardation. The field now uses the term *intellectual disabilities.* The word "retard" has acquired a good deal of stigma over the years (search YouTube for "the r word"). In this book you will see both terms (*intellectual disabilities* and *mental retardation*) used, but we will do our best to use "mental retardation" only when it is used in a historical document or reference.

Naturally, within special education there is an emphasis on the prevention of disabilities and on starting as early as possible to provide the help that children and families need. **Early intervention** is the provision of services (instruction, therapies, and supports) to children from birth to age 3 and their families. Its goal is optimizing each child's learning potential and daily well-being and increasing that child's opportunities to function effectively in the community (Cook, Klein, & Tessier, 2008). We use the term *at risk* to describe those infants and young children who have a greater than average likelihood of developing a disability because of factors such as extreme prematurity, chronic poverty, or early medical problems. Some educators also use the term to describe older students who may be more likely to drop out of school; in this book, however, we use it to describe infants and young children only.

❓ Pause and Reflect

In her book, *The Language Police* (2003), Diane Ravitch decries the use of people-first language because she thinks it is convoluted and indirect. What is your stand on this issue? Is this kind of language necessary? How might it be overdone? ●

Prevalence of Exceptional Children

Prevalence figures reflect how many students need special services. These figures are used to allocate funds, to determine whether there are enough teachers, and for many other purposes. In the fall of 2009, there were 5,882,157 children from age 6 to 21 receiving special education services in the schools in the U.S. and outlying areas (Data Accountability Center, 2009). Figure 1.1 shows the breakdown of students by disability group. In recent years, numbers of students in some categories (for example, learning disabilities and intellectual disabilities) are decreasing slightly, and numbers in others, such as autism, other health impairments (which now includes attention deficit disorder), and developmental delay, are

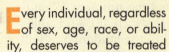

A CLOSER LOOK Eliminating Stereotypes: Words Matter!

Every individual, regardless of sex, age, race, or ability, deserves to be treated with dignity and respect. As part of the effort to end discrimination and segregation—in employment, education, and our communities at large—it's important to eliminate prejudicial language.

Like other minorities, the disability community has developed preferred terminology—*people-first language*. More than a fad or political correctness, people-first language is an objective way of acknowledging, communicating, and reporting on disabilities. It eliminates generalizations, assumptions, and stereotypes by focusing on the person rather than the disability.

As the term implies, people-first language refers to the individual first and the disability second. It's the difference between saying *the autistic* and *a child with autism*. While some people may not use preferred terminology, it's important that you don't repeat negative terms that stereotype, devalue, or discriminate, just as you'd avoid racial slurs and say *women* instead of *gals*.

Equally important, ask yourself if the disability is even relevant and whether it needs to be mentioned when referring to individuals, in the same way racial identification is being eliminated from news stories when it is not significant to the story's content.

What should you say?

Be sensitive when choosing the words you use. Here are a few guidelines on appropriate language.

- Recognize that people with disabilities are ordinary people with common goals for a home, a job, and a family. Talk about people in ordinary terms.

- Never equate a person with a disability—such as referring to someone as *retarded*, *epileptic*, or *quadriplegic*. These labels are simply a medical diagnosis. Use people-first language to tell what a person HAS, not what a person IS.

- Emphasize abilities, not limitations. For example, say a man walks with crutches, not that he is crippled.

- Avoid negative words that imply tragedy, such as *afflicted with*, *suffers from*, *victim of*, *prisoner*, and *unfortunate*.

- Recognize that a disability is not a challenge to be overcome, and don't say that people succeed in spite of a disability. Ordinary accomplishments do not become extraordinary just because they are done by a person with a disability. What is extraordinary are the lengths people with disabilities have to go to and the barriers they have to overcome to do the most ordinary things.

- Use *handicap* to refer to a barrier created by people or the environment. Use *disability* to indicate a functional limitation that interferes with a person's mental, physical, or sensory abilities, such as walking, talking, hearing, and learning. For example, people with disabilities who use wheelchairs are handicapped by stairs.

- Do not refer to a person as *bound to* or *confined to* a wheelchair. Wheelchairs are liberating to people with disabilities because they provide mobility.

- Do not use *special* to mean *segregated*, such as special schools or buses for people with disabilities, or to suggest that a disability itself makes someone special.

- Avoid cute euphemisms such as *physically challenged*, *inconvenienced*, and *differently abled*.

- Promote understanding, respect, dignity, and a positive outlook.

People-first language

People-first language recognizes that individuals with disabilities are—first and foremost—people. It emphasizes each person's value, individuality, dignity, and capabilities. The following examples provide guidance on what terms to use and which ones are inappropriate when talking or writing about people with disabilities.

rising. While the number of students receiving special education services is now declining slightly, it has increased dramatically since 1975, when the federal law now known as IDEA was passed. In the 2008–2009 school year, 13.2 percent of prekindergarten through secondary students in the United States received special education services (U.S. Department of Education, 2011).

People-First Language to Use	Instead of Labels that Stereotype and Devalue
• people/individuals **with disabilities** an adult who has a disability a child with a disability a person	• the handicapped the disabled
• people/individuals **without disabilities** typical kids	• normal people/healthy individuals atypical kids
• people with **intellectual and developmental disabilities** he/she has a cognitive impairment a person who has Down syndrome	• the mentally retarded; retarded people he/she is retarded; the retarded he/she's a Downs kid; a Mongoloid; a Mongol
• a person who has **autism**	• autistic
• people with a **mental illness** a person who has an emotional disability with a psychiatric illness/disability	• the mentally ill; the emotionally disturbed is insane; crazy; demented; psycho a maniac; lunatic
• a person who has a **learning disability**	• he/she is learning disabled
• a person who is **deaf** he/she has a hearing impairment/loss a man/woman who is hard of hearing	• the deaf
• person who is deaf and **does not speak**	• is deaf and dumb mute
• a person who is **blind** a person who has a visual impairment man/woman who has low vision	• the blind
• a person who has **epilepsy** people with a seizure disorder	• an epileptic a victim of epilepsy
• a person who **uses a wheelchair** people who have a mobility impairment a person who walks with crutches	• a person who is wheelchair bound a person who is confined to a wheelchair a cripple
• a person who has **quadriplegia** • people with paraplegia	• a quadriplegic the paraplegic
• he/she is of small or **short stature**	• a dwarf or midget
• he/she has a **congenital disability**	• he/she has a birth defect
• accessible **buses, bathrooms,** etc. reserved **parking** for people with disabilities	• handicapped buses, bathrooms, hotel rooms, etc. handicapped parking

Source: Prepared by the Texas Council for Developmental Disabilities: http://www.txddc.state.tx.us. Revised 02/07.

A recurrent and serious problem in our field is the disproportionate representation of students from traditional minority groups in special education services—particularly the overrepresentation of African American males in the intellectual disabilities and emotional disturbance categories (Skiba et al., 2008). We will discuss this issue in depth in Chapter 2.

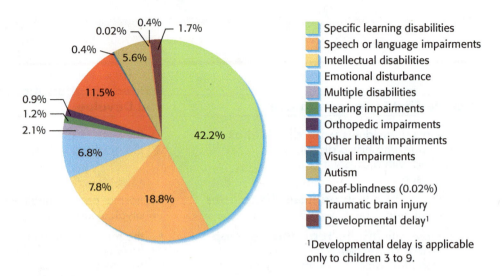

FIGURE 1.1

Percentage of students ages 6 through 21 served under IDEA, Part B in the U.S. and outlying areas, by disability category: fall 2009

Source: U.S. Department of Education, Office of Special Education Programs, Data Analysis System (DANS). Available at http://www.ideadata.org.

Foundations of Special Education

There have always been exceptional children. Gershon Berkson (2004) discovered in his review of disabilities in prehistory and early civilization that ". . . individuals with mental and physical disabilities have been members of society since the emergence of Homo sapiens and probably well before that" (p. 195). But documented attempts to teach people with disabilities are relatively recent. The first known attempts came in the sixteenth and seventeenth centuries, when priests and other religious men and women taught small groups of children who were deaf and blind children—usually the offspring of the aristocracy (Moores, 2001).

Early History: Great Teachers and Their Legacies

A series of curious, innovative, and dedicated men and women in Europe and the United States pioneered the teaching techniques that are the foundation of special education. The work of **Jean-Marc-Gaspard Itard** in France was followed in Europe by that of **Edouard Seguin** and **Maria Montessori**; in the United States **Samuel Gridley Howe** and **Anne Sullivan Macy** were among the pioneers. Figure 1.2 provides more detail on these early teachers and some of their noteworthy students. Visit the Education CourseMate website that accompanies our book at **www.cengagebrain.com** for more information and resources on great teachers of the past.

Later History: Advocates for Social Change

After an initial surge of interest within the United States in the education of children who were deaf, blind, or had intellectual and developmental disabilities, school services for children with disabilities plateaued for many years. Families of children with disabilities either kept their children at home without going to school or placed them in institutions. It was not until the 1960s that two events converged to re-ignite national interest in the needs of children with disabilities. The first of these was the election of John F. Kennedy as president in 1960. Kennedy had a sister, Rosemary, with intellectual and developmental disabilities, and he was openly committed to improving the quality of life for people like Rosemary. He did two concrete things to accomplish this goal: He established the President's Commission on Mental Retardation, a group of expert researchers and practitioners who identified the issues and priorities in the field, and he supported the use of federal funds to educate teachers of children with disabilities. Kennedy's greatest contribution was less concrete. His acknowledgment of disability in his family and his dedication to improving services for people with disabilities played a large part in lessening the stigma of and adding prestige to the career of teaching children with disabilities.

Kennedy's sister Eunice, who died in 2009, pushed her brother toward many of these accomplishments. Her influential *Saturday Evening Post* article from 1962 told Rosemary's story and explained the family's commitment to the rights of people with disabilities (read it at **http://www.eunicekennedyshriver.org/articles/saturday_evening_post**). She began the Special Olympics in 1968. **Eunice Kennedy Shriver's** adult children have continued the family tradition; Tim now runs the Special Olympics, and Anthony is the founder of Best Buddies, an organization that supports friendships between people with intellectual disabilities and those without.

The other event of the 1960s that influenced families and other advocates of children with disabilities was the civil rights movement, and the passage of the 1964 Civil Rights Act, which set the stage for advocacy for the civil rights of people with disabilities. The political and social demands of African Americans for equal rights and access to opportunities at all levels of society provided an example of what could be accomplished on behalf of disenfranchised groups by families and groups working with children with disabilities.

How Does a Teacher Refer a Child for Special Education Services?

Fourth-grade teacher Mike Costello is concerned about the progress of one of his students. Visit Chapter 1 on the CourseMate website and watch the video case entitled "Students with Special Needs: The Referral and Evaluation Process." Can you think of any additional information that might help Mike?

The Kennedy family's commitment to improving services for people with disabilities helped lessen the stigma of intellectual disability.

The Kennedy children in Hyannisport, Massachusetts around 1925. From left: Rosemary, John, Eunice, Joe Jr. and Kathleen. Rosemary was the inspiration for Eunice and John's commitment to people with intellectual and developmental disabilities.

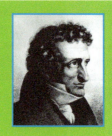   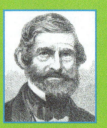  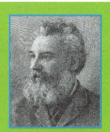

Jean-Marc-Gaspard Itard (1775–1838)	**Thomas Hopkins Gallaudet (1787–1851)**	**Laurent Clerc (1785–1869)**	**Samuel Gridley Howe (1801–1876)**	**Edouard Seguin (1812–1880)**	**Alexander Graham Bell (1847–1922)**
Physician, teacher to Victor, patriarch of special education.	After research and travel in Europe, Gallaudet started the first school for the deaf in the United States.	French teacher of deaf children, deaf himself, came to the United States with Gallaudet to teach in the first American school for deaf children.	Howe started the first "special school" and advocated on behalf of children with disabilities.	Itard's student was inspired by his mentor's work to do more for children with disabilities in Europe and the United States.	Known as an inventor, Bell always thought of himself as a teacher of speech to deaf children.
(Bridgeman Art Gallery @ Archives Charmet)	(Gallaudet University Archives)	(Gallaudet University Archives)	(© The Granger Collection)	(Courtesy of the National Library of Medicine, Prints and Photographs)	(© The Granger Collection)

— The Teachers —

FIGURE 1.2

Great Teachers and Their Students

> With normalization, people with disabilities have the opportunity to lead typical lives.

> Deinstitutionalization has helped end the segregation of people with intellectual disabilities from the community.

> P.L. 94-142, now known as IDEA, requires that children 3 to 21 with a disability be provided a free and appropriate public education in the least restrictive environment.

In 1972, Wolf Wolfensberger articulated the principle of **normalization**—that people with disabilities should have the opportunity to lead a life as close to normal as possible. This philosophy implies that no matter how severe an individual's disability, he or she should have the opportunity to participate in all aspects of society. The normalization principle, which is "deeply embedded in services to individuals with disabilities" (Harry, Rueda, & Kalyanpur, 1999, p. 123), implied that special institutions for people with intellectual and developmental disabilities, which tended to be segregated from the community, should be deemphasized. This movement, known as **deinstitutionalization,** has led to the establishment of many small group homes and other community-based residential facilities in towns and cities.

Historical Events Pave the Way to Inclusion

In schools, the application of the concept of normalization has led away from segregation—the education of exceptional children in special schools or separate buildings—and toward the goal of education in the **least restrictive environment** (where the child with a disability has the most interaction with nondisabled children that is appropriate—see the next section for more information on this). After the landmark special education legislation P.L. 94-142 (now known as the Individuals with Disabilities Education Act or IDEA) was passed in 1975, educators used the term *mainstreaming* to describe the participation of children with disabilities in the general education classroom. Today, the word **inclusion** is used. Inclusion refers to the placement of a child with disabilities in the general education classroom, with the supports that child needs also provided there. IDEA is amended by Congress every few years, and each time there is renewed emphasis on educating students with disabilities in less restrictive environments. In particular, the law encourages opportunities for children with disabilities to participate in general

Anne Sullivan Macy (1866–1936)

Helen Keller's beloved "Teacher" who taught her to communicate.

(© AP Photo)

Maria Montessori (1870–1952)

The first Italian woman M.D. Based her work with children with disabilities on that of Itard and Seguin.

(© Hulton-Deutsch Collection/CORBIS)

Victor, the "wild boy of Aveyron" (c. 1788–1828)

Today he would be described as having intellectual disabilities.

(© The Granger Collection)

Laura Bridgeman (1829–1904)

Deaf and blind, Laura was taught to read and write by Samuel Gridley Howe.

(© The Granger Collection)

Helen Keller (1880–1968)

She became a widely admired writer, speaker, and public figure despite being deaf and blind.

(Bettman/CORBIS)

Their Students

education settings and in the general education curriculum. Inclusion of children with disabilities in such settings is important because it *raises expectations for student performance, provides opportunities for children with disabilities to learn alongside their nondisabled peers, improves coordination between regular and special educators, and increases school-level accountability for educational results* (National Center for Education Statistics, 1999).

In practice, there appears to be a continuum of inclusion in today's schools, ranging from full-time, complete membership of the student with disabilities in the general education classroom to part-time participation for nonacademic subjects and activities. The practice of inclusion makes considerable demands on both the general educator and the special educator. The collaboration that must occur is often new to both, and it is a skill that requires time, patience, and willingness. Certainly, not everyone is in support of inclusion—in fact, the practice can be quite controversial. Some special educators strongly believe that inclusion should simply be one option in the continuum of program options and that the individual needs of the child, rather than a "one-size-fits-all" philosophy, should determine the child's placement (see Figure 1.3). Court decisions over the past several years have affirmed the need for the continuum of program options (Yell, 2011). According to the U.S. Department of Education:

> In fall 2007, some 95 percent of 6- to 21-year-old students with disabilities were served in regular schools; 3 percent were served in a separate school for students with disabilities; 1 percent were placed in regular private schools by their parents; and less than 1 percent each were served in one of the following environments: in a separate residential facility, homebound or in a hospital, or in a correctional facility. (U.S. Department of Education, National Center for Education Statistics, 2010).

Inclusion refers to placement of a child with disabilities in the general education classroom, with the supports that child needs also provided in the classroom.

The practice of inclusion requires collaboration between the general educator and the special educator, as well as time, patience, and willingness.

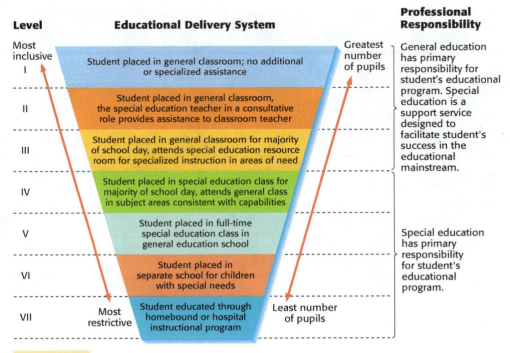

FIGURE 1.3

Learning Environments for Exceptional Children: The Continuum of Program Options

Source: Hardman Drew & Egan, HUMAN EXCEPTIONALITY, 10e page 31. Copyright 2011 Cengage Learning.

General educators have sometimes objected to inclusive practices, maintaining that they are not prepared to meet the individual needs of children with disabilities, that the practice is too time-consuming, and that it takes time from other children. But many special educators believe that the history of placement in segregated settings like a special school or even a special day class has interfered with the social and academic growth of children with disabilities and has also limited the opportunities of children who are not disabled to learn from those who are. Research suggests that the majority of general educators and administrators support the idea of inclusion, given the appropriate supports and collaborative practices (Avramdis & Norwich, 2002). In Idol's (2006) evaluation of four inclusive programs, teachers were positive about educating students with disabilities and working collaboratively with other teachers in inclusive programs but expressed preference for the support of another adult in the classroom, whether a special education teacher or an instructional assistant. In Horne and Timmons' (2009) qualitative study, teachers expressed the need for more planning time and professional development as their students' needs became more diverse. Effective inclusion requires positive attitudes and a willingness to collaborate on the part of all the professionals involved—and often the student and family as well. Our hope is that this book, and the course it accompanies, will help any member of the collaborative team—teacher, parent, psychologist, counselor, therapist, nurse—have a clearer picture of students with disabilities and the supports they need to succeed in the general education classroom.

Regardless of your personal experiences or beliefs about inclusion, it is important to understand what the "best practices" for including children with disabilities in general education classrooms are. They rest on the assumptions that all teachers receive appropriate preparation and education about meeting the needs of children with disabilities and that the appropriate supports are provided to both the student with disabilities and the teacher.

A good day at school for all children means having fun with friends.

? Pause and Reflect

In less than 40 years, schooling options for families have changed from none—particularly for families of children with more severe disabilities—to a range of settings, including general education. Put yourself in the shoes of a parent of a child with a disability. What do you think you would want for your own child? ●

Legislation

Federal law now mandates that children with disabilities be educated in the "least restrictive environment"—the setting that gives the child the greatest number of options for interactions with nondisabled peers and the same opportunities as those peers. Let's take a look at the specific pieces of legislation that pertain to the education of exceptional children.

● *Public Law 94-142*   The law that has had the most profound impact on children with disabilities is Public Law (P.L.) 94-142, formerly known as the Education for All Handicapped Children Act (1975) and now known as the **Individuals with Disabilities Education Act (IDEA).** It requires that every child between the ages of 3 and 21 with a disability be provided a free, appropriate public education in the least restrictive environment.

Before P.L. 94-142 was passed in 1975, only one-fifth of the children with disabilities in the United States were enrolled in school programs at all (U.S. Department of Education, 1995); the remainder were excluded from school, received inappropriate education, or were housed in institutions that did not provide educational programs. Now we are much closer to enrolling all children with disabilities in appropriate educational programs, although this is still an elusive goal. Congress has amended the law several times (see Table 1.3); as a result of the 1975 law and its amendments, children with disabilities and their families have well-defined rights, and those rights begin at birth or the point at which disability

Teaching Strategies & Accommodations

Supports for General Education Teachers

A synthesis of research studies on inclusion from the 1990s identified the following supports needed by general education teachers who are including students with disabilities in their classrooms:

- **Time.** Teachers report a need for one hour or more per day to plan for students with disabilities.

- **Training.** Teachers need systematic, intensive training—as part of their certification programs, as intensive and well-planned in-service trainings, or as an ongoing process with consultants.

- **Personnel resources.** Teachers report a need for additional personnel assistance to carry out objectives. This could include a half-time aide and daily contact with special education teachers.

- **Materials resources.** Teachers need adequate curriculum materials and other classroom equipment appropriate to the needs of students with disabilities.

- **Class size.** Teachers believe that their class size should be reduced to fewer than twenty students if students with disabilities are included.

- **Consideration of severity of disability.** Teachers are more willing to include students with mild disabilities than students with more severe disabilities. By implication, the more severe the disabilities in the inclusive setting, the more the previously mentioned sources of support would be needed.

Source: T.E. Scruggs & M.A. Mastropieri, Teacher perceptions of mainstreaming/inclusion, 1958–1995.

Since the 1990s, focus has turned from general supports that teachers need in order to include students with disabilities to supports that they need to participate in specific school-wide programs that have the potential to benefit *all* students. Among these are three-tiered models of intervention, such as school-wide positive behavior support (Lane, Kalberg, & Menzies, 2009) and Response to Intervention programs (Haager, Klingner, & Vaughn, 2007). These models will be described more fully in later chapters in this book, but they are both prevention programs that assume a strong layer of primary prevention in the general education classroom. Under these models, teachers must monitor student progress, offer preventative interventions (Fuchs & Fuchs, 2007), use evidence-based practices (Foorman, 2007), and all the while offer a rigorous classroom curriculum! Ongoing professional development and supports from collaborating professionals (such as the special education teacher) must accompany the expanded responsibilities of the general education teacher. These needs may be greater for secondary teachers than for elementary teachers, since they teach so many more students during the typical school day. The ultimate success of inclusion efforts, then, may well depend on the extent to which such supports are made available.

Source: Exceptional Children, 63(1), (1996), 72.

is identified. See the *Closer Look* box on page 20 for the principles that are the foundations of IDEA.

A child must meet two criteria to qualify for special education services under IDEA: He or she must have one of the 14 disabilities listed earlier in this chapter, and he or she must require special education and related services because the disability adversely affects his or her educational performance. The need for special education is determined through formal and informal assessment, which establishes whether the child's progress is behind that of typical children the same age. Not all children with disabilities do require services; many attend school without any modifications to their program. For example, some children with chronic health impairments do not require special services to keep up in school, despite frequent absences.

Why Was IDEA Needed?   In 1970, five years before Congress passed the original law, only one in five children with disabilities attended school. Some states had laws

© AP Photo/The Herald, Dan Bates

Inclusion of children with disabilities extends to all activities within the school—not just the classroom.

excluding children who were deaf or blind and children with emotional disturbance or mental retardation from school (U.S. Department of Education, 2003). Here is an excerpt from a report from the federal Office of Special Education and Rehabilitative Services in the Department of Education: "Before the enactment of Public Law 94-142, the fate of many individuals with disabilities was likely to be dim. Too many individuals lived in state institutions for persons with mental retardation or mental illness. In 1967, for example, state institutions were homes for almost 200,000 persons with significant disabilities. Many of these restrictive settings provided only minimal food, clothing, and shelter. Too often, persons with disabilities, such as Allan, were merely accommodated rather than assessed, educated, and rehabilitated.

ALLAN'S STORY

Allan was left as an infant on the steps of an institution for persons with intellectual disabilities in the late 1940s. By age 35, he had become blind and was frequently observed sitting in a corner of the room, slapping his heavily callused face as he rocked back and forth humming to himself. In the late 1970s, Allan was assessed properly for the first time. To the dismay of his examiners, he was found to be of average intelligence; further review of his records revealed that by observing fellow residents of the institution, he had learned self-injurious behavior that caused his total loss of vision. Although the institution then began a special program to teach Allan to be more independent, a major portion of his life was lost because of a lack of appropriate assessments and effective interventions.

Table 1.3 How Has IDEA Changed? The Law and Its Amendments

Year	Name	Noteworthy Provisions
1975	P.L. 94-142 (original law) Education for All Handicapped Children Act	A free and appropriate public education in the least restrictive environment for all students with disabilities aged 5 to 21.
1983	P.L. 98-199 Education of the Handicapped Act Amendments	Expanded incentives for preschool special education programs, early intervention, and transition programs.
1986	P.L. 99-457 Education for the Handicapped Act Amendments	Extended all provisions of the law to children aged 3 to 5. Provided incentives to the states to establish early-intervention programs for infants and toddlers from birth to age 3.
1990	P.L. 101-476 Education for the Handicapped Act Amendments	Changed name of law to Individuals with Disabilities Education Act (IDEA). Added two new categories of disability: autism and traumatic brain injury.
1991	PL 102-119 Individuals with Disabilities Education Act Amendments	Extended state timelines for implementing early intervention services.
1997	P.L. 105-17 Individuals with Disabilities Education Act Amendments	Required that students with disabilities participate in state and district testing. Increased emphasis on participation of students with disabilities in the general education curriculum. Detailed provisions on suspension, expulsion, and discipline for students with disabilities.
2004	P.L. 108-446 Individuals with Disabilities Education Improvement Act of 2004	Defines "high quality" special educators. Attempts to reduce paperwork. Allows states to use Response to Intervention to identify students with learning disabilities.

© Cengage Learning 2013

Unfortunately, Allan's history was repeated in the life experiences of tens of thousands of individuals with disabilities who lacked support from IDEA. Inaccurate tests led to inappropriately labeling and ineffectively educating most children with disabilities. Providing appropriate education to youngsters from diverse cultural, racial, and ethnic backgrounds was especially challenging. Further, most families were not afforded the opportunity to be involved in planning or placement decisions regarding their child, and resources were not available to enable children with significant disabilities to live at home and receive an education at neighborhood schools in their community"(U.S. Department of Education, Office of Special Education and Rehabilitation Services, 2003).

What Has IDEA Accomplished?   Today, intervention begins as soon as a child is identified with a disability, or as at risk of developing one (see Chapter 3). Exactly 269,596 infants and toddlers and their families received early intervention services in 2003 and over 6 million children and youth received special education and related services (U.S. Department of Education, 2005). While the law is not perfect, it has been the framework for many advances in the education of students with disabilities. The Department of Education (2010) identifies the following accomplishments of IDEA as the law marked the 35th year since its passage:

- **More young children with disabilities receive high-quality early interventions that prevent or reduce the future need for services.** *IDEA-*reported data indicate that rates of identification for young children with disabilities have been steadily increasing over the past 10 years. For infants and toddlers ages birth through 2, the number receiving services under Part C of *IDEA* has nearly doubled, from 177,281 in 1995 to 321,894 in 2007.

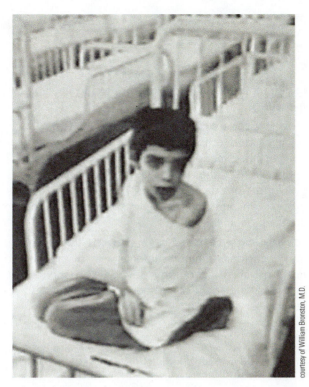

courtesy of William Bronston, M.D.

© Richard Hutchings/PhotoEdit

Thanks to changes in public policy and in law, the quality of life for children with disabilities has improved greatly since 1978, when the photo on the left was taken at Willowbrook State School in New York.

For children ages 3–5, the number receiving services under Part B of *IDEA* has increased by nearly 23 percent, from 548,588 in 1995 to 710,371 in 2007.

- **More children with disabilities are not only attending neighborhood schools but also are receiving access to the general education curriculum and learning a wide variety of academic skills.** In 2008, *IDEA*-reported data indicate that 5,660,491 students with disabilities were educated in general education classrooms for at least part of the day, depending on their individual needs. Thus, 95 percent of all students with disabilities were educated in their local neighborhood schools.

- **More youths with disabilities graduate from high school.** In school year 2007–08, *IDEA*-reported data indicated that 217,905 students with disabilities, ages 14–21, graduated high school with a regular diploma. There has been a 16-point increase in the percentage of students with disabilities graduating from high school since school year 1996–97.

- **More youths with disabilities are enrolled in postsecondary programs.** The rate at which youths with disabilities enrolled in postsecondary education rose from 14.6 percent in 1987 to 31.9 percent in 2005. Enrollment rates increased for both two-and four-year colleges, while enrollment rates decreased for postsecondary vocational, technical, and business schools.

- **More young adults with disabilities are employed.** Trends in the postsecondary employment of youths with disabilities are positive, with an increase of about 15 points in the percentage of out-of-school youths with disabilities who have worked for pay since leaving high school.

You can see that under federal law a great deal of emphasis is placed on what is called "categorical special education": providing services to children as if they fall into neat boxes, or categories. You may know from your own experience that this isn't the case in "real life"; children are much more complicated than that.

A CLOSER LOOK Foundations of IDEA

- **Zero reject.** No child, no matter how severely disabled, shall be refused an appropriate education by the schools.

- **Free, appropriate public education.** Each student is entitled to special education and related services in public school at no cost. At the heart of this component of the law is the Individualized Education Program (IEP). We further describe the IEP later in this chapter and refer to its use in the classroom throughout this book.

- **Least restrictive environment.** Each child must be educated with nondisabled peers to the maximum extent appropriate. We discuss the differing perspectives on this concept later in the chapter.

- **Nondiscriminatory evaluation.** Evaluation procedures must be conducted with fairness in the child's native language, using multiple measures.

- **Due process and procedural safeguards.** Families and school districts can exercise their Fourteenth Amendment rights to due process under the law; that is, they may resort to mediation and appeal procedures when they do not agree with one another over issues such as the child's placement.

- **Technology-related assistance.** IEP teams must consider whether students with disabilities need assistive technology devices and services in order to benefit from special education and related services.

Source: Adapted from M. Yell, *The law and special education* (3rd ed.). (Upper Saddle River, New Jersey: Prentice Hall, 2011).

You may find that, as you read through this book, the characteristics of a child you know are described in several different chapters. Keep in mind that the categories we use are for the convenience of lawmakers and educators; they are not iron-clad descriptors of the way children really learn and function. Harriet McBryde Johnson, who died in 2008, was a person who defied the application of categories. Let's allow her to speak for herself:

> It's not that I'm ugly. It's more that most people don't know how to look at me. The sight of me is routinely discombobulating. The power wheelchair is enough to inspire gawking, but that's the least of it. Much more impressive is the impact on my body of more than four decades of a muscle-wasting disease. At this stage of my life, I'm Karen Carpenter-thin, flesh mostly vanished, a jumble of bones in a floppy bag of skin. When, in childhood, my muscles got too weak to hold up my spine, I tried a brace for a while, but fortunately a skittish anesthesiologist said no to fusion, plates, and pins—all the apparatuses that might have kept me straight. At 15, I threw away the back brace and let my spine reshape itself into a deep twisty S-curve. Now my right side is two deep canyons. To keep myself upright, I lean forward, rest my rib cage on my lap, plant my elbows beside my knees. Since my backbone found its own natural shape, I've been entirely comfortable in my skin.

> I used to try to explain that in fact I enjoy my life, that it's a great sensual pleasure to zoom by power chair on these delicious muggy streets, that I have no more reason to kill myself than most people. But it gets tedious. God didn't put me on this street to provide disability awareness training to the likes of them. In fact, no god put anyone anywhere for any reason, if you want to know.

But they don't want to know. They think they know everything there is to know, just by looking at me. That's how stereotypes work. They don't know that they're confused, that they're really expressing the discombobulation that comes in my wake (Johnson, 2003).

In 2002, Johnson, who was a disability rights attorney in South Carolina, debated Peter Singer, the Princeton philosopher who believes in "selected infanticide"— the killing of babies born with disabilities (Kuhse & Singer, 1985; Singer, 1996). Johnson's story would qualify for inclusion in at least two chapters of this book—she was both physically disabled—and gifted.

Major Amendments to IDEA

Public Law 99-457.   In 1986, Congress amended P.L. 94-142 with P.L. 99-457. This amendment extended the provisions of P.L. 94-142 to all children between the ages of 3 and 5 through the Preschool Grants Program. Now states receiving federal funds under these laws *must* provide a free and appropriate public education to preschoolers with disabilities as well. In addition, states are provided incentives to develop early-intervention programs for infants with disabilities and those who are at risk for developing disabilities from birth through age 3. All states now provide early intervention for those infants. We will learn more about these provisions in Chapter 2.

Public Law 101-476.   The 1990 amendments used people-first language to rename the *Education of the Handicapped Act* the *Individuals with Disabilities Education Act (IDEA)*. This law also recognized the importance of preparing students for life and work after school. It mandated the creation of an Individualized Transition Plan (ITP) that would prepare each adolescent student receiving special education services for life after school.

> IDEA now mandates transition goals on the IEP for each student receiving special education from the age of 16.

Photo by Wade Spees

Harriet McBryde Johnson was an attorney in Charleston, South Carolina, and a fearless advocate for people with disabilities.

FIRST PERSON

David

David learned to jump rope last week.

It may not seem like much of an accomplishment for a strapping fourth-grader. By the time kids reach the fourth grade, haven't they mastered rope jumping and soccer and dodgeball and capture the flag?

Not all of them.

Jumping rope can be a source of pride for an awkward boy who has spent most of his time on the sidelines, watching other children . . . and for my daughter and her friends, who taught him how to play.

I don't know much about David. Only the stories my daughter tells.

He sits near the teacher, in the front row, and struggles through even the most basic tasks. He giggles when nothing's funny, speaks out when he hasn't been called upon, mumbles to himself. He has a distracting habit of constantly wringing his hands. He spends part of each day away from class, with a special teacher.

"I think he's handicapped," my daughter says, not as judgment but as explanation. It takes me back to my days as a reporter and all the stories I wrote on "mainstreaming"—the practice of teaching disabled students alongside other children, instead of isolating them in classes labeled "special ed."

Over the years I'd duly noted the pros and cons: the advocates' claims that disabled kids benefit by making friends and learning social skills from other children, and the critics' concerns that handicapped kids might be shunned or belittled or take up too much of a teacher's time. What neither argument acknowledges is what I see: that the benefits of this social experiment flow not just one way, but back from the disabled child to mine.

Because, while David might be struggling to learn, he is teaching without effort—providing his classmates with new opportunities each day to learn and practice patience, tolerance, kindness, ingenuity.

Public Law 105-17. The 1997 amendments to IDEA provided the most significant revision of the law since it was passed in 1975. The law was amended to require that students with disabilities participate in state and district-widve assessment (testing) programs, with accommodations when necessary; that the Individualized Education Program (IEP) process place increased emphasis on the participation of students with disabilities in the general education curriculum; and that general education teachers be involved in developing, reviewing, and revising the IEP.

P.L. 108-446 IDEA Improvement Act of 2004. The most recent amendments to IDEA continued an emphasis on providing access to the general education curriculum for students with disabilities, which the U.S. Department of Education (2010) calls "the civil rights issue of our time" (p. 16). Congress also placed greater emphasis on ensuring that special education teachers are "highly qualified," and took steps to reduce the disproportionate representation of students of color receiving special education services (see Chapter 2 for more on this issue). Based on the 2004 amendments, the states now can bypass the traditional methods of identifying students with learning disabilities and use a "Response to Intervention (RTI)" model.

I know it's not always easy, for him or for them. He is annoying at times, tagging along, interrupting conversations. I'm sure he tries the teacher's patience.

He fails, it seems, as often as he succeeds. That hurts, and he doesn't know how not to let it show. He cries sometimes. And on the playground, the older kids tease him.

But his classmates comfort him and rise to his defense. They encourage him when he's afraid to try something new. They teach him songs, tell him jokes . . . even if it means explaining the punch line over and over, until he understands it well enough to laugh.

And every day at recess, my daughter and her friends take out the long, red jump rope that David likes. They station him at one end, put the rope in his hand, take his arm and start it turning. Then as they jump, they swing their arms in big, wide circles, so David can keep pace by mimicking them.

Then it is his turn to stand alongside the rope and jump.

My daughter laughs with glee as she tells the story. I can imagine the grin on David's face, his fists clenched in determination, his pride as he launches himself airborne. And I can almost hear the shouts of his cheering section, yelling at him to lift his feet: *"Jump! . . . jump! . . . jump!"*

It has taken my daughter days longer than her classmates, but she finally has completed her computer lesson. Now everyone in class has finished and has received an award . . . everyone but David.

My daughter's sense of accomplishment is tinged by a tender sort of pity. "I wish everything wasn't so hard for David," she says, putting her award aside. "It's just not fair."

And I have to fight back tears . . . but not for David. You see, my daughter is no stranger to struggle. School has never come easy for her. She knows how it feels to be last, to be wrong . . . to miss the joke's punch line, to jump at the wrong time.

Fourth grade has been a good year for her. She has earned A's and B's, learned long division, won a solo in the school's musical, become a standout on her soccer team. But if you ask her now what she's proudest of, she's liable to tell you that it's teaching David that he can jump rope.

Because she has learned how one small achievement can lift you up, make you believe that big things are possible. And she wants David to learn that too.

Sandy Banks

Source: "Lessons from a Boy Named David" by Sandy Banks, *Los Angeles Times,* February 21, 1999.

So instead of comparing a student's ability with his or her performance on achievement tests and looking for a significant discrepancy, schools can try to teach the basics of reading using research-based methods and see if the student responds to that intensive intervention. You will learn much more about RTI in Chapter 5.

● *Section 504 of the Rehabilitation Act of 1973* Are you taking this class in a building that has ramps leading up to it? Are there elevators as well as stairs and escalators? In the elevators are there Braille cells next to the numerals indicating each floor? Is there a wide stall, a low sink, and a low mirror in the restroom? Is one of the public telephones set low on the wall? Are there plenty of special parking places for people with disabilities outside?

Let us hope that all these adaptations make your school building accessible to students, faculty, and staff with disabilities. Most public facilities have not become accessible out of the goodness of anyone's heart. They are accessible because of Section 504 of the Rehabilitation Act of 1973, a civil rights law requiring that institutions not discriminate against people with disabilities in any way if they wish to receive federal funds.

Section 504 of the Rehabilitation Act of 1973 requires that public facilities be accessible to people with disabilities.

Section 504 has had considerable impact on architecture and construction in the United States, since it requires changes in the design of physical access to buildings for public use. It has also been used to prohibit discrimination against a person simply because he or she is disabled. For example, if you had a newborn baby who needed corrective surgery to open a blocked trachea, would you hesitate to have the procedure performed? Well, that surgery cannot be denied to a baby with Down syndrome either, simply because she will have an intellectual disability. Section 504 prohibits discrimination on the basis of disability. To read more about disability rights laws, visit our accompanying Education CourseMate website at **www.cengagebrain.com.**

Students who may not qualify for services in the schools under the fourteen definitions in IDEA but still have a significant learning problem that affects their ability to perform in school may qualify for services under Section 504. Although there is no funding available under Section 504, it requires that the school create a special plan to accommodate the student's learning needs and create an accessible environment (Zirkel, 2009). For more information on how a child might be helped under Section 504, see **http://nichcy.org/laws/section504/.**

● *The Americans with Disabilities Act*   On July 26, 1990, President George H. W. Bush signed into law P.L. 101-336, the **Americans with Disabilities Act (ADA)**, with these words: "Today, America welcomes into the mainstream of life all people with disabilities. Let the shameful wall of exclusion finally come tumbling down." The ADA is civil rights legislation for people with disabilities, and it is patterned on Section 504 of the Rehabilitation Act of 1973. The provisions of the ADA cover four major areas: *private-sector employment; public services,* including public facilities, buses, and trains; *public accommodations,* including restaurants, hotels, theaters, doctors' offices, retail stores, museums, libraries, parks, private schools, and day-care centers; and *telecommunications,* making telephone relay services available 24 hours a day to people with speech and hearing impairments.

The ADA was amended in 2008 with the ADA Amendments Act. Since passage of the ADA in 1990, courts had interpreted the definition of disability under the ADA so narrow that relatively few individuals could meet it. To correct this, Congress passed the ADA Amendments Act, making clear the original legislative intent of the law. The ADA Amendments Act achieved the following:

- lowered the threshold for what constitutes "substantially limits a major life activity."
- clarified that the beneficial effects of "mitigating measures" should not be considered when determining the degree to which a disability impacts a major life activity.
- expanded the list of "major life activities" to include reading, thinking, concentrating.

As a result, more people (including those with learning disabilities) are now able to satisfy the definition of disability, gain access to reasonable accommodations, and be protected from discrimination. The homepage for the ADA is available at **http://www.ada.gov/.**

Review Table 1.4, which presents a summary of key legislation in special education.

Litigation

Behind the laws pertaining to the education of exceptional children and youth is a series of court cases initiated by parent and advocacy groups to improve services for children. Two important state court cases preceded the passage of IDEA and

> The ADA protects the civil rights of people with disabilities in four major areas: private-sector employment, public services, public accommodations, and telecommunications.

Table 1.4 Selected Foundations of Special Education and Civil Rights Law

1973	P.L. 93-112	Section 504 of the Rehabilitation Act
1975	P.L. 94-142	Education for All Handicapped Children Act (now known as IDEA)
1986	P.L. 99-457	IDEA amendments
1990	P.L. 101-336	Americans with Disabilities Act
1990	P.L. 101-476	IDEA amendments
1997	P.L. 105-17	IDEA amendment
2004	P.L. 108-446	Individuals with Disabilities Education Improvement Act
2008	P.L. 110-325	Americans with Disabilities Amendments Act

Note: The IDEA and its amendments are special education law; the Rehabilitation Act and the Americans with Disabilities Act are civil rights law.

© Cengage Learning 2013

addressed the need for schooling for children with disabilities who at the time were not provided with any education at all. In *Pennsylvania Association for Retarded Citizens (PARC) v. Commonwealth of Pennsylvania* (1972), the parents of children with intellectual disabilities sued to procure an education for their children. The courts decided in their favor and required Pennsylvania to provide a free, appropriate public education for students with intellectual disabilities. In *Mills v. the Washington, D.C., Board of Education* (1972), a similar decision was reached in regard to all children with disabilities in the District of Columbia.

Since the passage of P.L. 94-142, there have been several cases in which the courts have interpreted various aspects of the law. The first case to reach the U.S. Supreme Court, *Board of Education of Hendrick Hudson School District v. Rowley* (1982), concerned the question of what constitutes an "appropriate" education. The parents of Amy Rowley, a deaf child, requested that she have a sign language interpreter so that she could benefit fully from her placement in a general education class. The court wrote that an "appropriate" education did not mean that the student must reach her maximum potential, but that she have a reasonable opportunity to learn. Since there was evidence presented that Amy Rowley could derive some benefit from general education class placement without a sign language interpreter, the Court denied her that additional service.

In *Irving Independent School District v. Tatro* (1984), the Supreme Court explored the school's responsibility to provide catheterization, a medical procedure, to a child with spina bifida who needed this service in order to remain in school. The Court decided that since this procedure could be performed by people without medical training and the child needed it to remain in school, it should be considered a related service rather than a medical service, and the schools must provide it.

In 1988, the Supreme Court, in *Honig v. Doe,* ruled that a student receiving special education services cannot be excluded indefinitely from school and from receiving the services specified in the IEP (see the next major section). In addition, the student cannot be expelled from school if the behavior in question is related to his or her disability.

The 1999 *Garret F.* ruling by the U.S. Supreme Court ensures that any and all services necessary for a student with complex health-care needs are covered by IDEA, as long as a physician does not provide the services (Yell, 2011). Table 1.5 summarizes these and other court cases that have significantly affected special education.

PARC required Pennsylvania schools to provide a free and appropriate education to students with intellectual disabilities.

The *Rowley* and *Tatro* cases concerned the schools' responsibilities to provide "related services."

In *Honig v. Doe,* the Supreme Court ruled that a student receiving special education services cannot be expelled if the behavior in question is related to his or her disability.

Table 1.5 Important Litigation Involving Special Education

1954 *Brown v. Board of Education* In this case, the U.S. Supreme Court decided that the concept of "separate but equal" schools was unconstitutional and declared that all children must have equal opportunity for education.

1970 *Diana v. Board of Education* (California) This state case established that California schools could not place students in special education on the basis of culturally biased tests or tests given in the student's nonprimary language.

1972 *Pennsylvania Association for Retarded Citizens (PARC) v. Pennsylvania* This state case established the right of children with intellectual disabilities to a public education in Pennsylvania.

1972 *Mills v. Washington, D.C Board of Education* This case established that all students with disabilities were entitled to a public education in the District of Columbia.

1979 *Larry P. v. Riles* (California) In this state case, it was decided that IQ tests could not be used to identify African American students with intellectual disabilities.

1982 *Board of Education of the Hendrick Hudson Central School District v. Rowley* The U.S. Supreme Court, in its first decision interpreting P.L. 94-142, defined an "appropriate" education as one that provides a child with a reasonable opportunity to learn.

1984 *Irving Independent School District v. Tatro* The U.S. Supreme Court decided that procedures that could be performed by a non-physician (such as catheterization) qualified as related services, not medical services, and must be provided by the school district, so that a child can attend school and benefit from special education.

1988 *Honig v. Doe* The U.S. Supreme Court ruled that a student receiving special education services cannot be excluded from school indefinitely (expelled), particularly if the behavior is related to the student's disability.

1999 *Cedar Rapids Community School District v. Garret F.* The U.S. Supreme Court ruled that services related to a student's complex health-care needs are covered under IDEA as long as a physician does not provide them.

© Cengage Learning 2013

Pause and Reflect

The right of students with disabilities to a free and appropriate public education is the result of years of advocacy and hard work on the part of parents, professionals, lawmakers, and people with disabilities themselves. Our current system is certainly not free of problems, but it is also important to recognize the accomplishments of the last 35 years. How do you think the current system of providing services could be improved, for the benefit of students, their families, and their teachers?

Individualized Education

At the core of the laws pertaining to the education of exceptional children is the concept of **individualized education.** Each student should have a program tailored to his or her unique needs. IDEA and its amendments have instituted a system of planning that can now extend from birth to the post-school years. Table 1.6 describes the components of individualized education. In the following sections we'll look at each of these individualized programs.

Table 1.6 Key Components of Individualized Education

Relevant Ages	Description
	The IFSP: The Individualized Family Service Plan Must Include the Following Components:
Children birth to age 3 and their families	• A statement of the infant's or toddler's present levels of development (physical, cognitive, speech/language, psychosocial, motor, and self-help)
	• A statement of the family's strengths, needs, resources, and priorities related to enhancing the child's development
	• A statement of major outcomes expected to be achieved for the child and the family
	• The criteria, procedures, and timelines for determining progress
	• The specific early intervention services necessary to meet the unique needs of the child and family, including the frequency, intensity, and method of delivering services
	• Where in the natural environment (e.g., home, community) the services will be provided (if the services will not be provided in the natural environment, the IFSP must include a statement justifying why not)
	• The projected dates for the initiation of services and expected duration of those services
	• The name of the service coordinator overseeing the implementation of the IFSP
	• The procedures for transition from early intervention into the preschool program
	• The IFSP must be fully explained to the parents, and their suggestions must be considered. They must give written consent before services can start
	The IEP: The Individualized Education Program Must Include the Following Components:
Students ages 3 through 21	Each child's IEP must contain specific information, as listed within IDEA, our nation's special education law. This includes (but is not limited to):
	• A statement of the child's **present levels of academic achievement and functional performance**, including how the child's disability affects his or her involvement and progress in the general education curriculum;
	• A statement of measurable **annual goals**, including academic and functional goals;
	• A description of how the **child's progress** toward meeting the annual goals will be measured, and when periodic progress reports will be provided;
	• A statement of the **special education and related services** and **supplementary aids and services** to be provided to the child, or on behalf of the child;
	• A statement of the **program modifications or supports for school personnel** that will be provided to enable the child to advance appropriately toward attaining the annual goals; to be involved in and make progress in the general education curriculum and to participate in extracurricular and other nonacademic activities; and to be educated and participate with other children with disabilities and nondisabled children;
	• An explanation of the **extent, if any, to which the child will not participate with nondisabled children** in the regular class and in extracurricular and nonacademic activities;
	• A statement of any **individual accommodations** that are necessary to measure the academic achievement and functional performance of the child on state and district-wide assessments;
	• Note: If the IEP team determines that the child must take an alternate assessment instead of a particular regular state or district-wide assessment of student achievement, the IEP must include a statement of why the child cannot participate in the regular assessment and why the particular alternate assessment selected is appropriate for the child; and
	• The **projected date** for the beginning of the services and modifications, and the anticipated **frequency, location, and duration** of those services and modifications
	• A statement of transition services (ITP) needed by students who are 16 and over (or younger, if appropriate)

continued

Table 1.6 Key Components of Individualized Education *continued*	
The Transition Component of the IEP Must Include the Following:	
Students ages 16 through 21 (or younger, if appropriate)	• The student's postsecondary goals (what he or she hopes to achieve after leaving high school) • IEP goals that represent the steps along the way that the student needs to take while still in high school to get ready for achieving the postsecondary goals *after* high school; and • The transition services that the student will receive to support his or her achieving the IEP goals

Sources: Adapted from Legal foundations: The Individuals with Disabilities Education Act (IDEA), *Teaching Exceptional Children* (Winter 1993), 85–87; Writing the IFSP for Your Child (October, 2010), National Dissemination Center for Children with Disabilities: http://nichcy.org/babies/ifsp; The Short and Sweet IEP Overview (September 2010), National Dissemination Center for Children with Disabilities: http://nichcy.org/schoolage/iep/overview; and Transition to Adulthood (September 2009), National Dissemination Center for Children with Disabilities: http://nichcy.org/schoolage/transitionadult#contents.

The Individualized Family Service Plan

> The IFSP ensures that the youngest children and their families receive the services they need.

Exceptional children and their families can first receive individualized services through the **Individualized Family Service Plan (IFSP).** Congress, recognizing the importance of early intervention for young children within the context of the family, mandated that an IFSP be drawn up by an interdisciplinary team that includes family members. Table 1.6 lists the major components of the IFSP. It is meant to ensure that young children from birth to age 3, who are identified as having disabilities or developmental delay or who are at risk, receive the services they need to develop skills and prevent additional disabilities. It is focused on the child and his or her family, rather than just the child. Chapter 3 will discuss the IFSP in greater detail. For more on the IFSP, IEP, ITP, and other sample documents, visit our accompanying Education CourseMate website at **www.cengagebrain.com.**

The Individualized Education Program

> The IEP outlines the educational plan for each student.

The **Individualized Education Program (IEP)** is the basis for special education programming in preschool, elementary, middle, and high school. IDEA calls for a team of people to draw up a written IEP at a meeting called for that purpose. The team is typically made up of the parent(s), the special education teacher, the general education teacher, the school principal, and any specialists who have evaluated the child or have been providing services to that child. When it is appropriate, the student is also present at the IEP meeting. Other school professionals become involved, too, when the student needs supportive services: The school nurse, speech-language specialist, adaptive physical education teacher, and other school professionals may participate in the IEP process. According to the law, the IEP must have the components listed in Table 1.6. The National Dissemination Center for Children with Disabilities reminds us of the IEP's purpose:

> The IEP has two general purposes: to set reasonable learning goals for a child, and to state the services that the school district will provide for the child. The IEP is developed jointly by the school system, the parents of the child, and the student (when appropriate). (The Short and Sweet IEP Overview, **http://nichcy.org/schoolage/iep/overview**)

Table 1.7 The Basic Special Education Process Under IDEA

The writing of each student's IEP takes place within the larger picture of the special education process under IDEA. Before taking a detailed look at the IEP, it may be helpful to look briefly at how a student is identified as having a disability and needing special education and related services and, thus, an IEP.

Step 1. Child is identified by the family or the school as possibly needing special education and related services. The state must identify, locate, and evaluate all children with disabilities in the state who need special education and related services. To do so, states conduct "Child Find" activities.

Step 2. Child is evaluated. The evaluation must assess the child in all areas related to the child's suspected disability. The evaluation results will be used to decide the child's eligibility for special education and related services and to make decisions about an appropriate educational program for the child.

Step 3. Eligibility is decided. A group of qualified professionals and the parents look at the child's evaluation results. Together, they decide if the child is a "child with a disability," as defined by IDEA.

Step 4. Child is found eligible for services. If the child is found to be a "child with a disability," as defined by IDEA, he or she is eligible for special education and related services. Within 30 calendar days after a child is determined eligible, the IEP team must meet to write an IEP for the child.

Step 5. IEP meeting is scheduled. The school system schedules and conducts the IEP meeting.

Step 6. IEP meeting is held and the IEP is written. The IEP team gathers to talk about the child's needs and write the student's IEP. Parents and the student (when appropriate) are part of the team.

Step 7. Services are provided. The school makes sure that the child's IEP is being carried out as it was written. Parents are given a copy of the IEP. Each of the child's teachers and service providers has access to the IEP and knows his or her specific responsibilities for carrying out the IEP. This includes the accommodations, modifications, and supports that must be provided to the child, in keeping with the IEP.

Step 8. Progress is measured and reported to parents. The child's progress toward the annual goals is measured, as stated in the IEP. His or her parents are regularly informed of their child's progress and whether that progress is enough for the child to achieve the goals by the end of the year.

Step 9. IEP is reviewed. The child's IEP is reviewed by the IEP team at least once a year, or more often if the parents or school ask for a review. At that time, the IEP is updated to reflect goals that have been met, and new goals are identified.

Step 10. Child is re-evaluated. At least every three years the child must be re-evaluated. This evaluation is often called a "triennial." Its purpose is to find out if the child continues to be a "child with a disability," as defined by IDEA, and what the child's educational needs are.

Source: Adapted from A Guide to the Individualized Education Program at http://ed.gov/parents/needs/speced/iepguide/index.html#process AND:

For more detail, see The Basic Special Education Process under IDEA 2004 at www.nichcy.org/wp-content/uploads/docs/10steps.pdf/.

Transition Goals in the IEP

As noted earlier, the IDEA mandated transition services for all students receiving special education services. Transition services are those that prepare the student for life after school, whether independent living, work, further education, or another option. Transition plans are now required from the age of 16, but can be added to the IEP for students from the age of 14, if appropriate.

> Transition goals help prepare students for life and work after school.

Pause and Reflect

The concept of *individualized education* may be the primary difference between special education services and general education. It would be a wonderful luxury if *every* child could have an IEP—a program of schooling designed to address and improve areas of weakness and strength. Do you think all children should have an IEP? What are the arguments for and against that idea? •

A CLOSER LOOK   Discipline Under the IDEA

States, schools, and communities are understandably very concerned with school safety these days. Providing safe environments in which children can learn, free of drugs and violence, is one of education's top priorities. In keeping with that concern, it's not surprising that IDEA includes provisions that address the discipline of children with disabilities in school settings and at school functions.

IDEA's discipline provisions were first introduced in the 1997 amendments and have been retained in the 2004 amendments, where they've been streamlined. Even so, they remain complex, spelling out the authority of school personnel to take disciplinary action when the student violating the code of conduct is a student with a disability. Under certain conditions, the actions that schools can take include removing students with disabilities from their current placement, placing them in an interim setting, or, if appropriate, suspending or expelling them. This authority may be exercised only in specific circumstances, which you can read about at http://nichcy.org/schoolage/placement/disciplineplacements/.

- The law requires the IEP team to conduct a "manifestation determination" once a disciplinary action for a student with a disability is contemplated. The IEP team must determine—within ten calendar days after the school decides to discipline a student—whether the student's behavior is related to the disability. If the behavior *is not* related to the disability, the student may be disciplined in the same way as a student without a disability, but the appropriate educational services must continue.

- Schools may suspend students with disabilities for up to ten school days, if such alternatives are used with students without disabilities, BUT. . .

- Schools must continue to provide educational services for students with disabilities whose suspension or expulsion constitutes a change of placement (usually more than ten days in a school year).

- Schools may remove students with disabilities to appropriate interim alternative educational settings (IAES) for behavior related to drugs, guns, and other dangerous weapons for up to 45 days.

Sources: Adapted from B. Knoblauch & K. McLane, An overview of the Individuals with Disabilities Education Act Amendments of 1997 (P.L. 105-17), *ERIC Digest* (1999 update, E576, EDO-99-4) and *School Discipline* (September 2010) at http://nichcy.org/schoolage/placement/disciplineplacements/.

Educational Setting

The least restrictive environment, which may be different for each child, allows the most interaction with nondisabled peers.

IDEA requires that each school district provide a range of program options for students with disabilities. As you saw in Figure 1.3, these programs range from what is considered the least restrictive to the most restrictive environment. Remember that the concept of "least restrictive environment" is based on the opportunities available for interaction between the student with a disability and nondisabled peers. In practical terms, this means that a family attending an IEP meeting must have the option of choosing from this range of programs in order to obtain the most appropriate education for the child. (Figure 1.3 provides examples of those settings.) The family and the school district must come to an agreement about the setting in which the child's educational needs can most appropriately be met.

The concept of the least restrictive environment was originally envisioned as a relative one—that is, one that must be interpreted anew for each student on the basis of his or her unique learning characteristics. Some professionals today, however, interpret the least restrictive environment in a more general fashion and argue for the inclusion of all students with disabilities in the general education classroom, along with curricular adaptations and the collaboration and teaming of professionals from special and general education. Others call for maintaining the continuum of educational services as represented in Figure 1.3. Let's consider an example.

CASE STUDY

Ana is a student who has engaged in violent and self-destructive behavior. These behaviors have decreased in the special school for students labeled emotionally disturbed that she has been attending, but this is considered a relatively restrictive setting for Ana, since she has no opportunity there to interact with her typically developing peers. At her IEP meeting, her family and teachers decide that Ana's educational goals could best be reached in a less restrictive setting: a special class for students labeled emotionally disturbed on an elementary school campus. There she will have opportunities to participate in social and academic activities with her peers, with her special-class teacher planning and overseeing those experiences. With success, she will have the opportunity for more and more interactions with others.

Advocates of inclusion might suggest that Ana be placed at her grade level in her neighborhood school, with a special education teacher or instructional aide available to monitor her behavior and make curricular adaptations as they are needed. They would argue that only with the models of appropriate behavior available in the general education class and the opportunities for meaningful social interaction provided there can Ana be motivated to change her behavior. This picture of inclusion can succeed only if professionals from special and general education team up to provide individualized educational services for Ana and each included student.

The majority of students identified as exceptional *are receiving their instruction primarily in the general education classroom* (see Figure 1.4). A number of different kinds of programs have been developed to ensure that these students and their teachers receive the support they need. Many involve **collaboration**

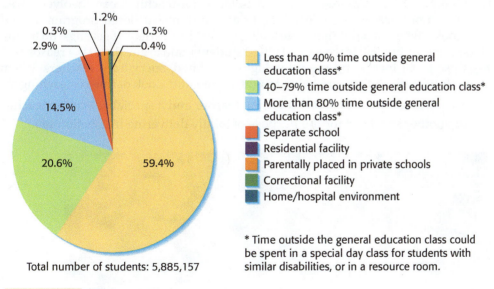

Less than 40% time outside general education class*

40–79% time outside general education class*

More than 80% time outside general education class*

Separate school

Residential facility

Parentally placed in private schools

Correctional facility

Home/hospital environment

Total number of students: 5,885,157

* Time outside the general education class could be spent in a special day class for students with similar disabilities, or in a resource room.

FIGURE 1.4

Percentage of students ages 6 through 21 with disabilities receiving special education and related services under IDEA, Part B, by educational environment: fall 2009

Source: U.S. Department of Education, Office of Special Education Programs, Data Analysis System (DANS). OMB#1820-0517: Part B.

Notes: Includes data from 50 states, the District of Columbia, and outlying areas.
Separate school includes both public and private separate school facilities. Residential includes both public and private residential facilities.

A CLOSER LOOK · Defining Characteristics of Collaboration

- Collaboration is *voluntary*. People cannot be forced to use a particular style in their interactions with others.

- Collaboration requires *parity* among participants. Each person's contribution is equally valued, and each person has equal power in decision-making.

- Collaboration is based on *mutual goals*. Professionals do not have to share all goals in order to collaborate, just one that is specific and important enough to maintain their shared attention.

- Collaboration depends on *shared responsibility* for participation and decision-making. Collaborators

must assume the responsibility of actively engaging in the activity and in the decision-making it entails.

- Individuals who collaborate *share their resources*. Sharing resources of time, knowledge, and materials can enhance the sense of ownership among professionals.

- Individuals who collaborate *share responsibility for outcomes*. Whether the results of collaboration are positive or negative, all participating individuals are responsible for the outcomes.

Source: Adapted from M. Friend & L. Cook, *Interactions: Collaboration skills for school professionals* (White Plains, NY: Longman, 2007), pp. 6–11.

Most exceptional students receive the majority of their instruction in the general education classroom.

between the special educator and the general educator—the foundation for successful inclusive practices. Marilyn Friend and Lynne Cook (2009) define collaboration as "a style for direct interaction between at least two coequal parties voluntarily engaged in shared decision-making as they work toward a common goal" (p. 6). The Closer Look box, "Defining Characteristics of Collaboration," describes the key characteristics of collaboration.

In inclusive settings, special and general educators also work together in team-teaching situations. **Co-teaching,** also called team-teaching, can involve shared instruction of a lesson, a subject area, or an entire instructional program. Friend and Cook (2009) point out that co-teaching is used in a variety of settings, including classrooms for English learners and gifted students, and argue that it is a reasonable response to an increasing press for highly qualified, specialized teachers. When students with disabilities are being taught, Friend and Cook define co-teaching as

the partnering of a general education teacher and a special education teacher or another specialist for the purpose of jointly delivering instruction to a

Co-teaching in an inclusion class can be an enjoyable learning experience for the special educator and the general educator.

© Ellen B. Senisi

diverse group of students, including those with disabilities or other special needs, in a general education setting and in a way that flexibly and deliberately meets their learning needs. (p. 11)

Kohler-Evans (2006) has referred to co-teaching as a "professional marriage." You will read more about this version of marriage in the next chapter.

Another arrangement is the **teacher assistance team** (also known by many other names, such as the *student support team*) (Buck, Polloway, Smith-Thomas et al., 2003). This is a group of teachers and other school professionals (such as school counselors) who work together to assist the general education teacher. Under some circumstances, a team concentrates on keeping children in the general education classroom instead of referring them to special education; a team like this is sometimes known as a **prereferral intervention team.** In other situations, team members provide consultation to teachers or direct services to students who are identified as having special needs but who are placed in the general education classroom.

These arrangements are designed to maintain the student's instruction within the regular classroom. Other kinds of services for students with special needs are called **pullout programs,** since they involve the student leaving the classroom to receive specialized instruction. The traditional organization of the resource room, for example, involves students leaving the general education classroom for specialized instruction in academic areas of need. In many parts of the country, however, this practice is changing, and the resource teacher is operating on the **consultation model**—meeting with teachers to plan instructional adaptations for students as well as providing direct instructional services within the general education classroom. Some other examples of traditional pullout programs are speech and language services, orientation and mobility for students with visual impairments, and physical therapy for students with physical disabilities. Table 1.8 describes the settings in which special education is provided.

> Co-teaching can involve shared instruction of a lesson, a subject area, or an entire instructional program.

> The prereferral intervention team works to keep students in the general education classroom.

Table 1.8 Settings for Delivery of Special Education Services

General education classroom	With supports as needed.
Resource room	A special education teacher provides instruction or support to identified students, either in the general education classroom or in a separate room.
Special classes in elementary or secondary schools	These classes group children by exceptionality—gifted, deaf, learning disabled—and a specialist teacher instructs them together. Individual students may leave the special class for part of the day to receive instruction in the general education classroom, but the majority of their time is usually spent in the special class.
Special schools	Designed exclusively for students with exceptionality. The related services that the students need are usually housed under the same roof. Special schools may be public or private.
Residential schools	Special schools where the students live during the school year. This is considered the most restrictive educational environment for exceptional students, since they have no opportunity to interact with their nondisabled peers.
Home- or hospital-based instruction	Provided by a special education teacher to students who, because of chronic illness or other needs, are taught at home or while they are hospitalized.

ASSISTIVE TECHNOLOGY FOCUS

What Is Assistive Technology?

To ensure effective team decision-making, IEP team members must help family members understand that assistive technology includes both devices and services.

An *assistive technology device* is defined in the Individuals with Disabilities Education Act (IDEA) of 1997 as "any item, piece of equipment, or product system . . . that is used to increase, maintain, or improve the functional capabilities of children with disabilities" (U.S. Code, vol. 20, sec. 1401 [25]). Examples of frequently used devices in classroom settings include:

This young girl benefits from using a slantboard on her classroom desk—straightforward assistive technology.

- Simple communication boards and wallets
- Sophisticated electronic communication devices
- Mobility aids, such as long canes and powered wheelchairs
- Expanded or adapted keyboards, touch windows, and speech recognition systems
- Magnification devices and computer screen reading adaptations

An *assistive technology service* is defined as "any service that directly assists an individual with a disability in the selection, acquisition, or use of an assistive technology device" (U.S. Code, vol. 20, sec. 1401 [25]). Examples of assistive technology services provided in the public schools include physical therapy, occupational therapy, and speech therapy.

Source: Phil Parette and Gale A. McMahan (2002). Excerpt from What should we expect from assistive technology? Being sensitive to family goals, *Teaching Exceptional Children, 35* (1) (2002), 56–61.

In today's schools, virtually all students with disabilities are receiving their education in a regular school building: The U.S. Department of Education (2010) put that number at more than 95.9 percent of students aged 6 to 21. At the classroom level, 48 percent spent less than 21 percent of their time outside the general education classroom (see Figure 1.4). The number of students receiving educational services in public and private separate school facilities, public and private residential facilities, and homebound or hospital settings decreases every year.

Sound challenging? Yes, it is challenging for all of us. But our commitment to normalization and inclusion for all students—especially, in our case, students with disabilities—requires that we give it our best effort. This book is about preparing you to make that effort, and helping you to recognize and ask for the supports that you and your students need.

SUMMARY

- Special education can be understood as services providing an individualized educational program to meet a student's unique learning needs.
- When describing exceptional students, we distinguish between a disability (which refers to a student's condition) and a handicap (which refers to a limitation imposed by his or her environment). We also use people-first language,

which decreases the negative impact of the labels that are commonly used to categorize exceptional children in school.

● Exceptional children make up about 13 percent of the school-age population, but advances in their education have been made only recently. Despite pioneering work by early advocates and educators, it was not until the civil rights movement of the 1960s that significant movement toward full acceptance and participation in society by people with disabilities began.

● In 1975 Congress passed a law that revolutionized education for students with disabilities. That law, the Individuals with Disabilities Education Act, is known as IDEA. IDEA and the Americans with Disabilities Act, passed in 1990, guarantee people with disabilities specific educational and civil rights. Among the most important are the individualized education program and the continuum of educational settings ranging from the least to the most restrictive environment.

● Progress has also been made through litigation. Court cases before and after the passage of IDEA in 1975 influenced its contents and interpretation.

● The options for educational settings for students with disabilities include general education classrooms, resource rooms, special classes, special schools, residential schools, or other placements such as home or hospital.

● Both students and teachers need support from others—family and other school professionals—in order to make inclusion work.

KEY TERMS

special education (page 3)
exceptional (page 3)
disability (page 3)
handicap (page 3)
people-first language (page 7)
early intervention (page 7)
Jean-Marc-Gaspard Itard (page 10)
Edouard Seguin (page 10)
Maria Montessori (page 10)
Samuel Gridley Howe (page 10)
Anne Sullivan Macy (page 10)
Eunice Kennedy Shriver (page 11)
normalization (page 12)
deinstitutionalization (page 12)
least restrictive environment (page 12)

inclusion (page 12)
Individuals with Disabilities Education Act (IDEA) (page 15)
Americans with Disabilities Act (ADA) (page 24)
individualized education (page 26)
Individualized Family Service Plan (IFSP) (page 28)
Individualized Education Program (IEP) (page 28)
collaboration (page 31)
co-teaching (page 32)
teacher assistance team (page 33)
prereferral intervention team (page 33)
pullout programs (page 33)
consultation model (page 33)

USEFUL RESOURCES

● *Teaching Exceptional Children* is a journal of the Council for Exceptional Children, and it is filled with practical ideas for teachers based on research from the field.

● D. Hayden, C. Takemoto, W. Anderson, and S. Chitwood, *Negotiating the special education maze: A guide for parents and teachers* (4th ed.) (Bethesda,

MD: Woodbine House, 2008) is a guide to helping parents and teachers understand the special education system.

- M. K. Cohen et al., *Survival guide for the first-year special education teacher,* revised (Upper Saddleback River, NJ: Prentice Hall, 2004). Developed by teachers who survived their first five years in the special education system, this guide offers tips on many aspects of teaching, from organizing your classroom to managing stress.

- Council for Exceptional Children (CEC) website available at **www.cec. sped.org.** CEC is the major professional organization in special education, serving children with disabilities through their families, teachers, and other advocates.

- B. D. Bateman and M.A. Linden, *Better IEPs: How to develop legally correct and educationally useful programs* (4th ed.) (Arlington, VA: Council for Exceptional Children, 2006). This book provides help with complying with the legal mandates of the IEP by following a three-step process.

- You will find a treasure trove of information for teachers and families about children with disabilities, the law that guides their education, and their educational needs at the *National Dissemination Center for Children with Disabilities* website: **http://www.nichcy.org.**

- *Wrightslaw* is a website devoted to information about special education law and advocacy for children with disabilities. It's at **http://www.wrightslaw. com.**

- *The IRIS Center* has developed a collection of resources for teachers and other school professionals to help them work effectively with students with disabilities. Start with the module called *What Do You See? Perceptions of Disability* (**http://iris.peabody.vanderbilt.edu/da/chalcycle.htm**), which will help you examine your own attitudes toward people with disabilities. Another module related to the content of this chapter is *The Pre-Referral Process: Procedures for Supporting Students with Academic and Behavioral Concerns* at **http://iris.peabody.vanderbilt.edu/preref/chalcycle.htm/.** If you have never used an IRIS module, click on *Navigating an IRIS Module* in the purple column on the right on each module's front page.

 PORTFOLIO ACTIVITIES

All of the following activities will help the student meet

 CEC Initial Content Standard 1: Foundations, and Initial Content Standard 9: Professional and Ethical Practice.

1. Begin a portfolio journal in which you reflect on your own attitudes and feelings toward people with disabilities. Which of your feelings are based on experiences, and which on media reports or stereotypes? What do you hope to learn from this course that might change your attitudes?

2. Volunteer at a service agency that serves children with disabilities in the age range that interests you. Call your local United Way, March of Dimes, or children's hospital, and ask about volunteering opportunities. Include your responses to this experience in your portfolio journal.

3. How do people in your community refer to exceptional individuals? During the first few weeks of this term, keep a file of newspaper clippings of articles that relate to exceptional individuals, special education, or related

services. What types of issues are discussed? What types of language are used? What conclusions can you draw about the role of exceptional individuals in the community, their acceptance, and their visibility? Include these clippings in your portfolio.

4. Observe media coverage of people with disabilities or issues important to them. Do newspapers and television newscasts cover these topics in a fair and unbiased manner? Write a letter to the editor suggesting more coverage or more positive coverage, perhaps concerning access, bias, aging, employment, or medical advances. Include your letter in your portfolio.

 To access Portfolio Activities for this chapter and other useful study resources including an interactive eBook, related web links, quizzes, flashcards, and videos, visit the Education CourseMate website at www.cengagebrain.com.

Making Special Education Work for All Children

Learning Objectives

After reading this chapter, the reader will:

- Describe three key characteristics of the population of students receiving special education services.

- Explain the concerns over disproportionate representation of students from culturally and linguistically different groups in special education services.

- Identify the major goals for students receiving special education services in inclusive settings.

- List several curricular and instructional methods designed to meet the needs of diverse learners.

- Discuss the roles of different forms of assessment of students with disabilities in the schools.

- Describe the components of the Framework of Support for students with disabilities.

A trip to India several years ago provoked my (Nancy Hunt's) reflections on the status of American children with disabilities. India is a gorgeous county with the largest and densest population in the world. Disability among both children and adults is very visible there, especially physical disabilities and blindness. There are effective and long-standing programs to meet individuals' needs, but not nearly enough for all. There is a national law similar to IDEA, requiring the education of students with disabilities, but it is not enforced. So there are literally millions of children and families whose needs for education and an improved quality of life are not being met. A very canny young girl said to me, as she begged, "Madame, you are lucky. You are so lucky, Madame." I have thought of her words many times since then.

In the United States we often complain about the inadequacies of our system for educating children with disabilities. Pick an area—the IEP, family involvement, assessment, related services—and search for it on Google Scholar. You will find a wealth of journal articles documenting the problems. Of course, that too is the American way. We identify problems in order to find solutions, and to improve the status quo. But in India I was reminded that we *are* lucky. We have federal laws that require the free and appropriate public education of every child with a disability—and they are enforced. We have a system for the education of their teachers, which is rigorous and widely available. Families are invited to participate in their child's education at every turn. New technologies help our students read and communicate with increasing effectiveness. Our system is propelled by American values of human rights and equality for all. It is not perfect, but I believe that its existence is something to be proud of.

This chapter will identify some of the problems in our education system for children with disabilities, particularly the **disproportionate representation** of some groups of children in special education services. But it also will introduce to you some of the solutions that professionals have identified since the passage of IDEA in 1975, such as the inclusion of children with disabilities in general education classrooms and the services and supports that allow them to remain there. Our profession invites you to enter the fray. Help us identify the problems, but offer solutions to them too, on behalf of all children attending American schools.

The Students in Special Education

The students receiving special education services are very much like any other group of American schoolchildren, except for three important factors. The first is related to **gender:** boys outnumber girls by a 2 to 1 ratio. Figure 2.1 shows this graphically.

> Boys are significantly more likely to receive special education services than girls.

The preponderance of males is more evident in the so-called "judgment" categories of disability—those which are not physically observable and require a judgment as to whether they occur. As an example, about 80 percent of students labeled emotionally disturbed and about 70 percent of those identified as learning disabled are males (U.S. Department of Education, 2006). One set of explanations for these gender differences in identification of students for special education is sometimes known as "the three B's" (Coutinho, Oswald, & King, 2001): *biological differences* between girls and boys (see, for example, Becker, Berkley, Hampson, Herman, & Young, 2007); *behavioral differences* between girls and boys; and *bias* in special education referral and assessment procedures (Arms, Bickett, & Graf, 2008; Coutinho & Oswald, 2006).

Internationally, disability occurs more often in females than in males (World Health Association, 2011), and there is concern that girls with disabilities are less likely to be educated, and that they experience greater degrees of stigma and discrimination than boys (United Nations Convention on the Rights of Persons with Disabilities, 2006). (See A Closer Look for more information on global disability.)

FIGURE 2.1

Gender of students aged 6–21 served under IDEA, Part B in the U.S. and outlying areas

Source: U.S. Department of Education, Office of Special Education Programs Data Analysis Systems (DANS), OMB #1820-0043: "Children with Disabilities Receiving Special Education Under Part B of the Individuals with Disabilities Education Act," 2009. Data updated as of July 15, 2010.

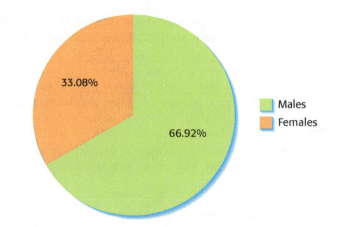

The disabilities more likely to be identified around the world, however, are the "non-judgment" disabilities—those that are observable and related to physical functioning, such as blindness (which is much more common in countries with inadequate health care systems), deafness, and mobility-limiting physical disabilities. But in the United States, where the larger categories of students receiving special education services are the "judgment" categories, boys dominate.

The second area where students in special education are somewhat different from the rest of American schoolchildren is in their socioeconomic status. You will read in Chapter 3 that poverty is a significant risk factor for disability. In 2000, Fujiura and Yamaki found that 28 percent of children with disabilities lived below the federal poverty threshold, as opposed to 16 percent of children without disabilities. So families of children with disabilities are more likely to be poor, and poor families are more likely to have children with disabilities.

The last factor has to do with ethnicity. Children from American Indian/ Alaska Native and African American backgrounds are overrepresented in special education services, and underrepresented in programs for students identified as gifted and talented. Our next topic pulls together those three differences: the overrepresentation of boys, children from poor families, and specific cultural/ racial backgrounds within special education classrooms and programs.

? Pause and Reflect

Many people are fascinated and puzzled by the fact that boys outnumber girls in most special education categories. What do you see as some of the possible school-based reasons for the preponderance of boys in special education services? Are there conditions that could be changed to improve outcomes for boys? ●

Disproportionate Representation of Minority Children

Special education professionals continue to be concerned about the disproportionate representation of students from culturally diverse backgrounds in special education services.

The issue of disproportionate representation of minority children in special education has a long history, grounded in the history of racial discrimination within the United States (Smedley, 2007; Skiba et al., 2008), and it has not yet been resolved (Harry & Klingner, 2006). Let's review the background on this important issue. What would you expect the racial breakdown of students receiving special education services to look like? In the United States, where in the 2009-10 school year 54 percent of the school-age population was white, 17 percent African American,

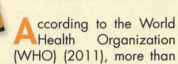

A CLOSER LOOK   Disability Around the World

According to the World Health Organization (WHO) (2011), more than a billion people around the world live with some form of disability, or about 15 percent of the global population—and the number is growing. About 95 million of that number are children aged 0 to 14; 13 million of those children have a "severe disability."

WHO uses a broad definition of disability:

The *International Classification of Functioning, Disability and Health* (ICF) . . . defines disability as an umbrella term for impairments, activity limitations, and participation restrictions. Disability refers to the negative aspects of the interaction between individuals with a health condition (such as cerebral palsy, Down syndrome, depression) and personal and environmental factors (such as negative attitudes, inaccessible transportation and public buildings, and limited social supports). (p.6)

Here are some excerpts from the WHO/World Bank *World Report on Disability* (2011):

The number of people with disabilities is growing. This is because populations are aging—older people have a higher risk of disability—and because of the global increase in chronic health conditions associated with disability, such as diabetes, cardiovascular diseases, and mental illness. . . . Patterns of disability in a particular country are influenced by trends in health conditions and trends in environmental and other factors—such as road traffic crashes, natural disasters, conflict, diet, and substance abuse. (p.7)

Among other factors reported:

- Women with disabilities are dually handicapped, by gender discrimination as well as disability barriers.
- School enrollment rates differ among impairments, with children with physical impairments generally faring better than those with intellectual or sensory impairments.
- Those most excluded from the labor market are often those with mental health difficulties or intellectual impairments.
- Disability disproportionately affects vulnerable populations. Results from the *World Health Survey* indicate a higher disability prevalence in lower income countries than in higher income countries.
- Children from poorer households and those in ethnic minority groups are at significantly higher risk of disability than other children.

In Chapter 3 we will discuss risk factors for disability, and you will notice that many of the risk factors we discuss—prematurity and low birth weight and exposure to environmental toxins, for example—occur more frequently in poor countries.

—————
To read a summary of the WHO/World Bank report, go to http://whqlibdoc.who.int/hq/2011/who_nmh_vip_11.01_eng.pdf.

22 percent Latino, 5 percent Asian, 1.2 percent American Indian/Alaska Native and .7 percent members of two or more races (National Center for Education Statistics, 2011), shouldn't the representation in special education be approximately the same? In both the past and the present, this has not been the case, and the disparities between expectations and reality have presented a significant problem for our field. Table 2.1 shows the risk ratio for the five largest categories; you can see that the groups with the largest risk ratio (and therefore the greatest overrepresentation) are African Americans and American Indian/Alaska natives.

In a classic and often-cited article in *Exceptional Children,* Lloyd Dunn (1968) reported that a disproportionately high number of African American, American Indian, Mexican, and Puerto Rican children from low socioeconomic backgrounds were being placed in special education classes for students with mild intellectual disabilities (then the term mental retardation was used). Jane Mercer (1973) provided support for Dunn's findings when she reported that three times as many African American and four times as many Mexican American children were being placed in classes for students with mild intellectual disabilities as compared to their numbers in the general school population. This situation is referred to as **overrepresentation,**

Overrepresentation occurs when there are more students in a group than would be expected from the population.

Table 2.1 Risk Ratios for Disabilities within Racial/Ethnic Categories

	American Indian/ Alaskan Native	Asian/ Pacific Islander	African American (not Hispanic)	Hispanic	White (not Hispanic)
All disabilities	1.35	0.48	1.46	0.87	0.92

Note: A *Relative Risk Ratio* value of 1.0 indicates equal representation; values between 0 and 1 indicate underrepresentation; and values greater than 1 indicate overrepresentation (Coutino & Oswald, 2006).

Source: From R.J. Skiba, A.B. Simmons, S. Ritter, A.C. Gibb, M.K. Rausch, J. Cuadrado, & C.G. Chung (2008). Achieving equity in special education: History, status, and current challenges. *Exceptional Children 74*(3), 269. Drawn from U.S. Department of Education, Office of Special Education and Rehabilitative Services (2006). *26th annual report to Congress on the implementation of the Individuals with Disabilities Education Act, 2004.* Washington, DC: Westat.

or a representation greater than would be expected based on the actual number of students from that group in school. Figure 2.2 illustrates the overrepresentation of students from the largest "minority" groups in three special education categories over the last 30 years. African-American and American Indian students have been overrepresented in those categories throughout that time period.

The studies by Mercer and Dunn described above are nearly thirty years old. But the overrepresentation and underrepresentation of individuals from certain ethnic cultures in categories of special education persist today (Donovan & Cross, 2002; Harry & Klingner, 2006, 2007). Russell Skiba and his colleagues note that

FIGURE 2.2

Overrepresentation of students from the largest minority groups in three special education categories over the last 30 years

Source: A. L. Sullivan, E. A'Vant, J. Baker, D. Chandler, S. Graves, E. McKinney, & T. Sayles (2009). Confronting inequity in special education, Part I: Understanding the problem of disproportionality. NASP *Communiqué,* Vol. 38, #1. http://www.nasponline.org/publications/cq/mocq381disproportionality.aspx

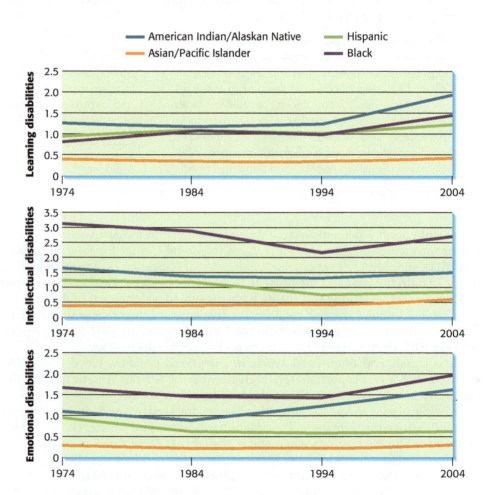

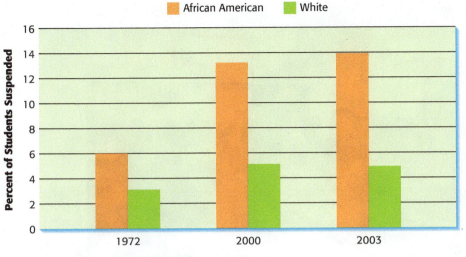

Note: Derived from U.S. Department of Education, 2004

FIGURE 2.3

Disproportionality in school discipline at the national level: 1972, 2000, 2003

Source: Russ Skiba (2008). *Changing the data, changing our minds: Disproportionality and improving schools.* Presented at the Office of Special Education Programs Project Directors' Conference, Washington, DC. Available at http://www.indiana.edu/~equity/resources.php/

despite the ongoing examination of the issues"... the full complexity of minority disproportionality has not yet been fully understood, nor has a clear or comprehensive picture emerged concerning the causes of disproportionality" (p. 265).

Russell Skiba and his colleagues (Skiba, 2008; Skiba et al., 2011) have also been studying the representation of African American and Latino students in school disciplinary actions. For over 30 years, research has indicated that African American students are significantly more likely than other groups to be referred to the school office for disciplinary action, suspended and/or expelled, or on the receiving end of corporal punishment. Skiba's study of disciplinary actions in 364 elementary and middle schools found that African-Americans receive harsher punishments than white students do for the same behaviors. Figure 2.3 shows the differences in school disciplinary rates between African American and white students across a 30-year period. These numbers are of particular concern because 30 to 50 percent of suspended students are repeat offenders, leading some to suspect that suspension serves as a reinforcement rather than a deterrent (Skiba, 2008). Suspension also correlates with school dropout rates and juvenile incarceration. A recent report analyzing discipline data for nearly one million secondary students followed for over six years in Texas indicates that 75 percent of middle and high school students with disabilities were suspended, expelled, or both at least once, compared to about 55 percent of students without a disability (Council of State Governments Justice Center, 2011). These figures will no doubt lead school districts all over this country to examine their practices.

Underrepresentation occurs when fewer students receive services than would be expected based on their representation in the general school population. African American, Hispanic, and American Indian students, for example, are underrepresented in gifted and talented programs.

Underrepresentation occurs when there are fewer students in a group than would be expected from the population.

African American and Latino children are underrepresented in programs for gifted students.

Factors Contributing to Over- and Underrepresentation

Why are some culturally diverse groups overrepresented in classes for children with disabilities, and others not? Do the statistics accurately reflect the incidence of exceptionalities among culturally diverse students? In addressing these questions, we must consider the referral, assessment, and placement process. We must also concern ourselves with the access these children have to educational services, along with environmental and poverty factors.

One factor in overrepresentation may be how culturally diverse children are referred to special education. Teachers most commonly refer children for

© AP Photo/Rich Pedroncelli

Teachers are influential judges of their students' problems and potential.

assessment, and referral is a subjective process, depending on local norms—that is, the child doing poorly stands out more in a class of children performing on grade level than within a class where all children are performing poorly (Donovan & Cross, 2002). The relatively high levels of referral for African American and Hispanic students initially led to the suspicion that bias caused teachers to refer students who were actually performing at an acceptable level. Recent research suggests that more subtle factors are at work when teachers make referrals (Harry & Klingner, 2006).

Another variable contributing to the overrepresentation of culturally diverse children in special education has been the use of assessment instruments that many believe are culturally biased, particularly the IQ test. There is a long history of debate about the appropriateness of IQ tests to determine eligibility for special education services, as you will see in the discussion of the *Larry P.* and *Diana* cases to follow, and there is little doubt that problems do occur. Misperceptions between the student and the evaluator, cross-cultural stereotyping, and item bias can lead to poor performance, particularly among students who have limited proficiency in English (Skiba et al., 2008). The National Research Council report on minority students in special and gifted education programs concluded that approaches more closely tied to the design of interventions, such as performance-based assessments (based on how students are actually achieving in school) and curriculum-based measures (based on whether or not the student is mastering the curriculum, or standards), will be better tools to determine student eligibility for special education (Donovan & Cross, 2002). But the authors of that report acknowledge that a movement away from IQ, with its long history of use, will require major changes in training and procedures—and greater changes in beliefs and attitudes:

Fair assessment of children from diverse backgrounds is challenging and complex.

> Even more daunting is the change required in the thinking of professionals and the public about disabilities—a change from assumptions of fixed abilities and internal child traits to new assumptions about the malleability of skills and the powerful effects of instruction and positive environments. (p. 287)

Poverty is a third factor that affects representation rates in special education classes, and poverty occurs disproportionately in African American, Hispanic, and American Indian families. Poverty jeopardizes nutrition, quality of medical care, and living conditions. Poor women must often work even when a pregnancy is at risk. These factors can contribute to children being born premature or with low birth weight. As you will learn in Chapter 3, children born at risk are more likely to develop learning problems and disabilities. In addition, poverty often contributes to stress and maternal depression, which affects the overall mental health of a family.

Finally, studies have demonstrated that children from poor environments are more likely to be exposed to lead and other environmental toxins, are more likely to be exposed to alcohol and tobacco in utero, and have micronutrient deficiencies (Donovan & Cross, 2002). For more information on how poverty affects children, visit the Children's Defense Fund website and our Education CourseMate website at **CengageBrain.com.** It is also important to keep in mind that poor children are more likely to attend schools in which there is a higher degree of teacher turnover, fewer experienced teachers, larger class sizes, and fewer resources (Skiba et al., 2008); in other words, "reduced educational resources and fewer opportunities for quality instruction" (p. 274). Harry and Klingner (2006) describe these and other related factors as **school-based risk.**

Lack of opportunity to learn because of adverse conditions within a school can be characterized as school-based risk.

Reasons for underrepresentation within special education classrooms are as varied as the reasons for overrepresentation and may differ according to ethnicity. The low national prevalence figures for Hispanics/Latinos in classes for students with intellectual disabilities and emotional disturbance, for example, may be related in part to the advent of bilingual education programs. These programs were only in their infancy at the time of the Dunn (1968) and Mercer (1973) studies, but they sometimes provide an alternative to special education programs. Aware that the language of instruction in special education is primarily English, bilingual teachers may be reluctant to refer students to special education out of a belief that their needs can better be met in a bilingual setting (Artiles, Harry, Reschly, & Chinn, 2002).

As with Latinos, there are several reasons why Asians may be underrepresented in classes for children with disabilities. (We should acknowledge here the tremendous diversity within the Asian culture—it is important to question generalizations knowing that these statements will not be true of all families who are identified as "Asian.") First, due to norms and beliefs within their cultures, some Asian parents are reluctant to seek external assistance for a child with disabilities (Chan & Chen, 2011). Parents may be hesitant to grant permission to school personnel to test their child or to consider special education placement. A second variable is the fact that, as a group (with some exceptions), Asians in the United States enjoy a relatively high standard of living. With the exception of the second wave of Southeast Asian immigrants beginning in 1978, most of the Asian immigrants entering the country have middle- or upper-middle-class backgrounds with a relatively high educational level. The children from these families are at less risk for special education placement than many of the children from cultural groups that experience poverty. In addition, educators may also have a tendency to stereotype Asian children as being very quiet. Thus, children who are seriously withdrawn may be passed off as having "typical Asian behaviors" and are not referred for possible special education services. Recent data suggests that there is a slightly higher incidence of autism and hearing impairment in Asian children (U.S. Department of Education, 2006).

The disproportionately low placement of American Indian, African American, and Latino children in classes for students labeled as gifted and talented is also an important issue. For a child to be placed in such a class, the child's potential must be recognized by someone, usually a teacher. He or she must then be referred, tested, and ultimately placed. A child will not be placed, however, if no one recognizes his or her abilities and makes a referral. We will discuss this issue at greater length in Chapter 14.

● *Litigation Relating to Over- and Underrepresentation*   A number of critical court cases have addressed the issues of overrepresentation in special education and the appropriate assessment and placement of students from culturally diverse backgrounds. The landmark *Brown v. Board of Education of Topeka, Kansas* (1954) decision set the stage for several important court cases concerning children with disabilities. In the *Brown* decision, the U.S. Supreme Court ruled that

In *Brown v. Board of Education,* the Supreme Court ruled that "separate but equal" schools were unconstitutional.

separate schools for African American and white students cannot be considered equal and are therefore unconstitutional. This ruling provided the precedent for parents and advocates who maintained that children with disabilities were being unfairly denied equal educational opportunities.

Diana v. Board of Education (1970) was a state class-action suit that addressed the overrepresentation of children from non-English-speaking backgrounds in special education classes in California. It was filed on behalf of nine Mexican American children who had been placed in classes for students with intellectual disabilities based on the results of IQ tests given in English. Advocates for the children argued that their assessment had been unfair, since it was not conducted in Spanish, their native language. The case was settled with the agreement that children must be tested in both their primary language and English when special education placement is being considered. When the children involved in the case were re-tested more appropriately, seven of the nine were no longer eligible for special education.

In *Larry P. v. Riles* (1979), the issue was the disproportionate number of African American students in classes for students with what was then referred to as *educable mental retardation* in California. The plaintiffs maintained that standardized IQ tests, which were used as the basis for placement of these students, were culturally biased against African American children. The *Larry P.* ruling eliminated the use of IQ tests to place African American students in classes for students with intellectual disabilities in California. As you have read, the overrepresentation of African American children in special education remains a cause of great concern, despite changes in assessment practices spurred by the *Larry P.* decision.

Table 2.2 lists and summarizes the key court cases we have described above. These cases are but a small sample of the numerous court decisions rendered on behalf of culturally and linguistically diverse students. They illustrate the inequities inherent in our educational system, many of which are so institutionalized that it often requires the threat of litigation to inspire changes.

IDEA reflects many of the decisions handed down by the courts through the years, and changes in the law have required that disproportionality be addressed by states and school districts. The provisions in IDEA require testing in the child's native language by trained professionals, nondiscriminatory assessment, due process, least restrictive environment, appropriate education, individualization, and confidentiality. In addition, IDEA provides certain procedural safeguards for language minority students by requiring written or verbal communication be provided to parents or guardians in the language of the home. All meetings or hearings must have a qualified translator. The IDEA 2004 regulations require states with high levels of disproportionality to use part of their IDEA funds for

Diana v. Board of Education mandated that children in California be tested in their primary language for special education services.

Larry P. v. Riles addressed the fairness of IQ testing for African American children.

Table 2.2 Selected Court Challenges to Inequity in Education

Case	At Issue	Outcome
Brown v. Board of Education of Topeka (U.S. Supreme Court, 1954)	African American children attended separate schools.	"Separate is not equal"; American schools ordered to desegregate.
Diana v. State Board of Education (California, 1972)	Children from non-English-speaking backgrounds were placed in special education classes based on their performance on IQ tests administered in English.	Children must be assessed for special education placement in their native language.
Larry P. v. Riles (California, 1972, 1979, 1984, 1986)	African American children were overrepresented in special education classes based on their performance on IQ tests.	Tests were deemed culturally biased and may not be used to determine eligibility for special education services in California.

early intervening services (such as Response to Intervention (RTI), described later in this chapter), with the expectation that those interventions might reduce disproportionality.

Skiba and his colleagues (2008) report research that describes the ease with which teachers talk about poverty, but the difficulty they have talking about race. They admonish us:

> ... educators and policymakers seeking effective interventions to close special education equity gaps must be willing to openly discuss and address issues of race, ethnicity, gender, class, culture, and language. (p. 280)

The multifaceted, complex nature of this issue demands additional serious study and a commitment on the part of all of us to assess our assumptions and our practices with minority students—particularly African American males.

? Pause and Reflect

Examining attitudes and practices related to race and ethnicity remains difficult in today's United States. We *all* have biases and hold unconscious stereotyped views about other groups. Have you had the opportunity to think about how your own values and beliefs about race have developed and changed since you were a child? Do you think your attitudes and values will affect your practice as a teacher or school professional? ●

The Challenges of Inclusion

As more children with disabilities are spending some or all of their school time in general education classrooms, we recognize that virtually all teachers may be teaching students with disabilities. The number of students with disabilities spending less than 21 percent of their time outside the regular (general education) class increased steadily in the 10 years between 1995 and 2004; see Figure 2.4 for an illustration (U.S. Department of Education, 2006). Therefore, each educational team—including special educators and general educators—works

> Increasingly larger numbers of children with disabilities spend the greater part of their day in general education classrooms.

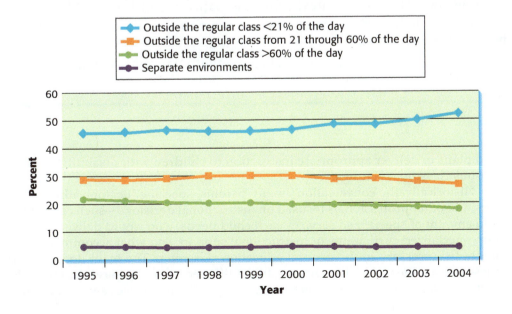

FIGURE 2.4

Percentage of students age 6–21 with disabilities by educational environment

Source: U.S. Department of Education, Office of Special Education Programs. Data Analysis System (DANS). OMB # 1820-0517: "Part B. Individuals with Disabilities Education Act. Implementation of FAPE Requirements." 1995–2004. Data updated as of July 30, 2005. These data are for the 50 states, District of Columbia, BIA schools, Puerto Rico, and the four outlying areas.

FIRST PERSON

Conflicting Thoughts About Inclusion

Ellen is the mother of Max, a young boy with cerebral palsy, and his little sister Sabrina. She blogs about her children at http://www.lovethatmax.com. Here, in excerpts from two blog entries from the same week, she illustrates the tension between "the special needs world" and a more integrated, inclusive experience for her son.

IN THE INNER CIRCLE, THERE IS NO "WEIRD"

Friday, I was filling out a form for a program I was taking Max to the next morning, sponsored by the local Arc. *(Author's note: The Arc is an advocacy organization for people with intellectual and developmental disabilities.)* The kids play games, do crafts, have lunch, hang out.

> Name: Max
>
> Nickname: Spaghetti Sauce Max
>
> Child likes: Best friend = Caleb, spaghetti, the color purple, trucks, cars, spaghetti, cars, coloring, did I mention spaghetti?
>
> Dislikes: Anything loud, any food
>
> Describe what motivates your child: Discussing spaghetti and sauce and repeatedly saying, "Max eats spaghetti with sauce." Also, anything purple.
>
> How does he/she calm down?: See above

As I wrote, I stepped outside of my head. And wondered whether the staffer reading the forms would think Max was . . . quirky. Weird, even. I find his obsessions cute and fascinating (mostly). But the act of writing them down made me ponder how someone else might view his spaghetti fixation.

I have been thinking a lot lately about how people see Max. This is not simply because I want him to fit in, so to speak. I ache for people to look beyond his disabilities and see the charming, funny, smart, complex kid I know. I want them to see *Max,* all of Max. Not just a child with cerebral palsy.

Then I got a grip: In the special needs community, there is no such thing as weird. For the people at the programs we go to, the teachers at Max's school, the therapists in his life, quirky is the *norm.* I may have a ways to go to get the world at large to see the wonderfulness of Max. But in the inner circle of special needs that we inhabit, he is who he is—and people usually adore him for it.

I finished up the forms and packed up some lunch in a container (one guess what it was). The next morning, Sabrina and I drove Max to his program. The woman running it glanced at his forms and smiled.

"Hello, Spaghetti Sauce Max," she said.

****

and plans to deliver appropriate instruction to children with disabilities across various classroom settings.

Historically, the conversation among parents, special educators, administrators, and other professionals focused on instructional decisions—such as the type and amount of specialized services each child needs, who would deliver instruction, specialized curriculum, or instructional support, and what accommodations might be necessary in the general education classroom. The team documented these instructional decisions in the child's IEP, recording all services, methods, materials, curricula, and assessment approaches. The IEP, as we saw in Chapter 1,

ARE WE TOO SUCKED INTO SPECIAL NEEDS WORLD?

Tonight, I got unnerved when I saw a new comment on the post about Max and sleepaway camp. The very wise Gina, who blogs at Inky Ed, is all about inclusion; she mentioned sending Max to a camp for all kids, not just "special" ones. Her little boy, Mac, is in a mainstreamed school in Australia.

CLICK. That was the sound of the proverbial lightbulb going on over my head.

THUD. That was the sound of my heart, dispirited that I hadn't thought of it myself.

I sent Gina a few messages on Twitter. "I wouldn't nag if I didn't think you had it in you to challenge your own thinking and be open to a different path for Max," she responded.

I have been thinking about nothing else since.

Every extracurricular activity in Max's life is geared toward kids with special needs: softball league, Sunday programs, school, probably camp. He has not one so-called typical friend.

Max is all special needs, all the time. And when it comes to bringing him up, so am I, it seems.

Am I doing Max wrong?

I'm thinking the answer is yes.

Trust me, I don't mean I'm a crappy mother for not having done inclusionary activities. Max has benefitted from the adapted ones we've tried. The personal attention and direction he gets from professionals and volunteers has helped him develop, gain confidence in himself and thrive. I am beyond grateful for them. I appreciate how they welcome Max, quirks and all, which I just wrote about. But it could do Max a world of good to be at activities with typical kids.

Months ago, I got recommendations for special needs camps from moms I know and Max's therapists. We applied to a sleepaway camp and also a day camp, got accepted. Like me, friends and family thought it could be good for Max. They didn't think about the potential for inclusion; why would they? It seems like a no-brainer that he'd benefit from camp for kids with special needs. I drank that camp Kool-Aid too.

No doubt, a special needs camp *will* be great for Max, especially because it's his first year at one. But including him in a typical camp could open up a whole new world for him. Realistically, it won't happen this summer. I'll have do to my research; I know of no camps that have a mix of kids. Calls will be made. Much convincing might have to be done. Much paperwork would definitely ensue. I'd need to find Max a one-on-one aide. But I don't just think I can pull it off—I *know* I can, because I will basically make *anything* happen for this child (excluding the other day when he asked to take a spaghetti bath).

Including Max in our local school isn't the right thing for him now; they aren't fully able to accommodate all of his therapies. But camp? That's a real possibility. Who knows, I might even be able to get him into Boy Scouts.

Tonight, I stepped out of Special Needs World and noticed places with other possibilities. I'm a little scared, a little how-are-we-gonna-do-this, but mostly, excited.

Source: Love That Max: A blog about kids with special needs (and parents who adore them), http://www.lovethatmax.com

---

described and provided education services, documented student progress, and established accountability.

While the IEP continues to be a critical component of special education programming, its role is changing—some question whether it will continue to be an integral part of how we plan for children in the future. Why? The separate, though often parallel systems of general education and special education practice are being challenged more vigorously than ever before due to new national educational requirements that apply to both general and special education. Most of these requirements have come about through educational reform,

> The role of the IEP is changing as emphasis is placed on access to the core curriculum.

Only by being around peers can an individual get to know other people of the same age. Here Eliza Schaaf rests during a painting project with a friend.

Source: http://www.mailtribune.com/apps/pbcs.dll/article?AID=/20110519/NEWS/105190334&cid=sitesearch&Template=photos

Federal law mandates that all American children have access to the core curriculum or content standards.

including the education act (P.L. 107-110) now entitled No Child Left Behind (NCLB). (Congress may change this title by the time you read this, since the law is due for reauthorization.) Like IDEA, the federal Elementary and Secondary Education Act (ESEA), originally passed in 1965 as a component of the federal "War on Poverty," is reauthorized and amended by Congress every several years. The "No Child Left Behind Act" (or NCLB) was the title of the 2001 amendments to ESEA.

Advocates of inclusion have identified two primary goals for students with disabilities in general education classrooms: access to the general education curriculum and social integration.

The Framework of Support: Goals for Students Receiving Special Education Services

Our definition of inclusion in Chapter 1 speaks not just of *placement,* but also of *supports.* Placement in a general education setting by itself will not usually improve educational achievement for a child with an IEP. The general education teacher cannot provide individualized education to one or more students without the help of other professionals—usually specialists in the disability area, and others providing related services—the special education teacher, speech-language pathologist, adaptive physical education teacher, orientation and mobility specialist, school nurse, and so on. Some of the supports for the general education teacher are described in the box in Chapter 1, "Support for General Education Teachers." But there is also a set of supports needed by the student with disabilities, which we describe in the **Framework of Support.** The framework outlines the supports necessary to help a student meet the major goals of education: access to the core curriculum and standards designated by each state, and **social integration**—inclusion, acceptance, and the development of friendships.

Inclusion must involve more than simply placement of a student in the general education classroom.

In Chapters 5 through 14 of our book, you will read about specific supports that may be appropriate for students with specific disabilities, but all of these are based on the basic principle of special education: individualized learning. This requires **differentiated teaching**—teaching that is designed to meet the individual needs of a student or small group of students. You can see that in order for the framework to be effective, *collaboration* between general educators, special educators, related service providers, and families must occur.

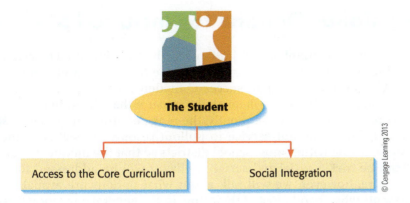

© Cengage Learning 2013

FIGURE 2.5

Goals for the student with
an IEP

Curriculum for Students Receiving Special Education Services

What should exceptional students learn in school? Curriculum options include the core general education curriculum; specialized curricula in areas such as social skills or study skills; specialized skills like those in the expanded core curriculum for students with visual impairments, or a **functional** or **life-skills** curriculum (which teaches some students the skills of everyday living that they may not acquire without explicit instruction). Traditionally, the IEP team determines what skills a student needs to be taught and the IEP serves as the curriculum blueprint for instruction. Figure 2.5 illustrates the goals of the framework of support.

Access to the General Education Curriculum

Today, however, special education can be defined as the services required by a student to facilitate access to the general education curriculum. According to federal law (IDEA and the Elementary and Secondary Education Act [ESEA]), all students must participate in the general education curriculum—teachers must even tie alternative curriculum content to the curriculum standards. ESEA includes tenets that require all states to develop curriculum standards and to develop tests that assess those standards, and many states have now adopted the national Common Core State Standards, which were developed by the National Governors Association and the Council of Chief State School Officers (Porter, McMaken, Hwang, & Yang, 2011).

Pause and Reflect

Before 1973, fewer than 50 percent of American children with disabilities attended school at all, and when they did go to school, they attended special, segregated schools for children with similar disabilities. Now virtually all American children with disabilities attend school, and most of them spend the majority of their school day alongside their nondisabled peers in "regular" classrooms. So much has changed in such a short time! Do you agree that the inclusion of children with disabilities in general education reflects traditional American values? What is the downside of such fast-moving social change? ●

Instructional Options for Included Students

The fact that greater numbers of students with disabilities have access to the general education curriculum poses a challenge for school professionals. What should teachers do to help them succeed? Evidence-based practices are a step in the right direction, but more is needed to ensure that all students will benefit from the core curriculum. Consequently, the range of program options discussed in Chapter 1, from itinerant service to pullout resource to self-contained programs, are available within most school districts so that the unique needs of each student can be met. Specialized service delivery will be addressed throughout this text—here, however, we will talk about what options are available for the many students who spend most of their time in the general education classroom. How can we, as either general or special education teachers, work together to target best practices for ALL of our students?

> Evidence-based practices are those teaching practices verified by research as effective.

Placing all students with disabilities in general education classrooms and adhering to standards will not address all the learning challenges that caused these children to be declared eligible for special education in the first place. In order for all students to learn in the general education classroom, a series of practices, instructional strategies, and supports must be in place for students with learning and behavioral challenges. First among them is special education itself. The National Dissemination Center (2010) quotes IDEA:

> By definition, special education is "specially designed instruction." And IDEA defines *that* term as follows:
>
> (3) **Specially designed instruction** means adapting, as appropriate to the needs of an eligible child under this part, the content, methodology, or delivery of instruction—
>
> (i) To address the unique needs of the child that result from the child's disability; and
>
> (ii) To ensure access of the child to the general curriculum, so that the child can meet the educational standards within the jurisdiction of the public agency that apply to all children. [§300.39(b)(3)]

Thus, special education involves adapting the "content, methodology, or delivery of instruction."

Special education—specially designed instruction—is part of the set of supports that most included students with disabilities will require in the general education classroom. And as far as is feasible, special education instruction should involve the use of scientifically proven or evidence-based instructional practices.

Evidence-Based Practices

NCLB made many sweeping changes in school practices; prominent among them was the expectation that schools use scientifically proven practices to teach students. The emphasis dictated by NCLB was on evidence-based practices to teach reading, but the search for curricula supported by research is now addressed by schools in all basic skills and content areas. The reason for the push for evidence-based practice is to ensure that students who fall behind are not failing because of an inadequate curriculum or poor teaching. The move toward evidence-based practice is designed, therefore, to address primary prevention—a reduction in numbers of children who are inaccurately identified with a disability—particularly a learning disability. An additional benefit of using evidence-based practices in schools is secondary prevention—those students who do end up being identified for special education may be performing better and possess more skills than they would if they hadn't received strong instruction. So what are evidence-based practices, how do we find them, and what are the issues surrounding their use?

● *Defining Evidence-Based Practices*   The U.S. Department of Education (2003) defines **evidence-based practices** (which are also sometimes referred to as "research-based practices") as "teaching practices that have been proven to work space." Sounds like a good idea, doesn't it? If we use a strategy or an instructional method with children, it should be backed by sound and valid educational research that demonstrates its effectiveness. But if you have studied educational research, you know that it is extremely challenging to conduct true experimental studies in schools, for many reasons. Schools are full of distractions and extraneous factors that may influence the outcome of a classroom study. If your reading intervention doesn't work, is it because of your teaching strategy, or something else that is happening during the school day? Did the children eat breakfast? Are they fluent users of English? Schools and classrooms are not laboratories. It is also difficult to randomly assign children to teaching conditions, and to assume that children within two different classrooms are comparable. (For more on these difficulties, see Berliner, 2002.)

Sam Odom and his colleagues (2005), in an introductory article to an influential issue of *Exceptional Children* on evaluating research for evidence-based practices, identify three additional challenges in conducting studies with students with disabilities, which is even "messier" (or more complex, according to these authors) than research with typically developing school-age children. First, there is tremendous variability within the group of students receiving special education services. Intellectual disabilities, deafness, or learning disabilities manifest themselves very differently in individual children, so it is hard to establish equivalent groups, which is important in most research designs. Odom et al. (2005) provide examples:

> Autism is now widely conceptualized as a spectrum consisting of four disorders. Mental retardation varies on the range of severity. Emotional and behavioral disorders consist of externalizing and internalizing disorders. Visual and hearing impairments range in severity from mildly impaired to totally blind or profoundly deaf. Physical impairment can be exhibited as hypotonia or hypertonia. Other health impaired may incorporate health conditions as distinct and diverse as asthma, epilepsy, and diabetes. Adding to this variability is the greater ethnic and linguistic diversity that, unfortunately, occurs in special education because of overrepresentation of some minority groups (Donovan & Cross, 2002). (Odom et al., 2005, p. 139)

The second complicating factor in conducting research on students with disabilities is the variety of settings in which they attend school. While you read earlier in the chapter that most students with IEPs spend at least part of their day in a general education classroom, there is a wide range of possibilities for their placement (see the continuum of educational settings, Figure 1.3), complicating the use of the classroom as the unit of research (Odom et al., 2005). Given these challenges, it is important to be extremely cautious in generalizing the results of a research study to students with disabilities as a group, or even to a sub-group. Again, Odom and colleagues:

> Complexity in special education has several implications for research. Researchers cannot just address a simple question about whether a practice in special education is effective; they must specify clearly for whom the practice is effective and in what context (Guralnick, 1999). (2005, p. 139)

A CLOSER LOOK Locating Research-Based Practices

As an educator, how do you find research-based practices to use with students? Our first suggestion: Go to the research literature! The most prominent journals in special education contain articles describing current research with students with disabilities and its implementation. Look at the reference list at the back of the book for the examples you see cited throughout this text, but among the most prominent are *Exceptional Children, Journal of Learning Disabilities, Journal of Special Education, Journal of Early Intervention, Intellectual and Developmental Disabilities*, and *Journal of Autism and Developmental Disorders*. Access to the full text of these articles is available through your university library. A few articles are available for free online; a search using Google Scholar will identify which ones you can access directly. Some authorities in the field are arguing for free access to all journal articles, so that parents and others who don't have access to a university library can read and use journal content. Others respond that if access to all articles was free, there would be no income generated to continue the existence of the journals. Other suggestions:

- The Beach Center for Families with Disabilities at the University of Kansas is developing a series of *Knowledge-to-Action Guides,* which will help family members find evidence-based practices and request their use at IEP meetings. These guides are available at the Beach Center website.

- The Institute for Education Sciences (IES) of the U.S. Department of Education has developed the *What Works Clearinghouse,* which describes the process used to evaluate the rigor of studies and the evaluation of the studies themselves. The partner site, *Doing What Works,* puts the evidence-based practices derived from those studies into action for teachers. See *Useful Resources* at the end of this chapter for the URLs for these sites.

- Practitioner-oriented journals, such as *Teaching Exceptional Children, Intervention in School and Clinic, Remedial and Special Education*, and *Language, Speech, and Hearing Services in Schools*, often "translate" research-based practices into usable practices for teachers.

Remember, researchers argue that evidence-based practices must be implemented with fidelity—in other words, carried out exactly as they were performed in the original study (Wolery, 2011). Otherwise we cannot expect to obtain the same results.

It is sometimes challenging to find evidence-based practices that can be replicated in the classroom with fidelity.

- *Finding evidence based-practices* Given those cautions, how do we find evidence-based practices that are valid and replicable for students with disabilities? See "A Closer Look" above. Most professional journals in both general and special education publish results of rigorous research that might generate practices for teachers, but it's not always easy to figure out how to replicate those practices yourself from the journal article. The researchers themselves argue that research-based practices must be implemented *with fidelity*—that is, exactly as they were performed in the original study (Odom, 2009; Wolery, 2011). This expectation sets an even higher bar for classroom teachers. Klingner, Ahwee, Pilonieta, & Menendez (2003) studied elementary school teachers who received professional development and ongoing support in implementing research-based practices in their inclusive classrooms. The teachers who were considered "high implementing" cited administrative support as the most important factor in their success. So it will be very helpful if your school administrator believes in the importance of using research-based practices!

Throughout this book, we specifically cite, discuss, and "translate" the results of research for your use. We hope that our references at the back of the book will encourage you to become an educated consumer of the special education research.

Universal Design for Learning

When we think about accessibility, typically we think of entering a building and the need to adapt existing structures to accommodate individuals with disabilities. That is known as *architectural accessibility*. But the concept of *access* has broadened to include gaining information from the curriculum. **Universal Design for Learning (UDL)** grew out of the idea of architectural accessibility. Here's the basic concept: Think of the way your college or university has changed over the years to become more accessible to students with limited mobility. These changes, such as curb cuts or elevators in every multi-story building, are necessary for people who use wheelchairs but helpful to many other people as well.

David Meyer, Anne Meyer and their colleagues at the Center for Applied Special Technology (CAST) came up with the idea of UDL. Here's how they described its inception:

> Our work taught us that when education fails, barriers to learning are likely found in the curriculum—not in individual learners, who fall along a continuum of diverse abilities, interests, and skills. As a result, the burden to adapt must, as a first step, be placed where it belongs: on the curriculum itself. (Meyer & Rose, 2006, p. vii)

So instead of developing a curriculum and then looking at ways to accommodate diverse learners, according to the principles of UDL the curriculum would be *created* with all learners in mind. UDL focuses on accessing the curriculum and eliminating curricular barriers to learning without lowering academic standards or restricting content coverage. Figure 2.6 provides examples of the three basic guidelines of UDL: provide multiple methods of presentation, multiple means of expression, and multiple means of engagement (CAST, 2011).

Universal design for learning is an approach to building curriculum that is accessible to all students.

Photo by Oli Scarff/Getty Images

Curb cuts, originally intended to help people who use wheelchairs, benefit many others as well.

Universal Design for Learning Guidelines

I. Provide Multiple Means of Representation	II. Provide Multiple Means of Action and Expression	III. Provide Multiple Means of Engagement
1: Provide options for perception	**4: Provide options for physical action**	**7: Provide options for recruiting interest**
1.1 Offer ways of customizing the display of information	4.1 Vary the methods for response and navigation	7.1 Optimize individual choice and autonomy
1.2 Offer alternatives for auditory information	4.2 Optimize access to tools and assistive technologies	7.2 Optimize relevance, value, and authenticity
1.3 Offer alternatives for visual information		7.3 Minimize threats and distractions
2: Provide options for language, mathematical expressions, and symbols	**5: Provide options for expression and communication**	**8: Provide options for sustaining effort and persistence**
2.1 Clarify vocabulary and symbols	5.1 Use multiple media for communication	8.1 Heighten salience of goals and objectives
2.2 Clarify syntax and structure	5.2 Use multiple tools for construction and composition	8.2 Vary demands and resources to optimize challenge
2.3 Support decoding of text, mathematical notation, and symbols	5.3 Build fluencies with graduated levels of support for practice and performance	8.3 Foster collaboration and community
2.4 Promote understanding across languages		8.4 Increase mastery-oriented feedback
2.5 Illustrate through multiple media		
3: Provide options for comprehension	**6: Provide options for executive functions**	**9: Provide options for self-regulation**
3.1 Activate or supply background knowledge	6.1 Guide appropriate goal-setting	9.1 Promote expectations and beliefs that optimize motivation
3.2. Highlight patterns, critical features, big ideas, and relationships	6.2 Support planning and strategy development	9.2 Facilitate personal coping skills and strategies
3.3 Guide information processing, visualization, and manipulation	6.3 Facilitate managing information and resources	9.3 Develop self-assessment and reflection
3.4 Maximize transfer and generalization	6.4 Enhance capacity for monitoring progress	
Resourceful, knowledgeable learners	**Strategic, goal-directed learners**	**Purposeful, motivated learners**

FIGURE 2.6

Universal Design for Learning Guidelines

Source: Adapted from National Center on Universal Design for Learning website http://www.udlcenter.org/aboutudl/whatisudl

Although UDL represents a general approach to curriculum development, it is a philosophy that is emerging in special education. Many of the principles of UDL are based in or revolve around the use of technology. But while UDL depends on new technologies to present materials in a variety of ways and to allow for varied ways for students to express themselves, it is not all about technologies. UDL simply envisions adding new technologies to the traditional ways of presenting information to students (such as lectures) and of student expression (such as speaking or writing). There are seven basic principles of UDL:

- **Equitable use.** Create materials that are accessible to everyone.
- **Flexibility in use.** Incorporate choice to appeal to individual likes and abilities.
- **Simple and intuitive use.** Choose designs that are uncomplicated and easy to understand.
- **Perceptible information.** Communicate necessary information clearly and effectively.
- **Tolerance for error.** The consequences of making a mistake are minimal.

- **Low physical effort.** Designs require minimal physical effort.
- **Size and space and approach and use.** Designs allow for easy use regardless of physical abilities or mobility (CAST, 2003).

Educators today are beginning to apply the principles and qualities of UDL in their everyday instruction. To incorporate Universal Design for Learning in your classroom, it helps to think of the broad goals or targets of UDL and how they can be translated into the design of your classroom environment and support strategies for all students.

In the Teaching Strategies box, "Example of Teaching U.S. History Using UDL," you can see how the three principles look when integrated into classroom instruction. To learn more about UDL and its applications for teachers, visit the website for Universal Design Education Online or the Education CourseMate website at **CengageBrain.com.** The *Useful Resources* section at the end of the chapter will also help you learn more about UDL.

Even if the principles of Universal Design for Learning were used to design all curriculum, there would likely still be a need for additional supports for some students. Assistive Technology will provide some of those supports.

Assistive Technology

As you read in Chapter 1, federal law requires that each student with an IEP be evaluated for a need for assistive technology. These technologies range from low-tech (for example, a plastic block placed around a pencil for a young child with a weak grip) to high-tech (an augmentative communication device that "speaks" for a nonverbal child, as an example). The range of technologies available to support the learning of students with disabilities is growing each day. Throughout this text, you will learn about many current forms of assistive technology used across today's classrooms and schools. Every chapter has a feature titled "Assistive Technology Focus." To use the terminology of Universal Design for Learning,

Teaching Strategies & Accommodations

Example of Teaching U.S. History Using UDL

A U.S. history teacher using the UDL approach might ask her students to construct an essay that compares and contrasts the industrial North and the agricultural South in the 1800s. Her focus is the thinking behind the essay, the methods of comparing and contrasting as a means to help her students gain a deeper understanding of the historical period and geographic locations.

The teacher emphasizes that there are many different approaches to constructing the essay and offers examples: outlines, diagrams, concept maps, digitally recorded think-alouds, and drawings. She uses tools supporting each of these approaches, so that students who need extra structure can choose the supports that work for them, and she creates templates with partially completed sections and links to more information.

Because this is a long-term assignment, the teacher breaks the research and the writing into sections and incorporates group sharing and feedback in the process to help students revise their essays as they work. The teacher also provides models by sharing the work of previous students who approached the same problem in varied ways.

Source: C. Hitchcock, A. Meyer, D. Rose, & R. Jackson (2002). Providing New Access to the General Curriculum: Universal Design for Learning. *Teaching Exceptional Children, 35* (2), 13. Copyright © Council for Exceptional Children.

assistive technology should allow students the means to express themselves and to be more engaged with learning.

Accommodations and Modifications

> An accommodation allows the student with a disability to access the curriculum.

Many students with disabilities can learn the same content, the same curriculum, or the same standard as other students, but they need additional support to master that material. These students require **accommodations.** Here's one definition of accommodation:

> An ***accommodation*** *is a change that helps a student overcome or work around the disability.* Allowing a student who has trouble writing to give his answers orally is an example of an accommodation. This student is still expected to know the same material and answer the same questions as fully as the other students, but he doesn't have to write his answers to show that he knows the information (National Dissemination Center for Children with Disabilities, 2010).

Some of your peers in this education course may have disabilities (or you may have one yourself). Those disabilities may be visible (it's difficult not to notice a student using a wheelchair or a sign-language interpreter) or invisible (students with learning disabilities do not look different from anyone else). They take the same course you do. The content is the same. But they may need more time to complete their work, or a quiet room to answer exam questions in, or captions on the videos that your professor uses. Those are examples of accommodations—the supports a person requires in school to master the same material that everybody else does.

> A modification changes the standard, or what is taught.

A **modification,** on the other hand, changes the standard or the content being learned in some way. Students in higher education do not typically have the curriculum modified, but school-age students with severe cognitive disabilities, for example, might require curricular modifications. Figure 2.7 is a school worksheet listing accommodations and modifications for a student with traumatic brain injury.

A student's IEP must specify the accommodations that should be made for him or her in the general education classroom. These terms can be confusing. We talk about supports, accommodations, modifications, and adaptations (adaptations and modifications are used synonymously). The National Dissemination Center for Children with Disabilities addresses this issue with some humor:

> You might wonder if the terms ***supports, modifications,*** and ***adaptations*** all mean the same thing. The simple answer is: No, not completely, but yes, for the most part. (Don't you love a clear answer?) People tend to use the terms interchangeably, to be sure, and we will do so here, for ease of reading, but distinctions can be made between the terms. Sometimes people get confused about what it means to have a *modification* and what it means to have an *accommodation.* Usually a ***modification*** means *a change in what is being taught to or expected from the student.* Making an assignment easier so the student is not doing the same level of work as other students is an example of a modification. (National Dissemination Center for Children with Disabilities, 2010)

You will see examples of these terms throughout this text.

Accommodations & Modifications in the Elementary Classroom
For a Student with Traumatic Brain Injury

Student: _____ Teacher: _____ Grade: _____ Today's Date: _____
Presenting Concerns: _____
Birth Date: _____ Date of Injury: _____

Consider Student's Environment
- [ ] Post class rules (pictures & words)
- [ ] Post daily schedule (pictures & words)
- [ ] Give preferential seating
- [ ] Change to another class
- [ ] Change schedule (most difficult in morning)
- [ ] Eliminate distractions (visual, auditory, olfactory)
- [ ] Modify length of school day
- [ ] Provide frequent breaks
- [ ] Provide place for quiet time
- [ ] Maintain consistent schedule
- [ ] Provide system for transition
- [ ] Position appropriately
- [ ] Explain disabilities to students
- [ ] Use color-coded materials

Consider Curricular Content & Expectations
- [ ] Reduce length of assignments
- [ ] Change skill/task
- [ ] Modify testing mode/setting
- [ ] Allow extra time
- [ ] Teach study skills
- [ ] Teach sequencing skills
- [ ] Teach visual imagery
- [ ] Teach memory strategies
- [ ] Write assignments in daily log
- [ ] Teach semantic mapping
- [ ] Teach peers how to be helpful

Consider Method of Instruction
- [ ] Repeat directions
- [ ] Increase active participation

Consider Method of Instruction—(Continued)
- [ ] Teacher circulate around room
- [ ] Provide visual prompts (board/desk)
- [ ] Provide immediate feedback (self correcting seat work)
- [ ] Point out similarities to previous learning/work
- [ ] Use manipulative materials
- [ ] Use frequent review of key concepts
- [ ] Teach to current level of ability (use easier materials)
- [ ] Speak loud or slow or rephrase
- [ ] Preteach/Reteach
- [ ] Highlight/underline material
- [ ] Use peer tutor/partner
- [ ] Use small group instruction
- [ ] Use simple sentences
- [ ] Use individualized instruction
- [ ] Pause frequently
- [ ] Discuss errors and how they were made
- [ ] Use cooperative learning
- [ ] Use instructional assistants
- [ ] Encourage requests for clarification, repetition, etc.
- [ ] Elicit responses when you know student knows the answer
- [ ] Demonstrate & encourage use of technology (instructional and assistive)

Consider Student's Behavioral Needs
- [ ] Teach expected behavior
- [ ] Increase student success rate

Consider Student's Behavioral Needs—(Continued)
- [ ] Learn to recognize signs of stress
- [ ] Give nonverbal cues to discontinue behavior
- [ ] Reinforce positive behavior (4:1)
- [ ] Use mild, consistent consequences
- [ ] Set goals with student
- [ ] Use key students for reinforcement of target student
- [ ] Use group/individual counseling
- [ ] Teach student to attend to advance organizers at beginning of lesson
- [ ] Provide opportunity to role pay
- [ ] Use proactive behavior management strategies
- [ ] Use schoolwide reinforcement with target students

Consider Assistive Technology
- [ ] Adaptive paper
- [ ] Talking spell checker/dictionary
- [ ] Concept mapping software/templates
- [ ] Magnetic words, letters, phrases
- [ ] Multimedia software
- [ ] Keyguard for keyboard
- [ ] Macros/shortcuts on computer
- [ ] Abbreviations/expansion
- [ ] Accessibility options on computer
- [ ] Alternative keyboards
- [ ] Communication cards or boards
- [ ] Voice output communication device
- [ ] Portable word processor
- [ ] Enlarged text/magnifiers
- [ ] Recorded text/books on tape/talking books

Consider Assistive Technology—(Continued)
- [ ] Scanned text with OCR software
- [ ] Voice output reminders
- [ ] Electronic organizers/reminders/pagers
- [ ] Large display calculators
- [ ] Voice input calculators
- [ ] Math software
- [ ] Picture/symbol supported software

Other Considerations
Home/School Relations
- [ ] Schedule regular meetings for all staff to review progress/maintain consistency
- [ ] Schedule parent conferences every _____
- [ ] Daily/weekly reports home
- [ ] Parent visits/contact
- [ ] Home visits
Disability Awareness
- [ ] Explain disabilities to other students
- [ ] Teach peers how to be helpful
- [ ] In-service training for school staff
Additional Resources
- [ ] Wisconsin Assistive Technology Checklist
- [ ] Therapists, nurse, resource teachers, school psychologist, counselor, rehab facility, parents, vision teacher, medical facility

Confield, T. & Swanson, K. (2006) Wisconsin Traumatic Brain Injury Initiative—adapted from Wisconsin Assistive Technology Initiative (Reed & Canfield, 1999), (Reed 1991)

FIGURE 2.7

School worksheet listing accommodations and modifications for a student with traumatic brain injury

Differentiated Instruction

Differentiated instruction allows changes in content, process, or products of learning as needed by individual students.

Differentiated instruction is a term that originated in education of gifted students (Tomlinson, 1999), but has been adopted for a wide range of learners. At its most basic level, differentiating instruction means "shaking up" what goes on in the classroom so that students have multiple options for taking in information, making sense of ideas, and expressing what they learn. In other words, a differentiated classroom provides different avenues to acquiring content, processing or making sense of ideas, and developing products.

Differentiation can involve changes in the content of what is learned, the process of how it is learned, or the product of learning. Unlike Universal Design for Learning, it does not address the design of the curriculum; instead, it allows a teacher to modify her practices or expectations for an individual student or a small group within the classroom. We will refer to differentiated instruction throughout the text, especially in Chapter 14.

Three-Tiered Models

Pyramid models depict levels of intensity of instruction.

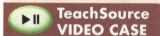

TeachSource VIDEO CASE

When Do "Problems" Become Disabilities?

African American students are three times more likely to be labeled with mental retardation (now called intellectual disabilities) than other groups. Visit Chapter 2 on the CourseMate website and watch the video clip entitled "Minority Students Mislabeled as Having a Disability." How do teachers decide when a language or a behavior problem is a disability?

Response to Intervention is an increasingly common set of instructional practices represented in a tiered model.

The last ten years have brought a new way of thinking about providing services to all students in schools, and it is often represented graphically in the shape of a pyramid. The idea is this—at the bottom of the pyramid is Tier One, and ALL students receive the services at that level. It could be a rich, challenging, standards-based reading or math program, or a structured system of rewarding positive behavior for the whole school, or whatever the basic level of the system being described might be. The greatest number of students receives this level of service, so it's the largest section of the pyramid. Tier One services are accompanied by progress monitoring (described more completely on page 61), which assesses how each student is performing. If the results of progress monitoring indicate that one or more students are not making acceptable growth, then they move to Tier Two, where more intensive services are provided in the areas of need. We assume that most students improve in Tier Two and ultimately return to the Tier One program. But for those who do not make progress in Tier Two, there is Tier Three—the most intensive, individually designed set of services.

● *Response to Intervention* The most familiar three-tiered model is known as **Response to Intervention,** or **RTI.** While an RTI model can be used in any subject area, it is most frequently used to describe a model of intervention for students who are not making progress in reading, which has been the focus of national concern (National Reading Panel, 2000; Snow, Burns, & Griffin, 1998). The 2004 amendments to IDEA (see Chapter 1 for a review) allow states to determine whether students are eligible for the largest special education category, that of learning disabilities, through a Response to Intervention (RTI) program. So instead of what is sometimes called a "wait until they fail" model, where schools must demonstrate that a student has a significant discrepancy between ability and school achievement, schools may now try to teach the student the reading skills needed through intensive individual or small-group instruction before they are referred to special education services, and often in kindergarten or first grade.

The principles of RTI include multiple tiers of intervention; use of evidence-based practices in all tiers; use of progress monitoring and problem-solving/decision making, and differentiated instructional intervention at each level. Tier One is universal instruction, Tier Two is targeted instruction, and Tier Three is intensive instruction (Center for RTI in Early Childhood, 2011).

You will read more about RTI in Chapter 5. Many of you are likely to work within an RTI program, whether you plan to become a general education or a special education teacher. While RTI is considered part of general education, in many schools general and special education teachers collaborate to plan and provide interventions.

● *School-Wide Positive Behavior Support*   When a three-tier model is used to describe interventions to improve students' behavior, it is known as positive behavioral interventions and supports (PBIS) or, when applied in an entire school, as **school-wide positive behavior support** (SWPBS). In SWPBS, the first step involves members of the school community (usually including students) deciding on a set of reasonable rules or standards for good behavior for the whole school. (Positive behavior support models always state desired behaviors in positive terms; so rather than "No running in the hallways," the rule would be "Walk in the hallways.") After the behavior standards have been identified and implemented, that becomes Tier One—all students are expected to meet those standards. For students who have difficulty meeting the behavior standards of Tier One, Tier Two provides more intensive incentives for meeting the standards, individualized for each student. Again, we would expect that most students would respond positively and return to Tier One. But for those few who do not, Tier Three services are the most intensive, individually designed behavior interventions (Lane, Menzies, Bruhn, & Crnobori, 2011).

Figure 2.8 shows the academic and behavioral tiered models side by side, and illustrates the likelihood that fewer students will need the most intensive supports. According to the model, 95% of all students would respond to Tier One and Tier Two Interventions.

One way to look at these methods for supporting students with disabilities is in another pyramid model—we are big on these in special education! In Figure 2.9 you can see the model applied to some of the instructional practices we have been discussing. All students can benefit from Universal Design for Learning, and as you move higher on the pyramid, fewer students need the practices listed; the fewest students will need Assisitive Technology. Students without IEPs

> School-wide positive behavior support sets behavior standards for every student.

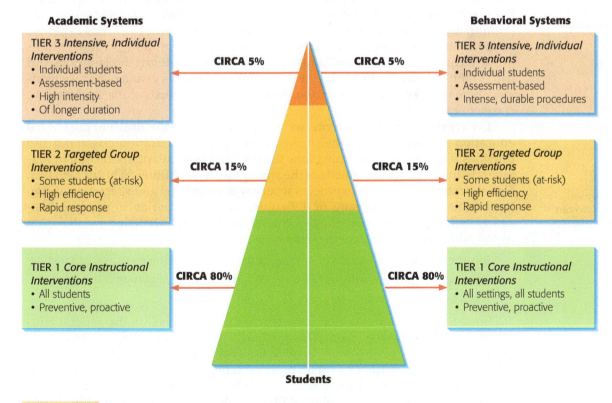

FIGURE 2.8

Tiered prevention models

Source: National Association of State Directors of Special Education (2005)

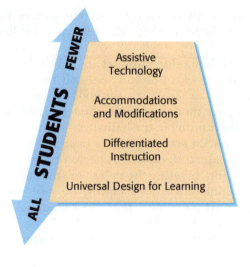

FIGURE 2.9

Instructional practices and the students they benefit

Source: From Universal Design for Learning: Creating a Learning Environment that Challenges and Engages All Students (p. 9). http://iris. peabody.vanderbilt.edu/udl/ chalcycle.htm. IRIS Center, Vanderbilt University. Used with permission.

will benefit from UDL and differentiated instruction; those requiring accommodations and modifications and assistive technology are likely to have IEPs.

Teacher-Directed Practices

As we've discussed, the general education curriculum may present obstacles for students with disabilities. Some of these obstacles can be addressed through curriculum design, or accommodations, and others can be addressed through differentiated instructional strategies. Yet another way to address students' needs is educational collaboration—between teachers or among peers. Chief among the teacher-directed instructional alternatives are *consultation, collaboration, coteaching, and classroom tutoring*. In all these options, the teacher who has expertise in special education or a specific area of instructional support, such as educational technology or mobility, comes into the general education classroom and works with the classroom teacher or student. Some schools employ all these models, whereas others select one or two, depending on the needs of the students and classroom teacher.

Let's review some of the terms we've been using. In **consultation,** the special education teacher observes the student in the general education classroom and provides suggestions concerning how the teacher might adapt instruction or materials to meet the specific needs of the student with disabilities in his or her class. **Collaboration** describes the process whereby both general and special education teachers identify the problems or difficulties a child is experiencing and work together to find intervention strategies. Friend and Cook (2009) define collaboration by including some of its essential elements:

> Interpersonal *collaboration* is a style for direct interaction between at least two coequal parties voluntarily engaged in shared decision-making as they work toward a common goal. (p. 7)

Sometimes, the special education teacher works alongside the general education teacher in the classroom. This method, called **co-teaching,** has many different forms. Co-teaching could involve the special educator teaching a specific subject area to the entire class (math or social skills) or teaching a specific group of students that includes a student with a disability (often a subject such as reading or a content area requiring reading skills). See the accompanying Teaching Strategies box, "Co-Teaching Models," for a description of the various co-teaching formats. Less than 10 years ago, little research on co-teaching existed (Murawski & Swanson, 2001); however, recent studies have found that it can be a very effective

Consultation occurs when the special education teacher acts as "expert" on the needs of the student with disabilities.

Collaboration is based on parity—equality between teachers or among school professionals.

Teaching Strategies & Accommodations

Co-Teaching Models

One person teaching in classroom

1. One teacher prepares materials and offers strategies but does not actually teach in the classroom. This model frequently coexists with all the other models.

2. One teach–one observe: One teacher observes a student in the classroom and perhaps takes data, evaluates student responses to instruction, etc. One teacher provides classroom instruction. Could be occasional or structured.

Two teachers in classroom: one supplementing general instruction

1. One teach–one drift: One teacher circulates around the room helping students with particular needs, and the co-teacher instructs the entire group. Can be most beneficial when roles are reversed regularly.

2. Alternative teaching: One teacher provides remediation, enrichment, or specialized instruction for students who need it, while the other provides instruction for the rest of the group. This may be done occasionally, on an as-needed basis, or as regular alternative reading instruction, for example.

Two teachers in classroom: both delivering general instruction

1. Station teaching: Curriculum content is broken into components; each teacher teaches one part of content to a group of children, then students switch to the other teacher. Could also include cooperative learning or an independent group station.

2. Parallel teaching: Class is broken into two groups of students; each teacher teaches the same content material to one group of students. (Teachers should take care not to separate all special education students into one group.)

3. Team teaching: Both teachers deliver the instruction together at the same time, sharing leadership in the classroom. This may be done for one class a day or more, but it should be consistent across time so that students perceive both teachers as the teachers in charge.

Source: Adapted from M. Friend (2005). *The power of 2: Making a difference through co-teaching* (2nd ed.). Port Chester, NY: National Professional Resources, Inc.

---

method for meeting students' needs (e.g., Magiera, Smith, Zigmond, & Gebauer, 2005; Murawski, 2006; Rea, McLaughlin, & Walther-Thomas, 2002; Scruggs, Mastropieri, & McDuffie, 2007). However, as with any paradigm shift, change is difficult and barriers are common. Teachers have reported a variety of frustrations with co-teaching; they include lack of training (Mastropieri et al., 2005); lack of administrative support (Dieker, 2001; Rea, 2005); and a lack of parity in the classroom (Dieker & Murawski, 2003; Spencer, 2005). Dr. Lynne Cook, a noted expert on co-teaching, clarified that "co-teaching is not simply having two teachers in a classroom with one acting as a glorified paraprofessional or an in-class tutor for one or two students" (Spencer, 2005, p. 297), and yet that is exactly what many teachers complain is occurring (Weiss & Lloyd, 2002).

> In co-teaching, the general and special education teachers teach in the same classroom.

A final alternative occurs when a teacher, peer, or older student tutors the student with a disability within the classroom setting.

Peer-Directed Practice

Although several models of peer-tutoring and cooperative learning strategies have been suggested as means of integrating students with disabilities into general education classes, few have strong research supporting their effectiveness. Teachers believe there is much potential in these types of interventions, however,

Peer tutoring can foster feelings of success in both students.

and report that cooperative learning and peer tutoring are the most useful approaches for working with multicultural students with disabilities (Utley et al., 2000). One peer-tutoring program that has been well researched and found to be effective for many students with mild disabilities is Peer-Assisted Learning Strategies (PALS) (McMaster, Fuchs, & Fuchs, 2006). PALS, outlined in the accompanying Teaching Strategies box, is based on the Class-Wide Peer Tutoring

 **Teaching Strategies & Accommodations**

Peer-Assisted Learning Strategies (PALS)

Preparation

PALS involves preparation of students: Teachers prepare students with a series of scripted lessons. Students are grouped into dyads; typically, one student is a stronger reader than the other. Reading material is selected that is at the lower reader's level.

Implementation

PALS sessions are implemented three times a week, for 35 minutes each session. Students receive points for correct performance and appropriate tutoring when necessary. Both students participate in tutoring activities, but the stronger reader begins the session. No answer keys are provided.

Activities

- **Partner reading.** The peer tutor, and then the other student, each read the text for five minutes. The peer tutor stops the reader when an error occurs and asks the student to try to figure out the mistake. If the reader cannot do this in four seconds, the tutor supplies the word. Then the sentence is re-read by the student who made the error.

- **Paragraph shrinking.** The students read the text aloud, stopping at the end of each paragraph to state the main idea and eventually presenting it in no more than ten words. The tutor prompts the identification of the main idea by asking questions. He or she asks the other student to try again if the response is incorrect and to shorten the response if it is too long.

- **Prediction relay.** The reader makes predictions about the content of a half page of text and then reads the text. While this student is reading, the tutor corrects errors, evaluates predictions, and presents the main idea of the text. The correction procedures used in the first two activities are included in this activity, and the tutor solicits new predictions if he or she deems the initial ones unreasonable.

Source: D. Fuchs, L. S. Fuchs, & P. Burish (2000). Peer-assisted learning strategies: An evidence-based practice to promote reading achievement. *Learning Disabilities Research and Practice, 15,* 85–91.

Program (Greenwood, Delquadri, & Hall, 1989) and designed to focus on reading instruction in general education classrooms. What distinguishes PALS from other classroom tutorial programs is the use of structured peer interactions, including specific task strategies, and the incorporation of effective instructional practices.

The PALS program was created for students in grades two through six, but it has since been adapted for use by many other groups, including English language learners with learning disabilities (Saenz, Fuchs, & Fuchs, 2005).

Peer models bring students together to assist one another.

? Pause and Reflect

As you prepare to become a teacher, you often imagine having your own classroom—what you would do to organize the class, how you would create learning opportunities, and the ways you and your students interact. Co-teaching involves sharing your classroom and your students, and may involve compromise to determine learning strategies and activities. Can you imagine participating in a co-teaching setting? What do you think would help make co-teaching an attractive option for you? ●

Assessment

Assessment, or evaluating student performance, is an integral part of education in general, and special education in particular. You will see the word *assessment* often throughout this text—often with reference to assessment used for identification and placement. Assessment is at the heart of special education practice; teachers must determine what a student knows and needs to know in order to individualize instruction. There are other reasons for assessing children and many types of assessment instruments or tests.

Purposes of Assessment

Two major purposes for assessing students are related directly to special education: (1) to evaluate or identify the student's need for special education or other support services if he or she is referred, and (2) to assess for purposes of instruction: learning where to begin instruction, monitoring a student's performance, and evaluating the effectiveness of instruction. The second type of assessment allows for teachers to provide appropriate and individualized instruction to students with disabilities. In contrast to these types of assessment, some testing is done on a large scale. State and national tests—largely achievement tests—have been used to provide parents and teachers with a sense of how their children are performing relative to other students in the state or across the country. Often, these scores are provided in percentiles to allow consumers a better means of comparison.

Assessment can determine eligibility for special education services or help to evaluate and plan instruction.

In the wake of the educational reform movement, testing has taken on increasing importance. Testing may be used as educators seek to set and maintain high-performance standards in the classroom, and to demonstrate that each school or school district is performing as expected. Instead of a test simply providing information that can be used to target instruction, tests are now employed to determine what child is eligible for certain classes, who passes to the next grade, and which students graduate from school (Salvia, Ysseldyke, & Bolt, 2009). Students' test scores are also used now to grade schools, evaluate school districts, and determine the effectiveness of teachers and school administrators. When the consequences of testing are great—when students can fail, principals can lose their jobs, and schools can be considered "failing"—we say that tests are used to make high-stakes decisions. Today, tests completed for the purpose of making these important and critical decisions have come to be known as *high-stakes tests.*

High-Stakes Testing

High-stakes testing has become the driving force in school reform and draws both praise and criticism. Some people praise the current use of **high-stakes testing** because they feel it promotes a standardized curriculum, provides a uniform level of expectations for students across schools, and helps parents to evaluate effective schools (Heubert & Hauser, 1999). On the other hand, many criticize the use of high-stakes testing because of the traditionally poor performance of students with disabilities, English language learners, and students who are members of minority groups. Disparities in the test performance of students in these groups may result in inappropriate tracking and lower expectations. In addition, the performance differences appear to result in more grade retention and higher drop-out rates, not necessarily increases in student learning (Horn, 2003).

The instructional benefits of high-stakes testing for students with cognitive and academic disabilities appear to be limited. Additionally, because of the importance of the IEP as an assessment tool as well as an instructional plan, many students with disabilities have not participated in statewide assessment, in the form of achievement tests, over the years. In 1997 IDEA reflected concern about schools' lack of accountability regarding the education of students with disabilities by requiring schools to include children with disabilities in their assessment system and to report results. Although schools could attend to the scores of students with disabilities, they were not actually held accountable for the degree of progress students with disabilities were making each year. This complacence changed drastically with the requirements of the No Child Left Behind Act of 2001 (NCLB). As we've indicated earlier, this law asserts that *all* children must make a year's worth of progress each year at their grade level. By law, every child in grades three through eight takes a statewide content-area test in reading and math. Each student receives a score, and although the terms used to grade scores may vary from state to state, the bottom line is that each student must demonstrate proficiency, or a passing grade, in each area. States are responsible for developing their own tests and competency scores. Each school is responsible for demonstrating that all children regardless of poverty, ethnicity, or level of disability can make adequate yearly progress.

The scores of most students with disabilities must be counted by each school and school district, and a few additional rules have been set forth, including:

- Accommodations for testing must be provided when necessary. Accommodations may include increased time allowed to complete tests, or taking the test in a room separate from the rest of the class.
- At least 95 percent of all students must participate in state tests.
- Scores of tests taken below grade level (to match the student's instructional level) cannot be counted.

Statewide assessments are based on the educational standards established by each state, and because schools must demonstrate the progress each child makes, participation in the general education curriculum for all children is critical. Consequently, several questions and concerns have been raised by advocates for children with disabilities. Because the NCLB requirements seem to dictate participation in testing and the curriculum, some professionals and parents are concerned about the continued importance of the IEP in preserving individualized educational programs. For many, the big picture emphasis of NCLB is contradicted by the individualized focus of the IEP (Olson, 2004). For others, it seems incongruous to expect children with academic or cognitive disabilities to make a year's work of progress each year—particularly when failure to progress in the general education curriculum is necessary for identification in many categories of special education. A number of organizations developed guidelines and position papers hoping to preserve the rights of individuals in the testing system, to assure test validity and accurate reporting, and to emphasize the importance of using test scores in a responsible manner (National Center for Learning Disabilities, 2011).

In addition to the effects of testing on individuals with disabilities, great concerns have emerged about the effects of high-stakes assessment on the interactions among administrators, teachers, and students in general education and special education. Federal law is requiring general education to attend to the performance of students with disabilities for the first time (Olson, 2004). On the one hand, we can perceive this attention as a good thing—the performance of students with disabilities is no longer irrelevant and can no longer be ignored. On the other hand, a school needs to demonstrate that all groups of kids make adequate yearly progress. If the students with disabilities don't make that progress, neither will the school as a whole—regardless of how the other students do.

● *Alternative assessment* The law recognizes that there are some children with severe cognitive disabilities who cannot take the standard test, and it allows one percent of them to take alternative assessments determined by the states. In addition, the law recognizes that general education curriculum standards must be modified for some students with "persistent academic disabilities." When those standards are modified, those students take alternate assessments based on the modified standards. Only two percent of the total student population can fall into this category; decisions about which assessments students take are made at the IEP meeting (U.S. Department of Education, 2006). These percentages could be modified or even eliminated when Congress reauthorizes the Elementary and Secondary Education Act (NCLB) (Shah, 2011).

Progress Monitoring

Assessment of student learning has long been a hallmark of special education practice. Think of it this way: How do you know whether a student is reaching the goals of the IEP without ongoing assessment? The research-based practices we describe in this chapter and throughout the book must be monitored on a regular basis to make sure they result in student learning. Fuchs and Fuchs (n.d.) describe three purposes for **systematic progress monitoring:** to identify students in need of additional or different forms of instruction, to design stronger instructional programs, and to achieve better learning outcomes for their students. Progress monitoring involves ongoing assessment of student learning in a specific area such as reading, mathematics, or spelling; it should be done at least monthly, and more often when needed. Teachers can use curriculum-based measures to monitor their students' progress (Stecker, Fuchs, & Fuchs, 2005), or a range of tools designed by others to measure student progress (see the National Center on Response to Intervention website for a list of such measures).

Progress monitoring is an essential component of Response to Intervention (RTI) models. Without progress monitoring, how would teachers know whether the students receiving Tier Two interventions were learning—that is, responding to the intervention?

Progress monitoring helps determine whether interventions result in student learning.

FIGURE 2.10

The Framework of Support

Source: Families and Advocates Partnership for Education (FAPE), School accommodations and modifications. Reprinted with permission from PACER Center, Minneapolis, MN, (952)838-9000, http://www.pacer.org

? *Pause and Reflect*

The extent to which students with disabilities participate in standardized state testing will probably continue to change. As you reflect on the advantages and disadvantages of including the vast majority of students with disabilities in these assessment programs, what direction should these changes take? Can you think of regulations or criteria that you would use to determine if students should or should not participate in high-stakes assessment? ●

The Framework of Support for Students with Disabilities

The Framework of Support is a visual model that depicts the school supports necessary for students with disabilities' learning.

Now we are ready to complete our Framework of Support. The framework shown in Figure 2.10 depicts some of the supports necessary to help a student with a disability learn through access to the core curriculum. In this chapter, we have identified some of the instructional means for reaching that goal: universal design for learning, differentiated instruction, accommodations, and assistive technology.

Who Provides the Supports?

Typically, the general education teacher is viewed as the expert in the content of a grade level or an academic subject, and the special education teacher provides knowledge of the supports and the skills involved in implementing them (although there is often a good deal of crossover in what those two groups of teachers know and do). In addition to those primary individuals in a student's school life, there are also related services professionals who may provide additional supports to a student. **Related services** are those extra intensive learning experiences that the student needs to benefit from his or her education. They

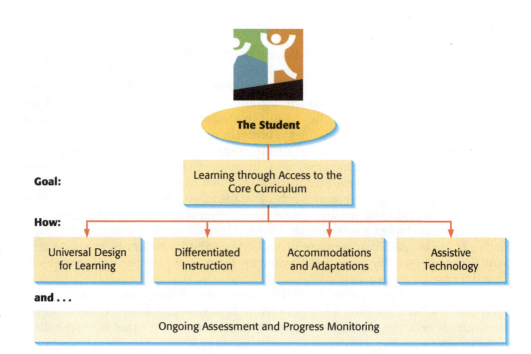

School Nurse

Occupational Therapist

Orientation &
Mobility Specialist

Interpreter

School Psychologist

Counselor

Speech-Language Pathologist

Physical Therapist

Adaptive Physical Education
Teacher/Recreation Therapist

FIGURE 2.11

The related services professionals working with children with IEPs in the schools

Source: http://www.edweek.org/ew/articles/2011/05/25/32henig_ep.h30.html?tkn=NONF%2BUZQnL
3kpUsqfpaOq4502zWLe%2f%2FKuH1%2F&cmp=ENL-EU-VIEWS1.

are provided by specialists, some of whom you see in Figure 2.11. Related services are written into each student's IEP. They are based on each student's needs,
and are different for each student. Ideally, teachers and related service providers
work together to achieve the student's IEP goals and master academic content.

In spite of the emphasis on serving students with disabilities in the general
education classroom with a series of supports, other service delivery options, such
as the resource room and self-contained classrooms, continue in most schools.
The new emphases on curriculum standards and high-stakes testing will make
it exceedingly difficult, however, for students to receive general education curriculum content in special education settings, and for the curriculum for most
children with disabilities to be anything but academic and standards-based. Children with severe disabilities are exempt from high-stakes testing and, therefore,
may continue to participate in curriculum that is functional in nature, emphasizing life skills, such as preparation for work activities, social interaction skills,
and exposure to domestic and recreational activities. What will happen to the
middle-school or high-school child who is reading on the second-grade level and
still has difficulty writing a legible paragraph? Where can he or she receive the
instruction in life skills needed? What will schools teach such a student if he or
she is exposed only to an academic curriculum and fails state achievement tests
year after year? These are the types of questions posed by special educators, parents, and students in the face of educational reform. We've discussed many of the

proactive strategies—approaches to curriculum and instruction—that attempt to facilitate learning and allow for many students to be more successful in school. The fact remains, of course, that there are many unanswered questions to the dilemmas facing schools and families as they continue to negotiate appropriate and individualized instructional programs for students with disabilities.

? Pause and Reflect

As you can see, the emphasis on educational programs in public schools may be greatly and immediately affected by public policy and national legislation. What educational rights for children, both with and without disabilities, do you believe should be protected by or identified through law? •

SUMMARY

- Students receiving special education services are disproportionally male. They are also more likely to be students of color from lower socioeconomic backgrounds. It is important not to overgeneralize, however, and assume that all students with IEPs fall into these categories.
- Special education professionals continue to be concerned about the disproportionate representation of students from culturally diverse backgrounds in special education services, particularly that of African American males.
- Progress has been made through litigation. Cases such as *Diana v. Board of Education* and *Larry P. v. Riles* challenged assessment practices that may help explain the disproportionate representation of students from minority groups in special education.
- Most children with disabilities participate in the general education curriculum, which is now a standards-based curriculum. High-stakes testing is tied to the curriculum standards.
- Special education instruction should be based on research-validated practices.
- Universal Design for Learning is a philosophical approach to creating a curriculum that is more accessible to all students.
- Assistive technology allows students to express themselves and participate more fully in their education.
- Differentiated instruction allows teachers to individualize based on the differing needs of students.
- Teachers use a variety of approaches, including co-teaching, to provide special education services to children with disabilities in general education classes.
- High-stakes testing is used in schools not only to evaluate individual student progress, but also to evaluate the performance of subgroups of students and to rate the success of schools.
- Both students and teachers need support from others—family and other school professionals—in order to make inclusion work.
- The Framework of Support provides a model for the kinds of supports that students with disabilities may need.

KEY TERMS

Disproportionate representation (page 39)

Overrepresentation (page 41)

Underrepresentation (page 43)

School-based risk (page 45)

Framework of Support (page 50)

social integration (page 50)

differentiated teaching (page 50)

functional or life-skills curriculum (page 51)

evidence-based practices (page 53)

Universal Design for Learning (UDL) (page 55)

accommodations (page 58)

modifications (page 58)

adaptations (page 58)

differentiated instruction (page 60)

Response to Intervention (RTI) (page 60)

school-wide positive behavior support (page 61)

consultation (page 62)

collaboration (page 62)

co-teaching (page 62)

Assessment (page 65)

high-stakes testing (page 66)

systematic progress monitoring (page 67)

Related services (page 68)

USEFUL RESOURCES

- The Institute of Educational Sciences of the U.S. Department of Education has established the *What Works Clearinghouse,* an online repository of studies that have passed the rigorous examination of experts in research design (**http://ies.ed.gov/ncee/wwc/**). While much of the research reviewed does not include students with disabilities in the subject pool, there are sections on students with learning disabilities and early childhood education for students with disabilities. Even more useful for teachers is the partner site, *Doing What Works* (**http://dww.ed.gov/index.cfm**), which explicitly identifies research-based practices for teachers and helps them translate those practices for their own use.

- Visit the Center for Applied Special Technology (CAST): **www.cast.org.** This center is a not-for-profit organization that focuses on creating opportunities for accessibility for all people via technology. The contributors to CAST engaged in much of the pioneering research in the Universal Design for Learning.

- Wolfgang Preiser and Elaine Ostroff (2011). *Universal design handbook* (2nd ed.). New York: McGraw-Hill. This book contains the American and international standards, American with Disabilities Act code requirements, and ideas for increasing accessibility in areas such as communication, transportation, Internet use, and buildings.

- There are several excellent websites on RTI. Among the best are the RTI Action Network (**http://www.rtinetwork.org**), the National Center on Response to Intervention (**http://www.rti4success.org**), and the Center for RTI in Early Childhood (**http://www.crtiec.org**).

- The IRIS Center has five online modules on RTI. For the purposes of this chapter, the most helpful module is the overview, which can be found at **http://iris.peabody.vanderbilt.edu/rti01_overview/chalcycle.htm.**

- The Office of Special Education Programs (OSEP) Technical Assistance Center on Positive Behavioral Interventions and Supports has lots of helpful information for teachers and families at **http://www.pbis.org.**

- The National Dissemination Center for Children with Disabilities offers more information on "Effective Practices in the Classroom and School" at **http://nichcy.org/schoolage/effective-practices,** and "Assessment and Accommodations" at **http://nichcy.org/research/ee/assessment-accommodations/.**

- The online "newspaper" *Disability Scoop* calls itself "the premier source of developmental disability news." It is a broad and reliable source of news about all ages of people with disabilities. Find it at **www.disabilityscoop.com.**

 PORTFOLIO ACTIVITIES

1. Visit your state's Department of Education website and review the schools' testing reports. Compare the passing scores of two school districts or of schools within one district. Summarize the performances of the schools as a whole and the performances of various subgroups reported. Note whether any reference is made to students with IEPs or alternate assessment.

CEC This activity will help students meet CEC Initial Content Standard 8: Assessment.

2. Examine the curriculum used for science at the middle-school level. Consider the principles of Universal Design for Learning and describe at least five ways you could create a curriculum more accessible for students with disabilities.

CEC This activity will help students meet CEC Initial Content Standard 10: Collaboration.

3. Review the early elementary-level reading standards for your state (Grades 1–3). Use the descriptions of academic challenges in reading that you may find in Chapters 4, 5, 7, and 8 of this text to identify the additional skills you will need to teach these standards to children with mild to moderate academic disabilities.

CEC This activity will help students meet CEC Initial Content Standard 7: Instructional Planning.

4. Create a notebook of articles and firsthand descriptions of special education programs delivered in a general education setting. Record and compare the models of instruction used by the teachers and the strategies or materials that you find particularly interesting and potentially useful in your own classroom.

CEC This activity will help students meet CEC Initial Content Standard 5: Learning Environments and Social Interactions.

 To access Portfolio Activities for this chapter and other useful study resources including an interactive eBook, related web links, quizzes, flashcards, and videos, visit the Education CourseMate website at CengageBrain.com.

CHAPTER 3

Risk Factors and Early Intervention

Learning Objectives

After reading this chapter, the reader will:

- Understand the concept of *risk* as it applies to the development of young children.

- List and explain the biological risk factors that can affect the development of young children.

- List and explain the environmental risk factors that can affect the development of young children.

- Describe how some disabilities might be prevented.

- Define and describe *early intervention* for young children at risk, with developmental delays, and with disabilities.

- Appreciate the importance of relationships in the healthy development of young children.

Happily, the great majority of pregnancies result in healthy babies. Yet each woman, each couple conceiving a child, also takes a chance that the child will develop differently from "the norm" and as a result have special needs that require extra help and support at home and at school.

Why do some pregnancies produce children with special needs? Why do some children who have difficult starts in life do just fine, whereas others who begin life under ideal circumstances develop problems? The answers are complicated—many times no medical or psychological expert can answer them for bewildered parents. But in this chapter we will describe some of the circumstances that place a child at risk for the development of a disability.

The information in this chapter should have meaning for you as a teacher or other professional working with exceptional children. First, it should help you decide whether the cause of a student's disability has any bearing on the kind of instruction or support that you will provide. Second, it should help you give more complete information to family members who come to you for advice and counsel. This information will be relevant to each of the specific disabilities discussed later in the book. We encourage you to review this chapter as you learn about children with specific disabilities.

We also expect that this information will have personal meaning for each reader. Some of you may be making decisions about whether or when to begin a family. Others may be watching your own children have children. We hope that the information presented here will help you to plan for a healthy family and to make intelligent, well-informed decisions that may enhance the possibilities for a healthy baby. Ultimately, the message of this chapter is that we can all have an impact on the prevention of disabilities in children. Each one of us has a responsibility to do whatever is within our power to *prevent* disabilities in the children of our country—and that is part of what this chapter is all about.

Terms and Definitions

Imagine this scenario: You are a teacher in a high school for pregnant teenage girls. One of your students, Amanda, is 16 years old, has juvenile diabetes, and, at six months pregnant, is refusing to eat healthy foods. She has a history of difficulty keeping her blood sugar under control. Amanda is frequently lethargic, and, although academically capable, she is barely engaged with her class work. At a meeting of school professionals to discuss her situation, the school nurse states emphatically to the group: "Look, this is a high-risk pregnancy—both Amanda and her baby are at risk. We have to do all we can to get this girl on track, for both of them!"

We hear the term *at risk* used frequently. People may be at risk for a heart attack, for failing a class, or for dropping out of school. In the story told above, Amanda's health appears to be at risk. Her baby, though, will be exposed to many risk factors, both biological (poor maternal health and nutrition) and environmental (young, single mother). These factors may affect his status at birth, and his performance in school when he is older. In this chapter, we will focus on risk to the fetus and the developing child. We will define the term *risk* in this context. Psychologist and researcher Claire Kopp (1983) defined **risk factors** as "a wide range of *biological and environmental conditions* [emphasis added] that are associated with increased probability for cognitive, social, affective, and physical problems" (p. 1). Biological conditions generally arise from factors related to pregnancy or maternal and child health, such as low birth weight, exposure to drugs or toxic substances, or a chromosomal abnormality. Environmental conditions include negative influences in the child's physical or social surroundings *after* birth, such as extreme poverty, child abuse, or neglect.

> The presence of risk factors increases the probability of adverse outcomes but does not guarantee them.

> Many factors—known and unknown—can place a child at risk for the development of a disability.

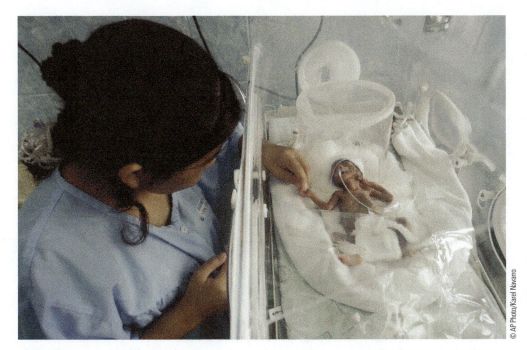

Premature infants like this little girl look so fragile that we are amazed that they survive. Most this size do, but they are at risk for chronic illness and disability.

The second part of Kopp's definition contains a crucial concept. These conditions are *associated with increased probability* for a variety of later problems. It is more likely that these problems will occur if there are risk factors present—but the presence of one or more risk factors *does not guarantee* poor development in children. The severity of the risk factor as well as the nature of the environment in which each child grows will determine whether developmental problems will occur.

Some children overcome both biological and environmental hurdles and, because of their own characteristics and the support that they receive from adult relationships, emerge as strong and productive adults. You will see, however, that the existence of clusters or combinations of risk factors makes it more likely that developmental problems will occur and that *early intervention*—comprehensive, individualized services provided to children from birth to age 3 and their families—can have a significant positive impact on a child's development.

> Clusters or combinations of risk factors in a young child's history make it more likely that developmental problems will occur.

❓ Pause and Reflect

The material in this chapter should have applications to your own life, both personal and professional. Can you think of individuals you have known who might at one time have qualified as "at risk"? ●

Types of Risk

Since the concept of risk is wide-ranging, it is helpful to have a framework within which categories of vulnerable infants can be described. We will use the categories of **biological risk** and **environmental risk** to describe the potential impact of specific factors on young children (see Figure 3.1).

> Risk factors are biological or environmental conditions associated with cognitive, social, affective, and physical problems.

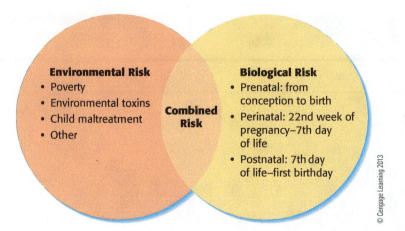

Environmental Risk
• Poverty
• Environmental toxins
• Child maltreatment
• Other

Combined Risk

Biological Risk
• Prenatal: from conception to birth
• Perinatal: 22nd week of pregnancy–7th day of life
• Postnatal: 7th day of life–first birthday

© Cengage Learning 2013

FIGURE 3.1

Types of risk

Biological Risk

Biological risk exists when events occur before, during, or after birth that may be associated with damage to the child's developing systems, increasing the likelihood that he or she will experience developmental problems. Biological risk factors can be divided into three categories that correspond with the earliest periods of development (Kopp, 1983): the **prenatal period,** from conception to birth; the **perinatal period** (which overlaps with the prenatal period somewhat), from the 22nd week of pregnancy through the seventh day of life (Nguyen & Wilcox, 2005); and the postnatal period. The **postnatal period,** for our purposes, will include part of the neonatal period (birth through the 28th day of life) and be defined as the seventh day of life through the first birthday. Definitions of some of these terms vary in the medical literature, and you can see that there is some overlap between periods. Rather than worrying about the exact days of the time period, focus on the larger concepts of before birth (prenatal), the time during pregnancy when a child might survive birth (perinatal), and the first year of life (postnatal) when you read and use these terms.

The accompanying A Closer Look box describes two ways to lower risk for developmental problems during pregnancy.

> Biological risk exists when prenatal, perinatal, or postnatal events increase the likelihood that the child will experience developmental problems.

● *Prenatal Factors*   Prenatal factors are those that affect embryologic and fetal development before birth. Adverse prenatal events often account for the most severe developmental outcomes among the infants who survive them. If they have their impact during the **first trimester** (first three months) of pregnancy, they may compromise the organs and body parts developing at that time; if they occur later in pregnancy, they may affect the growth and differentiation of those organs that are still developing, such as the brain and central nervous system. Prenatal factors include maternal illnesses and maternal use and abuse of substances, including drugs and alcohol. These factors—alcohol, drugs, illnesses, infections, and so on—are often called **teratogens,** substances that can cause birth defects. We will discuss some of the most common factors that research tells us can affect embryologic and fetal development during pregnancy (see Figure 3.2). The nearby A Closer Look box, "Newborn Screening," describes the screening of newborns for some of the genetic, metabolic, and hormonal diseases that exert their influence during the prenatal period.

> Teratogens are substances that can cause birth defects.

Maternal Illness and Infection   Not every illness of the pregnant mother will affect her unborn child, but some illnesses and infections are known to have a devastating impact on embryologic and fetal development. (In Figure 3.3 you will see when particular organs in the fetus are especially vulnerable.) As an example, let's look at **rubella** (sometimes called "German measles"), a highly contagious virus. Rubella is particularly damaging if contracted by a woman during the first

A CLOSER LOOK   Lowering Risk during Pregnancy: What You and Your Partner Can Do

Consume folic acid

What you need to know:

Folic acid, a B vitamin, helps prevent birth defects of the brain and spinal cord when taken before the end of early pregnancy. It is available in most multivitamins, as a folic-acid–only supplement, and in some foods.

What you can do:

Take a multivitamin with 400 micrograms of folic acid every day before pregnancy and during early pregnancy, as part of a healthy diet.

Eat a healthy diet that includes foods that contain folate, the natural form of the vitamin. Such foods include fortified breakfast cereals, dried beans, leafy green vegetables, and orange juice.

If you have already had a pregnancy affected by a birth defect of the brain or spinal cord, ask your health care provider how much folic acid you need. Studies have shown that taking a larger dose of folic acid daily can reduce the risk of having another affected pregnancy. The larger dose needs to be taken at least one month before pregnancy and in the first trimester of pregnancy. The recommended dose in this case is 4 milligrams (4,000 micrograms).

_____

(*Source:* http://www.marchofdimes.com/Pregnancy/folicacid.html)

Avoid hazardous substances

What you need to know:

Some substances and chemicals—such as solvents, paints, cleaners, and pesticides—can cause birth defects or increase your risk of miscarriage.

Substances to watch out for include cigarette smoke, lead (in water and paint), carbon monoxide, mercury, solvents, paint, paint thinners, benzene, and formaldehyde.

What you can do:

If you must live or work around these substances, minimize your exposure:

- Make sure your workplace is well ventilated.
- Wear appropriate protective gear, such as gloves or a face mask.
- Let someone else paint the baby's room and stay away until the fumes are gone.
- Check with your local water authority or health department if you are worried about the quality of your tap water. You can also drink bottled water while you are pregnant or trying to conceive.
- Be careful when handling fluorescent lightbulbs. If broken, they may release mercury.

_____

(*Source:* http://www.marchofdimes.com/Pregnancy/stayingsafe_hazardous.html)

For more information, visit the March of Dimes website: http://www.marchofdimes.com/pregnancy/pregnancy.html

---

16 weeks of pregnancy. It can result in blindness, deafness, heart malformation, and/or intellectual and developmental disabilities in surviving infants, depending on the fetal organ developing at the time the rubella virus strikes. Moores (2001, p. 106) describes the impact of the virus:

> If a pregnant woman contracts rubella, particularly during the first trimester (three months) of pregnancy, the virus may cross the placental barrier and attack the developing cells and structures of the fetus, killing or crippling the unborn child. The virus can kill growing cells, and it attacks tissues of the eye, ear, and other organs.

Fortunately, immunization against rubella has virtually eliminated this disease as a cause of disability in the United States; it still constitutes a threat in parts of the world where immunization is not widely available (National Organization for Rare Disorders, 2011).

Illness of the mother during pregnancy can cause damage to the developing fetus.

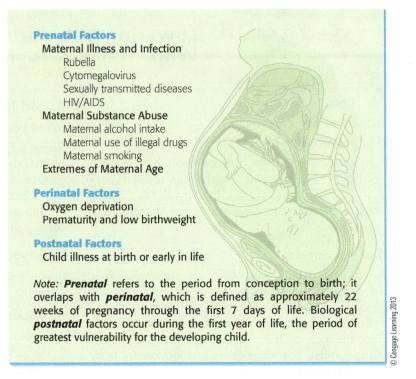

Prenatal Factors
Maternal Illness and Infection
Rubella
Cytomegalovirus
Sexually transmitted diseases
HIV/AIDS
Maternal Substance Abuse
Maternal alcohol intake
Maternal use of illegal drugs
Maternal smoking
Extremes of Maternal Age

Perinatal Factors
Oxygen deprivation
Prematurity and low birthweight

Postnatal Factors
Child illness at birth or early in life

Note: **Prenatal** refers to the period from conception to birth; it overlaps with **perinatal**, which is defined as approximately 22 weeks of pregnancy through the first 7 days of life. Biological **postnatal** factors occur during the first year of life, the period of greatest vulnerability for the developing child.

© Cengage Learning 2013

FIGURE 3.2

Examples of biological risk factors

Cytomegalovirus (CMV) remains the most common congenital viral infection in the United States (**congenital** refers to a condition the child is born with). Approximately 1 in 750 newborns are infected at birth because of transmission of the virus from their mother during pregnancy (Centers for Disease Control and Prevention, 2010). Most women with the virus acquire it from the blood or

A CLOSER LOOK Newborn Screening

Every state and U.S. territory routinely screens newborns for certain genetic, metabolic, hormonal, and functional disorders. Most of these birth defects have no immediate visible effects on a baby. However, unless detected and treated early, these disorders can cause physical problems, intellectual and developmental disabilities, and, in some cases, death.

"Screening" means testing to see if a baby is more likely than other babies to have a disorder. Newborn screening tests don't tell if a baby definitely has a disorder. That kind of test is called a "diagnostic" test. If a baby's screening tests show abnormal results, it does not mean the baby definitely has a disorder. It means that diagnostic testing is needed.

Fortunately, most babies get a clean bill of health when tested. However, about 5,000 babies each year are found to have these serious conditions and more than 12,000 to have hearing impairment. In cases like these, early diagnosis and proper treatment can make the difference between healthy development and lifelong disability.

The *Newborn Screening Task Force* report (2000) recommends that families be educated about newborn screening and involved in informed decision-making from the outset. Once a condition has been diagnosed, they should be made aware of the short- and long-term characteristics of the condition, treatment goals, and the health care and social service resources that are available. Newborn screening can save lives and prevent illness and disability, but it comes with the responsibility of education and follow-up treatment.

For more information about newborn screening, visit The March of Dimes' website at http://www.marchofdimes.com/.

_____

(*Source:* Adapted from http://www.marchofdimes.com/Professionals/education_newbornscreening.html)

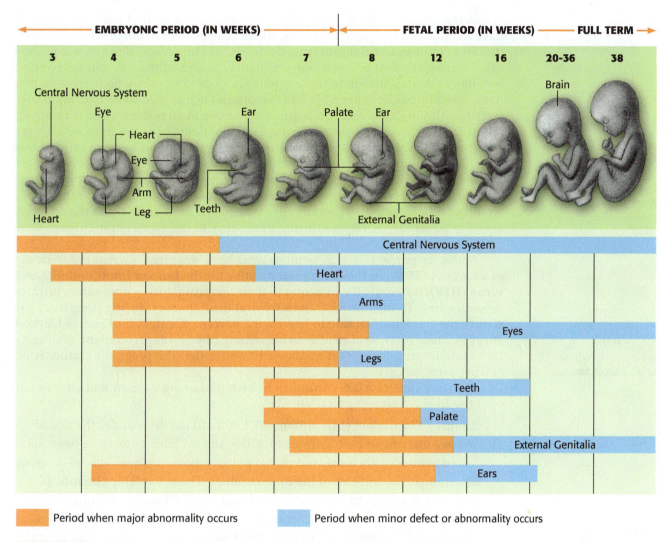

| EMBRYONIC PERIOD (IN WEEKS) | | | | | FETAL PERIOD (IN WEEKS) | | | | FULL TERM |

Period when major abnormality occurs   Period when minor defect or abnormality occurs

Sensitive periods in prenatal development

Source: K. L. Moore (1998). Adapted from *Before we are born* (5th ed.), Elsevier.

urine of infected children, which is one of the reasons why frequent hand washing and wearing gloves when coming in contact with bodily fluids are so important for those who care for young children. The virus can result in the infant's death or in aftereffects such as intellectual and developmental disabilities, visual impairment, and hearing loss, which may not manifest themselves until later in the child's life. For more information about cytomegalovirus, visit the Centers for Disease Control website or the Education CourseMate website that accompanies this text.

Sexually transmitted diseases (STDs) affect a mother and her partner, and can have serious implications for their child. The term "STD" denotes the more than 25 infectious organisms that are transmitted through sexual activity. The most common STDs among pregnant women in the United States are bacterial vaginosis, genital herpes, chlamydia, trichomoniasis, gonorrhea, viral hepatitis, HIV, human papillomavirus (HPV), pelvic inflammatory disease, and syphilis (Centers for Disease Control and Prevention, 2010). Active infection with STDs during pregnancy may result in a range of serious health problems among infected infants, including severe central nervous system damage, congenital malformations, and death (Bell, 2007). For example, a mother with syphilis may have a child with congenital syphilis, which can result in death or severe intellectual and developmental disabilities, deafness, and blindness. If the illness is identified during the first trimester of pregnancy, harm to the fetus can be avoided, but many infants with congenital syphilis are born to women who receive no prenatal care. Herpes, another STD, has symptoms such as cold sores and vaginal infections. Although the risk of transmitting herpes to an unborn child is relatively low, if transmission does occur during a vaginal delivery, it can have severe consequences for the infant, such as neurological, vision, and hearing impairment (Bell, 2007). Other STDs, including chlamydia, can also affect fetal development and the health of the newborn. STDs are a particular risk for adolescents and can be difficult to detect, since they are silent (there may be no obvious symptoms) in women. Left untreated, STDs can cause infertility. Learn more about the effects of sexually transmitted diseases during pregnancy at the Centers for Disease Control website.

> When STDs are identified and treated during the first trimester of pregnancy, harm to the fetus can be avoided.

About 25 percent of U.S. women who have **acquired immune deficiency syndrome (AIDS),** or those who test positive for the **human immunodeficiency virus (HIV),** transmit HIV infection to their offspring during pregnancy, birth, or breastfeeding. Treatment with antiretroviral drug therapy during pregnancy can reduce the transmission rate to less than 2 percent (Centers for Disease Control, 2010). Because early treatment is so important, physicians recommend testing for HIV early in pregnancy; that assumes, however, that the pregnant mother is receiving prenatal care.

> AIDS and HIV can be transmitted during pregnancy, birth, and breastfeeding.

The incidence of AIDS continues to be high among women and children all over the world. According to UNICEF:

> Roughly 17.5 million (14.6 million–20.9 million) children under the age of 18 have lost one or both parents to AIDS, and millions more have been affected, with a vastly increased risk of poverty, homelessness, school dropout, discrimination, and loss of life opportunities. These hardships include illness and death. Of the estimated 2 million (1.7 million–2.4 million) people who died of AIDS-related illnesses in 2008, 280,000 (150,000–410,000) of them were children under 15 years old. (Source: http://www.childinfo.org/hiv_aids.html)

In the United States, people of African American and Hispanic/Latino origin have particularly high rates of HIV/AIDS. Fortunately, the number of diagnoses of pediatric HIV/AIDS in the United States has declined significantly as medical care of HIV-positive pregnant women has become more aggressive and successful (**http://www.avert.org/usa-statistics.htm**). The same is not yet true in developing countries around the world. Table 3.1 describes the risk factors for HIV/AIDS. You probably think you know what they are, but take a look—you may be surprised at what is on the list. While this list was written about risk factors for African Americans, the group with the highest incidence of HIV/AIDS in the U.S., it also applies to many other Americans.

Maternal Substance Abuse Maternal drug use during pregnancy can place the health and development of the fetus at risk, and it remains a major public health problem; about one in ten pregnancies are affected by drug and/or alcohol use (Boris, 2009). Doctors recommend that even the most common legal drugs, whether they are over-the-counter or by prescription, should not be taken by pregnant women or be taken only with a doctor's recommendation. Many over-the-counter or prescription drugs have been associated with birth defects, particularly congenital malformations such as heart defects, ear damage, and cleft lip and palate. The effects of others on the developing fetus have not been adequately

Table 3.1 Risk Factors for HIV/AIDS

Sexual risk behaviors, such as unprotected sex with multiple partners, with a partner who also has other sex partners, or with persons at high risk for HIV infection.

Injection drug use can facilitate HIV transmission through the sharing of unclean needles. Casual and chronic substance users may be more likely to engage in unprotected sex under the influence of drugs and/or alcohol.

The presence of certain *sexually transmitted diseases (STDs)* can significantly increase the chance of contracting HIV infection. A person who has both HIV infection and certain STDs has a greater chance of infecting others with HIV.

The socioeconomic issues associated with *poverty*, including limited access to quality health care, housing, and HIV prevention education, directly and indirectly increase the risk for HIV infection and affect the health of people living with HIV.

Lack of awareness of HIV status. In a recent study of men who have sex with men (MSM) in five cities, 67 percent of the HIV-infected African American MSM were unaware of their infection.

Stigma also puts too many African Americans at higher risk. Many at risk for HIV infection fear stigma more than knowing their status, choosing instead to hide their high-risk behavior rather than seek counseling and testing.

(*Source:* Adapted from http://www.cdc.gov/hiv/topics/aa/index.htm/)

investigated by researchers (American College of Obstetricians and Gynecologists, 2008).

Medical professionals' caution about over-the-counter and prescription drugs comes in part from the experience of many Europeans with **thalidomide** in the late 1950s. Thalidomide was prescribed to pregnant women for nausea; over time it was learned that taking the drug during the first trimester of pregnancy often caused shortened or missing arms and legs in the fetus (Graham & Morgan, 1997). The thalidomide experience taught medical researchers and practitioners that they must carefully monitor drugs ingested during patients' pregnancies.

> The thalidomide tragedy of the 1950s demonstrated that great care must be taken with all drugs during pregnancy.

But what effects do the illegal drugs used today have on infants? Babies of mothers who have used cocaine, heroin or methadone, marijuana, PCP, or amphetamines (substance-abusing mothers who use combinations of drugs as well as alcohol are referred to as **polysubstance abusers**) appear to be at significant risk, and are particularly vulnerable to the effects of an unstable environment. Women who abuse drugs are often unable to provide a safe and stable environment for their children.

> Polysubstance abusers are those who use a combination of drugs as well as alcohol.

Among the drugs used by women of childbearing age, cocaine and marijuana may be the most common. Babies prenatally exposed to cocaine are more likely to be born early and to have a low birth weight and a smaller head circumference. Singer and her colleagues (2002) found that children prenatally exposed to cocaine had significant cognitive deficits and experienced a doubling of the rate of developmental delay during the first two years of life.

The long-term effects of exposure to illegal drugs on development are still being debated, but most researchers agree that preschool and school-aged children who were exposed to drugs *in utero* are at risk for emotional, behavioral, and attentional difficulties (Boris, 2009). In a recent review of the literature (2007), Bono and her colleagues concluded that prenatal exposure to cocaine *in itself* has only subtle effects on child development, but substance abuse significantly affects the family environment: Mothers who use cocaine are more likely to smoke, use other drugs and alcohol, and are less likely to have good nutrition and adequate prenatal care. In addition:

> Parental substance abuse is also associated with a deprived postnatal environment, which often includes homelessness, poverty, several custody changes, low parental education, and parental psychopathology (Phelps, Wallace, & Bontrager, 1997; Singer et al., 2002). These associated risk factors often lead to poor parent-child interactions, and generally inadequate caregiving, which may compound the subtle effects of cocaine exposure and raise the developmental risk for children in all competency areas, including cognition, language, and behavior. (Burnstein, Stanger, Kamon, & Dumenci, 2006; Nair et al., 1997)

The long-term effects of prenatal drug exposure on the child are difficult to predict.

More than half the women who are dependent on cocaine will experience physical abuse, STDs, or separation from their children by imprisonment (Hans, 1999). It is likely that the effects of the troubled home environment that often accompanies substance abuse are responsible for the poor outcomes seen in some of these children, particularly in their language development. The factors that help children's language flourish—consistent attention and responsiveness from adults—are missing in their lives (Bono et al., 2007). The substance-exposed children who are most likely to develop problems in life are those who also experience additional environmental risk factors. These children are examples of the doubly vulnerable—those who experience both biological and environmental risk. As we will see later in this chapter, exposure to multiple risk factors can change the brain architecture of the very young child, leading to school problems and health risks in adulthood (National Scientific Council on the Developing Child, 2007).

Every time we revise this book, new drugs are being used by women of childbearing age. It may take years for research to document the effects of those drugs on infants and young children who have been exposed to them *in utero*. So, never assume that drug use during pregnancy is harmless—assume the opposite. For more information on the effects of the "drugs of the moment," visit the National Institute on Drug Abuse website.

Maternal alcohol intake during pregnancy can have grave effects on the developing fetus. For surviving children, it can result in **fetal alcohol syndrome disorders (FASD)**. FASDs are a group of developmental disabilities associated with maternal alcohol intake during pregnancy. The most severe form of FASDs is fetal alcohol syndrome (FAS). The child with FAS has altered facial features, such as a small head, widely spaced eyes, upturned nose, large ears, and a small chin; he or she will also have developmental delays in language and cognition, and may have behavioral problems such as oppositional and defiant behavior, poor judgment, and social withdrawal (Wunsch, Conlon, & Scheidt, 2002). Some children have the cognitive and behavioral characteristics associated with FAS but not the physical abnormalities; they are said to have **alcohol-related neurodevelopmental disorder (ARND)**. **Alcohol-related birth defects (ARBD)** may include organ malformations and hearing problems. These fetal alcohol spectrum disorders occur in nearly 1 in 100 births worldwide, making them one of the leading causes of preventable intellectual and developmental disabilities today (Ismail, Buckley, Budacki, Jabbar, & Gallicano, 2010). Although not all children of women who drink alcohol experience these significant aftereffects, researchers have not identified a "safe" level of alcohol intake during pregnancy. The Centers for Disease Control summarize the findings this way: **FASDs are 100 percent preventable if a woman does not drink alcohol during pregnancy**. There is no known safe amount of alcohol to drink while pregnant. There is also no safe time during pregnancy to drink, and no safe kind of alcohol (Source: **http://www.cdc .gov/ncbddd/fasd/index.html**).

TeachSource VIDEO CASE

What Happens When Language Does *Not* Develop?

The most common reason for the referral of toddlers into early intervention is language delay. When you visit Chapter 3 on the CourseMate website and watch these two videos about young children and language, you will see what normal language development looks like in early childhood. What are the implications for children and their families when language does *not* develop as it should?

Maternal alcohol use during pregnancy can result in fetal alcohol syndrome or alcohol-related neurodevelopmental disorder.

© AP Photo/Michael Conroy

These triplets are getting the intensive interaction with their father that will help them develop well, despite the risk that accompanies multiple births.

Smoking   In the United States, about 18 percent of women smoke—and about ten percent of pregnant women smoke (March of Dimes, 2008). Most of us realize that smoking damages the smoker's health, but prenatal exposure to tobacco also has a serious impact on the developing fetus. Maternal cigarette smoking during pregnancy is the single most important cause of low birth weight (Kids Count Data Brief, 2009); pregnant women who smoke have a relatively high number of complications that can result in the death of the fetus, premature delivery, and physical abnormalities. Children of women who smoke during pregnancy are more likely to experience sudden infant death syndrome (SIDS) and have asthma (American College of Obstetricians and Gynecologists, 2008). According to the March of Dimes, a national organization which invests in and advocates for the prevention of prematurity and low birth weight:

> Cigarette smoke contains more than 2,500 chemicals. It is not known for certain which of these chemicals are harmful to the developing baby, but both nicotine and carbon monoxide play a role in causing adverse pregnancy outcomes. (2008)

Smoking can result in pregnancy complications as well as low birth weight and physical abnormalities in the infant.

Extremes of Parental Age   Mothers at the beginning and at the end of their reproductive span are at the greatest risk for potential pregnancy problems. Young mothers, particularly those in the earliest teenage years, are more likely to have pregnancy complications resulting in prematurity or low birth weight, as well as other medical complications that could endanger the life and health of their babies (Chen et al., 2007). Among the biological factors that place the infants of adolescent mothers at risk are poor maternal nutrition and low weight gain, a higher likelihood of sexually transmitted diseases, and, most important, limited access to prenatal care (March of Dimes, 2009). The children of very young mothers are also considered at risk because of the characteristics of their caregiving environment—their young mothers are less likely to finish school and have little work preparation; they may be less responsive to their baby's cues and are more likely to be accused of child abuse and neglect (Hans & Thullen, 2009).

Young mothers and older mothers are at risk for different pregnancy complications.

Table 3.2 Risk of Down Syndrome

Mother's Age	Chance of Having a Baby with Down Syndrome
20 years	1 in 1,600
25 years	1 in 1,300
30 years	1 in 1,000
35 years	1 in 365
40 years	1 in 90
45 years	1 in 30

Source: D. S. Newberger (2000). Down syndrome: What you need to know when you're pregnant. *American Family Physician.* 2000 August 15;62 (4) pg. 837–838.

One in five American women now have their first baby at age 35 or older (American Society for Reproductive Medicine, 2009). While most women over 35 have healthy pregnancies, they are more likely to have a child with **Down syndrome,** a condition caused by an extra 21st chromosome that results in intellectual and developmental disabilities and physical anomalies in the child (see Table 3.2 and Chapter 6). Since the older a mother is, the more likely she is to have a baby with Down syndrome, the American Medical Association recommends that pregnant women aged 35 and older undergo amniocentesis or other prenatal testing. But nowadays the physicians recommend that women of every age have a noninvasive screening for Down syndrome (Barclay, 2007). We will discuss prenatal testing procedures later in the chapter in the section on prevention of disabilities.

Women over 35 are also more likely to have health problems such as diabetes and high blood pressure, which can complicate a pregnancy. Older mothers, however, are also more likely to have access to early and consistent prenatal medical care, and, given such care, many potential pregnancy complications can be managed, and a healthy baby is born. Early and ongoing prenatal care can minimize the effects of maternal age.

Paternal age Students often ask the question "What about fathers?" Until recently, we have known very little about the potential risk associated with advanced paternal age. Recent research suggests that increased age of the father may be associated with decreased fertility and a greater likelihood of pregnancy complications (Sartorius & Nieschlag, 2009), as well as higher incidence of autism (Reichenberg et al., 2006) and schizophrenia (Miller et al., 2010) and relatively poor performance on neurocognitive tests in childhood (Saha et al., 2009). Also, investigations of exposure to toxic substances in the environment have intensified because of the conviction of many veterans of the Vietnam War that their exposure to the defoliant Agent Orange increased the number of birth defects such as spina bifida and the incidence of childhood cancer in their offspring.

While the age of 40 is considered "advanced" in some studies, the definition of "advanced" paternal age is not clear-cut; the relationship is linear (the older the father, the greater the risk). Because many couples are waiting until they are older to have children, this will continue to be an important area of research until more conclusive boundaries are identified.

● *Perinatal Factors* Perinatal factors are those that occur from about the 22nd week of pregnancy to the 28th day of infant life (definitions of perinatal vary in the research literature; Nguyen & Nowak, 2005). It is here that medical research and technology have had a profound impact on both the survival and the quality of life of small and sick babies. Nevertheless, perinatal stresses still increase the risk status and, at times, call for special treatment and follow-up.

Oxygen Deprivation   For a variety of reasons during pregnancy, labor, delivery, and newborn life, the infant can experience **hypoxia,** or a decreased availability of oxygen in the body tissues. Hypoxia can cause cells in the brain to die, resulting in brain damage and sometimes death. The long-term effects of oxygen deprivation can be severe or minimal, but among the disabling conditions associated with prolonged hypoxia (also known as perinatal asphyxia) are cerebral palsy, intellectual and developmental disabilities, seizures, visual and auditory deficits, and behavioral problems. Most affected infants, however, experience mild episodes of hypoxia and therefore do not develop disabilities (Levene & Chervenak, 2009). The incidence of disabilities like cerebral palsy caused by perinatal asphyxia is much higher in developing countries where women are more likely to give birth unattended.

> The perinatal period ranges from the 22nd week of pregnancy to the 28th day of life.

Prematurity and Low Birth Weight   Many of the prenatal risk factors discussed above increase the likelihood of **prematurity** and **low birth weight** (see Table 3.3). Most readers know those terms, but let's define them precisely. The average length of pregnancy, or gestation, is 40 weeks. Babies born before 37 weeks' gestation are called premature, or preterm. Although the timing of a birth is important, the baby's weight may be even more crucial. Babies born weighing less than about five and a half pounds (2500 grams) are said to be low birth weight. Those weighing three and a half pounds or less are considered **very low birth weight.** Babies born at 25 weeks gestation or less, usually weighing under one pound, are at the "threshold of viability"—their survival and their health are severely threatened (McDonald, 2002; Pignotti & Donzelli, 2008). Even full-term babies can be low birth weight; thus, prematurity and low birth weight may be independent of one another. Think of it this way: A premature baby, born at 34 weeks' gestation, might already weigh six pounds; a baby born on her "due date" might weigh only four pounds. For an example of how premature birth affects children and families, visit the Education CourseMate website at **CengageBrain.com** to read "The Story of Lucy and Nell."

> Premature babies are born before 37 weeks' gestation.

> Low birth weight babies weigh less than five and a half pounds.

What are the dangers of premature birth? Premature babies are more likely to be low birth weight, and the lower the birth weight, the more likely a baby will have serious complications or die. In fact, low birth weight is a factor in 65 percent of infant deaths. Premature babies' systems are sometimes not ready to function independently. They need to gain weight but often have not developed the ability to coordinate sucking and swallowing, and their intestines are not yet ready to digest food normally, so feeding and weight gain are complicated. Their immature immune systems make them very vulnerable to infection. In addition, the lower the

Table 3.3 Risk Factors for Prematurity

Inadequate prenatal care	Multiple gestation births
Poor nutrition and weight gain	History of previous premature pregnancies
Maternal infections	Smoking
Adolescent mother	Substance abuse
Poverty	Congenital anomalies or injuries to the fetus
Acute and chronic maternal illness	Problems of the cervix and the placenta

Source: K. Rais-Bahrami, B. L. Short, & M. L. Batshaw (2007). Premature and Small-for-Dates Infants. In M. L. Batshaw (Ed.) *Children with Disabilities*, (6th ed.). Baltimore: Paul H. Brookes.

birth weight, the more likely it is that the baby will develop complications of prematurity, such as respiratory distress syndrome (extreme difficulty in breathing), brain hemorrhage (bleeding), and retinopathy of prematurity (an eye condition that can lead to blindness), all of which place their long-term development at risk.

Advances in **neonatology,** the study of newborns, have dramatically changed the prognosis for even the tiniest surviving premature babies. The specialized care given to these fragile infants in the **neonatal intensive care unit,** the area of the hospital that provides care for sick and premature newborns, has ensured the survival of many babies who, even a few years ago, would have died. Until recently, babies weighing three and a half pounds and under (now called very low birth weight) routinely died; now most are routinely saved. The limits of survival have changed dramatically over the last few years; currently, the majority of infants born at twenty-four or more weeks' gestational age survive. Most of those babies weigh less than two pounds; the smallest survivors weigh around one pound. New drugs that successfully treat respiratory distress syndrome are helping to increase those numbers (Bradbury, 2002). However, premature babies are much more likely than full-term babies to have conditions such as cerebral palsy, intellectual and developmental disabilities, seizures, and vision and hearing impairments.

The number of premature survivors with disabling conditions increases as the birth weight drops. From 10 to 30 percent of very low birth weight babies who survive are chronically ill or disabled. Their disabilities range from school learning problems, particularly those related to hyperactivity and attention, to severe disabilities (Reichman, 2005).

The rate of premature birth in the U.S. rose more than 20 percent between 1990 and 2006 but dropped slightly in 2008. Still, one in eight American births result in premature babies (March of Dimes, 2011). Prematurity is a serious public health problem in our country.

● *Postnatal Factors*   Among the postnatal biological factors of the first year of life that place a child at risk for school learning problems are *chronic diseases and infections* and *severe nutritional deficiencies.* Among the diseases that can place a young child's learning at risk are asthma or chronic lung disease, meningitis (a life-threatening bacterial or viral infection), HIV, and ongoing ear infections (chronic otitis media). You will learn more about how chronic illness can affect learning in Chapter 13.

Nutritional deprivation is usually associated with extreme poverty, and it is difficult to separate the effects of poor nutrition from the other deprivations of poverty (Isaacs, 2007). In many developing countries, however, there is dramatic evidence that malnutrition, and particularly iron deficiency, alters brain development in children (Donovan & Cross, 2002). In short, there is little doubt that chronic poor nutrition can affect brain development and thus cause learning problems in school.

Environmental Risk

The category of environmental risk includes risk factors related to the surroundings in which the child develops. Environmental factors can influence development at any stage. They can influence biological development during pregnancy and neurological development during childhood and adulthood. We will first discuss events that may affect the environment of the mother before her child's birth, and therefore the development of the fetus.

● *Environmental Factors That Influence Prenatal Development*

Radiation   Studies from Hiroshima and Nagasaki, as well as ongoing observation of the aftereffects of the fire at the nuclear reactor at Chernobyl, suggest

---

Margin notes:

Advances in neonatology and high-risk infant care have ensured the survival of many low birth weight babies.

Diseases like meningitis and conditions like chronic otitis media can result in disabilities that affect school performance.

Environmental risk includes all the risk factors related to the environment in which the child develops.

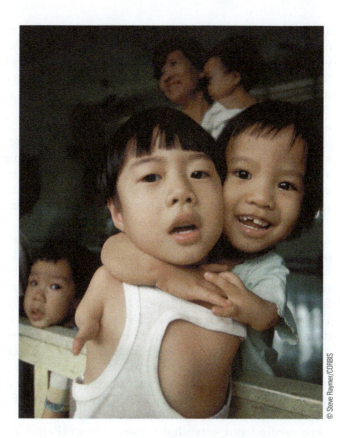

The mothers of these young children in Vietnam were exposed to Agent Orange, resulting in significant birth defects in their children.

a strong relationship between exposure to radiation in pregnant women and physical and psychological problems in their offspring (Kolominsky, Igumnov, & Drozdovich, 1999).

The effects of radiation depend on the level of the exposure and the stage of fetal development at the time of exposure. Weeks 2 through 15, when organs are being formed, are the most vulnerable time (Williams & Fletcher, 2010). Diagnostic X-rays that a pregnant woman might experience are rarely strong enough to harm the fetus (Centers for Disease Control and Prevention, 2005).

Neurotoxins Chemicals and metals that can cause damage to the nervous system are called neurotoxins, and like other teratogens they may have a particularly devastating effect on the developing fetal nervous system. Pregnant women whose workplaces or homes involve exposure to lead, mercury, cadmium, pesticides, radiation, or organic solvents must take care to protect themselves or seek workplace protections, since exposure to these and other substances has been linked to reproductive loss and intellectual and physical disabilities in children (Schroeder, 2000; Till, Koren, & Rovet, 2008). There is increasing concern among the public and professionals about the link between environmental neurotoxins and disability.

> Neurotoxins damage the developing central nervous system.

● *Postnatal Environmental Factors* After birth, environmental factors continue to influence how a child develops. The characteristics of the child's immediate caregiving environment are vital to optimal development. That environment must provide protection from exposure to dangerous toxins and disease as well as opportunities for learning and social growth and a stable home and family. We'll look at each of these areas.

Most researchers agree that the impact of biological risk events can be lessened or made worse by the characteristics of the environment. For example, although AIDS is classified as a biological risk factor and occurs in all sectors of our population, it is more likely to occur among those living in poverty. When we discussed prenatal exposure to drugs earlier in this chapter, we noted that the effects of a chaotic home environment can be as damaging (or more damaging) than the drug exposure. Children who are "at risk" develop as they do because of a complex interaction between their risk history and their caregiving environments.

Other agents within our environment can cause problems for children that may affect their school learning. Some of these, such as exposure to radiation, we are aware of, although hard data verifying the effects of these substances on the developing nervous system in children are difficult to come by. The toxins that we know most about are the heavy metals, particularly lead and mercury.

Lead   Lead exposure is an insidious teratogen because it has no symptoms and often is unrecognized, yet "Approximately 250,000 U.S. children aged 1 to 5 years have blood lead levels greater than 10 micrograms of lead per deciliter of blood, the level at which CDC recommends public health actions be initiated" (Centers for Disease Control and Prevention, 2010).

> Early exposure to lead is associated with a greater likelihood of school problems.

The early research of Needleman and his colleagues demonstrated that children with high lead levels have decreased IQ scores and poorer language and attention skills; their teachers find them more distractible and less well organized and persistent (Needleman et al., 1979). Long-term follow-up of these children indicated that early lead exposure is associated with a substantially elevated likelihood of having a reading disability, dropping out of school, delinquent behavior, and adult criminality (Needleman et al., 1991, 1996). Studies around the world have verified and extended these findings (Bellinger, 2008; Lidsky & Schneider, 2003). Tragically, exposure to lead is a major reason that millions of children around the globe do not live up to their full potential (Grantham-McGregor et al., 2007).

The primary source of lead in our environment is the remnants of lead paint, which is now outlawed. Chips and dust from old lead paint still contaminate the air in many neighborhoods, particularly in dense urban areas where old buildings are deteriorating. Infants and young children crawl and play in lead dust and then can ingest it as they put their hands in their mouths. Other sources of lead are traditional home health remedies such as *azarcon* and *greta*, which are sometimes used for upset stomach or indigestion in the Hispanic community; imported candies; imported toys and toy jewelry, pottery and ceramics, and drinking water contaminated by lead leaching from lead pipes, solder, brass fixtures, or valves (CDC, 2010). Although poverty significantly increases the risk of lead exposure, excessively high levels of lead are found in children of all social classes and racial backgrounds.

Other Environmental Toxins   Many of us are suspicious about the effect of environmental toxins on children, but research in this area is notoriously difficult to conduct. How does the researcher separate the effects of a toxic substance present in the environment—the air, water, soil, home, and community—from the effects of anything else? Some of the substances that have been studied are mercury, polychlorinated biphenyls (PCBs), pesticides and herbicides, organic solvents, environmental tobacco smoke, and endotoxins (toxic substances made by certain types of bacteria). These substances are **neurotoxins**—substances that adversely affect the structural or functional components of the nervous system (Center for Children's Health and the Environment, 2002). As such, they could have a relationship to the rising number of cases of attention deficit disorder, autism spectrum disorders, and other developmental disabilities, as well as asthma and cancer (Landrigan et al., 2002). The key word here is *could*—the research is not yet conclusive.

For example, small amounts of mercury are found throughout our environment, and mercury exposure has been found to have adverse affects on the development of the fetal neurological system during pregnancy and on the developing child (Evans, 2006). Human exposure to small amounts of mercury can come from eating fish and a range of other factors (Davidson & Myers, 2007). It appears that few children are exposed to enough mercury to cause any toxic developmental influence, but the science is still developing around this issue.

There are, no doubt, other substances within our environment that cause damage to the developing nervous system in children that have not yet been identified. One recent review of the literature identified excessive levels of noise, crowding, housing and neighborhood quality, and other aspects of the child's physical environment as potential mediators of child health and development (Evans, 2006). Many of the causes of childhood learning problems, as we shall see in future chapters, are unknown.

Accidents   Accidents or unintentional injuries are examples of environmental risks, and they are the major cause of death and physical impairment in children (Borse et al., 2008). Car accidents are the most common, but accidents may also happen on bikes, in swimming pools, and anywhere else that active, curious young children play and explore. Boys are almost twice as likely to be involved in accidents as girls (Borse et al., 2008). Accidents that involve head trauma, oxygen deprivation, or spinal cord injury can cause severe physical disability as well as learning and behavior problems. Lee, Harrington, Chang, and Connors (2008) found that children with developmental disabilities (in this case autism, ADD/ADHD, psychopathology, and other medical conditions) were more than twice as likely as unaffected children to experience an injury requiring medical attention. Teachers and caregivers must be extremely watchful and observant of children's play areas.

> Accidents are the most common postnatal risk factor.

The characteristics of the social environment are also crucial for optimal development: the nature of the medical technology available to support a sick newborn or child, the availability of public health services in the community, and the emphasis on educational achievement within the society as a whole. The next part of our discussion of environmental risk concentrates on the social aspects of poverty. You will see that there is a great deal of overlap among these areas, and they are often interrelated.

Poverty   Many people have achieved success in life despite being raised in poverty, but there is little doubt that poverty is a significant risk factor—perhaps the greatest of all. What is it about living in poverty that leads to poor outcomes for children? The obvious answer, lack of access to good medical care and nutrition, as well as to experiences and opportunities, is only partly right.

> Poverty—which can include both economic and social factors—is a major cause of environmental risk.

Millions of children live in poverty all over the world. Grantham-McGregor et al. (2007) examined the relationship between poverty, child growth (limitations in child growth are known as stunting), and cognitive potential in children in developing countries, and here they explain the implications of these factors for the development of nations:

> We have made a conservative estimate that more than 200 million children under 5 years fail to reach their potential in cognitive development because of poverty, poor health and nutrition, and deficient care. Children's development consists of several interdependent domains, including sensory-motor, cognitive, and social-emotional, all of which are likely to be affected. However, we focus on cognitive development because of the paucity of data from developing countries on other domains of young children's development. The discrepancy between their current developmental levels and what

FIGURE 3.4

Hypothesised relations between poverty, stunting, child development, and school achievement

Source: Reprinted from Child Development in developing countries 1: Developmental potential in the first 5 years for children in developing countris, Sally Grantham-McGregor, Yin Bun Cheung, Santiago Cueto, Paul Glewwe, Linda Richter, Barbara Strupp, and the International Child Development Sterring Group. *Lancet,* 2007; 369: 60–70. With permission from Elsevier.

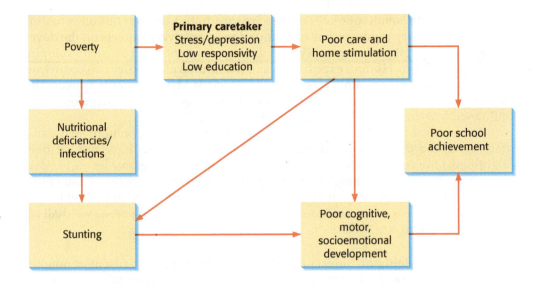

they would have achieved in a more nurturing environment with adequate stimulation and nutrition indicates the degree of loss of potential. In later childhood these children will subsequently have poor levels of cognition and education, both of which are linked to later earnings. Furthermore, improved parental education, particularly of mothers, is related to reduced fertility, and improved child survival, health, nutrition, cognition, and education. Thus the failure of children to fulfill their developmental potential and achieve satisfactory educational levels plays an important part in the intergenerational transmission of poverty. In countries with a large proportion of such children, national development is likely to be affected. (Grantham-McGregor et al., 2007, p. 60)

Figure 3.4 depicts a model of the interaction among these factors.

While economic conditions for families are largely better in developed countries like the United States, poverty is still a serious threat to child well-being. Poverty rates in the U.S. have increased over the last five years, and a disproportionate majority of the poor are children under age five (Duncan & Magnuson, 2011). The children of poverty are more likely to die in childhood, to be in special education programs, and to drop out of school; the girls are more likely to become pregnant during adolescence and the boys to engage in criminal behavior. Children who live below the poverty level are less likely to be in good health than those above the poverty line. They are also more likely to have limitations in their activity because of a chronic health condition (for example, asthma or diabetes) (Health Indicators, 2011). Children with disabilities are more likely to live in poor families, and people with intellectual disabilities are more likely to live in poverty than their nondisabled peers (Emerson, 2007). The nearby A Closer Look box provides more details on child poverty in the U.S.

Biologically normal infants who live in poverty may be at risk for problems of development because of characteristics of their caregiving environment. McLloyd (1998) identified some of the risk factors associated with persistent poverty: higher rates of perinatal complications, reduced access to resources that might buffer the effects of those complications, increased exposure to lead, and less home-based cognitive stimulation. These inadequacies are more likely to exist in impoverished families—money *does* buy health care, food, and quality day care for working or absent parents—but they are by no means exclusive to poor families.

A CLOSER LOOK   Childhood Poverty in the United States

Although the United States is home to 406 billionaires and countless millionaires, a baby is born into poverty every 32 seconds, 2,692 each day. Children are the poorest age group in America—every fifth child is poor. One in 12 children lives in extreme poverty (earning just half or below the annual poverty level of $22,050 for a family of four). The gap between rich and poor in the United States is the largest on record. The *richest 10 percent* of households with children received *38 percent* of the nation's income in 2006, the highest amount in three decades, while the *bottom 20 percent* received only *five percent* of the nation's income. Poverty could be eliminated for everyone for less than $140 billion, and all families with children for less than half that amount. Ending poverty is a crucial step to dismantling the cradle-to-prison pipeline.

- In 2008, as the recession was just beginning, 14.1 million children were poor, an increase of 2.5 million children (1.6 million of them in extreme poverty) since 2000.

- More than 5.6 million children are in families living at half the poverty level or less. For a family of four that is $919 a month, $212 a week and $30 a day. Children in extreme poverty increased by 1.6 million between 2000 and 2008.

- There are more poor Hispanic children than Black, American Indian/Alaska Native, or Asian/Pacific Islander. Black and Hispanic children are more than twice as likely to be poor as white, non-Hispanic children.

- Children in female-headed families are the most likely to be poor—four times as likely as children in married-couple families.

- Nearly 70 percent of poor children live in families where at least one family member works.

- More than half of all poor children live in eight states (California, Texas, New York, Florida, Illinois, Georgia, Ohio, and Michigan), and more than half of all children in extreme poverty live in these states plus Pennsylvania.

- Child poverty rates range from 30.4 percent in Mississippi to 9.0 percent in New Hampshire.

- There are almost as many poor children living in the suburbs as there are in urban areas. Additional information from the 2010 Census:

  - A total of 15.5 million children, or one in every five children in America, lived in poverty in 2009. Over five million of these children were under the age of five. Poverty is defined as an annual income of below $21,954 for a four-person family.

  - Of these children, almost half—6.9 million—lived in extreme poverty, defined as an annual income of less than half of the poverty level ($10,974 for a family of four). 2.4 million children living in extreme poverty in 2009 were under the age of five.

  - Children of color continue to suffer disproportionately from poverty:

    - 4 million Black children—more than one in three—live in poverty.

    - 5.6 million Hispanic children—one in three—live in poverty.

    - 4.9 million white, non-Hispanic children—more than one in ten—live in poverty.

(*Sources:* Children's Defense Fund, *The State of America's Children 2010 Report,* http://www.childrensdefense.org/child-research-data-publications/data/state-of-americas-children-2010-report.html/; *Millions More Children Living in Poverty: Now Is the Time to Act and Invest in the Future of Our Children,* http://www.childrens-defense.org/newsroom/cdf-in-the-news/press-releases/2010/millions-more-children-living-poverty.html)

Most of us can cite several examples of people who grew up in such circumstances who have reached significant levels of achievement in our society. Garbarino (1990) made the point that some families are economically impoverished but have a "socially rich family environment": family members, neighbors, and friends who provide support for both children and parents—the "informal helping relationships" that are the foundation of some communities. Other families are both economically and socially impoverished. According to Garbarino (1990, p. 90),

these are the environments in which prenatal care is inadequate, intervals between births are often too short, beliefs about child care too often

This billboard illustrates the living conditions that many U.S. children and families endure due to poverty and homelessness.

Source: http://www.horizonsforhomelesschildren.org/Newsroom_Billboard_Sept_06.asp

dysfunctional, access to and utilization of well-baby care inadequate, early intervention for child disabilities inadequate, and thus in which child mortality and morbidity are rampant.

These conditions are more likely to occur in our inner cities, where families must also live with the reality of frequent violence that respects no target—not even a small child. The stresses in such communities can become unbearable; neighbors may be afraid and distrustful of one another, and little sense of community may exist.

Social impoverishment can occur at every economic level, but more affluent families can pay for supportive services when they are not available through friends and family. Many poor families, frequently headed by single mothers, are left with few resources to help with the considerable stresses of childrearing.

Families come in all shapes, sizes, and configurations. We can no longer assume that a child will grow up in a traditional nuclear family, nor do we insist that there is one "right" way to raise children. We do know, however, that certain characteristics of the caregiving environment appear to help children develop optimally. Emotional and physical safety, responsive and sensitive caregivers, and stability of family members are all tied to the healthy development of children.

We will discuss issues related to families in the next chapter. But here it is important to describe two characteristics of families that place the child at risk: maltreatment and family instability.

Child Maltreatment   Child maltreatment can consist of physical abuse, sexual abuse, psychological (or emotional) abuse, or neglect, and is a major public health problem throughout the world (Gilbert, Widom, Browne, Fergusson, Webb, & Janson, 2009). In fact, reports of the murder, abuse, and neglect of children are as old as recorded history and appear in all cultures. Maltreatment during childhood can result in externalizing and internalizing behavior problems (see Chapter 8 for more information on this topic), cognitive delay, and low school achievement (Dubowitz & Bennet, 2007), as well as a range of problems in adulthood, such as mental health problems, drug and alcohol abuse, risky sexual behavior, obesity, and criminal behavior (Gilbert et al., 2009). It is a major risk factor for death, disability, and poor health and social outcomes in adulthood.

Child abuse may be responsible for some cases of intellectual and developmental disabilities, physical disability, and emotional disturbance in the United States today.

Children with disabilities are at increased risk of maltreatment, but this is a chicken vs. egg situation—does child abuse cause the disability, or are children with disabilities more likely to be abused? Hibbard and Desch (2007) address the issue of increased risk:

> . . . several elements may increase the risk of abuse for children with disabilities. Children with chronic illnesses or disabilities often place higher emotional, physical, economic, and social demands on their families. For example, a physical disability that causes difficulty in ambulation can place a child at risk of accidental falls. Therefore, much closer supervision will be needed, which itself can be stressful. Parents with limited social and community support may be at especially high risk of maltreating children with disabilities, because they may feel more overwhelmed and unable to cope with the care and supervision responsibilities that are required. Lack of respite or breaks in child care responsibilities can contribute to an increased risk of abuse and neglect. Finally, the added requirements of special health care and educational needs can result in failure of the child to receive needed medications, adequate medical care, and appropriate educational placements, resulting in child neglect. (p. 1020)

One study found that 24 percent of maltreated children received special education services at an average age of eight years (Jonson-Reid, Drake, Kim, Porterfield, & Han, 2004). Children are likely to be identified by the child welfare system before they are identified by special education. Since child maltreatment is such a significant risk factor for disability, Jonson-Reid and her colleagues (2004) suggest that maltreated children receive early intervention services to help prevent later disability, as well as school and mental health problems. To learn more about child abuse, visit the American Academy of Pediatrics' website at **http://www. aap.org/healthtopics/childabuse.cfm/.**

In many states, teachers are mandated to report suspected child maltreatment, so being informed about risk factors and reporting requirements is crucial. (See also "Useful Resources" at the end of this chapter.)

Family Instability   Although we now know that the two-parent family is not a necessary condition for optimal child growth and development, it does seem clear that children need at least one stable caregiver throughout their childhood in order to develop well (Werner & Smith, 1982). That caregiver may not be a parent; often, a grandmother or other relative can provide the ongoing stability a child needs. Children who experience many changes in the adult makeup of the household appear to do less well in school (Hunt, 1982) and may be at greater risk for dropping out of school and engaging in criminal behavior.

It is important to emphasize that the existence of one risk factor alone does not ensure developmental problems. Rather, those problems occur because of multiple risk factors, most often a combination of biological and environmental events.

Research on risk factors has shown us that children with some of the previously described biological risks, such as prematurity, are more vulnerable to environmental stresses than other children are. It is the combination of biological and environmental risk factors that places the developing child in jeopardy for future school problems.

Developmental problems most often stem from a combination of biological and environmental risk factors.

Family Structure   In a review of the data linking poverty and disability in children, Fujiura and Yamaki (2000) noted that the greatest concentration of poverty is found among single-parent households. Together, the environmental risk factors of single parenthood and poverty, likely to be linked, become a significant predictor of childhood disability. Since both of these factors are more likely to occur in traditional minority groups, minority children are at disproportionate risk for disability, which may contribute to their disproportionate representation in special education (which we discuss in Chapters 2 and 6).

Single parenthood is a difficult topic. We all know many individuals who were raised by single parents and who have done very well in life. Some of our readers likely are single parents, struggling to become teachers or other professionals so that the lives of their children can be improved. Our intention is not to discourage their efforts—there are many exceptions to these findings.

But there are built-in challenges for the single parent. He or she can be many things, but two adults is not one of them. Children who grow up with two parents, or extended family members living in their homes, have the benefit of a relationship with more than one caring and caregiving adult. It means that there are two people to talk with, ask for help from, get angry at, and learn about adulthood from. Single parenthood decreases the amount of adult attention available to the child (Donovan & Cross, 2002), and ultimately increases the likelihood of poverty and disability. As we will see in Chapter 4, the presence of family often increases the social and emotional supports for both children and parents.

School Factors   Some children are at risk for poor achievement and identification with a disability label simply because of the poor quality of the schools they attend. Schools in low-income neighborhoods, for example, are more likely to have fewer fully-credentialed teachers, more teacher turnover, fewer resources, and are more likely to be considered by the federal government as failing. The opportunities for children in these schools to learn and to become engaged are fewer. In a three-year study based on 679 observations, Harry and Klingner (2006) found that the weakest classrooms were located in schools that served the lowest-income African American students, and described the teaching in these classrooms as "extremely weak."

> What do we mean by "extremely weak" teaching? We mean classrooms in which teachers were often distraught or angry; where rough reprimands, idle threats, and personal insults were common; and where teachers' attempts to curb out-of-seat and off-task behavior were either sporadic and ineffective or unduly harsh. In these classrooms, instruction was frequently offered with no context, no attempt to connect with children's previous learning or personal experience. Here, rote instruction took the place of meaningful explanation and dialogue. Often, poorly-planned lessons were at the heart of the problem. (p. 56)

Wouldn't you think that any student coming from such a classroom would be more likely to withdraw or act out, or to drop out of school? Might they ultimately be more likely to be identified as having emotional and behavioral disorders, mild intellectual disabilities, or learning disabilities? We cannot discount these possibilities as we look for reasons for the over-identification of African American males in these special education categories.

The poor quality of schooling can be a risk factor for disability and dropping out.

Pause and Reflect

You have just read a long section with many examples of risk factors—not a complete list, but just the best-known examples. Can you think of other biological or environmental risk factors that affect child development? Is there research evidence supporting your examples? •

Prevention

It remains a frustration for many professionals that despite the fact that so much is known about how to prevent childhood disability, it continues to occur in the United States and around the world.

Major Strategies for Prevention

Many American women take steps to prevent disability during pregnancy and the early life of their children without thinking much about it. Giving birth in a hospital is a preventative step, though we often take its value for granted. You will recognize some of the strategies for prevention which follow—but have you thought about why doctors and public health experts recommend them? By keeping children healthy, they prevent many of the disabilities that we discuss in this book from occurring. Researchers and developmental experts have identified important steps that can prevent disabilities and other childhood health problems, and we will discuss them in the following section.

● *Immunization*—**vaccination** against infectious diseases—starts in the first year of life and should continue through early childhood. Children are inoculated against diphtheria, tetanus, pertussis (whooping cough), measles, hepatitis A and B, mumps, rubella, and polio, among other diseases (*Source:* **http://www.cdc.gov/vaccines/recs/schedules/default.htm**). An effective, wide-reaching immunization program can virtually eliminate these diseases, many of which can also harm pregnant women.

> Immunization, or vaccination against infectious diseases, is a prevention strategy that should be available to every child.

Recently some families have become concerned about the safety of childhood vaccines, especially the purported link between autism and childhood immunization. Despite the fact that many reputable scientific studies have demonstrated that there is not a causal relationship between childhood vaccines and autism (Offit, 2008), some parents are refusing to have their young children vaccinated. As a result, we are seeing more cases of childhood diseases such as measles. These diseases may threaten the lives of the children who contract them and members of their communities—and cause disabilities (Omer, Salmon, Orenstein, deHart, & Halsey, 2009). Parents with concerns about vaccines should be encouraged to weigh the disadvantages of refusing vaccination, and confer with their pediatrician or family doctor before making the decision to refuse vaccination for their children. For more information about immunization and vaccines, visit the Center for Disease Control's website.

© ChinaFotoPress/Getty Images

Many of us hate "shots", but they prevent diseases that routinely caused the death of children before the vaccines were developed.

● *Genetic Counseling*   Couples who have reason to be concerned they might have a child with a disabling condition will find that **genetic counseling** can provide them with helpful information. With information from a couple's family and personal health history, a genetic counselor can often discuss the likelihood that their child will inherit a genetic condition. (See the accompanying A Closer Look box: *What Is a Genetic Counselor?*) Some of the most common conditions identified through genetic counseling and testing are Down syndrome, Fragile X syndrome, sickle cell anemia, and Tay Sachs disease.

The role of the genetic counselor is a neutral one; the counselor provides prospective parents with information and possible options, but the parents are then left to make their own decision about whether or not to have a child. The prospective parents must often make difficult choices, since rarely can a genetic counselor guarantee what the outcome of a pregnancy will be.

● *Early Prenatal Care*   The easiest, most routine step that a pregnant woman can take to reduce the risk for her baby may also be the most effective. Early **prenatal care,** the care an expectant mother receives from her physician during pregnancy, can provide a prospective mother with crucial but routine tests and observations that can drastically affect her baby's health. Blood tests that rule out the presence of sexually transmitted and other diseases, information about proper nutrition and activity level during pregnancy, and counseling and treatment based on the prospective mother's needs significantly lower the level of risk in each pregnancy.

Despite the effectiveness of early prenatal care as a preventive measure, thousands of women give birth each year without ever seeing a doctor or visiting a clinic. Many of them are young, and most of them are poor. Babies born to women who do not receive prenatal medical care are more likely to be premature or sick at birth. There is also a higher likelihood of miscarriage, stillbirth, and early infant death in these pregnancies (Vintzileos, Ananth, Smulian, Scorza, & Knuppel, 2002).

● *Prenatal Testing*   For those who have received genetic counseling or are concerned about the health of their growing fetus, two procedures can provide more information: **amniocentesis** and **chorionic villous sampling (CVS).**

Amniocentesis was the first technique developed for prenatal diagnosis. It is performed between the fourteenth and eighteenth weeks of pregnancy by inserting a needle through the mother's abdomen into the amniotic sac and withdrawing less than one ounce of amniotic fluid. The amniotic fluid contains cells shed by the fetus, and these are cultured. A karyotype (a study of the number and description of the fetal chromosomes) is generally available in two weeks or less. Examination of the fetal chromosomes can lead to identification of chromosomal abnormalities such as Down syndrome. Evidence of neural tube defects like spina bifida can be seen in the analysis of the amniotic fluid cells. The risk to the fetus and the mother from amniocentesis is quite low.

In CVS, which is performed between the eighth and tenth weeks of pregnancy, a thin catheter is inserted through the vagina into the uterus and used to remove a small portion of the cells from the chorion, part of the developing placenta (Schonberg & Tifft, 2007). Those cells, which contain genetic material from the fetus, are cultured. In two to three days a karyotype is obtained. Evidence of Down syndrome and other relatively common genetic abnormalities can then be determined. According to the March of Dimes (2007), CVS and amniocentesis carry about the same rate of risk—1 in 200 pregnancies or less end in miscarriage after these tests, if they are carried out by an experienced medical team.

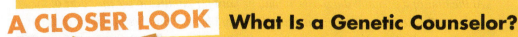

A CLOSER LOOK   What Is a Genetic Counselor?

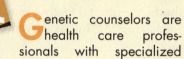

Genetic counselors are health care professionals with specialized graduate training in the areas of medical genetics and counseling. Genetic counselors usually work as members of a health care team, providing information and support to families who have members with birth defects or genetic disorders and to families who may be at risk for a variety of inherited conditions.

How can a genetic counselor help me?

Genetic counselors can help you to make informed, personalized decisions about your genetic health. As genetics professionals, they can help identify your potential genetic health risks, give you information about genetic conditions and inheritance patterns, discuss genetic testing options, help you understand your genetic results, and provide support throughout the process.

Here are some common reasons people speak with genetic counselors:

- I have a family history of a certain health condition; is there a genetic test I can take to find out if I'm at risk?
- My partner and I are planning a pregnancy; what types of testing are available to us?
- I have a known genetic mutation in my family; what can I do?
- I have a medical condition and want to learn whether I could pass it to my children.
- Can you help me share my genetic information with my relatives, or with my doctors?

Genetic counselors can also work with your physicians or other health care providers to make sure your genetic information is effectively considered in your overall health care.

What happens when I see a genetic counselor?

Most genetic counseling is provided in person to an individual, couple, or family, typically in a clinic or doctor's office. Depending on the specific reason for your consultation, the genetic counselor may:

- Review your personal and family medical history
- Identify possible genetic risks and discuss inheritance patterns
- Review appropriate testing options
- Discuss prevention strategies, screening tools, disease management
- Provide genetics-related information and reliable resources
- Provide supportive counseling that may help you with topics that arose during the consultation.

In some cases you may speak with a genetic counselor once. In other cases you may work with your counselor over time. As questions about your genetic health arise, genetic counselors are available to help.

How can I get the most out of a genetic counseling appointment?

A little preparation before your appointment can help you get the most out of your genetic counseling visit.

- Ask your relatives about medical conditions in the family
- Gather any medical records related to your concerns
- Bring a list of written questions to your appointment

You may not be able to get all the details, but the more information you have, the more your genetic counselor can help.

Is my genetic information protected?

Yes. Many people are not aware that both federal and state laws are in place to protect personal genetic information. Although these laws do not address genetic privacy across the board, they provide many important protections.

(*Source:* Abridged from the National Society of Genetic Counselors, "PatientFAQs," http://www.nsgc.org/Home/ConsumerHomePage/PatientFAQs/tabid/338/Default.aspx)

One mother who had prenatal testing before the birth of her daughter, who has spina bifida, reminds us that prenatal testing is often helpful no matter what a couple's views are on the termination of pregnancy:

I will always be grateful that when I finally gave birth to my daughter, it was in a setting where she could get the best of care from the moment of her first breath, and that my husband and I were fully prepared to welcome her into our lives with open arms.

At the time of a prenatal diagnosis, it may be hard for families to see the value of the opportunity they have been given, but ultimately I believe families and their children benefit most by knowing about problems as early as possible. (Reichard, 1995, p. 131)

Newer and less invasive methods of prenatal testing may ultimately replace amniocentesis and chorionic villous sampling, but as we write, these remain the tests that are most commonly used.

Early Intervention as Prevention

As we have emphasized, the presence of risk factors does not guarantee a developmental delay or disability. Today's developmental science theorizes a much more complex interaction between genes and experiences (Sameroff, 2010; Shonkoff, 2010). Early intervention plays an important role in preventing additional deficits in children who are at risk. The next pages will describe early intervention and the role it can play in the child's development.

Pause and Reflect

Do you notice any attempts in your own community to prevent disabilities? What might they be? ●

Early Intervention

Early intervention may lessen the effects of risk factors on a child by enlisting the support of a team of professionals and family members in the child's care and development. What is early intervention? What are its goals? These are vital concerns for the parents or caregivers of a child with a disability, or a child at risk for developing a disability.

First, think for a moment about what it would be like for you and your partner to come home from the hospital with a newborn with an identified disability—perhaps a baby who is blind, has Down syndrome, or spina bifida (these are the kinds of significant conditions that can be identified at birth). Besides the sadness that you would likely experience, you would probably be looking for information about your baby's condition, and wondering how and when you could begin to help the baby overcome the obstacles that life might put in her path. If you are lucky, the hospital social worker would refer you to the agency that coordinates early intervention services in your state—and you could begin to receive the help and support you need.

Early intervention is a set of individualized services for a young child with disability or developmental problems and his or her family, most often provided in the home, which is designed to lessen the impact of the disability on the child's development and provide informational, material, and emotional support to the family (McWilliam, 2010). Early intervention services can be provided by a range of professionals, but often the early intervention specialist is a special educator working collaboratively with other professionals—a physical therapist, occupational therapist, or infant mental health specialist, for example, depending on the needs of the child and family. These services are provided to children between birth and age three.

The focus of contemporary early intervention is on the caregiver as much or more than on the child! The idea behind it is this: Children need interventions that go on throughout their daily lives, not just once a week when the home visitor comes. So the early intervention professional models strategies for helping the child during the visit, then coaches the caregiver to use the same strategies. These strategies are sometimes called "routines-based" (McWilliam, 2010), because they

Prenatal testing and diagnosis can help a family and the medical team be prepared for the birth of a child with a disability.

Early intervention is the set of services provided to children from birth to age 3 and their families that is designed for their unique characteristics and needs.

Infants and toddlers from birth to age three are eligible for early intervention services.

are integrated or "embedded" into the child's daily routines of eating, playing, bathing, and so on.

The Case Study below provides an example of how this would happen.

CASE STUDY

Keisha, the home visitor, arrives to visit Jeremy and his 18-month-old son Frankie, who is blind in one eye and has low vision in the other. (Frankie may have usable vision in both eyes, as you will see in Chapter 12. *Blind* does not always mean totally blind.) Jeremy is feeding Frankie as he sits in the high chair, and neither one of them is happy! Frankie is struggling to wrest control of the spoon from his father, but Jeremy tells Keisha that he doesn't think it's appropriate for Frankie to feed himself, since he can't see the food on the tray well and is likely to make a huge mess. Keisha watches for a few moments and chats with Jeremy and Frankie. She remembers that Jeremy wanted an outcome on Frankie's IFSP that he would become more independent during his daily routines.

After a few moments, Keisha reminds Jeremy of his wish that Frankie become more independent, and he chuckles as he remembers his statements at the IFSP meeting. Keisha asks him if he's open to a couple of suggestions, and Jeremy agrees to listen. First,

Keisha asks Jeremy if he has a dark placemat around the house, and he finds a black plastic one. Keisha puts it on the high chair tray. Then, she asks Jeremy if there is a relatively non-messy food that Frankie likes. He suggests small pineapple chunks. So Keisha puts pineapple chunks on the black plastic mat, and the contrast between the yellow pineapple and the black mat makes it easier for Frankie to see the chunks. Then Keisha says to Frankie, "You find one and eat it!" He hesitates, so after waiting a bit, Keisha says, "Look down on the tray," and gently guides Frankie's hand to a piece of pineapple. She then withdraws her hand and Frankie puts the chunk in his mouth, smiles with recognition, and chews and swallows it. Keisha then turns control over to Jeremy, and after he watches Frankie eat a few more pieces, he says to him, "Here's the spoon; you can use the spoon if you want!" Frankie happily bangs the spoon on the tray, then allows Jeremy to guide him as he pushes a pineapple chunk onto the spoon and into his mouth. "Mission accomplished!" thinks Keisha.

Other key elements of early intervention are:

- It is *family focused,* conducted in partnership with family members.
- It is *individualized,* or designed to meet the unique needs of each child and family.
- It is *interdisciplinary,* since children benefit from the expertise of a variety of specialists, including physical therapists, occupational therapists, nutritionists, social workers, physicians and nurses, speech therapists and audiologists, and others.
- But it is also cross-disciplinary and *collaborative,* since services should be coordinated with one another.
- It is primarily provided in *natural environments,* or those places that most closely resemble places that typical infants would be, such as the home.
- It is described for each child in the *Individualized Family Service Plan* (IFSP).

> Family involvement and family support are the foundation of effective early intervention.

> The law requires that infants and toddlers receive services in *natural environments* to the greatest extent possible.

Eligibility for Early Intervention

As you learned in Chapter 1, early intervention services for infants and toddlers and their families are authorized by IDEA. The law identifies three groups of children aged birth to 3 who may be eligible for early intervention services. They are:

- Children with developmental delay
- Children with an identified physical or mental condition that carries a high probability of developmental delay
- Children who are medically or environmentally *at risk* for developmental delay if early intervention is not provided

ASSISTIVE TECHNOLOGY FOCUS

Assistive Technology for Infants and Toddlers

Research shows that assistive technology (AT) can help young children with disabilities learn valuable skills. For example, by using computers and special software, young children may improve in the following areas:

- social skills, including sharing and taking turns
- communication skills
- attention span
- fine and gross motor skills
- self-confidence and independence

Q: Why is AT important?

A: Many of the skills learned in life begin in infancy. AT can help infants and toddlers with disabilities learn many of these crucial skills. In fact, with AT, they can usually learn the same things that nondisabled children learn at the same age, only in a different way. Communication skills at this age are especially important because most of what an infant or toddler learns is through interacting with other people, especially family members and other primary caregivers. AT is also important because expectations for a child increase as those around them learn to say, "This is what the baby can do, with supports," instead of, "This is what the baby can't do." With AT, parents learn that the dreams they had for their child don't necessarily end when he or she is diagnosed with a disability. The dreams may have to be changed a little, but they can still come true. In addition, by using the right type of AT, some negative behaviors may decrease as a child's ability to communicate increases. Some common examples of AT include wheelchairs, computers and computer software, and communication devices.

Q: What types of AT devices can infants and toddlers use?

A: There are two types of AT devices most commonly used by infants and toddlers: switches and augmentative communication devices. There are many types of switches that can be used in many different ways. Switches can be used with battery-operated toys to give infants opportunities to play with them. For

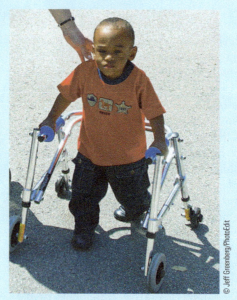

Using a support walker allows this boy to explore the playground.

example, a switch could be attached directly to a stuffed pig so that every time an infant touches the toy, it wiggles and snorts. Switches can also be used to turn many things off and on. Toddlers can learn to press a switch to turn on a computer or to use cause-and-effect (interactive) software.

Children who have severe disabilities can also use switches. For example, a switch could be placed next to an infant's head so that every time she moved her head to the left, a musical mobile hanging overhead would play.

Augmentative communication devices allow children who cannot speak or who cannot yet speak to communicate with the world around them. These devices can be as simple as pointing to a photo on a picture board or they can be more complicated—for instance, pressing message buttons on a device that activate prerecorded messages such as, "I'm hungry."

Source: PACER Center, Inc. Families and Advocates Partnership for education (FAPE) Project. Used with permission from PACER Center Inc., Minneapolis, MN, (952) 838-9000. www.pacer.org. All rights reserved.

Early intervention includes efforts to improve the child's performance in all major functional areas—language, cognition, fine and gross motor skills, and social-emotional development. And because research shows that early intervention yields significant results (Cook, Klein, & Tessier, 2008; Guralnick, 1997; McWilliam, 2010), the availability and comprehensiveness of early intervention programs can have a great impact on the lives of children who are at risk and those with disabilities.

> Research documents the effectiveness of early intervention services.

The Assistive Technology Focus box in this chapter features assistive technology used with infants and young children, and the Teaching Strategies & Accommodations box focuses on early intervention strategies.

Models for Early Intervention Programs

Early intervention services are generally delivered through either a home-based program, in which the early intervention specialist provides services to the family in its own home, a center-based program, in which the family brings the child to an early intervention center, or a program for young children within their community, such as day care. Often, services to infants and medically fragile toddlers are provided in the home; as children grow older and stronger, they are more likely to attend a program in the community.

> Early intervention can be provided in the family home, at an early intervention center, or in the community.

The 1997 amendments to IDEA specified that whenever possible, services be provided to children in **natural environments.** In a Division of Early Childhood position statement (1998), a natural environment is "one in which the child would spend time if he or she did not have special needs" (p. 1). As a result of this mandate, services are likely to be provided in play groups, day care, libraries, parks,

Teaching Strategies & Accommodations

Elements of Effective Early Intervention

High-quality early intervention programs can improve a wide range of outcomes and yield long-term benefits that far exceed program costs. Some of the major factors that have been found by the research to maximize the likelihood of promoting positive outcomes for vulnerable young children, their families, and society as a whole are listed below:

- Intervention is likely to be more effective and less costly when it is provided earlier in life, rather than later.

- Key factors to quality in early childhood programs include: the expertise of staff and their capacity to build warm, positive, responsive relationships with young children; small class sizes with high adult-to-child ratios; age-appropriate materials in safe physical settings; language-rich environments; and consistent levels of child participation.

- Early, secure, and consistent relationships with caring, trustworthy adults contribute significantly to healthy brain development.

- For maximum impact on later academic success and mental health, early childhood programs should give the same level of attention to young children's emotional and social needs as they give to children's cognitive skills.

The best early intervention programs will reflect these elements. For the standards of practice advocated by the Division of Early Childhood of the Council for Exceptional Children, see S. Sandall, M. L. Hemmeter, B. J. Smith, & M. McLean, (Eds.). (2005). *DEC Recommended Practices: A Comprehensive Guide for Practical Application in Early Intervention/Early Childhood Special Education.* Longmont, CO: Sopris West.

_____

(Adapted from E. Shaw and S. Goode (2008). *Fact Sheet: Vulnerable Young Children*. Chapel Hill: The University of North Carolina, FPG Child Development Institute, National Early Childhood Technical Assistance Center. This document appears at: http://www.nectac.org/~pdfs/pubs/factsheet_vulnerable.pdf)

Table 3.4 Mission and Key Principles for Providing Early Intervention Services in Natural Environments

MISSION

Part C* early intervention builds upon and provides supports and resources to assist family members and caregivers to enhance children's learning and development through everyday learning opportunities.

KEY PRINCIPLES

1. Infants and toddlers learn best through everyday experiences and interactions with familiar people in familiar contexts.

2. All families, with the necessary supports and resources, can enhance their children's learning and development.

3. The primary role of a service provider in early intervention is to work with and support family members and caregivers in children's lives.

4. The early intervention process, from initial contacts through transition, must be dynamic and individualized to reflect the child's and family members' preferences, learning styles, and cultural beliefs.

5. IFSP outcomes must be functional and based on children's and families' needs and family-identified priorities.

6. The family's priorities, needs, and interests are addressed most appropriately by a primary provider who represents and receives team and community support.

7. Interventions with young children and family members must be based on explicit principles, validated practices, best available research, and relevant laws and regulations.

*Part C is the section of IDEA describing early intervention services.

Source: Workgroup on Principles and Practices in Natural Environments, 2007. http://www.nectac.org/~pdfs/topics/families/Finalmissionandprinciples3_11_08.pdf

and other places in the community where young children and their caregivers can be found. The focus on natural environments flows from the principle of normalization we discussed in Chapter 1—in this case, young children in early intervention should be doing what their peers are doing, and they should be provided services in "normal" settings. Table 3.4 lists the key principles of early intervention as recently identified by a working group of experts.

The Role of the Family in Early Intervention

With the growing appreciation of the importance of viewing the child within the context of the family, the focus of early intervention has shifted from the child to the entire family system. This broadened focus is reflected in the law, which mandates that each family receive an **Individualized Family Service Plan (IFSP),** a written account of the personal and social services needed to promote and support each family member for the first three years of the child's life. Here's how the National Dissemination Center for Children with Disabilities describes the components of the IFSP to parents:

> The IFSP is written not just for the child, but for the family.

Your child's IFSP must include the following:

- your child's present levels of functioning and need in the areas of his or her physical, cognitive, communication, social/emotional, and adaptive development;

- family information (with your agreement), including the resources, priorities, and your concerns as parents, and those of other family members closely involved with the child;

- the major results or outcomes expected to be achieved for your child and family;

- the specific services your child will be receiving;

- where in the natural environment (e.g., home, community) the services will be provided (if the services will not be provided in the natural environment, the IFSP must include a statement justifying why not);

- when and where your son or daughter will receive services;

- the number of days or sessions he or she will receive each service and how long each session will last;

- whether the service will be provided on a one-on-one or group basis;

- who will pay for the services;

- the name of the service coordinator overseeing the implementation of the IFSP; and

- the steps to be taken to support your child's transition out of early intervention and into another program when the time comes. (National Dissemination Center for Children with Disabilities (2010). *Writing the IFSP for your child*. Retrieved from **http://nichcy.org/babies/ifsp/.**)

Most families need information related to their child's condition, assistance in learning to identify their child's unique cues, guidance in handling the child in a more therapeutic and easy manner, and referrals for other services. The focus of early intervention is typically on facilitating and coordinating this range of activities so that the family may experience more satisfying and rewarding relationships with the child and the child may develop well (Chen & Klein, 2008).

Let's look at another hypothetical baby who would be eligible for early intervention services, Lea, who has Down syndrome. Down syndrome carries with it an extremely high probability of intellectual and developmental disabilities, and often involves physical abnormalities (such as organ abnormalities) as well.

CASE STUDY

Lea is 8 months old and is recovering from heart surgery that successfully repaired a congenital heart defect. In the next year, Lea's physical health must be monitored closely to ensure her complete and successful recovery. Her family will need help facilitating Lea's speech and language development, which is usually delayed in children with intellectual and developmental disabilities. Lea is not sitting or crawling, which suggests a delay in her motor development, and we know that her cognitive development is likely to be delayed. Because of Lea's varied needs, the design of her intervention program, or the outcomes on her IFSP, will benefit from the input of a team consisting of health care professionals, a speech-language specialist, a physical therapist, and a teacher skilled in activities that will facilitate cognitive development. And we haven't even mentioned her parents' needs for information about her disability and development!

Lea will receive weekly home visits from an early intervention specialist and a speech-language pathologist, and her parents will take her to physical therapy twice weekly. Lea's parents will be given the name of their local Down syndrome parent group, and respite care will be provided so that they can attend the meetings. The team expects that Lea will be attending a center-based early intervention program or a play group in the community by the time she is 18 months old, with one or both of her parents attending with her. (See Figure 3.5 for excerpts from Lea's IFSP.) With the help of an **interdisciplinary team** of professionals, Lea's parents will make sure that she is off to a healthy start in life.

Family Strengths

Lucia and Omar Dean are totally committed to their first child, Lea. Mr. Dean has worked for United Parcel Service for five years. Mrs. Dean recently resigned from her job as a social worker to be a full-time mother. Their families are in a distant state, but the Deans are a part of a closely knit religious community, and have a great deal of support from friends.

Family Resources, Priorities, and Concerns

Mr. and Mrs. Dean have been focused on Lea's health after her heart surgery, and they are relieved that she is recovering well and beginning to move around more. They are unsure about what to expect from Lea, and frequently leave her alone in her crib to rest. Mrs. Dean has decided not to return to work so she can be with Lea, and she is very eager to get some ideas about how she can help her daughter. Mr. Dean is worried that his wife will be lonely at home, since their families live far away.

Outcomes

1. Lea's parents will learn more about Down syndrome and meet other parents of children with Down syndrome through participation in a parent-to-parent support group.
2. Lea's parents will feel confident in their ability to facilitate their daughter's healthy growth and development, particularly in the area of communication skills.
3. Lea will begin to use pointing and vocalizations to indicate her needs.
4. Lea's parents will learn more about the impact of her surgery and recovery on Lea's overall development, particularly her motor development.
5. Lea will sit and crawl independently.

FIGURE 3.5

Excerpts from an IFSP for Lea, an 8-month-old with Down syndrome

Note: On a complete IFSP, outcomes would be tied to strategies, criteria for measuring whether outcomes have been reached, service type and frequency, responsible agency, and so on. You can see a complete IFSP by visiting our website through CengageBrain.com.

© Cengage Learning 2013

? Pause and Reflect

In each state, a different agency is responsible for services to children from birth to age 3. What is the agency in your state? How do parents find early intervention services in your state or country? •

Identification and Assessment of Infants at Risk

Three groups of infants and toddlers are eligible for early intervention services under the law.

Since most states have developed early intervention programs for infants and young children under IDEA, criteria must be designed to identify children who are eligible for these services. Remember that three groups of young children (from birth to age 3) are eligible for early intervention services:

- Those with an identified condition related to developmental disability, such as hearing or vision loss or Down syndrome
- Those who are experiencing developmental delay in motor, cognitive, communication, psychosocial, or self-help skills
- Those who are at risk for significant developmental delay because of biological and/or environmental events in their lives

Clearly, young children with identified disabilities are eligible. Also eligible are those children described as developmentally delayed. It is the group of children we discuss in this chapter, those who are categorized as biologically and environmentally "at risk," who have presented the most significant problems to the state teams working on eligibility criteria, and based on our previous discussions in this chapter, we can begin to see why. We have developed a considerable list of biological and environmental risk factors, and there are many others we do not have the space to present. Deciding which risk factors or how many factors will qualify a child for services has presented a major challenge to the states. Many states require that multiple risk factors be used to qualify children for programs, since we know that as risk factors multiply, their combined effect is likely to be greater than that of any single factor.

Techniques for Identification and Assessment

We obtain information about a child's risk status from a number of sources: hospital and health records, family interviews, observation of the child, developmental and health screenings, and diagnostic assessment. **Screening** refers to quick and efficient procedures whereby large numbers of children can be evaluated to determine whether more in-depth assessment is required; screenings of young children's development, hearing, vision, and overall health can identify children with a high probability of delayed development. **Diagnostic assessment,** an in-depth look at the child's development, provides a more definitive picture of whether the child has special needs; in diagnostic assessment, formal assessment tools are used by a multidisciplinary team, with considerable input from the child's family.

Use of screening and diagnostic assessment tools, however, does not lead to the identification of all children eligible for early intervention; in fact, many children who are eligible never receive services because they are not identified in the first three years of life. Many of us in the special education field lament the lost opportunities for the children and families when the child's difficulty is not identified until kindergarten or later. In order to increase the likelihood that eligible young children will be identified for services, IDEA allows for the use of "clinical judgment," or the informed opinion of an experienced professional, to identify children for early intervention (Bagnato, McKeating-Esterle, Fevola, Bortolamasi, & Neisworth, 2008).

Clinical judgment, combined with results of screening and formal assessment, is widely used by early intervention practitioners to verify (or refute) the results of standardized assessments, which are sometimes not nuanced enough to identify developmental problems of very young children—remember, we are talking about infants and toddlers! Bagnato and his colleagues (2008) conclude that there is an evidence base for using clinical judgment to identify young children who are eligible for early intervention services, but it should be used under the following conditions:

- When conventional, standardized, norm-referenced measures are inappropriate, ill-advised, or unavailable
- When team members believe that the child's performance on traditional measures is at odds with their own ongoing observations and judgments about the child

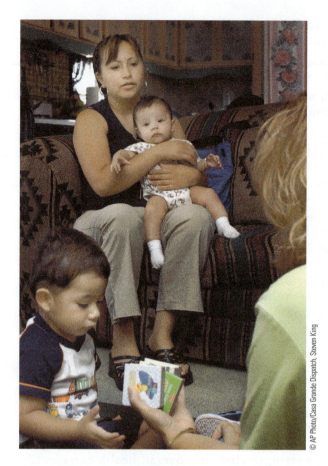

The most important part of a home visit may be the early intervention specialist "coaching" the child's mother so she is skilled and comfortable helping her child.

- When the child's capabilities are "low-threshold" and inconsistently exhibited and observed

- Whenever parents are integral participants in the assessment process—namely, always

- When teams seek to unify and facilitate team decisions about child characteristics and advocate for specific programmatic and intervention needs (Bagnato et al., 2008, pp. 346–347)

Multiple types of data from multiple sources, especially the family, should be used for good decision-making.

No one source of information should be used to make any decisions concerning a child's eligibility for services; "best practices" in assessment demand that multiple types of data from multiple sources be used for good decision-making. (This is a refrain you will hear repeatedly in this book. Think about it in your own case: Would you like one test score to determine what happens to you throughout your school life?) Foremost among these sources is the family. Their "clinical judgment" about their child's functioning and needs must be part of the decision about eligibility.

Can Disabilities Be Predicted from Risk Factors?

Despite the large number of studies that identify biologically at-risk infants and follow their development over time, researchers have found that their ability to predict which children will develop disabilities is relatively poor. Children with severe disabilities, often caused by massive central nervous system insult, are an exception to this rule. They can be identified by physical and health features very early in life, but they are the very small minority. Fortunately, many of the early complications of biological risk status are transient; that is, they disappear over time. Many infants can and do recover from the trauma of premature birth and early medical complications.

But, once again, the child's ability to recover from these early experiences appears to be mediated by the caregiving characteristics in his or her environment. We can begin to see why early intervention for infants at risk must focus on the infant within the context of the family.

The Resilient Child

The impact of risk factors varies a great deal in different children, families, and environments. For example, there are many healthy young children doing well in school today who were born at very low weight; other low birth weight children are striving to overcome disabilities ranging from mild learning disabilities to severe intellectual and developmental disabilities. Many children grow up in poverty and go on to lead productive adult lives; others develop school problems that lead to their dropping out of school or to special educational programming. On the other hand, few children born with serious chromosomal abnormalities grow up without developmental delays (although many of them can, as we shall see, become productive citizens).

So far in this chapter, we have identified a large number of biological and environmental risk factors that increase the likelihood of poor developmental outcomes in children. No single risk factor satisfactorily predicts or explains what will happen to a child, but the accuracy of our predictions increases with the number of risk factors that the child experiences, and the most vulnerable children of all are those who experience both biological and environmental risk factors. In fact, most children who experience a series of biological risk factors (with the exception of those that clearly damage the central nervous system) but grow up in a stable, supportive environment develop very well.

As we have written throughout this chapter, risk factors increase the likelihood that a child will have developmental problems, but many children escape their impact. Researchers have looked for explanations of that variability. One theory from the 1980s was that certain children were *resilient*; with the help of stable relationships they were able to overcome the odds against them. More recently, knowledge of the impact of early experiences on the developing brain (Shonkoff, 2010) has led to a greater understanding of the impact of risk.

All of us have stressful experiences, but stress during the first years of life seems to have significant effects on the structures of the developing brain (National Scientific Council on the Developing Child, 2005). Scientists describe three levels of physical responses to stress that they now believe can have an impact not only on early development, but on health throughout the lifetime. *Positive stress* describes the mild physical reactions to normal stressful experiences. For a baby, this could mean separation from the primary caregiver or frustration. Positive stress is necessary for healthy development; infants recover from stress and learn from it in a relationship with a nurturing, reliable caregiver. *Tolerable stress* refers to physiological responses to significant life events (divorce, homelessness, violence) which might affect the young child's developing brain unless they are "buffered" by a responsive adult relationship which allows the child to adapt and cope with the stress (Shonkoff, 2010). **Toxic stress** is much more significant, and it is considered toxic since there is no adult to buffer it:

> Toxic stress refers to strong, frequent, and/or prolonged activation of the body's stress-response systems in the absence of the buffering protection of stable adult support. Major risk factors include extreme poverty, recurrent physical and/or emotional abuse, chronic neglect, severe maternal depression, parental substance abuse, and family violence. The defining characteristic of toxic stress is that it disrupts brain architecture, adversely affects other organs, and leads to stress management systems that establish

relatively lower thresholds for responsiveness that persist throughout life, thereby increasing the risk of stress-related disease or disorder as well as cognitive impairment well into the adult years. (Shonkoff, 2010, p. 360)

Toxic stress affects the physiology—the brain architecture—of the young child, and cumulative or repeated toxic stress appears to have dramatic immediate and long-term effects. Figure 3.6 illustrates this point; children with six or seven risk factors have a 90 to 100 percent chance of experiencing a developmental delay (Scientific Council on the Developing Child, 2005).

> Exposure to multiple toxic stressors early in life can harm the child's long-term development and health.

The Importance of Relationships

For those of us committed to the healthy future of children, the numbers in Figure 3.6 are alarming and overwhelming. But there is a positive message in this work, and it too is verified in the science: The stress arising from these adverse experiences can be buffered or mitigated within a supportive and nurturing relationship.

Stable, caring relationships are essential for healthy development. Children develop in an environment of relationships that begin in the home and include extended family members, early care and education providers, and members of the community. Studies show that toddlers who have secure, trusting relationships with parents or non-parent caregivers experience minimal stress hormone activation when frightened by a strange event, and those who have insecure relationships experience a significant activation of the stress response system. Numerous scientific studies support these conclusions: providing supportive, responsive relationships as early in life as possible can prevent or reverse the damaging effects of toxic stress. (In Brief: The Science of Early Childhood Development, **www.developingchild.harvard.edu.**)

In the words of the distinguished developmental psychologist Urie Bronfenbrenner: . . . *in order to develop normally, a child requires progressively more complex joint activity with one or more adults who have an irrational emotional relationship with the child. Somebody's got to be crazy about that kid. That's number one. First, last, and always* (National Scientific Council on the Developing Child, 2004).

> Children with responsive and consistent caregiving have the best chance of recovering from the effects of risk factors.

A series of National Research Council reports has further emphasized the critical role played by the relationships that children experience as they grow. These researchers conclude that "the weight of successful development in the early years falls most heavily on the child's relationships with primary adult caregivers." And, despite their diversity, children require certain things from their relationships in order to flourish:

A. a reliable, supporting relationship that establishes a sense of security and safety,

B. an affectionate relationship that supports the development of self-esteem,

C. responsiveness of the adult to the child that strengthens the child's sense of self-efficacy, and

D. support for the growth of new capabilities that are within the child's reach, including reciprocal interactions that promote language development and the ability to resolve conflicts cooperatively and respectfully (Donovan & Cross, 2002, p. 121).

The fact that there are children who can experience many stressful biological and environmental events and emerge as healthy, competent adults—with the help of consistent relationships—provides us with hope and encouragement. Teachers, after all, have important relationships with children too. And teachers must take a hopeful stance in order to continue their challenging work with children in high-risk situations. We must use the results of research to support other children and families so that they, too, can develop protective personal characteristics despite stressful caregiving environments.

Resilient children can overcome the odds and become healthy, productive adults.

SUMMARY

- Risk factors include a wide range of biological and environmental conditions associated with increased probability of developmental problems in young children.

- Risk factors can be categorized as biological risks and environmental risks. Biological risks are a threat to a child's developing systems and can include diseases, maternal substance abuse, and oxygen deprivation. Environmental risk stems from damaging physical and social surroundings of the child and his or her caretakers, such as exposure to lead, accidents, or limited access to health care.

- Some steps that help prevent risk status and disability include immunization, genetic counseling, prenatal care, and prenatal testing. Early intervention is another means of preventing the negative impact of risk factors.

- Early intervention consists of a comprehensive set of services for infants and toddlers aged birth to 3 and their families that is designed for their unique needs and built on the unique strengths of each child and family. Early intervention has a strong family focus and can consist of services offered by a range of professionals across disciplines.

- Children at risk can pose a challenge for early intervention personnel because the range of possible risk factors is so great and because the presence of one or more risk factors does not guarantee a developmental delay. Techniques used to identify children for early intervention include screening, diagnostic assessment, and clinical judgment.

- It must be remembered that no absolute predictions can be made regarding children at risk. Some children are exceptionally resilient and succeed despite seemingly large odds. A strong bond with a caregiving adult and emotional support from other family members can help a child overcome biological and environmental stresses.

- Healthy development and learning take place in the contexts of loving relationships between children and their caregivers.

KEY TERMS

risk factors (page 74)
biological risk (page 75)
environmental risk (page 75)
prenatal period (page 76)
perinatal period (page 76)
postnatal period (page 76)
first trimester (page 76)

teratogens (page 76)
rubella (page 76)
cytomegalovirus (CMV) (page 78)
congenital (page 78)
sexually transmitted diseases (STDs)
    (page 79)

acquired immune deficiency syndrome (AIDS) (page 80)

human immunodeficiency virus (HIV) (page 80)

thalidomide (page 81)

polysubstance abusers (page 81)

fetal alcohol syndrome disorders (FASD) (page 82)

fetal alcohol syndrome (FAS) (page 82)

alcohol-related neurodevelopmental disorder (ARND) (page 82)

Alcohol-related birth defects (ARBD) (page 82)

Down syndrome (page 84)

hypoxia (page 85)

premature (preterm) (page 85)

low birth weight (page 85)

very low birth weight (page 85)

neonatology (page 86)

neonatal intensive care unit (page 86)

neurotoxins (page 88)

vaccination (page 95)

genetic counseling (page 96)

prenatal care (page 96)

amniocentesis (page 96)

chorionic villous sampling (CVS) (page 96)

early intervention (page 98)

natural environments (page 101)

Individualized Family Service Plan (IFSP) (page 102)

interdisciplinary team (page 103)

screening (page 105)

diagnostic assessment (page 105)

clinical judgment (page 105)

toxic stress (page 107)

USEFUL RESOURCES

- The American Academy of Pediatrics has a website that provides information about childhood diseases and psychosocial risk factors in children. Visit **http://www.aap.org/family.**

- *Kids Health* is a website from the Nemours Foundation that offers detailed explanations of prenatal tests and the reasons they are important. Information is available for children and teenagers on health issues too. Visit **http://kidshealth.org/.**

- Some of the country's foremost researchers on the effects of environmental toxins on children have written a book for families: P. Landrigan, H. L. Needleman, & M. Landrigan (2002). *Raising Healthy Children in a Toxic World: 101 Smart Solutions for Every Family.* Emmaus, PA: Rodale Press. Dr. Landrigan's work at Mount Sinai Hospital in New York is represented at the web page of the Children's Environmental Health Project, where you can find reliable information about exposure to environmental toxins.

- The Centers for Disease Control (CDC) have developed the CDC National Prevention Information Network (NPIN), devoted to disseminating information about the prevention of HIV/AIDS, sexually transmitted diseases, and tuberculosis. The web address is **http://www.cdcnpin.org.** The site has separate sections on children and youth; many resources are available in Spanish.

- Premature Baby-Premature Child is a website for families of children born premature. It's at **http://www.prematurity.org.**

- Two organizations committed to the development of high-quality professionals who will work with our youngest children are the Division of Early Childhood of the Council for Exceptional Children at **http://www.dec-sped.org** and the National Association for the Education of Young Children (NAEYC) at **http://www.naeyc.org.**

- Early childhood special educators at the Frank Porter Graham Center at the University of North Carolina have developed a series of online modules called CONNECT which introduce and demonstrate topics in early intervention. Find them at **http://community.fpg.unc.edu/.**

- The National Early Childhood Technical Assistance Center (NECTAC) is a consortium of six organizations providing assistance to early childhood specialists. Visit their website at **http://www.nectac.org.**

- Zero to Three is an organization devoted to the healthy development of infants and toddlers. The website has good information for both parents and professionals. Visit **http://www.zerotothree.org** or write to the organization at 734 15th St. NW, Washington, DC 20005.

- The Centers for Disease Control and Prevention has two publications for parents as part of its "Learn the Signs, Act Early" program, which seeks to improve early identification of children with autism and other developmental disabilities. The booklet, "Milestone Moments," includes milestone checklists and tips to help parents support their child's development from 2 months to 5 years. The second publication, a brochure called "Track Your Child's Developmental Milestones," includes a checklist of key milestones from 6 months to 4 years and a message for parents about what to do if developmental concerns arise. They are available online at **http://www.cdc.gov/.**

- The *Tots-n-Tech* Research Institute identifies low- and high-tech products and adaptations for the youngest children with disabilities at **http://tnt.asu.edu/.**

- For more in-depth information on many of the topics in this chapter, visit the *National Center on Birth Defects and Developmental Disabilities* website at **http://www.cdc.gov/.**

 ## PORTFOLIO ACTIVITIES

 These activities will help the student meet CEC Initial Content Standard 2: Development and Characteristics of Learners.

Each of us has a personal and a social responsibility to help prevent disability in our communities. Here are some ways for you to help:

1. Participate in fundraising and awareness campaigns.

- Pledge or organize a team of volunteers for a fundraising event. Major fundraising organizations such as the March of Dimes, the United Way, UNICEF, the United Cerebral Palsy Association, or the Cystic Fibrosis Foundation would love your help.

- Working as a class, design posters illustrating risk factors and related prevention strategies for display in a community education program.

- Hold a "risk awareness" education day at your local high school or community center.

Write up the results of these activities and include pictures for your portfolio.

2. Promote early prenatal care and early recognition of risk and disability.

- Invite a genetic counselor from a local hospital to come and speak to your class or your parent group.

- Find out about the low-cost prenatal care services in your community and, in a small group, devise a plan to publicize them.

- Find out where you can refer parents who are concerned about their child's early development in your town or city. Make a list for your school and local pediatricians.
- Visit a neonatal intensive care unit. Write a narrative report of what you observed and present it to your classmates.

Write up the results of these activities and include pictures for your portfolio.

3. Compile a resource guide for families of young children in your community. Include information about the risk factors described in this chapter and agencies in your area that might help families who experience such risk factors. Make your resource guide part of your portfolio.

 To access Portfolio Activities for this chapter and other useful study resources including an interactive eBook, related web links, quizzes, flashcards, and videos, visit the Education CourseMate website at CengageBrain.com.

CHAPTER 4

Families of Children with Disabilities

Outline

Learning Objectives

After reading this chapter, the reader will:

- Begin to appreciate how a family's background, experiences, and culture color their response to their child's disability.

- Begin to understand how their own life experiences, and the values and beliefs stemming from those experiences, influence their perceptions of families.

- Reflect on how the birth of an exceptional child affects the family.

- Understand the legal basis for family involvement in special education.

- Appreciate some of the ways in which an exceptional child contributes to the strength and richness of a family.

Defining a family today is more difficult than it used to be. Although for many of us the family unit still consists of two or more blood relatives residing together, there are plenty of exceptions: foster families (those created by the courts) and adoptive families are two that come to mind. For those of us living far away from relatives, close friends can create the kind of company and support that an extended family might.

Each family's cultural background—its combination of values, beliefs, history, traditions, and language—helps determine its response to the birth and raising of children, and to the birth and raising of a child with a disability. In the United States, a nation formed from the melding of thousands of groups from all over the world, the possibilities for variation in beliefs and traditions about child rearing are nearly endless. And it is within this context that most of our readers will work, often with families whose values, beliefs, history, traditions, and language will be very different from their own. This chapter is designed to help you begin to learn about families of children with disabilities and to reflect on how their traditions and beliefs form their responses to their children and to you, the teacher. Without such reflection, there is no foundation for real partnership with families.

Terms and Definitions

The traditional definition of *family* is people living together who are related by birth, marriage, or adoption.

How would *you* define family? Your own experiences and cultural background will color your definition. Families of exceptional children have their own ideas about child rearing, relations with the school, and disability colored by similar experiences. First we will define **family** in the traditional manner, as the U.S. Census Bureau (2010) does: A family is a group of two people or more related by birth, marriage, or adoption and residing together. Beyond this, you can expect to encounter many variations. According to Census Bureau definitions, a **household** is one or more people, including members of a family and others, who live under the same roof. An **extended family** consists of relatives across generations who may or may not live together. Many African American families, for example, report having "a wide network of kin and community" (O'Shea et al., 2001, p. 53) that provides them with support. "*My family, my folks, my kin,* and *my people* are terms used by many African Americans to identify their blood relatives and to denote relationships with special friends or 'cared for' individuals who are not related" (Goode, Jones, & Jackson, 2011, p. 155). So for many, the definition of family goes beyond biology. In fact, many of our students over the years have identified a broad and inclusive definition of family similar to this one:

> Families include two or more people who regard themselves as a family and who carry out the functions that families typically perform. These people may or may not be related by blood or marriage and may or may not usually live together. (Turnbull, Turnbull, Erwin, Soodak, & Shogren, 2011, p. 6)

One line in that definition bears exploration. Family members carry out various *functions* for one another. You are no doubt a member of a family—what functions do you carry out for other family members? Do you drive your grandmother to her doctor's appointment, or pick up groceries for your mother? Do you include your sister's dirty clothes when you do your own laundry?

Maybe you are a parent yourself. When we become parents we often feel shock as we realize how much there is to do for a new baby, or how many functions we must perform, like feeding, bathing, diapering, shopping, driving to appointments, buying and administering medicines, and so much more! Families take care of one another, and often that involves a good deal of work.

One of the goals of this chapter is to determine how a family changes or adapts when they have a child with a disability. How do those family functions change? Is it more work if a child has a disability? More stress? First let's listen to some parents tell us about their experiences. The nearby excerpts are taken from two parent blogs.

Clearly, it is not always the biological parent who raises the exceptional child. It may be one biological parent, a grandparent, a foster parent, another relative, or a family friend. Acknowledging these diverse possibilities, many professionals prefer to use the term **caregiver** to refer to the person who assumes that role. That term seems relatively impersonal to us, so in this chapter we use the word *parent* generically, to include all those caregivers who assume the responsibilities traditionally associated with being a parent.

We have been using the term "cultural background" without defining the term culture. In many ways, this chapter is about the intersection between family and culture. And **culture** means different things to different people. Most anthropologists define culture broadly, as ways of perceiving, believing, evaluating, and behaving (Goodenough, 1987). Culture can be seen as a series of norms or tendencies that are shared, interpreted, and adapted by a group of people. The characteristics of a given culture may be described as specific behaviors or life patterns; however, every person is an individual, and groups of individuals within a culture represent a *range* of characteristics (Hanson, 2011). Culture, therefore, may guide the way you think, feel, behave, dress, and eat, but it does not ensure that every member of a culture will do things in the same way. The word culture can also be used to describe many of the shared behaviors we experience in different parts of our lives. For example, the shared language, dress, communication patterns, and food preferences of our ethnic background, as well as the behavioral, ethical, social, and dietary guidelines of our religion, reflect two aspects of culture. The cultural backgrounds of our own families and the families we work with will influence beliefs about child rearing, education, and family life, as well as attitudes toward an exceptional family member. Even the way we praise—or don't praise—our children is culturally embedded (Bayat, 2011). According to one useful definition, culture is *a framework that guides life practices* (Hanson, 2011). While you have no doubt read and discussed the concept of culture in other books and classes, for this book we will use that last broad definition as our own.

> The perception of disability is rooted in the values of the culture.

© Jeffery Salter/Redux

> Parents usually set the tone for the rest of the family in terms of attitudes towards having a child with a disability.

FIRST PERSON

What Is it Like to Have a Child with a Disability?

Ellen and Dave's baby boy turned blue after birth and ended up in the Neonatal Intensive Care Unit (NICU):

"My body was healing from the c-section and I still wasn't able to walk, so Dave kept going to see Max, who was in an incubator. I forced myself to get up in the early evening. As we waited at the elevator bank to go to the NICU, there was a doctor standing there. Glasses, young, a little nerdy. He nodded at us. "Did they use forceps during your delivery?" he suddenly asked me. I'd never seen this doctor before and thought it was a bizarre question (as it turned out, Dave had spoken with him in the NICU). I figured maybe he was looking for people for some research project or something. "No," I said. "Why?"

"Because your baby is having seizures," he answered.

And that's the moment when I went from the happiest day of my life to the most devastating one. I couldn't have imagined how much worse things were going to get."

****

Seven years later, Ellen has become a fearless advocate for her son and other children with special needs:

"My son, Max, is 7 years old. He has cerebral palsy, which affects his ability to talk and use his hands. The cerebral palsy does not affect his sense of humor, his eagerness to play with other kids, his love for all things sweet, his curiosity about the world. He is a kid like just any other kid.

The cerebral palsy does not make him some angel boy, either. He has meltdowns when you don't buy him a toy he wants, he's been known to hit you when he gets mad, he pulls his sister's hair. In those ways, he is also a kid just like any other kid.

But that's not always people's perceptions. Some see him as a kid *unlike* any other kid.

I've had people ask if he likes to play with trucks or bubbles, as if he is *playing* impaired.

I've had mothers ask if he ever fights with his sister, as if he is incapable of sibling rivalry.

I've had mothers say things to their kids, in front of Max's face, along the lines of, "Honey, you can play with him; just pretend he's like a baby." As if Max couldn't hear.

Once, a stranger remarked, "Oh, that's so great he likes ice cream!" as if his disabilities affect his potential for pleasure and joy.

I know that people don't mean to be mean-spirited when they say these things. Often, they are trying to be inclusive. But in the process of doing so, they end up making Max seem like an "other"—as in, a kid who is not just another kid. And they teach their own, typical children the same.

My son has special needs. But at heart, he is not special. He is a kid just like any other kid. Please treat him that way."

Source: Ellen's wonderful blog is *Love That Max: A Blog About Kids with Special Needs (and the Parents Who Adore Them)* at http://www.lovethatmax.com/.

Working with Families

For some teachers, working with families is the most complex part of their job. All the research in both special and general education indicates that children have more success in school when their parents are involved in their education. But in too many schools across the nation there is an "us" versus "them" mentality about families. In fact the general public sees some disabilities as caused by the home environment (Tremaine Foundation, 2010). Blaming families for their child's disability is almost always erroneous, and it is counterproductive to working in partnership, which is based on respect and trust.

As you read in Chapter 3, in the field of early childhood special education we advocate for **partnerships** with families, in which there are shared goals and equal "expertise" about children (Turnbull, Turnbull, Erwin, Soodak, & Shogren, 2011). It's a model that promises collaboration and cooperation, and often it delivers those outcomes. We also advocate **family-centered practices:**

> *Family-centeredness* characterizes beliefs and practices that treat families with dignity and respect; individualized, flexible, and responsive practices; information sharing so that families can make informed decisions; family choice regarding any number of aspects of program practices and intervention options; parent-professional collaboration and partnerships as a context for family-program relations; and the provision and mobilization of resources and supports necessary for families to care for and rear their children in ways that produce optimal child, parent, and family outcomes. (Dunst, 2002, p. 139)

But too often, by the time a child reaches school age, these values and practices have disappeared, bogged down by the logistics of school personnel and family members' meetings, children riding the bus to school, and requirements for participation in IEP meetings that sometimes seem to set up both schools and families for disappointment.

Yet when I look back on my career teaching children (this is Nancy Hunt writing), many of my most satisfying and happiest learning experiences came from getting to know the parents of my students. The Weinribs of New York, for example, were a Deaf couple who communicated largely through American Sign Language (ASL). Yet the patience they had with my beginner's ASL and the warmth and respect they showed me despite my inexperience still touches me. Or Mr. Lopez in Los Angeles, patiently explaining that his daughter's language limitation was only in English, not her native Spanish, despite the fact that she was hard of hearing.

Not every parent is patient and warm, and not every parent has the time or inclination to explain their child—nor should they be expected to do those things. Many parents seem very different from each of us—they may have a lot more money or a lot less money; they may speak a language or wear clothing or have religious beliefs that we do not understand. But instead of being put on the defensive or feeling personally criticized when parents don't fit our "ideal" of how they should behave, it's important to examine where our own notion of "ideal" comes from, and how our own experiences color our perception of others. See the nearby First Person box in which Janice Fialka provides her thoughts and perspectives about her son's teachers.

> Self-examination is the first step to becoming culturally competent.

Developing Cultural Competence

To be able to work effectively with diverse parents, it is important for teachers to be aware of their own attitudes toward people from diverse groups, and to be aware of the cultural assumptions on which beliefs are built. Professionals who

A Letter from a Parent of a Child with Disabilities

I believe that as professionals you can make a difference in our lives as parents of children with special needs.

You have the opportunity not to be intimidated when we blow off steam. You should not personalize these angry negative feelings. The great challenge for you is to give us the opportunity to fall apart once in a while.

You have the opportunity to decrease our profound sense of loneliness. . . . So often we want to talk about "it," but few people appear to want us to talk. You will often be the ONE person who will say: Tell me more. And then what happened? And how did that feel?

You have the opportunity to help us know our child. In the beginning, most of us know very little about their special needs. . . . You can model for us how to say the words, how to tell others. You can take us into our children's lives.

You have the opportunity to share books, pamphlets, and resources. Take the articles out of your file cabinets and off the shelves and spread them to the parents who have no idea where to find the stories and facts about our children.

You have the opportunity to help us recognize and celebrate our victories. They are often small for the "normal" population to appreciate. You know that awful-sounding "grunt" made by our child is truly a miracle. Often it is only you that knows that a new movement is significant and indicates a renewed sense of hope.

You have the opportunity to remind us how far we have come and how much we have accomplished. You, often more than our closest friends, know the details of our successes. Over and over, you can highlight those changes and celebrate the growth.

You have the opportunity to allow us those moments when our souls fall into deep despair. We will, at times, feel that we cannot and don't want to continue for another moment.

You can give us the space to be in that dark place. It is one of the greatest "interventions" you can give us.

If at times you can do some of these suggested activities, then you will have the opportunity to help us feel hope. We must feel hope if we are to get to our next appointment, or to face the next birthday party or to use the words *special needs*.

Partnership is a collaboration. Plopped right in the middle of that word you will find the word *labor*. Partnership is labor. It is hard work. You are the midwives helping us to give birth to a new relationship. Let us begin.

—Janice Fialka

Janice Fialka is the mother of two children, Micah (who has developmental disabilities) and Emma. This excerpt is published in a collection of her writings entitled, *It Matters: Lessons from My Son*. To obtain a copy of this book or receive information about Fialka's speaking engagements, contact her by e-mail at ruaw@aol.com.

Source: J. Fialka (1996). Excerpted and adapted from *You Can Make a Difference in Our Lives. DEC Communicator, 23* (1), 8.

work in schools must begin to develop **cultural competence:** "respect for difference, eagerness to learn, and a willingness to accept that there are many ways of viewing the world" (Hanson, 1998, p. 493). Cultural competence is a lifelong process, not a set of skills that can be learned from a book (Lynch, 2011).

Our cultural and ethnic identities help to shape our beliefs and practices, and who we are as individuals and family members. Our definition of culture is broad—it includes not just linguistic or ethnic differences, but differences in religion, political affiliation, sexual preference, and many other important factors. Our identities are not the script for our behavior, but they do provide a texture and a richness—and they can bind us together in groups or separate us from one another. Knowledge and understanding of, sensitivity to, and respect for these cultural differences can significantly enhance the effectiveness of service providers in the helping professions (Hanson, 2011).

Hanson and Lynch (2004) describe three steps that we should take to move toward cultural competence. The first is *self-awareness*—the process of identifying one's own values and their origins, as well as one's own biases. "Our own beliefs, biases, and behaviors are so ingrained that we often fail to recognize that they simply represent our own worldview, not the way that all people view the world" (Hanson & Lynch, 2004, p. 154).

Next, we must learn more about others' *cultural and sociocultural perspectives*. This takes curiosity, interest, and time, but is an important part of becoming an educated citizen. And last, *apply one's self-awareness and the information learned about other cultures in practice*. We must use the information we acquire in order to serve our students effectively—for example, designing interventions or homework assignments that are compatible with families' worldviews.

I would add two more steps to those suggested by Lynch and Hanson. My first is to *avoid perpetuating stereotypes*. There is so much variation within cultural groups that stereotyping misses out on much that is interesting or nuanced in human behavior. Are you the same as everyone else in your state, with your gender or your religious beliefs? Avoid making blanket statements that characterize everyone in a group as the same. And last (inspired by Hanson and Lynch), *suspend judgments*. I can still hear my father's voice in my ear, paraphrasing Matthew in the New Testament—"Judge not, lest ye be judged." Judging

Cultural competence involves respect, willingness to learn, and appreciation of the many different ways of viewing the world.

Teachers must strive to achieve cultural competence with families, and avoid stereotyping.

parents for their behavior implies that you think you are right and they are wrong, which assumes the superiority of your culturally determined values. Families will feel your judgments when you talk with them, whether you state them overtly or not.

Regardless of their economic status, language skills, or educational level, parents are greatly concerned about the welfare of their children. They, better than anyone else, know the child's characteristics, strengths and weaknesses, and perceptions of the school. Cultivating a working relationship with diverse parents requires respect for these understandings.

In special education, our work with families begins early, particularly if a disability is discovered when the child is quite young. As we discussed in Chapter 3, the development of the Individualized Family Service Plan (IFSP) involves planning not only for the child but also for the family. Therefore, our ability to communicate and relate to the family, to identify the information that parents need, and to integrate our educational and social interventions with the participation preferences of the family are critical aspects of support for families (McWilliam & Scott, 2001). Our knowledge of how a family perceives not only a disability but also special services can affect the type of programming we plan and the extent to which services such as assistive technology are used (Parette & McMahan, 2002).

Harry and colleagues (Harry, Kalyanpur, & Day, 1999; Kalyanpur & Harry, 1999) urge school professionals to build bridges between the values and experiences of families and those of the special education system by operating within a framework of **cultural reciprocity**—a two-way process of information sharing and understanding that can be truly reciprocal and that can lead to genuine mutual understanding and cooperation. See the accompanying Teaching Strategies and Accommodations box, "Four Essential Steps for Developing a Posture of Cultural Reciprocity," to learn more about establishing such a framework for working with families.

Cultural reciprocity is built on mutual respect and information sharing.

A Cuban college student in a Miami teacher preparation program was required to attend a social event with one of her students and his or her family in order to reflect on cultural reciprocity. She arranged to attend church with Jack, an African American boy, and his family:

> "I was very nervous. I was on my way to a Baptist church in a predominantly black neighborhood. My stomach was in knots . . . I am of Catholic faith and was not sure what to expect. As I waited for the family, many people looked at me as if I were lost. I really did not fit in, I stood out like a sore thumb . . . I felt as if I were intruding. As people stared at me, I simply smiled and said, "Hello." I just wanted to disappear. When I saw Jack's family, I felt more comfortable. They welcomed me very warmly, and Jack shook my hand for the first time. It was then I felt I was in a very warm atmosphere. The church felt like one big family—very different from the church I regularly attend. At my church, when people walk in, they are very quiet and very careful not to make the slightest noise. At Jack's church, everyone was happy and no one whispered. This made me feel good. Jack's family interacted with everyone. I noticed that everyone greeted Jack—just like everyone else. No one treated him differently. Jack was accepted as he was. . . . What I saw was a close-knit community that was accepting of Jack's disability.
>
> Many times we make assumptions about people based on race, religion, and other factors. . . . I thought people in the church would not be accepting of me because of my race and my religion—but I was wrong!" (*Council for Exceptional Children*, 2001, p. 4).

Teaching Strategies & Accommodations

Four Essential Steps for Developing a Posture of Cultural Reciprocity

Step 1: Identify the cultural values that are embedded in your interpretation of a student's difficulties or in the recommendation for service.

Step 2: Find out whether the family being served recognizes and values these assumptions, and, if not, how their view differs from yours.

Step 3: Acknowledge and give explicit respect to any cultural differences identified, and fully explain the cultural basis of your assumptions.

Step 4: Through discussion and collaboration, set about determining the most effective way of adapting your professional interpretations or recommendations to the value system of this family.

_____

Source: B. Harry, M. Kalyanpur, & M. Day. (1999). *Building Cultural Reciprocity with Families: Case Studies in Special Education* (pp. 7–11). Baltimore: Paul H. Brookes.

Moving outside our own circles and experiences and into those of our students enriches our own lives and helps us understand cultural reciprocity.

Approaches to Studying Families

Families are so basic to human life and functioning that they are studied in almost every discipline. Whether you are an economist, a philosopher, or a biologist, there is likely to be a framework for considering families. In special education, we often borrow from theories of other disciplines to understand family life and to write and teach about families—to describe them, and the impact on the family of a child with a disability, in a way that makes sense to our students.

The Family Systems Approach

Family systems theory is a framework that comes from sociology for understanding the family as an interrelated social system with unique characteristics and needs. It is based on the assumption that an experience affecting one family member will affect all family members (Turnbull & Turnbull, 2001).

The **family systems approach,** illustrated in Figure 4.1, suggests that each family has its own characteristics, interactions, functions, and life cycle, and the interaction within each family is unique. Family characteristics include the characteristics of the exceptional child, such as the nature, degree, and demands of the child's exceptionality, as well as the family itself—its size, socioeconomic status, ethnicity, religion, and so on. Family interactions are the relationships between and among family members; often, they are very much affected by a child's exceptionality. Family functions include all the tasks and responsibilities of family members. The family life cycle is the experiences of the family over time.

The family systems approach provides a helpful framework for viewing the child in the context of his or her family, in all its uniqueness and complexity, including the components related to traditions, values, and belief systems that we call culture. If you draw your own family map (see Figure 4.2), you will find that the components of family systems theory will come to life.

> The *family systems approach* assumes that what happens to one family member affects all family members.

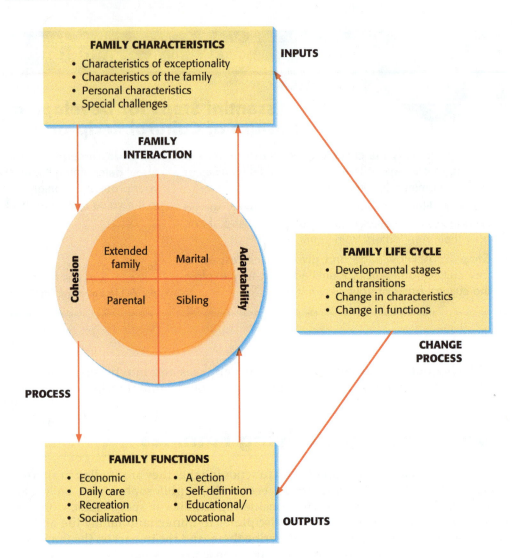

FIGURE 4.1

Family Systems Conceptual Framework

Source: Turnbull, A.P. Turnbull, H.R., Erwin, E., Soodak, L., & Shogren, K. (2011). Families, Professionals, and Exceptionality: Positive outcomes through partnerships and trust (6th ed.). Upper Saddle River, NJ: Merrill/Prentice Hall.

Ecocultural Theory

Ecocultural theory requires that we recognize each family's daily routines and activities.

Another framework through which the family and home can be studied is **ecocultural theory,** which is based on two fundamental premises. First, families are in the process of adapting to the environment in which they live. This adaptation is based on the family's goals, dreams, and beliefs, as well as the physical, material, and sociocultural environment in which they live. The interaction of these two forces makes up the "ecocultural niche" of the family. The second premise is that to understand the influence of this ecocultural niche on the individuals within the family, one must look at the family's daily routines and activities. Activities are defined and analyzed by the following five dimensions: the people present; the cultural goals, values, and beliefs of the participants; the motives, purposes, and intentions that guide the family's activities; the nature of the tasks involved; and the scripts, routines, and patterns of behavior used during the activities (Bernheimer, Gallimore, & Weisner, 1990; Dingle & Hunt, 2001). Analysis of these family activities and routines can help us "weave interventions into the fabric of everyday life" (Bernheimer & Keogh, 1995). Ecocultural theory is the framework for "routines-based" early intervention practices (McWilliam, 2010).

An example of the application of ecocultural theory comes from Bernheimer and Weisner (2007), who followed 102 families of children with disabilities for 15 years, listening to their descriptions of their daily lives. Using

DIRECTIONS FOR THE FAMILY MAP

1. *Decide what family* you will picture (family of origin or procreation). If you have more than one family you may do both.

2. *Trace and cut out circles* on a plain piece of paper, making enough for yourself and each person or set of persons or things you want to include. *There are no restrictions on whom you include or how you symbolize them* (parents, siblings, neighbors, pets, your father's golf game—whoever or whatever has a significant effect on the family). If you wish, you may vary size, shape, or color of the units to express yourself more fully.

3. *Label each circle.* A single circle may have only one name or more than one if you see those people/things as a unit.

4. *Arrange the circles* on the colored paper provided so they express the relationships you observe in your family. When you feel comfortable with the total arrangement, firmly glue them in place.

5. Draw any *boundary or connecting lines* you feel complete the picture.

6. Attach a *page explaining what you have done.* Explain who the components are (age, sex, relationship to you, why included), why you arranged them as you did, the meaning of any connecting or boundary lines, and any special use of size, shape, or color.

7. Finally, *list any people you left out* that you might logically have included and *explain why* you left them out.

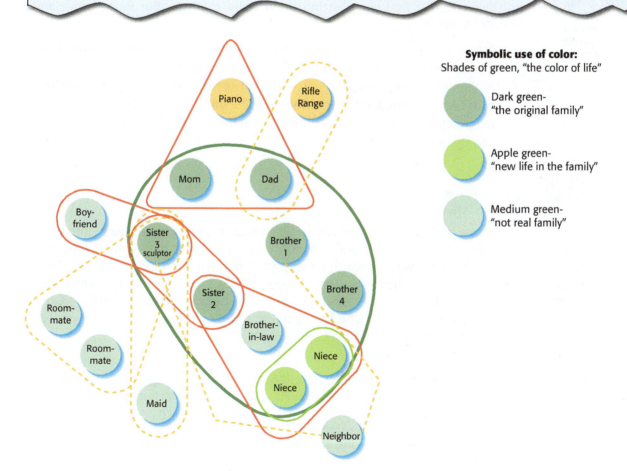

Symbolic use of color:
Shades of green, "the color of life"

Dark green—"the original family"

Apple green—"new life in the family"

Medium green—"not real family"

FIGURE 4.2

Complex Subsystems: Example of a family map

Source: Nancy V. Wedemeyer & Harold D. Grotevant (1982). Mapping the family system: A technique for teaching family systems theory concepts. *Family Relations,* Issue 8204, 31: 2, 185–193. (The authors would like to acknowledge Dr. Vivian Correa of Clemson University, who suggested the use of this article to teach family systems theory.)

ecocultural theory as the backbone of their work, they found that the families made many accommodations (changes made or not made to the family's daily routines) because of their child with a disability. Accommodations were related to families' cultural values and goals. Some families find that focusing on routines that appear similar to those of other families is important to them (normalization values); other families are driven to find the ideal plan for their individual family (familistic values). Here's an example of how they described possible issues:

> Families of children with disabilities may find it easier to maintain a hectic schedule of driving the child to a variety of community activities if they have strong "normalization" values; parents with strong familistic values, on the other hand, will have trouble sustaining a daily routine that is driven primarily by the demands of their high-pressure careers. (Bernheimer & Weisner, 2007, p. 196)

Part of the value of this work is that it breaks down each family's many "functions" into a detailed story of their daily lives and the accommodations they make for their child with a disability. This kind of family description then becomes the foundation for suggesting interventions for families—giving them ideas about infusing teaching and learning into their daily routines. But Bernheimer and Weisner caution us:

> If there is one message for practitioners from our parents and from our longitudinal studies, it is that no intervention, no matter how well designed or implemented, will have an impact if it cannot find a slot in the daily routines of an organization, family, or individual. The intervention (the information and practices that make it up) must fit into the existing beliefs and practices already in place. (p.199)

> Theories of how families operate help us see the child and family in a wider view, in this case, part of a system or interrelated group, which usually maintains an orderly and productive daily routine that supports each family member's functioning.

▶❚❚ TeachSource VIDEO CASE

What Are the Benefits of Family-School Partnerships?

It can be very satisfying for teachers to have productive relationships with families that result in good outcomes for the students. Visit Chapter 4 on the CourseMate website and watch the video entitled "Students with Special Needs: The Importance of Home-School Partnerships." See how Sophia Boyer's partnerships paid off for Nathanielle and Raulito. How comfortable do you think you will be working closely with parents in similar situations?

? Pause and Reflect

It may be helpful to apply the family systems conceptual model (see Figure 4.1) to your own family. Start with a family map (see Figure 4.2), which will help you reflect on your relationships with your relatives and close friends. Then think through the family systems model for your own family, remembering this basic idea: What happens to one member affects all members. Can you identify an event in one family member's life that had an impact on the rest of the members of your family? ●

As you read the next section, it will be important to keep in mind that many disabilities are **social constructs** viewed very differently by families from diverse cultural backgrounds. A social construct is the way in which an idea or concept is *constructed*—described and valued—within a culture. For example, in the United States, where there is a strong emphasis on educational achievement and many opportunities for education, not being able to read becomes a major problem— hence the category and label *learning disabilities*. Deafness, blindness, and physical disabilities are not social constructs in themselves, but attitudes toward them are socially constructed, or determined by the values and practices within a culture. What families think about what we call a disability may be strongly influenced by their early experiences of normal behavior, and their views may be much broader than those of the schools.

Family Reactions to Disability

We all have fantasies about our unborn children—which are soon erased by the experience of having a real child. We may think of an adorable toddler holding our hand and walking contentedly by our side. We may look at other people's children behaving irritably or having a temper tantrum and think, "*My* child will never behave like that." We may picture our future offspring winning the science fair, writing the great American novel, or competing in the Olympics.

Most of the time, our children don't fit those fantasies. They may excel in ways that surprise us and show no interest in areas in which we imagined they would achieve. We seldom live up to our own dreams of being perfect parents, either. Our children love us anyway, and we usually come to accept each other, imperfect as we all are.

The discovery that a child is exceptional may come at birth or soon after, or it may come later in a child's life—perhaps, as with giftedness or learning disabilities, at school age. Although parents may experience similar feelings at either point, the age of the child does appear to make a difference in the family's initial response. First we will discuss early diagnosis. Keep in mind that the more severe the disability, the earlier it is likely to be identified.

When a child with a disability is born into a family, the family's expectations are violated in at least two ways. First, the child may not look like or behave like the child they imagined. The doctor's predictions about the future may be dour and depressing or frightening in their vagueness. Grandparents and friends may not know how to react and may offer no congratulations, send no flowers, make no phone calls. Instead of imagining a bright future for the child, the parents imagine the worst—or don't know what to imagine. The family's cultural background may also influence how grandparents and extended family respond to the birth of a child with a disability. For some it may bring dishonor, with the sense that the parents have done something wrong for such a thing to happen; others accept disability as something that "just happens" (Klein & Chen, 2001).

> Severe disabilities are likely to be identified earlier in the child's life.

Second, the parents' expectations for caring for the child may not correspond to reality. Nearly all families underestimate how much work is involved in having a new baby and how much of their own lives they are required to give up. Although all newborns are demanding, a baby with a disability may have special equipment, require special feeding techniques, be particularly irritable or fussy, and not respond predictably to being cared for. As a result, first-time parents may not be able to benefit from advice from friends and relatives, and experienced parents may not be able to rely on their experiences with their other children for some aspects of caregiving.

When their children are identified with a disability, families who have access to other parents of children with a similar disability are fortunate: They can often provide both emotional support and specific ideas for easing the burdens of child care. Organizations founded by parents of children with a specific disability, such as the ARC, the Cystic Fibrosis Foundation, Autism Speaks, or the Down Syndrome Congress, are often a great help to families with newly identified young children. See our companion Education CourseMate website at **www.cengagebrain.com** for a list of useful organizations.

> National and local organizations can provide both information and support to families.

When parents of exceptional children look to the future, their dreams and expectations may also be violated. During childhood, the parents may be required to advocate for their child to ensure that he or she receives an appropriate educational program. As an adult, their child may still need their care. Parents must prepare for what will happen to that child—no matter what age—when they die.

This is not what we bargain for when we begin to dream about having a child. But it is not the catastrophe that it might seem to be at first glance, either. Many

© Jonathan Nourok/PhotoEdit

Not all family functions involve work! Here a mother and her son enjoy kayaking together.

families become stronger and wiser for the experience of having an exceptional member. As usual, those virtues do not arrive without pain and struggle.

As an illustration, let us consider the story of a hypothetical family.

Akil and Isabel's baby is whisked away from them the minute she is born and soon surrounded by green-coated medical personnel who work over her quietly but urgently for many minutes. Returning from the huddle, their ashen-faced obstetrician tells them that their baby appears to have Down syndrome and is having difficulty breathing. The doctors suspect that she has a heart problem, and she is being taken to the neonatal intensive care unit, where she will undergo tests and be evaluated.

Before they can think about what questions to ask, Akil and Isabel are in the recovery room, looking at each other. Down syndrome? Doesn't that mean intellectual problems? And a heart problem? Will she survive? Do we want her to survive? Will she need surgery? Why is this happening to us?

Professionals must be aware that it is difficult for parents to take in a lot of information in an emotional situation.

In describing the experience of learning that their child had a disability, many parents remember the initial feeling as one of *shock.* Parents sometimes describe themselves as standing over the situation, looking down on it and watching themselves. These feelings can be short-lived or persist for some time. Because of this, professionals are encouraged to repeat the information they have about the baby or child at another time, or in a different way, as often as possible over the first few days. It is crucial for professionals to be available to parents as they ask questions and as the import of the news slowly dawns on them.

As the shock diminishes, parents may begin to feel a deep *grief.* Their "dream child" is gone, and they don't know what they are left with. This is a feeling that many parents continue to experience for a long time, although it is not a constant feeling. For many, this grief is alleviated by the beginnings of an attachment to their child. Let's go back to our hypothetical situation.

Late that night, Akil and Isabel are able to visit their new daughter in the neonatal intensive care unit. The doctors have told them that their baby has a congenital heart defect that will require open-heart surgery. Although the baby is wearing a heart monitor and receiving some oxygen through a nasal tube, the nurse takes her out of her incubator and places her in Isabel's arms. "She's adorable!" Akil and Isabel exclaim with surprise as they notice her fuzzy hair, her smooth skin, her tiny hands. Akil notices that her nose is small and her eyes appear to have an upward slant. She opens those eyes, and suddenly the baby and her parents are looking at each other for the first time. Despite the sadness and anxiety in their hearts, Akil and Isabel fall in love with their new daughter. They decide to name her Angelica.

Another feeling that parents must often struggle with is *anger.* They look at friends and family members with normal, healthy babies and wonder why their baby couldn't have been that way. They look for someone to blame for their dilemma, and if they find no one, they may turn the anger inward and blame themselves, often without reason.

Despite the pain, most parents eventually reach a point at which they accept the fact that their child has a disability. Although feelings of anger, guilt, and sadness do not disappear, the parents are able to recognize and rejoice in their child's progress and to act as advocates for their child.

Our story of Akil and Isabel is a hypothetical example of a family learning shortly after their child's birth that she has a disability. In some instances, early diagnoses like these do occur. Some disabilities are present at birth and are identified immediately or in the first few days of life. For many other families, however, the knowledge that their child has a disability comes much later. Learning disabilities, for example, typically do not appear until the child is in school and must begin to learn to read. Children with autism may develop normally for the first months of life. Parents may suspect that something is wrong, but they sometimes have difficulty getting professionals to confirm their suspicions. The worry that something is wrong with their child is very stressful for parents; they often veer back and forth between reassurance and deep anxiety.

> Feelings of shock, grief, and anger may recur throughout child rearing, but most parents ultimately accept and adjust to their child's disability.

Factors Affecting Families' Reactions

We know a great deal about families and how they work from our own experiences, and the components of the family systems approach provide us with a conceptual framework for discussion. Foremost among these is the first component, **family characteristics,** which includes the characteristics of the exceptional child as well as the family itself. Let us examine how knowledge of family characteristics has specific implications for families of a child with a disability.

● *Characteristics of the Child's Exceptionality* Clearly, various abilities and disabilities will have differing effects on family life. For one thing, the *nature* of the exceptionality will determine the family reaction. The child who is deaf challenges the family to alter their communication system; will family members use sign language or speech for communication? If the choice is sign language, is each family member willing to take on the commitment of attending sign language classes? The child who is chronically ill places financial as well as emotional stress on the family; the child with a learning disability requires extra academic support and may cause a family to examine the emphasis they place on school achievement.

> The nature of the child's disability has an influence on family life.

The *degree* of exceptionality may also have an impact on the family reaction. Children with more severe disabilities may look and behave quite differently from other children. Although on one hand these factors might stigmatize a family, on the other they clearly communicate that the child has a disability, relieving the family of the need to explain. Some disabilities, such as deafness and learning disabilities, are "invisible"; they are less likely to be apparent from looking at the child. Families of children with disabilities often describe the stress and frustration that accompany the constant explanations of their child's disability that are

> Parents are often required to explain their child's disability to others.

expected by family, friends, and strangers. Berry and Hardman (1998) provide a poignant example of family stress in their excerpt from Kathryn Morton's description of grocery shopping with her daughter Beckie: "I took her shopping with me only if I felt up to looking groomed, cheerful, competent, and in command of any situation. . . . To look tired and preoccupied with surviving . . . would have turned both of us into objects of pity" (Morton, 1985, p. 144).

The *demands* of the exceptionality will also affect the family's ability to respond. Children who are medically fragile—needing special equipment such as ventilators, oxygen, or gastrointestinal tubes—present great caregiving demands on a family. Children in wheelchairs or those who use other equipment require special accommodations in their homes. Children with behavior and emotional disorders may be destructive of themselves, of others, or of objects within the home. Each exceptionality places its own unique constraints on family life (Hauser-Cram et al., 2001). Even giftedness is no exception; the needs of the talented child for lessons, tutoring, or special attention may create difficulties for other children in the family.

Parents of children with autism often experience special stresses because of their children's unconventional behavior and their intensive caregiving needs. Although the growth in the number of children with autism (see Chapter 9 for more information on this) has brought more public knowledge of this unique disability, parents are still exposed to high degrees of stress. Smith and colleagues (2009) examined the daily diaries of 96 mothers living with their adolescent and adult children with autism, and found they experienced significantly higher degrees of stress than their counterparts without children with autism—more arguments with family members and more stressful events at home. These authors describe the mothers as a particularly vulnerable group, and hope that their research will lead to more sources of support for the mothers.

Research that focuses on a specific group can always be criticized for who it leaves out. One father, for example, responding to a description of the Smith et al. study on the website *Disability Scoop* wrote: "What about dads? I guess we aren't active caregivers so we don't count. Give me a break. Hey researchers, WAKE UP!" (Source: http://www.disabilityscoop.com/2009/11/10/autism-moms-stress/6121/) It's also worth noting that this research focused solely on white American mothers, so we cannot assume it applies to mothers from other groups.

> **Disabilities place varying demands on family members.**

● *Characteristics of the Family* In addition to the nature and demands of the child's exceptionality, each family has qualities and characteristics that make it unique. Among these characteristics are **family configuration** and family size. Family configuration refers to the adults present in the family. These can include one or both parents, stepparents, or foster parents, and extended family members such as grandparents, aunts, uncles, cousins, or family friends. There may be one adult living with the child or many. For children of working parents, the caregiver during the parents' work hours may also be essential to the family configuration. Children who experience many changes in family configuration (such as several foster placements) appear to be particularly vulnerable to school problems later in life (Werner & Smith, 1982; Zetlin & Weinberg, 2004). Related to family configuration is family size, which usually refers to the number of children in the family. Issues for only-child families may be quite different from those of larger families. Where brothers and sisters are involved, we must consider their needs in light of their exceptional sibling.

Another important family characteristic, one determined by income, education, and employment, is its **socioeconomic status (SES),** which may affect the family's ability to participate in the child's educational program. Although most families have periods of financial strain, for some it is a more chronic problem

> **Socioeconomic status is determined by family income, education, and employment.**

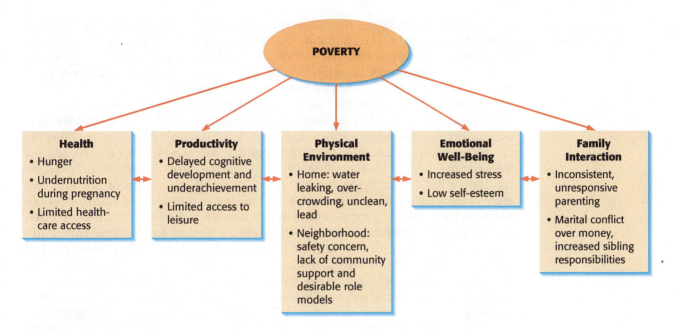

FIGURE 4.3

Impacts of poverty on five family life domains

Source: J. Park, A. P. Turnbull, & H. R. Turnbull (2002). Impacts of poverty on family quality of life in families of children with disabilities. *Exceptional Children,* 68 (2), 154.

than others. As this is being written, 22% of all children in the United States live in families whose income is below the poverty line, and 1 in 12 children lives in extreme poverty (Children's Defense Fund, 2010). Typically, even greater numbers of children with disabilities live in poverty (DeNavas-Walt, Proctor, & Smith, 2011). As we noted in Chapter 3, poverty can affect a child's health and nutrition as well as access to experiences. Park, Turnbull, and Turnbull (2002) describe the impact that poverty can have on **family quality of life.** These authors define family quality of life as family members having their needs met, enjoying their life together as a family, and having opportunities to pursue and achieve goals that are meaningful to them. Figure 4.3 illustrates the impact of poverty on family well-being that Park, Turnbull, and Turnbull describe. As one mother explained it:

> "If you have no money, it's very difficult to be—to do—to be together, to do fun things, to be at peace, to come home to a haven. . . . Because if you have no money, the bills not paid, you not gonna rest when you get home. You might have a good family, you know, a good husband, whatever. But, you don't have money, all that can go down the drain, so . . . money provides a way of release. You can go on a vacation, maybe, once a year, whereas if you don't have money, you won't be able to do that. You can—you can pay your bills. Whereas if you don't have money, you won't be able to do that. And when you can't do those things, you have this feeling of insecurity which floods over into other problems, emotionally. Anger, bitterness, and then it jumps off on the other family members and you got chaos." (Park, Turnbull, & Turnbull, 2002, p. 151)

Another important characteristic is the *language* of the family. Whether it be Spanish (the most common language spoken in American homes after English)

The language spoken in the home is an important family characteristic.

(Shin & Kominsky, 2010), American Sign Language, Chinese, Swahili, Gujerati, or another language, the child's home language will affect your ability to communicate with family members. In 2006, the Los Angeles Unified School District's Home Language Survey identified 91 different home languages used by pupils in the district, which is the second largest in the United States.

The home language is just part of the complexity of each family. As we have seen, a family's cultural background has a profound effect on its worldview and on its attitudes toward an exceptional child. A child with a disability may be perceived quite differently from culture to culture. Many American Indian groups, for example, believe in accepting all events as they are; this value is based on the Indian belief that these events occur as part of the nature of life, and one must learn to live with the good and the bad in life (Joe & Malach, 2011). As the result of such values, attitudes toward children with disabilities are often open and accepting; difference and disability may be viewed as a natural part of life (Dorris, 1989). Other groups define a broad spectrum for "normal" behavior and therefore have difficulty with a school label such as "intellectual disabilities" for their child (Harry, 1992a). In some Latino cultures, strong beliefs in the powers of good and evil, reinforced by religious beliefs, may lead a family to believe that the birth of a child with a disability has resulted from a curse put on the child or the effects of an evil spirit (Zuniga, 2011). Families with Anglo-European roots are more likely to resort to a traditional scientific explanation to understand the cause of a child's disability.

Cultural background may also influence a family's perception of what its role is in connection to the school. Moreno and Wong-Lo (2011) point out, for example, that while many Chinese families are very invested in their child's education and success, and often provide extra opportunities for learning for their children (for example art and music lessons, tutoring, extra homework), most of their efforts occur outside of the school day. These families may not see it as their role to participate in school events and meet the definition of "parent involvement" as it exists in American schools.

But each of us must take care not to make blanket assumptions about families' beliefs and practices based on their cultural background. According to Zuniga, "The central principle is to view each family as an individual unit to ascertain what meaning they ascribe to the illness or disability. Assumptions should not be made without first getting to know the family since so many variables contribute to views on causation and disability, particularly related to children" (p. 217).

A study by Cho, Singer, and Brenner (2000) described the responses of Korean and Korean American mothers to their child's disability:

> Without exception, all parents reported that the news that their children had disabilities precipitated an initial crisis. Several mothers described feelings of shame, self-blame, sorrow, denial, and anger. For example, a Korean American mother stated, "I was furious and ashamed to have an autistic child." A Korean mother reported, "I was hopeless and lost the meaning of my life when I learned that my daughter has autism." Many of the mothers described how they cried on and off during the first several months following the initial diagnosis. The duration of the initial crisis for parents could not be calculated because parents could not recall the precise time when the crisis was resolved. . . . (p. 241)

These parents, like many others, reported that they resolved their initial negative feelings and developed positive and loving views of their children. Those feelings returned, however, during times of stress, particularly when their child exhibited challenging behaviors. The authors point out that, for these parents, the process of resolving their feelings, "was complex, including mixed positive and negative emotions during the same time period and return of earlier emotional and cognitive reactions" (Cho, Singer, & Brenner, 2000). As you know from your own experiences, people don't just feel one way, but often have several conflicting emotions, and they come and go and come again, precipitated by events in our lives.

Ecocultural theory would caution us not to focus solely on crisis in family life; most families continue with their established life routines and adapt and adjust to the demands of caring for their child (Bernheimer & Weisner, 2007).

Religious background is another family characteristic that will affect the perception of disability. Churches, temples, and other religious communities often provide a significant source of support for families, and religious beliefs can shape a family's strategies for coping with a disability (Blacher & Baker, 2007; Parakeshwar & Targament, 2001).

> A family's religious beliefs can provide them with comfort and support.

Impact of Exceptionality on Family Functions

Think about the list you may currently have—either in your head or written down—of "things to do." Going to the bank, shopping for groceries, registering for a class, buying a book, calling a friend to arrange an outing, having your eyes examined—all these tasks are related to personal needs. If you are a parent, your own list is probably at the bottom of an infinite list of things to do for other family members.

Families with exceptional children are often responsible for complex **family functions,** which include all the tasks the family performs to meet its needs. Family finances can be strained by the need for ongoing professional evaluation and services. Taking care of the everyday needs of an exceptional child can be a full-time job in itself: Feeding, dressing, toileting, and transporting a child with a severe disability is labor-intensive. The socialization and self-definition needs of parents are often sacrificed to the needs of children, and families are expected to devote a great deal of time and energy to the educational and vocational needs of their exceptional child. When the needs of other family members are not met, stress may result.

> Family functions include all the life tasks the family performs to meet its needs.

When you work with the family of an exceptional child, you must take into account the needs of the entire family and the responsibilities for fulfilling other family functions that the parents must already shoulder. These responsibilities are challenging for any parent and sometimes feel overwhelming even in economically secure two-parent families; they are compounded in single-parent families and in those families where economic strains are real. Your expectations for families of children who are exceptional must be tempered by your appreciation of the responsibilities involved in meeting their overall needs. Your most useful suggestions to parents will help them incorporate effective strategies for facilitating their child's development into their daily routines; there will also be times when you can offer families additional supports to cope with the demands of their family life and the stress that results from unmet needs.

Exceptionality and Family Interactions

All the relationships within families can be touched by the presence of a child with exceptionality. Traditionally, conventional wisdom assumed that relationships would be affected negatively. More recently, researchers have begun to examine the possibility that the presence of such a child can affect **family interactions** in positive as well as negative ways, and we have consequently begun to alter many of our long-held assumptions and views.

> Family interaction describes the relationships among family members.

● *Within the Family* Research on the lifespan of a typical marriage suggests that most marital partners report a decrease in satisfaction with marriage in the years following the birth of children (Twenge, Campbell, & Foster, 2003). With the presence of any child adding to strain in a marriage, researchers have historically assumed that the birth of a child with a disability creates a great burden: "The history of research in this area is marked by a longstanding and almost pervasive belief that the birth of a child with a developmental disability is a tragedy entraining lifelong hardship for families (Risdal & Singer, 2004, p. 95)—what these researchers call the "tragedy metaphor." Risdal and Singer's meta-analysis of 13 studies addressing the impact of having a child with a disability on marital satisfaction concluded that

> There is a detectable overall negative impact on marital adjustment, but this impact is small and much lower than would be expected given earlier assumptions about the supposed inevitability of damaging impacts of children with disabilities on family well-being. (p. 101)

While having a child with a disability can increase family stress, most families remain together despite those strains. In fact, some couples report that their marriage is strengthened by the presence of their child with a disability (Turnbull, Turnbull, Erwin, Soodak, & Shogren, 2011).

● *Between Parents and Children* Researchers have identified some differences in parent-child interaction when the child has a disability or is at risk for the development of a disability. (The interaction between mothers and their children is studied much more frequently than that of fathers and their children.) These differences vary according to the characteristics of each mother and each child and appear to change somewhat over time, particularly during the first year of life. In general, it appears that mothers of young children with disabilities dominate the communication interactions with their children more than mothers of children

© John Griffin/The Image Works

Loving and stable relationships are the foundation of learning.

without disabilities, perhaps because it is more difficult to interpret infant cues and responses (Cook, Klein, & Tessier, 2008), or perhaps simply because their children talk less, since many children with disabilities have delayed language development. Kelly and Barnard (2000) believe that what is more important than the number of times the mother speaks to the child is whether the mother—or adult—and the child are responding to one another—with words or without—in contingent, sensitive, and empathic ways.

● *Among Siblings*   What happens to the brothers and sisters of children with exceptionalities? Do they suffer from lack of parental attention? Are they given too much responsibility for caregiving? Unsurprisingly, recent research on this topic finds both positive and negative effects. Among the positive effects reported by parents are an increased tolerance for difference, a caring and compassionate nature, and increased maturity; among the negative are a sense of embarrassment and ostracism by their peers (Dyke, Mulroy, & Leonard, 2009), which is most prevalent during the teenage years. But Heller and Kaiser (2008) conclude:

> Generally siblings across the lifespan often regard their experiences as a sibling positively. Siblings report affection and positive regard for their brothers and sisters with disabilities, attribute high levels of empathy and altruism as deriving from their relationship with sibling, and on the whole, appear to be as well adjusted and successful as individuals who have typically developing brothers and sisters. (Heller & Kaiser, 2008, p. 7)

There may be differences across diverse groups in how siblings respond to their experiences with a brother or sister with a disability. Lobato et al. (2011) noted that siblings in Latino families have greater responsibility for child care than those from other groups. When they have a sibling with a disability they are more likely to be absent from school and have lower educational performance than the non-Latino sibling group. These authors speculate that siblings may miss school to translate for their parents at medical appointments.

Most professionals today believe that it is important to invite siblings to participate in decisions concerning their brother or sister with a disability, and sometimes to help with the exceptional child's educational programs. Of course, teaching is not appropriate for every sibling; some will enjoy the process and some will not. But many brothers and sisters are natural teachers of their exceptional siblings, and the family benefits from these positive interactions. See the nearby First Person Box by a young woman who describes what it has been like growing up with her brother Micah.

● *The Extended Family*   Families with effective support systems seem to cope better with the stresses of daily life (Garbarino, 1990). For many, this group includes extended family members who provide help and support. The extended family includes grandparents, aunts, uncles, nieces, nephews, and other relatives. Extended family members may live with the parents and child or apart from them. They can be respite caregivers as well as sources of emotional (and sometimes economic) support to overstressed parents. Family support programs should consider the impact of a child with a disability on grandparents as well as on more immediate family members. Many parents of children with disabilities worry about how their own parents will accept their grandchild (Seligman & Darling, 2007).

Sources of Support

During their toughest times, families find support from each other, extended family members, friends, their communities, their churches, temples, and synagogues, and sometimes from counselors and therapists. Some are considered

Brothers and sisters of children with disabilities can participate in their siblings' care and education.

Reflections from the Sister of a Young Man with Disabilities

Sometimes as I watch kids with special needs in my high school I wonder, "Are they being treated fairly? Are kids respecting them?" My brother Micah is 19 years old and has some developmental disabilities. I often find myself wondering about what his life was like in high school. He loves to run, watch the news, and surf the web. I, Emma, am 15 years old. I enjoy playing my trumpet and playing soccer.

Living with a brother with special needs has been an experience, and it continues to provoke new challenges and accomplishments for both of us. I believe I am a more compassionate, understanding, and most importantly more accepting because I am a sibling of "a Micah." I say "hi" to anybody walking the streets, just like my brother does. I learned that from him. I am a caring person. Not only do I make sure I turn my homework in on time, but I also care about my brother. As my family has learned over time and we do continue to learn, we ask Micah questions that do not involve just a "yes" or "no" answer. Although sometimes it takes an

extra few seconds, I try to think of questions like, "How was your day?" or, "What did you do?" It challenges Micah and allows me to focus on one thing.

The hardest part about being a sibling at this age is hearing classmates use the word "retarded." When I hear that word, a sharp pain goes through my chest. It hits right at home. It bothers me because when people use that word, they are using it as a put-down. Kids and adults don't realize it is unacceptable to use the "r" word to describe a person or thing. When someone uses the word, I usually tell them that it is not cool to say that and it is unacceptable. I don't say anything about my brother because I have found that when I do people just say, "I didn't mean it towards him." Sometimes I don't say anything because sometimes I am just too tired of saying it.

Granted, I am not a perfect sister. When I was young, I knew my brother, Micah was special. He had friends. He was on a soccer team. Everyone seemed to know him. He was my

natural supports—those that are part of everyday life such as family members and friends. Others are **formal supports**—individuals who provide support in their professional role, such as teachers, counselors, or early intervention specialists (more on these supports in Chapter 7). When a family has a child with a disability, there are additional options that can help a family withstand stress and worry. The following are some examples.

Support groups can provide comfort and information for parents.

● *Parent-to-Parent Support* Parents often find their best support from other parents with children like theirs. One effective model for parent support is the **parent-to-parent model,** which links experienced parents of young children with disabilities to parents who are new to the programs and processes. Through phone conversations and meetings, experienced parents listen, comfort, and share their experiences with others who are just beginning to learn about their children. Parents who have had similar experiences are often the most empathic and knowledgeable source of support for new parents.

At times, organizations, school programs, or agencies offer support groups for parents of children with similar disabilities or ages. These groups may have

older brother. In the second grade, as I got older I began to understand the "needs" sides of his specialness. I wanted to change him. I tried hard too. I thought if I helped him with his homework, took him away from the television, helped him with his reading, than he would change and be like the fifth grader he was "suppose to be." He didn't. As I grew older, I became more knowledgeable. I knew more; I realized his special needs were permanent. When I began fifth and sixth grade, I hated having a "different" brother. He was embarrassing. I didn't like how he stuttered, how he rode a training-wheel bike at age 13, or how I sometimes was like the older sibling. I wanted a *normal* brother. I would avoid him. I would go over my friends' houses instead of my friends coming to my house. My parents helped me A LOT. My mom would let me talk to her at night, allowing me to let out my frustration. My dad bought a bike without training wheels so it wouldn't bother me when Micah wanted to ride a bike. This new bike turned out to be not only a match for me, but for my brother. Everyone in our neighborhood wanted to ride his cool bike. He continues to ride it today.

My parents got my brother involved in a lot of activities so he didn't come home right after school. Some weekends he even went away to youth group events. They also started a "circle of friends" when he was in elementary school, where a group of Micah's peers would get together and do activities. These made things better. It allowed me time with myself and special weekends with my parents.

Now in high school after going through many phases as a sibling, I have made the realization that Micah is Micah. Yes, I continue to go back to the phase of embarrassment, not understanding, and sometimes I try to change him. But most of the time I enjoy Micah as my older brother. I love how I can discuss politics and current events with him. We play basketball and soccer. We wrestle. I have taught him to be more assertive. When I first began to push him around like *normal* siblings do, my parents were concerned. They didn't want me hurting him. Despite their influence I continued to "push him around." Now when I shove him he gives me a big shove back, and it doesn't bother me one bit because I know that ALL brothers and sisters fight. And that is the kind of relationship I want to have with my brother.

Emma Fialka-Feldman

Source: Adapted from B.A. Boyd and V.I. Correa (2005). Developing a framework for reducing the cultural clash between African American parents and the special education system. *Multicultural Perspectives, 7*(2), 3–11. Reprinted by permission of Taylor & Francis Group, http://www.informaworld.com

a specific goal, such as teaching advocacy skills, or they may be formed to provide parents with an opportunity to get to know other parents who have similar concerns. Parents often feel most comfortable among a group of peers and can discuss their very private fears and worries about their children with other parents who may have shared their experiences and feelings. Participation in support groups appears to help many parents feel less isolated; often parents report that until they participated in a group they felt they were the only people in the world with their problems. Participation in groups can also help parents form a network of new and understanding friends, and this helps families fulfill the often neglected socialization function that we previously mentioned.

Support groups are common in early intervention programs, somewhat less so in school-age programs, and almost nonexistent for parents of older children and adults. Parents of older children and adults with disabilities often need information, communication, and sharing as well, and programs designed to meet their needs could fill a void that leaves many parents isolated. Technology has provided a boost to parent-to-parent support through the thousands of parent sites on the Internet. The list of family resources available on the Education

A CLOSER LOOK   Why All This Emphasis on *Support*?

Throughout this book, you will read the word "support" hundreds of times, until you take for granted that people in special education provide support to students with disabilities and their families, as well as to general education teachers who work with them. Why do you think we choose this word and this concept to describe what we do, or what we expect others to do?

Let's start with some background. In its early history, special education professionals were very patriarchal (whether they were men or women!)—they were the experts, they knew how to help, they knew what was best for the child. "Good parents" were those who behaved as the professionals expected them to behave. With the advent of Public Law 94-142 (now IDEA) in 1975, and the paramount value it placed on parents as the lead actors in the decision-making process, professionals such as Carl Dunst (2007), and

many others who followed, started to advocate for family-centered practices and partnerships with families. So, rather than a top-down model, where professionals as experts bestowed their knowledge on family members, we started to see parents as experts too. We moved toward a partnership model in which parents were the experts on their child and the decision-makers, and the role of professionals became one of providing support to parents, which enabled them to make informed decisions and carry them out.

Professionals write about support in different ways. As you read in Chapter 3, early intervention specialists try to provide emotional support, material support, and informational support (Jung, 2010; McWilliam & Scott, 2001). But at the bottom of this idea, and of the use of the word support, the belief that parents are the experts, and parents are in charge—and it is our role as professionals to support the decisions they make on behalf of their children.

 CourseMate website that accompanies this text will help you connect the families of exceptional children with other families and sources of support.

● *Respite Care*   For many families, the constant vigilance and caregiving required by a son or daughter with a disability can become overwhelming. A young child with intensive medical requirements, for example, may need to have equipment cleaned, adjusted, and monitored throughout the day; parents may even sleep lightly, perhaps with an intercom to the child's room next to them, in order to hear any "beeps" from equipment, indicating that the child (or the equipment) is having a problem. The child may be on several different medications or require special treatments that must be administered day and night. The child's care can be so complex that parents cannot simply leave the child with a babysitter. Children with unusual or demanding behavioral characteristics, such as those typical of some children with autism, for example, can also be particularly difficult to care for.

Most parents benefit from spending some time without their children in order to build up their spirits for the relentless requirements of being a parent. This is the case for parents of *all* children. For some families of children with very intensive caregiving needs, this time is much more difficult to obtain, and single-parent families are especially hard-hit. It is for families like this that the concept of **respite care** was developed. In respite care, trained substitute caregivers take over the care of the family member with a disability for a period of time that can range from an hour to a weekend. Respite care is usually provided in the family home, but it can also occur in the caregiver's home or in another facility such as a day care center or group home. Families from culturally diverse backgrounds may not be comfortable with the notion of respite care or may prefer to have extended family members provide it. In those cases, the wishes of the family should be respected; some states allow family members to be paid for providing respite care.

Respite care may not be widely available all over the country for families of children with disabilities; when it is provided, however, families report that it positively benefits their families and helps reduce stress levels (Strunk, 2010).

Family members respond to the presence of disability in a child in many ways, depending on family characteristics such as cultural values and beliefs, and the characteristics of the child's disability. Sources of support for families can consist of their religion, other family members, and other parents. What about you? What are your sources of support during difficult times? ●

The Role of the Family in Special Education Services

As we saw in Chapters 1 and 2, the laws pertaining to the education of children with disabilities (IDEA and its amendments) call for parent partnership during every stage of the educational process. Parents choose to collaborate with professionals to varying degrees—some participate a great deal, some not at all.

The concerns of families with exceptional children change as their children grow and develop, moving from infancy through the school years. Sometimes, their children receive special education services from the first year of life through age 21. Let us take a look at the programs available for children with disabilities throughout the school years, and the provisions and expectations for parent involvement within those programs.

Parents have the right to be informed, to consent, and to participate in placement and program decisions.

The Parents' Rights

Built into IDEA (see Chapter 1) is an acknowledgment of the parents' *right to be informed and to consent.* Before a child can be evaluated to determine whether he or she is eligible for special education services at all, parents must receive a written assessment plan that thoroughly describes, in clear, everyday language, what kind of evaluation will be conducted and for what purpose. They must sign and return the assessment plan before an evaluation can take place. In fact, parents' right to an informed consent must be considered at every educational decision point for their child. Ask yourself these questions when considering how this operates in the school in which you teach, or will teach:

- Are the written materials that explain procedures and alternatives available in the parents' native language? Verbally translating or paraphrasing this information may not constitute informed consent.

- Are the explanations on those written documents suitably simple and straightforward enough for a layperson to comprehend? Educators, like many other professionals, are notorious for their use of jargon; sometimes, we are so immersed in it that we assume that everyone else understands it too.

- Do parents understand that they have the option *not* to consent? Sometimes, professionals who talk with parents do not emphasize this information, or it is "buried" in consent forms.

Parents also have *the right to participate in placement and program decisions* through the Individualized Education Program (IEP) process. Parents are equal members of the IEP team. They can express preferences for where their child will attend school and what the primary goals and objectives of their child's educational program will be. If parents do not agree with the IEP team's recommendations, no change in placement or program can be made until the disagreement has been settled.

When parents and school personnel disagree about a child's evaluation, placement, or program, parents must be informed of their **right to due process.** Either the parents or the school may call for a hearing (usually called a **due process hearing**) in order to resolve the conflict. **Mediation** must be available to families and the school district before they go to a due process hearing, although participation in mediation in order to resolve disputes is voluntary. At the due process hearing, both parties may be represented by lawyers and have the opportunity to call witnesses who will testify for their point of view. The decision is made by an impartial hearing officer. Usually, both parties accept the decision of the hearing officer, but if either side still strongly disagrees, the decision can be appealed to the state educational agency and to state and federal courts.

> Due process procedures help parents and schools resolve disagreements about the child's schooling.

Because of the many opportunities for parent participation that IDEA provides, some professionals assume that parents are under an obligation to play a role in this process. This assumption is not correct. Parents also have the *right not to participate* in this educational decision-making. Some parents are not comfortable in such a situation; others are not able to take part, and so they waive their rights. Cultural considerations come into play here too. Parents from some cultural groups may prefer to leave educational decision-making to the schools. When parents choose not to become involved in the IEP process, you must be sure that they understand all their options. Perhaps transportation is difficult for them, and telephone participation would be easier. Has it been made clear to them that an interpreter will be available? And is the interpreter competent and experienced? Several studies of special education processes with parents of English learners indicate that there is a scarcity of interpreters available for non-English-fluent parents (Hardin, Mereoiu, Hung, & Roach-Scott, 2009; Klingner & Harry, 2006), and the interpreters are not always familiar with the terminology of special education (Cho, Singer, & Brenner, 2000). This factor may be related to a family's discomfort with attending school meetings.

> Parents who are not involved in their child's education may be up against barriers to participation that school professionals do not understand.

Teachers sometimes equate parents' noninvolvement in schooling with noninvolvement with the child who has a disability (Klingner & Harry, 2006; Prater, 2002). This is usually an inaccurate perception. Parents of children with disabilities, especially those with more severe conditions, have strenuous demands on their time and energy; they may see the time the child is in school as their only respite. In addition, family factors such as lack of child care, lack of a support system, or an inflexible work schedule may make participation in the child's educational programming nearly impossible for some families (Bauer & Shea, 2002).

Kalyanpur, Harry, and Skrtic (2000) examined the cultural underpinnings of the legal mandate for parent participation in special education law, and noted that it is based on three core values of American culture: equity, individual rights, and freedom of choice. But not all parents grew up with those ideals, and some may not subscribe to them. In addition, they may not have the "cultural capital" (the knowledge of how things work derived from experiences over time) required to navigate the educational system: language fluency, access to networks of support and information, access to school authorities, and so on. Again, as professionals, we must analyze the values and beliefs—often taken for granted—that underlie our expectations for children and families.

The earlier work of Harry and her colleagues (1992b, 1995) identified some of the factors that may contribute to the relatively low level of participation in special education procedures on the part of African American families. Harry's

Parents' Rights to Participate in Their Child's Education Under IDEA

One of IDEA's foundational principles is the right of parents to participate in educational decision-making regarding their child with a disability. The law is very specific about what school systems must do to ensure that parents have the opportunity to participate, if they so choose.

Parental rights of participation can be summarized as follows:

- Parents have the right to participate in *meetings* related to the evaluation, identification, and educational placement of their child.

- Parents have the right to participate in *meetings* related to the provision of a free, appropriate public education (FAPE) to their child.

- Parents are entitled to be members of any group that decides whether their child is a "child with a disability" and meets *eligibility* criteria for special education and related services.

- Parents are entitled to be members of the team that develops, reviews, and revises the *individualized education program* (IEP) for their child.

If neither parent can attend the IEP meeting, the school must use other methods to ensure their participation, including individual or conference calls.

- Parents are entitled to be members of any group that makes *placement* decisions for their child.

If neither parent can attend the meeting where placement is decided, the school must use other methods to ensure their participation, including individual or conference calls, or video conferencing.

The document addresses parents directly:

You are not *required* to participate, however; that is your choice. What IDEA guarantees is that you are given the *opportunity* to participate. The rest—whether to participate, how much to participate—is up to you. Parents vary in the amounts and ways in which they become involved in their child's education; many have written eloquently about its challenges and benefits. It's especially interesting to note that successful partnerships between schools and families grow over time in a climate of mutual respect and consideration, where there's a strong common focus on the well-being of the child.

Let's take a look now at *how* the school system will ensure that you have the opportunity to participate, if you so choose. It all begins with what IDEA calls providing *prior written notice*.

What's prior written notice?

Prior written notice refers to messages that you'll receive from the school system at specific times. At its heart, prior written notice is meant to inform you, as parents, as fully as possible about any actions the school system is proposing to take (or refusing to take) with respect to:

- your child's identification as a "child with a disability" as defined by IDEA and State policy;

- your child's evaluation;

- his or her educational placement; and

- the school system's provision of FAPE to your child.

Prior written notice includes notifying you of upcoming meetings far enough in advance to ensure that you have the opportunity to attend and scheduling those meetings at a mutually agreed-on time and place.

What else should I know about prior written notice?

Parents may also find it useful to know that IDEA requires that prior written notice be:

- written in language understandable to the general public; and

- provided in the native language of the parent or other mode of communication used by the parent, unless it is clearly not feasible to do so.

If the native language or other mode of communication of the parent is not a written language, the school must take steps to ensure that—

- the notice is translated orally or by other means to the parent in his or her native language or other mode of communication;

- the parent understands the content of the notice;

and

- there is written evidence that these requirements have been met.

Information in this table is excerpted from *Parent Participation: Q&A on IDEA, 2009* by the National Dissemination Center for Children with Disabilities. To read the complete document, go to http://nichcy.org/schoolage/qa-series-on-idea/qa2.

longitudinal study identified several factors that discouraged the parents' participation and advocacy for their children:

- *Late notices and inflexible scheduling of conferences.* Despite mandated timelines, parents did not always receive notice of meetings in a timely manner.
- *Limited time for conferences.* Meetings averaged only 20 to 30 minutes in length unless parents expressed many concerns.
- *Emphasis on documents rather than participation.* According to Harry and her colleagues:

  When parents were asked how they perceived their role in the conferences, the majority consistently replied that their main role was to receive information about their child's progress and to sign the documents. . . . Observations revealed that parents' participation in conferences usually consisted of listening, perhaps asking a question (usually regarding logistical issues such as transportation), and signing papers. A typical view, expressed by one mother, was: "They lay it out [the IEP]. If you have questions, you can ask them. Then you sign it." (p. 371)

- *The use of jargon.* The use of unexplained technical terms by professionals can have a silencing effect on parents and may cloud their understanding of information and decision-making.
- *The structure of power.* When conferences are structured so that professionals report and parents listen, there is an implication that power lies in the hands of the professionals. Practices such as these violate the spirit of the law when they diminish parents' incentive to participate as partners in assessment, planning, and placement issues regarding their children.

Boyd and Correa's (2005) "Framework for Reducing the Cultural Clash between African American Parents and the Special Education System" provides some suggestions for reducing those barriers. We have listed them in the nearby "Teaching Strategies and Accommodations" box.

Before Formal Schooling: The Early Years

In Chapter 3 we described the **early intervention** services that can be provided when a child under the age of 3 is identified with a specific disability or developmental delay, or is considered at risk for the development of a disability. Parents of young children in early intervention services are typically concerned with meeting the day-to-day needs of their child and learning more about the implications of their child's developmental status or disability. As we discussed in Chapter 1, the strengths and needs of the family are identified in the **Individualized Family Service Plan (IFSP),** which is developed cooperatively by the family and the family service team.

During the School Years

Starting school is an important event in every child's life, and it means adjustments for every family. For parents of typically developing children, school entry usually means that they will play less of a role in their child's education. Although they will help with homework, confer with teachers, and possibly attend school meetings, the decisions about what their child will learn, how he or she will learn it, and where learning will take place are all made by the school. This process is quite different for parents of a child with a disability. Under the provisions of IDEA, educational decisions, including those relative to program planning and placement, are made by a team that includes one or both parents. This process may begin as early as age 3, when a child who has been in an early intervention program or who has been recently identified with a disability transitions into a

IDEA allows parents to stay actively involved in the education of their children with disabilities through participation on the IFSP team.

The teacher is reviewing IEP goals with this boy and his father. Working as a team will increase the likelihood of success.

preschool program. The transitions from home to preschool, and from preschool to kindergarten, require coordinated planning by the IEP team.

● *The Parent-Teacher Relationship*   The laws mandating educational programs for exceptional children require that parents and professionals work together, or collaborate, to meet the best interests of the child. Although most teachers see the importance of this collaboration, some may not have the skills or the persistence needed to help parents become involved.

Harry (1992b) suggests that new roles for parents need to be developed to restructure parent-teacher communication:

- *Parents as assessors.* Parents' participation in the assessment processes that occur before the IEP meeting legitimizes their roles as providers of meaningful information about their children.

- *Parents as presenters of reports.* A parent report could be a formal part of the process, signaling to parents that their input is valued and necessary.

- *Parents as policymakers.* Harry recommends school-based, advisory parent bodies for special education programs, as well as active recruitment of parents as teachers' aides.

- *Parents as advocates and peer supports.* Parents serving in policymaking and support roles within schools may be more inclined to share their learning with other parents.

Schools traditionally have difficulty engaging parents in meaningful participation (beyond back-to-school night, the school picnic, or fundraising), then complain about lack of parental involvement. This is particularly true as children move into middle and secondary school. Perhaps Harry's suggestions for meaningful parental involvement would increase participation for all parents. Continuing to focus on "family-centered practices" (Dunst, 2002) throughout the school cycle might also encourage more family members to participate. Despite gains, most schools and school districts have a great deal of readjustment to do before parents feel like true partners in their children's education.

> Meaningful parent involvement may involve the schools' promotion of new roles for parents.

Leaving School

When the young person with a disability has completed school or reached age 22 (IDEA allows for schooling through age 21, or until the student has graduated from high school), the family must face a new bureaucracy and new issues.

Teaching Strategies & Accommodations

Family- and Culture-Centered Practices

Boyd and Correa (2005) promote "Family- and Culture-Centered Practices" to encourage the participation of African American families in school activities on behalf of their children with IEPs. The concept of matching services to characteristics of a particular cultural community could be used with other groups as well.

Characteristics of family- and culture-centered practices

Logistical supports:

- Provide transportation to and from meetings
- Schedule meetings during early morning or evening times when families might be able to attend a meeting
- Send multiple reminders home about scheduled meetings and parent-school activities
- Call parents to invite them and remind them of the scheduled meetings
- Meet outside of the school campus in a local community center, church, synagogue, or mosque

Informational supports:

- Offer aid and assistance that is culturally normative to the parent

- Use clear language and terms when describing the child's strengths and needs
- Provide families with family-friendly written materials (bullet formats; short in length; in non-professional language; basic reading level)
- Provide enough time at meetings to explain all aspects of the education plan
- Approach the family from a strength-based model
- Focus the meeting on what the parent or family members want for their child
- Use parents in the assessment process and have them present their reports at the meetings
- Actively involve them in the process of developing goals and objectives for their child
- Convey a sense of cooperation and joint responsibility for solving problems

Emotional supports:

- Incorporate the family's natural supports and networks into professional services instead of supplanting them
- Conduct information-gathering interviews with families, asking about their goals, needs, priorities, values, and beliefs related to their child

How will the child, now a young adult, spend his time? Is she prepared for employment? Can he find a job? How will she spend leisure time? What kinds of friendships and relationships will he have? Will there be a place for her in the community? Where will he live? Most of these issues confront any young adult seeking to separate from the family and achieve a sense of personal identity and independence, but they often assume a special degree of intensity and poignancy when faced by young adults with disabilities.

In 2010, Easter Seals, a national organization which works on behalf of people with developmental disabilities, polled parents of adult children with disabilities. The study report describes the rationale for surveying parents:

> After age 21, young adults with disabilities "age out" of the services and supports provided by law through the school system. Whatever help families living with disabilities may have received through childhood simply, and quite suddenly, goes away. In its stead, families are often met with heightened concerns about their adult child's immediate needs for employment, housing, independence, transportation, social interactions, recreation, health care, and financial security.

- Communicate often with the parent about positive aspects of their child's educational progress
- Reinforce parent's efforts to assist in the educational process and the well-being of their children
- Ask the family during meetings how they are feeling about what is being discussed
- Train parent liaisons to serve as "culture brokers" for families communicating with the school
- Invite family's relatives and/or friends to join the parent at school meetings
- Find time to meet and learn more about the parents' close relatives and friends
- Convey a sense of cooperation and joint responsibility for solving problems
- Conduct meetings with a more personal and informal discourse
- Identify the family's expectations regarding disabilities and developmental milestones for the child
- Identify past experiences of the child or the family that could influence their current perception of the special education process

Community supports:

- Support the use of community liaisons or family advisory councils

- Support parent-to-parent advocacy activities
- Connect with local black churches and black fraternities and sororities for assistance
- Connect with African American professional organizations and service organizations (e.g., Urban League, NAACP, NCNW)
- Establish networks with African American leaders in the community
- Encourage parents to serve on parent advisory committees (PACs) in their child's school or other schools in the community as a way to influence school and district policies on special education
- Make linkages with African American community-sponsored educational programs within the school
- Provide African American families with information about community resources
- Volunteer to serve on African American community programs and organizations
- Share information about special education programs at your school with African American community program planners

Source: Adapted from B. A. Boyd and V. I. Correa (2005). Developing a framework for reducing the cultural clash between African American parents and the special education system. *Multicultural Perspectives*, 7 (2), 3–11. Reprinted by permission of Taylor & Francis Group, http://www.informaworld.com

FINDINGS FROM THE EASTER SEALS SURVEY

- Only 11 percent of parents of adult children with disabilities report their child is *employed* full time (or 19 percent part time), while 48 percent of parents of adults without disabilities report the same (or 24 percent part time).
- Just 6 in 10 parents of adult children with a disability (61 percent) rate their child's *quality of life* as excellent or good, compared to 8 in 10 for parents of adults without a disability (82 percent).
- Huge gaps exist in parents of adults with disabilities' assessment of their child's ability to manage their own *finances* (34 percent vs. 82 percent of parents of adults without disabilities) and have the life skills necessary to *live independently* (30 percent vs. 83 percent of parents of adults without disabilities).
- Almost 7 in 10 adults with disabilities (69 percent) *live with their parent(s)* or guardian, and only 17 percent live independently—compared to more than half of adult children without disabilities (51 percent).
- While some adult children with disabilities work (30 percent) or go to school (29 percent), nearly half (43 percent) stay at home each day.

ASSISTIVE TECHNOLOGY FOCUS

Family Goals Determine Ultimate Success of Assistive Technology

Generally thought to be helpful to any student whose needs seem to require them, assistive devices or services are useful only if the student's family wants them. A study at Southeast Missouri State University (Parette & McMahan, 2002) focused on the need for IEP teams to be sensitive to family concerns, goals, and expectations for their child with disabilities. This is particularly important in the case of culturally and linguistically diverse families.

In establishing assistive technology (AT) goals, IEP teams need to consider certain factors relating to the family's perception of their child's disability and also their ability to understand and implement the devices. Some families, for instance, prefer that their children remain dependent on family and community resources rather than have them gain independence by means of the AT device or service. Some families may want their children to be included with their peers, but others may be afraid that the device will mark their child as out of the ordinary, and still others may feel doubly stigmatized by the AT, already having to cope with the stigma of their minority status.

The key to successful implementation of AT in the IEP is to consider the appropriateness of the device or service for a particular child, within the context of the family. The researchers formulated a detailed list of family goals and expectations regarding AT, potential positive and negative outcomes, and possible IEP responses in light of those outcomes. They also provide

Adapted equipment makes all kinds of childhood experiences accessible.

a helpful set of questions team members can pose to families regarding acceptance of the device within the family and community, expectations of results to be gained from its use, and the resources available within the family concerning its implementation.

For more information, see P. Parette and G. A. McMahan (2002), What Should We Expect of Assistive Technology: Being Sensitive to Family Goals, in *Teaching Exceptional Children*, 23 (1), 56–61. This article contains the list of recommendations for dealing with family goals and expectations when considering applying an AT.

Source: Adapted from the ERIC/OSEP Special Project (2003). *IDEAs that work: News brief.* http://www.hoagiesgifted.org/eric/osep/newsbriefs/news32.html.

The study found that on every measure, parents of adults with disabilities have significantly higher levels of concern than parents of adult children without disabilities.

Remember that the values and beliefs of the family will also affect their expectations for their adult child. Working in a culturally reciprocal manner with families is important at every stage of your student's life.

Transitions to Work and Higher Education

> Transition planning helps parents plan for their exceptional child as an adult.

Although many in special education equate **transition** with employment opportunities, Halvorsen and coworkers (1989) broadened the concept to include the needs of the whole person across all life areas. Transition planning helps parents understand how their exceptional child will live as an adult.

In the past, many families had to make the difficult decisions about the needs of their young adult child with little help. To compound the problem, few alternatives were available for quality residential and employment opportunities for young adults with disabilities. Over the past fifteen years, however, the federal government has turned its attention to post-school choices for individuals with disabilities (Will, 1984), and since 1990, special education professionals have been required to focus on providing transition services to families at times of change. Preparation for the transition from school to work must begin long before school ends. In fact, many experienced parents and professionals believe that for some students, particularly those with severe disabilities, preparation should begin very early in the child's schooling (Falvey, 2005).

The services for students with disabilities provided since the passage of IDEA in 1975 have led to an increased number of those students attending higher education programs (U.S. Office of Special Education, http://www2.ed.gov/offices/OSERS/Policy/IDEA/overview.html). Section 504 of the Rehabilitation Act of 1973 and the Americans with Disabilities Act (1990) require that higher education opportunities be extended to all qualified individuals with disabilities. You will read more about transition planning in the chapters to follow.

Family Concerns for the Future

The future of their children with disabilities is often a source of great concern for parents, and the Easter Seals (2010) study we described above documents some of the reasons for their worry. Many parents, recognizing that they are not immortal, worry about what will happen to their child when they are no longer able to take responsibility for his or her care. The recent upsurge in the number of children identified with autism has raised the level of public questioning about what will happen to those children as they become adults (Chasson, Harris, & Neely, 2007). For a look at what parents of individuals with disabilities fear most, see Figure 4.4.

Participation in the process of transition planning can allay some of the natural anxiety about future options (Greene, 2011). Along the way, the parents become aware of the resources available to help plan for the long-term future of their son or daughter. Families need information and support to confront the intricacies of financial planning and government benefits, guardianship, making a will, and finding and evaluating residential options for their son or daughter. Decisions relating to these crucial areas should be made, whenever possible, with the input of the son or daughter with a disability and should be based on his or her personal preferences. Even individuals with the most severe disabilities have ways of communicating personal preferences, and family members are most likely to be able to interpret their signals.

> Many families worry about the future life of their child with special needs.

Positive Aspects of Disabilities for Families

The ties that bind family members usually persist throughout a lifetime. When a son or daughter has a disability, those ties may involve more responsibility for decision-making and caregiving than a family anticipates. But despite these responsibilities, and despite the stresses and strains that can accompany them, many family members describe the benefits gained by living with a son or daughter or brother or sister with a disability. According to Ann and Rud Turnbull (1990, p. 115) and their colleagues, families have identified six of the ways in which young people with disabilities make positive contributions to their families:

- Being a source of joy
- Providing a means of learning life's lessons
- Giving and receiving love

> An exceptional child can affect family relationships in positive ways.

A majority of parents of adults with disabilities have *multiple fears* for their son/daughter after their death, whereas a strong majority of parents of adults without disabilities cite *no fears* for their son/daughter after their death.

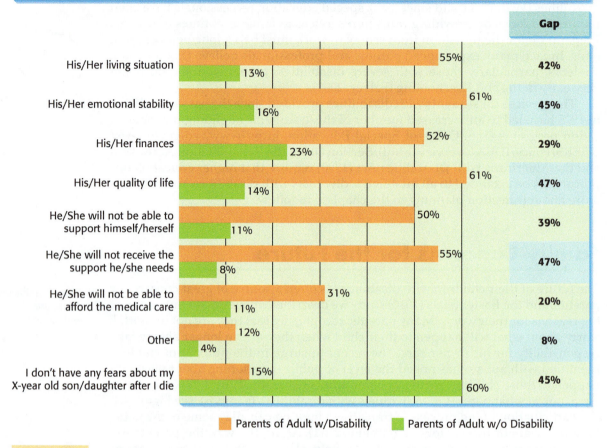

FIGURE 4.4

Fears of parents of adults with disabilities

Source: Easter Seals Disability Services: Living with Disabilities Study, p. 43

- Supplying a sense of blessing or fulfillment
- Contributing a sense of pride
- Strengthening the family

Parents in the Easter Seals study (2010) reported both positive and negative experiences in having an adult child with a disability. Among the benefits to raising and caring for a child with a disability through adulthood:

- Patience
- Respect, acceptance of others
- My son/daughter is a wonderful, loving person
- Made me aware, knowledgeable
- Appreciate life to the fullest
- Empathy, compassion
- Became an advocate for people with disabilities
- Met others with similar experiences
- Made us/me strong, a better person
- Our family bonded, became closer

Blacher and Baker (2007) conducted two studies in an attempt to apply a more rigorous empirical model to the concept of positive impact, and found in both families of young adults with severe intellectual disabilities and families with younger children (those with developmental delays and those typically developing), mothers and fathers were less likely to describe the positive impact when the child had behavior problems. Latino mothers were more likely to report the positive impact of their young child with developmental delay than were Anglo mothers. The authors speculated this cultural difference may reflect beliefs of many Latinos related to disability, family, and religion.

Although it is important to stress that the journey isn't easy and families must be supported through their very real times of crisis, professionals in special education are finding that, given support, information, and strategies from professionals and other parents, most families can come to recognize and experience the positive contributions made by their family member with a disability. Our role is to support and inform families in that process.

? Pause and Reflect

The "shoes test" (Turnbull & Turnbull, 2001) is helpful in determining how you interact with parents of students with disabilities. Put yourself in their shoes. How would you like to be treated? ●

SUMMARY

- Definitions of "family" vary; each family may define the term differently.

- Professionals in schools are increasingly called on to work with families and students from a variety of cultures. It is crucial that we begin to examine our own cultural experiences and attitudes so that we can respectfully engage family members with diverse backgrounds and experiences in a framework of cultural reciprocity.

- Theories of family life, such as the family systems approach and ecocultural theory, shape our understanding of families and the demands of family life.

- The family systems approach uses the characteristics, interaction, functions, and life cycle of each family to describe its unique dynamics, including the initial reaction to the child who is exceptional, the child's impact on the family, and the family's ability to cope and find support.

- The initial reaction to a child with a disability may be influenced by the nature and degree of the disability, family size and socioeconomic status, and cultural and religious background.

- Some of the most important sources of support for parents are parent-to-parent support groups, respite care, and early intervention and special education services.

- IDEA provides a series of rights and opportunities so that parents can participate in decisions related to their child's schooling.

- Parents continue to play a key role through the school years. They have the right to be informed and to consent to the evaluation of their child, and to participate in placement and program decisions through the IEP process. Families are the focus of transition services for planning for their child's future needs.

● Like all children, those with disabilities may have a positive or a negative effect on the family system. Many parents emphasize the positive aspects of having a child with a disability.

KEY TERMS

family (page 114)
household (page 114)
extended family (page 114)
caregiver (page 115)
culture (page 115)
partnerships (page 117)
family-centered practices (page 117)
cultural competence (page 119)
cultural reciprocity (page 120)
family systems approach (page 121)
ecocultural theory (page 122)
social constructs (page 124)
family characteristics (page 127)
family configuration (page 128)
socioeconomic status (SES) (page 128)

family quality of life (page 129)
family functions (page 131)
family interactions (page 131)
natural supports (page 134)
formal supports (page 134)
parent-to-parent model (page 134)
respite care (page 136)
right to due process (page 138)
due process hearing (page 138)
mediation (page 138)
early intervention (page 140)
Individualized Family Service Plan (IFSP) (page 140)
transition (page 144)

USEFUL RESOURCES

● The *National Dissemination Center for Children with Disabilities* (**http://www. nichcy.org/FamiliesAndCommunity/**) has an excellent page for families, which provides access to high-quality information on topics like networks of help, knowledge of the law, and disability itself. Their monthly email newsletter, *News You Can Use*, keeps the reader up to date on topics related to children with disabilities and their families (**http://www.nichcy.org/ News/Pages/**).

● *The Pacer Center* provides support for families to participate in all phases of their child's education. Many of their publications are available in Spanish and Hmong, as well as English. Visit them at **http://www.pacer.org.**

● Authors Deirdre Hayden, Cherie Takemoto, Winifred Anderson, and Stephen Chitwood (2008) have written *Negotiating the special education maze: A guide for parents and teachers* (4th ed.). Rockville, MD: Woodbine House. The book is a step-by-step guide for parents of exceptional children as well as teachers and other professionals. Its emphasis on the collaborative relationships among special education providers is highlighted by many practical checklists, examples, and guidelines.

● John W. Nadworny and Cynthia R. Haddad (2007) have written *The Special Needs Planning Guide: How to Prepare for Every Stage of Your Child's Life*. Baltimore: Paul H. Brookes. These authors are financial planning experts who advise families about how to plan for each stage of the life of their child with a disability.

- *Exceptional Parent* magazine publishes articles especially for families of children with disabilities and provides a forum for the exchange of information by families with children with rare or unusual conditions. Write them at 65 E. Rte. 4, River Edge, N.J., 07661 or go to **http://www.eparent.com.**

- *The Sibling Support Project* is devoted to providing peer support and information to brothers and sisters of family members with disabilities and health care needs. Their *Sibshops* are workshops for brothers and sisters, and their excellent website and blog describe their services and give siblings a place to express themselves. Find them at **http://www.siblingsupport.org/.**

- *The Sibling Slam Book: What It's Really Like to Have a Brother or Sister with Special Needs* Edited by Donald J. Meyer and available online through Woodbine House: **http://www.woodbinehouse.com/.**

- *Family Village* is a web-based organization that integrates information, resources, and communication opportunities on the Internet for persons with cognitive and other disabilities. Visit them at **http://www.familyvillage. wisc.edu.**

- *Family Voices* is an organization composed of families and others interested in children with special health care needs. Go to **http://www.familyvoices.org.**

- The *Family Center on Technology and Disability* offers a range of information about assistive technology used with children. Visit them at **http://www. fctd.info.** Look for the *FCTD Family Information Guide to Assistive Technology & Transition Planning* while you're on the site.

- *Parent to Parent USA* (P2PUSA) is a national non-profit organization committed to promoting access, quality, and leadership in parent-to-parent support across the country. **http://www.p2pusa.org/.**

- The *IRIS Center* has an excellent online module, *Collaborating with Families,* which describes many of the needs and issues of families of children with disabilities. Go to **http://iris.peabody.vanderbilt.edu/fam/chalcycle.htm/** for a look.

Books by Parents of Children with Disabilities:

- Sandra Z. Kaufman. (1999). *Retarded Isn't Stupid, Mom!* Baltimore: Paul H. Brookes. This well-regarded book about the author's own experiences with her daughter Nicole has been updated to include descriptions of Nicole's experiences as an adult.

- Dana Buchman and Charlotte Farber. (2007). *A Special Education: One Family's Journey Through the Maze of Learning Disabilities.* New York: Da Capo Press. Fashion designer Dana Buchman and her daughter describe a privileged family's response to learning disabilities.

- Jane Bernstein. (2007). *Loving Rachel: A Family's Journey from Grief.* Champaign, IL: University of Illinois Press. Jane's daughter Rachel is blind and has additional disabilities as well. Jane writes about Rachel again as she becomes an adult in *Rachel in the World: A Memoir* (2010), University of Illinois Press.

- Lynn Kern Koegel and Claire LaZebnik. (2004). *Overcoming Autism: Finding the Answers, Strategies, and Hope That Can Transform a Child's Life.* New York: Penguin. This book is co-written by a parent and a professional.

- Jennifer Graf Groneburg. (2008). *Road Map to Holland: How I Found My Way Through My Son's First Two Years with Down Syndrome.* New York: NAL Trade. Jennifer Groneburg and her husband had premature twins, one of whom has Down syndrome. The title of this book is inspired by Emily Perl Kingsley's well-known essay, "Welcome to Holland." See it at **http://www.ndsccenter. org/resources/holland.php/.**

PORTFOLIO ACTIVITIES

1. Interview the parent or parents of a child or young person with a disability. How much of the caregiving role does the parent currently undertake? Have the demands of caregiving increased or decreased during the past ten years? Have the parents sought support services, or do they rely on informal support from other family members, volunteers, and so forth? After completing the interview, record and summarize your results and present them to your classmates. Brainstorm some possible resources for the family. Write an IFSP for the family for your portfolio—no matter what their child's age! Using the IFSP rather than the IEP will help you put focus on the family's needs.

   CEC This activity will help the student meet CEC Initial Content Standards 1: Foundations and 10: Collaboration.

2. What are the cultural groups (other than your own) represented in the area in which you live? Draw up a list of things you could do, based on what you have read in this chapter, to become more familiar with the values, traditions, and beliefs of those cultures. Present your list to your classmates, and include it in your portfolio.

   CEC This activity will help the student meet CEC Initial Content Standard 3: Individual Learning Differences.

3. Are you acquainted with the family of an exceptional child? If so, how do the components of the family systems approach apply to this family? Are they useful in identifying areas where services might be provided? Do they help you recognize the family's specific strengths and needs? Use the family systems framework to write a brief description of this family. If you're not familiar with a family yourself, read a book written by the parent of an exceptional child and apply these questions to that family. Some good choices might be found in the list we supply above. Include your work in your portfolio.

   CEC This activity will help the student meet CEC Initial Content Standards 1: Foundations and 2: Development and Characteristics of Learners.

    To access Portfolio Activities for this chapter and other useful study resources including an interactive eBook, related web links, quizzes, flashcards, and videos, visit the Education CourseMate website at CengageBrain.com.

PART 2

LEARNING ABOUT THE POTENTIAL OF EXCEPTIONAL CHILDREN

The chapters in Part II emphasize learning about the characteristics of individuals with specific abilities and disabilities. In addition to information on each category of exceptionality, Chapters 5 through 14 focus on helping you to understand educational programming options for each group of students. These chapters address several aspects of educational programming—including placement, assessment, and the selection and use of appropriate teaching strategies.

Part Outline

Children with Learning Disabilities

Learning Objectives

After reading this chapter about students with learning disabilities, the reader will:

- Describe the definition of a learning disability and discuss reasons for alternative methods of identification.

- Explain the role of Response to Intervention (RTI) in the evaluation of learning disabilities.

- Describe how the learning characteristics of individuals with disabilities affect academic performance in the areas of reading, language arts, and mathematics.

- Understand and explain the most effective approaches for presenting information to students with learning disabilities.

- Identify ways to modify materials to facilitate accessibility for students with learning disabilities.

- Reflect on the need for instruction and curriculum to address the specific learning characteristics of an individual child, including the relationship among instruction, assessment, and student performance.

In this chapter we discuss students with learning disabilities, the largest group of children served in special education and the group most likely to be included in general education classes. Although these students require special education services, their learning needs are often balanced by excellence in other areas of life, and their ability to reach their potential can be dramatically enhanced by appropriate teaching and learning strategies.

Do you remember having to read aloud in school as a kid? Or sitting in a difficult math class, afraid of being called on to work out a problem at the board? Many of us remember vividly the feelings of panic, fear, and anxiety that those situations evoked, particularly if we were not good readers or if we were not confident in our understanding of geometry. Even now we can remember what it is like to feel inadequate in school. Some students feel this way in school every day. The most ordinary classroom tasks may be problematic for them. These students feel as you would—frustrated and confused about their inability to understand and perform in the classroom. Although they have average intelligence, they do not usually do well in school. Many students with learning disabilities read very poorly, and reading competently is the keystone of success in school. Let's find out more about these students.

Terms and Definitions

Children with learning disabilities have probably always existed, but for many years educators failed to recognize their unique problems and characteristics. In 1963, a group of parents met in Chicago and invited the noted special educator Dr. Samuel Kirk to address them. When Kirk described the "specific learning disabilities" that their children shared, the parents seized on that term to describe and unite their children (Lerner, 1993). Although the term *learning disabilities* has been used for almost 50 years, the definition of learning disabilities continues to evolve.

The Federal Definition

A number of definitions of learning disabilities have been put forth over the years; most of them are quite general in order to accommodate the wide range of beliefs related to the origins of learning disabilities. The most widely used definition of **learning disabilities** was originally written in 1968 by the National Advisory Committee on Handicapped Children. It was slightly adapted for inclusion in Public Law 94-142 (1975), now Public Law 101-476, the Individuals with Disabilities Education Act (1990). It reads:

> "Specific learning disabilities" means a disorder in one or more of the basic psychological processes involved in understanding or using language spoken or written, which may manifest itself in an imperfect ability to listen, think, read, write, spell, or to do mathematical calculations. The term includes such conditions as perceptual handicaps, brain injury, minimal brain dysfunction, and developmental aphasia. The term does not include learning problems which are primarily the result of visual, hearing, or motor handicaps, of mental retardation, of emotional disturbance, or of environmental, cultural, or economic disadvantage. (USDOE, 1977, 65083)

● *Key Elements in the Federal Definition* The federal definition emphasizes that the performance of students with learning disabilities is often tied to their ability to receive or express information. Reading, writing, listening, and speaking are some of the ways we take in information or communicate what we know. The

The current federal definition of learning disabilities refers to a disorder in one or more of the basic psychological processes of understanding and using language.

Students with learning disabilities do not achieve at their age and ability levels in one or more specific areas.

academic areas listed in the definition illustrate how this disability can be manifested. It is important to note that a child may have a learning disability in all of the skill areas mentioned, or just in one area. For example, a student may find it difficult to learn to read and spell, yet do quite well in math. Some individuals can speak and write in an organized and effective manner, yet become quite confused when dealing with number concepts and algorithms. Knowing that a child has a learning disability tells you only that the child is experiencing some difficulty processing information. You must learn much more about the child before you can tell how much difficulty he or she is experiencing, or what impact the disability has on specific academic subjects or tasks.

The definition also outlines what learning disabilities are *not*, in an element of the definition that has come to be known as the **exclusion clause:** "The term does not include learning problems which are primarily the result of visual, hearing, or motor handicaps, of mental retardation, of emotional disturbance, or of environmental, cultural, or economic disadvantage." Because a number of other disabilities or life situations may also cause problems in learning, some professionals feel that it is important to ensure that the difficulties a child is experiencing not be attributed to the fact that he or she comes from a deprived family or suffers from another disability. This clause can be used to help prevent the improper labeling of children from distinct cultures who have acquired learning styles, language, or behaviors that are not compatible with the academic requirements of schools in the dominant culture. The federal law goes on to state that a student has a learning disability if he or she:

> A diagnosis of learning disabilities calls for a comprehensive evaluation of learning abilities and academic performance.

1. Does not achieve at the proper age and ability levels in one or more of several specific areas when provided with appropriate learning experiences, or

2. Has a severe discrepancy between achievement and intellectual ability in one or more of the following areas: (a) oral expression, (b) listening comprehension, (c) written expression, (d) basic reading skill, (e) reading comprehension, (f) mathematics calculation, and (g) mathematics reasoning.

Both of these elements of the law—poor progress when given appropriate learning experiences and a severe discrepancy—now carry equal weight when it comes to defining and identifying children with learning disabilities. The addition of Response to Intervention (RTI) in the 2005 IDEA reauthorization and a nationwide movement in school programming has lead to a change in emphasis from a focus on the severity of a discrepancy to a focus on appropriate instruction. Let's discuss this in more detail.

Definition Issues and Response to Intervention

Historically, the most important element of the federal definition of learning disabilities, as far as identification goes, is that the students demonstrate a severe **discrepancy** between achievement, or their performance in school, and their intellectual ability or potential. For example, a 9-year-old child with an average IQ who reads on the first-grade level would be exhibiting a discrepancy between what we expect (reading on the third-grade level) and the way he or she performs (reading on the first-grade level). This discrepancy is determined by examining the differences between scores on intelligence and achievement tests. Although the extent of discrepancy differs among states and even among school districts, a significant discrepancy is usually defined as one or two grades below expected performance level or one to two standard deviations below average performance.

From 1975 to 2005, a significant discrepancy was the cornerstone of the process for identifying students with learning disabilities. This changed with the reauthorization of IDEA in 2005, which includes the Response to Intervention (RTI) option for determining resistance to effective educational strategies.

Because of the great increase of students identified as having a learning disability during this time period, from approximately 800,000 students to 2,877,000 (U.S. Department of Education, 1991; 2003), concern was expressed in the field that ineffective instruction greatly contributed to over-identification and inappropriate identification of learning disabilities. The RTI process focuses on a student's ability to respond to appropriate and evidence-based interventions. One way the process does this is to improve core and supporting curricula. Consequently, RTI has been adopted by an increasing number of schools across the country, and is gaining acceptance as a step in the assessment process for students with learning disabilities. **Progress-monitoring data,** a component of RTI models, is important evidence on the progress of all students through a core curriculum, and through curriculum in subsequent tiers of instruction. Schools now have a choice and can focus on students' response to appropriate instruction, or on documenting a severe ability-performance discrepancy, before conducting the comprehensive assessment to determine if a child has a learning disability.

Although you've learned about RTI in Chapter 2, it is important to look at the process closely here. Figure 5.1 provides an illustration of the RTI service continuum. The premise of RTI is that an evidence-based core curriculum is provided to all students in Tier 1—the general education classroom. Progress monitoring will identify those students who are responding and those who aren't. Approximately 80 percent of students will be successful in Tier 1. Those students who are not successful will receive supplemental, small-group instruction, or Tier 2. Approximately 75 percent of this group of students (or 15 percent of the total population of students) will be successful in Tier 2. Those students who are not successful (about 5 percent) will be eligible for intensive, individualized services in Tier 3. In some models, students must be identified as needing special education (typically as students with learning disabilities) before moving to Tier 3. In other models, students can receive intensive services first in Tier 3a (before special education) and then in Tier 3b (special education). Still other models will label these service levels Tier 3 and Tier 4. In all instances, progress-monitoring data will provide important information for the comprehensive evaluation that is part of the identification process for special education.

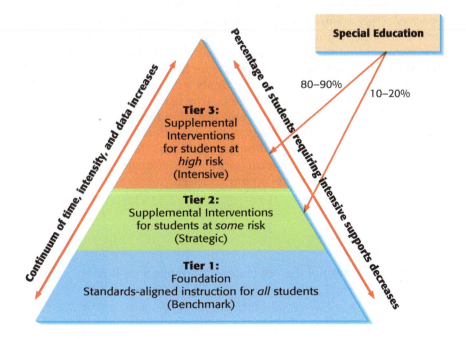

FIGURE 5.1

Representation of academic services for RTI models from the RTI Action Network

Source: Copyright 2011 by RTI Action Network, a program of National Center for Learning Disabilities, Inc. All rights reserved. Reprinted with permission. For more information, visit www.RTINetwork.org

A CLOSER LOOK

Thinking About Response to Intervention (RTI) and Learning Disabilities

In this short manual, the Division of Learning Disabilities summarizes the definition and purposes of RTI, tiered instruction, and progress monitoring, and explains how the procedures can mesh with the legal requirements for identifying and serving students with learning disabilities.

A few of the key points addressed in this manual are:

- The goal of Tier 1 instruction is to rule out lack of appropriate instruction as the reason for inadequate progress.

- Most of the RTI process is implemented by general education teachers. Classroom teachers will be responsible for delivering evidence-based curricula, and progress monitoring—all of the activities leading up to special education services.

- Teachers of students with learning disabilities may provide consultation, but typically will offer special education to identified students—a role no different than it was before RTI.

- Parents can continue to act as an advocate for their children and can request an eligibility evaluation at any point in the RTI process.

- A comprehensive evaluation for learning disabilities should include:

  a. Reviews of the RTI data on student performance

  b. Observational data on student performance

  c. Medical information, if relevant

  d. Data related to the exclusionary clause of the definition

  e. Data from standardized and informal measures of academic performance

  f. Identification of the student's strengths and weaknesses and the rationale for identification of a learning disability (if applicable)

(*Source:* Division for Learning Disabilities (2007). *Thinking About Response to Intervention and Learning Disabilities: A Teacher's Guide.* Arlington, VA: Author.)

Many professionals in the field already fear that as a result of misinterpretations of No Child Left Behind (NCLB), schools are neglecting to provide important, intensive support for all students with learning disabilities (Fuchs & Fuchs, 2009). An additional fear is that the construct of learning disabilities will be oversimplified through the RTI process and perceived as chronic underachievement instead of a complex processing difference. This fear is driven by the concern that schools increasingly are using progress-monitoring data (indicating underachievement) as the major component of a comprehensive evaluation and ignoring other aspects of the evaluation. The Division of Learning Disabilities of the Council for Exceptional Children has published a guide for implementing RTI while addressing the need for careful evaluation of students with learning disabilities. We look at a few key points of that manual in the nearby feature, A Closer Look: Thinking About Response to Intervention (RTI) and Learning Disabilities.

The subjectivity and changeability of the definition of learning disabilities, as well as the definitions of other disabilities, remind us that the term "disability" is relative, and the definition of the term *learning disability* may change with increasing social and academic demands on our children.

Pause and Reflect

Why do you think the number of children identified as having learning disabilities has increased so much in the past few decades? In your opinion, will RTI affect the number of students identified each year?

FIRST PERSON

Valeska

Valeska—a young woman with a learning disability who has worked hard to achieve her life goals.

Source: Succeeding in College and Work: Students with Disabilities Tell Their Stories. Watch Videos at http://humancentereddesign .org/neada/site/student_videos. Funded by Department of Education through NIDRR Grant # H133A060092.

Valeska is a young woman in her early twenties. After struggling with learning and later behavior problems in her youth, she decided to work hard to fulfill her goal of becoming an early childhood educator. After attending technical college and a postsecondary program designed for students with learning disabilities, Valeska has achieved her dream. Here are some of her words:

> I have no memory of not having a learning disability... I think that both my parents knew that something was wrong, or different when I was a baby. . . . I know that has made a huge difference in my life, that I had parents who were aware that something was going on. . . . that I had early, early intervention. I have this bunch of skills . . . but I need assistance in this other thing. . . My view of disabilities is that all disabilities are gifts. And if there is a reason I went through that experience I did in high school, if my learning differences are a gift, I need to know how to use it. That is why I'm in school—to learn how to use my gift. In English something interesting happened. It seemed like in every class someone came up to me for help. In the back of my mind I'm thinking—do you know who you are asking? And then I realized I could actually help people—other students. And that was kind of amazing. For a long time I was defined. . . it was my identity, my disability. Now, I know that it is a part of me, but it is not me. I'd like everybody to know that . . . that other people with differences or what have you—that it's not you.

Image courtesy of the Institute for Human Centered Design's New England ADA Center

Causes of Learning Disabilities

By virtue of its definition, a learning disability is not diagnosed until a student has experienced an academic problem in school or is not progressing at the same rate as same-age peers. Typically, a learning disability is identified in the early elementary years after a student does not progress in one or more subjects at the expected rate. In a great majority of cases, the cause of an individual's learning disability is unknown. This is true despite a vast amount of research investigating the possible causes of these disabilities. The speculation and research about the causes of learning disabilities can be grouped into two categories: **internal factors,** such as organic, biological, or genetic factors, and **external factors,** sometimes referred to as environmental factors. Keep in mind, however, that when we are talking about possible causes of learning disabilities, we are referring mainly to hypotheses rather than facts.

> In most cases, the cause of a child's learning disability cannot be determined.

Internal Factors

Below is a brief overview of some of the internal or physiological factors that are known to cause learning disabilities.

● *Brain Damage/Neurological Differences*   Since the brain is the center of learning, many professionals have assumed that students with serious learning problems have some type of brain damage. Although this explanation made sense intuitively, there was very little clear biological evidence. Today there is renewed interest in neurological evaluations and brain research in the area of learning disabilities. One reason for this interest is advanced technology, which has allowed us to get new information about our brains. For example, some findings suggest that there are differences in the structure, symmetry, or activity levels of at least one hemisphere of the brain for individuals with and without learning disabilities. Bigler (1992) used a procedure called magnetic resonance imaging (MRI) to obtain a picture (similar to an X-ray) of the brains of individuals who had severe reading disabilities and also of some people who did not have learning disabilities. He found that some of the individuals with learning disabilities had structural irregularities in the left hemisphere of their brains. This structural difference was not present in all the individuals with disabilities, so Bigler could not draw any definitive conclusions.

Neurobiology helps us to see how the brains of students with reading disabilities are similar to and different from the brains of students without reading disabilities. In Figure 5.2 we see evidence of how the brain distributes effort when automatic word reading doesn't occur (Shaywitz & Shaywitz, 2008).

Current research in this area focuses on the different ways individuals with learning disabilities, particularly reading disabilities, process information while

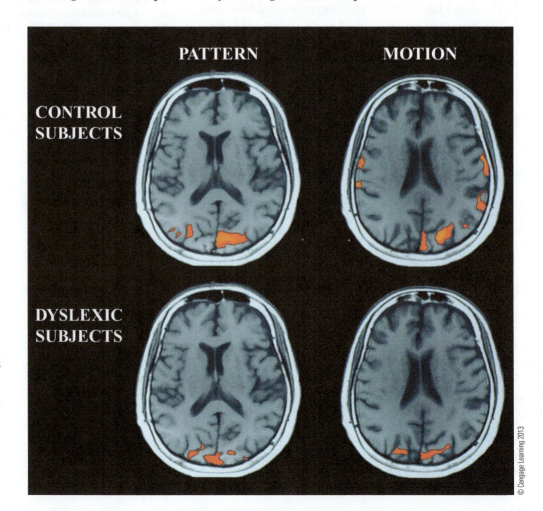

FIGURE 5.2

A sample MRI that compares individuals with dyslexia and a neurotypical control group.

Source: Sally E. Shaywitz, M.D.; Bennett. Dyslexia: The Science of Reading and Dyslexia [Internet]. Version 22. Knol. 2008 Sep 8. Available from: http://knol.google.com/k/sally-e-shaywitz-md/dyslexia/PTVo4Rev/pkT5pA

© Cengage Learning 2013

reading. We now can see the differences in brain activity between poor and fluent readers while they are reading text (Shaywitz & Shaywitz, 2001; Shaywitz & Shaywitz, 2008). It is the evidence that instruction can change brain activity—to train skills mirrored by changes in neurological pathways—that is currently exciting researchers and other special education professionals. Some researchers (Simos et al., 2007; Temple et al., 2003) found that providing structured instruction, particularly in the areas of phonemic awareness (e.g., rhyming), can change the way the brains of children with reading disabilities process information.

● *Other Physiological Factors*   Medical researchers have suggested that other physiological factors have a role in causing learning disabilities. Many possible causes have been proposed over the years, including malnutrition and biochemical imbalances such as allergies or the inability of the blood to synthesize a normal supply of vitamins (Cott, 1972; Feingold, 1975). None of these theories, however, stood up to scientific experimentation (Arnold, Christopher, & Huestis, 1978; Kavale & Forness, 1983).

When we look back on the birth histories of students with learning disabilities, we do see that many of them experienced more **perinatal stress** than other babies. That is, during the perinatal period (from the 22nd week of pregnancy through the seventh day of life) there were more traumatic events in their lives, such as difficult or prolonged labor and delivery, hypoxia during the birth process, low birth weight, or illness. Many babies with those same problems, however, do not have learning difficulties later in life, so perinatal stresses cannot be the sole cause of learning disabilities.

Several researchers have postulated that learning disabilities are inherited. As a teacher, you will often hear the parent of a child with learning disabilities say, "I had that same problem when I was in school—we just didn't have a name for it then." Although you may discover a lot of anecdotal evidence for inheritance, the empirical evidence is in dispute. The strongest evidence of a genetic basis for learning disabilities comes from studies of identical twins reared apart, which showed that both twins were likely to have a learning disability if one twin had a learning disability (De Fries, Gillis, & Wadsworth, 1993: Wood & Grigorenko, 2001), and studies of the rate of disability occurrence within families (Lewis, 1992; Shalev et al., 2001). Much more conclusive research needs to be done, however, before a link between heredity and learning disabilities can be established.

External Factors

If we look at learning disabilities as differences in the way a child learns or the way a student approaches learning, we may see the interaction between the student and the environment as a cause of learning disabilities. Some people believe that children identified as having a learning disability are really those children who require a different type of instruction, method of presenting information, or levels of support in the classroom. In other words, if teaching procedures and task requirements were different, the students might not have a disability at all. Today, some educators believe that other external factors, such as inappropriate instruction, materials, and curricula, contribute to learning disabilities (Wallace & McLoughlin, 1988). This theory is attractive to many people because many students with learning disabilities *can* learn when they receive direct, systematic instruction. As we mentioned earlier, concerns related to the need for appropriate instruction currently are receiving a lot of attention. Although skills that are missing or weak can be taught, instruction cannot remove a learning disability; it remains a lifelong problem (Gerber & Reiff, 1994). Since learning disabilities range along a continuum from mild to severe and consist of many different types, it is probably foolhardy to search for *one* cause of a complicated group of learning problems (see the accompanying Closer Look box, "Possible Causes of Learning Disabilities").

TeachSource VIDEO CASE

How Can Teachers Build Their Students' Self-Confidence?

Students with learning disabilities look and act like all the other kids—their challenges are subtle but serious, and their academic difficulties often spill over into the social arena. Visit Chapter 5 on the CourseMate website and watch the video entitled "Chris: Instructional Interventions for a Student with a Learning Disability." See how Chris's teacher builds on his interests and aptitudes to create learning experiences that have positive effects on his self-esteem. How will you determine what your students' interests are?

No link between heredity and learning disabilities has yet been proven.

Pause and Reflect

Often, children who have difficulty in school are relieved when they receive a diagnosis of learning disabilities. Before, they couldn't understand what the problem was—now, they have an explanation, even if they don't know the cause. Do you think knowing the cause of a learning disability is important to what we do in the classroom? Why or why not? ●

Characteristics of Individuals with Learning Disabilities

In this section, we will examine some of the ways learning disabilities can affect individuals. We will focus first on how people with learning disabilities receive, process, and produce information—in other words, how they learn. We will then look at the possible effects of learning disabilities on basic academic skills and on social behavior.

Learning Disabilities and Cognition: Approaches to Learning

The learning styles of children with learning disabilities may be incompatible with school requirements.

As you remember, the federal definition of learning disabilities specifies that it is "a disorder in one or more of the basic psychological processes involved in understanding or using language." In this definition, *language* refers to the symbols of communication—spoken, written, or even behavioral. Although *psychological processes* is a vague term, think of it as referring to all the things we do when we take in information (listen, read, observe), try to learn information (classify, remember, evaluate, imitate), and produce information (speak, write, calculate, behave). Students with learning disabilities potentially have learning differences that relate to learning efficiency (strategy use and rate) and psychological processing (Kavale & Forness, 2000). These psychological processes are aspects of *cognition*, the wide range of thinking skills we use to process and learn information.

A CLOSER LOOK Possible Causes of Learning Disabilities

Internal factors

The following causes have been suggested, but little hard data are available:

- Brain damage
- Malnutrition and biochemical imbalances
- Perinatal stress
- Genetics: Genetics research provides the most promising avenue for identifying a cause for learning disabilities, as current research focuses on attempts to identify genes that may be responsible for learning differences (Wood & Grigorenko, 2001).

External factors

Many educators believe that external factors are major causes; others believe that they predispose children to learning disabilities. Major external factors include:

- Learning style
- Classroom factors (lack of motivation; inappropriate materials, methods, and curriculum)
- Environmental stressors (personal pain, family instability, poverty)

In this section, we will look at five cognitive processes: perception, attention, memory, metacognition, and organization. These processes are vital to our ability to understand and use language. All students who have difficulty learning are probably experiencing a problem in one or more of them. Although everyone uses the same basic processes to learn information, we don't always use them the same way or with the same degree of efficiency.

● *Perception* **Perception,** as defined here, is the ability to organize and interpret the information we experience through our senses, such as visual or auditory abilities. Perception is important to learning because it provides us with our first sensory impressions about something we see or hear. When we hear a note or sound, we are able to identify and appreciate its uniqueness. When we see the letter *B*, we identify its structure (overall shape), orientation (direction of the letter), and component parts (one straight line and two curved lines). Later, if we observe the letter *D*, we are able to see that *D* has its own set of properties, and some are similar to those of *B* and some are different.

A student relies on his or her perceptual abilities to recognize, compare, and discriminate information. The ability to hold the image of a letter, word, or sound is necessary before information can be recognized, recalled, or applied. Let's look at an example of a young child who is just learning to read. If this child has difficulty discriminating sounds, she may confuse similar sounds, such as those made by the letters *m* and *n*. This confusion may make it difficult for the child to decode words by "sounding them out" and to make the connection between written letters and spoken sounds. In her mind, the relationship seems to change; sometimes she sees *m* and hears *mmm*; other times she sees *n* and hears *mmm*. This means she may begin guessing when asked to read a word such as *man*. (Is it *man, nam, nan,* or *mam*?).

Some children with learning disabilities reverse letters, words, or whole passages during reading or writing. Occasional letter or word reversal is typical of all young children. Children with learning disabilities, however, may continue to have difficulty with letter and word orientation and therefore continue to reverse letters and words throughout elementary school. Children who reverse words while reading typically reverse words that can be read in either direction (*saw* and *was*). You will seldom see a child try to read *firetruck* as *kcurterif*. The most common letter reversals are also those that are letters in either direction (*b* and *d*). If we think about how close these two letters are in the alphabet and recognize that often they are taught close together, we can understand why children often reverse them. The child hasn't had time to learn one completely before he or she is introduced to the other.

● *Attention* The importance of attention to learning seems fairly obvious to most of us. It is the underlying factor in our ability to receive and process information. How can you take notes on a lecture if you can't tell what's important? How can you work a long division problem if you can't stay on task? **Attention** is a broad term that refers to the ability to focus on information. Many students with learning disabilities experience some level of attention difficulties. Students who experience severe attention difficulties may also be identified as having **attention deficit disorder (ADD)** or **attention deficit/hyperactivity disorder (ADHD).** Attention deficit disorder will be discussed in more detail in Chapter 8; this is a distinct disorder that can stand alone or coexist with many other categories of disability, including learning disabilities.

Attention deficits are one of the disorders teachers most frequently associate with individuals with learning disabilities. Many teachers describe their students with learning disabilities as "distractible" or "in his/her own world." These teachers are talking about kids who have trouble coming to attention and maintaining attention; something appears to be interfering with their ability to get on task and stay focused. Sometimes the students are distracted by things in the classroom; other times they are subject to internal distractions, such as random thoughts or ideas.

> Learning disabilities can affect cognitive processes—thinking skills used to process information.

> Attention deficits are frequently associated with individuals with learning disabilities.

Programs that incorporate peer tutoring allow each student to build on his or her academic and social strengths.

Teachers are also perplexed or frustrated when a child seems to be paying attention, but doesn't follow directions or can't summarize the main idea of a story. These problems may be a result of difficulties with **selective attention,** the ability to zero in on the most important part of a piece of information. For example, given the directions "Circle the correct answer," Keisha focuses on the fact that the word *circle* is underlined and proceeds to underline her answer. She attends to an inappropriate cue.

Again, once we understand the types of difficulties that can result from attention deficits, we can begin to restructure our teaching presentations to circumvent some of these problems or to teach some new attention skills. When children have difficulty attending to a task for a long period of time, we can address their work load. The accompanying Teaching Strategies box, "Teaching Strategies for Students with Attention Difficulties," offers some suggestions for instruction.

● *Memory* If perception and attention are the skills that form a foundation for learning, then memory is the major vehicle for acquiring and recalling information. Think of all the memorizing that children must do during their years in school. **Memory** involves many different skills and processes. Some of these processes are used to organize information for learning; these are called **encoding processes.** When individuals encode information, they use visual, auditory, or verbal cues to arrange material; thus, encoding relies heavily on skills such as perception and selective attention. Students with learning disabilities who experience difficulty in perception and attention are also likely to have problems remembering correctly because they may be encoding partial, incorrect, or unimportant information.

Students with learning disabilities may experience deficits in **working memory**—the ability to store new information and to retrieve previously processed information from long-term memory (Gathercole, Alloway, Willis, & Adams, 2006; Cochran & Ewers, 1990). Deficits in working memory translate into difficulties in the classroom. Students who don't use memory strategies try to learn information that is not broken down into manageable parts or that

Encoding processes organize information so it can be learned.

Students with learning disabilities often show deficits in working memory—the ability to store and retrieve information.

Teaching Strategies & Accommodations

Teaching Strategies for Students with Attention Difficulties

Maintaining attention

- Break long tasks or assignments into smaller segments. Administer the smaller segments throughout the day, if a shorter assignment isn't acceptable.
- Present limited amounts of information on a page.
- Gradually increase the amount of time a student must attend to a task or lecture.

Selective attention

- Use prompts and cues to draw attention to important information. Types of cues include:
  1. Written cues, such as highlighting directions on tests or activity sheets
  2. Verbal cues, such as using signal words to let students know they are about to hear important information
  3. Instructional cues, such as having students paraphrase directions or other information to you
- Teach students a plan for identifying and highlighting important information themselves.

---

is unconnected to any previous knowledge. This makes it difficult for them to transfer the information into long-term memory and to retrieve it later on.

It is important to teach students memory strategies. Sometimes teachers try to associate materials with pictures, key words, or context clues to help students remember a number of facts or the relationships between them. Although many students with learning disabilities do not use tools for remembering, you can teach them some of these tools (see the accompanying Teaching Strategies box, "Memory Strategies").

● *Metacognition* **Metacognition,** the ability to monitor and evaluate performance, is another area in which students with learning disabilities often experience difficulty (Johnson, Humphrey, Mellard, Woods, & Swanson, 2010; Wong, 1991). Metacognition is the ability to identify and select learning skills and techniques to facilitate the acquisition of information; to choose or create the setting in which you are most likely to receive material accurately; to identify the most effective and efficient way to process and present information; and to evaluate and adapt your techniques for different materials and situations. These skills are also referred to as **executive functions.** Metacognitive skills are critical to all aspects of learning. These skills supply many of the keys to learning from experience, generalizing information and strategies, and applying what you have learned.

Because most of these skills focus on planning, monitoring, and evaluation, students who do not have them may appear to plunge into tasks without thinking about them and never look back once they're done. Practicing a book report before delivering it to the class, making an outline of a paper before you begin writing, and jotting down the key points you want to make on an essay question before you begin writing all illustrate how metacognition can affect performance. As you probably know from personal experience, the students who practice, outline, and make notes are more likely to have coherent presentations or answers.

Fortunately, metacognitive skills can be taught. One technique that helps students plan, monitor, and evaluate—**self-monitoring**—is described in the accompanying Teaching Strategies box, "Teaching Self-Monitoring." Self-monitoring teaches students to evaluate and record their own performance periodically.

> Lack of metacognitive skills may hinder competent learning.

Teaching Strategies & Accommodations

Memory Strategies

Remember this number: 380741529

Look quickly at the number written above, then cover it completely with your finger. Wait one minute and try to say the number out loud. Check your accuracy, but then ask yourself a more important question: What did I do to try to remember that long string of digits?

If that experiment didn't work, think of this situation. You run into a classmate at a restaurant and she gives you her phone number as she is leaving. You left your phone in the car and you don't have a pencil and paper. How do you remember the number?

In either one of those situations, you probably used one of the following memory strategies:

- *Chunking* is the grouping of large strings of information into smaller, more manageable "chunks."

Telephone numbers, for example, are "chunked" into small segments for easier recall; remembering 2125060595 is much harder than remembering (212) 506-0595.

- *Rehearsal* is the repetition, either oral or silent, of the information to be remembered.

- *Elaboration* is the weaving of the material to be remembered into a meaningful context. The numbers above, for example, could be related to birthdays, ages, or other telephone numbers.

- Another useful memory strategy is *categorization*, in which the information to be remembered is organized by the category to which it belongs. All the animals in a list, for example, could be grouped together for remembering.

Written or auditory cues are provided for students, which prompt them to check their behavior.

- *Organization*   If we look at the many behaviors we consider to be characteristic of individuals with learning disabilities and examine the processes we have just discussed, we can see that the underlying thread is difficulty in **organization.** Because organization is a term we all use often, it is a useful and familiar framework to apply to learning disabilities.

Difficulties in organization can affect the most superficial tasks or the most complex cognitive activities. The simple acts required to come to class with a paper, pencil, and books; to get a homework assignment home and then back

Teaching Strategies & Accommodations

Teaching Self-Monitoring

The following procedure teaches self-monitoring of attention, defined as attention to task. The same technique can be used for a variety of skills.

- Teach students the difference between "on-task" and "off-task" behavior. Model the different behaviors and have students demonstrate them to you.

- Provide students with written or auditory cues (a timer; a tone, chime, or beep) that prompt them to check their behavior.

- Have students stop what they are doing when they hear the cue, ask themselves if they are paying attention, and record their response.

- Gradually fade the cues, then the recording sheets, as students learn to self-monitor independently.

to school; and to copy math problems on a piece of notebook paper all rely on organizational skills. These may seem to be minor problems that can be easily addressed. Next to attention deficits, however, these simple problems of organization are mentioned most often by classroom teachers as sources of difficulty. It is important to recognize, however, that many students with learning disabilities cannot plan effectively. To some extent, metacognitive skills play a role in organization. Students must be able to understand the need to have a system of organization and develop a plan for carrying it out.

Classroom interventions designed to improve organizational skills usually provide students with specific actions or guidelines for organized behavior. Examples include having a single notebook with designated places for homework, paper, and pencils; developing a list for students' lockers that identifies what is needed for each class; and preparing a standard end-of-the-day checklist for students to use in ensuring they have all required materials. Strategies like these have helped counteract the day-to-day organizational problems of many students with learning disabilities. Figure 5.3 is an example of a homework contract designed to address organizational skills and performance monitoring at the same time (KidTools, 2011). We will look more closely at complex organizational problems involving writing and thinking skills when we discuss academic interventions.

Learning Disabilities and Academic Performance

Before we look at the effects of learning disabilities on academic performance, let's review the processes involved in cognition. Perception, attention, memory, metacognition, and organization are the five key processes we've discussed. Together, they enable us to receive information correctly, arrange it for easier learning, identify similarities and differences with other knowledge we have, select a way to learn the information effectively, and evaluate the effectiveness of our learning process. If a student has problems doing any or all of these things, it is easy to see how all learning can be affected. We will look at three basic skill areas—reading, language arts, and math—and show how difficulties in these areas can affect other types of learning as well.

> Reading is the most difficult skill area for most students with learning disabilities.

Homework Contract

Class: Social Studies   Due Date: Friday

Assignment	Goal	Done?
Do worksheet on Missouri map	Do all questions and make corrections	☐ Yes ☐ No _____ Signature
Write first copy of speech on jesse James	Notes on paper	☐ Yes ☐ No _____ Signature
Plan my Jesse James costume	List of clothes	☐ Yes ☐ No _____ Signature
Bonus 10 bucks for school raffle	**Penalty** Stay in at recess untill all are done	

_____ (Student)   _____ (Teacher)   _____ (Witness)

Name: Jessica Wilson   Date: 9/15/2009

FIGURE 5.3

Organizational Aid: KidTools Homework Contract

Source: Fitzgerald, Gail (2011). KidCoach: The KidTools™ Support System. [URL: http://kidtools.org] © 2011 The Curators of the University of Missouri, a public corporation. All Rights Reserved.

● *Reading*   Reading is the most difficult skill area for the majority of students with learning disabilities. The term *dyslexia* is often associated with reading difficulties in students with learning disabilities. Although this term was initially used to refer to a specific and severe reading disability with clear neurological origins, the word often is used today, by some educators, to refer to more generalized reading disabilities (Shaywitz & Shaywitz, 2001). Because reading is necessary for almost all learning, the student with a reading disability often experiences difficulty in many other subjects as well. In addition, the emphasis on oral reading in the early school years may make the child with a reading disability reluctant to read, so he or she may progressively fall further behind in reading skills. Teachers are often faced with the challenge of not only trying to teach a child to read, but also motivating the child to *try* to read. A student with a severe reading disability may be reading on the first- or second-grade level, even though he or she may be 10, 11, or even 15 years old. As you can imagine, trying to inspire a teenager to "keep trying" in reading when he or she is so far behind can be a painful and difficult process.

If you think about everything you do when you read, you realize that it is a very complex process. To examine the potential effects of learning disabilities on reading, let's look at the major skills involved in the reading process. In 2001, the National Reading Panel (National Reading Panel, 2001) identified five major areas of reading instruction supported by research. These five areas are:

- phonemic awareness (the ability to hear and manipulate sounds)
- alphabetic principle (using sound-symbol relationships to decode and read words)
- fluency (the rate of reading correctly—usually measured as number of correct words read per minute)
- vocabulary knowledge (direct and indirect instruction of word meaning)
- reading comprehension (understanding what is read)

> Teaching reading to students with learning disabilities involves a structured presentation of phonics skills and rules.

In this section we will first look at word analysis skills, which will include not only phonemic awareness and alphabetic principle, but also reading sight words

A CLOSER LOOK   English Language Learners Who Struggle with Reading: Language Acquisition or Learning Disabilities?

Researchers interested in this question carefully reviewed an extensive amount of research that looked at how to differentiate the reading difficulties experienced by young children learning to speak English from those experienced by young children with reading disabilities. Importantly, they looked at implications for research, referral, assessment, and instruction. Below are some of the instructional recommendations for young children who are English Language Learners manifesting difficulty in early literacy skills:

- Combine phonological awareness with other reading and language development activities (whether instruction is in the student's first language or in English).

- Provide explicit vocabulary instruction to facilitate reading comprehension in the student's first and second language.

- Teach and encourage the use of reading comprehension strategies in the student's first and second language.

- Help students develop a strong foundation in their first language as a way to promote literacy in both their native language and English.

(*Source:* Klingner, J. K., Artiles, A. J., & Barltell, L. M. (2006). English language learners who struggle with reading: Language acquisition of LD. *Journal of Learning Disabilities, 39,* 108–128. Reprinted by permission of SAGE publications.)

and other skills involved in decoding text. Then we will look at reading fluency and, finally, vocabulary and comprehension.

Word Analysis   In order to identify written words, we use a number of different skills. Some of the most important **word-analysis** skills include the ability to hear and manipulate sounds (phonemic awareness), to associate sounds with the various letters and letter combinations used to write them (alphabetic principle), to immediately recognize and remember words (sight-word reading), and to use the surrounding text to help figure out a specific word (context clues).

If students do not have basic phonics skills, they cannot sound out words and will be very limited in the number of words they can read. This is particularly true given that many of these same skills are required in other word-analysis strategies, such as reading sight words. Research suggests the importance of assessing and teaching very young children skills in the areas of phonological and phonemic awareness (Foorman et al., 1998; Lonigan, Schatschneider, & Westberg, 2008). There appears to be an important relationship between a young child's ability to hear and distinguish among sounds and his or her later ability to read. The National Early Literacy Panel identified six skills that were good predictors of early reading ability—alphabet knowledge, phonological awareness, rapid automatic naming of numbers, rapid automatic naming of objects or colors, writing, and phonological memory (Lonigan, Schatschneider, & Westber, 2008). Researchers and teachers are investigating the most effective way to teach young children these important skills (Torgesen, 2000). (See the accompanying Teaching Strategies box about teaching young children who are at risk for developing reading disabilities).

The most frequently recommended approaches to teaching reading to elementary students at risk for reading disabilities include a structured presentation of phonics skills and rules, or direct instruction (Carnine, Silbert, Kameenui, & Tarver, 2010). Because the students cannot identify sound/letter associations and patterns on their own, it is necessary to present these associations in a very clear way and provide students with lots of opportunities to practice and remember them.

If students cannot sound out words, they will try to memorize words or guess the words from the surrounding text (using context clues). Memorizing every word, when you are first learning to read, is quite challenging for students with learning disabilities who have difficulties with memory and selective attention. Learning most sight words, unless they are always in a specific context (such as the word stop on a stop sign) requires being able to identify and recall the aspects of the word that make it unique and to associate the correct sounds with the words.

Poor readers tend to use context clues as their major word-analysis strategy. If you don't know the word, you look at the pictures or surrounding words and guess. Although context can be helpful when you come across one or two words that are difficult to decode, using context to figure out 50 or 60 percent of the words in a passage is ineffective. Some students try to guess their way through an entire story. Reading programs for students with learning disabilities often try to prevent or eliminate guessing by controlling the words students are expected to read so that only words the child knows how to decode are presented in stories; they also eliminate pictures and other cues from initial reading passages. Once the child gains confidence in her ability to use other word-attack skills and uses them effectively, then the use of context clues—which will become quite valuable when the student begins reading complex material—can be encouraged.

Fluency   Any child who has been asked to read aloud has faced the performance pressure to read in a smooth and accurate fashion in front of the rest of the class. **Reading fluency,** most frequently defined as the rate of accurate reading (correct

Many students with learning disabilities depend heavily on context clues for guessing words.

Students need to develop strategies that will help them remember material and self-check their understanding of it.

Teaching Young Children at Risk for Reading Disabilities

A review of research over the past 15 years shows that early literacy skills of young children are strong predictors of early reading ability. Research also demonstrates that young children can significantly improve their early literacy skills when receiving appropriate instruction, thereby greatly increasing their chances of becoming better readers (Marshall, Brown, Conroy, & Knopf, 2011). Here we highlight some of the important findings by researchers in teaching early literacy skills.

- Systematic and explicit instruction in early literacy skills is most beneficial for young children at risk for reading difficulties. The greater the risk, the more explicit the instruction may need to be (Kamps et al., 2008; Simmons et al., 2011).

- Students with the greatest need (children most behind during screening) may require more time in instruction than children with less risk, particularly for certain skills (Simmons et al., 2007).

- In addition to explicit instruction and increased time in instruction, at-risk students were able to gain significant vocabulary skills when there was also a decrease in the size of the instructional group and an increase in instructional intensity. Instructional intensity is defined by the authors as increased opportunities for response and practice, and increases in feedback to the students on their responses (Loftus et al., 2010).

- Best practice for young children at risk for reading disabilities (children performing low on literacy screening measures) includes instruction in phonological awareness and alphabetic principle, letter knowledge, and shared, interactive storybook reading (Justice, Kaderavek, Fan, Sofka, & Hunt, 2009; O'Connor, Bocian, Beebe-Frankenberger, & Linklater, 2010; Simmons et al., 2007).

- Kindergarten children with poor language skills—regardless of the source of poor language (experience, cognitive development, English language learner)—all responded to programs based on best practice in early literacy instruction (O'Connor, Bocian, Beebe-Frankenberger, & Linklater, 2010).

words per minute), is more than a status symbol for children; it is an important indicator of reading ability. As you might expect, a child who has difficulty in word analysis will also have difficulty reading fluently. Obviously, the ability to recall information quickly, or rapid naming, is a fundamental component of reading fluency. Historically, interventions to improve reading fluency have focused on having students practice reading a piece of text orally several times (called repeated readings). Although repeated readings represent the most frequently employed fluency intervention, they have not yet been determined to meet current criteria for evidence-based practice (Chard, Ketterlin-Geller, Baker, Doabler, & Apichatabutra, 2009). Other interventions focus not only on trying to improve the rate and accuracy of oral reading, but also on strengthening the ties between fluent reading and comprehension. Students are sometimes taught strategies that involve previewing text, summarizing paragraphs, reading with inflection, or monitoring errors to improve not only fluency but comprehension as well (Allinder et al., 2001; Vaughn et al., 2000). Reading fluency, most typically oral reading fluency (number of words read correctly per unit of time), is one aspect of reading that, although once neglected, is now featured prominently in more reading programs. This can be attributed to two major reasons. First, reading fluency was identified as one of the five most important areas of reading instruction by the National Reading Panel (NRP, 2001). Second, oral reading fluency is the curriculum-based measurement used most frequently today in progress monitoring of elementary reading performance.

Some children with reading disabilities benefit from individual and small-group instruction.

Reading Comprehension   Students with learning disabilities may experience difficulties in **reading comprehension** because they lack the skills required for understanding text and have poor word-analysis skills. The child who has difficulty with reading fluency will have trouble understanding the gist of sentences and passages. It is important to adjust your expectations for comprehension if the child has difficulty in the actual reading of material. It is better to teach or assess reading comprehension skills on material the students can decode fluently or that is presented orally.

In addition to word-analysis skills, a number of other factors can affect a child's ability to comprehend text. First, vocabulary knowledge may be a critical component of understanding written text. If a child doesn't know what many of the words in the text mean, obviously she will have difficulty understanding a passage or a chapter. Literal comprehension of material—the ability to identify specifically stated information—requires the ability to select important information from unimportant details, to organize or sequence this information, and to recall it. The ability to select and categorize information is also necessary for organizational comprehension, which includes identifying main ideas.

For more advanced comprehension activities, such as interpreting text, evaluating actions in a story, predicting consequences, and relating text to personal experience, students with learning disabilities can experience difficulty because of the role-taking skills required in some of these tasks and a reluctance to go beyond what is specifically stated in the text. Many difficulties in reading comprehension can also be traced to the lack of specific strategies used to help remember material or to self-check understanding (Berkeley, Mastropieri, & Scruggs, 2011; Mastropieri, Scruggs, & Graetz; 2003). If you are reading a book that is not particularly interesting, you may find after you've read a few pages that you haven't actually taken in anything you've read. If you are reading this book to prepare for a test, you may go back and reread the material, perhaps stopping every so often to paraphrase what you've read, rehearse the important points, or ask yourself questions to see if you really do understand it. All these learning strategies, which are essentially memory and metacognitive skills, help you to comprehend the text, and they become increasingly important as reading material becomes denser and more complex. Students with learning disabilities who do not use these active strategies are unlikely to have good comprehension.

Vocabulary words are typically taught directly in content-area courses. Students also can acquire new vocabulary words indirectly by spending more time reading and by listening to language more complex than their own—either through conversation or written texts. In order, however, for students to learn the specific vocabulary words necessary to understand content-area material or to apply to a specific novel or textbook, direct instruction is the way to go. Evidence-based practices include the explicit instruction of vocabulary and may include direct instruction of words—relying on memorization, discrimination, and practice using the word(s)—or may involve the use of cognitive strategy instruction—verbal associations, acronyms, keywords, etc.—to help students remember what words mean (Jitendra, Edwards, Sacks, & Jacobson, 2004). Perhaps you remember using similar strategies to remember the distinction between certain confusing content vocabulary words—ectoderm, mesoderm, and endoderm for example. Stop for a minute and think of how you could use illustrations, verbal associations, or other cues to help students remember what each of these terms mean. Take a look at Figure 5.4 to see a technology-based example of vocabulary instruction that can be used for reading as well as for written language. Many of the word prediction software packages, or word reading software, also include the option of highlighting words to get a quick and simple definition.

Many teaching strategies that focus on broader aspects of reading comprehension emphasize the use of specific plans or behaviors to help students review material and check their comprehension periodically (Berkeley, Mastropieri, & Scruggs, 2011). Some techniques involve identifying and highlighting key information in the text, or recording the information using story maps or other graphic organizers (Proly, Rivers, & Schwartz, 2009). Usually, the teacher will model these skills and then teach the student how to extract the key information necessary for good comprehension. Similar techniques are used to help students

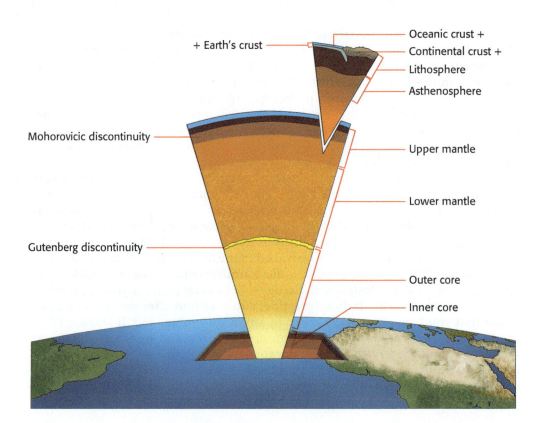

FIGURE 5.4

The Earth is formed of three concentric layers: the core, the mantle and the crust; these are separated by transition zones called discontinuities

Source: Illustration from "The Visual Dictionary" © QA International, 2003.

Teaching Strategies & Accommodations

Suggestions for Teaching Reading Comprehension

- **Predictions.** Predictions can be based on pictures, headings, subtitles, or graphs. They can be used to activate students' prior knowledge before reading, to increase attention to sequencing during reading, and can be evaluated after reading to help summarize content.

- **Questions.** Questions can be asked before reading to help students attend to important information, or students can be taught to transform subtitles or headings into questions to ask themselves as they read. Having students make up questions to ask each other after reading is a good alternative to the typical question-answer period, and helps students develop study skills as well.

- **Advance organizers or outlines.** You can prepare an advance organizer on the text to help focus students' attention on key material in the text. Students can review the organizer before reading and take notes on it while reading. When it is completed, the students have a study sheet to review.

- **Self-monitoring or self-evaluation.** When students begin reading longer text selections, they can learn to stop periodically and paraphrase the text or check their understanding. This can be done by using an auditory self-monitoring tape recorder or by randomly placing stickers or other markers throughout the text. When the student reaches the sticker, it is time to think about what he or she has just read.

at the secondary level identify important information from textbooks, which are frequently several grade levels above their reading level. By using specific comprehension strategies and the conventions of the text (headings, vocabulary words, questions in text), students can find and retrieve essential information (see the accompanying Teaching Strategies box, "Suggestions for Teaching Reading Comprehension").

Reading continues to be the biggest obstacle faced by most students with learning disabilities. For this reason, the type of reading instruction used is critical. Because more and more students with learning disabilities are served in general education classrooms, teachers must investigate ways to provide reading skill instruction, particularly for young children, in a classroom setting.

● **Language Arts** In this section, we will look at three general areas: spelling, spoken language, and written language. Because of the close ties of some of these skills to reading ability, they tend to be areas of great difficulty for many students with learning disabilities.

Spelling Spelling requires all the essential skills used in the word-analysis strategies of phonics and sight-word reading. The student must either know specific sound and letter relationships or be able to memorize words. The difficulties students with learning disabilities have in learning and applying rules of phonics, visualizing the word correctly, and evaluating spellings result in frequent misspellings, even as they become more adept at reading. It is not uncommon to find the same word spelled five or six different ways on the same paper, regardless of whether the student is in the fifth grade or in college (for example, *ther, there, thare,* and *theyre* for *their*).

Many students with learning disabilities are asked to spell many words they cannot yet read. When this occurs, the students cannot be expected to succeed. If at all possible, it is best to combine spelling lessons with reading lessons. Use the sounds and words involved in reading as the sounds and words studied in spelling lessons. This will increase the probability that students will learn to spell

It is best to combine spelling lessons with reading lessons.

with more confidence, and they will have many opportunities to practice sounds and words. For students of all ages, learning to evaluate spellings and developing a consistent mental representation of the word are critical skills. Recommended spelling strategies include teaching students to visualize the whole word while studying. Common spelling activities used by many classroom teachers, such as writing the words five times each, are useless if the student is copying the word one letter at a time. If students are encouraged to write the word, spell the word aloud, visualize the word, spell the word aloud without looking at it, check the word's spelling, write the word without looking, and then compare their word to the original, the task will help develop needed memory and metacognitive skills.

Spoken Language   Many students with learning disabilities experience difficulties in spoken or oral language, which can affect academic as well as social performance. These may include problems identifying and using appropriate speech sounds, using appropriate words and understanding word meanings, using and understanding various sentence structures, and using appropriate grammar and language conventions. Other problem areas include understanding underlying meanings, such as irony or figurative language, and adjusting language for different uses and purposes, called **pragmatic language skills** (Troia, 2011).

Pragmatic language skills enable the child to use language effectively in different settings and for different purposes. This includes **functional flexibility,** or the ability to move easily from one form of language to another to accommodate various settings or audiences (Simon, 1991). Functional flexibility requires the individual to identify the type of language appropriate to the setting, to anticipate the needs of the audience, and then to adjust language structure, content, and vocabulary to meet these needs. It also requires an understanding that different types of language are used for different purposes. Individuals with learning disabilities may have difficulty with pragmatic language because they have difficulty attending to the cues (for example, other students' behavior) found in various settings. This can cause a problem if they don't pick up on when it is important to use respectful language, when it is OK to be relaxed and informal, or when it is appropriate to laugh or tell jokes. Students with learning disabilities may not monitor their effectiveness in communicating and therefore may not adjust their language to the setting.

Written Language   Students with learning disabilities often have great difficulty in written language or composition. Specific problems include inadequate planning, structure, and organization; immature or limited sentence structure; limited and repetitive vocabulary; limited consideration of audience; unnecessary or unrelated information or details; and errors in spelling, punctuation, grammar, and handwriting (Carnine, 1991; Mercer, Mercer, & Pullen, 2010;). Deficits in pragmatic language skills can also affect performance in written language (Troia, 2011). Students with learning disabilities also lack the motivation and the monitoring and evaluation skills often considered necessary for good writing (Newcomer & Barenbaum, 1991). When we look at the skills necessary for good writing and consider the characteristics of students with learning disabilities, the types of difficulties we have identified are not surprising.

"Phillip's Story" is the first installment of a story (and its translation) written by a boy who has a learning disability in written language and reading (see Figure 5.5). Phillip is entering the sixth grade next year; he is a bright kid who enjoys wrestling, playing the violin, and building things with his father and brother. As you can see, his spelling doesn't get in the way of his storytelling, yet it will pose quite a challenge for him in middle school.

For most students with learning disabilities, the educational emphasis for written language is on the development and use of organizational and metacognitive

> Interpreting oral language correctly involves reading nonverbal cues, which can be difficult for students with learning disabilities.

> Wain i upin my linch dox
> wine I up ina my lick box I fond ege
> thing that fond. So the inev day I went
> to ologaint and he hamp tono watthe
> creaswar. He card up his frind and
> he sid laik me see the doy so h hetold
> Me wat it was. and he said it was
> aneuses but i the itwasand ithet
> I was ski. sond the sant sad com
> dack and we will go ttoseewat
> it is. thenexday i went back
> and It was clads but Iner wer
> the keeP was Kept Igotthe
> Keee and I unp the dry and
> I was seeing a noat onthedsk
> It said I am atthe Otɓ sants
> I be backinaour but I wainyou
> to bether wan i com back. wen
> I was want I was look arnd
> and i liok arnd the biski fond a
> pradr that hada lot of phindnods
> on it. I wand out afthe bory and...

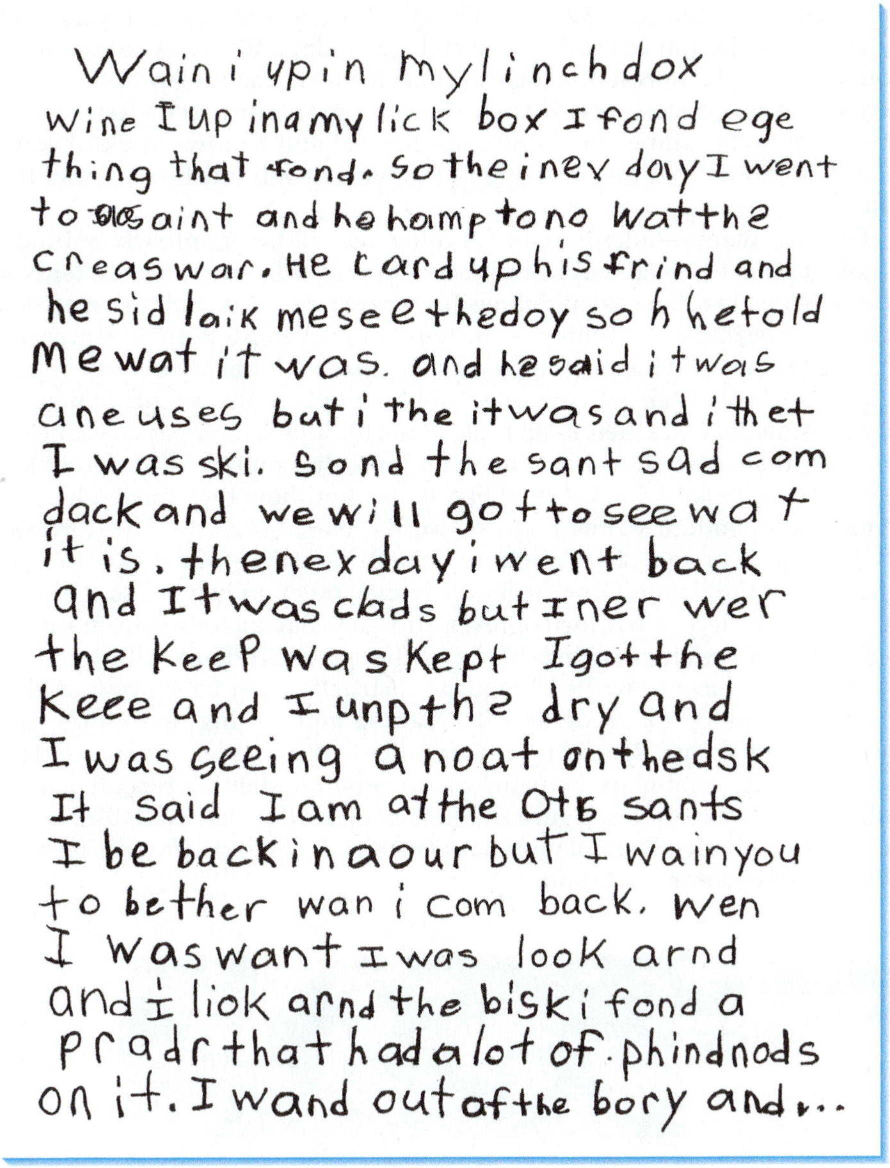

When I Opened My Lunch Box

When I opened my lunch box I found an egg thing that flobbed. So the next day I went to a scientist and he happened to know what the creature was. He called up his friend and he said let me see the boy so he told me what it was and he said it was chicken but I thought it was a snake. So the scientist said come back and we will go to see what it is. The next day I went back and it was closed but I knew where the key was kept. I got the key and I opened the door and I was seeing a note on the desk. It said I am at the other scientist. I will be back in an hour but I want you to be there when I come back. When I was waiting I was looking around and I looked around the desk I found a paper that had a lot of phone numbers on it. I ran out the door and . . .

FIGURE 5.5

Phillip's Story

Source: Phillip DeKraft, copyright 2003.

Students with learning disabilities may have difficulty planning, organizing, and writing their papers.

skills (Graham, Harris, & Olinghouse, 2007). From the first paragraph a child writes, to a major paper written by a college student, the ability to organize and sequence thoughts, present a logical, cohesive text, and review and edit writing is critical. Word processors and spell-check programs are used often by students with learning disabilities to address mechanical and handwriting problems, but the words chosen and the structure of the writing still must come from the students themselves.

Because many students with learning disabilities approach writing tasks without a plan, instructional techniques often include providing students with a series of steps to follow as guidelines for writing. Some techniques may be quite specific; for example, students may be taught to develop a graphic representation of their thoughts and ideas to help them organize material before they begin writing. One example is an activity called webbing or creating a concept map. In this activity, students write their main topic in the middle of their paper—for example, cats. They then draw lines from the main topic that represents different subtopics (what cats look like, what they like to eat, and how they move). Under each subtopic, the student writes notes or words related directly to it (for example, soft, furry, long or short hair, different colors). Now the student can use this web to help write the paper: Other techniques may be more general so that they can be used in a variety of writing contexts, and they may include steps for planning, checking, and revising writing. Many of the needs students with learning disabilities might have in written language instruction can be supported via technology. Technology for students with reading and writing disabilities can take many different forms. Recall Figure 5.4 earlier in the chapter, which uses technology to develop vocabulary by using pictures (strengthening receptive language skills). Another example is Figure 5.6—a science writing tool available from CAST (Center for Assistive Technology) that assists with task-specific writing activities and expressive communication.

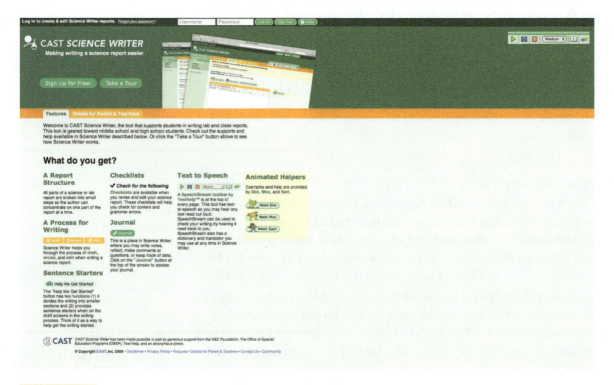

FIGURE 5.6

Center for Assistive Technology (CAST) Science Writer

Source: http://sciencewriter.cast.org/welcome;jsessionid=EBA2B ADFA71659ED47C9B759EBAB59CC

● *Mathematics* Although in the past, difficulties in math have not received the same attention as problems in reading and language arts, students with learning disabilities often have a number of problems in this area. Specific problem areas include difficulty understanding size and spatial relationships and concepts related to direction, place value, decimals, fractions, time, and difficulty remembering math facts (Lerner, 1993; Mabbott & Bisanz, 2008). Remembering and correctly applying the steps to mathematical algorithms (for example, how to divide) and reading and solving word problems are significant problem areas (Cawley et al., 1996; Harris, Miller, & Mercer, 1995). Many students with disabilities use concrete and simple approaches to solving math problems (for example, counting) rather than more abstract, cognitive strategies (Jimenez Gonzalez & Garcia Espinel, 2002), yet recent research suggests that students have a deeper contextual understanding of mathematics than is revealed in their simple problem-solving skills (Vukovic & Siegel, 2010). Like all students, many students with learning disabilities also make simple computational errors because of inattention to the operation sign, incorrect alignment of problems, and omission of steps in the algorithm, or not checking or reviewing work.

Current recommendations for instruction in mathematics include beginning your teaching, even of complex concepts, at the concrete level (materials that can be held and moved), then gradually moving to the semiconcrete level (pictures or graphics), and finally moving to the abstract level (numbers only) (Harris, Miller, & Mercer, 1995; Mercer, Mercer, & Pullen, 2010). It is important for teachers to realize that advanced mathematical concepts, such as decimals, may take much more time to teach than they anticipate (Woodward, Baxter, & Robinson, 1999). The memorization of basic math facts—addition, subtraction, multiplication—is a significant challenge for many students with learning disabilities in math. These students, in addition to working on memory strategies, may also rely on calculators to bypass laborious efforts to complete simple multiplication problems so that they may engage in more advanced problems-solving. For instruction in algorithms, word problems, and complex functions, the use of step-by-step written plans, or strategies for students to follow, helps them develop organization, memory, and evaluation skills. Instruction in mathematics can move from presenting simple algorithms for addition or subtraction to presenting more complex skills, such as solving algebraic equations (Maccini & Hughes, 2000; Mercer, Mercer, & Pullen, 2010; Montague, Warger, & Morgan, 2000).

The need to identify an appropriate range of evidence-based practices in teaching mathematics is resulting in an upsurge of research in the best ways to teach mathematics in general, including strategies for teaching students with learning disabilities. Fuchs, Fuchs, Powell, Seethaler, Cirino, and Fletcher (2008) outlined seven principles of effective instruction for students with math disabilities. These seven principles are: "instructional explicitness, instructional design to minimize the learning challenge, strong conceptual basis, drill and practice, cumulative review, motivators to help students regulate their attention and behavior to work hard, and ongoing progress monitoring" (Fuchs et al., p. 86). These principles focus on the basic principles of direct instruction and reflect the type of support necessary in both curriculum and instruction so that content is sequential and specific, and skills are explicitly taught, mastered, practiced, and applied. In Figure 5.7, you will find two examples of the use of strategies instruction related to mathematical problem-solving. First is the Star Strategy, which illustrates a fairly complex but linear and explicit approach to solving math word problems. Second are simple "counting up" strategies that are embedded in a more complex curriculum. Both of these examples stress important ideas for instruction—delineating very specific activities to perform the algorithm and each component skill, and including decision-making components and regulatory steps in the strategy when necessary.

> It is important to review and assess math concepts and strategies constantly so that students can build on previous skills.

> Mathematics instruction for students with learning disabilities should move from concrete, to semi-concrete, to abstract levels.

STAR Strategy

1. **S**earch the word problem.
   a) Read the problem carefully.
   b) Ask yourself questions: "What facts do I know?" "What do I need to find?"
   c) Write down facts.

2. **T**ranslate the words into an equation in picture form.
   a) Choose a variable.
   b) Identify the operation(s).
   c) Represent the problem with the **Algebra Lab Gear** (CONCRETE APPLICATION).
      Draw a picture of the representation (SEMI-CONCRETE APPLICATION).
      Write an algebraic equation (ABSTRACT APPLICATION).

3. **A**nswer the problem.

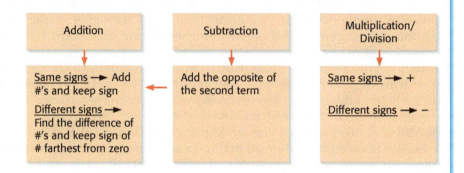

4. **R**eview the solution.
   a) Reread the problem.
   b) Ask question, "Does the answer make sense? Why?"
   c) Check answer.

FIGURE 5.7A

Star strategy

Source: P. Maccini & C.A. Hughes (2000). Effects of a problem-solving strategy on the introductory algebra performance of secondary students with learning disabilities. *Learning Disabilities and Practice,* 15, 10–21. Reprinted with permission of Blackwell Publishing Ltd.

Counting Up Addition

1. Put the bigger number in your head and say it.
2. Count up the smaller number on your fingers.
3. Your answer is the last number you say.

To ADD, you can reverse the numbers!

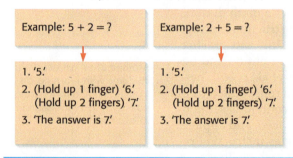

Counting Up Subtraction

1. Put the minus number in your head and say it.
2. Count up your fingers to the number you started with.
3. Your answer is the number of fingers you have up.

To SUBTRACT, do not reverse the numbers!
The minus number always goes first.

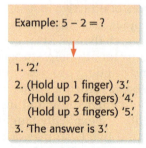

FIGURE 5.7B

Embedding problem-solving strategies: Counting up addition and subtraction

Source: Powell, S.R., Fuchs, L.S., & Fuchs, D. (2010). Embedding number combinations practice within word-problem tutoring. *Intervention in School and Clinic,* 46(1), 22–30. (page 27). Reprinted by permission of SAGE Publications.

Learning Disabilities and Social and Emotional Development

Although you may typically think of students with learning disabilities as individuals who have difficulty in academic tasks, it is important to realize that most social behaviors also involve learning. The characteristics that interfere with a student's acquisition of reading or writing skills can also interfere with his or her ability to acquire or interpret social behaviors (Kavale & Forness, 1996). For example, individuals may have difficulties correctly interpreting or responding to social situations, reading social cues, and acting impulsively without identifying the consequences of behavior or recognizing the feelings and concerns of others (Bryan, 1991; Carlson, 1987; Schumaker & Hazel, 1984). Research suggests that first-grade students with reading problems were much more likely to have difficulties with self-control and task attention, and to have externalizing or internalizing behavior problems, than first graders without reading problems (Morgan, Farkas, Tufis, & Sperling, 2008). It isn't hard to imagine that if a child isn't successful in reading or any other academic task, he or she will let the teacher know through his or her behavior.

> Students with learning disabilities may have difficulty acquiring and interpreting social behaviors.

Certainly, not *all* students with learning disabilities have problems with social behavior; however, many students with learning disabilities have problems relating to others and behaving acceptably at school. It is important to note that although some difficulties in social behavior may be related to learning characteristics, still others may be tied more directly to academic failure. The 16-year-old reading on the second-grade level may search for attention, acceptance, and control by engaging in inappropriate or even antisocial behavior. The search for a peer group, susceptibility to peer pressure, and problems anticipating consequences of actions may all contribute to the fact that adolescents with learning disabilities are often considered at risk for juvenile delinquency. Studies suggest that over half of the adolescents in the juvenile justice system have a disability—including learning disabilities (Bullis et al., 2002). McNamara and Willoughby (2010) found that adolescents with learning disabilities not only engaged more frequently in some risk-taking behaviors (smoking, marijuana use, acts of delinquency, aggression, and gambling), but they also continued to increase some of

© iStockphoto/Morgan Lane Studios

Normal variation makes it hard to tell which children will develop learning disabilities.

these behaviors more rapidly over time. What first seemed to be a school problem can quickly escalate into a social problem with severe consequences.

Having difficulty in academic work may also cause emotional distress. Of most concern is the self-esteem of students with learning disabilities. Research suggests that students with learning disabilities may not perceive themselves in a positive way—their self-esteem and academic self-efficacy is lower than those of children without learning disabilities and these feelings are related to subsequent effort in school tasks (Bryan, 1991; Lackaye & Margalit, 2006). It has long been hypothesized that educational settings influence students' self-concept, and that pulling out children for specialized instruction would negatively affect children's perceptions of themselves. In an analysis of studies that compared students' self-concepts, Elbaum (2002) found that there were no predictable relationships between placement and self-concept in children with learning disabilities. Some children felt better when they received support services in the general education classroom, and some preferred going to a resource setting. Studies suggest, however, that many students with learning disabilities have their own peer group, and they tend to have lower social status among their peers as a whole (Estell et al., 2008).

As you read through all the characteristics of individuals with learning disabilities, perhaps you thought, "Wow, I have difficulty with my organizational skills" or "My five-year-old reverses letters." It is very common to see yourself, your parent, or your child in almost any description of individuals with learning disabilities. Why? Because we've looked at all the basic learning processes and academic skills, and, as we said earlier, all learning ability is on a continuum. Very few people are perfectly efficient learning machines, and not everyone relies on the same skills to learn information well.

Pause and Reflect

What characteristics did you see that reflect your own learning characteristics or those of your students? Can you identify things you've done either as a student or a teacher to address those specific learning characteristics? ●

Teaching Strategies and Accommodations

How to assess and teach students with learning disabilities is a question that has been asked and debated for the past four decades. Many different philosophies can be found in the variety of educational programs for students with learning disabilities. In this section, we present assessment and teaching procedures that reflect what research suggests is best practice in the field. We will look at two major instructional approaches: direct instruction of specific skills and strategy instruction. Teaching models combining direct instruction and strategy instruction appear to be the most effective model for students with learning disabilities (Swanson, 1999). When integrated, these approaches reflect a similar philosophy about how students should be taught (direct instruction) and skills students should be taught (strategy instruction). We also will look at the instruction of support skills for students with learning disabilities, reflect on considerations for culturally diverse populations, and look at specific recommendations for adapting materials and presentations for students with learning disabilities.

Assessment for Teaching

There are two major purposes for assessment of students with learning disabilities. First, we assess in order to *identify* students who need special services and to determine the placement that best suits each child. Recall that we discussed this process in Chapter 1. Next we assess in order to *plan* the student's instructional program—to answer the question "What do I teach?" Assessment also allows us to evaluate the effectiveness of the program and the progress that the student is making; in fact, it can serve a variety of purposes.

● *Formal Assessment* **Formal assessment** involves the use of standardized tests, the results of which can be used to compare the student's performance with that of his or her same-age peers. These tests assess the student's performance in math, reading, and several basic skill areas, and yield scores that reveal grade level and standing relative to other students. Although the information yielded by these tests may be useful in diagnostic contexts, it is not detailed or specific enough to provide a foundation for instructional planning. For that purpose, many teachers rely on informal measures.

● *Informal Assessment* **Informal assessment** refers to direct measures of student performance and student progress in academic or behavioral tasks. There are many ways for a teacher to obtain information using informal assessment. Among them are *observations* of the student's work habits—for example, identifying the amount of time a child is able to pay attention to a task or activity. Observations can provide some information about why the child is unable to do well in certain tasks. For example, you might notice that a child works very rapidly on certain tasks and never reflects on or checks his or her work. You may notice that the child spends large amounts of time playing with the buttons on his or her shirt, or writing, erasing, and rewriting his or her words. This information may help you target specific areas for intervention.

Observations can also help prepare students to move into regular classroom settings. Because classroom teachers may have specific behavioral or learning requirements, the special education teacher or another professional can conduct an informal observation of the regular classroom into which the child will be placed. By noting specific requirements, such as length of seatwork time, types of tests, and behavior rules and requirements, the special education teacher can prepare the student for his move in a more effective manner.

Another important source of student performance data is **curriculum-based measurement (CBM).** A curriculum-based measure is a single, brief probe that can be used periodically to reflect student performance in a basic skill area (Deno, 1985). By using the informal curriculum-based assessment to assess a child's reading, writing, or math skills, the teacher can observe how the child approaches the task, as well as the specific types of difficulties he or she is experiencing. Because curriculum-based measurement is a key element in Response to Intervention models, many schools incorporate it as a means of measuring the progress of all students in the core curriculum. For students with learning disabilities, the use of curriculum-based measures provides a convenient means for teachers to keep track of how students are responding to what we are doing instructionally. Most important, of course, is how we respond to that data and adjust instructional strategies or curricula to meet students' needs. Typically, reading curriculum-based measures include oral reading fluency (correct words read per minute) and maze procedures for secondary students (grade-level text with 20 percent of words missing—students select the correct word from multiple choices). Other measures have been created for spelling, vocabulary, arithmetic, and written language. Most of these are based on the number of correct items or connected items performed in a certain time period. There are sources for curriculum-based measures in reading, mathematics, and written language that can be used by all schools, and some are free of charge. Two of the most frequently used sources are DIBELS: Dynamic Indicators of Basic Early Literacy Skills and AIMSWEB. Visit the Education CourseMate site at **www.cengagebrain.com** to connect with these sources.

This special educator is providing individualized direct instruction to a student during a math lesson.

Regardless of the type of curriculum-based measure used, research clearly suggests that teachers who use curriculum-based measures can see greater gains in students' achievement. These gains are dependent, however, on teachers using the data effectively and adjusting instruction responsively (Stecker, Fuchs, & Fuchs, 2005).

Direct Instruction

In direct instruction, specific academic skills are taught using proven techniques.

The term *direct* is used in this text to refer to a philosophy and approach to teaching students with learning disabilities. **Direct instruction** commonly refers to (1) the identification and instruction of specific academic skills and (2) the use of teaching techniques that have been empirically demonstrated to be effective with students with learning difficulties. The identification and instruction of specific skills may seem to be a fairly obvious approach to teaching, but it represents a departure from many popular teaching approaches. The philosophy behind direct instruction is that any specific processing disabilities the child demonstrates can be managed through effective teaching procedures, and that the most efficient use of instructional time is to focus on the academic skills in need of remediation.

Direct instruction teaching methods address the organization and presentation of instruction. The direct instruction approach includes a number of presentation techniques designed to maximize student attention and involvement in learning (Carnine et al., 2006). The approach is very teacher directed and includes an initial presentation based on the teacher first *modeling* the skill or response, then providing guided practice (*leading*), and, finally, eliciting independent student responses (*testing*). Direct instruction provides students with positive examples of a response or strategy. Exposure to positive examples promotes the probability of correct responding and helps to eliminate confusion related to poor directions or student misinterpretation of the task. The modeling and leading steps are eliminated as instruction in a specific skill progresses (Engelmann & Hanner, 1982).

Direct instruction appears to be the most effective means of teaching students with learning disabilities (Adams & Engelmann, 1996; Rosenshine & Stevens, 1986) and is identified as an evidence-based practice. Some of the commercial programs based on this approach include Corrective Reading—Revised (Engelmann et al., 1999) and Reading Mastery Plus (Engelmann et al., 2002). Figure 5.8 is an excerpt from Reading Mastery II, Fast Cycle, a direct instruction program (Engelmann & Bruner, 1995). All the commercial direct instruction programs contain specific scripted lessons for teachers and incorporate the teaching techniques just described. Other materials contain direct instruction techniques, including a variety of computer software and multimedia and DVD programs. These programs use direct instruction to involve students in more active learning (Hayden, Gersten, & Carnine, 1992).

For more information on direct instruction programs and techniques, visit the National Institute for Direct Instruction's website **www.nifdi.org/**.

Strategy Instruction

A strategy can be defined as a set of responses that are organized to perform an activity or solve a problem (Swanson, 1993). In this section we will focus primarily on the strategy approaches used most often by teachers of students with learning disabilities. In addition to academic skills instruction, we will see that strategies are also used to teach specialized skills, adaptive skills, and life skills.

A **strategy instruction** approach to teaching students with learning disabilities involves first breaking down the skills involved in a task or problem—usually a procedure such as writing a paper—into a set of sequential steps. The steps are prepared so that the student may read or, later, memorize them in order to

> Strategy instruction teaches specific skills by organizing steps, providing prompts, and focusing on metacognitive skills.

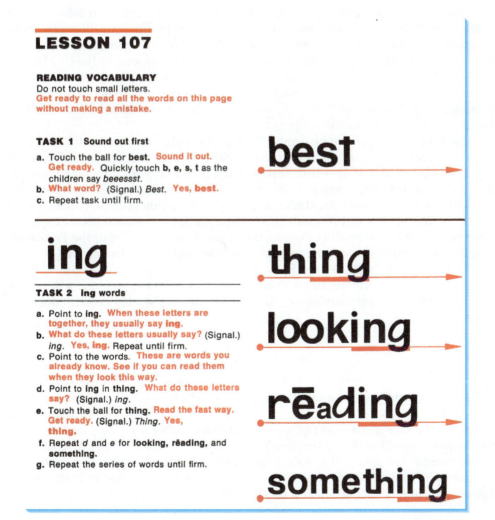

FIGURE 5.8

Excerpt from Reading Mastery II: Fast Cycle

Source: Siegfried Engelman and Elaine C. Bruner (1995). *Reading Mastery II: Fast cycle,* Rainbow Edition, Presentation Book C, p. 165. © 1995, McGraw-Hill. Reprinted with permission.

perform the skill correctly. Some strategies are developed so that the first letters of all the steps form an acronym to help students remember the purpose of the strategy and the steps involved. Many strategies also include decision-making or evaluative components designed to help students use metacognitive skills (Graham, Harris, & Olinghouse, 2007).

Strategy training involves more than just the presentation of steps, however. Careful assessment and direct instruction, including sufficient opportunities to practice the strategy, are considered essential in most strategy instruction. Students should first observe how to use the strategy, practice, and receive feedback before attempting to use it on their own. Strategies have been developed to address the needs of students with learning disabilities in a wide range of areas. Test-taking skills, study skills, reading comprehension, written composition, anger control, and math problem solving are all possible target areas for strategies. Some research suggests that the use of strategy instruction can be an important learning tool for students with learning disabilities. For example, elementary and secondary students with learning disabilities are found to write more reflective, complex, and well-written essays when using writing strategies (Graham & Harris, 2005; De La Paz et al., 2000). Students with disabilities who were taught to use strategies to complete math word problems improved their ability to complete the problem and arrive at the correct answer (Owen & Fuchs, 2002). Learning strategies have even been integrated successfully with some computer software to assist in the decision-making and problem-solving skills of older students with reading disabilities (Hollingsworth & Woodward, 1993).

The strategy instruction approach is intuitively appealing to educators. It teaches specific skills in a manner that controls for potential problems in a student's ability to identify important information or steps, organizes the steps for the student, provides a continual prompt for remembering, breaks the task into its component parts, and often focuses on metacognitive skills. One of the most well-known curricula designed for students with learning disabilities is the Learning Strategies Curriculum, which was developed at the University of Kansas Institute for Research in Learning Disabilities.

Each component of the Learning Strategies Curriculum contains a sequence of steps for learners to follow and practice so they can perform tasks such as writing a paragraph or taking a test. Teachers are provided with a series of specific guidelines for teaching students how to perform these strategies. As we usually see with strategy instruction, students are taught not only specific behaviors but also how to evaluate and monitor their performance. For examples and specific information on teaching the Learning Strategies Curriculum, visit the Education Coursemate website to accompany this text at **www.cengagebrain.com.**

In Figure 5.9, McLesky and Warrant (2011) synthesize best practice for teaching students with learning disabilities. In this synthesis you will recognize elements of direct instruction, curriculum content, strategy instruction, and assessment.

Special Skills Instruction

Teachers must tailor the social skills curriculum to their students' particular environment.

Many students with learning disabilities may receive instruction in specialized skills such as study skills or social skills. Instruction in these skills may be the only type of service required by some students with learning disabilities; for others it may be one component of a more comprehensive set of support services. Sometimes special skills instruction is incorporated into the regular classroom curriculum; other times, these skills are taught in special education settings—for example, in a resource class. This section gives an overview of instructional approaches to teaching study and social skills.

Components of High-Quality, Intensive Instruction for Elementary Students with Learning Disabilities

a. Grouping

- Instruction should be provided to small groups of students (e.g., from one to three students for optimal results)
- Students should have similar instructional needs

b. Instructional Design

- Instruction should focus on a small group of clearly defined skills and/or concepts
- Instruction should be provided using an instructional sequence and materials that meet individual student needs
- Instruction should be well structured and provide explicit information with concrete examples, models, and demonstrations

c. Delivery of Instruction

- Allow an appropriate pace and sufficient time for student mastery of targeted skills, with redundant instruction as necessary
- Provide cognitive support through the use of carefully sequenced lessons, control of task difficulty, and providing models and scaffolding that ensure a high level of student success
- Provide emotional support through encouragement, feedback, and high levels of student success
- Provide students with opportunities to practice and respond (i.e., guided practice)

d. Independent Practice

- Provide practice directly related to the skills being taught
- Students should achieve a high success rate during independent practice
- Independent practice should be actively supervised
- Independent practice should continue until responses are automatic

e. Progress Monitoring

- Monitor student progress weekly or biweekly to evaluate the effectiveness of the intervention, and ensure students are making sufficient progress
- Provide students with feedback regarding their individual progress

Sources: Fletcher and Vaughn (2009), Foorman and Torgesen (2001), Gersten et al. (2009a, b), Rosenshine and Stevens (1986), Swanson (2008), Swanson (2001), Swanson and Hoskyn (1998), Torgesen (2000, 2002).

FIGURE 5.9

Educational programs for elementary students with learning disabilities: Can they be both effective and inclusive?

Source: McCleskey, J., & Waldron, N.L. (2011). Educational programs for elementary students with learning disabilities: Can they be both effective and inclusive? *Learning Disabilities Research and Practice,* 26, 48–57. Table 1: Page 50 . Reprinted by permission of John Wiley and Sons.

● *Study Skills*   As we have seen throughout this chapter, the difficulties experienced by many students with learning disabilities revolve around the ability to receive, process, and express information effectively. Study skills instruction addresses these areas as they relate directly to classroom activities. The purpose of teaching study skills is to give the student a set of tools for performing required classroom activities, not to teach the content of a specific course. Study skills instruction for students with learning disabilities might include teaching techniques for reading and remembering material in content-area texts, taking and reviewing notes, taking essay or multiple-choice tests, and preparing reports or projects. Students learn and practice these skills on materials from a variety of content areas. Study skills are frequently taught through the use of strategy training. The strategies are usually general enough so that they can be applied to many different types of tasks and content areas. For example, a strategy taught for taking an essay exam should work in any type of essay exam (English, history, science, or psychology). Other instructional techniques include teaching students to use graphic aids, such as charts, to apply time management and general

Study skills instruction provides practice on different types of work so that students can use the skills in many classes.

ASSISTIVE TECHNOLOGY FOCUS

Technology Tools for Improved Learning

For many students with learning disabilities, technology becomes an important avenue for accessing and producing information. Students with difficulty reading or writing—as well as those who have difficulties organizing content—find many supportive resources through technology. Here, we look at two important avenues that teachers can explore to help students with learning disabilities use technology to more efficiently take in or produce information. Example 1 is a table that describes free software that can be used in classrooms to provide text-to-speech options. This software can be used to read text aloud—an important

option for students who may be working in higher-level content but reading at a lower level (Berkeley & Lindstrom, 2011). Example 2 illustrates a test development/test delivery system (NimbleTools Assessment Systems) that teachers can use to incorporate technology into test design (Russell, Hoffmann, & Higgins, 2009). Many additional opportunities for integrating technology into students' instructional and assessment programs can be found, at all levels of cost. See the CAST Sciencewriter example and Kid-Tools contract earlier in the chapter to see other examples of assistive technology in action.

Text-to-Speech Options	Features	Web Link	Free?
Software programs with TTS options			
Microsoft Word (as part of Windows XP/Microsoft Office)	Text/background colors and contrast; reading rate; dynamic highlighting	http://support.microsoft.com/kb/306902	Yes
Adobe Read Out Loud (as part of Adobe Reader)	Text/background colors and contrast; reading rate; voice options	http://www.adobe.com/enterprise/accessibility/reader6/sec2.html	Yes
Web browser add-ons or plug-ins			
Firefox or Thunderbird (owned by Mozilla)	Text/background colors and contrast	https://addons.mozilla.org/en-US/firefox/tag/text%20to%20speech	Yes
Internet Explorer	Text/background colors and contrast; reading rate; dynamic highlighting	http://support.microsoft.com/kb/306902	Yes
Stand-alone software programs			
ReadPlease (for Windows XP-based operating systems) and Reading Bar 2 (Internet Explorer)	Text background colors and contrast; reading rate; voice options	www.readplease.com	Low-cost and free version available
NaturalReader (for various programs/browsers, Mac and Windows)	Reading rate; voice options	http://www.naturalreaders.com	Low-cost and free version available

FIGURE 5.10A

Example 1. Technology for the struggling reader: Free and easily accessible resources.

Source: Berkeley, S., & Lindstrom, J. H. (2011). Technology for the struggling reader: Free and easily accessible resources. *Teaching Exceptional Children,* 43 (4), 48–55. (From article–Table 1. Free or Low-cost text-to-speech options on page 55.)

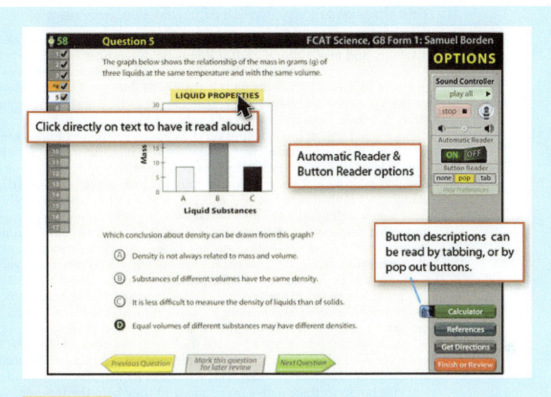

FIGURE 5.10B

Example 2. NimbleTools: A universally designed test delivery system.

Source: Russell, M. Hoffman, T., & Higgins, J. (2009). Nimble Tools: A universally designed test delivery system. *Teaching Exceptional Children.* 42(2), 6–20. Figure 1.

organization aids to study behavior; to use structure or content outlines for taking notes; and to use alternative tools, such as tape recorders and computers (Minskoff & Allsopp, 2003).

As you learned in the previous section, curricula such as the Learning Strategies Curriculum include strategies for teaching study skills, and new strategies are continually being developed and evaluated. For example, Hughes et al. (2002) found that a strategy for completing homework assignments (the PROJECT strategy) was very effective in giving adolescents a plan to use with weekly schedules and assignments across classes. Strategies such as these help to address the organizational challenges that are particularly problematic in middle and high school because of the number of courses, books, and assignments. Of course, a published curriculum is not necessary to teach study skills. If students are receiving a special course or series of classes in study skills, however, it is definitely helpful for the teacher to have an organized plan of instruction. Many teachers of students with learning disabilities develop original study skills curricula by drawing on existing programs and research and then adapting and applying those objectives and instructional techniques to the specific needs of their students. One of the most important goals of study skills instruction is to provide extensive practice on different types of work and to prompt the students to use the skills in other classes. Boyle and Weishaar (2001) found that high-school students learning a strategy for notetaking in content classes needed instruction and practice in using the strategy before applying it in their classes. These activities help to ensure that students will actually use the skills to do their coursework, which, of course, is the purpose of study skills instruction.

Considerations for Culturally Diverse Learners

It is difficult to have a learning disability; it is more difficult to have a learning disability and face cultural and/or linguistic differences in a classroom setting. As teachers, we must consider how cultural and linguistic differences affect the needs of individual students with learning disabilities. The characteristics may be the same, but additional challenges are faced by the students, and teaching strategies must be evaluated accordingly. For example, if students in your classroom are not native English speakers, they may speak and understand English at different levels of proficiency. Obviously, it is important for you to know each child's level of English proficiency in both receptive and expressive language. The way you present information to students can help to facilitate their understanding of both directions and content. Many of the teaching techniques we have just described, such as using clear, simple instructions, providing examples, and using response signals or cues, are quite helpful. Holding and pointing to the material you are presenting and modeling the way to answer questions provide context by giving the student cues about what is required (Fueyo, 1997). The students will be looking to you for prompts, and the direct instruction format can provide needed modeling and guided practice. The specific difficulties encountered in reading and writing by students who are learning two languages may also require adjustments in how we teach these basic skills. In fact, many bilingual special educators advocate the use of the whole-language method of instruction, or direct instruction in a literature-based context, for students who are not native English speakers. These types of instruction allow students to use relevant books in their native language, and they help the teacher evaluate the student's performance in higher-level thinking, planning, and conversational skills (Lopez-Reyna, 1996).

Recent research suggests that the direct instruction approach to teaching phonological awareness and other reading skills may be quite important for bilingual children and that the same instructional strategies appear to benefit all students at risk for reading disabilities (Lonigan, Schatschneider, & Westber, 2008; McKinney et al., 2000; O'Connor, Bocian, Beebe-Frankenberger, & Linklater, 2010). Gunn and coworkers (2000) found that a structured direct instruction reading program resulted in significant gains in skills such as word attack, vocabulary, and comprehension for young Hispanic children, even those who spoke little or no English, when compared to children who did not receive the intervention. The specific-skill instruction characteristic of most special education programs appears to be quite important; however, any instructional method needs to be supported with motivating literature and with extensive opportunities to read, write, and discuss content in both native and new languages to facilitate development in both (Gersten & Woodward, 1994).

> Many educators suggest supplementing direct instruction with motivating literature when teaching reading for bilingual students.

Adapting Classroom Materials

One of the best ways for teachers to address the needs of students with learning disabilities is to adapt instruction and materials. Although the way a textbook or worksheet looks may seem relatively inconsequential, students with learning disabilities face many unnecessary obstacles because of the way material is presented. Adaptation of materials may be as simple as redoing a skills sheet or as complex as restructuring a curriculum. An understanding of the basic approaches to learning by students with learning disabilities is necessary, as are time, motivation, and knowledge of course content. As we look at some basic guidelines, remember that you can make a number of different adaptations. If you keep in mind that students with learning disabilities often have difficulty perceiving, attending to, and organizing important information, you can go a long way in identifying what adaptations are needed. Couple this knowledge with the basic concepts of direct instruction discussed earlier, and you will be able to teach students with learning disabilities in a more effective manner. Our focus in this section is mainly on adapting written materials typically used in regular class instruction—materials that are not developed with students with learning disabilities in mind. We will look at organizing lessons from textbooks, preparing for lecture and reading activities in content areas, and general ideas for worksheet and test construction.

> Lesson plans from a teacher's manual often have to be modified.

● *Modifications for Lesson Planning*   Many textbooks include teachers' manuals to assist in the presentation of instruction. Too often, however, the lessons in the manuals are brief and potentially confusing because of the amount and structure of the content. You may need to modify these lessons before you present them to the class. The accompanying Teaching Strategies box, "Strategies for Lesson Planning," offers specific suggestions for modifying your lessons for students with learning disabilities. Keep them in mind as you review manuals before planning your lessons.

● *Modifications for Lectures and Reading Assignments*   In many content courses, particularly at the middle- and high-school level, the teaching format may be limited to lecturing by the teacher and independent reading by the student. Even if projects or other activities are a regular part of the class, much of the material essential for tests and passing the course comes from the student's ability to identify and organize important information from what is presented orally or in the textbook. Adaptations, therefore, focus on clarifying important information and providing a clear organizational structure.

Teaching Strategies & Accommodations

Strategies for Lesson Planning

1. *Identify all the new skills being taught in the lesson.* More than one is too many. Sequence the skills according to the hierarchy of content and choose the first one in the sequence.

2. *Identify the preskills the student needs.* If the text does not provide a review of the preskills, prepare one.

3. *Review the introduction and actual teaching part of the lesson.* A surprising number of textbooks include very little instruction.

- Is the skill or concept clearly identified and described at the beginning of the lesson?

- Are there plenty of positive examples of the skill or concept being taught? Are there also negative or incorrect examples that require the student to discriminate and actually identify the fundamental parts of the skill?

- Think of a rule or cue to help the student learn the skill more efficiently.

4. *Look at the opportunities for practice presented in the manual and student text.*

- Is there a lot of guided practice and opportunity for response before the student has to work alone? Practice with the teacher gives the student a chance to learn the skill and allows the teacher to correct any errors right away. You may have to develop some practice examples.

5. *Examine application exercises or "written practice" activities.*

- Do the independent activities reflect the skill that was taught?

- Are the language and reading requirements appropriate for your student?

- Is the right amount of independent work provided? Is there enough practice to show you that the student has mastered the skill, but not so much that the amount is overwhelming?

Lectures Adaptations for lectures involve helping students with learning disabilities identify important information and take notes in an organized way. Some ways to help students do this include:

- Providing students with an advanced organizer, such as an outline of the lecture, or with some questions to read before the lecture begins. The students can review the organizer and be better prepared to listen for key information.

- Preparing a simple outline that includes major topics but has room for the students to take notes under the different headings. This will help students organize and see the relationship between various pieces of information.

- Reviewing key vocabulary before the lecture begins or writing critical information on the board or on an overhead. Specifically tell students that information written on the board is important.

- Teaching students to recognize and identify the clues used most frequently to identify important information.

- Stopping every so often and asking students to paraphrase or talk about the topic.

Reading Assignments Adaptations for written texts include many of the same ideas just listed. Suggestions include:

- Providing advance organizers before reading, including both outlines and questions about the materials, to help students read for important content. A number of content textbooks present questions or "what you will learn" guidelines at the beginning of chapters. If these exist in your text, remember to show students how to use them.

- Reviewing, highlighting, or boxing vocabulary or facts before reading.

- Cueing students to stop reading after every paragraph or every few paragraphs to review the material. The review could consist of written or oral paraphrasing or answering questions prepared for the different sections of the text.

- Teaching students to develop questions themselves about the text, for use during or after reading.

- Having students answer questions reviewed at the beginning of the passage, having them paraphrase, and asking them to fill in outlines or other advance organizers after they finish reading the text.

- Using other activities, such as the webbing technique discussed in the section on written language, or developing pictures or other graphic representations of content.

Advance organizers or outlines can help students identify important information in lectures and take organized notes.

For students who are able to understand grade-level content but who read at a far lower grade level, interaction with the regular classroom text may be quite difficult. For these students, adaptations of content-area texts may include simplifying instructional content so that the reading requirements are reduced and only key information is presented. Classroom teachers or special education consultants or resource teachers may want to prepare annotated outlines that present only essential information. In some instances, this technique may be very difficult because of the density of the text (U.S. history or chemistry, for example). Alternatives include taping the lectures, persuading someone to record the text on tape, attempting to find a simpler version of the text (some programs have two levels of textbooks), or using a peer or adult tutor to read the text.

● *Modifications of Worksheets and Tests* Much evaluation and practice in the classroom takes place through written performance. The content, structure, and appearance of worksheets and tests are important because they affect the ability of students with learning disabilities to perform as well as they can. The guidelines we provide in this section are simple ones designed to call the student's attention to relevant information and to remove confusing or distracting information. They may be used when creating your own material or when adapting existing material.

Directions should be simple and clear.

- Use bold print, capital letters, or other means of highlighting important words in the directions.
- If more than one type of direction is necessary for different sections on the worksheet or test, make certain the sections are clearly separated from each other. Each set of directions should be clearly identifiable and immediately precede the related section.

The *appearance* of the material should be organized and uncluttered.

- Avoid unnecessary pictures. If a picture or graphic is necessary to answer a question (for example, a map or a graph), make sure that the questions related to the graphic are on the same page and adjacent to the questions if possible.
- Make sure all writing is clear and legible and that adequate space is provided for responses.
- Break up long tests or exams into different sections to help students organize responses (and possibly to prevent them from skipping or omitting questions). If possible, allow room for answers directly under the questions. Try to minimize the amount of page flipping the students have to do. Students do need experience in standardized test formats (for minimum competency tests, basic skills tests, or SAT exams), so specific practice in these types of tests must be provided. Understand, however, that these formats are difficult for students with learning disabilities and may need to be introduced carefully.

Although types of questions or written activities will vary depending on grade level or subject area, the *format* of the presentation is always important.

- Avoid long columns of matching items—the ones that require drawing all those lines between the items on both sides of the paper. Either use another format or break the list into sections.
- Essay questions will create problems for many students with disabilities, and some guidelines may be necessary (outline, approximate number of sentences, strategy for answering essay questions).
- Some students with poor reading and writing skills may need to have the test read to them or have the whole test or worksheet on tape so that reading and writing are not necessary.

When preparing tests or other written assignments, it is important to remember that the goal of the assessment is to evaluate the students' knowledge of the subject matter. You don't want other skill difficulties to interfere with your understanding of what each student has actually learned.

Curriculum

It is beyond the scope of this chapter to discuss curriculum in any detail; however, many educators have suggested the need to restructure curricula to present content effectively to students with learning disabilities and to encourage the development of higher-order thinking skills (Carnine, Silbert, Kameenui, Tarver, & Jungjohann, 2006). Curriculum, whether you select or develop it,

> Directions on tests and worksheets should be simple and clear.

A CLOSER LOOK · Growing Up with Learning Disabilities

Although a learning disability can be a significant challenge, it is not necessarily an obstacle to success and accomplishments in adult life.

- Many students with learning disabilities graduate from high school with a diploma and go on to postsecondary education. Although research a decade ago suggested that more students with learning disabilities drop out of high school and fewer attend community colleges or four-year colleges than students without disabilities (Murray et al., 2000; Scanlon & Mellard, 2002), some recent research implies that the gap has closed. The gap in postsecondary experiences as well as employment opportunities appears to be closing (Seo, Abbott, & Hawkins, 2008).

- Perceptions of self and school experiences may figure significantly in postsecondary opportunities. Irvin et al. (2011) found that students in rural areas, with or without learning disabilities, who had negative or low perceptions of school, were less likely to pursue postsecondary options and, therefore, were less likely to go to college.

Because more students with learning disabilities had negative school perceptions, they were less likely to pursue college.

- Recent research suggests that students with learning disabilities who held two or more jobs in high school were almost twice as likely to be working or participating in postsecondary education after graduation as those who did not work (Berry, Lindstrom, & Vovanoff, 2000). Perhaps early work experience allows students to develop skills that help promote success later in life.

- Successful adults with learning disabilities take control of what is happening to them. Showing students how to use learning tools to create change and facilitate self-reliance may increase their probability for success (Gerber, Ginsberg, & Reiff, 1992).

- Personal attributes, including self-awareness, proactivity, and perseverance, are critical factors in achieving adult success. Students entering postsecondary placements need to be able to determine what services they need (Mull, Sitlington, & Alper, 2001; Raskind et al., 1999).

should reflect the components of effective instruction, as well as sequential presentation of content. References to important elements of curriculum, such as sequence, presenting one skill at a time, examples, and structure, can be found in the guidelines for direct instruction, and in the academic characteristics sections presented earlier in the text. Researchers also found that organizing curriculum around the concept of "sameness" helps students learn more effectively (Engelmann, Carnine, & Steely, 1991). The underlying principle is using the same strategy or conceptual model for approaching all tasks in a skill or content area. For example, Kinder and Bursuck (1991) suggest that a model based on organizing knowledge into a "problem-solution-effect" structure should be applied to all social studies content. In this example, students organize their notes from text and lectures according to the problem-solution-effect rubric. By trying to organize content according to a basic structure or a few sets of structures, you can reduce the memory load for students and help them organize complex information.

A number of different teaching strategies and accommodations were presented in this section. It is important to consider two major points as you reflect on your own teaching ideas and plans for the classroom. First, consider that the interaction between students' abilities and teaching strategies is very important. If students have difficulty attending to information, then you must determine how to address that attention problem in your instruction and through your accommodations. If a child is not making progress in your reading program, you must figure out why and *adjust* the way you are teaching. Second, the teaching strategies presented here reflect current research and best practice—not just for students with learning disabilities, but for many children without learning disabilities as well. Not all children require or even benefit from such structured instruction, but many do—think about the ways these instructional strategies can be integrated into general education classrooms to support children or to present complex content.

? Pause and Reflect

How can you adapt your teaching methods to address such issues as distractibility? Can you think of ways you could use direct instruction or strategy instruction to teach in a specific content area? ●

SUMMARY

- Students with learning disabilities demonstrate a discrepancy between potential and achievement that cannot be attributed to other disabilities or to environmental or cultural factors. Schools are no longer required to use this discrepancy during identification.

- Response to Intervention (RTI) is a school-wide approach to preventing the inappropriate identification of students with learning disabilities.

- Although there is no single known cause of learning disabilities, internal and external factors may be involved.

- Learning disabilities can affect five major cognitive processes: perception, attention, memory, metacognition, and organization. Difficulties with each of these processes can lead to problems in academic areas such as reading, language arts, and mathematics.

- The social difficulties often caused by learning disabilities may stem from problems in learning appropriate behavior, or from repeated failures in school that lead to low self-esteem, helplessness, or acting out.

- Students with learning disabilities are assessed formally and informally to determine their academic skills.

- The most widely used instructional techniques for students with learning disabilities are direct instruction, strategy instruction, and special instruction in study and social skills.

- Many classroom materials and presentations can be modified for students with learning disabilities. When these students are included in regular classrooms, general and special educators must collaborate in making the necessary modifications and providing instruction.

KEY TERMS

learning disabilities (page 153)

exclusion clause (page 154)

discrepancy (page 154)

progress-monitoring data (page 155)

internal factors (page 157)

external factors (page 157)

perinatal stress (page 159)

perception (page 161)

USEFUL RESOURCES

- *Children of the Code:* **http://www.childrenofthecode.org/.** This self-described "Social Education Project" includes videos, interviews, and text related to reading disabilities and the state of reading education today. The website also includes access to professional development materials (e.g., DVDs, events). Many prominent educators and political figures are featured.

- *Association for Direct Instruction:* **http://www.adihome.org.** This organization provides information, assistance, and support to educators interested in using direct instruction and/or ordering related materials.

- *National Center for Learning Disabilities (NCLD):* **http://ncld.org.** Contact: 381 Park Avenue South, New York, NY, 10016, (212) 545-7510.

- *The Gram.* Newsletter of the Learning Disabilities Association (formerly ACLD): **http://www.ldanatl.org/about/index.asp.** Contact: 4156 Library Road, Pittsburgh, PA, 15234, (412) 341-1515. This newsletter provides information about current legislation, educational programs, and research in the area of learning disabilities.

- *LD OnLine:* **http://www.LDOnLine.org.** This is a comprehensive website on learning disabilities, and the official website of the Coordinated Campaign for Learning Disabilities.

- *National Center to Improve the Tools of Educators (NCITE):* **http://www.uoregon. edu/~ncite.** Contact: 805 Lincoln Street, Eugene, OR, 97403-1211, (541) 346-1646. This site offers numerous publications on academic skill instruction, a curriculum, and related research.

- *National Institute of Child Health and Human Development (NICHD).* Contact: Dr. G. Reid Lyon, National Institutes of Health, 6100 Executive Boulevard, Room 4B05, Bethesda, MD, 20892, (301) 496-6591: *www.nichd.nih.gov.* Publications related to understanding learning disabilities, reading and learning disabilities, and other areas of research are available at this location.

- *Reading and Learning Disabilities*: National Reading Panel (NRP): Teaching children to read: **http://www.nationalreadingpanel.org/.** The report of the NRP can be obtained from this site.

- *The Division for Learning Disabilities of the Council for Exceptional Children:* **http://www.TeachingLD.org.** This website provides information on conferences, research updates, and organization publications. An interesting feature is interactive forums with experts in specific areas of learning disabilities.

PORTFOLIO ACTIVITIES

1. Interview a school psychologist in a local school district or the consultant in the area of learning disabilities at your state department of education. Identify the state criteria for identifying students with learning disabilities. Compare and record the ways these criteria can be interpreted by school districts across your state. Discuss the role of Response to Intervention in the identification process.

CEC This activity will help the student meet CEC Content Standard 2: Development and Characteristics of Learners.

2. Select a lesson from a textbook in your content area. Adapt the material along the lines suggested in the text. What specific changes did you make? Who is the intended audience for your revised version of the lesson? Can you envision making these types of modifications in your classroom?

CEC This activity will help the student meet CEC Content Standard 3: Individual Learning Differences. Portfolio Activity 2: Standard 4: Instructional Strategies.

3. How do successful adults with learning disabilities cope with the demands of their jobs and lives? Interview an adult with a learning disability. Invite him or her to talk to your class about the strategies he or she has used to succeed in life. What types of strategies are described? How might they be used by your future students?

CEC This activity will help the student meet CEC Content Standard 3: Individual Learning Differences.

4. Why are course content, teacher presentation, and the student's place in the classroom all vital to consider when planning a class that welcomes a student with learning disabilities? Based on what you've read in this chapter and your own experience, list classroom modifications in each of these areas that would be effective for all students. Be sure to consider social and academic aspects of the class when listing your modifications

CEC This activity can help the student meet CEC Content Standard 5: Learning Environments and Social Interactions.

To access Portfolio Activities for this chapter and other useful study resources including an interactive eBook, related web links, quizzes, flashcards, and videos, visit the Education CourseMate website at CengageBrain.com.

CHAPTER 6

Children with Intellectual Disabilities

Outline

Learning Objectives

After reading this chapter about students with intellectual disabilities, the reader will:

- Understand the terminology and definitions related to intellectual disabilities.

- Describe the role of adaptive behavior in the definition of intellectual disabilities.

- Identify and describe some of the known causes of intellectual disabilities.

- Identify and discuss some of the learning characteristics of individuals with intellectual disabilities.

- Identify and describe the range of educational goals that may be appropriate for individuals with intellectual disabilities.

- Examine the importance of the community as an educational setting for individuals with intellectual disabilities.

- Describe teaching methods and materials that can be used to help students with intellectual disabilities achieve their learning potential.

Students with intellectual disabilities demonstrate a range of abilities. Many are included in high-stakes testing and the general education curriculum. In this chapter, we will look at how curriculum and teaching strategies are modified to help these students reach their potential in academic and life skills. We will also focus on the community as a source of instructional materials, employment, and independent living arrangements—both during and after the school years. Throughout this chapter, we will address changing perceptions toward and expectations for individuals with intellectual disabilities.

Perhaps more than any other term used in the field of special education, the term *mental retardation* conjures up specific images of individuals or groups of individuals. The feelings and images aroused by this term have long been of concern to individuals, parents, and professionals. As of October 2010, the term "mental retardation" officially changed in the federal law (see A Closer Look, "What's in a Name" below).

A CLOSER LOOK   What's in a Name?

Throughout history, the terms used to describe students with intellectual disabilities have changed. Typically a term is used because it fits the scientific or social constructs of the era. Over time, however, this term may acquire negative or pejorative connotations as it is used out of context. Examples include the once-acceptable and now painful-to-hear terms "moron" and "imbecile." For well over 50 years, the term "mental retardation" has been used to refer to individuals with intellectual disabilities. In spite of changes in language over the years, including using person-first terminology, this term has remained. Many youth in our country also use the term "retarded" as a general descriptor of people, things, and events. Individuals with intellectual disabilities, parents, siblings, friends, professionals and other advocates have worked to change the term mental retardation since it is now in the social vernacular as a pejorative term rather than a descriptive one. No one wants to describe people using that term anymore. Recently, individuals and organizations, including the National Down Syndrome Society, the American Association on Intellectual and Developmental Disabilities (AAIDD), the Arc, and Special Olympics, to name a few, participated in a campaign "Stop Using the R Word!" One problem, however, was that the term remained in the federal law, so it was used in schools and by both education and legal professionals. This unhappy fact was changed in October 2011. President Obama signed federal legislation officially changing the term "mental retardation" to "intellectual disabilities." The legislation, known as Rosa's law, is named for Rosa Marcellino, a Maryland girl with Down syndrome. Now, people are working to break the habit. March

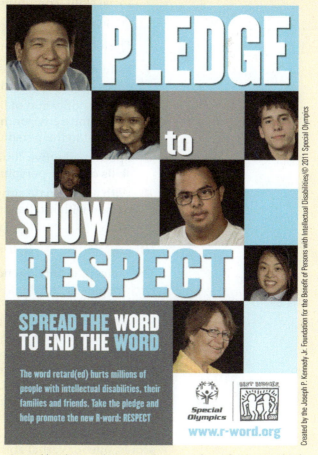

Created by The Joseph P. Kennedy Jr. Foundation for the Benefit of Persons with Intellectual Disabilities.

http://www.r-word.org/

10, 2011 was declared "Spread the Word to End the Word Awareness Day!" We hope you, too, will think before you speak, and use terms that convey respect towards all people.

As you read this chapter, we ask you to keep two basic concepts in mind. First, each individual with intellectual disabilities is just that—an individual. You must let go of any negative preconceptions you may have related to how children with intellectual disabilities look, how they act, or what they can achieve. Second, each and every child has promise; thus, you must identify the specific skills and interests that need to be encouraged and strengthened.

Terms and Definitions

Intellectual disabilities are characterized by subaverage intellectual functioning and deficits in adaptive behavior.

The definition of **intellectual disabilities** has been revised numerous times to reflect our evolving understanding. The federal definition, adopted in 1993, with terminology changed in 2010, is as follows:

> Intellectual disabilities refers to substantial limitations in present functioning. It is characterized by significantly subaverage intellectual functioning, existing concurrently with related limitations in two or more of the following applicable adaptive, or life-skill areas: communication, self-care, home living, social skills, community use, self-direction, health and safety, functional academics, leisure, and work. Intellectual disabilities manifests before age 18.

> The following four assumptions are essential to the application of the definition:

1. Valid assessment considers cultural and linguistic diversity as well as differences in communication and behavioral factors.

2. The identification of limitations in adaptive skills occurs within the context of community environments typical of the individual's same-aged peers and is indexed to the person's individualized needs for supports.

3. Specific adaptive limitations often coexist with strengths in other adaptive skills or other personal capabilities.

4. With appropriate supports over a sustained period, the life functioning of the person with intellectual disabilities will generally improve.

Intelligence and General Cognitive Functioning

The concept of intelligence is critical to the definition of intellectual disabilities. Each reader of this book will have different ideas about what constitutes intelligence. Researchers, too, have difficulty agreeing on a definition of intelligence. It is what psychologists call a *construct*, defined by theorists and test makers and determined by their ideas, beliefs, and cultural values. Even though no universal agreement exists on what constitutes intelligence, a number of tests have been developed to measure it. The **Stanford-Binet Intelligence Scale** and the **Wechsler Intelligence Scale for Children, Third Edition (WISC-III)** are the two tests most widely used by American psychologists to assess intelligence. These tests include a number of subtests and yield a composite score, the score we typically refer to when we state a student's IQ. The WISC-III also yields two major subscores, one for verbal ability and one for performance ability. The intelligence test scores for the population at large can be represented in what is often described as a bell-shaped curve (see Figure 6.1). This distribution, also known as the normal curve, illustrates the range of scores that can be expected in any representative population. An average intelligence test score of 100 represents equivalence between mental age and chronological age.

The phrase *subaverage intellectual functioning* in the American Association on Intellectual and Developmental Disabilities' definition refers to performance on one or more intelligence tests resulting in an IQ score of about 70 or below. It is possible, however, for a student with an IQ score higher than 70 to qualify as

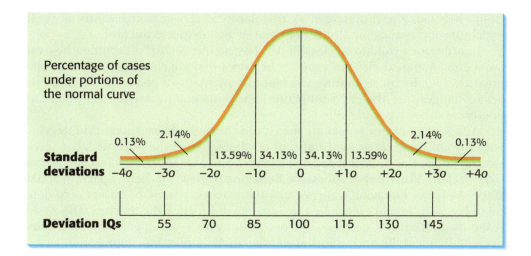

FIGURE 6.1

Theoretical distribution of IQ scores

Source: S. A. Kirk & J. J. Gallagher (1988). *Educating Exceptional Children* (6th ed., p. 11). Boston: Houghton Mifflin.

having intellectual disabilities if there are clear deficits in adaptive behavior. Conversely, it is possible for a student with an IQ score of 65 not to be identified as having intellectual disabilities if he or she has good adaptive behavior. A critical point to remember is that the word *significantly,* which is used in the federal definition ("significantly subaverage intellectual functioning"), is subject to professional interpretation. It can also be decided that a child no longer has intellectual disabilities if gains are made in adaptive behavior or in measured intelligence level. The term *intellectual disabilities* can thus refer to a current state of functioning or performance rather than a permanent condition.

Adaptive Behavior

Adaptive behavior, the other key element of the AAIDD definition, includes those social, maturational, self-help, and communicative acts that help each individual adapt to the demands of his or her surroundings (Beirne-Smith, Ittenbach, & Patton, 2002). Behaviors are *age-appropriate* and *situation-appropriate;* that is, they are different at each age and in each situation. Adaptive behaviors present a more comprehensive picture of a child's abilities than do IQ scores alone. Let us examine some examples of adaptive behaviors found in different developmental periods to see how they vary.

The most rapid and dramatic changes in adaptive behavior occur during the infancy and preschool period. The infant learns to reach, roll over, sit, stand, walk, and run; to finger-feed and then to use a spoon and drink from a cup; to draw others into close social relationships; and to communicate—first through vocalizing, and then, gradually, through understanding and repeating single words, two words together, short phrases, and finally sentences that increase in length and complexity. By preschool, many of these milestones have been mastered. The child becomes toilet-trained, and then many of the adaptive behaviors focus on social goals: learning to play and interact successfully with other children and with new adults, sharing, and making friends.

In the elementary school years the child must become socialized to the expectations of school and learn to adapt to those demands: to sit quietly until spoken to, to raise a hand to be recognized, and to follow the teacher's directions. Other adaptive behaviors are refinements of earlier milestones in motor, social, and language development; also included are academic skills that apply to everyday functioning in the environment, such as reading danger and warning signs. Adaptive behavior is not easy to measure. Expectations for age-appropriate and situation-appropriate behavior may differ from city to city, state to state, and culture to culture. Geography, local behavior norms, and cultural differences all interact to determine if a

Expectations for appropriate behavior may differ from place to place and culture to culture.

child's behavior is appropriate in a particular locale. These factors contribute to the variability of classification status from one school district to the next.

In order for a child to be classified as having intellectual disabilities, he or she must demonstrate deficits in adaptive behavior that are comparable to the child's measured IQ. By incorporating the measure of adaptive behavior, the definition acknowledges that the child functions in various environments and potentially possesses many types of skills.

Adaptive behavior is usually measured through observation and interviews with the child's parents, guardians, or teachers. Two of the most widely used instruments are the **AAMR Adaptive Behavior Scale** (Nihira, Leland, & Lambert, 1993) and the **Vineland-II Adaptive Behavior Scales** (Cicchetti, Sparrow, & Balla 2005). Adaptive behavior scales enable the teacher, parent, or observer to determine the child's competence in a wide range of functional behaviors. The AAMR Adaptive Behavior Scale measures two major areas—independent performance of daily living skills and inappropriate or maladaptive behaviors, such as self-abuse or destructive behavior. The Vineland Adaptive Behavior Scales, Interview Editions, measure the domains of communication, daily living skills, socialization, motor skills, and maladaptive behavior. Figure 6.2 shows a section from one of these scales.

Manifestation During the Developmental Period

> Intellectual disabilities must be identified before age 18, but a child can show gains in adaptive behavior or measured intelligence.

Intellectual disabilities must be present before the age of 18. This criterion is included in the AAMR definition to distinguish intellectual disabilities from conditions in which adults suffer from impairment of brain functioning, such as from a head injury or stroke. The great majority of people with intellectual disabilities—about 80 to 85 percent—are "invisible": They do not look "different." These individuals have mild intellectual disabilities, and most of them are integrated naturally into the community. This fact adds to the difficulty of determining accurate prevalence rates and reveals one of the reasons why many children aren't identified until they reach school. Children with moderate intellectual disabilities, however, are more likely to exhibit distinguishing physical or developmental characteristics and therefore are more likely to be identified at an early age or at birth. Often the delay of certain developmental milestones, such as walking, the onset of speech, and the acquisition of self-help skills, alerts the parents and physician. Only about 7 to 10 percent of the people with intellectual disabilities fall into this category.

Classification Issues

> There are varying degrees of intellectual disabilities.

Scientists and educational professionals differentiate among individuals with varying degrees of intellectual disabilities. As with most categories, or groups of exceptional individuals who share a common label, there is tremendous variety within the group of people identified as having intellectual disabilities.

The American Association on Intellectual and Developmental Disabilities (AAIDD) uses the terms *mild, moderate, severe,* and *profound* to denote degrees of intellectual disabilities. People with mild intellectual disabilities may require support services to enable them to graduate from high school, obtain appropriate job training, and get married and raise a family. Most individuals with mild intellectual disabilities easily blend in to school and work environments. People with moderate intellectual disabilities typically require support services and often supervision to enable them to live and work in independent or semi-independent community settings. People with moderate intellectual disabilities have characteristics that are probably those you think of when you hear the term *intellectual disabilities*.

Individuals identified as having severe or profound intellectual disabilities require more extensive educational services. In this chapter, we will discuss the needs of students with mild and moderate levels of intellectual disabilities. You will learn about individuals with severe and profound intellectual disabilities in Chapter 7.

Daily Living Skills Domain, *continued*

Response Options: 2 = Usually, 1 = Sometimes or Partially, 0 = Never, DK = Don't Know

☎ Telephone Skills ● Rules, Rights, and Safety ⊘ Time and Dates ▼ Job Skills ▦ Computer Skills
$ Money Skills ☺ Restaurant Skills ☐ Television and Radio 🚌 Going Places Independently

Check for Comment below

1–3 →	☎	1	Demonstrates understanding of function of telephone (for example, pretends to talk on phone, etc.).	☎	2	1	0	DK
	☎	2	Talks to familiar person on telephone.	☎	2	1	0	DK
	☐	3	Uses TV or radio without help (for example, turns equipment on, accesses channel or station, selects program, etc.).	☐	2	1	0	DK
			Scoring Tip: You may mark "N/O" for No Opportunity if there is no TV or radio in the home.		N/O			
4 →	$	4	Counts at least 10 objects, one by one.	$	2	1	0	DK
	●	5	Is aware of and demonstrates appropriate behavior while riding in car (for example, keeps seat belt on, refrains from distracting driver, etc.).	●	2	1	0	DK
	$	6	Demonstrates understanding of the function of money (for example, says, "Money is what you need to buy things at the store"; etc.).	$	2	1	0	DK
	●	7	Uses sidewalk (where available) or shoulder of road when walking or using wheeled equipment (for example, skates, scooter, tricycle, etc.).	●	2	1	0	DK
5, 6 →	⊘	8	Demonstrates understanding of function of clock (for example, says, "Clocks tell time"; "What time can we go?"; etc.).	⊘	2	1	0	DK
	●	9	Follows household rules (for example, no running in the house, no jumping on the furniture, etc.).	●	2	1	0	DK
	▦	10	Demonstrates computer skills necessary to play games or start programs with computer turned on; does not need to turn computer on by self.	▦	2	1	0	DK
			Scoring Tip: You may mark "N/O" for No Opportunity if there is no computer in the home.		N/O			
	☎	11	Summons to the telephone the person receiving a call or indicates that the person is not available.	☎	2	1	0	DK
	$	12	Identifies penny, nickel, dime, and quarter by name when asked; does not need to know the value of coins.	$	2	1	0	DK
	●	13	Looks both ways when crossing streets or roads.	●	2	1	0	DK
7 →	⊘	14	Says current day of the week when asked.	⊘	2	1	0	DK
	●	15	Demonstrates understanding of right to personal privacy for self and others (for example, while using restroom or changing clothes, etc.).	●	2	1	0	DK
	●	16	Demonstrates knowledge of what phone number to call in an emergency when asked.	●	2	1	0	DK
	⊘	17	Tells time using a digital clock or watch.	⊘	2	1	0	DK
8 →	$	18	States value of penny (1 cent), nickel (5 cents), dime (10 cents), and quarter (25 cents).	$	2	1	0	DK
	$	19	Discriminates between bills of different denominations (for example, refers to $1 bills, $5 bills, etc., in conversation; etc.).	$	2	1	0	DK
	●	20	Obeys traffic lights and *Walk* and *Don't Walk* signs.	●	2	1	0	DK
	⊘	21	Points to current or other date on calendar when asked.	⊘	2	1	0	DK
	$	22	Demonstrates understanding that some items cost more than others (for example, says, "I have enough money to buy gum but not a candy bar"; "Which pencil costs less?"; etc.).	$	2	1	0	DK
9–11→	⊘	23	Tells time by the half hour on analog clock (for example, 1:30, 2:00, etc.).	⊘	2	1	0	DK
	☎	24	Makes telephone calls to others, using standard or cell phone.	☎	2	1	0	DK

COMMUNITY

Comments _____

FIGURE 6.2

A sample page from the Vineland Adaptive Behavior Scales (2nd edition) that includes ratings of Daily Living Skills.

Source: Extract from the Vineland Adaptive Behavior Scales, Second Edition (Vineland-II). Copyright © 2005 NCS Pearson, Inc. Reproduced with permission. All rights reserved.

An ongoing classification issue in the area of intellectual disabilities is the overrepresentation of students from minority populations among those classified as having intellectual disabilities, particularly mild intellectual disabilities. Children who are African American, and to a lesser extent, children with Native American and Hispanic heritage, are overrepresented in classes for children with intellectual disabilities even when poverty is controlled—the trend exists even in wealthy districts (Civil Rights Project, 2002). As you learned in Chapter 1, representatives from minority groups have objected to the use of IQ tests with children from both racial and language minority backgrounds (*Larry P. v. Riles, Diana v. State Board of Education*) because they believe that these children do not have equal access to the middle-class American cultural experiences that may be measured by norm-referenced IQ tests. Both the law and good practice dictate that no one test should ever be the sole grounds for diagnosis of a disability or for special class placement. Other factors, such as teacher and school authority bias, the influence or lack of influence of parents from minority backgrounds, the unequal distribution of school resources, and interpretations of actions related to testing policies, are all considered part of the complex overrepresentation issue (Civil Rights Project, 2002).

> Increasing cultural awareness in teachers may help address overrepresentation of minority students in classes for students with intellectual disabilities.

Because referrals for assessment are initiated by classroom teachers, some attempts to stem the overrepresentation of minority students in classes for children with intellectual disabilities involve increasing the cultural awareness and cultural competence of teachers before actual testing takes place. For example, Craig et al. (2000) suggest the use of teacher assistance teams trained to recognize cultural differences and evaluate instruction. One of the anticipated consequences of the Response to Intervention process mentioned in Chapter 5 is that good instruction and curriculum-based assessment can help to overcome bias and reduce disproportionate identification of students from diverse cultural background. Figure 6.3 presents a recommendation of how RTI can be used with English language learners to make the system more effective by reducing the probability of inaccurate assessment and inappropriate placement decisions. The nearby A Closer Look box also examines this issue of disproportionate representation of minorities within the category of students identified with intellectual disabilities.

Prevalence

> With fewer children classified as having mild intellectual disabilities, the mild and moderate categories are merging.

> Approximately one percent of school-age children have intellectual disabilities; most are classified with mild intellectual disabilities.

A strict interpretation of the normal curve (see Figure 6.1) would suggest a prevalence rate of about 3 percent for intellectual disabilities; that is, 3 percent of the total population would be identified as having intellectual disabilities. According to the National Dissemination Center for Children with Disabilities, 545,000 children ages 6 through 21 were identified as having intellectual disabilities (NICHCY, 2011) and 6.5 million individuals of all ages have intellectual disabilities. Factors affecting the prevalence rate include the procedures and recommendations used in school referral processes, changes in federal and state regulations over time, and the identification and elimination of potential risk factors through early intervention.

? Pause and Reflect

In this section, we discussed the importance of adaptive behavior to the definition of intellectual disabilities. How do you think the ways we identify and measure adaptive behavior influence the composition of the population of children identified with intellectual disabilities? How could adaptive behaviors differ among various communities or cultures across the country and around the world? ●

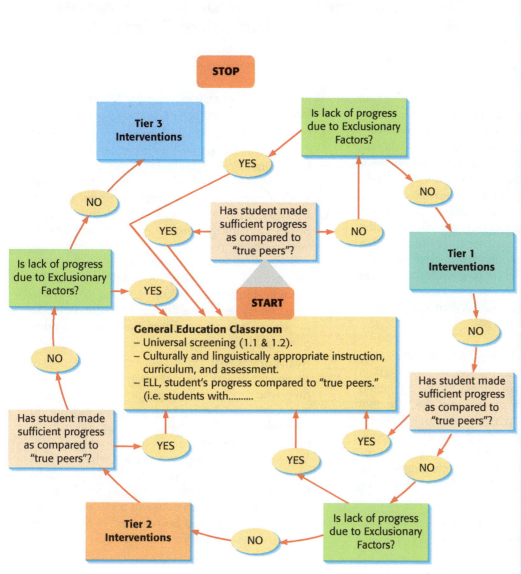

Tier 1 Interventions
– Review of student's ecology (i.e., educational history, language proficiency in L1 and L2, family education and literacy, acculturation level, SES, etc.).
– Interventions are developmentally, culturally, linguistically and experientially appropriate for targeted students and may be the classroom curriculum but a "double dose" or extension of classroom curriculum.
– Interventions provide by classroom teacher, instructional assistant or other specialist within the general education classroom in a small group.

Tier 2 Interventions
– Small group in or outside of general education classroom.
– Interventions are linguistically, culturally, and experientially appropriate.
– Interventions counter to address specific problem areas and progress is closely monitored.

Tier 3 Interventions
– Small Group or 1:1 instruction with alternative curriculum in alternative setting.
– Curriculum…and…instruction… address the specific deficit(s).
– Interventions must continue to be culturally, linguistically, and experientially appropriate.
– Standardized assessment in both L1 and L2 could be considered at this tier to identify learning profiles.

Decision-making point for special education consideration
– If the student has not made sufficient progress, a psychoeducational evaluation may be considered that links to interventions.
– Parent rights and consent are required for standardized assessments.
– All information must be provided to parents in their native language, including parent rights.
– Using a discrepancy formula approach for learning disability is appropriate for ELL students.
– Interpretation of standardized test data must be done within the context of the student's language proficiency in L1 and L2 acculturation level.
– IEP goals must consider the student's developmental, cognitive, cultural, and linguistic abilities.

"Exclusionary Factors" Disorders Not included (20 U.S.C sec. 1401(29)(cl))

Do the difficulties appear to be primarily the result of:
– vision?
– hearing?
– motor disabilities?
– mental retardation?
– emotional disturbance?
– environmental, cultural, or economic disadvantage?

Are the difficulties the result of lack of appropriate instruction in:
– reading, including the essential components of reading?
– math?
– the student's limited English proficiency?

FIGURE 6.3

RTI for English Language Learners flowchart

Source: Brown, J. E., & Doolittle, J. (2008). A cultural, linguistic, and ecological framework for Response to Intervention with English Language Learners. *Teaching Exceptional Children,* 40(5), 66–72. Figure 1/page 68 only.

A CLOSER LOOK   Disproportionate Identification of Students of Color and Intellectual Disabilities: Where Are We Now?

As we've discussed in earlier chapters, litigation and legislation related to protecting students of diverse racial, cultural, linguistic, and impoverished backgrounds from being inappropriately identified as needing special education services has been a hallmark of special education in the past three to four decades. Today, school-wide programs that provide evidence-based practices to all students, such as Response to Intervention approaches, are also intended to reduce inaccurate or inappropriate identification of any student, including students who have traditionally been overrepresented in disability categories (Skiba et al., 2008).

What do the experts think? What do the data suggest?

- **Importance:** The relationship between poverty, social class, and disproportionate identification of children of color must continue to be evaluated and understood. We don't know the role that each of these factors plays in over-identification. We cannot assume that the cause of disproportionate evaluation is poverty or social class, or that over-identification is not influenced by a student's cultural background (Artilles, Kozleski, Trent, Osher, & Ortiz, 2010).

- **Research:** Early research suggests that, in some schools, RTI systems do not result in disproportionate identification of children of color (VanderHeyden, Witt, & Gilbertson, 2007).

- **Evidence-Based Practices:** The importance of cultural context, as well as the context of school environment, must be recognized as research is conducted to determine and characterize evidence-based practices and classroom success. Interventions or curricula identified as evidence based with the general population may not reflect culturally responsive instruction—instruction that is relatable to children's social or linguistic background—or ecological validity (NCCREST Position Statement, 2005; Orosco 2010). In other words, evidence that an intervention works in general doesn't mean that it will mesh with any given child's language needs or cultural practices.

- **Measurement:** Early research on the use of curriculum-based measurement (CBM) with children who are English language learners suggests that CBM can be a valid progress monitoring measure in an RTI system, although much more research is needed (Sandberg & Reschly, 2009). Some researchers recommend that when we look at curriculum-based measures, we must realize that they represent more than just the student's ability. The interaction between a student and the environment can also be reflected in these measures (Artiles, Bal, & Thorius, 2010).

Causes of Intellectual Disabilities

Many causes of intellectual disabilities appear to be related to biological factors, but cause is uncertain in over 50 percent of cases.

There are a number of possible causes of intellectual disabilities, many of which can be linked to the risk factors described in Chapter 2. The AAIDD identifies four basic categories of risk factors: biomedical, social, behavioral, and educational (AAMR, 2002). Table 6.1 lists ten potential causes that relate to the four areas of risk factors. The list includes causes for all levels of intellectual disabilities. With the exception of category 9 (associated almost exclusively with mild intellectual disabilities), the conditions listed can result in any level of intellectual disabilities.

Biomedical Factors

Table 6.1 shows that many causes of intellectual disabilities appear to be tied to biomedical, or biological, factors, such as metabolic or nutritional disorders, post-natal brain disease, prenatal diseases, chromosomal abnormalities, perinatal/gestational conditions, and some psychiatric disorders. The more severe the level of intellectual disabilities, the more likely it is that a cause can be pinpointed. For

Table 6.1 Causes of Intellectual Disabilities

1. *Infections and intoxications.* Examples include rubella, syphilis, meningitis, and exposure to drugs, alcohol, or lead. The child may be exposed through the mother during pregnancy or may contract infections after birth. Unfortunately, fetal alcohol syndrome and drug addiction are major causes of intellectual disabilities.

2. *Trauma or physical agents.* Injuries to the child that occur before, during, or after birth fall into this category. Hypoxia (deprivation of oxygen) and injuries received through child abuse are examples.

3. *Metabolic or nutritional disorders.* Examples of these disorders include phenylketonuria (PKU), Tay-Sachs disease, and galactosemia. In disorders of this type, the child's inability to metabolize or tolerate certain elements in food results in brain injury.

4. *Postnatal gross brain disease.* This refers to tumors that occur after birth.

5. *Prenatal diseases or conditions of unknown origin.* Examples of conditions found in this category include hydrocephalus and microcephaly. Hydrocephalus refers to the presence of cerebrospinal fluid in the skull, which increases the size of the skull while causing pressure on the brain; microcephaly describes a condition in which the skull is significantly smaller than normal.

6. *Chromosomal abnormality.* Chromosomal abnormalities refer to an unusual pattern of genetic material on one or more of the child's chromosomes. Two of the more well-known syndromes associated with chromosomal abnormalities are Down syndrome and fragile-X syndrome. Both of these syndromes usually result in distinct physical characteristics and intellectual disabilities. Fragile-X syndrome is found mostly in males (because of the defective X chromosome). Females carry the chromosome and some may experience mild intellectual disabilities. In some instances, these syndromes appear as recessive genetic traits; in others (such as the most frequently occurring type of Down syndrome), the abnormality is associated with other factors, such as the age of the mother.

7. *Other perinatal/gestational conditions.* Two prominent examples in this category are prematurity and low birth weight. Although many infants do not suffer negative effects from these conditions, both prematurity and low birth weight are risk factors for intellectual disabilities. As you might expect, the more extreme these conditions are, the higher the level of risk.

8. *Presence of psychiatric disorders.* There is an increased risk of dual diagnosis of individuals with some psychiatric disorders, such as depression and intellectual disabilities.

9. *Environmental influences.* This category includes causes that are described as cultural-familial. We will describe this category in greater detail later in this section.

10. *Other unknown causes.* Because it is difficult to identify the causes of intellectual disabilities in many children, we suspect that there are causes that have yet to be discovered.

Source: H. J. Grossman (1983). *Classification in Intellectual Disabilities*. Washington, DC: American Association on Mental Deficiency.

persons with moderate or severe intellectual disabilities, biological causes can be pinpointed in 60 to 75 percent of the cases (Batshaw and Rose, 1997). Beirne-Smith, Ittenbach, and Patton (2002) point out that there is no certain cause in at least 50 percent of cases of intellectual disabilities. This is particularly true for individuals with mild intellectual disabilities.

As we mentioned in Chapter 2, prenatal care, genetic counseling, and appropriate immunizations can help prevent many disabilities, including intellectual disabilities. The medical community continues to identify ways to prevent or ameliorate intellectual disabilities through genetic research or very early (often prenatal) treatment. For example, the effects of hydrocephalus can be greatly minimized by surgery in which a shunt is implanted in the head of the infant prior to birth, allowing the fluid to drain away before brain damage occurs. Another example involves the identification of phenylketonuria (PKU), a metabolic disorder. All hospitals now require a test for PKU at birth. If the condition is present, the child is put on a specific diet and intellectual disabilities can be avoided. One clearly identifiable cause of intellectual disabilities is Down syndrome, an example of a

The relative importance of heredity and the environment in intellectual development has been debated for years.

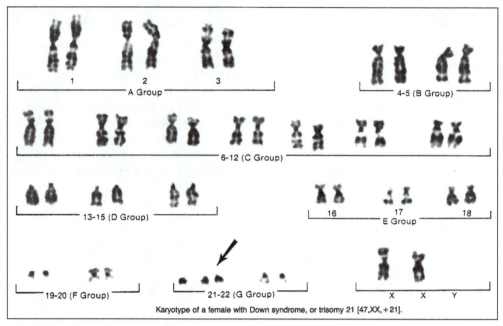

Karyotype of a female with Down syndrome, or trisomy 21 [47,XX,+21].

An extra chromosome can result from an incomplete division of the twenty-three pairs of chromosomes during the formation of an egg cell. The extra chromosome at the 21st position results in trisomy 21—the most common form of Down syndrome.

S. Pueschel [1983]. The child with Down syndrome. In Mel Levine, W. Carey, A. Crocker, & R. Gross (eds.), *Developmental Behavior Pediatrics.* Philadelphia: Saunders. Copyright 1983 by W.B. Saunders and Company. Reprinted by permission.

A CLOSER LOOK  Questions About Down Syndrome

1. What is Down syndrome? Although there are several types of Down syndrome, all types are a result of an extra copy or an extra part of the 21st chromosome in an individual's cells. This extra genetic material can result in intellectual disabilities and distinctive physical features and characteristics. Down syndrome is associated with congenital heart defects, gastrointestinal difficulties, and a variety of physiological concerns.

2. What causes Down syndrome? Down syndrome is the most common genetic condition. Estimates of occurrence range from 1 in 691 to 1 in 1,000 live births. Typically, we associate the occurrence of Down syndrome with increased maternal age. Although the incidence of Down syndrome is strongly correlated with the age of the mother, over 80 percent of children with Down syndrome are born to mothers younger than 35. Sometimes, Down syndrome is a chance occurrence.

3. What are the educational opportunities for children with Down syndrome? The possibilities for individuals with Down syndrome have increased greatly in the past few decades. Because of their distinctive physical characteristics, children with Down syndrome are identified at birth. Years ago, babies with Down syndrome were routinely placed in residential or institutional settings with little expectations for independent life in the community. Now, we know that most children with Down syndrome experience mild to moderate cognitive disabilities. All children, including those with Down syndrome, display a range of abilities. Some will do well academically, others will find community-based jobs or supported work, and others will become actors in television shows.

(*Sources:* Medline Plus, 2003; National Down Syndrome Society, 2011.)

For information, news, and research related to Down syndrome, visit the website of the National Down Syndrome Society.

chromosomal abnormality. Read A Closer Look, "Questions About Down Syndrome," to learn more about the effects of this condition on children and families.

Social, Behavioral, and Educational Factors

It often is difficult to pinpoint specific causal relationships between intellectual disabilities and general environmental factors. The effects of social and educational factors such as social interaction, cultural differences, and socioeconomic conditions on cognitive abilities often appear to be correlational in nature. For example, although poverty alone does not imply poor nutrition, poor health care, or a poor social environment, many of these risk factors do tend to occur together.

You may have heard about the ongoing debate over the role of environment versus the role of heredity in determining intelligence. Do smart parents have smart children because the children inherit intellectual ability, or do their surroundings encourage the fullest possible development of their intelligence? Could students with mild intellectual disabilities inherit low intellectual ability from their parents, or could a bright child be affected by adverse environmental conditions? The relative importance of heredity and the environment in intellectual development has been discussed, debated, and researched for many years.

The current thinking in this area represents a compromise. Each child probably comes into the world with a potential range of intellectual ability, and the environment in which the child is reared helps to determine the extent to which that ability is expressed (MacMillan, Semmel, & Gerber, 1994). In other words, it is likely that heredity and environment *interact* to result in the demonstrated intellectual ability of most children. Certainly, the environment (including teaching) can affect how any child's cognitive, behavioral, and physical skills develop throughout his or her lifetime.

When we look at the specific environmental and behavioral causes outlined by the AAIDD (also presented in Table 6.1), however, we see specific maternal behavior related to the use of intoxicants that can have clearly documented effects on unborn children. The link between these causes—maternal drinking, smoking, and drug use—can be easily and all too frequently linked to intellectual disabilities in children. Alcohol consumption by a pregnant woman frequently results in fetal alcohol syndrome (FAS), a syndrome often accompanied by intellectual disabilities, extensive behavior difficulties, and distinctive physical characteristics. FAS is now the leading cause of intellectual disabilities in this country.

Pause and Reflect

In this section, we discussed the importance of the child's environment as a source of support for his or her inherited potential. Think of the ways you might enrich a young child's environment to support social, physical, and cognitive growth. ●

Characteristics of Individuals with Intellectual Disabilities

Intellectual disabilities are developmental disabilities; that is, they affect a child's overall development in a relatively uniform manner. When we look at the effects of intellectual disabilities on any individual, we must keep in mind not only the obvious things, such as severity and complicating factors, but also the child's own personality and determination. Characteristics are generalized descriptions of behavior. Any specific characteristic we present may or may not occur in a certain individual with intellectual disabilities.

Cognitive Development

By definition, intellectual disabilities can be interpreted to mean a low level of cognitive ability. Intelligence tests are used to provide an overall measure of cognitive ability, and persons with intellectual disabilities are identified as having deficits in the ability to learn.

The ability to learn can be described in many ways. One aspect of learning is capacity—how much information can be processed at one time. Generally, children with intellectual disabilities process smaller amounts of information than their typically developing classmates. Another aspect of learning is the ability to engage in problem solving. Individuals with intellectual disabilities may rely on a limited set of problem-solving strategies, which can cause difficulty when new, different, or complex problems arise (Wehmeyer & Kelchner, 1994). Students with intellectual disabilities may also have difficulty using cognitive skills such as metacognition, memory, and attention.

● *Metacognition and Memory*   Most students with learning problems, including intellectual disabilities, have difficulty in the areas of metacognition and memory, particularly short-term memory. Metacognition refers to the ability to identify how one learns and to evaluate, monitor, and adapt the learning process. These difficulties in metacognition and memory, therefore, translate into problems in planning, evaluating, and organizing information.

Let's look at a student learning to use a calculator for multiplication. The student will say and practice the steps involved in pushing the calculator buttons several times (rehearsal, a memory strategy). He will determine if he needs more practice (performance evaluation, a metacognitive strategy). He will say the problem aloud as he enters it into his calculator (rehearsal, a memory strategy). He may then work the problem by hand to double-check his answer and his ability to use the calculator correctly (awareness of need to evaluate performance and method of evaluating performance, a metacognitive strategy). If he has done the procedure incorrectly, he might rehearse the skill some more or create some type of mnemonic device to help him remember the procedure (metacognitive awareness and memory strategy).

A student with intellectual disabilities is more likely to have difficulty realizing the conditions or actions that will help her or him learn or retain the material (Merrill, 1990). Given the calculator activity, the student might not think to practice or rehearse the process first, not think to evaluate her or his performance or know how to do it, and not realize that more practice or a new memory approach might be helpful. Because of these cognitive effects, we must focus instruction on *how* to learn as well as on *what* to learn so that the student can achieve the greatest possible level of independence.

Memory and metacognitive skills are sometimes closely related. Before students can use strategies for aiding memory, they must be aware that such strategies are needed. Consequently, a very important way to improve the learning abilities of students with intellectual disabilities is to teach a student when specific strategies for remembering should be used.

● *Attention*   Intellectual disabilities is often characterized by attentional deficits—the child has difficulty coming to attention, maintaining attention, and paying selective attention (Westling & Fox, 2000; Zeaman & House, 1963, 1979). In many instances, the problem is not that the child *won't* pay attention, but that he or she *can't* pay attention or doesn't know how to attend. It is possible, however, to minimize the effects of attentional deficits on learning.

A student with a deficit in coming to attention will experience difficulty focusing on the task at hand and, in the case of independent work, will have problems getting started. For some students this may be a result of having difficulty diverting their attention from distractions or previous activities. Other students may have difficulty recognizing the signs, directions, or task requirements for a new activity. It is often helpful for teachers to use clear and unambiguous signals that indicate the beginning or ending of activities and that specify task requirements. These signals may be phrases, such as "eyes on me," or actions, such as clapping the hands.

Many students with intellectual disabilities have a shorter attention span than other children their age. A child experiencing difficulty maintaining attention will do much better on long tasks (such as practicing problems in arithmetic) if the task is broken into shorter segments that can be done throughout the day rather than all at once. Sometimes, gradually increasing the amount of time a child is required to pay attention will help to lengthen a child's attention span. Children with intellectual disabilities, like all children, will be able to attend longer to material that is interesting and attractive.

A student with problems maintaining attention may need frequent direction to reorient him or her back to the task at hand. One way teachers try to deal with this problem is to establish a signal that can be used instead of constant verbal direction. A clap, or a tap on the board or desk, can be used to remind the child to refocus. Teachers also try different types of written cues, including colored marks, underlining, arrows, and so on, to help children focus on starting points in written material.

In the area of selective attention—attending to the key issues—students with intellectual disabilities often have difficulty identifying the critical aspects or content of information. A young child might not be able to identify the distinguishing characteristics or dimensions of a letter or word. An older student might miss the key words in the directions for a test.

Some ways you can accentuate important information for students include:

- Underlining key words, using color or exaggeration to help draw attention to the words
- Using key words to cue the student that what you are about to say is important
- Presenting less extraneous information during initial teaching
- Teaching the student to recognize and use the cues you have provided

> Teachers must focus instruction on *how* as well as *what* students learn.

● *Generalization* Most students with intellectual disabilities experience difficulty transferring skills from one context to another. In other words, once a student has learned a specific skill in the classroom using certain materials, he or she may have difficulty performing that skill another way, in another setting, or with other materials (Polloway & Patton, 1997). Sometimes, the problem of **skill transfer,** or **generalization,** can be relatively minor and easy to remedy. For example, some children simply become confused by a change in format or materials and just need to be told that they can use the same skill or strategy in the new situation. Another possibility is that the novel, or new, environments need to be adjusted in order to support the newly acquired skills. Children may be less likely to use a new skill (waiting and raising a hand to ask for a pencil), if it is not as efficient as an old one (getting out of a seat to take a pencil off the teacher's desk).

> Generalizing, or transferring skills from one setting to another, is often difficult for students with intellectual disabilities.

You can maximize the potential for generalization by incorporating real-world materials into your instruction. For example, a student who has learned all the basic addition and subtraction skills may not realize that those same skills can be used to balance a checkbook, so you might have students practice using real checkbooks. Use real materials whenever they are readily available—it makes learning more meaningful for all students and helps to address the problem of poor skill transfer.

The child with moderate intellectual disabilities may experience a great deal of difficulty understanding that the pencil-and-paper addition he or she does in the classroom is the same basic skill used in counting money or adding up points in a board game. For students with moderate intellectual disabilities, the use of actual materials to teach needed or desired skills has even more importance. Teachers should never assume that a generalization of responses will occur without specific instruction. See Teaching Strategies, "Strategies for Enhancing Cognitive Skills," for a summary of instructional strategies.

Language Development

> Children with intellectual disabilities may experience a delay in language development.

One early sign of mild or moderate intellectual disabilities is a delay in the acquisition of communication skills. Children with intellectual disabilities acquire language at a slower rate than other children, usually have limited vocabularies, and tend to use a restricted number of sentence constructions. Speech problems are also found more frequently in children with intellectual disabilities. A survey of services provided to elementary-age students with mild intellectual disabilities found that 90 percent of the population surveyed had been identified as needing speech or language services, especially in the area of articulation (Epstein et al., 1989). Structural differences, such as tongue size or facial musculature, can affect the way some individuals pronounce certain sounds.

Physical Development

The physical health and motor skills of individuals with intellectual disabilities are more likely to be affected as the degree of intellectual disabilities increases. Thus, people with moderate intellectual disabilities are more likely to have noticeable physical differences than those with mild intellectual disabilities. The same rule holds true when we consider the existence of additional disabling conditions, many of which, like cerebral palsy and epilepsy, involve physical ability and overall health. The greater the degree of intellectual disabilities, the more likely it is that another disabling condition will accompany it.

> People with intellectual disabilities may have physical health problems.

Some of the specific syndromes that cause intellectual disabilities result in accompanying physical impairments. The most common of these, Down syndrome, frequently results in structural heart defects, which in most cases can be corrected surgically. The incidence of hearing and visual impairments in children with Down syndrome is also considerably higher than in the general population. Although at one time these physical disabilities greatly shortened the prospective

Teaching Strategies & Accommodations

Strategies for Enhancing Cognitive Skills—Metacognition and Memory

- Teach memory strategies, such as rehearsing and chunking information, if students are not using them.
- Teach students when to use memory strategies or provide cues for using them.

- Gradually increase the amount of time you expect children to attend to a task.
- Accentuate key content and directions for the students through the use of response prompts or cues.

Attention

- Establish clear signals to orient students to the task or lesson.
- Break up long instructional segments or tasks into several short sessions.

Generalization

- Teach students to use the skills they have learned in one class in other classes or settings.
- Use real-world materials to help students generalize basic skills to realistic situations.

life span of people with Down syndrome, medical technology has enabled most individuals to live well into adulthood.

Many students with mild intellectual disabilities require no extra programs or assistance to participate in sports or physical education activities. Other students, however, require more specialized physical activities, such as adaptive physical education, that include specific activities designed to improve strength and coordination. For many students, specific instruction in games or activities such as swimming or racquetball may be part of their educational program. Education geared not only to the activity itself, but also toward appropriate independent behavior in a gym or pool setting is important to helping students learn patterns of behavior that can be used both during the school years and into adulthood (Modell & Valdez, 2002). Many communities have organized activities designed specifically for persons with intellectual disabilities or other disabilities, such as Special Olympics. These programs provide additional opportunities for persons with mental and physical disabilities to compete in track and field events; however, integrated activities are always preferable to segregated ones.

Social and Emotional Development

Research has indicated some variability in the extent to which students with mild intellectual disabilities are accepted and liked by their peers (Siperstein, Leffert, & Widaman, 1996). It is important to remember that every child or adolescent, with or without intellectual disabilities, has personal and physical characteristics that can assist or detract from that individual's popularity and acceptance.

> Students with intellectual disabilities may have difficulty interpreting social cues.

Students with intellectual disabilities may display delays in the development of communication skills (Wehmeyer & Kelchner, 1994). Children with intellectual disabilities also may have difficulty interpreting social cues, particularly if multiple cues are presented at once, or if incongruent cues and behaviors are present (Leffert, Siperstein, & Millikan, 2000). All these characteristics can contribute to ineffective interaction with others, but they can be addressed, in part, through specific instruction in communication and social skills. Some research suggests that the educational placement of students with intellectual disabilities can affect their social acceptance by peers. For example, Buysse, Goldman, and Skinner (2002) found that young children with disabilities are more likely to have typically developing friends if they are in preschool settings that include large numbers of children without disabilities.

Most social behaviors are learned, just as other skills are learned. Sometimes, students with mild and moderate intellectual disabilities display **immature behavior,** which generally reflects an inability to control emotions and delay gratification. Students with immature behaviors may have a low tolerance for frustration, cry easily, and do socially inappropriate things (Epstein et al., 1989). These behaviors may indicate a lack of appropriate social learning.

Studies have demonstrated that the behavior of students with mild and moderate intellectual disabilities can be changed through behavior modification techniques and social skills instruction. With instruction, students can learn appropriate behaviors by modeling the behavior of peers in the classroom. This can pay off in improved social relations with others and an improved perception of self.

Many children with intellectual disabilities may have the skills to perform appropriately, or according to the social norms in school or recreational settings, but they may display a lack of self-control or self-management of their performance. Self-control, self-awareness, and self-management of behavior are among the chief concerns of parents of children with cognitive disabilities (Kolb & Hanley-Maxwell, 2003). Many recent instructional programs demonstrate that students with mild and moderate intellectual disabilities can learn self-management strategies to improve behaviors, ranging from recording and evaluating performance of academic tasks, to initiating appropriate social interaction, to improving on-task behaviors in the classroom (Firman, Beare, & Lloyd, 2002; Hughes et al., 2002;

Children learn social behavior from each other as they participate in everyday school and play activities.

Mithaug, 2002). We discussed self-monitoring in Chapter 5, and the same types of procedures were not only found to be effective in teaching students to manage behavior, but also easy to implement in classrooms. Evidence of current applications of self-management can be found in the Assistive Technology Focus box on p. 223.

Effects on the Family

The realization that a child has intellectual disabilities may be either sudden or gradual, as you learned in Chapter 3. Sometimes, when a child is very ill at birth or when recognizable physical signs are present, the parents know about their child's disability before they leave the hospital. More often, however, the clues come slowly. The child may not sit, stand, and walk at the expected ages and may not understand language or use words at the expected times. But there are many differences in the way children develop, and parents often postpone acknowledging that their child is different from others.

> Most children with mild intellectual disabilities are first diagnosed at school.

It is in the school environment that most children with mild intellectual disabilities are identified and the effects on the family are fully realized. Parents may confer with their child's teacher or receive a letter from the school administrator requesting permission to assess their child for possible provision of special education services. A discussion with the school psychologist after testing, or during the IEP meeting, may be the first place that the parents hear the words *intellectual disabilities* applied to their child.

For some parents, diagnosis, labeling, and the provision of special services will come as a relief; they usually are the ones who have suspected that their child has learning difficulties. Others will react negatively to the term intellectual disabilities. These words evoke a special set of reactions from parents, perhaps because most people have little knowledge of intellectual disabilities or of persons with intellectual disabilities. Skinner et al. (1999) found that a majority of Latino mothers who wrote narratives about their relationship with their children with intellectual disabilities reported that the children brought about positive change in their lives and were also viewed as a blessing from God. Although both cultural and religious background may influence a parent's reaction to a child with a disability, ultimately, each parent reacts in his or her own way.

> Many parents of children with intellectual disabilities find that support groups help them manage stress and access resources.

Because the most identifiable causes of intellectual disabilities increasingly are related to substance abuse by parents, parent reactions often now include responsibility and guilt. Some parents assume responsibility for their child's disability without cause; others clearly can link their behavior to their child's intellectual disabilities. Often, mothers who abuse drugs or alcohol during pregnancy lose their children, at least temporarily, through the courts and foster care system.

Another possible cause of negative reactions by parents is that their concept of intellectual disabilities includes an inability to learn and limited potential for a fulfilling life. It can be particularly difficult for parents who have perceptions of this type to attach the label of intellectual disabilities to their child—a child who seemed just like all the other children until he or she reached school. Accepting intellectual disabilities, for many parents, involves a significant adjustment in their expectations and hopes for the child. Of course, these adjustments are often based on the parents' perceptions of intellectual disabilities rather than their knowledge. Once parents acquire a more realistic concept of intellectual disabilities, they are often able to raise their expectations and focus on the strengths and abilities of their child.

Greg and Tierny Fairchild have a young daughter, Naia, who has Down syndrome. The Fairchilds share their life—their decisions, struggles, and many joys—through words and pictures. The following excerpt from *Choosing Naia: A Family's Journey* (Zuckoff, 2002) gives a glimpse of Greg's thoughts as he contemplates the future for his daughter:

> His basket filled with food and diapers, Greg ambled toward the Stop & Shop checkout line. It was morning, and the store wasn't crowded. He could have chosen any line, but he was drawn to one in particular. He placed his groceries on the moving belt and looked past the cashier to a smiling young woman at the far end of the counter. "Hello," Greg said. The young woman looked up from her work as a bagger. "Hi," she said sweetly. Greg wished he could tell her all the things in his heart. He wished he could ask a hundred questions about her life, her job, her family. How she got to work each day. Where she lived. What she did for fun. He wished he could ask about the friends he hoped she had. He wished he could tell her about his six-month-old daughter. He said none of those things. It would have seemed odd, intrusive. So he left it at hello. When her work was done and his groceries were neatly packed, Greg said, "Thanks." He gave her a warm smile. She smiled back. The bagger's name was Sarah, and she had Down syndrome. (p. 207)

Parents of children with intellectual disabilities, like most parents of children with disabilities, often seek support from parent groups, gain knowledge from classes, books, and journals, and become aware of available services through contact with schools, associations, and service agencies (see the Useful Resources section at the end of this chapter). In fact, parents of children with specific conditions, such as Down syndrome or Prader-Willi syndrome, often find that they must play the role of "expert" in presenting information specific to their children's syndrome to the educational community (Fidler, Hodapp, & Dykens, 2002). Balancing parenting roles and responsibilities and using resources effectively are important life-management strategies used by parents of children with disabilities (Scorgie, Wilgosh, & McDonald, 1999). Unfortunately, little research has been done to identify interventions that can be used to provide emotional support to families (Friend, Summers, & Turnbull, 2009).

The presence of a child with intellectual disabilities can affect family interactions and relationships. A common concern of parents is that children with intellectual disabilities will monopolize their attention and disrupt sibling relationships. Individuals with moderate intellectual disabilities may demand more time of their parents than do other children. For example, it may take young children longer to acquire independence in skills such as eating and toileting, and parents may spend more time in schools with older children due to IEP development, curriculum planning, and behavior management issues. All families respond to these demands differently. Overall, the research in this area seems to suggest that siblings of children with intellectual disabilities find ways to get the attention and social interaction they need (Stoneman et al., 1988). The interactions of siblings within families reflect

© Jeff Greenberg/Photo Edit

the added child-care responsibilities of older siblings, and the sibling relationships are often characterized by a strong caregiving or dominant role on the part of the sibling without intellectual disabilities. As individuals with intellectual disabilities continue to receive educations that increasingly stress independent activities and functional skills, it will be interesting to see how sibling relationships change.

? Pause and Reflect

Teachers often assume that once a skill is learned, the child will be able to apply it in all situations. Yet, one of the characteristics of children with intellectual disabilities is difficulty in generalizing or transferring new skills from one situation or task to another. Consider the many ways you can prompt students to apply skills in other settings. ●

Teaching Strategies and Accommodations

Educational programs for many students with intellectual disabilities emphasize preparing students for life after school.

Teachers are expected to provide meaningful educational experiences—experiences that will help prepare students for life on their own—and to do it in the most inclusive setting possible. In many educational settings, the classroom teacher is responsible for the majority of service delivery to students with intellectual disabilities. Interaction, communication, and professional cooperation between the special education teacher and classroom teacher are becoming the most important factors in the successful educational experience of students with intellectual disabilities. Many current and upcoming educational issues, therefore, focus on the cooperative nature of educational programming and the development of challenging educational environments for full inclusion.

Early Intervention

Although diagnosis of severe intellectual disabilities is typically made at birth or within the first year of life, children with moderate or mild intellectual disabilities are more likely to be identified at a somewhat later age. The advent of Public Law (P.L.) 99-457, however, stresses early identification of children with disabilities and provision of appropriate services.

P.L. 99-457 (see Chapter 1) states that children identified as developmentally delayed, at risk, or having an identified disability between birth and the age of 3 are eligible to receive services. Most students in this age range receive services from the agency designated by the state to handle infant programs. Identified 3- and 4-year-olds are eligible for preschool programs through the local educational agency. As you might expect, one of the goals of early intervention is to reduce the effects of intellectual disabilities on learning and basic skills acquisition. Early educational programming can provide students with a head start in basic skills and provide positive and successful learning experiences. In spite of our goals as educators, however, some research indicates that 93 percent of preschool children identified as having mild intellectual disabilities were still receiving special education services in the fourth grade (Delgado, 2009). Interestingly, although still in special education, over half of the children in this study were identified with another disability "label" by the fourth grade. This does illustrate how difficult it is to identify mild disabilities accurately at an early age and how important it is to keep expectations for all children high.

Curriculum

Curriculum options for students with mild and moderate intellectual disabilities range from the basic learning skills (reading and math) and content-area skills (science and social studies) taught in the regular classroom, to functional life skills designed to help students learn the work, domestic, or leisure skills needed for independent living. Curriculum decisions should be based on the anticipated outcomes, or expected goals, of education for the individual student. The focus should be on the individual's abilities and preferences, and not on the particular level of intellectual disabilities. For example, the anticipated outcome for a student who is capable of doing class work in the regular class and has a high level of basic skills may be to graduate and receive a high-school diploma. This student may be best served by taking basic academic courses in the regular curriculum, which might also include some vocational classes and training. The anticipated outcome for another student might be to live and work in a supervised community setting. This student would follow a full-time curriculum devoted to life skills, which might include training in social skills; interpersonal communication; domestic skills such as cooking, managing finances, and cleaning; using community transportation; and prevocational and vocational preparation, including on-the-job training.

It is important to keep in mind this wide range of potential outcomes and personal interests and abilities as we examine curriculum options for students with mild to moderate intellectual disabilities. The three types of curriculum we will discuss are academic content, life skills, and transition programs. Although these are examined separately, you will see that many students could benefit from all three types of programs.

● **The Core Academic Curriculum**   Although you may not think of academics when you think of the term intellectual disabilities, you may be surprised to know that many students with mild intellectual disabilities participate in general education classes for all or part of the school day. In elementary school, students may attend basic content classes and receive extra support in reading or math through in-class instruction or through a resource program. Some students will benefit more than others from general instructional programs. In middle or secondary school, some students will continue in academic classes in pursuit of an academic diploma. Others will take courses that are less academic and more vocational in nature to best address their individualized educational goals.

Is a student with intellectual disabilities expected to acquire the content delivered in the general education classroom? For example, is a student with intellectual disabilities in a 10th-grade biology class expected to do the same lab work, read the same text, and complete the same tests as the other students in the class? There

The focus of a student's instruction will often determine his or her educational setting.

 TeachSource VIDEO CASE

How Do We Build Successful Experiences for Included Students with Intellectual Disabilities?

Students with intellectual disabilities can meet goals for access to the core curriculum and social integration in inclusive classrooms. Visit Chapter 6 on the CourseMate website and watch the video case "Lauren and Beth: Serving Students with Special Needs in Inclusive Learning Environments." Watch two different teachers and mothers discuss how to build success for a 5-year-old and a 14-year-old. What do you see as the essentials for successful inclusion?

is no single answer to that question—the response depends on the student and the course. In general, though, many students with mild intellectual disabilities do participate in the general education curriculum. Because students with mild intellectual disabilities participate in high-stakes assessments based on the general education curriculum, they spend more time working in the core curriculum than ever before. Accommodations or adaptations of content are typically necessary, particularly as students get older and the material becomes more abstract and difficult. Most of these accommodations should reflect an emphasis on the academic skills necessary for students to meet their life goals and independence. For example, science content could focus more on self health care and management, or plant care and gardening, especially if a related career is possible.

The extent to which an individual student participates in the core curriculum, versus or in addition to the other curricular emphases presented below, is a point of professional debate. Many believe that participation in the core curriculum is essentially the mandate of both NCLB and IDEA. Some argue that the core curriculum, even if the content is "watered down," is good preparation for postsecondary opportunities and jobs, and reflects high expectations and, consequently, higher performance. Others argue that we are spending time teaching skills that are minimally useful to many students with intellectual disabilities (e.g., algebra, English literature) while neglecting to teach skills critical for independent living. Future research will continue to evaluate programs and postsecondary outcomes for students with intellectual disabilities in order to provide more direction for educators (Bouck, 2009; Walker, Uphold, Richter, & Test, 2010). What do you think?

Functional academics are basic academic skills, such as reading, writing, and arithmetic, taught in the context of real-life or community activities. For example, reading skills might be presented within the context of reading menus, movie listings, clothing labels, signs, and directions; and arithmetic skills within the context of paying for food in restaurants or grocery stores, using a soft drink machine, planning a weekly budget, or balancing a checkbook. Functional academics taught in a separate class setting are more likely to be tied to specific tasks—for example, a class that focuses on cooking and the related reading, math, and health skills corresponding to planning, shopping for, and preparing meals. This type of curriculum should be integrated with using the target skills—for example, actually measuring ingredients for baking—so that the content is meaningful. At the elementary level, a functional curriculum would focus on content related to independent performance in home and community environments (preparing snacks, finding video games, keeping track of the baseball score, choosing a movie).

Older children with mild intellectual disabilities and many students with more moderate levels of intellectual disabilities tend to have a curriculum plan that focuses more comprehensively on the skills necessary for everyday life. Although these students may experience a range of school experiences, most of their education may be guided by a life-skills curriculum.

● *Life-Skills Curriculum* A **life-skills curriculum** is intended to provide the skills necessary to maximize a student's ability to live and work independently. Because students with moderate intellectual disabilities may require support and have difficulty in transfer or skill generalization, they often can benefit from a comprehensive curriculum that includes self-care skills, community access skills, social interaction and communication skills, physical and motor development (including recreation and leisure skills), and specific job training (Beirne-Smith, Ittenbach, & Patton, 2002; Drew, Logan, & Hardman, 1992.)

Instruction in a life-skills curriculum encompasses the essential areas of everyday life. These areas are referred to as *domains*. Although you may see different terms used to describe these areas, they can be identified as domestic, recreation and leisure, vocational, and community living. The development of the curriculum involves:

> A functional or life-skills curriculum provides the skills necessary for students to live and work independently.

> The curriculum for students with moderate intellectual disabilities emphasizes self-care skills, social interaction, recreation and leisure skills, and job training.

- Looking at the specific skills that the student needs in these areas
- Identifying the specific skills in which the student needs instruction
- Providing that instruction within the context of the particular domain

In other words, the curriculum is generated by the student's environment rather than by a list of skills found in basal texts or regular curriculum guides. To identify the components of a curriculum, the teacher must assess the environment by observing and recording the exact skills needed in a specific home, recreation, or potential work setting. Once these skills are identified, the teacher will determine which ones the student already knows how to perform. Instruction will focus on those skills the students cannot yet perform independently. (See Teaching Strategies, "Environmental Assessment of Skills for Instruction," for an example of curriculum planning.)

Instruction involves presenting the skill in a naturally occurring context and integrating it with other skills found in that setting (Snell & Brown, 2000). All instruction is useful, meaningful, and motivating to the student; teaching is focused on usable skills that can be practiced often.

Teaching Strategies & Accommodations

Environmental Assessment of Skills for Instruction

Student: Patricia Kelly, age 16
Environment: Home
Domains: Domestic/vocational
Rationale: Patricia is responsible for watching her two younger siblings (ages 8 and 10) every day from 3:30 to 5:30. Many of the skills required can also be used as a basis for employment in child-care fields. All the skills can be used to address future parenting needs.

Area 1: Recreation—skills for instruction

Suggest activities appropriate for indoor play.
Check toys and play materials to make sure they are safe and age appropriate.
Check on children playing indoors every 15 to 20 minutes if they are not within sight.
Keep children in sight or hearing distance at all times when they are playing outside.
Recognize and prohibit rough or dangerous outside play.
Guide children in their selection of after-school snacks or prepare suitable snacks for them.
Play with children.

Area 2: Child management—skills for instruction

Know household rules for indoor/outdoor play.
Remind children of rules when they return from school.

Enforce rules.
Know and use only management strategies suggested by parents.
Know and use a few plans or "tricks" for diverting children's attention.
Give accurate report of children's behavior to parents.

Area 3: Safety—skills for instruction

Identify and clear away unsafe debris, broken toys, etc., both inside and outside the house.
Check premises to ensure that potentially harmful materials are out of children's reach (matches, choking hazards, cleaning materials).
Be familiar with and experienced in administering emergency first aid procedures.
Know how to administer emergency procedures when a child is choking.
Distinguish between a mild incident and an emergency, and act according to plan.
Read labels to determine if a substance is poisonous.
Locate and use fire extinguisher and know fire evacuation plan.
Locate and call appropriate persons in case of concern or emergency (includes neighbor, parents, local emergency number).

Community-based instruction allows students to receive instruction in meaningful and motivating settings.

The community itself is playing an ever-increasing role in curriculum content for students with intellectual disabilities. One goal of **community-based instruction** is placing students in job settings that are found in their local community. In addition, the community provides opportunities for the functional application of basic skills. For example, teachers can use menus, job applications, store names, movie theater marquees, bank books, bowling scorecards, and city maps (to name a few items) from the local community to assist in developing skills that can be used immediately and practiced repeatedly in the student's home environment. The regular classroom teacher should find that using these resources facilitates learning and provides motivation for all the students in the class.

A third role for the community is to serve as a source of activities. A series of local activities—using the post office, visiting the doctor and dentist, applying for a job, using the public recreation center, and eating at a favorite restaurant—could be the basic curriculum components for the school year, and all the academic, social, communication, and self-care skills needed for each activity could be taught as the class participated in that activity.

● *Transition Programming*   Many people with mild intellectual disabilities integrate themselves successfully into the life of their community with little or no outside assistance. They find jobs and do them well; they marry and begin their own families. Others, though, continue to need the help and support of social agencies. More and more, emphasis is being placed on the skills that young people need to make the transition from school to the working world. There is also a focus on the factors related to quality of life: social adjustment and integration into all aspects of the community. Research suggests the importance of community employment and living to the self-esteem of individuals with intellectual disabilities (Griffin et al., 1996). The educational experiences that address the movement from school to work and from home or residential school to independent community living are referred to as **transitional programming.**

Transitional programming addresses the experiences students need to move on to life after school.

All secondary students with intellectual disabilities now have a separate component of their IEP that identifies and describes the transition training they will receive. The 2004 reauthorization of IDEA [20 U.S.C. 1416(a)(3)(B)] mandates a more comprehensive, measureable, and specific transition plan than earlier versions of the law, resulting in more research on the identification and promotion of effective transition practices. The importance of transition in the curriculum of

During community-based instruction, a student learns work skills while he is on the job.

© Dana White/Photo Edit

students with intellectual disabilities is likely to continue to increase as specific needs of adults with mild intellectual disabilities are identified. Greater cooperation between the educational system, the business world, and adult social agencies will help to improve transition services.

Many professionals assert the importance of the student's voice in effective transition programming. **Self-determination,** which describes the active role the student takes, includes decision-making and self-advocacy, which may need to be taught to students with intellectual disabilities. Many educators feel that a deep level of participation by the student is critical to a successful transition plan (Devlieger & Trach, 1999; Hasazi, Furney, & DeStefano, 1999). Spencer and Sands (1999) found that student, school, and family factors, including job-related skills, ability to self-regulate, and family environment, were related to the level of student participation in transition plans. High levels of self-determination are also linked to students' success in the general education curriculum (Agran, Wehmeyer, Cavin, & Palmer, 2010). Although self-determination is increasingly considered an important area for instruction at the secondary level by both general and special education teachers (Carter, Lane, Pierson, & Stang, 2008), many parents, particularly those of diverse cultures, are not aware of the meaning of the term. Educators planning on incorporating self-determination components of instructional programs (e.g., goal-setting, self-management, problem-solving, self-advocacy) should inform not only students, but also parents of the importance of self-determination skill instruction in school and at home.

Transitional programming has become an integral part of the educational plans of most students with intellectual disabilities. Research specific to the adjustment of students with intellectual disabilities to the world of work suggests that more comprehensive and long-range transition support is necessary (Neubert, Tilson, & Ianacone, 1989). Steere and Cavaiuolo (2002) provide a specific example of an educational plan for independent employment and living (see Figure 6.4).

In the past couple of years there has been an explosion of interest in the development of postsecondary programs for individuals with intellectual disabilities. Perhaps increased participation of students with intellectual disabilities in the core academic curriculum, more experiences with inclusion, or just greater expectations are at the root of this new program emphasis. Whatever the reason, almost all states in the United States now have at least one postsecondary program—some at community colleges, some at technical colleges, and many at large state colleges and universities. Typically, these programs allow students to take college-level courses and engage in work internships, live on campus, and enjoy college service and social activities. Federal resources help to support these initiatives and include the development of the Center for Postsecondary Education for Individuals with Intellectual Disabilities and the Consortium for Postsecondary Education for Individuals with Developmental Disabilities, as well as support for websites, including the widely used "Think College! College Options for People with Intellectual Disabilities." It is exciting to see how, in a few short years, the opportunities for college students with and without disabilities have expanded to include postsecondary experiences. These programs are typically self-supporting, so they are expensive. Depending on the program, the major focus may be vocational or having a "typical college" experience. Not surprisingly, research suggests parents are more concerned about employment outcomes and students are more interested in college life (Griffin, McMillan, & Hodapp, 2010). Research on how students do when they exit postsecondary programs is in the beginning stages. Clearly, transition plans for students planning on entering postsecondary programs will require preparing for areas such as getting around a large campus, managing unstructured times and different schedules, self-management, study skills, and displaying appropriate behavior in different sizes and types of classes. Read about one college student, Bryann Burgess, in "A Closer Look: Postsecondary Transition."

Many students with intellectual disabilities are now candidates for postsecondary college-based programs.

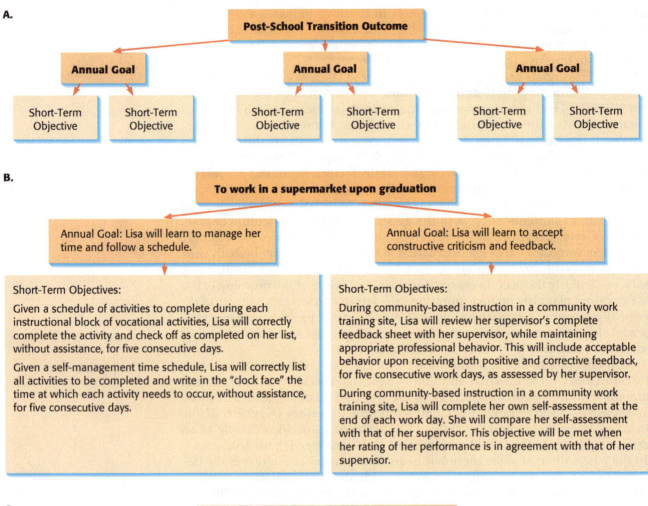

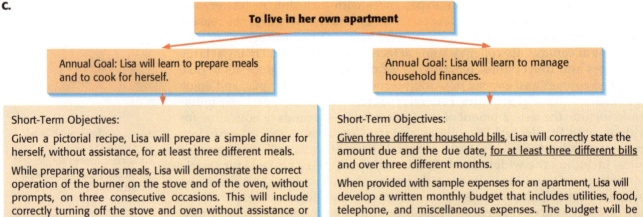

FIGURE 6.4

Educational plans for post-school living: (A) Relationship of post-school outcomes
to annual goals and short-term objectives; (B) Employment transition example;
(C) Community-living transition example

Source: Steere and Cavaiuolo (2002). From Connecting outcomes, goals, and objecties in
transition planning. *Teaching Exceptional Children,* 34 (6) July/August 2002, pp. 56–57.

Delivery of Instruction

We see many commonalities in the instructional procedures used for students with mild and moderate intellectual disabilities. A basic instructional technique focuses on the clear and straightforward presentation of tasks that have been carefully analyzed and sequenced. The process of breaking down a task or skill into its component parts is called **task analysis** (Alberto & Troutman, 2003). Teachers must be able to identify the skills required to complete a certain task (from preparing a sandwich to reading a newspaper article) and to develop an appropriate instructional sequence to teach them. The steps of a task analysis can be taught using a variety of techniques ranging from physical guidance, to the use of verbal prompts, to observational learning. The level, or intensity, of instruction is directly related to the level of support required by the student. Researchers are constantly evaluating the most effective, most efficient, and least intrusive way to teach specific skills.

> Teaching students with intellectual disabilities includes focusing on task analysis, a clear presentation of carefully sequenced tasks.

Prompts are clues or guides that maximize the probability that a student will answer correctly or attend to the appropriate material. Prompts are an important aspect of instruction in special education and are used extensively during initial instruction. If you underline the key word in a series of directions, you are prompting the student to attend to that key word. If you model the correct way to sound out a word, you are providing a prompt for the correct response. Prompts are then faded, or eliminated, over time. Prompts for teaching students with intellectual disabilities may begin as physical prompts, such as a guiding hand, and then gradually move to verbal or visual prompts, such as a suggestion or picture. They may occur before or during skill performance; the timing of the prompt may have implications for skill acquisition and generalization. For example, Singleton et al. (1999) found that prompts occurring before skill performance resulted in quicker skill acquisition, and prompts occurring during skill performance facilitated maintenance and generalization.

Many teachers focus on prompting students' awareness of their learning. Students with moderate intellectual disabilities may need content-specific prompts, such as a series of pictures or photographs to remind them of what needs to be done. For example, a picture of a student raising his hand might prompt classroom behavior, or the words "wash, soap, dry" on the clothes' basket might prompt someone to follow the correct steps for doing the laundry. Browder and Minarovic (2000) found that nonreading students with moderate intellectual disabilities were able to use sight-word prompts and self-instruction to initiate work tasks in competitive employment settings. In another interesting study, Le Grice and Blampied (1994) taught students with moderate intellectual disabilities to operate a video recorder and personal computer using color videotapes of a familiar staff member doing the steps of the skill. The videotape served as a sequenced series of prompts corresponding to the task analysis. We are only touching on the types of prompts that can be used in the classroom. The important thing to remember is that prompts can be easily integrated into regular classroom instruction. Recent applications of technology-based prompt systems used for vocational training are highlighted in the Assistive Technology Focus box on the next page.

Cooperative learning is a strategy that provides children of various skill levels with a task to complete together. The teacher must structure the activity to allow each child to make a significant contribution to the task. Cooperative learning is a good strategy to keep in mind when teaching students with intellectual disabilities in an integrated classroom (Sonnier-York & Stanford, 2002). Peer tutoring or peer support programs are related strategies for teaching students with intellectual disabilities in general education settings. When teachers provide structured activities for peer tutoring groups, this increases the amount of time all students are academically engaged during a classroom period and can improve

A CLOSER LOOK Postsecondary Transition

Bryann Burgess is getting ready to begin her senior year at the University of South Carolina, as part of their CarolinaLIFE program. CarolinaLIFE is one of many new programs across the country that provides postsecondary opportunities for individuals with intellectual disabilities. Bryann, whose interests and talents are in music and theater, is interested in teaching music and drama to young children. Bryann is privileged to be in the third year of a teaching apprenticeship with Mrs. Alison Trotter, a teacher in the Kindermusik International program. Alison keeps a blog of their mutual learning experience, and we share part of that blog, written a few weeks into the internship, with you below. Bryann and Alison are friends, co-opportunities in our community.

From the blog: Notable accomplishments:
September 22, 2009

My Goals for Bryann this week:
For Bryann to lead a circle dance with scarves
Lead the hello song/matching pitches w/each child

During this training session, we worked on many aspects of teaching. We sang the hello and goodbye song together, worked on matching pitches as before, we talked about the importance of time out, and taking children to the bathroom.

One issue that Bryann was hesitant and nervous about was discipline. "What if they don't listen to me, or do what I tell them to do?" And this is a very valid issue, I believe, for any teacher who is starting out.

I addressed these issues in the following ways, beginning with simply finding ways to attain their attention. Once we get the child's attention, then we can re-direct. We talked about how those two aspects follow hand in hand and how to react in certain situations.

I. Discipline

A. *Step 1: Getting their Attention*
  1. *Physically getting down on the child's level, engaging in eye contact, hand on shoulder*
  2. *Turning off the lights and counting to 3*
  3. *"Magic Fingers up High, Magic Fingers down low"*
  4. *"Put your hands in your lap"*
B. *Step 2: Redirecting their behavior*
  1. *"Instead of running, let's use our walking (running, skipping, jumping, dancing) feet. Can you show me your dancing feet?"*
  2. *"Instead of screaming, let's use our inside voices. Can you whisper like me?"*
  3. *"Instead of hitting, can we give each other a hug?"*

their academic performance (Copeland et al., 2002; Mortweet, 1999). Research emphasizes the importance of the special educator's presence in the general education classroom to support the general education teacher when students with moderate to severe intellectual disabilities are served in inclusive settings (Snell & Janney, 2000). The special educator can work with the general education teacher to provide appropriate levels of attention, instruction, and behavior management to all the students in the classroom.

Students receiving instruction in a functional curriculum also have many learning experiences that require attention, remembering, and organizing. These activities can range from something as simple as learning a telephone number and address to remembering the steps involved in following a recipe, writing a check, or going shopping for groceries. Instruction also needs to be sequenced and structured carefully, with reliance on prompts to illustrate how to do the task as well as when to do it. Basic instructional guidelines are found in the Teaching Strategies box, "Simple Strategies for Teaching Students with Intellectual Disabilities."

It is important for all educational programs and other school activities to emphasize the importance of socialization and friendships between all students.

We acted out most of these ideas, role-playing me as a teacher, then her as the student. And even incorporated some imaginary students as well into the mixture. We worked on different ways to pass out the rhythm sticks, followed by introducing the song or activity. We also switched back and forth, me being the student, her being the teacher—and ended up being quite hilarious. But, it's a very good learning technique and I'm sticking to it!

I asked Bryann if she felt comfortable in assisting/supervising the children in the bathroom one at a time. She greatly hesitated and wasn't too wild about the idea. She was also a little apprehensive about the children getting out of control in the class. Both of these are very good issues to be able to have talked about with her and all the more to overcome them. I reminded her of the "life's a dance" country song, and how it's exactly the same way with teaching. Sometimes you lead the children, and sometimes you follow their lead.

"Life's dance you learn as you go
Sometimes you lead, sometimes you follow
Don't worry about what you don't know
Life's a dance. You learn as you go"

I encouraged her to have courage, and step out...and that's exactly what happens in Week 2 of our application class . . . to be continued . . .

Source: http://notableaccomplishments.blogspot.com

Interaction with peers is a major focus of education—an important consideration for successful community integration in later years as well as during school. Students in self-contained programs may be mainstreamed into lunch or arts classes in order to provide at least minimal interactions with peers. Many educators, however, feel that more complete assimilation in regular classes is necessary. Sometimes, the need for special instruction and training must be weighed against the philosophy of integration and the need for social interaction as educators and parents try to decide on the most appropriate program for an individual child.

Materials

Because of the issue of skill transfer and generalization, the types of materials used in instruction can be very important, particularly when life skills or vocational skills are being taught. Both simulated materials and real-life materials have their uses. If you were teaching sight words found in the environment, an example of a simulated material would be the word *exit* printed in red capital letters on a rectangular card placed over the doorway of the classroom. An alternative

ASSISTIVE TECHNOLOGY FOCUS

Technology in Community Environments

A promising area of technology use for students with intellectual disabilities is instruction in independent living skills. Recent research focuses on cues provided via technology to prompt and reinforce performance of new skills or behaviors in community settings. This technology helps to increase the independence of individuals with intellectual disabilities in home and community environments.

- **Independent Living/Cooking:** Mechling, Gast, and Fields (2008) used a portable DVD with a seven-inch screen to teach cooking skills to young adults with moderate intellectual disabilities. The young adults used self-management strategies to play video segments and prompt steps of the cooking process. They prepared grilled cheese, ham salad, and hamburger helper (microwave) in their apartment kitchens. Mechling, Gast, and Seid (2010) conducted a similar study using a Personal Digital Assistant (PDA) to teach cooking skills via self-prompting using video, customized pictures of the cooking environment, and auditory prompts.

- **Independent Living/Community Transportation:** Mechling and O'Brien (2010) found that using computer-based video instruction to teach bus-riding skills to individuals with moderate intellectual disabilities could not only teach specific community-based skills, but that the instruction could take place via simulation, thereby reducing the need for actual community-based instruction. By using video-simulation that included recordings from a first-person perspective, verbal cues, visual landmarks, and videos of the bus route, three

Photo courtesy of Kiba Technologies, LLC

A Cyrano Communicator, like this one, can be used to guide a student's performance of work-related skills by giving him picture and/or verbal prompts.

young adults with moderate intellectual disabilities transferred bus-riding skills to community settings.

- **Independent Living/Recreation:** Hammond, Whatley, Ayres, and Gast (2010) taught students with moderate intellectual disabilities to use an iPod for fun and recreation—skills that we sometimes forget are as important as any others! The middle-school students learned via video modeling to watch movies, listen to music, and look at photographs on their iPods.

---

would be to use the real thing and conduct your lesson using the actual exit sign over the door at the end of the hallway. Because not all teachers are able to take their students into the community for training on a daily basis, teachers and researchers have looked at ways to combine the use of simulated materials with real materials in natural environments. For example, Morse and Schuster (2000) found that a combination of community-based instruction and simulation training using a picture story board, a board on which representative pictures or cutouts are used for illustration, resulted in successful instruction and maintenance of grocery-shopping skills. Branham et al. (1999) found that a videotape of individuals modeling certain skills, such as mailing a letter and cashing a check, was an even more effective addition to community-based instruction than classroom simulation. As our knowledge of the most effective ways to combine alternative instructional strategies with community-based instruction grows, we increase opportunities for teaching a wide range of important life skills.

Instruction using real materials can help students generalize skills.

Teaching Strategies & Accommodations

Simple Strategies for Teaching Students with Intellectual Disabilities

- Teach students in small groups (three or four students).
- Teach one concept or skill at a time.
  Teach steps or strategies for learning (a plan for remembering or sequencing information).
- Provide ample opportunity for practice (practice often, but don't overload).

- Use prompts to promote correct responding (examples, modeling, physical guidance).
- Teach skills that are meaningful and can be practiced often.

The use of real materials in natural environments is, however, a critical component of effective instruction for many students with intellectual disabilities. Real materials can motivate as well as facilitate generalization. As we've mentioned, using an actual checkbook folder and checks may be a good way to practice subtraction and addition skills that can easily be integrated into the regular curriculum. Many schools have had success at integrating the more functional objectives of a student's curriculum into their regular classroom curriculum.

Personal and Civil Rights

The history of educating individuals with intellectual disabilities includes acts and philosophies that ignore personal and civil rights. Today, many legal and ethical dilemmas remain unresolved. Many adults with intellectual disabilities have to fight for access to fair housing, for the right to marry and have children, and for the opportunity to work in community settings.

It is difficult for most persons with intellectual disabilities to wage an effective campaign for personal rights, since the mental competence of the individual is often determined to be unknown or insufficient and the parents or other legal surrogate must legally represent the individual. Often, the wishes of the parent and the individual may be different, resulting in decisions that are at odds with the individual's preferred outcomes. Another issue that received a lot of attention is the fact that until litigation In 2002, (U.S. Supreme Court, Atkins v. Virginia), individuals with intellectual disabilities were not considered a protected class and could be eligible for the death penalty. The apparent inequities in the legal system and the potential for abuse through representation suggest that advocacy is an important function for everyone interested in the fair treatment of *all* people.

> The battle for personal and civil rights for people with intellectual disabilities is not yet over.

? Pause and Reflect

Most of us would agree that the basic goals of education are to prepare us for independent work, life in society, and personal satisfaction. These goals are no different for individuals with intellectual disabilities. What are some things you could do and changes you could make in your home or in your place of work to support the individual independence of a person with cognitive disabilities?

A CLOSER LOOK   Employment Opportunities

People with mild intellectual disabilities continue to face serious problems finding meaningful work. From the mid-1980s to the mid-1990s, hourly wages increased, as did the employment rate, but 65 percent of individuals with cognitive disabilities remained unemployed (Frank & Sitlington, 2000; Wehman, West, & Kregel, 1999). Data comparing the first and second National Longitudinal Transition Survey indicated that individuals with intellectual disabilities surveyed four years after high school completion showed a reduction in the percentage of employed youth from 46.5 percent in 1990 to 29.8 percent in 2005 (Newman, Wagner, Cameto, Knockey, & Shaver, 2010). There was a corresponding increase from 8 percent to 20 percent of students enrolled in postsecondary programs, but even with this trend, the employment data are not increasing significantly over time. Employment options for persons with disabilities, from most to least segregated, include (1) sheltered employment, (2) supported employment, and (3) independent competitive employment in community settings.

Sheltered employment

In sheltered employment, individuals with intellectual disabilities are in segregated work settings, usually set up as assembly-line workshops, in which individuals work on assigned contracts, often receiving payment on a piecework basis; that is, getting paid for each task or product that is finished.

Supported employment

In supported work settings, people are placed in jobs that are either located in integrated settings or that facilitate social integration. The term *supported* refers to the training, supervision, and financial assistance that is provided to the individual and the employer in the work setting. There are a number of different models for supported employment, including the mobile work crew, the enclave, and supported jobs (Kiernan & Stark, 1986).

- The **mobile work crew** is a group of individuals with disabilities who learn a specific trade or set of skills that can be applied in the community, such as gardening and catering.
- An **enclave** is a small group of individuals with disabilities who are placed in a work setting, usually within a large business or corporation. They receive on-the-job training and support from job coaches, schools, or social service agencies and from within the corporation.
- The **individual supported job model** involves one-to-one coaching and teaching of a single individual in a job setting. In an individual supported job model, a job coach, or employment specialist (Wehman & Targett, 2002) provides on-site training and ongoing problem solving.

Independent competitive employment

Most students with mild intellectual disabilities, and many with moderate intellectual disabilities, will find independent competitive employment. Agencies such as vocational rehabilitation may be tapped, but often individuals seek and get jobs independently. Tools to identify and evaluate work performance, employee satisfaction, and needed support for both employers and employees are the focus of research designed to promote long-lasting and satisfying community employment for individuals with disabilities (Brady & Rosenberg, 2002).

SUMMARY

- The AAIDD definition of intellectual disabilities includes three criteria: sub-average intellectual functioning, impairments in adaptive behavior, and manifestation during the developmental period.

- Intellectual disabilities are usually classified as mild, moderate, severe, or profound. Eighty to eighty-five percent of students with intellectual disabilities have mild intellectual disabilities. The causes include both biological and environmental factors.

- Students with intellectual disabilities may have trouble learning how to learn (metacognition), remembering, coming to and maintaining attention, and generalizing. Language development may be delayed, although most differences are quantitative rather than qualitative. Students may be smaller and more prone to health problems, although physical differences generally are not visible. Students may also exhibit inappropriate social behavior.

- Parents and siblings adjust their familial roles to accommodate a child with intellectual disabilities. Siblings often spend more time on child care, though not at the expense of peer relationships.

- A functional curriculum emphasizes independent functioning and incorporates academic skills, such as reading, in a real-life context. Teaching strategies that can be used by regular or special educators include task analysis, the use of prompts, cooperative learning, and the use of concrete materials. Computers provide drill and practice, word processing, tutorials, and other instructional assistance.

- Transition programs are designed to help students achieve as much independence as possible through employment, living arrangements, and social relationships.

KEY TERMS

intellectual disabilities (page 196)

Stanford-Binet Intelligence Scale (page 196)

Wechsler Intelligence Scale for Children, Third Edition (WISC-III) (page196)

adaptive behavior (page 197)

AAMR Adaptive Behavior Scale (page 198)

Vineland-II Adaptive Behavior Scales (page 198)

skill transfer (page 207)

generalization (page 207)

immature behavior (page 209)

functional academics (page 214)

life-skills curriculum (page 214)

community-based instruction (page 216)

transitional programming (page 216)

self-determination (page 217)

task analysis (page 219)

prompts (page 219)

cooperative learning (page 219)

mobile work crew (page 224)

enclave (page 224)

individual supported job model (page 224)

USEFUL RESOURCES

- American Association on Intellectual and Developmental Disabilities (AAIDD) (formerly AAMR), 444 North Capitol Street, Washington, DC, 20001-1512, (202) 387-1968. This website (**http://aamr.org/**) provides extensive information and resources about intellectual disabilities, including research, books, policy, events, and a wide range of other services.

- ARC National Headquarters, 500 East Border, Suite 300, Arlington, TX, 76010; (817) 261-6003 (**www.thearc.org**). Information about programs and national policies affecting individuals with intellectual disabilities and the ARC newsletter can be obtained from ARC headquarters.

- *The Capitol Connection Policy Newsletter.* Published by the Division on Career Development and Transition (**http://www.dcdt.org/**), the Council for Exceptional Children, 1920 Association Drive, Reston, VA, 20191. This newsletter addresses interdisciplinary policy and practice in career preparation and transition to postsecondary education, employment, and responsible citizenship for special learners.

- Center for Applied Special Technology (CAST), 39 Cross Street, Peabody, MA, 01960, cast@cast.org. This center provides information on assistive technology resources and educational applications.
- *Down Syndrome News.* Newsletter of the National Down Syndrome Congress (**http://www.ndsccenter.org/**), (800) 232-6372. This newsletter can serve as a source of information and support for professionals, parents, siblings, and individuals with Down syndrome.
- *Graduating Peter.* Gerardine Wurzburg, State of the Art, Inc., 2002. This excellent documentary, originally shown on HBO, chronicles the life of an adolescent with Down syndrome and the lives of his family as he attends inclusive programs in middle school and high school.

 PORTFOLIO ACTIVITIES

1. Visit your local high school and make an appointment with a job coach for individuals with intellectual disabilities. Try to arrange an observation of a community-based job training session. Describe the observation and record the specific instructional strategies used by the job coach, the methods of job evaluation, and the social interaction between the trainee and his or her colleagues.

CEC This activity can help the student meet CEC Content Standard 7: Instructional Planning and Standard 4: Instructional Strategies.

2. Send out a survey to local business people to find out their needs and attitudes regarding disabilities. Present data from the survey that address the following questions: Would they want to hire a person with a disability? What types of jobs would they suggest for individuals with intellectual disabilities? What would the employers' expectations be? Support? Pay? Security?

CEC This activity can help the student meet CEC Content Standard 5: Learning Environments and Social Interactions.

3. Visit a local college program for students with intellectual disabilities. Visit with the students, faculty, and staff. Record or transcribe your interviews. Find out what type of contacts students have within the university community (for example, college social events, sports, clubs or organizations, riding university transportation). Discuss the students' and their peers' views on the value of living on campus and preparation for independent living.

CEC This activity can help the student meet CEC Content Standard 3: Individual Learning Differences.

4. Observe several secondary or elementary classrooms in a local school. Identify the teaching strategies and materials used in the classroom. What adaptations might the teacher have to make to accommodate and support a student with mild or moderate intellectual disabilities? Talk with the teacher to see what types of instructional adjustments he or she may have made in the past. Create a notebook of suggested teaching strategies, materials, and adaptations for use in your classroom.

CEC This activity can help the student meet CEC Content Standard 4: Instructional Strategies.

 To access Portfolio Activities for this chapter and other useful study resources including an interactive eBook, related web links, quizzes, flashcards, and videos, visit the Education CourseMate website at CengageBrain.com.

CHAPTER 7

Children with Severe Disabilities

Learning Objectives

After reading this chapter, the reader will:

- Describe the roles of both physical and social integration in the inclusion of individuals with severe disabilities into school and the community.

- Describe the ways a teacher can identify skills to be included in a student's life-skills curriculum.

- Describe the importance of choice in determining instructional goals for students with severe disabilities.

- Identify ways an educational team can prepare a transition plan that will enable the student with severe disabilities to move to an integrated setting.

- Identify the community living options available to individuals with severe disabilities.

All children with disabilities experience significant challenges in their lives. Children with severe disabilities, however, face the greatest and most comprehensive challenges—typically both cognitive and physical. Today, the outlook and opportunities for individuals with severe and profound disabilities are greater than you might think—certainly greater that many parents and professionals ever anticipated. Someone with severe intellectual disabilities may be living in a home down the street from you, or may be the young man bagging groceries in your neighborhood grocery store. However, many of us are not afforded, nor do we seek, the opportunity to interact in a meaningful way with people who have severe disabilities. Although programs that prepare persons with severe disabilities to work, live, or interact with other members of the community are steadily increasing in both quantity and quality, there are still not enough of them. Often, schools provide our best models of integration; unfortunately, sometimes they demonstrate only segregation and a lack of tolerance. Schools can select programs, curricula, and activities that promote and develop knowledge, acceptance, and interaction among all individuals, including those who have severe disabilities. In this chapter, we introduce educational strategies designed to maximize these students' potential, and raise questions about the protection of their rights.

Terms and Definitions

Individuals who are identified as having severe disabilities may display a variety of primary disabilities. In this section, we will look briefly at a general description of severe disabilities as well as the definitions of severe and profound intellectual disabilities—terms included in the broader term *severe disabilities*.

Severe Disabilities

TASH: Equity, Opportunity, and Inclusion for People with Disabilities, a professional and family organization designed to provide advocacy and services for individuals with severe disabilities, describes people with severe disabilities in the following resolution statement:

> TASH addresses the interests of persons with disabilities who have traditionally been excluded from the mainstream of society. These persons include individuals with disabilities of all ages, races, creeds, national origins, genders, and sexual orientation who require ongoing support in one or more major life activity in order to participate in an integrated community and enjoy a quality of life similar to that available to all citizens. Support may be required for life activities such as mobility, communication, self-care, and learning as necessary for community living, employment, and self-sufficiency. (TASH, 2000)

> Individuals with severe disabilities require extensive support in major life activities.

Although most disabilities can range in intensity from mild to severe (for example, learning disabilities, behavior disorders), the term **severe disabilities** is used in this chapter to refer primarily to individuals who have severe or profound intellectual disabilities. The life supports and educational programs required by these individuals are typically more extensive than those required by individuals with other types of disabilities.

Severe and Profound Intellectual Disabilities

The federal definition of **severe intellectual disabilities** includes an IQ of less than 40 and the manifestation of deficits in adaptive behavior, with both areas of deficit originating during the developmental period—before the age of 18. **Profound intellectual disabilities** vary only in the range of the IQ score, which is 20 and

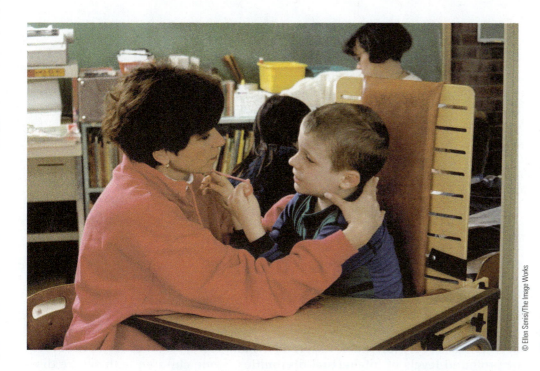

© Ellen Senisi/The Image Works

Communication, in all its forms, is the basis of all learning.

below. It is sometimes very difficult to determine the extent of intellectual disabilities in an infant. This is particularly true when the child also has severe health or sensory impairments. Thus, the extent of intellectual disabilities often cannot be determined until the child is much older. As you might expect, however, IQ scores, which are highly correlated with academic success, don't tell us much about individual children or adults when we are looking at scores of 30 or 18. IQ scores at this range do not yield information useful in providing educational support in everyday living skills. So, typical test information provides us with little usable data.

Another way for educators, parents, and the community to describe individuals with severe and profound disabilities is to evaluate levels and types of supports needed for individuals to live their fullest lives in included settings. In this approach to disability, we focus on how we can make things happen, rather than on a test score or behavior scale. The focus on external supports guides educational programming today, and is supported by the American Association on Intellectual and Developmental Disabilities (Luckasson et al. 2002). Kennedy (2004) identified the following content areas of support as critical to appropriate educational planning: communications, adaptive behavior, problem behavior, systematic instruction, family-centered practices, social relationships, sensory and motor needs, and collaboration.

Probably more than with any other group of students, it is important that we, as teachers, family, or friends, pay very close attention to what a student *can* do, and how he or she is trying to convey information. This is the information that will guide us in planning instruction—not IQ scores. Individuals with severe disabilities are dependent on the people in their environment to provide opportunities for communication, growth, and a sense of belonging. Education will focus on what we need to do to support each individual's development.

Prevalence

The number of students served in the schools with severe disabilities could be recorded in several places, including the areas of intellectual disabilities and physical disabilities. Typically, however, students with severe disabilities are identified through the category of multiple disabilities (NICHCY, 2011). Often, the prevalence estimates range between .5 and 2 percent of the population (Kennedy, 2004).

? *Pause and Reflect*

If you look at the general definition of severe disabilities and the definitions of severe and profound intellectual disabilities, you may notice a very basic difference. Professionals focus on the level of external support needed for individuals to participate in the community, and the federal definitions focus on individual performance or scores on assessment instruments. How do the different definitions cause you to look at the population of individuals with severe disabilities? Does an emphasis on external supports make you look at individuals with severe or multiple disabilities in a different way? ●

Causes of Severe Disabilities

There are numerous causes of severe and profound intellectual disabilities, including genetic syndromes, physical trauma, and disease. Most of the causes of intellectual disabilities presented in Chapter 6, such as fetal alcohol syndrome, may affect individuals differentially and can sometimes result in severe or profound levels of intellectual disabilities. Some children with severe disabilities happen to be born with a cluster of challenges, one of which is severe or profound intellectual disabilities. The genetic syndromes we discussed in the last chapter, including Down syndrome, Klinefelter's syndrome, Turner's syndrome, fragile-X syndrome, and Tay-Sachs disease, result in a number of common physical, behavior, and intellectual characteristics and may cause severe intellectual disabilities. The probability of having a child with some of these conditions can be determined through genetic counseling. Some, such as Down syndrome, can be detected through tests conducted during pregnancy, such as amniocentesis.

Other causes, such as physical trauma to the head caused by accidents or child abuse, can result in severe brain damage and intellectual disabilities. Medical abnormalities, for example, brain tumors, and diseases, such as meningitis, can also cause severe disabilities.

In most cases, the ways we teach students with severe disabilities will be the same regardless of the cause. As we mentioned, it is critical to attend to the particular skills and abilities of each child. However, there are times when knowing the cause of a disability can be important; for example, certain physical disabilities or health concerns are associated with specific syndromes, such as Down syndrome and cerebral palsy. As a teacher, you should become familiar with the characteristics of these conditions to avoid exposing your students to injury or health risks through some play or exercise activities. Sometimes, knowing the cause of severe disabilities can help teachers know what to expect and be better prepared for instruction (Hodapp & Fidler, 1999). For example, if we know that children with some syndromes are likely to show extreme self-abusive behavior, we will be better prepared both emotionally and instructionally to deal with these difficult circumstances.

Neither social and economic status, nor the general intellectual ability of the parents, seems to be related to the incidence of severe or profound intellectual disabilities. Medical technology enables many individuals with severe disabilities to live much longer than in previous years; however, infants born with severe and profound intellectual disabilities continue to be at high risk due to low birth weight and other complicating factors, such as respiratory complications, congenital heart defects, and accidental trauma (Hayes et al., 1997; Strauss et al., 1999).

My Friend Carolyn

It is said that beauty is in the eye of the beholder. In Carolyn's eyes, everything is beautiful. She is always so happy that beauty seems to generate into the hearts of everyone around her.

Carolyn Dadd, 15, has moyamoya disease. She cannot walk, talk, or feed herself, and she requires total care. She knows the people around her, though. I only wish more people could realize how capable she is.

I am 19 years old, and I have been Carolyn's sitter for the past seven years. I first met Carolyn when I was 12 and she was 9. I had never seen anyone quite like her. She was very small then, barely 60 pounds. Her smile was as deep as if it sank back into her soul. When we met she raised her hand in a gentle motion to touch my face and laughed as if there was a joke between us. Soon I found myself laughing too. That day started our friendship—one that I will cherish the rest of my life. It was obvious that Carolyn was different from anyone I had ever met, and that is exactly what I liked about her.

Jessica Morgan

Moyamoya disease is a progressive disease that affects the blood vessels in the brain. It is characterized by narrowing and/or closing of the carotid artery. This lack of blood may cause paralysis of the feet, legs, or upper extremities. Headaches, various vision problems, intellectual disabilities, and psychiatric problems may also occur.

Source: "Good Things Come in Small Packages" by Jessica Morgan. From *Exceptional Parent*, July 2000. Reprinted with the expressed consent and approval of Exceptional Parent, a monthly magazine for parents and families of children with disabilities and special health care needs.

Pause and Reflect

Probably the most challenging prospect facing new parents is the possibility of having a child with severe disabilities. Mothers and fathers may rack their brains trying to identify causes; some may wonder why they did not seek genetic counseling. It is impossible to know or even anticipate how you would react if you had a child with a severe disability—it is possible, however, to reflect on the importance of family and community. What community resources and activities could be identified to support students and their parents currently meeting the challenge of living with severe disabilities? ●

Characteristics of Individuals with Severe Disabilities

If you ask parents, siblings, and teachers of individuals with severe disabilities what the effects of those disabilities have been on the children themselves, you will get a wide range of answers. It is sometimes difficult to describe the effects of severe disabilities when you are personally involved. You keep thinking of the *person* with the disabilities—John is a hard-working student; Susan enjoys music; Mary is a little temperamental in the morning. Even when the disabilities are very challenging and sometimes overwhelming, you come to know and appreciate each individual.

Cognitive Development

The effects of severe disabilities on cognitive development are related partially to the learning experiences the person has throughout life, particularly in the early years. The frequent coexistence of physical or health impairments with severe cognitive disabilities often results in a reduction in the normal environmental interactions considered instrumental in the development of cognitive abilities. For example, an infant without severe disabilities, while lying in his crib, may accidentally hit the side of the crib with his hand and hear the noise it makes. After this happens a few times, the child will make the connection between his hand movement and the noise it makes against the crib. This is called an understanding of cause and effect. The realization that something you do can have predictable consequences is an important tool for learning to control and interact with the environment. Another example, recognized immediately by parents and infants, is the connection between crying and parental attention. The child may begin to hit his hand against the crib for the purpose of making the noise or cry in order to be held. He intentionally does something to get a specific result—attention from a parent. This purposeful behavior is referred to as a *means-end relationship.* The development of an understanding of cause and effect and of means-end relationships is critical for children to begin to explore their environments actively and with purpose; these skills are also considered important in language development (Iacono & Miller, 1989).

The child with severe or profound disabilities may experience difficulty learning these early skills in the typical way. A child with severe physical disabilities or with very delayed motor development may not be aware that it is her hand that is hitting the side of the crib—or she may not have sufficient motor control to direct it to happen again. A child with severe intellectual disabilities may be unable to understand that her mother appears two or three minutes after she has started crying. As a result, the child may have difficulty making a connection between the things she does and the results of these actions or behaviors. The infant, therefore, may not acquire these important behaviors unassisted and may not attempt to interact with the world around her. The child simply may not know that what she does makes any difference.

Children with severe disabilities, however, do learn communication to indicate wants and needs, and to participate in their community in different ways. Many students with severe intellectual disabilities will have limited ability to perform academic-type tasks, so education may not focus on academic areas. Individuals with profound intellectual disabilities may present educators or parents with great challenges in establishing specific communication skills, or teaching students to perform skills or tasks.

Physical Development and Health

Children with severe and profound intellectual disabilities are usually much below average in physical size and may experience a wide range of physical and health-related difficulties (McDonnell, Hardman, & McDonnell, 2003). As we have mentioned, intellectual disabilities to this degree of severity are typically accompanied by other disabilities. Infants born with severe and profound intellectual disabilities often experience significant delays in physical development. Because of this delay, the infant may have very limited physical movement at the beginning of life.

Sometimes, physical disabilities and health risks are associated with the specific syndrome or condition responsible for the intellectual disabilities. Children with Down syndrome, for example, may require heart surgery at a very young age because of congenital heart defects, and they are at risk for respiratory problems. Children with severe intellectual disabilities and cerebral palsy may have varying degrees of motor impairment; sometimes, the physical disabilities may

---

Understanding cause and effect and means-ends relationships is critical for most cognitive skills.

Children with severe and profound intellectual disabilities often experience health-related difficulties and severe delays in physical development.

Life skills are best learned in community settings.

affect mobility, speech, and regulated motor activity. A number of children will be prone to a seizure disorder such as epilepsy, although most types of seizures can be controlled or reduced by appropriate medication. Other syndromes or conditions may be degenerative in nature: The conditions will worsen over time, and the child's health will become progressively worse, until death occurs. An example we have already mentioned is Tay-Sachs disease.

In some instances, the physical development of the child with severe or profound intellectual disabilities is compromised as a side effect of extreme developmental delay. Intrusive procedures may be required on a regular basis to maintain comfort and sustain life. For example, a child who must be catheterized daily or fed through a stomach tube is exposed to more opportunities for infection and, therefore, illness.

A number of children with profound intellectual disabilities may not be independently mobile and thus may not use their limbs with any regularity. This can result in atrophy of the muscles. Other individuals may have mobility, but also may require guidance and instruction to participate in physical activity of either a therapeutic or recreational nature. Therapeutic physical activity, including physical therapy, can increase strength and flexibility and prevent some health problems (Green & Reid, 1999). Physical activities not only have obvious health benefits, but also can serve an important recreational function and contribute to independent movement and psychological well-being (Modell & Cox, 1999).

Language Development and Communication

Severe and profound disabilities can have extensive effects on an individual's language development and communicative abilities. Some people with severe or profound intellectual disabilities will have limited spontaneous oral language, others will not have functional oral language, and some, no oral language at all. The presence or lack of oral language does not, of course, imply that a child is not communicating. Research suggests that, by far, the most common form of expressive communication used by children with severe disabilities is direct behavior, such as dragging adults to the desired place or object, getting the desired object, or throwing away an undesired object (Harvey & Sall, 1999). Ineffective communication may result in aggressive behavior; other students may simply give up trying to communicate because of a lack of responsive partners (Downing, 2005). Once again we see the strong and obvious relationship between behavior and communication. Identifying and teaching reliable, usable, and meaningful avenues for communication is probably the single most important task of families and teachers of individuals with severe and profound disabilities.

New communication skills, whether they are verbal or nonverbal, must be as efficient and as easy to use as the behaviors students are currently using to communicate needs. In other words, the communication must be **functional communication**—easy to use and easily understandable (Ostrosky, Drasgow, & Halle, 1999). The Teaching Strategies box, "Guidelines for Developing Functional Communication Systems," on the next page, presents a set of guidelines for developing functional communication skills for individuals with severe disabilities.

Nonverbal communication systems include sign language and language boards or communication boards. On communication boards, words or symbols that represent possible needs and requests are placed on a lap board, and the person communicates by indicating the appropriate word or picture. Many people with severe and profound intellectual disabilities do find ways of communicating their wishes and controlling their environment by using nonverbal means.

Downing (2011), using the term multiple modes of communication, divided communication into nonsymbolic and symbolic communication, and aided and unaided communication. Figure 7.1, abstracted from her work, illustrates the context of these communication models.

> Many people with severe or profound disabilities can use a verbal or nonverbal communication system.

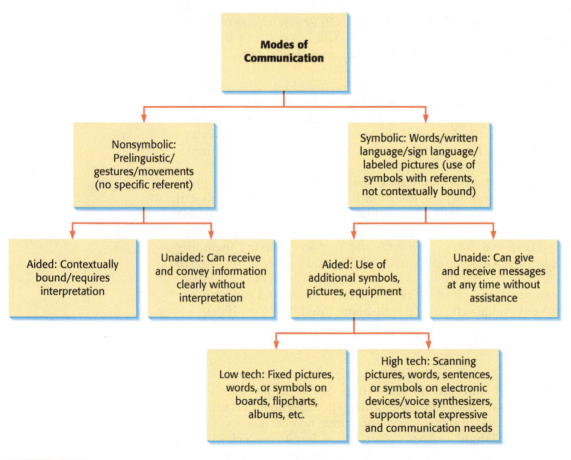

FIGURE 7.1

Multiple modes of communication

Source: Snell, Martha E., Brown, Fredda, *Instruction of Students with Severe Disabilities,* 7th Edition, © 2011. Adapted by permission of Pearson Education, Inc., Upper Saddle River, NJ.

Teaching Strategies & Accommodations

Guidelines for Developing Functional Communication Systems

1. Take advantage of the existing communication skills of students with severe disabilities.

- Observe the communication strategies students already use to communicate. Ask yourself: What forms of communication does this student consistently and intentionally use to communicate? Observe these forms across settings, routines, and activities.

- Build on existing types of communicative behavior by teaching socially desirable and functionally equivalent forms of behavior that are more easily understood by others.

2. Select functional communication targets and identify powerful teaching opportunities.

- When selecting communication targets, ask yourself: Will learning this behavior help the student become more independent?

- Select potential teaching opportunities that will likely result in high levels of motivation by capitalizing on current student-initiated communicative occasions.

3. Facilitate the widespread use of the new forms of behavior.

- Identify the situations in which students currently use their existing communication forms (for example, generalized use of the existing form).

- Determine the consequences that might be supporting this generalization.

- Teach the new communication form in all situations where the student currently uses the existing form. Careful attention to, and reflection on, one's own behavior and prudent observation of student behavior are necessary.

4. Ensure maintenance of the new behavior.

- When replacing existing forms of communicative behavior, take care to ensure that the new form requires less physical effort and produces reinforcement more rapidly and more frequently than the old one.

Source: M. M. Ostrosky, E. Drasgow, & J. W. Halle (1999). How can I help you get what you want? *Teaching Exceptional Children, 31*(4), 58.

Regardless of the method of communication selected, critical factors for effective communication include the preparation and interest of communication partners and an environment that supports individual interaction and communication (Butterfield & Arthur, 1995). Family interaction and support are critical, and the technical efficacy of a communication system must be weighed against the extent to which a family will encourage its use. In other words, the communication system must fit within the family dynamic and work for family members in order to be effective. Factors such as the weight and cumbersome nature of a communication board, the monotone sound and volume of a system using artificial language, and the simple visibility of assistive technology may interfere with a family's desired goals of social acceptance for their child and for themselves (Parette & McMahan, 2002). Because hand-held technology is now ubiquitous in our culture, the social acceptability of assistive technology for communication purposes is increasing rapidly.

Social Behaviors and Emotional Development

By definition, students with severe and profound intellectual disabilities will have deficits in adaptive behavior (Luckasson et al., 2002). The extent to which appropriate adaptive behaviors, such as self-help skills and general social skills, are acquired will vary according to the severity of the disability, the type and breadth of educational programming, and the environment in which the person lives, works, or goes to school. For example, improvements in some areas of adaptive behavior have been found when persons with intellectual disabilities live in group homes rather than institutional settings and work in competitive employment versus sheltered workshops (Felce & Emerson, 2001; Inge et al., 1988; Leher, Apgar, & Jordan, 2005).

Because the label *severe disabilities* can encompass a wide range of ability and performance levels, it is difficult to characterize "typical" social behavior. For a few persons, social development may be very limited, and target skills may include establishing eye contact or acknowledging someone's presence. Some individuals will have inappropriate behaviors, and interventions may then focus on reducing acting-out or tantrum-like behaviors (McDonnell, Hardman, & McDonnell, 2003). For others, social development goals may include appropriate social interaction in a community work setting. Often, a drawback to successful social interaction is the lack of a common communication system. Storey and Provost (1996) found that the use of communication books (essentially picture books) increased the amount of social interaction as well as interpersonal communication between individuals with severe disabilities and their nondisabled coworkers in a community work setting. The communication book provided a method everyone could use to "talk" to each other. Problems in communicative ability are also related to the presence of inappropriate or aberrant behavior (Sigafoos, 2000). Children with severe levels of aberrant behavior, such as self-injury, displayed fewer communication skills.

Although there is very little descriptive research available on the emotional development of persons with severe or profound mental disabilities, we know that all people experience an array of emotions. In some instances, we must learn to recognize the indicators of basic human emotions such as love, trust, fear, and happiness. For example, Yu and coworkers (2002) developed an observational recording system that allows observers to recognize distinct and reliable behavior indicators of happiness in individuals with severe and profound cognitive disabilities as they participate in work and recreational activities. The fact that researchers are devoting time to evaluating emotions such as happiness is an important sign the studies increasingly are focusing on improving the quality of life of individuals with severe disabilities. Some aspects of emotional development and expression are more easily observed. The management or appropriate demonstration of emotions such as anger or frustration is an important aspect of adaptive behavior. The development and nurturing of many emotions rest with the significant others in the person's life, including the family.

Pause and Reflect

As you think about the characteristics of individuals with severe disabilities, reflect on the important interaction between each person and his or her surroundings. Our expectations for individuals with severe disabilities—our ability to see children in schools and adults in community settings—is a result not only of philosophical changes, but also of our knowledge about the importance of appropriate environmental support. You are part of the environment—what is your role in supporting individuals with severe disabilities? ●

Effects on the Family

In this section, we will look at the joys and struggles of families of children with severe disabilities. We will also discuss the multiple roles that parents of children with severe disabilities must play.

Family Attitudes and Reactions

Many children with severe or profound intellectual disabilities are diagnosed at birth, or shortly thereafter, and families must immediately confront the prospect of rearing a child with a severe disability (McDonnell, Hardman, & McDonnell, 2003). As you might expect, reactions to this diagnosis and the onslaught of ensuing emotions vary greatly. Parents have many questions about what the future holds for them and their other children: How can I care for this child? What will happen to her when I'm no longer around? How will my other children react to their brother? Some of these questions will be answered in time, some can be answered through education, and some can never be answered.

You may see many differences in the lives of families that include an individual with severe disabilities. It is interesting to note, however, that mothers of youngsters with severe disabilities, like all mothers, hope and expect that their children will be able to achieve independence (Chambers, Hughes, & Carter, 2004; Lehmann & Baker, 1995). Although there are more services than ever before to assist families, many parents are concerned about the lack of community support and related services, such as respite care and speech therapy, that are available to them—services that are necessary for community inclusion and maximum independence for their child (Turnbull & Ruef, 1997). Parents of children with severe disabilities, especially those who have complex medical needs, are particularly vulnerable to stress. Factors such as availability of services, financial issues, care of other children in the family, and continuing medical care are weighed by parents as they try to make appropriate and life-altering decisions about caring for their child (Bruns, 2000; Timmons, Whitney-Thomas, Mcintire, Butterworth, & Allen, 2004).

Parents, of course, are not the only family members affected by the presence of a child with severe disabilities. Brothers and sisters will have their own reactions and ways of dealing with them. Reactions can range from resentment to extreme protectiveness; probably the whole spectrum of emotions will be experienced at some point during the sibling's lifetime. Although it is not unusual for siblings of children with intellectual disabilities to experience high levels of stress, many children develop very close relationships with each other (Stoneman, 2005).

> Most children with severe or profound intellectual disabilities are diagnosed at birth.

Family Roles in Education

The family of an individual with severe or profound disabilities can play an active role in educational programming from the very beginning. The passage of P.L. 99-457 in 1986 provided the legislative impetus needed for the establishment of federal programs for infants and young children with disabilities and their families (Campbell, Bellamy, & Bishop, 1988). The importance of early intervention and family responsiveness in the development of children with severe and profound intellectual disabilities, as well as any type of disability, has been recognized for a long time. Parents who learn how to encourage language or communication, or who are trained to provide at-home occupational therapy, will feel more competent in dealing with their child, and will help that child to build an important and perhaps critical learning foundation. Educators must incorporate parents' goals and priorities, particularly in areas such as communication, curriculum content, and educational procedures (Stephenson & Dowrick, 2000). Dunst (2002, p. 140) identified the following four critical components of family-centered intervention models:

> Early intervention programs provide crucial services for children with severe disabilities and their families.

1. Relational components
   a. Family friendliness/interpersonal skills
   b. Practitioner attitudes and behavior about family capabilities
2. Participatory components
   a. Family choice and action
   b. Practitioner responsiveness and flexibility

Keeping Sophia Healthy, Alive

The following newspaper article was written about the struggle to support a little girl born with a rare, degenerative disease called Niemann-Pick Disease. During her short life, Sophia's family created awareness of the challenges facing children and families with rare diseases or conditions that received little support from either research or financial sources. Although Sophia died in 2005, she—through her family—has made a lasting impact on her community and other families facing immense challenges. The website devoted to Sophia, Sophia's Garden, continues as a resource for families and as a source of information and updates about conditions similar to Sophia's: http://www.sophiasgarden.org/index.html.

If there is one clear thing about the quest to save 13-month-old Sophia Herzog Sachs' life, it is that it reaches out to us all. It includes Western pediatricians and Eastern herbalists. It includes neighbors as well as strangers. It includes prayer circles and those with just plain beliefs and wishes. The diagnosis is that this tiny charmer of a toddler with large brown eyes will die from Type A Niemann-Pick disease. And that is unacceptable to her parents, Karen Herzog, 42, and Richard Sachs, 49, who are Ashkenazi Jews—a population affected by the disease. In 20 years, Lucile Packard Children's Hospital at Stanford had not seen a single case. The nation's top center for what are called lysosomal storage diseases, the Mount Sinai School of Medicine, has seen only 40 cases in 20 years. None of the children lived. "It's awful," said Dr. Greg Enns, director of the Stanford genetics program and co-director of the University of California-San Francisco Lysosomal Disease Center, who spoke of telling the parents the shocking diagnosis. "As a pediatrician and as a parent, it is very difficult to see a family go through getting news like that." Not acceptable, the parents said again, and began their mission to seek life for their daughter. Niemann-Pick is an inherited metabolic disorder in which harmful quantities of a fatty substance accumulate in the spleen, liver, lungs, bone marrow and—in some patients, like Sophia—the brain. Referred to as a lysosomal storage disorder, it is named for physicians Albert Niemann and Ludwick Pick, who in the 1920s identified two forms of the disease. Sophia's condition is so rare that only one in 30,000 Ashkenazi Jews have it, said Enns, who has treated other similar lysosomal disorders. In the close-knit south Palo Alto community of Greenmeadow, Penny and Richard Ellson rushed across the street to Herzog and Sachs when they learned about Sophia. Herzog mentioned an organic garden to ease Sophia's digestive problems. Ellson got on the phone, and on June 8 about a dozen people—neighbors and strangers—showed up in Herzog and Sachs' back yard, including master gardener Marcia Fein of the Foundation for a Global Community. Following Fein's organic design, they dug flower beds and planted neat rows of organic vegetables and herbs. It is called Sophia's Garden. "

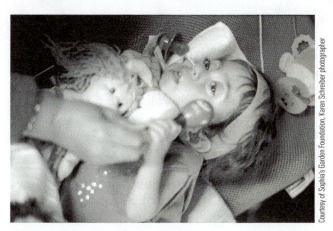

Courtesy of Sophia's Garden Foundation, Karen Schreiber photographer

Sophia: Surrounded by the people who love her and the toys she loves.

It has been very touching," Sachs said. But the garden is just a part of the action to help Sophia. "This is all a part of this larger picture to keep Sophia healthy and alive," said Sachs, president and creative director of Valley Design in Menlo Park. Sophia cannot crawl, but she babbles and has the look of a very curious little girl. "We feel her great energy and her wanting to be here," her mother says. In Sophia's room, where a long row of stuffed animals perch on top of a sofa, a tiny "altar" is filled with symbols of the diverse things that place the wind beneath people's wings. There are healing stones, a green Tibetan tara, tiny seeds from the Dalai Lama and a Buddha. On her crib are a Roman Catholic Mother Miraculous medal and an American Indian prayer wheel. The family has met with a rabbi, Chinese herbalists, shamans and a 94-year-old Chumash Indian healer. Last week, Sachs flew home from Paris, where he attended the third Scientific Lysosomal Storage Disorders Conference. He hopes Sophia can be included in a scientific trial. "We hit the ground rolling," Herzog said. "We have a window here to try to keep her well. They are gone by age 3." The plan to help Sophia is broad and

"integrative," Herzog explained, pulling out a black and red chart that has "Sophia's care" written in a center circle. Inside about 30 surrounding connected circles are words such as: pediatric neurology, traditional Chinese medicine, homeopathy, Tibetan medicine, Feldenkrais, physical and occupational therapy, chiropractic, feng shui, ayurvedic, rabbi, Jewish Center, Western and Eastern herbs and so on. Enns, who had never seen a Niemann-Pick Type A child until he met Sophia, said, "I applaud Sophia's family for being so persistent in their striving for the best care possible. They have her best interest in mind in trying to coordinate a complex team of physicians from all sides of the globe. I have a relatively open mind to other forms of therapy. Just because we don't understand how something works, doesn't mean that something can't work." But he also said he has "Western medicine-trained skepticism" and urges caution in ensuring that alternative treatments don't cause harm. Sophia's parents hope to establish a fund in her honor to encourage research and share information. Meanwhile, there is a daily whirlwind of e-mailing, organizing, documenting their own research and contacting research scientists from the home office that they call jokingly Sophia Central. It helps them not be simply terrified parents, they said, and most important, they think of Sophia not as dying, but healing.

Loretta Green

For additional information on Niemann-Pick disease, visit the National Niemann-Pick Disease Foundation, Inc. at http://www.nnpdf.org; the National Tay-Sachs and Allied Diseases Association, Inc. at http://www.NTSAD.org; the Genetic Disease Foundation at http://www.geneticdiseasefoundation.org.

Source: "PA Parents Try to Save Ill Daughter," by Loretta Green, *San Jose Mercury News,* July 1, 2002.

Teaching Strategies & Accommodations

Cultural Competence of Teachers of Students with Severe Disabilities

Classroom environment: Creating culturally responsive classrooms

- Become aware of your (the teacher's) role in the classroom and cultural identity.
- Create caring, safe classrooms.
- Arrange the physical environment for learning groups, ease of movement.
- Create and nurture learning communities.
- Learn if the cultures represented in your classroom have learning style preferences.

Family engagement

- Consider how your beliefs intersect with those of the cultures represented in your class.
- Identify any cultural differences in perceptions and meaning of disability while realizing that every parent will have a unique perspective.
- Discover how best to achieve open and honest communication with family, while respecting cultural patterns and providing families with choices.

Access to general education curriculum

- Expect competence in the classroom but design individualized, appropriate accommodations and modifications.

- Focus on the interests, talents, and strengths of each student.
- Ensure that the curriculum, regardless of type, is culturally relevant for individual students.

Evidence-based practices for students with significant support needs

- Make sure each student's methods of communication are integrated into the classroom routine; students must have a voice in the classroom.
- Use differentiated instruction and culturally responsive teaching; identify and provide what individual students need within the context of cultural preferences.
- Universal Design for Learning—use multiple methods of presenting and receiving information and multiple means of engaging students.

Source: Abstract of content summary from Harmon, C., Kasa-Hendrickson, C., & Neal, L.I. (2009). Promoting cultural competencies for teachers of students with significant disabilities. *Research and Practice for Persons with Severe Disabilities, 34* (3–4), 137–144.

Not everyone agrees with the present focus on the provision of early service in the home environment. Krauss (1990), for example, suggests that some families may resent the fact that the family must be evaluated before their child can receive services and may feel that their privacy is being threatened. Although you might think that most families would not feel this way, if you work with parents and families of infants or young children, it may be an important consideration to keep in mind. Understanding that families have different ideas of how they want to be involved and to what extent you, as a teacher, should offer recommendations is sometimes a hard lesson to learn. Cultural influences can also affect parents' perceptions and expectations. In the above Teaching Strategies and Accommodations box, "Cultural Competence of Teachers of Students with Severe Disabilities," we point out a few key steps for teachers as they work with students and families of different cultures.

One challenge faced by a number of families including children with severe disabilities is the realization that their child experiences a disability so unusual that there is little research, few educational resources, and no plan for parents to follow. When there is nothing for parents to do to support their child, they often experience frustration and despair, and search for interventions themselves. The

First Person feature, "Keeping Sophia Healthy, Alive," describes the fight waged by one set of parents determined to pull together all possible resources and interventions, no matter how unusual, to save the life of their little girl, Sophia, who has Niemann-Pick disease, a metabolic disorder.

? Pause and Reflect

In this chapter on severe disabilities, we've chosen to include a separate section on families. Think about the challenges of everyday activities with a child who has severe disabilities—going to the grocery store, visiting friends, attending religious services. Also think of how difficult life can be when you have specific goals and dreams for your child and the older he gets, the greater the obstacles. What kind of support do you think is necessary for parents to maintain optimism and enthusiasm as they meet the challenges of parenting a child with severe disabilities? ●

Teaching Strategies and Accommodations

As we mentioned earlier, terms and criteria do little to suggest specific ways for educating persons with severe disabilities and do not address the educational or health-related issues of individual children. It is important to visit a student's classroom or to meet with him or her to learn who the child is and what his or her specific educational needs are.

The future of children with severe disabilities will depend in part on the vision and commitment of their families, their teachers, and their peers—of people like you. The extent to which children with severe and profound levels of intellectual disabilities will become adults who are accepted, valued, and integrated into the mainstream of society is your responsibility as well as theirs.

The nature and content of educational programming for individuals with severe and profound levels of intellectual disabilities have changed significantly in recent years. Most of the changes have come about because of new or different educational philosophies and greater expectations and goals for children, adolescents, and adults with severe disabilities.

Earlier in this chapter, we mentioned that professionals in the field describe the educational needs of students with severe or profound intellectual disabilities in terms of supports in all domains of life. McDonnell, Hardman, and McDonnell (2003) identify two categories of environmental support that we can use to facilitate the integration, independence, and success of individuals with severe disabilities. The first category is **formal supports.** Formal supports are the legal requirements, organizations, and agencies that offer people with disabilities and their families protection, resources, and assistance. Formal supports serve as a structure for financial and governmental incentives to individuals and communities. The second category is **natural supports.** Natural supports are the opportunities, activities, and responses offered by family, friends, and neighbors. As you read through this section, you will see that these parameters are useful ways of looking at interventions and programs for individuals with severe disabilities. Formal supports can provide important evidence of society's responsibilities and efforts to create quality life experiences for individuals with disabilities. The natural supports, however, touch each individual personally and serve as the foundation for necessary changes and modifications in formal support networks over time.

Most evidence-based instructional strategies for teaching individuals with disabilities typically reflect a clear behavioral philosophy and focus on the analysis

New educational philosophies and higher expectations have changed educational programming for people with severe and profound intellectual disabilities.

of behavior. Specific interventions include the task analysis and prompt systems introduced in Chapter 6. The Teaching Strategies & Accommodations box, "A Brief Teaching Program Guide," provides a comprehensive example of teaching a young man to dress using these strategies.

Another important paradigm shift in recent years is toward self-determination. Person-centered planning, which allows individuals with severe disabilities to play an important role in decisions regarding their lives, is the underlying component of many educational programs (Michaels & Ferrara, 2006; Reid, Everson, & Green, 1999). Because of the importance of decision making in establishing personal input on life goals and activities, recent research is carefully examining ways to best tap into the preferences of individuals with severe disabilities. Discovering if Martin prefers bowling or watching videos, or if Anna likes orange juice or

Teaching Strategies & Accommodations

A Brief Teaching Program Guide

Brief Teaching Program Guide

Student: Adrian **School:** **Start Date:** February 26, 2009

Teachers: Ruth (teacher), Lindsey and Carmen (teaching assistants), MaryAnn (OT) **Aim Date:** April 20, 2009

Goal: Adrian will put on and take off his shirt, pants, jacket, hat, socks, and shoes; this does not include tying his shoelaces or doing fasteners other than zippers. He will put each clothing item on in 30 seconds or less and take each clothing item off in 20 seconds or less.

Objective(s):

First Objective: Adrian will take off his shirt, pants, jacket, socks, and hat (excluding fasteners).

Second Objective: Adrian will put on his shirt, pants, jacket, hat, and socks (excluding fasteners) and take each item off in less than 20 seconds.

Third Objective: Adrian will put on and take off his shirt, pants, jacket, hat, socks, and VELCRO shoes; this does not include fasteners. He will put each clothing item on in 30 seconds or less and take each clothing item off in 20 seconds or less.

Present level of performance: Adrian is able to put on and take off his coat and shirt with assistance because he is not able to zip or button the items. Adrian is not able to put on his hat, pants, shoes, or socks. Adrian is not toilet trained, although that is not part of this program; independent dressing is seen as a prerequisite for independent toileting.

Description of Assessment/Probe Procedure

Probes were completed during natural opportunities. During probe procedures, Adrian was given an instructional cue (varied according to clothing item) such as, "Put your coat on." The teacher then observed how he put the jacket on and recorded the data on the task analysis sheet. Adrian was never reinforced or prompted during probes. If Adrian asked for help he was told to try and complete the task himself. During baseline and intervention probes, a multiple-opportunity assessment was used. If Adrian performed a step incorrectly or if it took him longer than the 8-second latency period to initiate performance, then the assessor performed the step for him and marked it as an incorrect response for that step on the data table. Testing continued until the task was completed, regardless of the number of errors.

Stage of learning: Acquisition **Grouping arrangement:** One-to-one

Teaching times: During natural opportunities: before and after going outside, using the restroom, during P.E. **Teaching days:** Mondays and Thursdays **Test day:** Every fourth day

Setting: Special education classroom, restroom, gym

grape juice can be difficult if Martin and Anna simply take or do what is offered and don't have clear communication skills. Researchers are discovering systematic ways of presenting choices and creating response opportunities so that individual preference can be reliably and clearly demonstrated (Lancioni et al, 2008; Lim, Browder, & Bambara, 2001; Stafford et al., 2002). In addition to the obvious benefits of having a voice in determining what you are able to do during the day, there are other positive side effects of self-determination. For example, research suggests that having choices is associated with increased happiness (Mechling & Bishop, 2011) and improved job performance (Morgan, & Horrocks, 2011). Importantly, research has long demonstrated that choice is associated with increases in appropriate behavior and reductions in inappropriate behavior (Canella, O'Reilly, & Lancioni, 2005; Carlson, Laiselli, Slyman, & Markowski, 2008). As we see in the

Instructional cue: "Put your_____ on" and "Take your_____ off"

Prompt(s)/prompt system and latency: Constant time delay with a verbal + physical prompt. First two teaching sessions 0-second latency period, followed by 3 training days with a latency period of 4 seconds, after which the latency was increased to 8 seconds for 5 days. Probes were given every 4 days.

Materials: VELCRO shoes, coat with zipper, winter hat, socks, pants with fasteners (button and zipper), and T-shirt

Reinforcers: Listening to music and computer time

Description of the Teaching Procedures

Adrian was always instructed during natural opportunities, which created natural reinforcement because Adrian usually wanted to put on or remove his clothing in order to prepare for the next activity, such as recess. Instruction began with the instructional cue and ended when Adrian had removed the entire clothing item or put on the item properly without the need for adjustments.

If Adrian performed an error, he was immediately prompted, with a verbal plus physical prompt, to repeat the step correctly. Reinforcement was faded as Adrian's abilities increased and the latency period was extended. For example, when an 8-second latency period was reached, Adrian was not provided with the option of selecting a song if he performed the task because there was not time for problem behavior since Adrian had moved into the fluency stage of learning.

After Adrian was able to complete all of the steps in a task analysis independently, he transitioned to the fluency stage of learning and the practicum student began to time Adrian during dressing procedures. For this reason, the latency period never exceeded 8 seconds and if Adrian's progress was decreasing during the extended latency period, then it was shortened to either 4 or 0 seconds.

How will you teach the next relevant stage of learning (generalization, maintenance, fluency)?:

Fluency: After Adrian mastered a specific skill (putting on or removing one type of clothing), he then transferred to the fluency stage. During this stage, he was timed with a stopwatch whenever he was dressing or undressing. All clothing items were to be removed in 20 seconds or less and to be put on in 30 seconds or less.

Maintenance: Adults should refrain from assisting Adrian when he is dressing or undressing. In order to entertain this concept on a regular basis, adults should allow extra time in the schedule for dressing and undressing so that Adrian will be able to complete these tasks independently. Probes should be given every 2 weeks in the beginning and faded to monthly after 2 months.

Source: Snell, Martha E.,; Brown, Fredda, *Instruction of Students with severe disabilities*, 7th edition, © 2011. Adapted by permission of Pearson Education, Inc., Upper Saddle River, NJ 07458.

ASSISTIVE TECHNOLOGY FOCUS

Technology and Individuals with Severe Disabilities

Technological advances in the areas of communication and cognitive development have contributed significantly to the quality of life of individuals with severe and profound levels of intellectual disabilities. Technology has opened many avenues of communication not previously available to people with severe physical as well as cognitive disabilities. Both low-tech (communication boards) and high-tech (voice synthesizers) provide individuals with various options for communication (Light & Drager, 2007). Devices designed to augment communication needs also may serve to help develop speech or other language skills (Sulzer-Azaroff, Hoffman, Horton, Bondy, & Frost, 2009).

Technology is playing an emerging role as a means of delivering and enhancing instruction for individuals with severe disabilities. Langone and Mechling (2000) used a computer-based program to teach students with severe disabilities to recognize photographic prompts for appropriate language use. In recent years, wearable computers have been developed. When attached to glasses or headphones, these may provide exciting options for community-based instruction and for performance feedback. Hand-held electronic devices are also now widely used in instructional settings and for guiding students through school or vocational activities (Cihak, Kessler, & Alberto, 2008).

An emerging role of technology focuses on the ability of individuals with severe disabilities to participate in decision-making opportunities. As we discussed in the text, the self-determination and identification of individual preferences are important components in educational programming

(Wehmeyer et al., 2007). When personal preferences are tapped in areas such as food choice or in-school activities, tangible items can be used to elicit responses. Choices about work-related tasks or environments are more difficult because the opportunities cannot be presented visually to the student. Enter the CD-ROM. Through video clips of different work environments, individuals with severe disabilities can view work settings and see the various tasks that might be involved at each site. Morgan, Gerity, and Ellerd (2000) and Ellerd, Morgan, and Salzberg (2002) found that using videos through CD-ROM technology allowed a student with severe disabilities to identify preferential work environments and to choose preferred tasks when presented with up to five job choices. The use of technology to extend sound instructional principles to new areas reflects one of its best and most promising applications.

Technology Focus box above, technology is contributing to the programmatic emphasis on eliciting choice.

Although there is some disagreement among professionals about the rate or extent of some of the changes we will be discussing, we now recognize the importance and need for programs that emphasize normalization, social and physical inclusion, and life-skills curricula. Each of these areas will be discussed separately. As you will see, however, they are closely interrelated and together represent a continuing movement toward change for individuals with severe disabilities.

> The focus of normalization is that all people should lead lives that are as normal as possible.

Normalization

One of the forces behind educational change for individuals with all levels of intellectual disabilities was the movement toward normalization that emerged in the 1970s and 80s. The term **normalization,** or *social role valorization,* refers to an emphasis on conventional or normal behavior and attitudes in all aspects of education, socialization, and other life experiences (Wolfensberger, 1977, 1983). In other words, the focus of normalization is that all people should lead lives that are as normal as possible. For persons with intellectual disabilities, this movement has great implications. Wolfensberger (1977) defined two dimensions of normalization: (1) direct contact or interaction with typically developing individuals and (2) the way an individual with disabilities is described to others.

The first dimension involves the way we treat people with intellectual disabilities, and the things we decide to teach and encourage. It is important, for example, to consider a person's age and the usual criteria for normal behavior when we are interacting with someone or deciding what types of behaviors, skills, or recreational activities we will be teaching or doing. It may be easy and fast to feed a 10-year-old with severe disabilities, but it is not age-appropriate, and therefore, if it is at all possible, we should choose to implement a self-feeding program so that the child not only will become more independent but also will be expected to perform some of the skills of other children his or her age.

Sometimes, it may be beyond a person's physical or cognitive abilities to perform some self-care skills (eating, toileting, dressing) or other types of tasks with complete independence. In these instances, we encourage **partial participation:** we enable the student to perform the parts of the skill or task that are within his or her ability range (Snell, 1988).

The second dimension of normalization refers to the way we portray or present persons with intellectual disabilities to others. This dimension includes the way we may refer to a student in our class, the words or phrases we include in writing about or describing persons with intellectual disabilities, and the way we select clothing or hairstyles for our children or clients. The types of housing or educational environments in which we place persons with disabilities and the extent to which legislation protects and enforces basic human rights reflect our society's perceptions of individuals with disabilities. Persons with intellectual disabilities should live in environments and structures that approximate normal living arrangements and that include a small group of friends, family, or caregivers (Taylor, Racino, & Walker, 1992).

In general, the move toward a normalized existence for individuals with severe and profound intellectual disabilities depends on the increased willingness of the public to recognize and accept the humanity, value, and contributions of persons with intellectual disabilities. Normalization has served as a foundation for many of the major social as well as educational changes that we have observed in the area of intellectual disabilities over the past few decades. It is important for us, as educators, clinicians, and members of the community, to serve as advocates for normalized life opportunities for individuals with severe disabilities; it is also important for us to recognize the sometimes overwhelming challenges faced by families with members with severe disabilities.

Inclusion

One term you will hear or see repeatedly in any educational program description or curriculum for students with severe intellectual disabilities is *inclusion,* the incorporation of all individuals into the mainstream of society. There are several reasons why inclusion has become an important facet of instructional programming for individuals with intellectual disabilities. First, it is proposed that individuals are more likely to develop functional patterns of behavior and higher levels of functioning if they have the opportunity to interact with people without disabilities. Second, it is considered to be every individual's right to access the opportunities and facilities that the community has to offer to the greatest extent

People with severe intellectual disabilities may develop higher levels of functioning and independence when they interact with people without disabilities.

possible. Third, an emphasis on inclusion will provide many individuals with the direct training and experiences they will need in order to achieve full or partial independence (Stainback, Stainback, & Ayres, 1996).

Inclusion also involves the acceptance of individuals with intellectual disabilities by the community. Of course, acceptance and social interaction cannot be dictated, but they can be developed through encouragement, preparation, and opportunities. Obviously, it is easier to develop friendships and good working relationships with people who are living and working in the same environment as you are. It is also possible that early physical integration with typically developing peers will encourage the development of long-term friendships that will last through the school years. Interestingly, research suggests that students with severe disabilities who are included in general education classrooms are more likely to be accepted by nondisabled peers and less likely to be rejected by teachers than students with mild disabilities. Some research, however, suggests that these higher ratings of acceptance are related to nurturing attitudes of peers rather than true friendship behaviors and that although students with severe disabilities are less rejected, teachers are not confident that they can provide them with appropriate instruction (Cook, 2001; Cook & Semmel, 1999).

A key issue in inclusion is the extent to which people with severe intellectual disabilities should be integrated into the school or community. Many professionals suggest that total inclusion should be the goal. An example of total inclusion in the public school setting would be the placement of students with severe disabilities in regular classes in order to promote socialization experiences. In many full inclusion programs, teachers attempt to adapt the general education content for the student with severe disabilities (Siegel-Causey et al., 1998). Other professionals feel that inclusion to this extent may result in a reduced amount of needed educational programming for students with severe disabilities, and that curriculum decisions should be individualized and instruction should address the specific skills needed to maximize independent performance (Ayres, Lowrey, Douglas, & Sievers, 2011). In addition, some parents are concerned about their child's safety and emotional well-being in integrated environments and prefer, at least initially, less risky program options.

The attitudes of the nondisabled persons in the community, school, or work setting are critical to successful inclusion. Various educational programs have been developed to give nondisabled persons some knowledge about individuals with disabilities, and many teachers do take the time to discuss individual differences and specific disabilities with their classes.

> Integration is a natural outcome of community-based instruction.

Social interaction is an important part of school life. All students benefit from close personal friendships.

Curriculum

Curriculum for students with severe disabilities often looks different from the curriculum we might think of in typical school situations. Frequently, we will look at the student, project life outcomes, and then decide what skills or knowledge needs to be taught in order for the student to achieve those outcomes or life goals. As we look at curriculum options, therefore, we will be looking at the interaction between the student and his or her present and future environments.

● *The Functional Curriculum*   Most of the curricula currently used in instructional programs for individuals with severe and profound disabilities stress instruction in life skills and are designed to maximize independent functioning. A curriculum that emphasizes preparation for life and that includes skills that will be used by the student in home, school, or work environments is called a **functional curriculum.** A functional curriculum includes instruction in all of the important areas, or domains, of adult life: domestic, community, recreation and leisure, and vocational. All types of instruction, including training in self-help skills and communication skills, mobility training, physical therapy, and occupational therapy, are integrated so that they complement one another and focus on functional activities rather than isolated practice tasks (Snell & Drake, 1994). Each student must be taught the behaviors or tasks required in his or her home, work, or recreational setting (see the accompanying Teaching Strategies box, "Examples of Functional Curriculum Domains").

Instruction in language is an important part of the functional curriculum for most persons with severe or profound intellectual disabilities. This is especially true for individuals who will be going out to work or who are living in community settings. Caro and Snell (1989) have identified the following three major goals of programs designed to teach language or communication to persons with severe disabilities: (1) to increase the frequency of communicative behavior, (2) to expand the student's repertoire of communicative functions, and (3) to promote the spontaneous and generalized use of communication skills in everyday life. Instructional programs in language and communication must focus on functional communication, as we have already mentioned. Communication interventions should occur in natural environments, such as classrooms and playgrounds, and focus on purposeful communication, such as asking for a ball or a favorite snack.

Teaching Strategies & Accommodations

Examples of Functional Curriculum Domains

Domestic

Areas or subdomains: kitchen, bathroom, laundry room, bedroom

Community

Areas or subdomains: grocery store, bank, post office, restaurants, school

Recreation/Leisure

Areas or subdomains: park, YMCA, movie theater, bowling alley, fishing pond

Vocational

Areas or subdomains: specific job sites (hotel, restaurant, landscape)

Skill areas to be addressed across all domains: communication, transportation, social skills, attire, behavior expectations, word/sign/symbol recognition, area-specific skills (for example, using the stove, depositing money, bowling, greeting customers), decision-making skills

The technique that is frequently used to identify skills for instruction is called an **environmental inventory,** or **environmental analysis** (Nietupski & Hamre-Nietupski, 1987). An environmental inventory involves a visit to the settings in which the student has to function. The environment might be a group home, the cafeteria in an elementary school, the local park, or the neighborhood bus station. A list is made of the specific skills needed by the average person to be successful in that environment. Then the skills of the individual student are compared to the needed skills, and specific behaviors or tasks are targeted for instruction. By using this procedure, the curriculum truly prepares the student to be successful in current or future life situations and channels valuable teaching time into meaningful instruction.

● *Community-Based Instruction* One way that integration is incorporated into educational plans is through community-based instruction, which, as you learned in Chapter 6, involves actually conducting learning experiences in community settings. Students who are able to travel in the community will, for example, receive training on how to walk to their home or work site or how to take a bus. Instruction will take place on the very sidewalks or bus lines that the student will be using to travel. Community-based instruction provides students with direct training in skills they need to become integrated into society and also allows them to experience integration during the instructional process.

Transition Programming

As we've discussed throughout this text, *transition* refers to the process of preparing for and facilitating movement from one situation or place to another. In the area of severe and profound disabilities, the term usually refers to one of three types of movement: (1) movement from one level of school to another, (2) movement from a segregated school or home setting to an integrated or community-based school or residence, or (3) movement from school to a work setting, typically a work setting in the community. Both educational and philosophical movements in the field today have been directed toward preparing individuals with severe disabilities for integration in local communities. The need for advance planning and continual instruction in the skills and behaviors needed to maximize the potential for successful experiences in future environments has resulted in the development of specific programs and extensive research focused on the transition process. The individualized transition plan prepares the child with disabilities for new environments. Consequently, transition programming permeates the educational programs of essentially all individuals with severe disabilities. Figure 7.2 illustrates the six areas of adult life that should be addressed by transition programs. How do we know if our programs have been successful in these areas? How can we determine if someone is productive, happy, and healthy? A number of research investigations are conducted periodically to determine such factors as employment rates, graduation rates, and living arrangements of individuals with disabilities.

> The individualized transition plan prepares the child with disabilities for new environments.

● *Transition Between Levels of School* For the infant born with severe disabilities, transition programming in educational settings often begins immediately. As soon as the need for specialized services is recognized, interventions are put in place that are designed to prepare the child for success in future environments as well as the present one. Programs are available at day-care centers, through home-based instruction, and in preschools that are, in part, designed to help the infant or child move to an integrated setting or to prepare him or her for the next level of schooling.

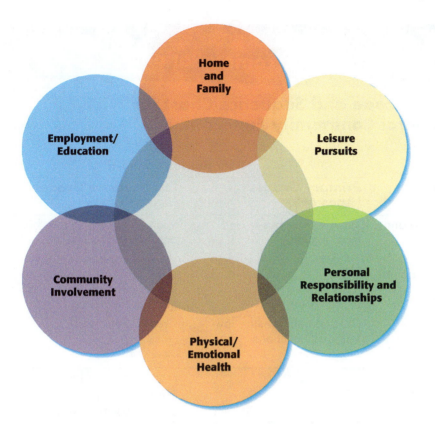

FIGURE 7.2

Domains of adulthood

Source: From *Life Skills Instruction: A Practical Guide for Integrating Real-Life Content into the Curriculum at the Elementary and Secondary Levels for Students with Special Needs or Who Are Place At Risk,* 2nd. Ed. (p.17), by M. E. Cronin, J. R. Patton and S. J. Wood, 2007, Austin, TX:PRO-ED. Copyright 2007 by PRO-ED, Inc. Reprinted with permission.

The process of preparation for a new school situation will take place as long as the child is in the school system. If a child is already in an integrated setting, the change from elementary school to a middle school, or from junior high school to senior high school, will need to be addressed in the curriculum. All children must learn to cope with the new physical environment, the usually larger number of students, and the progressively greater freedoms that are present as they go from first through twelfth grade. The individual with severe intellectual disabilities must be prepared to cope with these changes. For example, learning to use a locker may require a comprehensive instructional program (Felko et al., 1999). As we discussed in Chapter 6, some universities across the country participate in postsecondary programs designed to integrate students with disabilities into the college setting (Grigal, Neubert, & Moon, 2002). The Teaching Strategies box, "Danny's Schedule for Spring Semester at State University," provides a specific example of how university personnel can work together to create a viable postsecondary school environment for individuals with severe disabilities.

● *Transition from Segregated to Integrated Settings*   The education of students with severe or profound levels of disabilities has, historically, been segregated. The movement to end the practice of segregating students with severe disabilities is reflected in the transition plans of students of all ages. Many of these plans contain programming and educational goals intended to enable students to move to a partially or fully integrated school setting. In some instances, these goals may be to prepare students to move from a protective, residential setting to a classroom in the local public school. For other students, the goals may be to move them from a separate lunch held in their classroom to a fully integrated lunch with all the other students in the school, or for them to join the regular classroom for certain nonacademic or even academic subjects.

Teaching Strategies & Accommodations

Can Do: Scope and Sequence Chart for General Community Functioning

Goal Areas	Kindergarten (Age 5)	Elementary School	
		Primary Grades (Ages 6–8)	**Intermediate Grades (Ages 9–11)**
Travel	Walk or ride bus to and from school.	Walk or ride bus to and from school.	Walk, ride bus, or ride bike to and from school.
	Walk to and from school bus and to point in school (classroom, office).	Walk to and from school bus and to point in school (classroom, cafeteria, office, music room).	Walk to various destinations in school and in the community (neighborhood grocery store, mailbox).
	Cross street: stop at curb.	Cross street: familiar, low-traffic intersections.	Cross streets safely.
Community safety			Problem-solve if lost in new places.
			Use caution with strangers.
Grocery shopping			Buy two to three items at neighborhood store for self (snack) or classroom snack activity.
General shopping		Buy item at school store.	Buy item at school store.
Eating out	Carry milk/lunch money.	Carry milk/lunch money.	Carry milk/lunch money.
	Follow school cafeteria routine.	Follow school cafeteria routine.	Follow school cafeteria routine.
			Order and pay: familiar fast-food restaurants, snack stand.
			Buy snack/drinks from vending machine.
Using services	Mail letter at corner mailbox.	Mail letter at corner mailbox.	Mail letters.
		Use pay phone with help.	Use pay phone.

Source: A. Ford, R. Schnorr, L. Meyer, L. Davern, J. Black, and P. Dempsey (Eds.) (1989). *The Syracuse community-referenced curriculum guide for students with moderate and severe disabilities* (p. 78). Baltimore: Paul H. Brookes Publishing Co., Inc. Reprinted by permission.

Transition plans that include a focus on inclusion will probably contain many skills and experiences that address different aspects of communication, socialization, and independent movement. A student who has little or no experience interacting with nondisabled peers will not have the skills needed to benefit from new school situations. The transition plans may thus include trial experiences in the new school to help the student gradually become accustomed to the change.

Middle School (Ages 12–14)	High School (Ages 15–18)	Transition (Ages 19–21)
Walk, ride bus, or ride bike to and from school.	Walk, ride bus, or ride bike to and from school.	Walk, ride bus, or ride bike to and from home and community sites.
Walk to various destinations in school and in the community (store, restaurant, job site).	Walk to various destinations in school and in the community (store, restaurant, job site).	Walk to various destinations.
Cross streets safely.	Cross streets safely.	Cross streets safely.
Use public bus/subway for general transportation.	Use public bus/subway for general transportation.	Use public bus/subway for general transportation.
Problem-solve if lost in new places.	Problem-solve if lost in new places.	Problem-solve if lost in new places.
Use caution with strangers.	Use caution with strangers.	Use caution with strangers.
Buy items needed for specific planned menu.	Buy items needed for specific meal or special event.	Buy items needed for specific meal or special event.
Buy few items in store with limited money amount.	Shop for desired items in shopping center.	Shop for desired items in shopping center.
Purchase personal care items.	Purchase personal care items.	Purchase personal care items.
Budget/carry money for lunch/snacks.	Budget/carry money for lunch/snacks.	Budget/carry money for meals and snacks.
Eat in school cafeteria.	Eat in school/public cafeteria.	Eat in public cafeteria.
Order and eat in fast-food restaurants.	Order and eat in fast-food restaurants.	Order and eat in fast-food restaurants.
Buy snack/drinks from vending machine.	Buy snack/drinks from vending machines.	Buy snack/drinks from vending machines.
Use post office.	Use post office.	Use post office.
Use pay phone.	Use pay phone.	Use pay phone.
Ask for assistance in stores.	Ask for assistance in stores, information booths.	Ask for assistance appropriately in stores, information booths.

As you might expect, the success of a student's transition into an integrated environment will depend not only on the appropriateness of the educational program the student receives before the move, but also on the support the student receives once he or she is in the school. Cooperative planning between the student's present and future teachers will help to facilitate a smooth transition.

Successful transition into an integrated environment depends on appropriate educational programs and support.

Teaching Strategies & Accommodations

Danny's Schedule for Spring Semester at State University

Time	Monday	Tuesday	Wednesday	Thursday	Friday
7:00	Danny rides city bus to college campus				
8:00	Functional academics with special education teacher in classroom on college campus	Career planning or self-determination skills class with special educator	Free time—Danny gets to campus in time for weight training class	Career planning or self-determination skills class with special educator	Functional academics with special education teacher in classroom on college campus
9:00	Weight training class at fitness center	Ceramics class in art building	Weight training class at fitness center	Ceramics class in art building	Independent study and tutoring from special education intern at library
9:30					
10:00					
10:30		Travel training/ community skills training with teaching assistant and two other students		Travel training/ community skills training with teaching assistant and two other students	
11:00	Computer tutorial with special education intern (peer tutor)		Computer tutorial with special education intern (peer tutor)		Lunch with fraternity brothers
12:00	Lunch with other students and/or best buddy at student union food court	Lunch in community	Lunch with peer tutor at student union food court	Lunch in community	Review schedule for following week with special educator in classroom
1:00	Go to city bus stop on campus, go to job site	Travel training and go to SPCA for volunteer work with teaching assistant and two other students	Go to city bus stop on campus, go to job site	Travel training and go to SPCA for volunteer work with teaching assistant and two other students	Go to city bus stop on campus, go to job site
2:00	Works part-time at PetSmart		Works part-time at PetSmart		Works part-time at PetSmart
3:00		School bus picks Danny up on campus		School bus picks Danny up on campus	
4:00					
5:00	Parents pick Danny up from work		Parents pick Danny up from work		A friend picks Danny up from work

Source: M. Grigal, M. Neubert, & M. S. Moon (2002). Postsecondary options for students with significant disabilities. *Teaching Exceptional Children*, 35 (2), 68–73.

Although many school personnel are becoming more receptive to the integration process (Stainback, Stainback, & Stainback, 1988), parents, special education teachers, and others involved in transition plans should always anticipate the possible resistance of other educators, or sometimes family members. Letting people know exactly what to expect and ways to deal with potential difficulties will alleviate anxiety. Another factor critical to the successful movement of students with severe disabilities from segregated to integrated facilities is the role of parents. This role may change over time.

When it comes to decisions related to integrated placements, particularly if they involve changes in schools, parents may be concerned about the quality of programming in a new school or class situation and about the safety of their child, or they may be worried that their child will be rejected in the new situation. These feelings will be less pronounced if the parents have been planning

Courtesy of the Family Village Project

FIGURE 7.3

Family Village website

Source: http://www.family
village.wisc.edu/index.htmlx.

for transitional placements during the course of the child's life. Parents may find support, encouragement, and strategies for helping to prepare themselves and their children through support groups composed of other parents of children with similar disabilities who have experienced the same concerns. These support groups can be face to face or online, as evidenced by the screen shot of Family Village in Figure 7.3. Teachers and school administrators can help to get parents together if groups do not exist already in the community. Parents also might benefit from observing model programs that include integration and from communicating with personnel at the new school (Hanline & Halvorsen, 1989).

Transition from segregated to integrated settings can involve residential as well as school settings. For years, the vast majority of individuals of all ages who experienced severe or profound levels of intellectual disabilities lived in segregated residential facilities. Most of these were institutional or private settings such as nursing homes. During the past three decades, however, many of these individuals have moved to smaller and more integrated residences, such as group homes, or to live with their families. According to Taylor, Lakin, and Hill (1989), the number of children and youth in long-term residential facilities decreased from 91,000 to 48,450 in the years from 1977 to 1986. Similarly, according to the U.S. Department of Education's Data Accountability Center (2011), during the 2007–2008 school year, fewer than 15 percent of students with disabilities spent less than 40 percent of their time in a regular class. For students with multiple disabilities, however, that percentage was 46 percent—close to half of the students with multiple disabilities served by IDEA.

Transition to an integrated setting focuses on helping families keep and support their child in the home, and on enabling adults to live as independently as possible and to maximize interaction within the local community. Both the child who has been living at home and the child who has lived in a segregated facility must receive transition training for adult living. In many cases, it will be possible for individuals with severe intellectual disabilities to live in group homes or apartments in a community setting. People living in independent or semi-independent housing must be prepared emotionally and technically. The skills involved in cooking, cleaning, dressing, recreational activities, and transportation must be taught and will usually require extensive planning and instruction. Preparation for these skills and related ones must begin early, and then be extended to enable the individual to function in the specific home or apartment setting. See the Closer Look box, "Living Settings for Individuals with Severe Disabilities," on the next page for a description of the range of living options for individuals with disabilities.

● *Transition from School to Work*   Probably the most commonly perceived meaning of the term *transition* across the field of special education is the transition from school to work settings. Preparing students with severe disabilities to go into the work force, particularly the community work force, is a major educational goal.

Although transition programming from school to work begins at least five years before graduation from school, and clear transition plans are developed by age 16, preparation is often a major component of the curriculum throughout the student's educational experience (Noonan & Kilgo, 1987; Wehman et al., 1987). The transition process will encompass not only skills directly related to a work situation but also the necessary skills involved in social interaction, self-help areas, and transportation. Providing support in community-based settings involves some of the same processes and people discussed in Chapter 6. For example, job coaches go with students to the work site to provide on-the-job instruction.

An essential component of all school-to-work transition programs is community-based work experience. When possible, the student should try out several types of work experiences and play an important decision-making role in job selection (Brooke et al., 1995; Wehman et al., 1987). Research continues to refine instructional programs that will support students with severe disabilities in the community and foster the move towards paid employment. Carter, Trainor, Ditchman, Sweeden, and Owens (2009) found that participation in a muticomponent, school-based program resulted in the students being 3.5 times more likely to find summer employment than similar students not in the program. The program included conducting community conversations, engaging in community resource mapping, and identifying individuals to serve as community connectors and employer liaisons.

Supported employment is a desired goal for many young adults with severe disabilities and is often a transitional step between a high school internship and competitive employment. Moon, Simonsen, and Neubert (2011) conducted a survey of community rehabilitation providers to find their recommendations for skills students needed to begin supported employment services. A number of skills and domains were identified and ranked—at the top were skills that would fall under self-management (personal health/hygiene) and social/self-determination (follows rules, manages own behavior) skills. In addition, the importance of knowing how to access adult services—particularly making the transition into adulthood in terms of funding sources was a key recommendation. Continued business and community support is needed, of course, to provide adequate opportunities for supported employment to interested individuals (Brooke et al., 1995). In fact, research suggests that individuals with severe disabilities remain underrepresented in supported employment positions, compared to individuals with other, less severe, disabilities (Mank, Ciofi, & Yovanoff, 1998).

Teachers also should examine how to teach students to work independently in the employment setting. **Self-management procedures** have been taught to students with severe intellectual disabilities to facilitate independent performance (Lagomarcino & Rusch, 1989). These procedures include self-monitoring or recording of completed tasks and giving praise or other reinforcement to oneself when a task or step of a task has been completed. The self-monitoring and prompt systems are the same as those we examined in the Technology Focus feature in Chapter 6. Whether high tech or low tech, a step-by-step prompting system is a useful instructional strategy (Cihak, Kessler, & Alberto, 2008; Minarovic & Bambara, 2007). For example, a student might have a series of five photographs

Joining the community work force is a major educational goal for many students with severe disabilities.

Self-management procedures facilitate independent performance.

A CLOSER LOOK
Living Settings for Individuals with Severe Disabilities

Individuals with disabilities often want to live in independent, community-based homes. For many people, these goals are realized through independent living arrangements. For others, the goals are adapted to include the most independent and normalized setting possible.

Institutions

Large, segregated residential buildings known as institutions were used for years to house thousands of individuals with intellectual disabilities, mental illness, sensory impairments, or physical disabilities. After numerous cases of neglect and abuse in these institutions, a social and legal movement began in the 1960s and the 1970s to remove people from the institutional setting and relocate them in smaller, community-based settings. This movement, deinstitutionalization, led to the development of good community residential programs. However, the lack of existing support networks and adequate community-based housing also resulted in many people being displaced and homeless. Although institutions still exist, the buildings are often repurposed, and in most states are not considered as residential options.

Community-based residential facilities

Some individuals who in the past lived in segregated settings have moved directly and successfully into the community. People with disabilities such as severe intellectual disabilities may live in settings that range from nursing homes to community-based homes or facilities. Opportunities for community-based residences are continuing to increase for all individuals; however, the more complex an individual's health care and personal maintenance needs are, the more likely it is that the person continues to live in one of the more segregated settings, such as a nursing home. Often, these settings are able to employ support personnel, such as nurses and therapists, and have access to more elaborate medical equipment than a group home or apartment.

Intermediate-care facilities

An intermediate-care facility (ICF) is composed of a number of individuals with disabilities living together in a supervised setting. Some large ICFs do not provide for community integration, however, and may serve as permanent, segregated living settings for individuals with disabilities. These facilities may include cottage living or other congregated living options.

Small group homes house several adults with disabilities who live with a nondisabled person responsible for general supervision and coordination of activities. Such living situations require not only financial resources and trained personnel but also a receptive community. The resistance of some communities to the placement of group homes is one more obstacle to be overcome in the move toward normalized and independent living. The road to normalized socialization and integration within the community is an exciting option, but not an easy one.

Occasionally, individuals with severe or profound disabilities live in apartment settings. For example, one or more individuals with disabilities may live independently in an apartment, with only periodic visits from a counselor or case manager. Another option may be a person with a disability living with a roommate without a disability. (The roommate may be a residential care provider—or just a friend.) Apartment living is one step closer to an independent, normal living arrangement for many young adults but may be a challenging option for individuals who require more intensive supports in home settings.

Living with family

Another living option is the family home. Many individuals with disabilities continue to live in the family home during their adult years. Financial dependence, emotional dependence on the part of the family as well as the individual, and a lack of alternative living options may contribute to adults living in this setting.

that are used as prompts for the five steps needed to complete a task, such as setting a table in a restaurant. A self-recording procedure might involve putting a check or another mark beside each picture as the task is completed. Students who can learn to monitor themselves accurately will require less direct supervision over time and therefore may be more likely candidates for permanent employment opportunities. Figure 7.4 illustrates a series of instructional prompts in

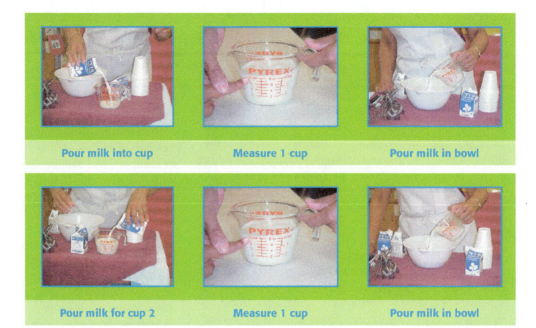

FIGURE 7.4

Picture prompts: making pudding

Source: Reprinted with permission of Dr. Cheryl Wissick, University of South Carolina.

the form of picture cues used to teach cooking skills to a class of middle-school students with severe disabilities.

Permanent employment in community settings is the ultimate goal of transition programming from school to work; it requires not only effective instructional techniques but also extensive coordination among the school, family, employers, and adult service agencies. Remember that the primary service providers for people with severe and profound intellectual disabilities will change from the school to adult agencies once the students reach the age of 22. Work-related goals that are intended to extend into the student's adult life must include the cooperation and participation of case managers from community service agencies.

Quality of Life

Ethical issues that have arisen in the area of severe and profound disabilities revolve around the basic rights of all individuals, such as the right to life, the right to treatment, the right to participate in the community, and the right to education. Professionals in the areas of medicine, education, and law have become involved with children with severe disabilities and their parents in attempts to resolve some of these issues and to find answers to some very disturbing questions. The fact that questions are raised at all relative to the human and constitutional rights of individuals with severe or profound levels of disabilities is difficult for many of us to understand.

Quality of life refers to the extent to which an individual can participate in, enjoy, and be aware of the experience of living. When a child with severe intellectual and/or physical disabilities is born, assumptions are also made about his or her prospective quality of life. Sometimes, these assumptions focus on whether or not the child's life is worth living, whether the mental or physical disabilities experienced by the child will enable him or her to have a meaningful life (Peushel, 1991). Often, these assumptions are accompanied by concern about the physical pain or discomfort the child is likely to experience, the prospect of a painful death later in life, or the likelihood of an existence characterized by endless surgical procedures and medical treatment. In other instances, the presence of moderate, severe, or profound levels of intellectual disabilities may lead to negative assumptions about the child's quality of life. All these considerations come into play when medical decisions are being made about whether or not to treat children with severe disabilities when life-threatening conditions occur. In some cases, the decision is made that, because of the prospect of poor quality of life, the infant should be allowed to die.

Most of the individuals who make decisions or provide guidance to parents about the potential quality of life for individuals with intellectual disabilities, including parents, physicians, and lawyers, have had little, if any, experience living, working, or spending time with persons with any degree of intellectual disabilities (Roberts, Stough, & Parrish, 2002; Smith, 1989). This lack of familiarity results not only in fear for the child's future, but often in misconceptions about the potential quality of life of individuals with varying levels of intellectual disabilities.

> Quality of life refers to the extent to which an individual is aware of, participates in, and enjoys life.

Quality of life is defined many different ways when used to measure adult outcomes. Halpern (1993) suggests that the major criteria for quality of life are (1) physical and material well-being, (2) performance of adult roles, and (3) personal fulfillment. Objective, quantitative evaluations, such as specific job requirements, are important tools for identifying target instructional skills in the environment that may lead to successful performance. Qualitative or descriptive analyses of an individual's performance and personal fulfillment also are considered necessary for an accurate picture of that person's quality of life. Dennis and colleagues (1993) suggest that there is no single definition of quality of life. They, too, recommend that an individual's performance be evaluated within the context of his or her environment, using indices that reflect that person's culture, family or support system, and personal preferences. These indices may be different for each person, reflecting those facets of life that are important to the individual and his or her significant others.

> Ethical issues in the area of severe disabilities include the right to life and the right to education.

? Pause and Reflect

In this section, we've examined some of the philosophical and practical components that contribute to effective educational programs for individuals with severe disabilities. As we've mentioned, the role of personal choice or preference—the voice of the individual—is finding increasing importance as educators and families work together to set goals, establish programs, and transition to other environments. Why do you think this emphasis on choice is so important? What does knowing individual preferences bring to our perceptions of individuals with disabilities—whether that choice seems as mundane as choosing between chocolate or vanilla ice cream or as relevant as choosing a restaurant or grocery store as a work environment? •

SUMMARY

- Severe intellectual disabilities is defined as an IQ score of 40 or below, and profound intellectual disabilities as an IQ score of 20 or below accompanied by deficits in adaptive behavior. Severe and profound disabilities are caused by a variety of genetic and environmental factors and are usually identified at birth.

- The effects of a severe disability on the child include cognitive difficulty in making connections between the action and the environment, relatively small physical size and high risk of health problems, delays in or lack of oral communication, and limited social skills.

- Parents of children with severe disabilities, like all parents, hope their children will lead happy lives as independently as possible.

- Educational issues include normalization, integration, and an appropriate life-skills curriculum. Normalization involves age-appropriate treatment and providing environments and representations of individuals that are as close to normal as possible. Integration refers to both physical and social integration. The functional curriculum emphasizes preparation for life and instruction in integrated skills useful in school, work, or home.

- Transitional programming for children with severe and profound disabilities includes preparation for changes in schools, for movement from a segregated to an integrated setting, and for work after school.

- Basic rights, including the right to life and to education, have been questioned for people with severe disabilities. These issues often revolve around perceptions of the individual's quality of life.

KEY TERMS

severe disabilities (page 228)

severe intellectual disabilities (page 228)

profound intellectual disabilities (page 228)

functional communication (page 234)

formal supports (page 241)

natural supports (page 241)

normalization (page 245)

partial participation (page 245)

functional curriculum (page 247)

environmental inventory (page 248)

environmental analysis (page 248)

self-management procedures (page 254)

quality of life (page 256)

USEFUL RESOURCES

- The AbilityHub is a resource center for new programs and products in assistive technology. Their Assistive Technology Solutions are available at **http://www.abilityhub.com**. Go to the section on cognitive disabilities to access information on new products appropriate for individuals with intellectual disabilities.

- PE Central-Adaptive Physical Education is available at **http://pecentral .org/adapted/adaptedmenu.htm.** This website is a resource page for articles or other printed information about adapting physical activities for individuals with disabilities.

- The Arc is an organization that provides information, resources, and training opportunities for people interested in learning more about individuals with cognitive disabilities. Go to its website at **http://www.thearc.org** for links to many helpful and informative sources related to the area of intellectual disabilities.

- The Association for Persons with Severe Handicaps (TASH) is located at 26 West Susquehanna Avenue, Suite 210, Baltimore, MD, 21204, (410) 828-8274. Visit the association's website at **http://www.tash.org.**

- Visit the website **https://www.disability.gov/** to learn about the rights of individuals with disabilities regarding housing opportunities, transportation, employment, and related legislation.

- The following book can provide guidelines to teachers and other professionals interested in developing functional curricula: Paul Wehman and John Kregel (Eds.) (2004). *Functional curriculum for elementary, middle, and secondary age students with special needs* (2nd ed.). Austin, TX: Pro-Ed.

PORTFOLIO ACTIVITIES

1. Visit teachers or transition coordinators in several local schools who specialize in working with individuals with severe or profound intellectual disabilities. Ask to observe the teacher working with students in community-based settings. Record your observations and compare the instructional strategies, types of tasks, and individual performance of the students in each setting.

CEC This activity will help students meet CEC Content Standard 5: Learning Environments and Social Interactions.

2. Identify a task you do frequently as part of your daily or weekly routine, such as doing laundry or preparing a meal. Carefully observe and write down all the components of that task, including specific behaviors and any decisions that must be made to complete the task. Develop a low-tech or a high-tech self-prompting system using pictures, symbols, or video clips.

CEC This activity will help students meet CEC Content Standard 4: Instructional Strategies. And Content Standard 7: Instructional Planning.

3. Locate several grocery stores or fast-food restaurants in your local community. Before visiting them, make a list of things you might need to know if you were teaching individuals with severe disabilities—for example, the location of specific food items, exits, and check-out lines in the grocery store; or methods of ordering, use of picture cues, and location of trays and condiments in the fast-food restaurants. Then visit each location. Create a chart or a graph of the similarities and differences at each location.

CEC This activity will help students meet CEC Content Standard 3: Individual Learning Differences.

4. Compare and contrast functional or life-skills curricula for people with severe disabilities. Obtain the curricula from local public and/or residential schools. Identify the characteristics all the curricula have in common and any significant differences. Create a rubric for critiquing life-skills curricula.

CEC This activity will help students meet CEC Content Standard 3: Individual Learning Differences. And Content Standard 4: Instructional Strategies.

 To access Portfolio Activities for this chapter and other useful study resources including an interactive eBook, related web links, quizzes, flashcards, and videos, visit the Education CourseMate website at CengageBrain.com.

CHAPTER 8

Children with Behavior Disorders

Learning Objectives

After reading this chapter, the reader will:

- Describe how behavior disorders are defined and classified.

- Identify techniques used to recognize and assess children with behavior disorders.

- Describe the importance of schoolwide processes in preventing the development of behavior disorders and demonstration of inappropriate behavior.

- Explain how behavior-management strategies can be used to prevent or manage inappropriate behavior in children.

- Describe the role of academic interventions in behavior management.

- Identify strategies you can use to help students learn to manage their own behavior.

In this chapter, you will learn how behavior disorders are identified and defined, the effects of these disorders on students and their families, and strategies that you can use to work with students who have them. We will also discuss some of the questions and problems surrounding the definition and identification of these disorders.

If you look at a crowd watching a baseball game or a soccer match, you will notice lots of people acting in a lot of different ways. Some people will stand up and yell, some may curse, one fan may be jumping up and down, and one fan may hide his eyes because he just can't look. One person may be ignoring the game and reading the newspaper. Many will stand up during exciting parts of the game and sit down during the rest, so that others can see. Most people appreciate or at least tolerate these behaviors in their fellow fans. If, in a fit of excitement, one man throws a cup of ice in the air, well, that can happen sometimes. But if someone runs down and jumps on the field—it is clear to everyone that a violation of appropriate behavior has occurred.

There are many differences in the ways people react to certain situations, act around other people, follow rules and regulations, and conform to society's expectations for behavior. As illustrated above, this is particularly true among adults, for we accept the fact that people choose their own lifestyles and behave in ways that are most comfortable to them. Typically, concern is voiced only when there appears to be a chance that someone will harm others or himself or herself, or does not appear able to cope with the daily activities of life.

Our outlook on conformity and acceptable patterns of behavior is different when we look at children, particularly children in school settings. The range of behaviors considered acceptable in school settings is limited so that children can benefit from educational programming. Our expectations of how children should feel and act are much more narrowly defined than are our expectations of acceptable adult behavior. Many children do, from time to time, behave in ways that appear to be out of bounds—beyond our typical standards of normal behavior. A child may get into a fight on the playground, or a teenager may come home from the shopping mall with purple hair and three eyebrow piercings. These children are not the focus of this chapter. As educators, we are concerned when inappropriate behavior persists, interferes with school performance, and appears harmful to the child or others.

Terms and Definitions

The children identified in this category of special education can be referred to in a number of ways. The terms used include *behavior disorders, severe emotional disturbance, emotional disturbance, emotionally handicapped,* and *behaviorally handicapped.* Professionals have many different opinions about which term is most appropriate; the term **behavior disorders** is used most frequently in the literature, but the term **emotional disturbance** is still used in the federal definition.

The Federal Definition

At the present time, the federal definition of emotional disturbance in IDEA includes two major criteria:

1. The term means a condition exhibiting one or more of the following characteristics over a long period of time and to a marked degree, which adversely affects educational performance.

    a. An inability to learn that cannot be explained by intellectual, sensory, and health factors;

    b. An inability to build or maintain satisfactory interpersonal relationships with peers and teachers;

    c. Inappropriate types of behavior or feelings under normal circumstances;

    d. A general pervasive mood of unhappiness or depression; or

    e. A tendency to develop physical symptoms or fears associated with personal or school problems.

2. The term includes children who are schizophrenic. The term does not include children who are socially maladjusted unless it is determined that they are emotionally disturbed (US Department of Education, *Federal Register* 42 [163], August 23, 1977, p. 42,. 478).

This definition, like most definitions in special education, is the source of much debate and discussion. A great deal of the controversy revolves around the ambiguity of the terms used as diagnostic markers, and concern that this ambiguity excludes children who require services. For example, phrases such as *inappropriate types of behavior* or *satisfactory interpersonal relationships* are difficult to translate into clear-cut measures of performance. It is not too difficult to imagine that different people would interpret these terms in different ways. As we look below at different ways to measure behavior, it will be easier to see some ways that behavior can differ from one person to another, and how terms such as "inappropriate" may be translated.

Measures of Behavior

Behaviors can differ in frequency or rate, intensity, duration, and age appropriateness. Measures based on these factors are used to determine whether behavior is considered normal or abnormal. In other words, abnormal behavior can be normal behavior that is performed to such a degree that it becomes atypical.

● *Rate*   **Rate** refers to how often a behavior occurs in a given time period. Most children occasionally get out of their seats without asking permission, or get into fights. A child who gets into a fight every day, however, or who gets out of his seat every two minutes would be demonstrating an unusually high rate of these behaviors.

● *Intensity*   **Intensity** refers to the strength or magnitude of the behavior. For example, if a child hits his fist against the desk because he becomes frustrated, he might just hit it loud enough to make a noise, or he could hit it so hard he breaks either his hand or the desk. One instance would be considered a normal response; the other, more intense behavior would be considered problematic.

● *Duration*   The length of time a behavior lasts is referred to as its **duration**. Any child might have an occasional temper tantrum or cry if his or her feelings are hurt. But a tantrum or crying spell that goes on for an hour or two will be considered differently than a ten-minute outburst.

● *Age Appropriateness*   **Age-appropriate behavior** refers to the fact that some behaviors are considered quite normal in children of a certain age but are considered problematic when they persist as the child ages or occur before they are expected. For example, clinging to a parent, throwing tantrums, or being afraid of monsters in the closet are behaviors we might expect from a 5- or 6-year-old, but not from a preteen.

    Some children with emotional or behavior disorders exhibit *unusual* behaviors—behaviors we do not typically see at any level in other children. Children with unusual behaviors usually have a more severe level of behavior disorders. Examples of this type of behavior include unusual patterns of language,

Many behavior problems take place outside of the actual classroom environment.

distinctive hand movements and walking patterns, and behaviors directed at harming oneself or others. We will look at these behaviors more closely when we discuss severe emotional or behavior disabilities later in the chapter.

An important point to keep in mind is that a single episode of what appears to be abnormal behavior does not mean that a child has a behavior disorder. Events within the child's life, as well as the changes and pressures of growing up, can result in an incidence of problem behavior, or perhaps even a few weeks in which the child seems to be exhibiting new and difficult behaviors. For example, we expect certain behaviors, such as talking back to parents and resisting being told what to do, to emerge during the beginning of adolescence. Although these behaviors may cause some difficulty in the family and at school, they reflect our expectations for teenagers. Educators are concerned about atypical behavior that exceeds expectations—that persists over several months and does not seem to have a readily identifiable cause (such as parents going through a divorce or a death in the family).

A single episode of abnormal behavior does not mean that a child has a behavior disorder.

Classifying Behavior Disorders

Behaviors are usually classified into groups or categories. Sometimes, this is done for the purpose of diagnosis, sometimes for assessment, and other times for placement and educational interventions. For the most part, behaviors that seem related in some way are grouped together. Often, children exhibiting one type of behavior in a group or cluster will exhibit others found in that same cluster. Those children may be identified as having a specific type of syndrome or disorder. Other children display behaviors from a number of different groups. A number of classification systems are used with children having behavior or emotional disorders. In addition to the various behaviors described in this section, we have included a separate section on attention deficit/hyperactivity disorder (ADHD) later in this chapter. Although ADHD is not technically a behavior disorder, it has been considered a disorder of behavior because of its historical relationship with hyperactive behavior. ADHD is not a separate category of special education under IDEA; however, it is a common diagnosis for students in general education classrooms and warrants a clear and thorough discussion.

● *The DSM-IV-TR System* One classification system is presented in *The Diagnostic and Statistical Manual of Mental Disorders of the American Psychiatric Association* (4th ed., 2000), known as **DSM-IV-TR.** This manual groups behaviors into diagnostic categories. In other words, the manual lists specific behaviors and other criteria that must be present before a disorder can be diagnosed. Because many behavior and psychiatric disorders are diagnosed on the basis of behavior alone, rather than by a specific test or medical diagnosis, these behavior descriptions can assist in the diagnosis of specific disabilities. Thus, a psychologist may collect observations and reports of a child's behavior in a number of settings over time and compare those behaviors to the categories in DSM-IV-TR to make a diagnosis.

> The DSM-IV-TR classifies behavior by diagnostic categories.

In some schools, the school or clinical psychologist makes the diagnosis of behavior disorders. In other schools, or in the case of a particular child, a psychiatrist or pediatrician may diagnose the disability. The professional status of the individual making a diagnosis is particularly important when severe problems are exhibited or when therapy or medication is part of the remediation process. For example, a physician will need to be involved for types of behavior disorders that may require drug therapy, such as depression or ADHD. An example of diagnostic criteria from DSM-IV is found in the section on ADHD in this chapter.

Visit the website of the American Psychiatric Association to learn more about applying the information from the DSM series, to see the research agenda for DSM-V (the upcoming version of the manual), and to learn more about current research in areas such as ADHD, depression, anxiety disorders, and autism. The new page on the APA website dedicated to DSM-V also provides information on the areas targeted for change in the new edition.

● *Educational Classification Systems* Other systems of classifying behavior are more informal and based on groupings of a more general nature. Rather than looking for specific disorders, we describe broad patterns of behavior or disorders, such as those described below. This type of classification system may be used for educational placement, service delivery, and program development. Although a classification system gives us an idea of the nature of a child's disability, it does not necessarily tell us the best treatment or educational procedures to use (Cullinan, 2002; Kauffman, 2001). As with all special education practices, appropriate interventions are selected based on the individual needs of each child.

Some of the systems currently used by schools and psychologists include scales based on the criteria found in the federal definition, such as the *Scale for Assessing Emotional Disturbance*, 2nd edition (Epstein & Cullinan, 2010). Other scales and assessment instruments are based on systems developed and researched by professionals in the field.

For example, Quay and Peterson devised a classification system based on extensive observations of children and the patterns of behavior that surfaced. They used six types of behavior as the basis for their classification scheme: conduct disorder, socialized aggression, attention problems-immaturity, anxiety-withdrawal, psychotic behavior, and motor excess. They developed the Revised Behavior Problem Checklist (Quay & Peterson, 1983, 1996), which reflects this classification system.

Achenbach developed the Child Behavior Checklist (Achenback & Edelbrak, 1979; Achenbach, 1991) that classifies behavior and then identifies these behavior clusters as either externalizing or internalizing behaviors. This framework continues to be the most frequently used rubric for classifying behaviors in the literature in emotional/behavioral disorders. **Externalizing behaviors,** also known as acting out or aggressive behaviors, encompass all those behaviors that are expressed overtly and that appear, in some way, to be directed toward others or the environment. These outwardly directed behaviors may represent impulsivity or a lack of self-control and can often be confrontational, aggressive, or disruptive. Children with externalizing behavior disorders typically stand out in a classroom because of the impact their behavior has on others. The child who throws tantrums or teases his or her neighbor will interfere with others' abilities to listen or participate in class; aggressive actions may result in more than one child on the floor or in tears.

Internalizing behaviors are self-directed behaviors, such as withdrawal, avoidance, or compulsiveness. A child with an internalizing behavior disorder may be sad or depressed, withdrawn or shy, or focused on disturbing fears or fantasies.

Because of the nature of internalizing behavior disorders, a child's problems may not be recognized immediately, if at all. Often, children with internalizing behavior disorders may slip through screening procedures, as well as the PBIS system, which will look initially at office referrals for screening; many children with internalizing behaviors won't engage in the type of behaviors that will require referrals. Research suggests, however, that risk factors for internalizing disorders can be identified in children between the ages of 2 and 5. These risk factors include parental psychopathology, parental stress related to parenting, and parent report of the child's internalizing disorders (Ashford, Smit, van Lier, Cuijpers, & Koot, 2008). The fact that so many of these risk factors are related to parents' concerns makes it more challenging to look at children in this cluster with typical screening instruments.

The child with an internalizing emotional disorder typically will not be a disruptive influence in the class and will not exhibit behaviors that draw attention from peers or the teacher. The student's avoidance of social interaction and the presence of fears or interfering thoughts, however, can affect his or her ability to perform in school and to establish social relationships. Recently, in light of the publicity given to adolescent suicides, more attention has been directed to identifying children with this type of disorder. Again, it is important to examine the degree and appearance of the behavior, as well as the effects on the child when trying to identify internalizing behavior disorders. Many young children will exhibit excessively shy behavior when encountering new experiences or people

> Some feel that many children with emotional or behavior disorders are not receiving needed attention.

Social acceptance by classmates is desired by every adolescent. The peer group can play an important role in identifying and supporting appropriate behaviors.

(such as the first day of school). We might also expect a period of depressed or withdrawn behavior when a traumatic event such as death, divorce, or a move has occurred in a child's life.

In the rest of this chapter, we will be using the Achenbach and Edelbrock classification system of externalizing and internalizing behaviors to look at the effects of behavior or emotional disorders on children and their educational needs. This system is the least complicated, encompasses all behaviors, and focuses on the fundamental difference in children's behavior patterns.

From the teacher's perspective, the system helps to emphasize the relevance of *both* types of behavior. Unfortunately, the behaviors found in the internalizing dimension are not recognized as easily or determined to be problematic even though these behaviors can have a profound effect on a child. As you might expect, teachers are more motivated to identify problems that disrupt the classroom and cause daily conflict than to recognize a problem such as depressed or withdrawn behavior that affects only the child in question.

● *Severe Behavior Disorders*   In the case studies we present throughout this chapter, we can see the great impact behavior disorders might have on a child's life. Yet the continuum of emotional or behavior disorders extends even further than what has been already described. Some individuals exhibit severe disorders of behavior—behaviors that require even more specialized attention and intervention, some of which are provided outside of the regular school setting. Others have unusual patterns of behavior, such as those found in autism (see Chapter 9), a psychiatric diagnosis such as childhood schizophrenia, or a combination of disabilities that also require specialized interventions and that can have profound effects on the individual's behavior in all areas of life.

Although children with very severe behavior disorders may have externalizing or internalizing behavior disorders, they exhibit behaviors that are markedly severe and intended to harm others or themselves. Other children in this category may be so withdrawn as to resist any semblance of normal social interaction. Their functioning may be severely inhibited because of withdrawal, disoriented thoughts, or depression. In general, these children require extensive and intensive educational assistance. Some children with severe disabilities receive educational services in public school settings, whereas others still are served, at least for a time, in segregated or residential facilities:

> One child, John, who is barely 8 years old, lives in a residential facility for children with severe behavior disorders. He is exceptionally bright yet works at a primer level. By the age of 7, John had stabbed his mother twice with a knife, pushed his younger brother down the stairs and off a high chair, and tried to set fire to his room on three separate occasions. Although most of the time John seemed to be a friendly, outgoing child, his behaviors were determined to be so potentially harmful that he was placed in the residential setting.

Behavior patterns similar to John's are among the most difficult for professionals and parents to handle. The child seems to be normal or above average in so many respects, yet exhibits incredibly hurtful behavior without any warning or apparent reason. Treatment for John will need to be very complex, and most likely it is outside of the realm of school personnel. Teaching him to recognize and control his impulses will be a key focus.

Other students with severe behavior disorders may be the target of their own destructive behavior:

> Rhonda is 17 years old. Although she has always been moody and aggressive, she was identified as having behavior disorders only a few years ago.

At that time, her behaviors became increasingly self-destructive and violent. She broke her hand by slamming it against her locker, gave herself cigarette burns on her arms, and, in the last year, made two suicide attempts. Although Rhonda was placed in a public school resource class initially, she was later placed in a residential setting for more intensive interventions and close supervision.

Such violent, self-destructive behavior is often interpreted as a plea for attention or a cry for help. Interventions for suicidal students include counseling, medication (when appropriate), helping them think more positively about themselves, teaching new and more positive ways to communicate anger, fear, or frustration, focusing on activities designed to demonstrate and accentuate their skills and abilities, and developing positive friendships. We constantly hear media reports of increasing numbers of depressed teenagers and alarming rates of youth suicide. There are a number of websites you can visit to find out more about these issues. The American Academy of Pediatrics website includes recent research data and suicide warning signs. Another website, About Teen Depression is targeted more toward parents. This website presents information on depression, alcohol, drugs, suicide, and treatment options.

The specific instructional strategies and therapies used for children with severe behavior disabilities will vary widely and must be tailored to the specific needs of the individual. In a number of instances, drug therapy will be a component of the treatment plan. In part, drug treatment is a response to recent discoveries that some disorders, such as certain types of schizophrenia or depression, appear to have a strong physiological component.

Prevalence

The prevalence rate of behavior disorders is estimated to be about 8.6 percent of the school-aged population with disabilities, although estimates have reached as high as 20 to 30 percent. In the United States and territories, 484,000 students, ages 3 to 21, were served for emotional disturbance during the 2003–2004 school year (NICHCY, 2011).

Although these numbers may seem large, they actually represent a figure far lower than most estimates of the true number of students with behavior disorders. The vague criteria in the definition and the subjective nature of assessment often make a definitive diagnosis difficult; therefore, the percentage of students identified with emotional disturbance in one state could be very different from the percentage of children identified in another. There are probably many students with behavior disorders who are not receiving needed special education services.

Pause and Reflect

Most children with behavior disorders are diagnosed based on the evaluations of teachers, parents, and school psychologists. When thinking about behavior disorders, it is helpful to understand your own ability to tolerate differences in behavior, as well as your perceptions of "too much" activity or "not enough" social interaction. What are your expectations of behavior for a child in your class? How flexible can you, or should you, be? ●

A CLOSER LOOK

Cultural Diversity and Serious Emotional Disturbance (SED)

Misperceptions abound

Because many people lack understanding and cultural sensitivity toward cultures different from their own, teachers, administrators, ancillary personnel, and students may misinterpret culturally based behaviors and may view them as behavior disorders. What teachers consider "discipline problems" are determined by their own culture, personal values, attitudes, and teaching style. More often than not, disciplinary problems seem centered on interpersonal discourse. Tension and negative consequences seem to intensify among the various communication styles of diverse ethnic groups when teachers and their students do not share the same cultural backgrounds, ethnic identities, values, social protocols, and relational styles.

Cultural inversion and other behavior

Culturally different behaviors are not equivalent to social-skills deficits or behavior disorders. Standardized or European American-based social-skills assessments may not adequately reflect the social competence of culturally different students. The quick, high-intensity responses of African Americans, for example, may be seen as hostile, rude, or hyperactive. Acting-out, disruptive behaviors do not automatically signal conduct disorder and, in some cases, may be more a manifestation of "cultural inversion" where students are resisting the label of "acting white" by refusing to follow the established expectations of the classroom culture.

Cycles of misinterpretation and fear

Cultural misunderstandings can have negative effects for both students and teachers. Researchers noted the occurrence of vicious circles, explaining that when students find their playful acts are misinterpreted, they become angry and intensify the roughness of their activities; the result is greater fear on the part of whites. Students may feel empowered and rewarded by the effects of their actions on whites, particularly females. This false sense of power may lead them to escalate those behaviors, most likely at the expense of more productive behaviors that relate to school success.

Excessive compliance or cultural expectation?

It also should be noted that exceptionally compliant behaviors are not necessarily indicative of the absence of some difficulty. For example, in one study Asian American students received positive teacher and peer ratings but also indicated they were least likely to question unfair rules or do anything if treated unfairly. This emphasis on conformity and "saving face" may cause teachers to make erroneous assumptions about the child's well-being and may lead to significant problems being overlooked.

Ecosystem importance

The tendency for some children to need more "wait time" or to be verbally unassertive (e.g., Native and Hispanic American children) may be interpreted as a lack of motivation or resistance to instruction. Researchers assert the need for an "ecosystemic" assessment, which takes an ecological approach to consider all aspects of the child's environment.

The issue of culturally relevant assessment for SED is probably most relevant for African and Asian American students who are proportionately overrepresented and underrepresented in SED diagnoses, respectively. Researchers recommend that one use norms based on members of the cultural group of the student being assessed and that evaluation materials be reviewed by people who know the child well and can provide culturally based interpretations of the child's behavior. Other suggestions for linguistically diverse students are to assess students in both languages, attend to verbal and nonverbal communication, and to focus on ways to support the student rather than on simply documenting student deficits.

Source: G. Cartledge, C. D. Kea, & D. J. Ida (2000). Anticipating differences—celebrating strengths: Providing culturally competent services for students with serious emotional disturbance. *Teaching Exceptional Children, 32* (2), 32.

Causes of Behavior Disorders

The causes of most behavior and emotional disorders are difficult to pinpoint. We often see children with very similar behavior patterns, yet very different learning and family histories. Sometimes, it is easy to pinpoint factors or situations that possibly contribute to behavior and emotional disorders; sometimes, there are no readily identifiable causal factors. Let's look at the following two examples of students with externalizing behavior disorders.

It is difficult to pinpoint the causes of most behavior and emotional disorders.

CASE STUDIES

Sandy, age 10, was identified as behavior disordered at age 7. At that time, she began demonstrating a number of problematic behaviors: She used extremely violent and obscene language toward her teachers and classmates; threw loud and long temper tantrums; hit her teacher and threw things when she was denied a request; and said cruel things to the other children in the class. She was failing the second grade. About two years later, it was discovered that Sandy had been the victim of sexual abuse by her mother's boyfriend. Although the abusive situation had ended, Sandy's behavior persisted. The identification of the specific cause could not, by itself, heal Sandy's emotional distress or end the behaviors that she had acquired and practiced over time.

Bill, age 13, was identified as having emotional or behavior disorders for the past five years. He is very active, always out of his seat, and moving around. Although he can be compliant and cooperative, he flares up easily, becoming resistant and confrontational with teachers and principals. Bill constantly fights with other children. He seems to see every interaction as a challenge and responds with anger and aggression. He failed fourth grade and is barely passing his classes now. Most of the students in school dislike and avoid him. Bill lives with his mother and they apparently have a good relationship. Although Bill's behavior has improved some during the past few years, he is socially rejected and behind academically, and he still resorts to violent interactions when frustrated or when he feels challenged in any way.

Although Sandy's inappropriate behavior had a clear time of onset, Bill is an example of a child with a long history of problem behavior. He has trouble interacting with adults and peers, and is not doing well in school. Bill seems to see things somewhat differently than other children; he feels others are out to get him, he can't control his temper, and he always uses aggression to respond. Why does Bill act this way? Does he live in a violent home or neighborhood? Does he have problems dealing with reality? Or is he just a bad kid?

There are no simple answers to these questions for many students with behavior disorders. Sometimes, we (as teachers) can speculate or make assumptions about the role of parents, peers, or temperament, but often this is all we can do. It is very difficult to determine why one child has a behavior disorder and another child in the same situation does not.

In spite of numerous theories and hypotheses about the causes of behavior disorders, all we can do with certainty is identify factors that seem to coincide with the occurrence of behavior differences. These factors can be grouped into two major categories: environmental and physiological. Environmental factors focus on the child's interactions with people and things external to him or her; physiological factors focus on the inner biology or psychology of the child. The accompanying Closer Look box, "Factors Associated with Behavior Disorders," summarizes these points.

A CLOSER LOOK   Factors Associated with Behavior Disorders

Environmental Factors
- Family factors
- Cultural factors
- School factors

Physiological Factors
- Organic factors
- Genetic factors
- Specific syndromes with behavior correlates

Environmental Factors

Environmental factors that may contribute to behavior disorders include family factors, cultural factors, and school factors. Family factors often revolve around the level and consistency of discipline; the history of violence and arrests in the family; and the way parents and siblings deal with feelings and each other. Children who experience consistent behavior management practices, including positive as well as negative consequences for behavior, have a clearer idea of appropriate and inappropriate behavior. In other words, just as in the classroom, it is important for children at home to know the rules and be expected to follow them. Some other possible contributors to children's behavior can be the modeling of aggressive behavior by family members, neglect, or traumatic events such as death or divorce. Remember, however, that the way individual children respond to factors such as these can vary considerably. Also, it is important to note that many children with behavior disorders seem to have very supportive and loving family environments.

Cultural factors may include cultural norms for accepted levels of deviant behavior. Webb-Johnson (2003) suggests that one of the reasons African American students are overrepresented in classes for students with behavior disorders is that many teachers misinterpret culturally acceptable behavior as inappropriate, leading to a cycle of attempted control by teachers and resistance by students. Some people suspect that other cultural factors influencing the occurrence of behavior disorders include the level of violence in the media. Figure 8.1 presents a diagram of the interaction between environmental risk factors and the development of inappropriate behaviors.

Physiological Factors

Physiological factors that may influence the development of behavior disorders include organic factors, such as dysfunctions of the central nervous system; genetic factors, such as a family history of schizophrenia; or specific syndromes, such as Tourette's syndrome, that are accompanied by unusual behavior patterns. A child's temperament has also been identified as a possible source of behavior differences. Again, with the exception of some syndromes with distinct behavior correlates, we must rely primarily on assumptions when dealing with physiological causes of behavior disorders.

It is interesting to note that a number of students receive drug treatment for behavior disorders. Although the cause of the behaviors may be unknown, certain drugs ameliorate symptoms for some people. Because drug treatments work on the symptoms rather than on the causes, drug therapy must be constant in order for the symptoms to stay suppressed. A prominent example is the use of drug therapy for attention deficit/hyperactivity disorder (ADHD). Although the exact

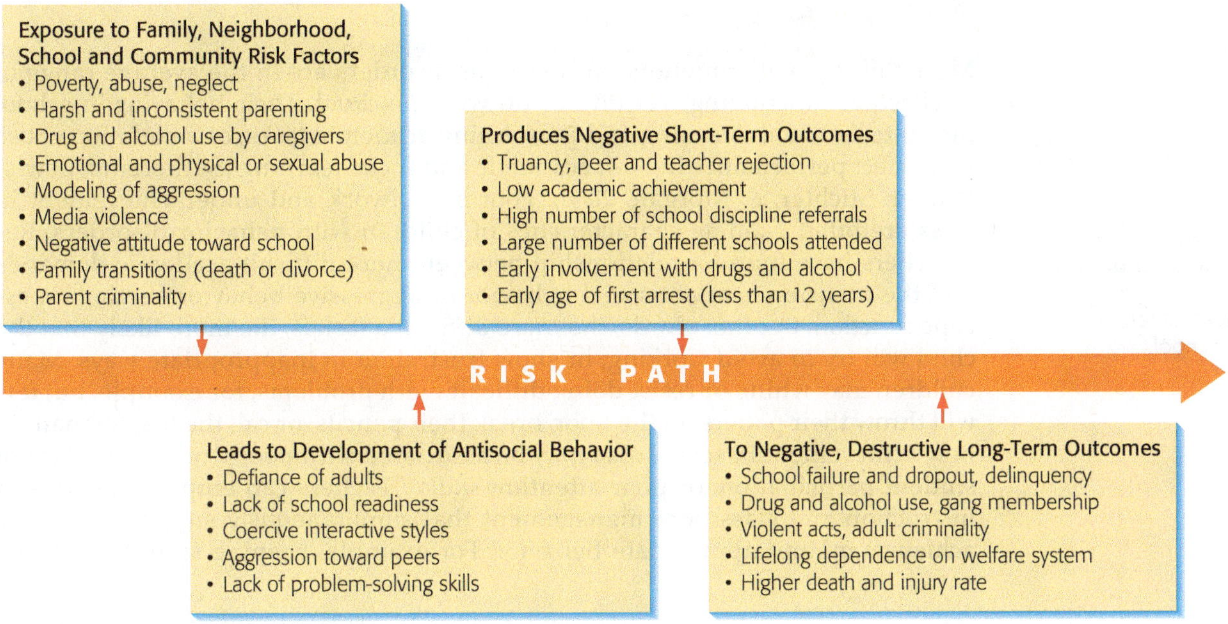

Exposure to Family, Neighborhood, School and Community Risk Factors
- Poverty, abuse, neglect
- Harsh and inconsistent parenting
- Drug and alcohol use by caregivers
- Emotional and physical or sexual abuse
- Modeling of aggression
- Media violence
- Negative attitude toward school
- Family transitions (death or divorce)
- Parent criminality

Produces Negative Short-Term Outcomes
- Truancy, peer and teacher rejection
- Low academic achievement
- High number of school discipline referrals
- Large number of different schools attended
- Early involvement with drugs and alcohol
- Early age of first arrest (less than 12 years)

R I S K   P A T H

Leads to Development of Antisocial Behavior
- Defiance of adults
- Lack of school readiness
- Coercive interactive styles
- Aggression toward peers
- Lack of problem-solving skills

To Negative, Destructive Long-Term Outcomes
- School failure and dropout, delinquency
- Drug and alcohol use, gang membership
- Violent acts, adult criminality
- Lifelong dependence on welfare system
- Higher death and injury rate

FIGURE 8.1

The path to negative outcomes

Source: J. Sprague & H. Walker (2000). Early identification and intervention for youth with antisocial and violent behavior. *Exceptional Children,* 66 (3), 391.

cause of this disorder is not known, certain drugs have been found to suppress its symptoms in some students. Young people with depression or who demonstrate psychotic behaviors may also receive medication. A medical model for treatment may be used with increasing frequency as we learn more about the role of physiological contributions to behavior disorders. Professionals stress, however, that effective programs may include medication in conjunction with behavior and educational interventions (Brown et al., 2005).

Pause and Reflect

As you can see from our discussion of causes of behavior disorders, it is often difficult to pinpoint a clear cause of a child's inappropriate behavior. Even when we do find a traumatic event or sequence of events that precipitated behavior at one time, our interventions focus on the here and now. Factors in current environments must be addressed before behavior can be changed. Do you find it surprising that often there is no clear cause of a child's behavior disorder? ●

Characteristics of Students with Behavior Disorders

Behavior and emotional disorders, by definition, affect the way children interact with those around them as well as the performance abilities of the children themselves. In this section, we discuss some of the specific ways the child's life can be affected by behavior disorders.

School Achievement

Most children with emotional or behavior disorders are in the average range of intellectual functioning, yet do not do well in school. Their behavior in school may interfere with learning and performing academic tasks, or a common cause may affect performance in both academic and social learning (Sutherland, Lewis-Plamer, Stichter, & Morgan, 2008). Poor schoolwork and underachievement in class are often cited as characteristics of children with behavior disorders. Researchers have found a relationship between more difficult academic demands and the occurrence of antisocial behavior or aggressive behavior serving an escape function. In other words, the more difficult a task is, the more likely that the child will try to avoid working, or show frustration in inappropriate ways. Many children may whine or resist doing difficult math problems, for example, but few will throw their papers on the floor, break their pencils, or call the teacher names. Low achievement in school also may be associated with poor work habits, lack of student participation, or poor attention skills. Teachers can employ methods of instruction and classroom management that simultaneously support academic achievement and appropriate behavior. For example, keeping students actively

> Most children with emotional or behavior disorders are in the normal range of intelligence but tend to do poorly in school.

FIRST PERSON

Jon: His Turn

Jon is a 13-year-old student with emotional/behavior disorders. Jon is in middle school; currently, he is in a self-contained class for students with behavior disorders. He was elated when he was asked to tell his story: Finally, we would listen.

I hope that this passage will help every E.D. teacher understand an emotional disability called "bipolar disorder", something that will haunt me for the rest of my life. I remember when I was first sent to an E.D. class it was September and I was going into fifth grade my first day was OK but as the days progressed things got much worse. I Started to get heavily depressed. Every day I went to school the biggest thought In my head was suicide but I could only keep it in my head for so long. It kept getting worse to the point that when I walk down the hall way to My classroom it was like walking into HELL! When I was in in kinder garden I got into trouble close to every day. My mother has told me about this many times. She

used to say many of my family members used to say that something was Not quite right with me. The year I entered the Third grade was the year that Will live in infamy for me. It was the year that the monster inside me broke free. I still was not on any meds and when the littlest things happened such as getting Punished or having a lot of pressure put on me I would start crying then I Could not stop and I start thinking the words in my head what if what if what if. After that I look at things around me and somehow I don't remember where I am. Now I am on meds and doing better. I'm slowly but surely digging myself Out of my hole. There is a kid in my class that ticks me off but other then that School is going great. In this entry I would liked to thank my mom my dad And my psychiatrist Dr. Davis thanks to them I'm doing much better.

Source: This is a true story though the names and identities have been changed to protect the privacy of the individuals depicted here. "Jon's story" is copied as originally written.

engaged during instruction, providing plentiful opportunities for students to respond during class, and offering consistent praise for good performance can create increases in both accurate academic responses and appropriate classroom behavior (Simonsen et al., 2008; Sutherland, Wehby, & Yoder, 2002).

In general, poor academic performance is an important and troubling characteristic of students with emotional and behavioral disorders. Lane, Barton-Arwood, Nelson, and Wheby (2008) found that both elementary and secondary students served in self-contained classrooms for students with behavior disorders were below the 25th percentile in the areas of reading, written language, and mathematics. In addition, Anderson, Kutash, and Duchnowski (2001) found the academic prognosis for reading performance of children with behavior disorders was actually worse than the prognosis for children with learning disabilities. In spite of the fact that they actually received more special education services than the children with learning disabilities, children with behavior disorders made little progress in reading between kindergarten and the end of elementary school. There is no clear reason for this lack of progress; however, we can speculate that the amount of time teachers spend on managing behavior, and the resistance of students with behavior disorders to academic requirements, may contribute to poor academic growth. One important result of the RTI and PBIS models is that research on evidence-based interventions that address both academic and behavioral needs of students is now recognized as an important priority (Lane, 2007). Much of the recent research, especially on small-group instruction for students at risk for behavior problems, focuses on strengthening academic skills as a way to engage students successfully and reduce behavioral issues.

> PBIS is a process designed to recognize and support appropriate behaviors and reduce inappropriate behaviors.

© Mary Kate Denny/PhotoEdit

Some children experience difficulty adjusting to the behavior requirements of social situations, which leads to inappropriate or aggressive behavior.

Social Adjustment

Children with emotional and behavior disorders by definition exhibit behaviors that affect their social and emotional development. Externalizing behaviors such as violence and aggression may be directed toward classmates, and many children with externalizing behavior disorders do not have the skills for reflecting on and restricting their behavior. As these children grow into adolescents, their lack of control can often lead to serious conflicts. The patterns of violent behaviors exhibited by students with behavior disorders may change as students age. Violent behavior patterns may consist of bullying at the elementary level, fighting at the middle-school level, and using weapons or drugs at the high-school level (Furlong & Morrison, 2000). Some subgroups of individuals with behavior disorders, particularly children identified with "callous-unemotional traits" such as a lack of empathy and guilt, may be particularly and consistently violent across childhood and adolescence (Frick & White, 2008). These individuals may demonstrate a stable rate of particularly aggressive behavior across time.

Internalized behaviors such as withdrawal or depression may result in the children being teased or rejected by classmates, and may cause great difficulty when interacting with others. Without education and intervention, the behaviors that characterize a behavior disorder will continue to affect the student after he or she leaves the school environment. Physical aggression in young boys suggests a higher likelihood of physical aggression and delinquent behavior in adolescents (Brody et al., 2003). What will happen when an aggressive child grows into an adult? Will he punch his coworkers or have a tantrum while driving or arguing with his girlfriend? If a student doesn't learn new ways to control and respond to anger or frustration as he or she grows older, the probability of encounters with the law increases.

High-school classes for students with behavior disorders often include students who have been in trouble with the law. The number of teens with behavior disorders who have gone through the legal system at least once varies greatly from area to area; however, students with this diagnosis appear at higher risk for arrest both during and after the school years (Cullinan, 2002). Patterns of aggressive, rule-breaking, and risk-taking behavior are often found in students with behavior disorders, and these behaviors set the stage for illegal activities.

Research has investigated patterns of drug use and dropout rates of junior and senior high-school students with and without behavior disorders. Students with behavior disorders are a particular risk for abuse of illegal substances such as alcohol, tobacco, marijuana, and hard drugs (Flory, Milich, Lynam, Leukefeld, & Clayton, 2003). Another issue addressed by research recently is bullying—which children are likely to become or be victimized by bullies. Although bullies have been around for generations, the intensity of bullying behavior, the new avenues for bullying opened up through electronic media, and the devastating results of some bullying episodes have brought this issue into focus like never before. Read A Closer Look, "Bullying" on page 276, for a more in-depth description of bullying behavior and for helpful resources.

> Many adolescents with behavior disorders have been in trouble with the law.

Language and Communication

As we look at the effects of emotional or behavior disorders on communication, we must remember that behavior *is* communication. Some behaviors are learned as a way of responding to situations or events, or as a way of getting a response; some are developed because an individual has no other effective means of expression; and some are developed to enable an individual to control a situation. When we talk about teaching students appropriate behavior, or reducing inappropriate behavior, we are also teaching students alternative ways of communicating information, feelings, or needs.

Inappropriate behavior does not necessarily imply that a student has poor language skills; in fact, some students with behavior disorders may be quite expressive and articulate. Research has found, however, that there appears to be a relationship between language development and some students with behavior disorders. For example, in a study conducted by Brownlie et al. (2004) adolescent boys with behavior disorders exhibited higher rates of general language impairment and report higher rates of arrests and convictions than adolescents without language impairments. Some students with behavior disorders are found to use fewer words per sentence, to have difficulty staying on a topic, and to have problems using language that is appropriate or meaningful in a given situation or conversation (Donahue, Cole, & Hartas, 1994). Students may also have difficulty organizing their thoughts to communicate effectively through oral or written language.

Language is crucial to academic performance, to interactions with peers and adults, and to the development of the sequential logical thought processes required in many self-management interventions; it is an important component of any educational program. Communication, however, involves more than language. Name-calling, tantrums, and turning over desks, like all behaviors, are ways of communicating. Teachers should always keep in mind the potential communicative intent of the *behaviors* students are exhibiting and be ready to provide appropriate alternatives—new ways of expressing how they feel or what they want—so they can successfully overcome their existing inappropriate communication behaviors.

The more teachers understand about the environments in which children are working, the more they can prepare the students to handle those emotional and behavior requirements.

Families

When someone you love, particularly your child, your brother, or your sister, does things to hurt him or herself or you, wreaks havoc in the house, throws tantrums in public, or stays in his or her room crying all day, a lot of emotions are raised. Behaviors like these not only affect your relationship with that individual; they are confusing—why is the behavior occurring? Are you doing something to cause the behavior or make it worse? How can you look past the behavior to see the child you love? The challenges faced by the families of children with behavior disorders are difficult; parents may feel helpless when the child they know and love sometimes becomes a child with behavior they can't understand.

● *Relationships with Children with Behavior Disorders*   The effects on the family of a child with behavior disorders can be significant. Some parents struggle with the feeling that they are responsible for their child's behavior problem; many parents find dealing with the child's behavior to be emotionally and physically exhausting. Some parents, and siblings as well, feel they have to focus all their attention on a child with behavior disorders; others try to ignore the behaviors. Because a child's behavior is often taken to be a reflection of parenting skill, a child with behavior disorders may cause a parent to feel embarrassed and guilty. Parents may try to "make it up" to the child, or conversely become angry with him or her. Try to remember this the next time you stare angrily at a parent whose child is crying in the grocery store. Parents may be faced continually with fear of what their child will do next, or with feelings of helplessness.

Because of specific stress factors and other individual needs of families, educational plans must take the family's needs into account. Some of the feelings of helplessness can be addressed when parents are given strategies to implement and carry over to the home, particularly in the area of dealing with crises—a need

A CLOSER LOOK   Bullying

As we think about students with emotional and behavioral disorders, we should consider children who, during their lives, could be either victims or aggressors. When we look at children who are aggressive towards or threaten other children, we are often looking at behavior that can be described as bullying. Bullying behavior is often in the news because of its disastrous effects. Whether one child or a group of children are doing the bullying, the consequences can be deadly for the victim, as sometimes the victimized child sees suicide as the only means of escape.

What is bullying?

Bullying can be defined many ways, but all definitions have some commonalities. These include:

1. Desire for control or power
2. Threatening or harmful behavior
3. Repetitive actions towards an individual or group of individuals (Stop Bullying, 2011)

What types of bullying are there?

1. Direct bullying: Direct bullying means that a bully, or group of bullies, is doing something to you directly. This could be verbal (calling you names, teasing you about the way you look, etc.). Direct bullying could also mean a physical interaction—the bully could be hitting you, pushing you, or taking something that belongs to you.

2. Indirect bullying: Indirect bullying means that the bully is doing something behind your back. He or she may be spreading rumors, posting pictures of you in the school or on Facebook, or writing graffiti about you (Medlineplus, 2011). A new term, cyberbullying, refers to this type of indirect bullying via electronic media such as Facebook, Myspace, Twitter, cell phones, and YouTube (National Crime Prevention Council, 2011).

Who does bullying?

Although bullying clearly is an inappropriate behavior, children or adolescents do not have to be identified with a behavior or emotional disorder to be a bully. Some students plan to frighten or dominate other children, and occasionally students find themselves caught up in a cycle of bullying. Research gives us some information about bullies, but it gives us a wide range of characteristics.

1. Historically, research on bullies has described bullies as quick to anger, impulsive, dominating, and seeing violence in a positive way. Bullies are frequently described as coming from families with troubled backgrounds, with inconsistent and violent parenting in the home. Bullies were found to have a higher incidence than children who were not bullies of substance abuse, as well as depression, attention deficit hyperactivity disorder, and conduct disorders. The relationship between bullying and social status, or popularity, as well as self-esteem was not clear. Recent studies suggest

frequently expressed by parents of children with behavior disorders. For example, a family may be concerned about the tantrums their 10-year-old displays in public places when he is unable to get his way. Embarrassed by their child, the parents typically give in to him so that he will stop creating a public scene. The parents feel manipulated by their child and helpless. The teacher may come up with a set of techniques for the parents to try. These may include a checklist for the child to keep for himself while out in public. If all the appropriate behaviors are checked off, the child could be eligible for some privilege or allowed to choose where to eat lunch. Other strategies include helping the parents develop consistent and firm consequences to implement if a tantrum should occur and taking the child on a number of short trips to places that usually do not result in problems (for example, the post office as opposed to the toy store) so that lots of praise and encouragement can be given when no tantrums occur.

Teachers often involve parents in programs designed to teach behavior.

● *Parents and Schools*   The family of the child with emotional or behavior disorders plays a critical role in the development and implementation of effective educational programs. Strong parent-teacher relationships may be particularly

some clarification on these issues—bullies may not be the homogenous group we once thought (Smokowski & Kopasz, 2005).

2. Not surprisingly, recent research confirms that children who bully have a higher incidence of aggressive and disruptive behaviors than other children; they also may have a higher incidence of sleep problems (which could have physiological or environmental origins) (O'Brien et al., 2011).

3. Young children who were bullies were found to be socially desirable playmates, particularly by other bullies and aggressive boys, and had relatively good leadership skills (Perren & Alsaker, 2006).

4. There may be subgroups of bullies for both boys and girls, including a subgroup that is popular and socially intelligent, a group that is moderately popular, and a group that is unpopular with low social intelligence. Each bully subtype may bully for different reasons—from gaining popularity to showing dominance to instinctual aggression (Peeters, Cillessen, & Scholte, 2010).

5. Children who have been both victims and bullies may experience different consequences from bullying behavior than children who are not victims, but "pure" bullies. Pollastri, Cardemil, and O'Donnell (2010) reported that the self-esteem of bully/victims in both boys and girls was much lower than that of students in the pure bully group.

Over time, however, girls in both groups, but especially the pure bully group, had significant increases in self-esteem, while boys in neither group had changes in self-esteem.

What do you do to stop bullying?

Tips for students

1. Avoid the bully.
2. Be brave and confident if you do see the bully: Try to ignore the bully, don't show you are scared, and don't try to bully back.
3. Try to walk with or be with friends.
4. Tell an adult you can trust about what is happening (KidsHealth, 2011).
5. In the case of cyberbullying, you may want to block communication with the bully and report the problem to the Internet service provider (National Crime Prevention Council, 2011).

How can you find out more information?

There are many websites devoted to bullying as well as other types of printed media. One child-oriented website that also has information for parents and teachers is Stop Bullying **(http://stopbullyingnow .hrsa.gov/)**, a website presented jointly by the U.S. Department of Health and Human Services and the Departments of Education and Justice. More information on cyberbullying can be found at the National Crime Prevention Council website.

important when the teacher and student are from different cultural backgrounds so that the parents believe the behavior goals are meaningful, and to ensure an absence of cultural bias in the goals the team selects (Cartledge, Kea, & Ida, 2000). If the parents do not buy into the child's behavior intervention plan, the child probably won't either. Many educators try to involve parents as much as possible when establishing consistent behavior-management strategies across home and school settings. Programs with a home-based component that include the delivery by parents of positive and negative consequences for behavior (privileges and restrictions) result in decreases in noncompliant and antisocial behaviors as well as in symptoms of depression in children (Eddy, Reid, & Fetrow, 2000; Rosen et al., 1990). Children are more likely to learn and apply new behaviors when they are receiving the same attention, consequences, and rules at home and at school.

> A key factor in consistent behavior management is communication between teacher and parent.

One major factor in consistent behavior management is the degree of communication between the teacher and the parent. Parents of a child with behavior disorders should keep in close contact with their child's teachers so they can be aware of how he or she is progressing and how they can stress the same behavior patterns at home. Many teachers have devised daily or weekly checklists or

© Mary Kate Denny/PhotoEdit

Children with behavior disorders may require certain levels of classroom structure to support appropriate school behavior.

behavior reports that are sent home to let parents know how the child behaved that day and what the parents can do to help reinforce good behavior. Parents may provide consequences for good school behavior, such as taking the child to a movie on Saturday afternoon after a week of good reports. This type of teacher-parent alliance may be particularly helpful with older children who value their weekend and afterschool time. In the Teaching Strategies and Accommodations

Teaching Strategies & Accommodations

Working Effectively with Parents

Teachers of students with challenging behaviors know that interventions that are supported and continued by parents are more likely to be effective and to be maintained over time. Five important steps towards teacher-parent collaboration are described below.

1. Teachers should understand the parents and family of their students—listen, learn family routines, and learn family goals.

2. Teachers should help parents understand the rationale behind a behavioral approach and explain important behavioral principles. Explain how these principles are operating within the context of the individual family.

3. Work with parents to design behavior interventions—identify antecedents and consequences, learn the child's learning history, and identify

together the types of supports that can and will be provided at home.

4. Teach parents to conduct interventions at home—include defining and recording behavior, options for responding to behavior, and teaching other family members. Teachers should actually teach these skills to parents using modeling and guided practice, and providing feedback on parent activities.

5. Teachers should help parents continue their involvement as interventionists by providing education support and assisting parents in locating support groups and additional resources.

(*Source:* Park, J. H., Alber-Morgan, S. R., & Fleming, C. (2011). Collaborating with parents to implement behavioral interventions for children with challenging behaviors. *Teaching Exceptional Children, 43,* 22–30.)

box, "Working Effectively with Parents," Park, Alber-Morgan, and Fleming (2011) pinpoint five strategies to use when collaborating with parents to implement effective behavior change strategies.

Pause and Reflect

As we look at the characteristics of children and adolescents with behavior disorders, it is clear that there often is a strong interaction between behavior and academic performance. Perhaps you are surprised that so many children with behavior disorders also experience learning difficulties. How do you think inappropriate behavior could affect academic learning or difficulty in academics could affect behavior? ●

Attention Deficit/Hyperactivity Disorder

As mentioned earlier, **attention deficit/hyperactivity disorder (ADHD)** refers to a disorder that affects an individual's ability to attend to or focus on tasks and that may involve high levels of motoric activity. As you can see on the next page in the A Closer Look box, "Diagnostic Criteria for Attention Deficit / Hyperactivity Disorder," the symptoms of ADHD are grouped into two major categories: (1) inattention and (2) hyperactivity-impulsivity. The number of symptoms a child displays in each category will determine if the child has primarily an attention disorder (ADHD, predominantly inattention type), a hyperactivity disorder (ADHD, predominantly hyperactive-impulsive type), or a combination (ADHD, combined type) (DSM-IV-TR, 2000). You may hear the term *attention deficit disorder* (ADD) used by teachers or parents to refer to the inattention type of ADHD, or as a general description of attention problems.

Assessment and Diagnosis

Historically, between 3 and 7 percent of children in the United States have been identified as having ADHD (DSM-IV-TR). However, recent research suggests an even higher prevalence rate in some places (CDC, 2011). The data from the National Health Interview Survey reports that 7.6 percent of students were identified as having ADHD between 2006 and 2008 (Goodwin, 2011), and others have data suggesting that those numbers have grown to 9.5 percent of children (Visser, Danielson, Perou, & Blumberg, 2010). The methods used to determine if a student has ADHD include interviews with the child, parents, and teachers, and the use of behavior checklists. If you look at the DSM-IV diagnostic criteria in the accompanying Closer Look box, you will note that all children display some of these behaviors at one time or another. As with all behavior disorders, the clinicians look at the degree to which these behaviors are performed and how the behaviors affect academic and social performance before reaching a diagnosis. ADHD is diagnosed in individuals of all ages; however, the symptoms must have been present before 7 years of age (DSM-IV-TR, 2000). Research suggests that between 60 percent and 80 percent of students with ADHD have an additional diagnosis— for example, learning disabilities or conduct-related behavior disorders (Austin, Reiss, & Burgdorf, 2007). Although assessment and diagnosis can be done by psychologists in the school setting, many children are referred to pediatricians for evaluation. Some parents prefer a pediatrician's evaluation because the doctor can rule out other possible causes for the behavior, and because drug therapy is often used, which must be prescribed by a physician.

A CLOSER LOOK   Diagnostic Criteria for Attention Deficit/Hyperactivity Disorder

A. Either (1) or (2):

1. six (or more) of the following symptoms of inattention have persisted for at least six months to a degree that is maladaptive and inconsistent with developmental level:

Inattention

a. often fails to give close attention to details or makes careless mistakes in schoolwork, work, or other activities

b. often has difficulty sustaining attention in tasks or play activities

c. often does not seem to listen when spoken to directly

d. often does not follow through on instructions and fails to finish schoolwork, chores, or duties in the workplace (not due to oppositional behavior or failure to understand instructions)

e. often has difficulty organizing tasks and activities

f. often avoids, dislikes, or is reluctant to engage in tasks that require sustained mental effort (such as schoolwork or homework)

g. often loses things necessary for tasks or activities (e.g., toys, school assignments, pencils, books, or tools)

h. is often easily distracted by extraneous stimuli

i. is often forgetful in daily activities

2. six (or more) of the following symptoms of hyperactivity-impulsivity have persisted for at least six months to a degree that is maladaptive and inconsistent with developmental level:

Hyperactivity

a. often fidgets with hands or feet or squirms in seat

b. often leaves seat in classroom or in other situations in which remaining seated is expected

c. often runs about or climbs excessively in situations in which it is inappropriate (in adolescents or adults, may be limited to subjective feelings of restlessness)

d. often has difficulty playing or engaging in leisure activities quietly

e. often is "on the go" or often acts as if "driven by a motor"

f. often talks excessively

Impulsivity

g. often blurts out answers before questions have been completed

h. often has difficulty awaiting turn

i. often interrupts or intrudes on others (e.g., butts into conversations or games)

B. Some hyperactive-impulsive or inattentive symptoms that caused impairment were present before the age of 7.

C. Some impairment from the symptoms is present in two or more settings (e.g., at school [or work] and at home).

D. There must be clear evidence of clinically significant impairment in social, academic, or occupational functioning.

E. The symptoms do not occur exclusively during the course of a pervasive developmental disorder, schizophrenia, or other psychotic disorder and are not better accounted for by another mental disorder (e.g., mood disorder, anxiety disorder, dissociative disorder, or a personality disorder).

———————

Source: American Psychiatric Association (2000). Diagnostic criteria for attention-deficit/hyperactivity disorder from *Diagnostic and Statistical Manual of Mental Disorders* (4th ed.).

Characteristics of Students with ADHD

The characteristics of children with ADHD will vary both across and within types of the disorder. When a child has inattention symptoms, his work may be messy, incomplete, and disorganized; directions may be forgotten or only partially followed; and he may be easily distracted and forgetful. The student with ADHD is likely to forget to bring pencils, paper, books, and lunch tickets to school—every day. Essentially, any activity that requires voluntary, sustained attention can be disrupted. For example, while you are giving directions for a test, the student may interrupt you to ask what is being served for lunch today. Long tasks or activities are particularly difficult, and the student may try to avoid them altogether. Your request for a student with ADHD to write a two-page essay in class could be met with (1) frequent trips to the bathroom or pencil sharpener; (2) a half-written sentence, with the student gazing out the window; (3) a "completed" essay consisting of three sentences and written in less than five minutes; or (4) the student attempting the task, crumpling up the paper, and sulking with his head on his desk. A student's attention deficits can eventually result in learning deficits because of difficulty attending to material long enough to learn and practice it.

The behavior of students who experience impulsivity/hyperactivity symptoms reflects high and constant levels of activity. They may react quickly to situations without considering the consequences, or they may shout out answers to questions without waiting for recognition or reflecting on their responses. The activity level demonstrated by many students with ADHD is much higher than that of other children, and it is constant. The child with hyperactivity symptoms is always moving—running, twitching, tapping, shifting, and jumping. Young children with ADHD may have a history of difficulty sleeping or eating (Fowler, 1995; Owens, 2005). The constant motion, combined with impulsivity, obviously is at odds with the behavioral requirements of school settings and often puts kids with ADHD at risk for accidents and social altercations. In addition to exhibiting impulsive behaviors, students with ADHD seem to be at risk for other risk-taking behaviors. Recent research found, in a longitudinal study, that both male and female adolescents with ADHD were significantly at risk for developing substance abuse (cigarettes, alcohol, drug use) disorders (Wilens, Martelon, Joshi, Bateman, Fried, Petty, & Biederman, 2011).

Educational Programs for Students with ADHD

Although ADHD is not a category of special education identified in IDEA, many students with the disorder do receive special education or other educational support services. Students with ADHD who do not have another identified disability may receive services under the IDEA category "Other Health Impaired" or, more typically, under Section 504 of the Rehabilitation Act of 1973. It is likely, therefore, that if you have a student with ADHD in your classroom, he or she will have an IEP that identifies specific accommodations and educational needs. Educational strategies for students with ADHD focus on attention, organization, behavior management, and self-management. The specific interventions used for students with ADHD overlap considerably with the strategies we discuss in each of these areas in both Chapter 5 and this chapter. Students with ADHD need structure, consistency, and clear consequences for behavior; direct instruction procedures for social behavior and academic skills, strategy instruction, and self-monitoring instruction are examples of types of interventions that can be useful for children with ADHD. It is important for teachers and parents to remember that students with ADHD need to learn specific skills for organizing, attending, and self-management.

Drug therapy is frequently a part of educational programs for students with ADHD. It is successfully used in many, but not all, cases to allow students time to think, reflect, and learn. Approximately 70 to 80 percent of students with ADHD respond to medication (Barkley, 1998; National Resource Center on ADHD, 2011). However, drug therapy does not *teach* students necessary skills, although it may give the students the time needed to learn them. If you have a student in your class who is receiving drug therapy for ADHD, it is important for you to provide feedback to the parents and physician about the effects of the drug. Often, physicians must experiment with dosages before finding the correct one; your input will be important. The most common drugs used are psychostimulants, particularly Ritalin, Dexedrine, and Concerta (Barkley, 1998; NIMH, 2011). Other drugs

▶❙❙ **TeachSource**
VIDEO CASE

How Do We Build Successful Experiences for Included Students with Emotional and Behavior Disorders?
Brittany and Trisha need significant supports to succeed in middle school. Visit Chapter 8 on the CourseMate website and watch the video case entitled "Brittany and Trisha: Teaching Strategies for Students with Emotional and Behavioral Disorders." Listen as their teachers and Brittany's mother describe the modifications and teaching strategies they use to address academic and behavior goals. Can you identify additional supports that might help these two students?

Drug therapy can be an important component of a treatment plan for some students with behavior disorders.

include nonstimulants such as some antidepressants (Prozac), and the atomoxetine (Straterra). Each child will react differently, and some side effects are indicated, so it is important to learn as much about each student's drug therapy regime as possible. To learn more about ADHD—including research, resources, facts, and policy issues—visit the website of Children and Adults with Attention-Deficit/Hyperactivity Disorder (CHADD).

Pause and Reflect

It is important for you, as an educator or as a parent, to reflect on how each child interacts with his or her environment, and how you can adjust the environment to address the child's behavior patterns. With ADHD, sometimes medication, or drug therapy, can help the child better benefit from behavior and academic environmental supports—it may make the child more receptive to instruction. How can classrooms be adjusted so they are helpful to children with ADHD?

Identification and Assessment

Identifying and assessing behavior disorders are not easy because of the ambiguity of the definition and the subjectivity involved in judging the appropriateness of behavior. For example, suppose I like my classroom busy and bustling, with chatter going on at all times, whereas you like your class perfectly still and quiet—no one moves without raising a hand. Further, suppose that little Bobby likes to roam around the class and talk. You and I will rate Bobby's behavior very differently. This point is important to keep in mind, because although there are many ways to assess behavior differences, including screening, rating scales, and psychological testing, the primary method of identifying students with emotional or behavior disorders is, increasingly, observations of the child's behavior.

● **Screening**   There is so much variation in what behaviors and emotional reactions are considered developmentally appropriate among young children that it is difficult to identify emotional or behavior disorders in the early years. Many educators, however, believe that early intervention is critically important for young children and their families, and that it can help to prevent the development of even more serious problems (Brayner & Stephens, 2006).

Today, a major component of intervention is the prevention of behavior disorders, resulting in screening procedures being applied in preschool settings. Young children with behaviors that greatly concern parents may be eligible for services under P.L. 99-457, as we discussed earlier, without being labeled behavior disordered.

- The purpose of screening is to identify children who exhibit behaviors that interfere with their classroom performance and academic achievement. Procedures designed to integrate screening and possible assessment for identification include parent questionnaires (e.g., Ages and Stages Questionnaires: Social Emotional), and behavior rating scales for teachers, caregivers, and other observers (e.g., Achenbach System of Empirically Based Assessment—Preschool Model; Behavior Assessment for Children, 2nd edition, BASC-2; Early Screening Inventory—Revised). Some of these screening tools including the Systematic Screening for Behavior Disorders—SSBD (1992), involve what the authors call a *multiple-gating procedure*. That is, there are three stages, or gates, of the screening and assessment process. In the first stage of the SSBD, teachers rank all their students according to two types of behavior patterns: **externalizing behaviors** (such as stealing, throwing tantrums, damaging property, using obscene language, or physical aggression) or **internalizing behaviors** (such as shyness, sadness, thought disorders). This step requires teachers to look at all their students, therefore increasing the teachers' awareness of and attention to specific behavior difficulties that some children might be experiencing.

- In the second stage, the three children who rank highest in the class on each of the two behavioral dimensions are assessed using comprehensive behavior-rating scales.

- If any of the children score beyond a certain point on the behavior-rating instruments, then the final stage, direct observation in various settings, occurs.

Positive Behavior Interventions and Supports

Prevention: The idea behind multiple gating—looking at different stages of assessment—is compatible with a schoolwide system of behavior change known as **Positive Behavioral Interventions and Supports** (PBIS). PBIS, an integrated system of assessment and intervention, was introduced in Chapter 2. PBIS focuses on developing coordinated, school-based change and incorporating consistent, positive interventions to create an environment that supports and recognizes appropriate behavior. The three-tiered model is designed to create school environments that clearly identify, teach, and support appropriate behavior while addressing the development of preventable behavior problems. Figure 8.2 provides

PREVENTING VIOLENT AND DESTRUCTIVE BEHAVIOR IN SCHOOLS: INTEGRATED SYSTEMS OF INTERVENTION

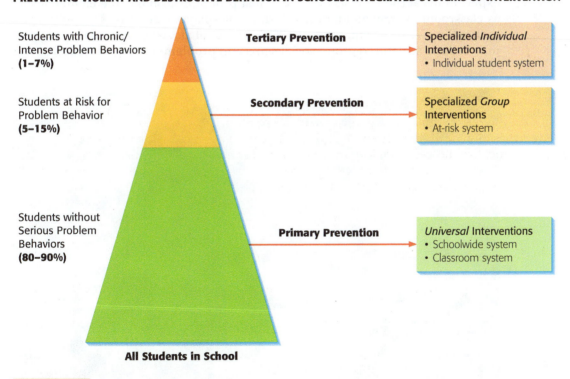

FIGURE 8.2

Multilevel system of schoolwide discipline strategies

Source: G. Sugai, J. R. Sprague, R. H. Horner, & H. M. Walker (2000). Preventing school violence: The Use of office discipline referrals to assess and monitor school-wide discipline interventions. *Journal of Emotional and Behavior Disorders,* 8, 94–101. Reprinted by permission of SAGE Publications.

another look at the three levels of intervention (and prevention) that we discussed in Chapter 2.

The focus on prevention by PBIS programs has led to researchers looking at not only behavior-change strategies, but also at academic interventions that might result in behavior change. As you read about recent academic research later in the chapter, you will see that many of these programs were developed to work within the PBIS system. In general, behavior in PBIS systems is measured by Office Disciplinary Referrals (ODRs). Recent research clearly demonstrates that PBIS systems, particularly at the Primary Prevention level, are very effective at reducing the number of ODRs in elementary, middle, and high schools (Barrett et al., 2008; Bradshaw et al., 2010; Muscott et al., 2008; Warran et al., 2006).

Primary prevention focuses on general, schoolwide programs—often called universal interventions—that are designed to prevent problems among all children. Secondary prevention targets specialized group interventions for students who are at risk for more severe problems or who already exhibit mild behavior problems. Tertiary programs include specialized individual interventions designed for students who are at great risk for serious problems or who are already demonstrating serious behavior problems (Sprague & Walker, 2000). For each level, the complexity of the intervention is matched to the severity of the target behaviors.

Early research suggests that the tri-level approach is an effective way to prevent or delay the onset of behavior problems for at-risk children. Universal interventions appear to reduce inappropriate and aggressive behaviors (Serna et al., 2000). Although the universal programs vary, most include both parent and school components. These schoolwide programs include identifying and reinforcing behavioral expectations for all students. Figure 8.3 gives an example of schoolwide expectations at the high school level. Most programs also include elements such as classroom management, peer tutoring, role-playing, and problem-solving activities (Frey, Hirschstein, & Guzzo, 2000; Kamps et al., 2000). Secondary programs may include structured group social skills and problem-solving activities, as well

> Prevention includes primary, secondary, and tertiary levels.

The hallway of an elementary school participating in schoolwide PBIS, covered with reminders of the behavioral expectations included in the Tier 1, or universal level of intervention (prevention).

Photo courtesy of PBIS

Behaviors	In the Classroom	Community: To and From School	During Assemblies
Be Respectful	**P** = Bad language, yelling, cutting people off, talking back, talking down, favoritism. **T** = Say something positive, ask for a conference, keep temper, count, teachers show interest in others.	**P** = Throwing trash in yards, walking on gardens, talking back to community members. **T** = Throw trash in can, walk on the sidewalk, let an administrator know about problems.	**P** = Being in wrong spot, booing, loud talking. **T** = Listen, participate, sit in correct spot, make encouraging/positive statements. State dislikes appropriately when given the opportunity.
Be Academically Engaged	**P** = Head down, no materials, not participating, not handing in assignments, not physically attending, tardy, disruptive. **T** = Make the class interesting, use variety, have supplies, have assignments, ask, be in uniform, be on time. Have a creative lesson. Have rewards.	**P** = Not being on time or in dress code, not attending school, hanging out during school hours. **T** = Be on time, be in dress code. Show your ID when asked.	**P** = Not following presentations, not listening. **T** = Use materials during the assemblies, follow along.

FIGURE 8.3

Sample grid of schoolwide expectations

Source: Sample of schoolwide expectations for a PBIS high school program
Morrissey, K. L., Bohanon, H., & Fenning, P. (2010). Positive Behavior Support: Teaching
and acknowledging expected behaviors in an urban high school. *Teaching Exceptional
Children*, 42, 26–35.

as group behavior management programs. Tertiary programs likely will focus on the Behavior Intervention Plan (BIP) that results from each student's functional behavioral assessment.

The PBIS system is somewhat parallel to the RTI system. The anticipated result of RTI is that fewer children will experience learning problems and fewer children will be misidentified with a learning disability because of poor instruction; the anticipated result of PBIS is that fewer students will experience behavior difficulties in school, and fewer will be identified with emotional or behavior disorders because of inappropriate or neglected behavior management. To learn more about PBIS systems, visit the OSEP Technical Assistance Center on the PBIS website, created by George Sugai and Rob Horner. At this website you will learn more about the goals and procedures of this research-based model and the latest information on evidence-based procedures.

Assessment for Identification

In addition to the IQ and achievement tests that are a part of all special education evaluations, a few specific types of instruments are employed if emotional or behavior disorders are suspected. After a child is referred, teachers, parents, and school psychologists observe him or her in school and home settings and complete **behavior-rating scales** designed to reflect patterns of behavior. Behavior-rating scales used frequently in the schools include the Conners' Behavior-Rating Scales and the Peterson-Quay Behavior-Rating Scales. An example from the Abbreviated Conners' Rating Scale for Teachers may be found in Figure 8.4.

Professionals urge that children be observed in a number of different settings, that ratings and observations be conducted by several different people, that observations be conducted over a period of time rather than during a single session, and that predisposing factors, including the influence of cultural differences

In the past month, this was...	0 = Not true at all (Never, Seldom) 1 = Just a little true (Occasionally)		2 = Pretty much true (Often, Quite a bit) 3 = Very much true (Very often, Very frequently)		
1. Leaves seat when he/she should stay seated.	0	1	2		3
2. Gets overly excited.	0	1	2		3
3. Has a short attention span.	0	1	2		3
4. Fidgets or squirms in seat.	0	1	2		3
5. Cannot do things right.	0	1	2		3
6. Begins a task or project without making a plan.	0	1	2		3

FIGURE 8.4

Disruptive Behavior Rating Scale – Teacher Form

Source: From Attention-Deficit Hyperactivity Disorder: A Clinical Workbook (2nd ed.), pg. 63–64, by Russell A. Barkley and Kevin R. Murphy. Copyright 1998 by The Guilford Press.

and family expectations, be considered during assessment (Executive Committee of the Council for Children with Behavior Disorders, 1998). Although there are recommendations for administering each behavior-rating scale, it is important to understand that there is no standard or uniform battery of tests, checklists, or procedures to follow for the identification of children or adolescents with behavior disorders. Each state education agency establishes its own guidelines and identifies the particular tests that can be used. Intelligence and achievement tests may be used to substantiate or rule out specific disability areas. Other assessment devices are largely subjective. All the information is examined to determine if the child has a behavior disorder. There is no specific test score, test average, or level of behavior agreed on by professionals as an appropriate criterion for identification.

Because classroom teachers play an important role in the identification of students with behavior or emotional disorders, it is important for them to understand the issues involved in defining and identifying children who fall into this category.

It is easy to see how the effects of personal bias and tolerance can influence behavior-rating scales. Each of the people involved in the rating process can have very different perceptions of what is normal or acceptable in terms of activity level or acting-out behavior; the raters may have different personal feelings toward the child, which could bias ratings; and the level of experience a rater has had with children can affect scoring—a parent with no other children might rate behavior differently than a parent with three or four other children.

Researchers have studied the effects of gender and cultural bias on behavior ratings and student referrals (Reid et al., 2000). Cultural bias is of particular concern due to the growing overrepresentation of some populations, particularly African American students, in the number of students identified as having behavior disorders, as well as overrepresentation in the numbers of school suspensions and expulsions (Webb-Johnson, 2003). The Closer Look box, "Cultural Diversity and Serious Emotional Disturbance (SED)," describes some of the factors to keep in mind when identifying and instructing children from culturally diverse backgrounds.

Visit the website of the Council for Children with Behavior Disorders to view assessment and instructional practices for working with culturally and linguistically diverse children, youth, and their families.

> Teachers' personal biases can affect the referral and assessment process.

Assessment for Instruction

Although behavior checklists and screening procedures may help identify students with behavior disorders, they may not provide specific information about instructional objectives. Educators will conduct functional behavioral assessments to obtain information that can be translated into instructional goals when students with disabilities exhibit problem behaviors. The 1997 IDEA amendments require that a **functional behavioral assessment** (FBA) be administered to students with behavior problems in order to identify strategies that are positive and replacement behaviors that can serve the same function as the problem behaviors (IDEA Amendments, 1997). See the Teaching Strategies box, "What Is a Functional Behavioral Assessment?" on page 288 for more information about this type of assessment. The information from the FBA will serve as the basis for a **behavior intervention plan** (BIP). The BIP should contain positive behavior support strategies designed to teach and reinforce appropriate behavior (Kauffman, 2001). The BIP becomes a part of the student's IEP and reflects both behavior goals and interventions. Fundamental components of the Functional Behavioral Assessment, and ultimately the behavior intervention plan, include observations of what happens before, during, and after behavior. These components are referred to as the ABC's of behavior observation: A = antecedent (what happens before the behavior); B = the behavior itself; C = consequence (what happens after the behavior). If you work in a school setting, it is likely you will be asked to conduct these observations. Figure 8.5 is one school team's summary of the ABC's for one student.

FBA - Sandra

Antecedents	Behaviors	Consequences
Math: Asked class to get ready for peer quizzing	Refuses to get with peer—says "I'm not doing this"	Goes to time-out
Geography: Class preparing to identify countries on class map—teacher asks her to study	Puts away map and refuses to study—say "buzz off" to teacher	Sent to office
Reading: Independent reading time	Reads more than any student in the class—very respectful	Teacher provides her with "A" grade and note to parents
Math: Class instruction, asked to state the next step in the problem	Told teacher to "drop dead"	Sent to office
Home Economics: Class working on their own recipes at their desks	Does research and studies—writes perfect recipes	No interaction— praised by teacher
Reading: Group reading of novel—take turns reading aloud	Refuses to follow along—closes book and sleeps	Teacher ignores so as not to disrupt group reading

FIGURE 8.5

ABC Chart for Functional Analysis

Source: T. M. Scott, C. J. Liaupsin, C. J. Nelson, & K. Jolivette (2003). Ensuring student success through team-based functional behavioral assessment. *Teaching Exceptional Children,* 34 (5), 16–21.

Teaching Strategies and Accommodations

> The curriculum for students with emotional and behavior disorders must address both behavioral and academic needs.

Educational planning and programming for students with emotional or behavior disorders involve several interrelated issues: early intervention, assessment, placing children with behavior disorders within the school system, choosing a philosophical approach, designing curriculum and instructional strategies to enhance learning, and handling discipline in the school.

Curriculum Focus

The curriculum for students with behavior and emotional disorders must address behavioral as well as academic needs. The teacher must include curriculum components that remediate behavior excesses or deficiencies as well as those

Teaching Strategies & Accommodations

What Is a Functional Behavioral Assessment?

According to the IDEA Amendments of 1997, all students with behavior problems served under IDEA must receive a functional behavioral assessment (Yell & Shriner, 1997). Brady and Halle (1997) describe a functional behavioral assessment as a way to determine the uses or functions of behavior. They identify the following components of a functional behavioral assessment:

1. Interviews: The student, parents, teachers, and other caregivers should be interviewed about the occurrence of the behavior and the surrounding circumstances.

2. Direct observation: The student should be observed in the setting or settings in which the behavior occurs. Observations should include what happens before, during, and after the behavior occurrence.

3. Analog probes: The observer should manipulate specific variables, such as the setting or the number of opportunities for interaction (e.g., between the student and teacher) to get a better understanding of when and why the behavior occurs.

What can we learn from a functional behavioral assessment?

1. When a behavior is most likely to occur: after lunch, during unstructured time, when the student is fatigued.

2. If something specific prompts the behavior: difficult seatwork, teacher correction, teasing.

3. What the student is trying to tell you: I want to be left alone, I want to get out of work, I am embarrassed, I love all this attention.

4. What usually happens after the behavior occurs: The student is ignored, put into time-out, or receives a lot of negative comments; the class laughs or works quietly; different consequences occur at different times of the day.

What do we do after a functional behavioral assessment?

In the IEP meeting, the teachers, parents, student (if appropriate), and other relevant personnel develop an appropriate behavior-management plan based on the information from the functional behavioral assessment. Answers to the following questions will be used to develop the plan:

1. Can changes in the student's environment (seating, method of teacher questioning, shortening assignments) help to prevent the occurrence of behavior?

2. What new behaviors (requesting, self-removal from setting) can the student use to satisfy the same communicative intent of the problem behaviors?

3. How can we prompt use of the alternative behavior (signals, self-monitoring, modeling)?

4. What consequences shall we provide for (a) demonstration of new behavior and (b) demonstration of problem behavior?

5. How can we evaluate behavior change?

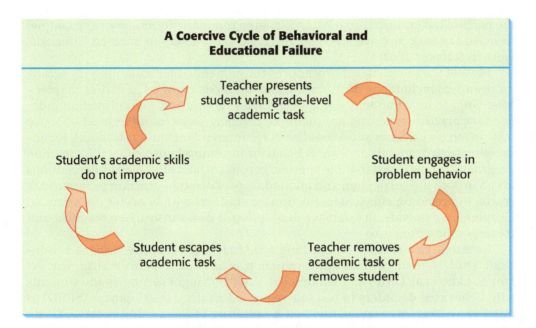

A Coercive Cycle of Behavioral and Educational Failure

Teacher presents student with grade-level academic task → Student engages in problem behavior → Teacher removes academic task or removes student → Student escapes academic task → Student's academic skills do not improve →

FIGURE 8.6

The hypothesized relationship between behavioral and educational failure

Source: McIntosh, K., Horner, R. H., Chard, D. J., Dickey, C. R., & Braun, D. H. (2008). Reading skills and function of problem behavior in typical school settings. *The Journal of Special Education,* 42, 131–147. Reprinted by permission of SAGE Publications.

that teach the regular school curriculum. To address both these major curriculum areas is quite a challenge for any teacher. Although the responsibilities of the classroom teacher and the special education teacher will vary depending on placement options and class size, the importance of collaboration in instruction and planning cannot be overemphasized.

Children with behavior disorders have the same placement options as other children with disabilities. These options range from the residential school to the regular classroom. Because of the nature of certain types of behavior disorders, such as aggressive and threatening behavior, some segregated service-delivery models have persisted in many school systems. These placement options are usually reserved as a last resort for students, usually adolescents, who are deemed unable to cope with the regular school environment.

The balance of instruction between academic skills, and interventions or programs designed to increase appropriate behavior is difficult to achieve. The extent of instruction in either area is generally dictated by the severity of the behavior disorder of the individual child. Most children with behavior disorders are now responsible for performing and succeeding in the general education curriculum. The ability of the special education teacher and classroom teacher to work together is a critical factor in the successful adjustment of these students in general education classes. Specific social skills or behaviors, such as moving around the classroom, completing class assignments, or speaking appropriately to adults, need to be targeted for instruction, and all individuals involved in educational planning must agree on them. Increasingly, however, professionals are focusing on the relationship between academics and behavior. Figure 8.6 illustrates the proposed relationship between academics and inappropriate behavior related to poor academic performance.

Academic Programming

We've already mentioned the importance of the function of inappropriate behavior. Research suggests that students with poor academic skills, particularly in reading, will more frequently demonstrate inappropriate behavior as a way to escape the class environment (McIntosh, Horner, Chard, Dickey, & Braun, 2008). This makes sense—students don't want to be in a situation in which they fail repeatedly and become embarrassed. The solution? Research suggests modifying

Direct instruction programs are recommended for students with emotional and behavior disorders.

the parts of the task that are most challenging (preteach vocabulary, for example) to make the task less aversive and the child more likely to succeed (Preciado, Horner, & Baker, 2009).

Most of the instructional procedures recommended for students with behavior disorders include the direct instruction methods outlined in earlier chapters. Modeling/demonstration, leading or guided practice, and then providing independent practice or testing are the three teaching steps found in most effective instruction plans. Stein and Davis (2000) recommend including strategies for addressing both academic and social behavior in comprehensive direct instruction programs. They suggest that the specific, consistent, and structured interventions found in both the curriculum and methodology of direct instruction programs are crucial to providing effective instruction for students with behavior disorders. In Chapter 5, we provide an extensive description of direct instruction practices and corresponding programs.

Research also focuses on teaching academic skills that are designed to include student-management and evaluation of academic performance. For example, Lane et al. (2010) and Sandmel et al. (2009) taught second-grade students with behavioral disorders to use self-regulated strategy development (SRSD) to improve writing, motivation, and self-monitoring of the writing process. Using very systematic instruction, the authors were able to improve students' writing skills, reported more strategic writing behavior and, anecdotally, increased social interactions by more introverted students. By conducting systematic lines of research in topics such as SRSD, we will learn specific ways to address needed academic skills while also managing behavior. Figure 8.7 provides an illustration of the SRSD used in this series of studies to teach writing as part of a Tier-Two intervention for these young students.

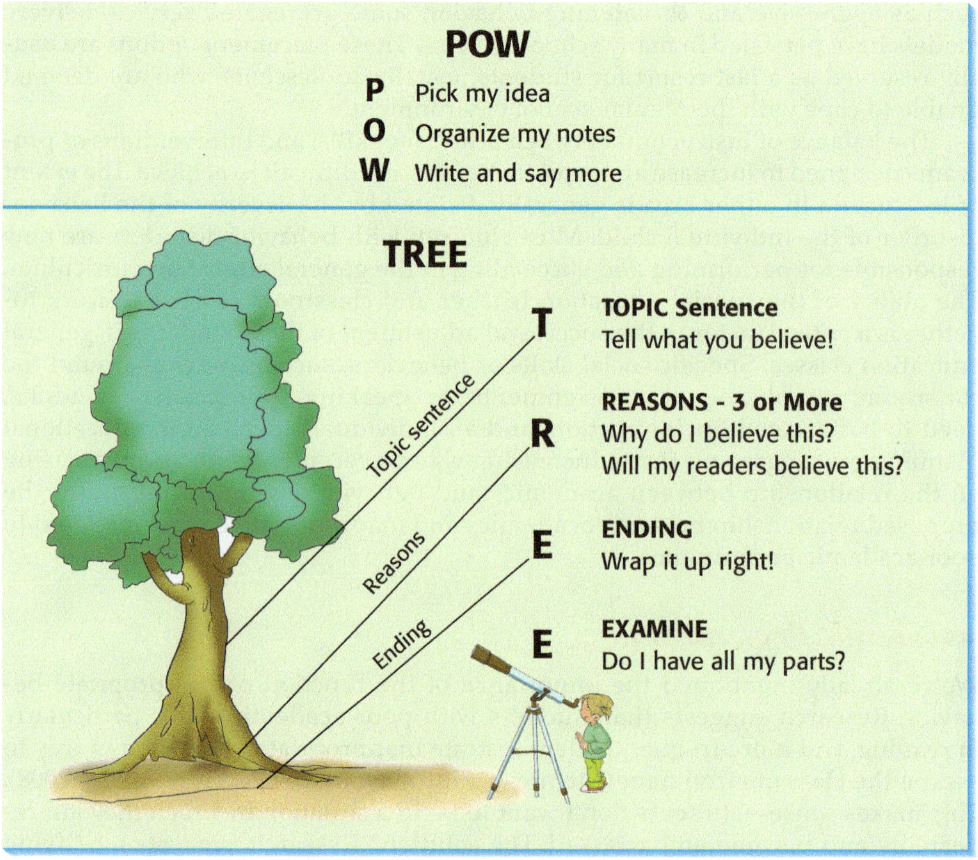

FIGURE 8.7

Self-regulated strategy development to teach writing skills to young students with behavior disorders

Source: Sandmel, K. N., Brindle, M., Harris, K. R., Lane, K. L., Graham, S., Nackel, J., Mathias, R., & Little, A. (2009). Making it work: Differentiating tier two self-regulated strategies development in writing in tandem with schoolwide positive behavioral support. *Teaching Exceptional Children, 42,* 22–33.

POW

P Pick my idea
O Organize my notes
W Write and say more

TREE

Topic sentence

Reasons

Ending

T **TOPIC Sentence**
Tell what you believe!

R **REASONS - 3 or More**
Why do I believe this?
Will my readers believe this?

E **ENDING**
Wrap it up right!

E **EXAMINE**
Do I have all my parts?

Teaching Strategies & Accommodations

Students Talk to Teachers and Give Some Teaching Suggestions

Rich curriculum

- Allow for more group activities and projects.
- Show enthusiasm when teaching.
- Allow for more discussion and expression of students in class.
- Relate the information to your students' lives (current and future).

Embracing positive behaviors

- Hold high expectations.
- Explain the "rules" clearly and provide consistent consequences regardless of labels or race.
- Encourage students to do their best regardless of their label or race.

Weaving student-centered connections

- Understand issues students face today.
- Get to know students and their families.
- Get to know students in and out of school.
- Communicate with students at their level.
- Identify and connect students with services within and outside the school setting.

Source: L. Owens & L. A. Decker (2003). How to spell success for secondary students labeled EBD: How students define effective teachers. *Beyond Behavior*, 12 (2), 21.

Clearly, educational professionals are recognizing the importance of academic assessment and effective educational interventions for children with behavior disorders. Much research is still needed in order to identify how to ensure that children with behavior disorders achieve academically. In the Teaching Strategies box, "Students Talk to Teachers," high-school students with behavior disorders give their own recommendations for teaching. When discussing the recommendations, one student said:

> Teachers need to remember that we are still kids and they were kids once too. We were born in a more violent world—we listen to different music—we will learn more responsibility, but we are kids now (Owen & Dreker 2003, p. 21).

Behavior-Change Interventions

Behavior goals for students with behavior and emotional disorders must be individualized to meet each student's needs; however, more general interventions designed to prevent behavior disorders may take place at the class or building level. These interventions can be described in terms of their intended effects. In the following sections, we examine three common curriculum goals and related teaching strategies: addressing inappropriate behaviors, developing appropriate cognitions, and teaching new behaviors.

Many interventions attempt to prevent the occurrence of behavior disorders.

● *Addressing Inappropriate Behavior* The current emphasis on prevention of behavior disorders, as well as the general societal concern about violence in schools, has led to new programs designed to reduce the probability of inappropriate behavior through the implementation of school-based programs such as PBIS. Prevention is not always possible, and sometimes inappropriate

© David Young-Wolff/PhotoEdit

Appropriate and engaging instruction is an important part of managing classroom behavior.

or violent behaviors must be addressed. In earlier sections we've discussed the importance of finding out the function of a behavior so that antecedents or consequences can be addressed to change the behavior. In the following sections, we discuss strategies for managing and teaching behaviors. Some students, however, will exhibit behaviors that call for immediate intervention on the part of the teacher so that a student will not harm himself or others. Strategies that teachers use in these instances, referred to as crisis intervention, must be carefully taught and governed by regulations (Carvillon et al., 2010). The most critical time to intervene in a crisis is the first minute, so teacher responses must be swift and calm (Bickel, 2010). The move from a philosophy of responding to inappropriate behaviors through punishment to preventing inappropriate behaviors in the first place is a significant philosophical change in the culture of working with students with behavior disorders. When prevention isn't enough, the profession has established clear guidelines for teachers to deal with crisis interventions (Bickel, 2010). If you teach children with emotional and behavioral disorders, it is important for you to become aware of these guidelines. For more information, consult the websites of the Council for Exceptional Children and the Council for Exceptional Children Division on Behavior Disorders. They have a series of policy statements as well as teacher guidelines on issues related to crisis intervention and restraint.

● *Developing Appropriate Cognitions*   One of the recurring problems experienced by children with behavior disorders is difficulty interpreting events realistically and determining socially appropriate responses. For example, Hartman and Stage (2000) interviewed students with behavior disorders who were assigned to in-school suspension. The interviews revealed that the students had reacted negatively to their perception that teachers deliberately provoked them. Studies like this one suggest the importance of interventions with a positive and reinforcing focus. They also suggest that students need instruction in skills to help them identify and cope with both real and exaggerated concerns and thoughts. Regardless of the cause, children who have retreated from social activities and relationships usually receive instruction that will enable them to make slow and nonthreatening steps toward appropriate social behavior.

Because of the possible role of a child's thoughts in behavior disorders, it is difficult for the teacher, who cannot observe these thoughts, to manage the behavior without student participation. One way to address this problem is to provide **self-management instruction.**

Instruction in self-management skills involves teaching children to pay attention to, monitor, and record their own performance (Harris, Friedlander, Saddler, Frizzelle, & Graham, 2005; Levendoski & Cartledge, 2000). For example, children record on a piece of paper every time they talk without raising their hand. Alternatively, children can record a mark for every five minutes they exhibit appropriate behavior such as time on-task or time without fighting. Self-management programs can involve the use of videotaping (Falk, Dunlap, & Kern, 1996) and role-play to assist in self-evaluation. Students can observe and record behaviors and practice giving alternative responses.

Currently, technology offers numerous resources for teachers and other educational professionals to use when developing self-management programs for students with behavior disorders. See the Assistive Technology Focus feature for a summary of a great technological resource for parents, teachers, and other professionals.

> Instruction in self-management skills teaches students to attend to and record their own performance.

● *Teaching New Behaviors*   Some programs focus on the instruction of new behaviors to take the place of the inappropriate ones. Interventions of this nature may involve teaching students problem-solving strategies to use when they begin to feel angry or upset. For example, a problem teachers often face is a child throwing a tantrum in the classroom when he becomes frustrated. Simply telling the child to stop, or even punishing the child, will not necessarily address the problem because the child who habitually has tantrums does not know what else to do when he gets frustrated. Therefore, the teacher can give him a signal when he starts to become angry. When he sees the signal, the student has three choices: He can count to ten and take a deep breath to calm down, he can raise his hand and ask the teacher for help, or he can get up and go sit in the reading corner for five minutes to relax. Now the child has options. Instead of throwing a book, he can choose an alternative behavior.

Other strategies may focus on addressing the school environment to promote positive and constructive social interactions among students. An interesting and simple example of this is prompting positive behaviors in all students in a classroom. For example, Nelson, Caldarella, Young and Webb (2008) created a classroom system using positive peer reporting (PPR) in the form of peer praise notes. Every week, each student in the class wrote a brief but positive note (e.g. "Great to sit with you at lunch today.") to class members. They found increased positive social interactions with withdrawn students, particularly if the students formed a special relationship with an important peer. Figure 8.8 illustrates a template of the positive peer note used in this research.

Viewing videotapes of appropriate behaviors, modeling by teachers and peers, and practicing appropriate responses are other activities that have been used effectively to teach new behaviors (Whalen, Franke, & Lara-Brady, 2011). Research has examined the role of peers in helping students with behavior disorders to learn appropriate anger-management behavior. Presley and Hughes (2000) found that high-school students with behavior disorders demonstrated appropriate anger-management behaviors in role-play after receiving a combination of individual instruction from peers, self-management instruction, and a

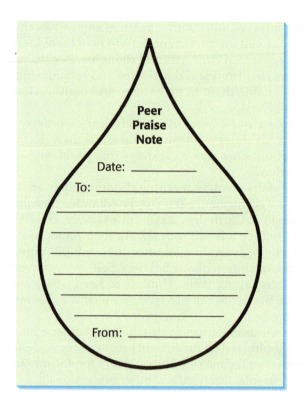

FIGURE 8.8

Example of praise note format used to encourage positive peer classroom interactions

Source: Nelson, J. A. P., Caldarella, P., Young, K. R., & Webb, N. (2008) Using peer praise notes to increase the social involvement of withdrawn adolescents. *Teaching Exceptional Children*, 41, 6–13.

traditional anger-control program. According to federal law, children cannot be punished for behavior that is a result of their disability.

Some behaviors (such as stealing and using obscenities) may seem more deliberate and manipulative and less a result of lack of control. Usually, behavior-management techniques that involve the application of specific consequences for appropriate and inappropriate behavior are used to address these types of behaviors. Although the predominant philosophy in behavior management is to focus on using positive interventions to teach new behaviors, punishing and exclusionary strategies (loss of recess time or time-out) are still used in many classrooms. All teachers must remember that negative approaches may produce negative reactions by students with behavior disorders; they should also realize that punishing a child does not tell him what he is supposed to do.

Regardless of your ultimate behavior goal for an individual student, several factors, such as consistency and clear consequences, are required for all behavior-management programs. It is also important for you, the parent, and the student to see the program as positive and practical. One of the many advantages of PBIS systems in schools is that the system helps to prepare all teachers and school staff to systematically look for and reinforce appropriate student behavior.

Discipline in the Schools

Most schools have established programs for the purpose of disciplining children who exhibit inappropriate behavior. These programs may include suspension, in-school suspension, time-out, corporal punishment, and expulsion. Children with externalizing behavior disorders may seem to be prime candidates for experiencing some of these disciplinary actions, but federal law states that children cannot be punished for their disability. In other words, if a child's behavior is considered to be related to his or her disability, that child should not be punished for it. The IDEA amendments of 1997 present some guidelines for addressing the behavior problems of students with disabilities, including those with behavior disorders.

☀ASSISTIVE TECHNOLOGY FOCUS

Technology Application for Students with Behavior Disorders: Self-Management Programs

Very little information is available in the literature on the effective use of technology for children with behavior disorders. Sources of information for teachers of students with behavior disorders are available on the Internet. One source of information is the Virtual Resource Center in Behavioral Disorders (VRCBD). The VRCBD is located on a website at the University of Missouri at Columbia (UMC) and is directed by Dr. Gail Fitzgerald and her colleagues. This site includes information and a link for ordering CDs for the Teacher Problem Solving Skills series. In this series, teachers can find interactive training materials that use authentic videos of children and classrooms and case-based activities to teach and provide practice in understanding, assessing, and developing educational plans for children with emotional and behavioral disorders. Supplemental training materials, archives of national online conferences, and access to online discussion groups are provided on this website. A related branch of this program is the Strategy Coach interactive software, designed specifically for adolescents. A screen shot from this website is illustrated in Figure 8.9.

FIGURE 8.9

This strategy is an example of software, described as an electronic performance support system (EPSS), to provide assistance to adolescents with social and academic behavior disorders.

Source: © 2004–2011 The Curators of the University of Missouri, a public corporation. All Rights Reserved.

One requirement is that a school review, called a **manifestation determination,** must be conducted after a school behavior problem has occurred, to determine if the student's behavior is related to the disability. If the ruling is that the behavior is not related to the disability, the student may be disciplined like any other child (IDEA Amendments, 1997; Yell & Shriner, 1997). In addition, children with behavior disorders must have a specific behavior-intervention plan, or BIP, including disciplinary procedures in their individual educational programs. Any disciplinary actions, such as suspension, that change the student's placement are limited to ten days. Exceptions include the possession of firearms or drugs in school or at school functions, which allows administrators to place the child in a temporary alternative educational setting for up to forty-five days (IDEA Amendments, 1997; Yell & Shriner, 1997).

> Schools must develop guidelines that enable them to implement discipline without violating students' rights.

Many adolescents with behavior disorders spend time in **alternative schools**-schools that are part of the public schools system, but established as a temporary placement for all students demonstrating significant behavior difficulties in their typical high school schools. Students may spend a few weeks to a year in these alternative schools. If students with an IEP are served in an alternative school, all of the protections we've just discussed need to be in place. There is little research supporting the effectiveness of alternative schools on changing behavior (Atkins & Bartuska, 2010). Some studies suggest that although most alternative schools include students with disabilities, almost half of them do not have licensed special education teachers and almost two-thirds report that the IEP team was not involved in placement decisions for the students (Washburn-Moses, 2011).

What effects do school-based programs have on behavior disorders? Few recent long-term outcome studies have been conducted on students with emotional and behavior disorders. The existing research does, however, suggest that students with behavior disorders often have a difficult transition from school to postschool environments. Young adults with behavior disorders often experience difficulties keeping and maintaining jobs and are also at greater risk for criminal behavior (Lane & Carter, 2006).

Research suggests that about half of all antisocial children become adjudicated as adolescents, and 50 to 75 percent of these adolescents go on to become adult criminals (Walker, Colvin, & Ramsey, 1995). This is dismal news, particularly when coupled with what we have already discussed about the high dropout rates of, and drug use by, adolescents with behavior disorders. With such concern about the prognosis for students with emotional and behavior disorders, it is easy to understand why there currently is such an emphasis on prevention.

? Pause and Reflect

Probably the most challenging aspect of working with students with behavior disorders is thinking of how we can create positive, supportive interventions rather than negative, punitive interventions to address inappropriate behavior. Why does understanding the antecedents and consequences of behavior help us to figure out an effective, positive plan for behavior change? ●

SUMMARY

- Federal law lists five factors for identifying children who are emotionally disturbed: unexplained inability to learn, inability to relate satisfactorily to peers and teachers, inappropriate behavior under normal circumstances, pervasive unhappiness or depression, and a tendency to develop physical symptoms or fears associated with school or personal problems.

- Behavior can be evaluated in terms of rate, intensity, duration, and age appropriateness.

- It is difficult to determine the prevalence of behavior disorders because of differences in instruments used to measure behavior, in terminology and interpretation of definitions, and in the subjectivity of behavior-rating systems.

- The causes of behavior disorders are not known; however, certain environmental and physiological factors seem to relate to differences in behavior.

- The effects of behavior disorders on the child include underachievement in school, difficulties with social adjustment, and difficulties in self-expression or communication. Effects on the family include parental anger, stress, and guilt; helplessness; and an increased risk of child abuse.

- Assessment techniques include screening instruments, observation, and behavior-rating scales. States establish their own guidelines for selecting and administering tests, and professionals interpret the results based on the nature of the specific case and their own expertise. A teacher's conscious or unconscious bias can cause problems in assessment.

- Many educators recommend direct instruction programs and strategies for teaching students with emotional or behavior disorders.

- Regardless of a student's placement, regular and special education teachers should share the same expectations for appropriate behavior and use a consistent behavior-management system. The major strategies for working with students with behavior disorders involve developing appropriate cognitions, teaching new behavior, and eliminating inappropriate behavior.

KEY TERMS

behavior disorders (page 261)

emotional disturbance
(page 261)

rate (page 262)

intensity (page 262)

duration (page 262)

age-appropriate behavior
(page 262)

DSM-IV-TR (page 264)

externalizing behaviors
(page 264)

internalizing behaviors
(page 265)

attention deficit/hyperactivity
disorder (ADHD) (page 279)

externalizing behaviors (page 283)

internalizing behaviors
(page 283)

Positive Behavioral Interventions
and Supports (page 283)

behavior-rating scales (page 285)

functional behavioral assessment
(page 287)

behavior intervention plan
(page 287)

self-management instruction
(page 293)

manifestation determination
(page 295)

alternative schools (page 295)

USEFUL RESOURCES

- Russel A. Barkley (2005). *Attention Deficit Hyperactivity Disorders: A Handbook for Diagnosis and Treatment* (3rd ed.). New York, Guilford Press. A comprehensive discussion of ADHD from one of the leading authorities in the field.

- Mary Fowler (2000). *Maybe You Know My Kid: A Parent's Guide to Identifying, Understanding, and Helping Your Child with Attention Deficit Hyperactivity Disorder* (3rd ed.). New York: Citadel Press. A classic manual designed to support parents of children with attention deficit / hyperactivity disorder as they learn about assessment, diagnosis, and treatment options.

- Positive Behavioral Interventions and Supports: Effective Schoolwide Interventions (**http://www.pbis.org/**). This OSEP Technical Assistance Center website offers many resources, information, technical assistance, and research on the PBIS process.

- George Sugai, Wayne Sailor, Rob Horner, and Glen Dunlap (Eds.) (2010). *Handbook of Positive Behavior Support*. Issues in Clinical Child Psychology Series. New York: Springer-Verlag. Guidelines for the development and maintenance of PBIS systems in schools.

- WrightsLaw: **http://wrightslaw.com/.** This site provides access to the latest updates in special education legislation and case law. This site is used frequently by both parent groups and school districts to get summaries and interpretations of recent legislation and litigation.

- Children and Adults with Attention Deficit / Hyperactivity Disorder (CHADD): **http://www.chadd.org/.** The CHADD organization and website are devoted to families of and individuals with attention deficit/hyperactivity disorder. It has many suggested strategies, activities, resources, and contacts for children and adults.

 PORTFOLIO ACTIVITIES

1. Find a school in your area that uses the Positive Behavior Interventions and Support (PBIS) system. Ask to observe the school and notice the postings of schoolwide behavioral expectations and the positive behavior reinforcement systems. Interview the school's PBIS coordinator and ask about how the process works in that school and what secondary and tertiary tier interventions they use.

  CEC This activity will help students meet CEC Content Standard 5: Learning Environments and Social Interactions.

2. Ask school guidance counselors or conflict-management specialists for suggestions of strategies and programs that teach students self-control and problem solving. Ask them for some examples of curricula related to self-management, social skills training, and affective development. Critique several of the curricula and determine which you could integrate into a general education classroom.

  CEC This activity will help students meet CEC Content Standard 4: Instructional Strategies.

3. How do your expectations of classroom performance affect the ways you perceive students' behavior? Using a teacher's behavioral checklist, visit several classrooms at various grade levels. Observe and record the behavior of a few children in each class. Afterward, compare your observations and ratings with those of the classroom teachers. Are your perceptions and observations similar to those of the classroom teacher? Evaluate your own biases and their effects on your ratings. Make a list of behaviors that you think will be important in your own classroom.

  CEC This activity will help students meet CEC Content Standard 2: Development and Characteristics of Learners and, CEC Content Standard 8: Assessment.

4. Interview a local pediatrician about the methods he or she uses to identify children with ADHD. Ask to see examples of behavior checklists and forms for classroom observations and parent interviews. Record the criteria the doctor uses. If possible, interview several pediatricians and compare their diagnostic methods.

CEC This activity will help students meet CEC Content Standard 2: Development and Characteristics of Learners and, CEC Content Standard 8: Assessment.

5. Observe a teacher conduct a functional behavior assessment for a student. Record the antecedents, behaviors, and consequences along with the teacher, and arrive at your own hypothesis about the function of the inappropriate behavior. Confer with the teacher and discuss his or her assessment. Identify suggestions for appropriate replacement behaviors.

CEC This activity will help students meet CEC Content Standard 3: Individual Learning Differences.

 To access Portfolio Activities for this chapter and other useful study resources including an interactive eBook, related web links, quizzes, flashcards, and videos, visit the Education CourseMate website at CengageBrain.com.

CHAPTER 9

Children with Autism Spectrum Disorders

Learning Objectives

After reading this chapter, the reader will be able to:

- Define and explain the different kinds of autism spectrum disorders.

- Outline some possible causes for autism spectrum disorders.

- Describe the relationship between communication and behavior, and explain why this relationship is so important when working with children with autism.

- Discuss how the goals of teaching students with autism compare to those of teaching other children.

- Identify the types of collaboration necessary to provide effective early intervention programs for young children with autism.

- Describe methods for determining the most effective interventions to use with individuals with autism.

- Identify the most important characteristics of effective teaching strategies.

Arguably, no other area of special education has been the subject of as much speculation and controversy as autism. In most areas of disability, we can easily see that individuals perform somewhere on an ability continuum in physical, cognitive, sensory, or emotional skills. We can observe our own or others' performances and logically understand deficits or exceptional abilities. Autism, however, sometimes seems to defy logic. The characteristic behaviors of autism, coupled with the apparently uneven distribution and range of deficits and abilities displayed by individuals with autism, seem to undermine a clear and rational explanation. Consequently, autism has been attributed to many different causes, and a wide variety of sometimes bizarre treatments has been explored through the years by confused parents and professionals. Although science is leading us ever closer to a good understanding of autism, many questions remain. We do, however, know that individuals with autism, like individuals with other pervasive disabilities, are in a better position than ever before to assume fulfilling and productive lives.

Educational programs for children and adolescents with autism focus on instruction in functional communication, appropriate behavior, social interaction, and life skills. In this chapter, we discuss historical and current theories about autism and review effective interventions.

Terms and Definitions

Autism is a lifelong developmental disability that is best described as a collection of behavioral symptoms. The extent and severity of those symptoms provide a range of diagnoses referred to as autism spectrum disorders.

Defining Autism

Although autism has been recognized as a syndrome for many years, it was not identified as a separate category of special education until the IDEA reauthorization of 1990.

Autism was identified as a special education category in 1990.

The following is the federal definition of autism:

Autism means a developmental disability significantly affecting verbal and nonverbal communication and social interaction, generally evident before age 3 that adversely affects a child's educational performance. Other characteristics often associated with autism are engagement in repetitive activities and stereotyped movements, resistance to environmental change or daily routines, and unusual responses to sensory experiences. The term does not apply if a child's educational performance is adversely affected primarily because the child has an emotional disturbance.

A child who manifests the characteristics of "autism" after age 3 could be diagnosed as having "autism" if the criteria in the above paragraph are satisfied. (IDEA, Part B, p. 34.300-6A)

The federal definition provides us with a general description of autism. As with all disability categories that rely on observational measures, the diagnosis of autism may be subjective. The *Diagnostic and Statistical Manual of Mental Disorders,* 4th Edition (DSM IV TR), published by the American Psychiatric Association (2000), contains complex diagnostic criteria that parallel and attempt to quantify the behavioral characteristics present in the federal definition of autism.

Diagnostic Criteria for 299.00 Autistic Disorder (from DSM IV R)

● *How Psychologists and Psychiatrists May Define Autism*

A. A total of six (or more) items from (1), (2), and (3), with at least two from (1), and one each from (2) and (3):

1. qualitative impairment in social interaction, as manifested by at least two of the following:

   a. marked impairment in the use of multiple nonverbal behaviors such as eye-to-eye gaze, facial expression, body postures, and gestures to regulate social interaction

   b. failure to develop peer relationships appropriate to developmental level

   c. a lack of spontaneous seeking to share enjoyment, interests, or achievements with other people (e.g., by a lack of showing, bringing, or pointing out objects of interest)

   d. lack of social or emotional reciprocity

2. qualitative impairments in communication as manifested by at least one of the following:

   a. delay in, or total lack of, the development of spoken language (not accompanied by an attempt to compensate through alternative modes of communication such as gesture or mime)

   b. in individuals with adequate speech, marked impairment in the ability to initiate or sustain a conversation with others

   c. stereotyped and repetitive use of language or idiosyncratic language

   d. lack of varied, spontaneous make-believe play or social imitative play appropriate to developmental level

3. restricted repetitive and stereotyped patterns of behavior, interests, and activities, as manifested by at least one of the following:

   a. encompassing preoccupation with one or more stereotyped and restricted patterns of interest that is abnormal either in intensity or focus

   b. apparently inflexible adherence to specific, nonfunctional routines or rituals

   c. stereotyped and repetitive motor mannerisms (e.g., hand or finger flapping or twisting, or complex whole-body movements)

   d. persistent preoccupation with parts of objects

B. Delays or abnormal functioning in at least one of the following areas, with onset prior to age 3 years: (1) social interaction, (2) language as used in social communication, or (3) symbolic or imaginative play.

C. The disturbance is not better accounted for by Rett's Disorder or Childhood Disintegrative Disorder.

Source: Reprinted with permission from the *Diagnostic and Statistical Manual of Mental Disorders,* Fourth Edition, Text Revision, (Copyright © 200). American Psychiatric Association.

For many years, parents had a difficult time getting a diagnosis of autism for their child because of the medical profession's lack of familiarity with the disorder and because of the complexity of the diagnosis. This is no longer the case, as professionals and parents are now very aware of autism and related characteristics. Today, receiving a diagnosis of autism may be complicated by the fact that

© Owner Owner/cultura/Corbis

Parents may notice a lack of eye contact or social interaction in their young children with autism.

there are a number of disorders related to autism, referred to as **pervasive developmental disorders (PDD)** or **autism spectrum disorders.** These terms refer to a collection of syndromes and conditions ranging from those in which only a few of the characteristics of autism are present or the characteristics are present in a very mild form, to autism itself. Over time, each of these syndromes were given specific names and the characteristics more clearly delineated. The following disorders are considered to be part of autism spectrum disorders. You can see how the symptoms of the disorders overlap:

Pervasive developmental disorders include autism and Asperger's syndrome.

- **"Classic" or Kanner's Autism**—As defined above, children exhibit severely disordered verbal and nonverbal language and unusual behavior patterns.

- **Asperger's syndrome**—This is one of the most common autism spectrum disorders. Estimates vary, but a Approximately 1 in 500 school-age children are diagnosed with Asperger's syndrome (Torpa, C.B., 2009). Individuals with Asperger's syndrome may have many of the social and behavioral characteristics of autism but, importantly, *without* any marked delays in language and cognitive development. They experience difficulties in social functioning and relationships, but not in intelligence or language skills. A child with Asperger's syndrome is likely to be a student who does very well in some academic areas, yet not so well in others. He or she may work well alone and love to use the computer and the Internet, but resist working in cooperative learning groups or on group projects. (Safran, 2002).

- **PDD-NOS (Pervasive Developmental Disorder-Not Otherwise Specified).** Also called "high functioning autism" or "atypical autism." Children experience nonverbal language difficulties but do not meet the criteria for other PDDs such as autism, Asperger's syndrome, or Rett's disorder.

- **Rett's disorder.** A rare genetic neurodegenerative disorder that primarily affects girls, resulting in loss of social skills, language, and motor development, accompanied by distorted hand movements.

- **Childhood disintegrative disorder.** After a few years of normal development, children regress progressively in all areas, including language, social development, and motor development (DSM IV TR, Kutscher, 2003).

Because autism has been the only category among the pervasive developmental disorders specifically identified in IDEA, it was important for parents to get a confirmed diagnosis of autism as soon as possible so that they could obtain appropriate services. This concern may be disappearing in the near future. The new *Diagnostic and Statistical Manual of Mental Disorders* (5th edition, DSM V) is scheduled to be published in 2012, and a proposed change is to consolidate the diagnostic categories to one: Autism Spectrum Disorders (ASD). A fundamental rationale for this change is the challenge of reliably distinguishing, in terms of diagnosis, among the different disorders on the autism spectrum (e.g., Tryon, Mayes, Rhodes, & Waldo, 2006). In fact, many parents and professionals now just use the term "Autism Spectrum Disorders" (ASD) instead of the various other diagnoses listed above.

Dual Diagnosis

Another difficulty in attempting to diagnose autism is the fact that it coexists with a number of other conditions, such as **fragile-X syndrome,** an inherited disorder caused by chromosomal abnormalities. Unlike autism, fragile-X syndrome is diagnosed through genetic testing. Affected children exhibit many of the same behaviors as children with autism, such as communication delays, stereotypic movements, perseveration, and hyperarousal. In fact, according to the National Fragile-X Foundation, about one-third of all children with fragile-X syndrome are clinically diagnosed with autism and approximately 20 percent of children with fragile-X also are diagnosed with PDD-NOS (Hagerman, Rivera, & Hagerman, 2008). Between 2 and 6 percent of individuals diagnosed with autism have autism caused by the fragile-X gene mutation (The National Fragile-X Foundation, 2011). It is important for children diagnosed with autism to receive the DNA testing necessary to determine if they have fragile-X, so that appropriate genetic counseling and perhaps targeted interventions can be provided.

Historically, we've been told that the vast majority of individuals with autism (80 percent) also have intellectual disabilities ranging from quite mild to profound. Some researchers have challenged this statistic, however, saying that (1) the face of autism has changed since much of the earlier work, and (2) little of that information was actually empirical evidence. Edelson (2006) suggests that surveys conducted in the last decade reflect a prevalence of intellectual disabilities between 40 and 55 percent, and suggests that much more research is needed before accurate statistics can be determined. Although the level of intellectual disabilities certainly affects the ultimate ability levels of individuals with autism, as well as the specific educational goals and expectations, it typically does not affect the general educational approaches used in the classroom or other educational settings. Levels of higher intelligence may, however, affect the focus of interventions—with more of an emphasis on social and communication instruction rather than cognitive and academic instruction (Freeman & VanDyke, 2006). Other common diagnoses that occur with individuals with autism and autism spectrum disorders are attention deficit / hyperactivity disorder in younger children (Simonoff, Pickles, Charman, Chandler, Loucas, & Baird, 2008) and depression in adolescents and adults (Sterling, Dawson, Estes, & Greenson, 2008).

Prevalence

Estimates of the prevalence of autism fluctuate and often include the entire spectrum of autism disorders. In general, it is estimated that between 1 in 80 and 1 in 240 (average estimate of 1 in 110 children) are diagnosed each year with autism or a related disorder (Center for Disease Control and Prevention, 2011). During the 2008-2009 school year, 0.70 percent of all students ages 3 through 21, or 336,000 students, were served as students with autism (U.S. Department of Education, 2010). The number of children identified as having autism has increased dramatically in recent years. For example, the number given above of children receiving service from IDEA doubled from the 2004–2005 school year to the 2008-2009 school year (USDOE, 2010). Of course, the relatively recent identification of autism as a separate category in special education is partially responsible for this increase: As school districts became more practiced and prepared in classification procedures, more children were identified. Some professionals, however, suggest that the rise in the number of children identified as having autism represents a true increase in numbers, and they speculate about possible environmental and medical causes.

? Pause and Reflect

It may surprise you to know that twenty-five or so years ago, most people had not even heard about autism. Today, people with autism are featured in movies, television shows, and all other aspects of the media. Most people have heard the term and have an idea of what constitutes autism. What do you think is behind these changes in public awareness? Does awareness lead to other changes? ●

Causes of Autism

Research is bringing us ever closer to answering the questions about the reasons for autism spectrum disorder and the unusual cognitive, behavioral, and communicative patterns that occur with it. Because of the unusual nature of the behaviors associated with autism, the disorder has been attributed to a wide range of possible causes.

Autism has been attributed to a wide range of possible causes.

Historical Opinions About Causes

Although theories about the causes of autism now rest firmly in the physiological realm—the neurological, genetic, and metabolic—this certainly was not always the case. Autism was first defined in the mid-1940s by Leo Kanner (1943), who identified a cluster of behavioral characteristics that are essentially the same as those used today to diagnose children with autism. Kanner speculated about a range of possible causes, but it was Bettleheim (1967) who felt strongly that autism was a psychiatric response to an unsupportive and deprived environment. Naturally, the person responsible for the young child's environment was the mother, and it was she who was held responsible for the autistic state of her young child. How? It was assumed at the time that the child's withdrawal from social contact, abnormal focus on objects rather than people, and delayed language development reflected a lack of appropriate socialization and loving behaviors from the mother. In fact, the term *refrigerator mother* was used to describe the mothers of young children with autism—cold, unfeeling, icy. So, if you were a mother forty or fifty years ago and had a young child with autism, not only did you have the great challenge of trying to teach your toddler how to talk and play and smile, you also had to shoulder the burden of responsibility for supposedly *causing* these learning problems.

Fortunately, all we have learned about the nature of autism in the past decade or so has almost erased the stigma on parents, although, unfortunately, we still see some interventions based on the concept of parents as the cause of autism.

Current Hypotheses About Causes

Although there is still much speculation in the field, today our hypotheses about the causes of autism focus on physiological differences. The search for physiological causes for autism began in the 1960s (Rimland, 1964; Scott, Clark, & Brady, 2000) and has received increasing support in the past few decades. Most scientists agree that the collection of symptoms constituting autism spectrum disorders are neurodevelopmental disorders originating before birth. In other words, it is likely that autism is caused by differences in the neurological system—beginning very early in the embryonic development of the child. Children with autism have specific differences in brain development, specifically in the brain stem (see Figure 9.1). Many also have specific genetic abnormalities. Although many genes appear to be associated with autism, no clear causal relationship between a specific genetic abnormality and the occurrence of autism has yet been established. Discovering the ultimate cause of autism will mean answering the following questions: What types of environmental or physiological insults to the fetus trigger the brain differences? What factors influence the variety and intensity of characteristics related to autism? Is there a clear set of identifiable risk factors? The answers to these questions will depend on further knowledge about specific genetic and chromosomal factors, and they may lead to the discovery of the importance of environmental factors. Investigations designed to

> Today, hypotheses about the causes of autism focus on physiological factors.

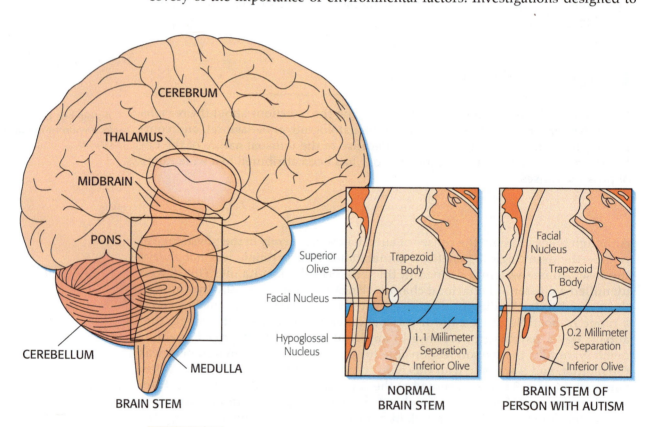

FIGURE 9.1

Autism's effects include changes to the brain stem, the region just above the spinal cord (*left*). The brain stem of a person with autism is shorter than a normal brain stem (*right*): The structures at the junction of the pons and the medulla (such as the facial nucleus and the trapezoid body) are closer to the structures of the lower medulla (the hypoglossal nucleus and the inferior olive). It is as though a band of tissue were missing. The brain stem of a person with autism also lacks the superior olive and has a smaller than normal facial nucleus. Such changes could occur only in early gestation.

Source: Adapted from © 1999 Terese Winslow.

examine possible neurochemical factors common to children with autism have found only elevated levels of platelet serotonin, a neurotransporter, but the implications of this finding are speculative and require replication (Lam, Aman, & Arnold, 2006).

Certainly, one of the puzzling factors about the onset of autism is that in close to 30 percent of children diagnosed, the defining characteristics don't appear until the child is a toddler, at which point some of the children begin to regress markedly in communication and social abilities. This phenomenon is referred to as autistic regression (Boyd, Odom, Humphreys, & Sam, 2010; Davidovitch et al., 2000), and presents one of the many challenges to prevention and early intervention. Although this characteristic may be attributed to genes that are active only during specific times of a child's development, it has fostered increased, yet unsubstantiated, speculation about direct environmental influences, such as childhood vaccines or prenatal exposure to diseases such as rubella.

No clear relationships between specific environmental factors and the onset of autism have ever been established, but the role of the world around us, including what is in the air and what we do in our homes, continues to be examined as we look for causes for autism. There are likely many. Research has long provided support for the theory that there is a genetic component to autism. For example, the chance of having autism if your brother or sister has autism is 2 to 8 percent (Heflin & Alaimo, 2007). You may know of a number of families that have more than one child with autism—these families even have a name—multiplex families. On the other hand, the most recent research presents twin studies that suggest, although genetics is still considered a factor in autism, it may be less of a factor than we originally thought. In a large, recent twin study—known as the California twin study—Hallmayer et al. (2011) found that although identical twins had a 60 to 70 percent chance of one having autism if the other one did, fraternal twins had a 20 to 30 percent chance of this occurring. Although these results certainly illustrate the genetic component, the fraternal twin dual diagnosis rate was higher than expected, and the identical twin dual diagnosis rate was lower than expected. Where do these results lead researchers? To more twin studies, but also to renewed emphasis on studying risk and the early environment—including perinatal factors.

? Pause and Reflect

The cause or causes of autism have eluded the professional community for many years, in part, because we were focused for too long on psychiatric rather than biological etiologies. You can see how the great increases in the number of children with autism would prompt additional research in this area. Why do you think that as we changed our perceptions of what causes autism, we also changed the nature of interventions we use with children and families? •

Characteristics of Individuals with Autism

Individuals with autism often demonstrate unusual patterns of learning, speech, and behavior. There is great variability in the amount and intensity of symptoms among children who are identified as having autism. Children described as having autistic-like behaviors usually have only a few of these characteristics.

Cognitive Characteristics

Many individuals with autism have intellectual disabilities and display unusual learning patterns.

Children with autism can be found at all levels of intellectual ability. As we stated earlier, although the data are changing, it appears that close to 50 percent of people diagnosed with autism are also diagnosed with intellectual disabilities. Individuals with autism, even those without significant intellectual disabilities, display unusual, uneven learning patterns, often consisting of relative strength in one or two areas of learning. Although a very small number of children with autism are truly gifted in one area, many do have learning strengths that are surprising in light of the child's overall level of functioning.

A child with autism may demonstrate ability in auditory memory, organization, or telling time and yet have extreme difficulty in other learning skills, such as reading or writing. For example, Michael, a young man with autism and moderate intellectual disabilities, has a sight-word vocabulary of only twenty-five words, yet can remember all the words to songs and commercials he heard over fifteen years ago. Although he cannot do even simple addition or subtraction when it is presented in number problem format, he can instantly add or subtract hours on his watch to accommodate changes due to Daylight Savings Time or Standard

FIRST PERSON

Kevin Sribnick

When Kevin was an infant, my parents thought he was deaf because he was so detached. One of my earliest memories was my father firing a cap pistol near Kevin to see if he would respond. He didn't. My parents took Kevin to doctor after doctor before he was diagnosed as autistic. I remember my mother saying she was happy to learn he wasn't deaf because there are so many wonderful sounds to hear. I suspect as Kevin got older and his inappropriate behaviors began to emerge, she had second thoughts about her preference. Kevin's early years were difficult for our entire family. He would only drink milk and would not eat until age 4. Finally my grandmother, who was visiting from New York, got him to eat solid food. As a young child, Kevin was quite destructive. I remember how distraught my mother was when Kevin used a lamp plug to scratch the surface of two new coffee tables she had recently brought home. From then on, she realized she would never be able to keep beautiful things in our

Kevin and Richard Sribnick at home.

home. Kevin would wander the house at night, frequently falling asleep wherever he happened to be when he finally closed his eyes. My brothers, sister, and I would take turns being responsible for finding him and bringing him to bed. Kevin would frequently have night terrors and the only way my parents could calm

Photo courtesy of Kathleen Marshall

Time, before his watch is adjusted. He also can easily convert "military time" to standard time (for example, 1400 hours to 2:00 p.m.). These skills alone are not exceptional (most of us can convert time), but they are surprising when compared to other skills with which Michael has difficulty.

We have seen that many children with cognitive or learning disabilities have difficulty with memory tasks. Children with autism spectrum disorder may have variable memory skills, but we do see some similarities with other children who have disabilities in some aspects of remembering. For example, individuals with autism, like children with learning disabilities and intellectual disabilities, do not appear to use active memory strategies such as organization and rehearsal of information. In general, kids with ASD seem to have difficulty with the information-processing aspects of memory—recognizing details and categorizing information (Renner, Klinger, & Klinger, 2000; Williams, Goldstein, & Minshew, 2006). Of course, the uncanny ability of a number of kids with ASD to remember particular types of information—particularly auditory information such as television or radio advertisements or songs, seems to tap into another area of learning.

---

him was to take him for a drive, often at 2:00 in the morning. As is true for so many other children with autism, he could not tolerate change and would frequently have tantrums when something familiar was moved from its usual spot. By trial and error we would try to figure out what was missing and put it back into place. Because Kevin did not have any outward signs of a disability, strangers didn't understand his bizarre outbursts. We were very defensive and protected him from annoyed stares and unkind comments.

Despite all these problems, we loved Kevin very much. It became an early ritual that before any of us blew out our birthday candles, we would wish for Kevin to get better. As Kevin got older, his behavior began to improve. He attended a school for children with mental and emotional disabilities and later worked in a sheltered workshop. Kevin learned to read simple phrases and add single digits. He became very close to me and would sit with me for much of the time while I studied for school. He also loved to swim. Being in the water always seemed to make him relaxed and happy.

Kevin lived at home until his mid-thirties. I would frequently keep him overnight on the weekends. We would make our supper together

and listen to music. We both enjoy music from the late 1960s. I don't think the Moody Blues have a more devoted fan than Kevin. Five years ago, Kevin had a serious illness requiring hospitalization. I have never been so frightened in my entire life, and realized just how much Kevin means to me. Fortunately, he recovered completely.

Kevin is now 48 and for the last nine years has lived in an apartment with a caregiver and another man with autism. He continues to work and has become more self-sufficient. Kevin doesn't talk very much but does express all of his needs and preferences. He has become quite flexible when things are different from what he expects. Kevin and I always have lunch together on Sunday afternoons. Now that he lives independently, I have the opportunity to see how others view him. I recently read his quarterly service plan. As I read about Kevin's preferences and strengths, I realized that my little brother had become his own man. This year, my birthday wish will be for something else. Kevin is fine just the way he is.

Richard L. Sribnick, M.D.

Source: Personal account.

Most typically developing kids have a good memory for things that happened to them. Children with autism, however, seem to recall events that happened to their peers better than they recall events that happened to themselves (Millward et al., 2000). This surprising learning characteristic seems incongruous with what we know about the social withdrawal of most children with autism. It is puzzling that children who don't seem to notice or may not interact with their classmates have such a good memory of what happens to the others around them.

Children with autism also may be very rigid in their demands for environmental sameness and dependent on exact routines during the day (Koegel et al., 1995; Lam & Aman, 2007). For example, Mateo, a student who catches the school bus at 7:15 in the morning, will always leave the house at 7:10 a.m. and walk the exact same number of steps each time. If he leaves early, Mateo will walk very slowly so that he arrives and boards the bus at exactly 7:15. Some individuals will insist on sameness in their house or classroom, or in the sequence of events involved in going on a shopping trip or preparing lunch. Perry, a young man with autism living in a group home, became incensed one day and began raging at his housemates. The counselor living in the group home spent the afternoon searching for the problem. What was different? Had something been moved in Perry's room? Finally, Perry told the counselor that it had to do with toilet tissue. There had been a sale and the counselor bought two extra packages of toilet tissue. It was too much for Perry—too different from what the bathroom usually held. Not all individuals with autism will exhibit this characteristic, and some will require sameness in routine or order for only certain things. As you might expect, this need for sameness may have significant implications when selecting instructional strategies and types of interventions. Once again, it is important to know and understand if and how this characteristic affects the child with autism in your classroom.

> Children with autism are often very rigid in their demands for environmental sameness.

Physical and Sensory Characteristics

Children with autism are usually described as average in appearance, if not as unusually attractive children. Most young children with autism look like any other typically developing young child. There are some physical characteristics that can be associated with autism spectrum disorder, including a number of features associated with the symmetry of the face (mouth, eyes, general facial asymmetry) and shape of the head (brachycephaly, prominent lower jaw) (Ozgen et al., 2011). These characteristics are truly minor, are not present in all children, and are difficult to observe unless one knows to look for them. Researchers also hypothesize that some physical characteristics could present evidence of risk factors rather than be results of ASD (Ozgen et al., 2011).

Many individuals with autism appear to be highly sensitive or reactive to certain sensory stimulation. In particular, many children with ASD have differences from typically developing children in the way they process information from all five senses (hear, see, smell, taste, touch), as well as the proprioceptive (reflex) or vestibular (balance) systems (Baker, Lane, Angley, & Young, 2007). This means that some individuals will appear highly sensitive and react strongly to loud noises, for example, or perhaps be unable to stand wearing a rough fabric—reactions can vary widely depending on each individual child. Research related to auditory responses suggests that although students with ASD scored similarly to typically developing children on auditory tests—in other words, there appear to be no physiological differences—they exhibited more reactive behaviors in response to sounds (Stiegler & Davis, 2010; Tharpe et al., 2006). It has often been hypothesized that oversensitivity to external stimuli is responsible for some of the unusual behaviors individuals with ASD may demonstrate (e.g., hands over ears, hand-flapping, toe-walking). Research continues to explore these relationships. The more we learn about the brain and children with autism, the closer we get to

▶❚❚ TeachSource VIDEO CASE

How Can Students with Autism Learn to Cope with Change?

As you have read, students with autism like predictable routines, but life in school is not always predictable. Visit Chapter 9 on the CourseMate website and watch the video case entitled "Rebecca and Ben: Creating Structured Educational Programs for students with Autism." Watch how Rebecca, a 5-year old with autism, and Ben, an older boy with Asperger's syndrome, learn to cope with change. What else could be done to help students with autism adjust to change?

answering questions about the relationship between sensory and physical characteristics and behavior.

Social Interaction

Individuals with autism typically demonstrate patterns of social behavior that reflect social withdrawal and avoidance of others. These patterns can include failure to make eye contact and to attend to others in the room, even if the other individuals are attempting to play with or talk to the child. The individual with autism simply may not react or may actively avoid other people's efforts at social interaction or communication. In fact, a characteristic description given by parents is that the child with autism appears to look through or past them (Maurice, 1993; Park, 1998). Historically, young children with autism were often misdiagnosed as being deaf, because their inattention was so marked that parents assumed they couldn't hear the noises around them, including their own names.

Many children with autism focus their attentions on objects instead of other people. They seem to disregard the desire for **joint attention**—the mutual sharing of experiences, activities, or even objects with friends, teachers, or parents (Scott, Clark, & Brady, 2000). As you can imagine, these characteristics can be particularly difficult for parents as they attempt to interact with and come to know their young child. Here is an example of one parent's observations:

> We start with an image—a tiny, golden child on hands and knees, circling round and round a spot on the floor in mysterious, self-absorbed delight. She does not look up, though she is smiling and laughing; she does not call our attention to the mysterious object of her pleasure. She does not see us at all. She and the spot are all there is, and though she is eighteen months old, an age for touching, tasting, pointing, pushing, exploring, she is doing none of these things. She does not walk, or crawl up stairs, or pull herself to her feet to reach for objects. She doesn't want any objects, instead she circles her spot. Or she sits, a long chain in her hand, snaking it up and down, up and down, watching it coil and uncoil for twenty minutes, half an hour, longer. . . . (Park, 1998, p. 30)

Not all individuals with autism are so completely withdrawn from social interaction with others, but most experience significant delays or deficits in social skills. A dual diagnosis of autism and intellectual disabilities suggests higher rates of poor adaptive behavior (Kraijer, 2000). Even those with less severe social deficits may have difficulty seeing things from the perspective of others and engaging appropriately in reciprocal social exchanges.

The importance of these characteristic social behavior patterns cannot be overestimated, because they affect virtually all areas of functioning—school, work, home, and play. For just about all individuals with autism and autism spectrum disorders, acquiring appropriate social skills and adaptive behavior comprises a substantial portion of their educational programming at any age. As we will see, appropriate social interaction is closely intertwined with language, communication, and behavior.

Language and Communication

Difficulties and delays with language and communication are the hallmarks of children with autism. As we've just mentioned, many toddlers with ASD don't engage in or initiate joint attention—seeing a dog outside, pointing to it, and urging mom to look at it too. Joint attention emerges about the same time as language and specific deficits in joint attention are related to delays in receptive and

> Many children with autism withdraw from social interaction or display significant deficits in social skills.

expressive language development (Murray et al., 2008). Some children with ASD have delayed speech; it is not unusual for a child with autism to begin saying words at the age of six or seven. Sometimes, a toddler may begin talking at a normal developmental rate and then stop using previously acquired speech around age two (Davidovitch et al., 2000). Some children with autism may not acquire verbal language at all. A nonverbal child may use gestures, vocalizations, or facial expressions to communicate (Stephenson & Dowrick, 2000). Sign language or language boards are often used with nonverbal students to provide a means of communication.

If individuals with autism acquire oral speech, their speech patterns may take unusual forms. One common example is **echolalia,** the repetition of speech sounds. For example, if you asked a child, "What is your name?" the child would respond, "What is your name?" The child also may repeat certain words over and over—the jingle from a television advertisement or a sentence he or she has overheard. Although echolalic speech may seem to be nonfunctional—that is, not used for a specific purpose such as asking a question—it often does represent an attempt at direct communication. The student does not use typical forms of interpersonal communication, but the *intent* to communicate may be there. In fact, echolalic responses can indicate an attempt at the turn taking required in reciprocal speech (Scott, Clark, & Brady, 2000). In other words, the child may understand that a response is required but be unable to formulate an appropriate response, so he simply repeats what was just said. For example, in an attempt to manage his own disruptive behavior, Kyle will say over and over the words he's heard so often—"Kyle, you've got to calm down." Although Kyle is repeating the words others have spoken, he uses them in a self-regulatory fashion—and calms himself down. Research continues to increase our knowledge base in this area, and interventions now include teaching students to adapt echolalic speech into useful, or functional, language.

Individuals with autism may present other types of language differences. Some may speak telegraphically, omitting articles, conjunctions, and tense markers ("Dan eat apple"). People with autism also may refer to themselves in the third person and avoid using pronouns altogether. As an example of both characteristics, Jim might say, "Jim watch TV" instead of "I want to watch TV." The speech of individuals with autism also is characterized by a flat or monotone quality.

As you can probably see, many individuals with autism have a difficult time with reciprocal language—the use of language to give and receive information. **Reciprocal speech** combines the social or pragmatic aspects of communication, such as eye contact and turn taking, with the mechanical requirements of communication. It also involves skills in both **receptive language,** that is, understanding and interpreting information, and **expressive language.** Much research has been devoted to the observation and development of reciprocal speech in young children with autism (Ingersoll & Schreibman, 2006; Kasari, Paparella, Freeman, & Jahromi, 2008; Simpson & Souris, 1988). Some investigators have found that structured interventions that emphasize social interactive skills with peers or adults can increase both social and communication skills (Hwang & Hughes, 2000). It makes sense that teaching language in the context of social interaction will facilitate the acquisition and generalization of both types of behaviors. See Figure 9.2 for a sample protocol for language instruction in pronoun use.

We still have much to learn about the receptive communication skills of individuals with autism. As we mentioned earlier, individuals with autism often do not respond to language directed toward them. Sigafoos (2000) conducted research that reinforced our knowledge base on the relationship of poor communication skills to inappropriate behavior. Interestingly, he found stronger correlations between inappropriate behavior and receptive communication than between inappropriate behavior and expressive language. In other words, children with autism may be even more frustrated by their inability to understand information than their difficulty

PROGRAM: Pronouns (I and You)

Program Procedure

1. *I*—Prompt the child to perform an action (e.g., physically guide the child to clap his or her hands) and say "What are you doing?" Prompt the child to say what he or she is doing with the correct pronoun (e.g., "I am clapping my hands"). Reinforce the response. Fade prompts over subsequent trials. Differentially reinforce responses demonstrated with the lowest level of prompting. Eventually, only reinforce correct, unprompted responses.

2. *You*—Sit across from the child. Establish attending and demonstrate an action (e.g., clap your hands). Say "What am I doing?" Prompt child to say what you are doing with the correct pronoun (e.g., "You are clapping your hands"). Reinforce the response. Fade prompts over subsequent trials. Differentially reinforce responses demonstrated with the lowest level of prompting. Eventually, only reinforce correct, unprompted responses.

3. *Randomize I and You*—Prompt the child to perform an action (e.g., give the child some juice to drink) and demonstrate an action (e.g., eat a cookie). Say either "What are you doing?" or "What am I doing?" Prompt the child to say what are you doing (e.g., "You are eating a cookie") or to say what he or she is doing (e.g., "I am drinking juice"). Fade prompts over subsequent trials. Differentially reinforce responses demonstrated with the lowest level of prompting. Eventually, only reinforce correct, unprompted responses.

Suggested Prerequisites:

Labels actions, possession, and pronouns (*my* and *your*).

Prompting Suggestions:

Model the correct response and use a time-delay procedure.

Question	Response	Date Introduced	Date Mastered
1. "What are you doing?" 2. "What am I doing?" 3. Either 1 or 2	1. Describes what he or she is doing with correct pronoun "I am…" 2. Describes what you are doing with correct pronoun "You are…" 3. Either 1 or 2		
1. I am			
2. You are			
3. Randomize I and You			
Helpful Hint: Be sure to ask your child to label pronouns in natural contexts.			

FIGURE 9.2

Teaching Pronouns I and You

*Source:*Pronouns (I and You). Note. From *Behavioral Intervention for Young Children with Autism: A Manual for Parents and Professionals* (pp. 133), by C. Maurice, G. Green & S. C. Luce (Eds.), 1996, Austin, TX: PRO-ED. Copyright 1996 by PRO-ED, Inc. Reprinted with permission.

in expressing themselves. This implies that teachers need to assess the clarity and efficiency of their own communication strategies during instruction—you may increase appropriate behavior through good communication with your students with autism. See Table 9.1, "Considerations in Developing Communication Skills."

Behavior

Individuals with autism may display a unique range of characteristic, sometimes disturbing, behaviors. Some are typical of the types of behaviors you might see in any child, but they occur at greater rates and intensities and at unexpected times.

Table 9.1 Considerations for Developing Communication Skills in Children with Autism

- Make the communication an integral part of the child's life in and out of school.
- Communication, rather than rote responses, should be the goal.
- Emphasize spontaneous speech, whether pictorial, gestural, or verbal.
- Give the child many opportunities to communicate in all settings.
- Any socially acceptable attempt to communicate should be reinforced in all settings.
- Communication goals should be part of any plan to change maladaptive behavior.
- Initial communication goals should target obtaining items and activities that the student finds reinforcing.
- Communication goals should be developmentally and chronologically appropriate.
- Work together with all significant people in the student's environment to make the communication training as consistent as possible.

Source: From SCOTT. *Student with Autism,* 1E. © 2000 Wadsworth, a part of Cengage Learning, Inc. Reproduced by permission. www.cengage.com/permissions

Examples include throwing tantrums, crying, yelling or screaming, and hiding. You might expect a typical two-year-old to throw a tantrum if you take a toy away, or a five-year-old to start crying if he is reprimanded for leaving his toys out overnight. You would not, however, expect a ten-year-old to throw a tantrum because a certain spoon is in the dishwasher, yet this is a behavior you might see from a child with autism.

One frequent cause of inappropriate behavior we've mentioned is the characteristic of rigidity, or need for structure, often present in children with autism. A common experience of parents of young children with autism is that the child will start crying or screaming because something is out of place. The parents and siblings then begin a long process of checking everything in the environment—every piece of furniture, book, lamp, rug—to identify and then fix the source of the child's dismay.

An unusual behavioral tendency demonstrated by some individuals with autism is the performance of repetitive patterns of behavior such as rocking, twirling objects, clapping hands, and flapping a hand in front of one's face. These repetitive, nonharmful behaviors are often referred to as **stereotypic behaviors,** or self-stimulating behaviors. Some people with autism display a number of stereotypic behaviors and perform them frequently, if not constantly. Others may engage in one or two behaviors, such as rocking, during periods of inactivity.

> Individuals with autism often engage in repetitive behaviors referred to as stereotypic behaviors.

Sometimes, the stereotypic nature of behavior is reflected in more disturbing actions. A few individuals with autism exhibit self-injurious or self-abusive behaviors, ranging from hand biting or head slapping to life-threatening behaviors such as head banging. The individuals seem oblivious to the pain and damage caused by these behaviors.

Why do individuals with autism display these behaviors, particularly harmful ones? Research suggests many possible reasons for self-injurious and other inappropriate behavior, including attempts at communication and efforts to manipulate the environment and avoid demanding or stressful situations (Chandler et al., 1999; Durand & Carr, 1985; Sigafoos, 2000). In other words, many of these behaviors have a definite use or function for the child with autism. Often, they

Individuals with autism often engage in in repetitive, stereotypic behavior, such as hand-flapping.

represent the individual's best effort to tell you how he or she is feeling and to achieve some control over his or her environment.

This knowledge of the relationship between behavior and communication is extremely important to those who make up the social support system of individuals with autism. Our first instinct as teachers is to try to eliminate inappropriate or harmful behavior. However, we must first assess the student's communicative intent and try to provide alternative behaviors or skills in language and communication when attempting to reduce inappropriate behaviors. Our job, therefore, is twofold: (1) determine the purpose or function of the behavior, and (2) identify and teach an appropriate, alternative behavior that will serve the same function. To accomplish these goals, we conduct functional behavioral assessments that include observations of the student performing the behavior in home, school, or play settings (see Chapter 8). This procedure has been found to be effective in replacing inappropriate behavior with appropriate behaviors for students with ASD (Campbell, 2003). A functional behavioral assessment can also determine when stereotypic behaviors are inherently or sensorially reinforcing (feels good) rather than socially reinforced (Ahearn, Clark, & MacDonald, 2007).

> Inappropriate behavior may reflect attempts by individuals with autism to communicate or to manipulate the environment.

Family Issues and Interactions

Several times throughout this chapter, we refer to issues and challenges faced by families of individuals with autism. It is difficult to talk about autism without including parents in the discussion. Parents have been substantial contributors to the knowledge base in the field, both as ethnographers and as sources of objective evidence on the effectiveness of various interventions. Unfortunately, most parents are forced into the roles of treatment evaluator, teacher, and, in some cases, intervention designer. Because of the dearth of practical information about living with children with autism, difficulty getting an early diagnosis, inconsistency in treatment recommendations, and lack of early intervention programs, parents took the reins and brought the needs of children with autism into focus. This effort by parents is still under way, but now many parents and professionals are working together, and parent advocacy has resulted in a renewed demand for objective, empirical proof of an intervention's effectiveness as well as increased interventions for very young children.

> Parents are major contributors to the knowledge base in the field of autism.

Historically, the literature written by parents was filled with concerns about the difficulties they experienced as they have tried to get an accurate diagnosis for their child (Maurice, 1993). Even when a child receives an early diagnosis, the process is never an easy one. Parents report finding compassion and honesty to be important characteristics of the professionals who are in the role of delivering the diagnosis of autism (Nissenbaum, Tollefson, & Reese, 2002). Today, issues such as securing appropriate insurance to pay for necessary services for their children tops the list of concerns for many parents.

Because early diagnosis is so critical, a number of screening tests have been developed that can be given in the home, doctor's office, or day care settings and can depend largely on parent input. The National Institute of Mental Health (NIMH) (2011) recommends that screening instruments routinely should be part of well-child check-ups. Some of the more common screening measures are the: Communication and Symbolic Behavior Scales (CSBS DP) (Wetherby & Prizant, 2002); Modified Checklist of Autism in Toddlers (MCHAT) (Robins, Fein, & Barton,

Teaching Strategies & Accommodations

The M-CHAT

M-CHAT

Please fill out the following about how your child usually is. Please try to answer every question. If the behavior is rare (e.g., you've seen it once or twice), please answer as if the child does not do it.

1. Does your child enjoy being swung, bounced on your knee, etc.? Yes No

2. Does your child take an interest in other children? Yes No

3. Does your child like climbing on things, such as up stairs? Yes No

4. Does your child enjoy playing peek-a-boo/ hide-and-seek? Yes No

5. Does your child ever pretend, for example, to talk on the phone or take care of a doll or pretend other things? Yes No

6. Does your child ever use his/her index finger to point, to ask for something? Yes No

7. Does your child ever use his/her index finger to point, to indicate interest in something? Yes No

8. Can your child play properly with small toys (e.g. cars or blocks) without just mouthing, fiddling, or dropping them? Yes No

9. Does your child ever bring objects over to you (parent) to show you something? Yes No

10. Does your child look you in the eye for more than a second or two? Yes No

11. Does your child ever seem oversensitive to noise? (e.g., plugging ears) Yes No

12. Does your child smile in response to your face or your smile? Yes No

13. Does your child imitate you? (e.g., you make a face—will your child imitate it?) Yes No

14. Does your child respond to his/her name when you call? Yes No

15. If you point at a toy across the room, does your child look at it? Yes No

16. Does your child walk? Yes No

17. Does your child look at things you are looking at? Yes No

18. Does your child make unusual finger movements near his/her face? Yes No

19. Does your child try to attract your attention to his/her own activity? Yes No

20. Have you ever wondered if your child is deaf? Yes No

21. Does your child understand what people say? Yes No

22. Does your child sometimes stare at nothing or wander with no purpose? Yes No

23. Does your child look at your face to check your reaction when faced with something unfamiliar? Yes No

_____

Source: © 1999 Diana Robins, Deborah Fein, & Marianne Barton.

1999); and the Screening Tool for Autism in Two-Year-Olds (STAT) (Stone, Coonrod, Turner, & Pozdol, 2004). Screening tools like these will help parents either allay fears about their child's development or allow for early follow-up and evaluation, if necessary. See Teaching Strategies and Accommodations, "The M-CHAT."

Once a diagnosis is obtained, parents are faced with a growing body of literature and testimonials about literally dozens of interventions, all of which should begin when the child is about 2 years old. So, sifting through the research and trying to find the intervention and desired service provider in the community as soon as possible become the next priorities. Of course, families with limited resources or those living in rural areas may experience even more difficulty finding appropriate services. It is no wonder that parent support groups and organizations such as the Autism Society provide valuable guidance and assistance as parents try to make their way through the intervention maze. Research suggests that social networks provide needed support to families of children with ASD—many of whom get much of their information about autism from other parents (Meadan, Halle, & Ebata, 2010). Visit the website of the Autism Society of America to learn more about advocacy, resources, research, and general information related to autism and autism spectrum disorders.

Once an intervention is chosen, the role of the parents and other family members will only increase. Almost all recommended interventions for young children with autism include intensive teaching, often within the child's home, and usually involving round-the-clock instruction, measuring, and evaluating by parents. So, by the time a child with autism is 3 or 4, his or her family will have devoted at least two to three years of nonstop searching, investigating, and teaching. Because of the intimate role parents play in service delivery, great care is taken to understand and incorporate their needs and educational concerns in areas such as communication priorities (Stephenson & Dowrick, 2000).

Obviously, finding and evaluating appropriate and effective interventions for their children is the priority for many parents of children with ASD, but often it is day-to-day life that causes stressors for families. Some young children with ASD have severe acting out episodes, some will engage in stereotypic behaviors, or some kids will suddenly engage in spurts of running and jumping that can make public interaction challenging, or make parents think twice about bringing kids to church or taking the family on a long car ride to the beach. If your child doesn't want to engage in social interactions and won't or can't communicate with other children, what happens at birthday parties, T-ball games, sleepovers, or play dates? Do you go and try to encourage some interaction even when your child fights it? Do you give up and go home? Most parents, over time, gradually introduce their child to a variety of social situations—once the family becomes more comfortable with life as they know it, others seem to become more comfortable as well. Each family learns to find their own way of incorporating difference into their lifestyle. In the meantime, families of kids with ASD continue to look for support, suggestions, and ideas of ways to help their son or daughter become active and make friends. Parent-centered websites, as we've discussed, are great places for parents to go for resources. See Teaching Strategies and Accommodations, "Physical Activities for Kids with ASD," to find a list of suggested physical activities that parents report their kids with autism have found enjoyable.

The majority of students with autism receive a functional, community-based curriculum.

Pause and Reflect

The social and behavioral characteristics of children with autism, as well as language skills, vary greatly from child to child, but always present challenges. How do you think you would react if a child with autism entered your family or your classroom? Where would you go for guidance and assistance? ●

Teaching Strategies & Accommodations

Physical Activities for Kids with ASD

Ten Sport Suggestions for Kids with Autism
by Carrie Bishop
May 01, 20 ll

Not one child with autism is alike. What works for one kid may not be ideal for the next. As parents consider introducing sports and athletics to their child with autism, Georgia Frey, associate professor in the department of kinesiology at Indiana University, encourages families to try lots of athletic activities before settling on one sport. First help the child gain physical confidence, and then they may have the self esteem and the drive to try other activities, including team sports.

Following are a few physical activities that area experts say may be fun for kids on the autism spectrum. Of course, parents know their child better than anyone. If they like sailing or skipping, so be it. It may not be on this list, but it may be right for the child. The possibilities for athletic fun is truly without limits.

© George Doyle/Stockbyte/Getty Images

Rock climbing: This sport helps kids learn to think ahead and problem solve.

Golf: On the green, kids have to wait their turns and let people play ahead of them.

Swimming: This whole-body sport is often sensory rewarding for kids with autism.

Track and field: Running is a great activity for the individual-minded athlete; however, be aware that the events often start with a loud bang from a gun that may not be good for some kids.

Martial arts: Taught in a highly structured environment, martial arts can help develop a child's self confidence, motor skills, and concentration.

Hiking: Hikes, even if it's as simple as walking the Monon Trail, can put kids in touch with nature, become a heart-healthy habit, and get them out and about amongst the community.

Bicycle riding: In addition to promoting a child's balance and coordination, riding bikes can be a great recreational activity the entire family can enjoy together.

Horseback riding: Not only is horseback riding good exercise, the interaction between the horse and rider can grow into an amazing relationship.

Gymnastics: With a good coach, kids can gain body awareness and learn to exert better control of their bodies.

Bowling: Lanes of bowlers may be loud, but it's an underlying roar of white noise versus the shrills and shrieks that come with other team sports. This can sometimes be easier for kids with sensory issues to take.

Source: Carrie Bishop, *Ten Sport Suggestions for Kids with Autism, Indy's Child Parenting Magazine,* May 1, 2011. Reprinted with permission.

Teaching Strategies and Accommodations

The recommended focus of curriculum and instruction for individuals with autism varies greatly depending on each child's abilities and needs. Individuals with autism and moderate to severe intellectual disabilities will require extensive behavior support and skills instruction, and will benefit from a functional, community-based curriculum that focuses on life skills. Other individuals with autism, those with mild intellectual disabilities or typical cognitive ability, may progress through a general education academic curriculum and receive less intensive behavioral, academic, and social support. Some students may require services only in the area of social skills or communication. In general, the areas of communication, socialization, and generalization of learning are particularly important in programs for individuals with autism and form the basis for most interventions.

As you might expect, students with autism may receive special education services at all levels of the service delivery continuum, depending on each student's individual strengths and needs. Many young children receive services at home, or attend a preschool program. As with all children with disabilities, decisions about educational settings for children with autism will be based on short-term and long-range educational goals for the child, and on his or her ability to perform in general education settings. You may find a child with autism and moderate intellectual disabilities served in a self-contained class or in a high-school vocational training program. Or, you may find a child with autism receiving academic instruction in the general education class, with accommodations for language and in-class instruction in social skills. You may notice there is no section in this chapter on academic characteristics or instruction. That is because students with ASD have a very wide range of abilities in academic areas, so it is impossible to characterize them in one way. There also has been little research on best teaching practice specific to children with autism. The approaches we've already covered in Chapters 5 through 8 address the practices currently used to teach academic skills to most students with autism spectrum disorders. Research, however, increasingly is addressing how best to teach academic skills to students with ASD. It is important to ensure that students with autism, regardless of the classroom setting, receive the level of instruction they require, particularly in the areas of social behavior and communication. These areas continue to be crucial throughout the transition plan of adolescents because they relate to job training and other preparations for life after school.

The Importance of Early Intervention

Although there is a great variety of available interventions for individuals with autism, the proponents of virtually all of them agree on one thing: the earlier the better. Early interventions for young children with ASD can be grouped into two types of evidence-based practices discussed by Boyd, Odom, Humphreys, and Sam (2010). The first type is called *focused interventions*—these are specific instructional strategies or interventions and include behavioral and naturalistic interventions. We look at several of these in the following sections. The other type of interventions, *comprehensive treatment models*, consist of theoretically based, multifaceted programs. The comprehensive treatment models can include focused interventions, but the efficacy of the program is evaluated based on the entire model, which may include parent, family, and community components.

Currently, there are general guidelines for the focus of early interventions designed for young children with ASD based on an analysis of early intervention research. The following recommendations for intervention were advanced by the National Research Council (2001):

1. Functional, spontaneous communication should be the primary focus of early education.

2. Social instruction should be delivered throughout the day in various settings, using specific activities and interventions planned to meet age-appropriate, individualized social goals.

3. The teaching of play skills should focus on play with peers, and additional instruction in appropriate use of toys and other materials.

4. Instruction aimed at goals for cognitive development should also be carried out in the context in which the skills are expected to be used, with generalization and maintenance in natural contexts as important as the acquisition of new skills.

Children with autism should receive intensive intervention at an early age.

5. Intervention strategies that address problem behaviors should incorporate information about the contexts in which the behaviors occur; positive, proactive approaches; and the range of techniques that have empirical support.

6. Functional academic skills should be taught when appropriate to the skills and needs of a child. (NRC, p. 221)

These elements can serve as guidelines for both teachers and parents as they search for comprehensive preschool programs. Because of the requirements of PL 99-457, school districts must provide programs for individuals over age 3 identified with autism or other developmental disabilities, and many districts offer educational programs for children between the ages of birth and 3 (see Chapter 3). Increased awareness of autism and related disorders leads to parents receiving earlier diagnoses for their children and, therefore, demanding a greater number of comprehensive services. State educational agencies will be able to identify the range and type of services available in specific communities. Table 9.2 provides some guiding questions for parents to help match interventions to the specific needs of a child.

As children become school-aged, they will move from early intervention programs to school-based programs. Some of the specific programs or approaches described below are designed primarily for young children (e.g., the Lovaas method), while other approaches or interventions are appropriate for children of all ages (applied behavior analysis, social skills instruction). As we look at the sample of interventions presented below, you will notice some differences and some similarities. As was done with early intervention programs, research on interventions for school-aged children with autism was evaluated to determine the fundamental elements of successful programs for all students with autism. You can see that the following components mirror, in a general way, the factors of successful early intervention programs.

These six components (Iovannone et al., 2003, p. 153) are:

- Individualized supports and services for students and families: include looking at parent and child preferences to establish goals for instruction
- Systematic instruction: carefully plan, deliver, and evaluate instruction and student outcomes
- Comprehensible and/or structured environments: include organizing and defining the classroom setting, using schedules, behavioral supports, and opportunities for choice
- Specialized curriculum content: teach functional skills based on individual assessment and emphasizing social, behavioral, and communication skills
- A functional approach to problem behavior: use Functional Behavior Assessment to identify the relationship between the environment and problem behavior, to develop positive interventions, and to teach appropriate and alternative behaviors
- Family involvement: Provide families with the opportunity to participate in educational programs to the extent they feel comfortable (Iovannone, Dunlap, Huber, & Kincaid, 2003)

Applied Behavior Analysis

Effective interventions for individuals with autism are based on applied behavior analysis.

The methods used most successfully for individuals with autism and other severe disabilities are based on the principles of applied behavior analysis (ABA) (Arick et al., 2003). As we discussed in Chapter 7, applied behavior analysis is not a specific intervention, but rather the application of scientific principles to the study of behavior. The application of ABA to intervention strategies focuses on clearly defining behavior within the context of the environment and then arranging the

Table 9.2 Criteria for Selecting Early Intervention Programs: Questions for Parents

1. *Does your child have the necessary prerequisite skills for this program?*

   When you choose a teaching program, ask yourself what skills your child may need to perform the response. For example, you may want your child to request in sentences, but she may not be able to repeat words. Breaking a skill down into its component parts can help you identify what other skills you may need to teach first.

2. *Is this program developmentally age-appropriate for your child?*

   Programs should loosely reflect a sequence of development that would be expected of a typical child. When identifying a skill to teach, ask yourself if another child of similar age could perform the same skill.

3. *Will this skill help to reduce problem behaviors?*

   Choose teaching programs that are likely to have a positive impact on your child's behavior. For example, teaching communicative responses such as pointing and gesturing yes and no may reduce problem behaviors that serve a communicative function.

4. *Will this skill lead to the teaching of other skills?*

   When choosing skills to teach, identify those that are likely to build on one another. For example, teaching your child to imitate sequenced gross motor actions (e.g., imitating two actions in the correct order) will probably lead you to teach your child to follow two-step verbal instructions.

5. *Is this skill likely to generalize?*

   Choose programs and target responses that your child will have ample opportunity to practice beyond the teaching sessions. For example, you are more likely to ask your child to "Shut the door," or "Turn on the light," throughout the day, as opposed to "Stomp your feet." Responses that are associated with naturally occurring positive consequences are more likely to generalize.

6. *Will your child acquire this skill within a reasonable time frame?*

   Priority should be given to teaching skills that your child is likely to acquire in a reasonable amount of time. For example, if your child does not speak, he will need to learn effective communicative responses. Your child can learn to point to desired items relatively quickly, in comparison to requesting in phrases. Skills that will be acquired in a reasonable time frame will be reinforcing for you, your child, and your teaching staff.

7. *Is this an important skill for you and your family?*

   Choose skills that will have positive implications for your child's participation in family activities. Although matching colors is an important readiness skill, teaching your child to identify family members will have a greater impact on your child's participation in the family.

8. *Is this a skill that your child can use throughout the day?*

   Choose to teach skills that are functional for your child. For example, learning to follow simple instructions, using yes and no, pointing to desired items, and completing play activities are useful for your child and can be incorporated into his or her day.

Source: From *Behavioral Intervention for Young Children with Autism: A Manual for Parents and Professionals* (p. 64), by C. Maurice, G. green and S.C. Luce (Eds.), 1996, Austin, TX:PRO-ED. Copyright 1996 by PRO-ED, Inc. Reprinted with permission.

environment and providing consequences for increasing or decreasing specific behaviors. First you determine the role or function that the student's behavior plays in his or her environment, and then you identify alternative behaviors that can serve the same function. New behaviors are taught through reinforcement-based opportunities for response. In other words, a specific skill, such as hand raising, could be taught to replace hand flapping, if teacher attention were the student's goal. The reason for the behavior is determined through a functional behavior analysis. The student would receive instruction in how and when to raise his hand. The teacher would carefully attend to the student whenever the appropriate behavior was performed—reinforcing the student's appropriate action. The occurrence of the original behavior (hand flapping) and the new, substitute behavior (hand raising) would be recorded and observed over time to determine if the reinforcement supplied by the teacher and others in the environment was resulting in increases in the desired, new behavior. Complex or multistep behaviors, such as some vocational tasks, may be taught in segments and then linked together. Other skills, such as getting dressed, are presented as a whole, with the student gradually increasing participation. Students with autism may require many instructional trials (discrete trials) and explicit training across environments. Visit our Education CourseMate website through **www.cengagebrain.com** to read more about applied behavior analysis in educational settings and to find more resources for further study.

● *The Lovaas Method*   The UCLA Young Autism Project, an intensive, three-year program for young children with autism, received much attention by parents and some professionals. This project uses interventions based on strategies developed by Ivar Lovaas over thirty years ago. The project developers present data that support significant change in children's cognition, language, and behavior (Smith & Lovaas, 1997). The project is based on the principles of applied behavior analysis; however, some professionals question the curriculum context (what skills are taught and where they are taught) and criticize the quality and validity of the program's experimental research (Gresham & MacMillan, 1997).

The Lovaas method, or discrete trial training, as this intervention is commonly called, requires intensive training of teachers or parents and begins when the child is 2 to 3 years of age. The trained interventionist provides intensive, discrete trial training with the child on a one-to-one basis in the child's home. A discrete trial is one episode in a set of repetitive instructional sessions, designed to teach a specific skill. Training is recommended for up to forty hours per week for a minimum of three years. Needless to say, this is an expensive and exhausting intervention approach, yet it is the treatment most commonly requested by parents of young children with autism. The existing empirical base of support has driven the widespread use of the program (Simpson, 2005). In fact, the Lovaas program, historically, has been one of the few specific educational approaches supported by the courts in litigation against school districts (Yell & Drasgow, 2000). Many school districts are attempting to create applied behavior analysis programs that provide substantial empirical support for learning, without requiring the expensive and limiting in-home training.

This pre-school aged child with autism is receiving home based, discrete trial training from a trained behavioral therapist. The girl's father is assisting during the session.

Environmental Interventions

Some methods of teaching students with autism focus exclusively on arranging the environment to provide support and extensive opportunities for behavioral expression. These interventions, or approaches, may be loosely defined, as they will emerge from the surroundings specific to each individual.

● *Project TEACCH*   The most prominent of the environmental intervention approaches is Project TEACCH (the Treatment and Education of Autistic and Related Communication Handicapped Children program) (Mesibov, 1994). The TEACCH program began as a statewide service delivery system in North Carolina over thirty years ago, and it has spread across the United States and Europe. The intervention emphasizes encouraging and maintaining existing behaviors and structured teaching of developmentally appropriate new skills, often using one-on-one instruction, and focusing on the individual interests and needs of the student (Dawson & Osterling, 1997). Structured instruction takes place in context to support performance within designated environments. Structured instruction refers here to a carefully organized classroom or work environment, clear directions and predictable work patterns, and the use of physical, verbal, and picture prompts to promote correct responses. Supports are gradually withdrawn as students become more independent.

A fundamental component of the TEACCH program is the close working relationship between the professionals in the program and parents and families (Scott, Clark, & Brady, 2000). The program focuses on early intervention but continues throughout adulthood, providing safe and interactive learning environments for individuals with autism. Intervention research supports the effectiveness of TEACCH programs in producing satisfaction in increasing independence, and in reducing problem behaviors among the families and children and adults with autism (Hume & Odom, 2007; Simpson, 2005), and it is considered a promising practice. To learn more about the TEACCH program, including recommended instructional strategies, visit their website.

● *Social Skills Interventions*   Although social skills training may be a component of many other types of instructional approaches, including applied behavior analysis and TEACCH, there is a current emphasis on training social skills as a distinct intervention. In addition, social skills interventions may comprise the major instructional emphasis for students with Asperger's syndrome or other autism spectrum disorders. Social skills may include initiating play activities, establishing eye contact, sharing toys, taking turns, and participating in cooperative recreational activities, such as games or reading stories. As noted in the recommendations of the National Research Panel, instruction in social skills and play skills should include peers. The emphasis of peer-focused social skills intervention involves creating an environment that simultaneously teaches and reinforces appropriate social behavior. Many of the social skills interventions for children with autism that include peers frequently incorporate peers in an instructional role. Usually the interventions include typically developing peers, but in some cases, peers with mild intellectual disabilities have participated in interventions. In the instructional role, peers receive training in modeling, prompting, and reinforcing the appropriate play behaviors and social interaction skills of children with autism (DiSalvo & Oswald, 2002: Kamps et al., 2002; Owen-DeSchryver, Carr, Cale, & Blakely-Smith, 2008). Terpstra, Higgins, and Pierce (2002) also recommend providing specific scripts for peer trainers, as well as incorporating environmental support such as well-designed play spaces, following a regular schedule and routine, and determining play preferences and motivational activities to serve as a basis for play and other social activities.

Language-Based Interventions

A few popular instructional programs for individuals with autism are designed to prompt communication and link pictures or written language with verbal communication. These programs focus on incorporating the personal needs and circumstances of the individual child into the instructional program. The goal of these interventions may be simply to achieve more effective communication, to improve social interactions—including student-initiated interactions, or verbal guidance of appropriate alternative behaviors. When communication is at stake—it is critical that we carefully look at what is most "usable" by the child and by teachers, friends, classmates, and, of course, family (Spencer, Peterson, & Gillam, 2008). There are many options for alternative or augmentative communication systems for children with ASD. Some children use sign language, some use technology (see the Assistive Technology Focus box below on VOCA), and many students in need of communication support use the Picture Exchange Communication System described below.

● *Picture Exchange Communication System*   The Picture Exchange Communication System (PECS) is a communication system based on teaching nonverbal children to use pictorial symbols to request information. Bondy and Frost (2001)

ASSISTIVE TECHNOLOGY FOCUS

Vocal Output Communication Aids

There are many useful and important applications of technology for individuals with autism. Many of these applications focus on augmenting communication through electronic communication boards that include voice output. These devices are known as vocal output communication aids (VOCAs). The VOCA may look like a regular communication board, but pushing the picture or symbol will result in a digitized or synthesized speech reading of the symbol. Some VOCAs are more complex and may not provide vocal output until an appropriate two-word combination or sentence is created. These may include a combination of words and symbols or pictures. In addition to basic communication functions, some boards also contain educational programs that can be used for more traditional instruction. For example, a program can ask the student to find the picture or symbol of a particular word, match words, or find the word or sentence that describes a specific picture. Most VOCAs are portable, and can be carried by the child or placed on a desk or mounted on a wheelchair. Recent research indicates that preschool and young children can learn to use VOCAs successfully to communicate by requesting items (Son, Sigafoos, O'Reilly, & Lancioni, 2006), and participating in play activities (Olive et al., 2007). These researchers

FIGURE 9.3

A **Voice Output Communication Aid** (VOCA) is an electrical device that assists people who are unable to use natural speech to express their needs and exchange information.

Source: http://www.axistive.com/what-is-a-voice-output -communication-aid.html.

found VOCAs and PECS to be equally useful and suggested that children and families select the communication option that fits them best.

formalized the PECS system and developed the training manual. The children gradually learn to combine the pictures to make picture sentences—eventually using language to accompany and, possibly, to replace the picture symbols. The PECS program uses a wide variety of pictures and an assortment of different picture boards on which to create phrases and sentences. Examples of PECS picture cards can be found in Figure 9.4. The picture boards are based on the concept of a traditional communication board; in this case, however, the emphasis is on student selection of the pictures and symbols used and the constant changing of these symbols to reflect immediate student needs. For students to use this technique, it must be an effective and efficient means of communication for the individual child; therefore, immediate responses by teachers, parents, and peers

FIGURE 9.4

Picture Exchange Cards (PECS) for selecting videos. The child can touch or move the cards (manual or electronic options can be developed) to complete the sentence. As the child grows up, or as his or her tastes change, new cards (PECs) can be added to or replace the old ones.

Source: Picture Exchange Communication System (PECS), http://pyramidproducts.com. Retrieved November 2003.

are necessary, particularly in the beginning of the program. Research suggests that young preschool children with ASD may find PECs easier to use than other technology-based communication aids (Beck, Stoner, Bock, & Parton, 2008). The popularity of these picture collections with young children with autism resulted in a number of other picture groups designed to be used either for expressive language by children with autism or as a means of conferring messages to children. For example, the Picture Literacy Project at the University of Kansas (2003) developed a series of noun and action-word symbols that could be learned and used either for receptive or expressive communication. There are many other sources of pictures available to teachers and parents, most at little or no cost.

● *Social Stories* Whereas the PECS system, and those like it, focus on symbols or pictures to foster language and social interaction, social stories are based primarily on verbal and written language. Gray (2003) created and defined social stories over a decade ago as a means of addressing the language and social needs of verbal children with autism spectrum disorders. In essence, a social story is a brief sequence of sentences designed to provide a self-instruction plan for the student. The social story uses four types of sentences, including descriptive sentences, perspective sentences, affirmative sentences, and directive sentences, to talk a child through specific situations, scenarios, or tasks. Each story is created by parents or teachers to reflect a specific challenge for the individual child. Sometimes, stories are designed to help a student engage in appropriate alternative behavior in problem situations; to prepare the child for a new experience, such as going to a new playground; or to help a child make decisions or remain calm. The complexity of the sentences, the length of the stories, and the vocabulary used will depend on the child. Winterman and Sapona (2002) found that the social story concept could be used by a nonverbal child with autism by utilizing picture communication symbols instead of sentences and creating picture stories.

Examples of social stories on a variety of topics are readily available to teachers and parents. Research is still continuing in the area of social stories—there is evidence of the effectiveness of social stories in teaching appropriate behavior, but more research needs to be done that conforms to the gold standard for determining evidence-based practices (Horner et al., 2005; Spencer, Simpson, & Lynch, 2008; Test, Richter, Knight, & Spooner, 2011). Figure 9.5 provides an example of a social story on the topic of line leader. To read more about social stories and to see additional samples of social stories, visit the website of the Gray Center.

Visual Supports

In addition to focusing on using language, both the PECS program and social stories teaching different skills involve the presentation of visual information—either in pictures or words. Visual supports of one type or another have provided a wealth of instructional strategies for many types of skills for individuals with ASD. Teachers often use visual schedules—pictures (photographs, drawings, icons) as reminders of the daily schedule or how to set the table, or what needs to be done to clean the reading corner (Meadan, Ostrosky, Triplett, Michna, & Fettig, 2011). For those children with little language, the visual medium becomes an important tool for instruction. Because we have such access to technology today, there are so many other options for making visual supports active and interactive. Visual activity schedules can be placed on a computer and incorporate PowerPoint, audio, video clips, and even interactive components (Stromer, Kimball, Kinney, & Taylor, 2006). Students can actually watch someone (or themselves) use the washing machine while they are washing their clothes, instead of just looking at picture prompts. Video-modeling is rapidly becoming a widespread instructional

Who Is Line Leader?

My name is Andrew. I am in the first grade. Sometimes, the children in my class form (one, two, three, etc.) lines.

The children in my class *stand* in a line when we are getting ready to go to another part of the school. Children do move a little when they stand in a line. Children may move to scratch, or fix their shirt, or their shoe. Sometimes, because they are standing close together, children may touch one another. Many times, it is an accident when children touch one another in line. They were not planning to touch another child.

The children in my class *walk* in a line to move safely in the halls. Walking in a line keeps children in order, too. If another group of students are walking in the hall going the opposite direction, the two groups can pass one another easily. That's why teachers have asked children to walk in lines for many, many years. It is a safe and organized way to move many children.

Usually, children stand and walk in lines for a short period of time. Once the children reach their destination, their teacher often doesn't need them to stay in the line anymore.

Sometimes, I may be the Line Leader. This means that the other children in my class will walk behind me.

Sometimes, I may be second, or third, or fourth, or another position.

Many children in my class like to be the Line Leader. My teacher knows who should be first in line. Teachers know about being fair, and try to make sure each child is Line Leader now and then.

It's important to follow directions about who is Line Leader. My turn to be Line Leader again gets closer every time the children in my class walk in a line!

Who Is Line Leader?

FIGURE 9.5

Sample social story by Carol Gray

Source: Carol Gray (2003). The Gray Center Website. Retrieved 7/5/11 from http://www.thegraycenter.org/social-stories/what-are-social-stories.

Teaching Strategies & Accommodations

Video-Modeling—A New Approach to Teaching New Behaviors

Teaching new behaviors to individuals with ASD—how to interact on the playground, how to take a community bus, or how to make a peanut-butter sandwich—often requires breaking down the task and teaching the behaviors step by step on site. Over the past few years, there has been a flurry of research activity on the use of video-modeling to teach these often complex and typically very important life skills. The success of these procedures with individuals with ASD is why there is now so much research in this area.

What is video-modeling?

Video-modeling is recording a behavior or social interaction or activity on video and using the video as an instructional tool.

What types of video-modeling are there?

1. Video prompting: If a student is learning a new and complex task, they can be shown one step of the task, complete it, look at another step, complete it, etc.

2. Video-modeling: A video is created of a peer doing the target activity or behavior. The video is shown to the student, who then is asked to perform the behavior. Students can watch the video repeatedly for practice.

3. Video self-modeling: The student who is learning the behavior models the target behavior and the watches the video and is asked to perform the behavior (Oglivie, 2011). If, for example, you were teaching the student to walk from the school to the bus along the walkway without repeatedly running into the driveway, you would verbally prompt the child or redirect as necessary until you reached the bus, while you or someone else is shooting the video. You would edit out the

Videos can be important tools to help teach new behaviors to children with autism.

redirection, the verbal prompts, and, of course, the trips to the driveway. Your end result would look like a smooth and correct walk to the bus that you could then use as your teaching model.

4. Does research support video-modeling? Yes—research indicates that video-modeling is an effective instructional tool for many individuals with ASD, including individuals with and without intellectual disabilities, children and adolescents (Bellini & Akullian, 2007), and students learning a variety of skills, including social skills (Bellini, Akullian, & Hopf, 2007; Oglivie, 2011); life skills (Keen, Brannigan, & Cuskelly, 2007); and play skills (Buggey, Hoomes, Sherberger, & Williams, 2011; Nikopoulos & Keenan, 2007). Research also suggests that while individual preferences will vary, students as a group didn't show a preference for videos in which the student or a peer served as the model (Mechling & Moser, 2011).

medium for students with ASD. Read Teaching Strategies and Accommodations, "Video-Modeling—A New Approach to Teaching New Behaviors," to learn more about this intervention.

Biochemical Interventions

Over the years, a number of interventions have focused on biochemistry, including diet-based interventions, vitamin-based therapies, and others. Most of these interventions lack supporting empirical data. The most recent of the proposed biochemical interventions involves the use of the gastrointestinal hormone secretin to reduce the symptoms of autism. In spite of personal testimony to the contrary, current research indicates that the administration of secretin produces no meaningful changes in the language or behavior of individuals with autism (Chez et al., 2000).

Pharmacological interventions, on the other hand, are widely considered to be an important part of treatment protocols for many individuals with autism. Although not a primary educational intervention, drug treatment is often used to address some of the concomitant symptoms of autism, such as hyperactivity, depression, seizure disorders, agitation, aggression, and self-stimulatory behaviors (Heflin & Alsomo, 2007).

> Pharmacological interventions are often a component of treatment protocols for individuals with autism.

In addition to the interventions we have described above, many other treatments have been proposed. These treatments run the gamut from new, promising approaches to historical, unsubstantiated interventions and everything in between. Some of these interventions focus on the suspected psychopathology of autism, and address parental acceptance of children's behaviors and increasing the child's comfort as he or she attempts to communicate (Heflin & Simpson, 1998). Although these interventions may show up in any given community, many do not have empirical support. Some of the interventions appear to be logical and helpful; others may appear idiosyncratic and quite far-fetched. Yet because parents are often desperate for answers, they may be drawn to unproven and often expensive treatments. The support of good, empirical research is the criterion that must be used by parents and teachers to select an appropriate educational intervention for individuals with autism.

Transition to Adulthood

Adults with autism have the same opportunities for independent performance at work and in residential settings as individuals with other disabilities. Because of the wide range of abilities of children identified with ASD, many individuals will attend high school, graduate, and go on to college or employment. Others may perform various types of work through competitive employment or supported work programs.

> Adults with autism have the same range of opportunities for independence in work and residential settings as individuals with other disabilities.

Of course, the particular social and behavioral characteristics of autism may present great challenges preparing for postschool environments, even for individuals without intellectual disabilities. In spite of the abilities of many students with ASD, almost half (43.57 percent) of adolescents with ASD had not graduated after eight years in high school (Shifter, 2011). Skills such as language use and appropriate social interaction may be targets for instruction throughout the lifetime of an individual. Instructional approaches such as applied behavior analysis and TEACCH are used through adulthood. Many adults with autism live with the family; others live semi-independently in group homes or apartments; and some adults live in more restrictive settings. Often, individuals with autism who live independently benefit from support services, even if it is only an occasional visit from a relative or care provider. Adults with ASD may seek out support groups. Jantz (2011) reports that adults with ASD may feel lonely, and seek out support groups as a source of social interaction, as well as a place to get information, advice, and structure. In the First Person box, a mother describes Jessy, her adult daughter with autism.

Adolescents and young adults with autism spectrum disorders, particularly those with Asperger's syndrome, like many other students with or without disabilities, are entering postsecondary education. Some students with ASD are entering alternative postsecondary programs, such as those described in Chapter 6, while others are simply going to college. Because many of the students with ASD who enter college will require support, a number of universities have established programs just for that purpose. For example, Wenzel and Rowley (2010) describe a year-long course they provide for college students with ASD (although others

FIRST PERSON

Jessy Park

Anecdotes must temper our yen for the miraculous, keep the account honest. Without them, Jessy's slow progress takes on too much of the aura of the success story everybody wants to hear. Suppose I say what is entirely true: that she has worked, rapidly and efficiently, for sixteen years in the Williams College mailroom; that she is hardly ever absent and never late; that she pays taxes; that she keeps her bank account accurately to the penny; that she has saved more money than any of her siblings; that increasingly she keeps house for her aging parents; that I haven't touched a vacuum cleaner in years; that she does the laundry, the ironing, some of the cooking, all of the baking; that she is a contributing member of her community and of her family. Who wouldn't hear, behind those words, others: miracle, recovery, cure? And I have as yet hardly mentioned the brilliant acrylics that seem to be, but are not, the crown of her achievements.

Indeed, they are remarkable. Black-and-white can convey the ordered exactitude of the outlines, the clarity and repetition of design elements, recalling the baby to whom shapes and colors were more significant than faces. There is no vagueness in her paintings, no dashing brush strokes, no atmospheric washes. It is hard-edge stuff, and always has been. Even in nursery school she never overlapped her colors, never scrubbed them together into lovely, messy mud. Her paintings then were as characteristic as these today, repetitive arrangements of shapes and patterns, always controlled, always in balance. What black-and-white can't convey is the incandescence of her colors, and even the finest reproduction could not convey their variety.

Jessy paints; paintings bring checks; the numbers in her bank account rise, as once the numbers rose (and occasionally fell) when she kept track of her behaviors on a golf counter. The checks are a significant motivator for her, as the growing recognition is for us, who must answer inquiries and learn to negotiate the world of galleries and shows social complexities forever beyond Jessy's ken. But for us, and for her, what's important about this demanding, absorbing activity, valued and rewarded by society, is not what it brings to her bank account or her reputation (a concept much harder to understand than stratification), but what it brings to her life. It interests people, predisposes them in her favor, encourages them to overlook behavior that needs overlooking. Autistic people need that. Yet its real meaning for her life is more ordinary: it gives her something to do.

Claira Claiborne Park

Source: Reprinted from *The American Scholar,* Volume 67, No. 2, Spring 1998. Copyright © 1998 by the author.

could request to attend) at the University of Connecticut through the Center for Students with Disabilities. This course is in seminar format and addresses different issues each week, such as goal setting, conversational skills, time management, giving and accepting criticism, and study skills. If you are in or remember your first year of college, I'm sure you are thinking a course like this would've been helpful!

As we've said many times in this chapter, individuals with autism and autism spectrum disorders display a great range of abilities, and learning and behavioral differences. Outcomes of educational programs for adolescents and adults will also vary greatly. Interviews with individuals who are clearly high-functioning adults with autism suggest that they have very strong opinions about what factors were important in facilitating their success, and that they would like to be considered experts and be asked to share their perceptions with the professional community (Hurlbutt & Chalmers, 2002). Input from individuals with autism spectrum disorders, information from parents and teachers, and continued longitudinal research will help us navigate the many interventions and resources focused on the area of autism.

? Pause and Reflect

In this section, we looked at many types of interventions—some very structured and intensive, others less so. If a student with autism were to be included in a general education program, which of these interventions do you think could be incorporated into the general education classroom? Do you think the age of the student would affect the type of intervention that could be more easily integrated with a teacher's typical teaching strategies? ●

SUMMARY

- Autism/Autism Spectrum Disorder is a lifelong developmental disability that is best described as a collection of behavioral symptoms. Symptoms include deficits in verbal and nonverbal communication, social withdrawal, repetitive and stereotypical behaviors, resistance to change, and unusual responses to sensory experiences.

- The cause of autism is not known; however, current research suggests that the cause or causes of autism are physiological factors. At one time, autism was thought to be an emotional or psychological disorder.

- Autism greatly affects the areas of communication, cognition, and social behaviors. Individuals with autism may display unusual speech patterns, such as echolalia, or may have no oral language. About 50 percent of people diagnosed with autism also have intellectual disabilities. Most individuals with autism display stereotypic behaviors, such as rocking, twirling of objects, or hand clapping.

- Early intervention is a key factor for improving the prognosis of children with autism. Parents, therefore, play an important role in the education of their young children.

- The most effective interventions for individuals with autism are based on principles of applied behavior analysis; these programs involve the systematic instruction of discrete skills.

- Technology plays an increasingly important role in the interventions used to teach social, vocational, and independent living skills to individuals with autism spectrum disorder.

- Young adults with autism may require support systems as they enter college and enter into the world of work.

KEY TERMS

autism (page 301)

pervasive developmental disorders
(PDD) (page 303)

autism spectrum disorders (page 303)

Asperger's syndrome (page 303)

fragile-X syndrome (page 304)

joint attention (page 311)

echolalia (page 312)

reciprocal speech (page 312)

receptive language (page 312)

expressive language (page 312)

stereotypic behaviors (page 314)

USEFUL RESOURCES

- Visit the Autism Society of America at **http://www.autism-society.org.** It is a national organization for parents, professionals, and individuals with autism. Branches exist in most states.

- The National Center on Birth Defects and Developmental Disabilities has websites designed to answer children's questions about specific disabilities. These Kids Quest websites include one on autism spectrum disorder. Visit **http://www.cdc.gov/ncbddd/kids/autism.html** for a great resource for kids, including general information, reflective questions, web links, and other websites about people with autism spectrum disorders.

- Go to Families for the Early Treatment of Autism at **http://www.feat.org.** This website provides information to families and advocates about early intervention options.

- Healing Thresholds: Connecting Community and Science to Heal Autism is a website service that has lots of helpful information for parents and teachers of individuals with autism. The website includes discussions of available therapies and available facts and new research. It also connects directly to your local area and lists doctors, dentists, therapists, etc. who work with individuals with autism in your neighborhood (**http://autism.healingthresholds.com/**).

- C. Maurice (1993). *Let Me Hear Your Voice: A Family's Triumph over Autism.* New York: Fawcett Columbine. This book tells one family's story about the emotional and physical struggle for appropriate interventions for two young children with autism.

- Paul and Judy Karasik (2003). *The Ride Together: A Brother and Sister's Memoir of Autism in the Family.* New York: Washington Square Press. In this interesting and touching book, two adult siblings of a man with autism recall the family experiences from early childhood to the present. An interesting aspect of this book is that both siblings do this, but in different ways. Judy writes the text, and Paul presents lengthy comic book-format presentations of their experiences with their brother.

- Research Autism: Improving the Quality of Life. This website from the United Kingdom evaluates the research on existing interventions for individuals with autism. A rating scale, similar to that used by the WhatWorks website, presents a consumer-friendly system for reviewing research evaluations and ratings (**http://www.researchautism.net**).

- Dawn Prince-Hughes (Ed.) (2002). *Aquamarine Blue 5: Personal Stories of College Students with Autism.* Athens, OH: Swallow Press. In this book, college students and university instructors with autism present essays about their academic life, academic abilities and disabilities, and social struggles and successes.

● Visit Rage for Order: The Paintings of Jessica Park at **http://www.jessicapark. com/index.html**. This website is dedicated to the life and work of Jessy Park—a young lady with autism who is an exceptional artist. On this website, you can view Jessy's artwork in full color, learn about upcoming art exhibits of her work, and preview the text of *Exiting Nirvana,* a book written by Jessy's mother, Claira Claiborne Park.

PORTFOLIO ACTIVITIES

1. Interview several pediatricians about the process they use to diagnose a child with autism. Discuss and compare the specific criteria each uses and the medical and educational recommendations he or she gives to parents.

   CEC This activity will help students meet CEC Content Standard 2: Development and Characteristics of Learners.

2. Attend a meeting of the Autism Society of America or an autism support group in your area. Talk with its members to identify the range and sources of services available in your area. Compile a list of these local activities, services, and contacts for parents of children with autism.

   CEC This activity will help students meet CEC Content Standard 5: Learning Environments and Social Interactions.

3. Observe or participate in a teaching session identified as applied behavior analysis, discrete trail training, or Lovaas training with a teacher or therapist who works with young children with autism. Describe how you think the training program does and does not address the specific characteristics of children with autism.

   CEC This activity will help students meet CEC Content Standard 3: Individual Learning Differences.

4. Identify the services local school districts provide for preschool children with autism. Visit the classrooms or teaching sessions for each type of program and compare them. How do they differ? Summarize each program you observe and discuss which ones you would recommend to parents and why.

   CEC This activity will help students meet CEC Content Standard 4: Instructional Strategies.

5. Visit a secondary school program that includes adolescents with autism. Map out the range of skills being instructed for each student with autism in the areas of communication, social skills, work skills, and academic skills.

   CEC This activity will help students meet CEC Content Standard 5: Learning Environments and Social Interaction.

 To access Portfolio Activities for this chapter and other useful study resources including an interactive eBook, related web links, quizzes, flashcards, and videos, visit the Education CourseMate website at CengageBrain.com.

CHAPTER 10

Children with Communication Disorders

Learning Objectives

After reading this chapter, the reader will be able to:

- Understand and articulate the definitions of communication, language, and speech, and the relationships among those terms.

- Define and describe the major categories of speech disorders in school-age children.

- Define and describe language impairment in school-age children and its relationship to school learning.

- Describe an array of teaching strategies for children with communication disorders.

- Explain the roles of members of the interdisciplinary team working with the student with communication disorders.

Most of you reading this book are highly verbal individuals. You know how to change your communicative style to talk in different ways to different people in different situations. You know that talking to a toddler and talking to the school principal require distinct and different communicative styles. You can express a wide range of meanings, often in subtle ways, take your turn at speaking in all the many different situations you experience in a day, manage the flow and direction of conversations with both familiar and less familiar conversational partners, and fix breakdowns in understanding when they happen—for example, by asking for clarification. When it comes to reading and writing, you know how to read differently for different purposes—you can skim an article online versus reading a textbook—and you know what to do when you don't understand what you have read. You also know how to write for different purposes and audiences, how to adjust your style and form of writing for the occasion, and how to revise your meanings when you think they may not be clear to the reader. You are an effective communicator. For you, communicating with others, either orally or through print, is relatively easy—at least in your native language.

Yet you have probably experienced difficulty in communication—the "fear and trembling" that can happen when a professor calls on you in class to answer a question, the frustration of having your speaking turn taken away when someone interrupts you, the inability to make sense of what you are reading, or the essay returned with a poor grade because the main ideas have not been communicated well.

Those who have experienced some disruption in the development and use of oral communication can experience similar difficulties every day—difficulties also reflected in their reading, writing, and spelling. Communication problems are common to many exceptional students studied in this book, such as those with intellectual disabilities, learning disabilities, or behavioral and emotional disorders. Communication issues are at the core of autism spectrum disorders, and students with a severe hearing loss or a physical disability may have difficulty acquiring effective oral communication skills.

The groups of students we describe in this chapter are different from other exceptional students. Most of them have normal sensory and motor functioning, and normal intellectual potential. Their primary disability involves the communication process. But their problems with communication are often subtle. In the following sections, we will examine the components of communication, language, and speech, and their development, and then look at how teachers work with students who have communication disorders.

Terms and Definitions

Communication, language, and *speech* are related terms. Since they constitute the foundation for teaching and learning in school, we will examine their meaning more closely.

Communication

Communication is the exchange of ideas, information, thoughts, and feelings (McCormick, Loeb, & Schiefelbusch, 2003). It involves two or more people interactively sending and receiving messages. Communication has many purposes, and its power cannot be overestimated: "No matter how one may try, one cannot *not* communicate. Activity or inactivity, words or silence all have message value: they influence others and these others, in turn, cannot *not* respond to these communications and are thus themselves communicating" (Watlawick, Beavin, & Jackson, 1967, p. 410).

We usually think of communication occurring through speaking, listening, reading, and writing. But it's important to think of communication as more than

Interactive storybook reading provides opportunities for children to communicate about things that are interesting to them with a responsive adult.

> We communicate— exchange ideas—through verbal and nonverbal behavior.

words. Don't pets communicate to their owners when they are hungry or hurt? Don't people communicate with their clothing, their movement, and their facial expressions? Even students with disabilities who lack the ability to speak express themselves in some way, as we will see in Chapter 13. Figure 10.1 displays some of the different types of communication.

Language

> Languages are governed by rules, and the rules are different in each language.

Language is the verbal system by which human beings communicate. As a system, it is bound by rules. Linda McCormick writes that "languages are abstract systems with rules governing the sequencing of their basic units (sounds, morphemes, words, sentences) and rules governing meaning and use" (2003a, p. 2). So different languages have different rules—of sequence; or order; of meaning; and of the ways language is used. For example, in Spanish adjectives usually come after nouns. In English we say "I like hot food." In Spanish: "Me gusta comida caliente," which, translated word for word, is "I like food hot." If a student's first

FIGURE 10.1

Types of communication

Source: M. Diane Klein, Division of Special Education and Counseling, California State University, Los Angeles.

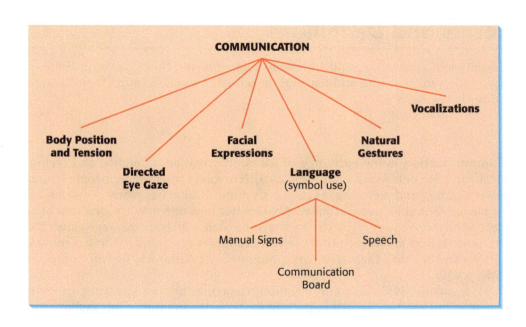

language is American Sign Language (ASL), he or she may omit articles (such as *a* and *the),* which are infrequently used in ASL, when using English. The rules of the first language of a student in your classroom will likely influence the way he or she learns English.

So an important feature of language is that it is rule-governed. This means that patterns of regularity exist in the form or structure of language, or what is often called its *grammar.* For example, if you were asked to complete the following sentence: "Here is a bik; here are two _____ ," you would most likely respond *biks,* demonstrating your knowledge of the rules of the English language (Berko, 1990). Linguists describe five interrelated components of language, each having a rule system: (1) **phonology:** phonological rules govern how we combine **phonemes,** the smallest units of sound, in permissible ways to form words; (2) **morphology:** morphological rules tell us how word meaning may be changed by adding or deleting **morphemes**—prefixes, suffixes, and other forms that specifically indicate tense and number, such as *-ed* to mark the past tense (miss*ed*) and *-s* to mark the plural form (dog*s*); (3) **syntax:** syntactic rules govern how words may be combined to form sentences; (4) **semantics:** semantic rules specify how language users create and understand the meaning of words and word combinations (McCormick, 2003a); and (5) **pragmatics:** pragmatic rules indicate how to use language appropriately within a social context in order to achieve some goal. Pragmatic goals might include finding information, fulfilling a need, or sharing a thought. All speakers of a language share the knowledge of how to use language in accord with the social rules of their speech community. Shared communication, called conversation or **discourse,** has specific rules for taking turns, responding appropriately, and managing topics. Figure 10.2 depicts the interrelationship of the primary components of language. They can be addressed separately, but are interrelated.

> The form and structure of language is its grammar.

> Language can be analyzed by its phonological, morphological, syntactic, semantic, and pragmatic components.

Speech

Speech involves the physical action of orally producing words. It is a product of complex, well-coordinated muscular activity from respiration to phonation to articulation. Just to say "pop," for example, requires 100 muscles coordinating their work at a speed of 15 speech sounds per second (Haynes, Moran, & Pindzola, 1990). Figure 10.3 shows the structures of the speech mechanism, and begins to give us an idea of how complex speech is. Every language uses a set of sounds, or phonemes, from a larger set of all possible sounds. Phonemes are not the same as letters; they are the sounds pronounced in the word. (For example, the word *beach* has five letters, but uses only three phonemes: *b, ee,* and *ch.)* Languages do not all have the same number of phonemes; English uses approximately 40 to 45.

> Speech is the oral component of language.

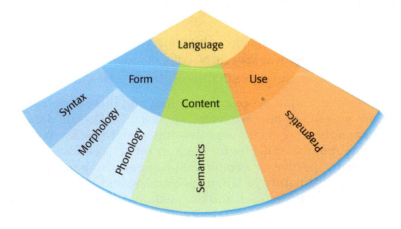

FIGURE 10.2

Components of language

Source: Owens, Robert, E., *Language Development: An Introduction* Fifth Edition, © 2001. pp. 19, 78–103. Adapted by permission of Pearson Education, Inc., Upper Saddle River, NJ.

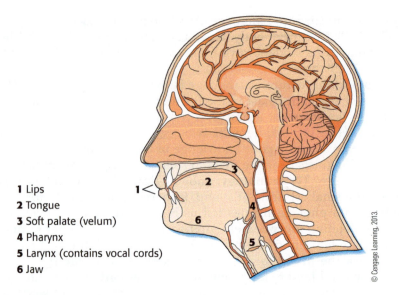

1 Lips
2 Tongue
3 Soft palate (velum)
4 Pharynx
5 Larynx (contains vocal cords)
6 Jaw

© Cengage Learning, 2013.

FIGURE 10.3

Structures of the speech
mechanism

Speech and Language Development

The next few pages cover very briefly what other books spend hundreds of pages explaining and discussing—the process of normal language development. Obviously, there is much more to learn about this subject than we can present here. If you have not learned this material through another course or your own reading, we have provided additional resources on normal language and speech development at the end of this chapter. The following brief overview provides the foundation for our understanding of communication disorders, which occur when language and speech do *not* develop as expected.

In about one thousand days, from birth to age 3, most children develop initial competence as oral communicators. How do children acquire communication skills so rapidly? What kinds of experiences must they have in order to learn to speak? How is their developing knowledge organized? How and why does this knowledge change during their school years? Theories of communication acquisition attempt to address these vital questions.

Language Acquisition

From the earliest times, humans have expressed curiosity about how language develops. According to Owens (2008),

> Psammetichus I, an Egyptian pharaoh of the seventh century B.C. with a difficult-to-pronounce name supposedly conducted a child language study to determine the "natural" language of humans. Two children were raised with sheep and heard no human speech. Needless to say, they did not begin to speak Egyptian or anything else that approximated human language. (p. 30)

The oral communication process is complex, and there is no agreement on a single theory explaining how we learn language. Most texts describe variations on five major theories of language development. These are summarized in Table 10.1. Contemporary strategies for teachers reflect a psycholinguistic or social interactional perspective, or a combination of both. Both perspectives stress the active, constructive nature of language learning and the interrelationships among biological, cognitive, social, and linguistic systems (Owens, 2008).

FIRST PERSON

"Don't pity me—I'm onto you!"

*T*ooner is the pen name of an adult with cerebral palsy who blogs at Accessibility in Canada (http://accessibilityincanada.blogspot.com/). Disabilities awareness is her passion. This is a guest blog she wrote for Love That Max, a blog that we have used excerpts from in earlier chapters of this book. It's perfect for this chapter because of Tooner's reflections on what it is like when your attempts to communicate are not understood.

The other day I was talking to two guys. One was nonverbal and one was verbal. The verbal one said "You know, he can't talk," about the nonverbal man. I replied, "Yes, I do know that but I still like to talk to him."

It seems that people don't recognize that just because someone is nonverbal, it doesn't mean they are not a person. Like Max, I have disabilities, which makes it hard for some people to understand me. My muscles won't always do what my mind tells them to.

Now that I have the help of my communication device, it makes it easier to have conversations and be clear about what I want. I use the Dynavox Dynawrite, a computer that can speak whatever I type. I also use it to communicate with my computer. It surprises me how some people still treat me as if I don't think for myself. One time, somebody asked my assistant if I could have ice cream and *I* said no because I know he was just offering it to me because I am in a wheelchair. He wasn't offering ice cream to everybody that walked by.

People don't always understand me. I'll say, "How's the weather outside?" for example and they'll say, "Your favorite color is *what*?" Sometimes, people pretend they do know what I'm saying even if they don't. It's

Tooner communicates by means of an augmentative communication device which converts what she types into speech.

funny because I always know when they don't understand.

I am an adult that does not like to be treated like a child. It bugs me when people think that I don't do anything or I'm lazy. I'm always excited to meet new people who treat me like the adult that I am. I really like it when people give me responsibilities and hold me accountable to get them done on time—just as everyone else is. Even though it may be hard to understand, I really like it when people talk to me instead of my assistant.

I'm always curious whether people have had experience with people with disabilities, but some people are more compassionate, I guess!

I would like to start a discussion on this. It's my passion to get people talking about issues like these because it makes me feel better and not as alone. How do other people tend to treat your child? If you are a person with disabilities, how do they treat you?

Source: Accessibility in Canada blog by Tooner.

Table 10.1 Models of Language Development

	Behavioral	Psycholinguistic-Syntactic	Psycholinguistic-Semantic/Cognitive	Sociolinguistic	Emergentists
Language form	Functional units (mands, tacts)	Syntactic units (nouns, verbs)	Semantic units (agents, objects)	Functional units: speech acts (requesting, commenting)	All components of language
Method of acquisition	Selective reinforcement of correct form	Language-acquisition device (LAD) contains universal phrase structure rules used to decipher the transformational rules of grammar	Universal cognitive structures help child establish nonlinguistic relationships later expressed as semantic relations	Early communication established through which child expresses intentions preverbally; language develops to express early intentions	Language acquisition is the result of a child's processing language with limited cognitive abilities
Environmental input	Reinforcement and extinction; parental modeling	Minimal	Cognitive relationships established through active involvement of child with environment	Communication interaction established first; parental modeling and feedback	Language input is the foundation for a child's cognitive processing

Source: Owens, Robert E., *Language Development: An Introduction,* 7th Edition, © 2008, p.57. Reprinted by permission of Pearson Education, Inc., Upper Saddle River, NJ.

> Theories of language acquisition attempt to explain one of the great mysteries of humanity—how we learn to talk.

Psycholinguistic theories are primarily concerned with mental processes within the child—what goes on inside the child's head. Often, psycholinguists study the child alone. *Social interactional theories* (called *sociolinguistic* in Table 10.1) assume that mental processes originate as social processes and are progressively internalized by the child through interactions with a caregiver or teacher. This conceptual framework emphasizes the interpersonal context in which the child participates—how adults support the child as they collaborate to accomplish goals. Emergentist theory suggests that grammar grows out of meaning (Owens, 2008), and emerges as a result of the brain's need to communicate through speech.

Although there is still disagreement about exactly how language is acquired, we do know when most children reach developmental milestones. There is variation in the age when individuals achieve these stages, but the process has a pattern and pace common among all languages and cultures. Table 10.2 summarizes five stages of language and communicative development from birth to age 12. For more information about language development, visit the American Speech-Language-Hearing Association (ASHA) website and the Education CourseMate website at **www.cengagebrain.com.**

The age boundaries between phases, as well as the ages for the appearance of particular behaviors, represent data that have been compiled from many children and then averaged—so in working with individual children, teachers should use this information only as a general guideline. It's also important to be cautious when applying milestones to children from cultural minority groups, or children who are learning English as a second language, because they have not typically been included in research studies.

You can see from the information in Table 10.2 how swiftly development proceeds during the first three to five years of life. For example, by approximately 12 months, the infant has become a highly social individual and has begun the transition to conventional first words. At 24 months, the child has begun to use

Table 10.2 Overview of Communicative Development: Birth to 12 Years

Age	Appearances
The examiner (1–6 months)	Responds to human voice; makes pleasure sounds (1 month)
	Produces strings of consonant-vowel or vowel-only syllables; vocally responds to speech of others (3 months)
	Smiles at person speaking to him/her (4 months)
	Responds to name; smiles and vocalizes to image in mirror (5 months)
	Prefers people games, e.g., peek-a-boo, I'm going to get you; explores face of person holding him/her (6 months)
The experimenter (7–12 months)	Recognizes some words; repeats emphasized syllables (8 months)
	"Performs" for family; imitates coughs, hisses, raspberries, etc. (10 months)
	Obeys some directives (10 months)
	Anticipates caregiver's goal and attempts to change it via persuasion/protest (11 months)
	Recognizes own name; engages in familiar routines having visual cues (e.g., bye-bye); uses one or more words (12 months)
The explorer (12–24 months)	Points to toys, persons, animals named; pushes toys; plays alone; begins some make-believe; has four- to six-word vocabulary (15 months)
	Begins to use two-word utterances (combines); refers to self by name; has about 20-word vocabulary; pretends to feed doll, etc. (18 months)
	Enjoys rhyming games; tries to "tell" experiences; understands some personal pronouns; engages in parallel play (21 months)
	Has 200- to 300-word vocabulary; names most common everyday objects; uses some prepositions (*in, on*) and pronouns (*I, me*) but not always accurately; engages in object-specific pretend play and parallel play; can role-play in limited way; orders other around; communicates feelings, desires, interests (24 months)
The exhibitor (3–5 years)	Has 900- to 1000-word vocabulary; creates three- to four-word utterances; talks about the "here and now"; talks while playing and takes turns in play; "swears" (3 years)
	Has 1500- to 1600-word vocabulary; asks many questions; uses increasingly complex sentence constructions; still relies on word order for interpretation; plays cooperatively with others; role-plays; recounts stories about recent experiences (narrative recounts); has some difficulty answering *how* and *why* (4 years)
	Has vocabulary of 2100 to 2200 words; discusses feelings; understands *before* and *after* regardless of word order; play is purposeful and constructive; shows interest in group activities (5 years)
The expert (6–12 years)	Has expressive vocabulary of 2600 words while understands 20,000 to 24,000 word meanings; defines by function; has many well-formed, complex sentences; enjoys active games and is competitive; identifies with same-sex peers in groups (6 years)
	Verbalizes ideas and problems readily; enjoys an audience; knows that others have different perspectives; has allegiance to group, but also needs adult support (8 years)
	Talks a lot; has good comprehension; discovers he or she may be the object of someone else's perspective; plans future actions; enjoys games, sports, hobbies (10 years)
	Understands about 50,000 word meanings; constructs adultlike definitions; engages in higher-order thinking and communicating (12 years)

Source: Owens, Robert E., *Language Development: An introduction,* 5th Edition, © 2001, pp.19, 78–103. Adapted by permission of Pearson Education, Inc., Upper Saddle River, NJ.

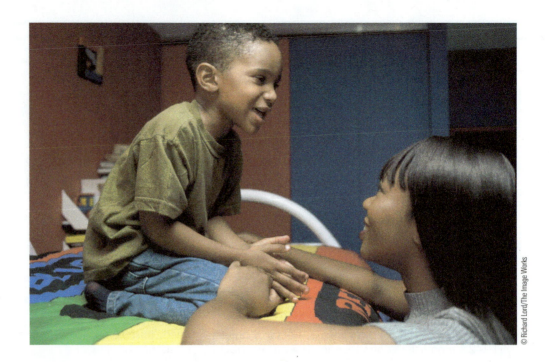

Children with language disorders may have no visible disability. Their challenges arise when they attempt to communicate.

two-word sentences, and at 48 months she is using complex utterances. Such rapid learning is possible, in part, because of the typical child's communicative environment. If you are a parent or teacher of a young child, you know that there is almost nothing more interesting in this world than observing language develop! It is estimated that by age 4, in everyday interaction, the average child has been exposed to 20 to 40 million words and has spoken 10 to 20 million words (Chapman et al., 1992). By age 5, the basic system of oral communication has been acquired. This system continues to grow in more sophisticated ways during the school years because it is influenced by two new tools the child learns for thinking and communicating: reading and writing.

Most children acquire the basic system of oral communication by age five, and it forms the foundation for reading and writing.

Some of you will work with children with disabilities and language delays who are not (yet) speaking. Table 10.3 may be helpful to you because it describes the building blocks of language as well as the sequence of expressive language development. Start from the bottom, and you will see that in order to begin to communicate, children must have the biological prerequisites; they must have access to a language model—someone around them who is talking; they must have some of the basic markers of cognitive development; they must have an intent to communicate, that is, a reason and a purpose to communicate, and the intention to do so; and they must have some social characteristics, such as the ability to take turns. Once those foundations are present, gestural communication can begin, followed by single spoken (or signed) words (Haynes, Moran, & Pindzola, 2012).

Speech Production

During the first six months of life, infants primarily produce vowel-like sounds with some glottal and back consonant-like sounds. At about 6 months of age their vocalizations begin to include more consonant-like sounds ("ba-ba-ba"). This stage is called *babbling*. These sounds tend to follow rather predictable patterns of development in all languages (Oller et al., 1976; Oller & Eilers, 1982). Social interactions with caregivers involving imitative vocal play and turn taking, along with developing cognitive capabilities such as increased memory span, play a role in the transition from babbling to speech, along with the increasing fine motor control necessary for phoneme differentiation.

Table 10.3 The Building Blocks of Language Development and Steps in the Language Acquisition Process

Source: From W. O. Haynes, M. J. Moran, & R. H. Pindzola, *Communication Disorders in Educational Settings*, p.59. Sudbury, MA: Jones and Bartlett Learning.

? Pause and Reflect

Many school-aged children have difficulties learning language—spoken or written. As the language needs of our students become more complex, teachers must know a great deal about how to develop vocabulary and concepts. How do *you* learn new vocabulary? How can you apply your own strategies to teaching your students? ●

Types and Characteristics of Communication Disorders

The IDEA definition of **communication disorder** is "a . . . disorder such as stuttering, impaired articulation, a language impairment, or a voice impairment that adversely affects a child's educational performance" (*Federal Register*, 1992). Disruptions to the communication process can affect language, speech, or hearing. Language disorders involve a delay in understanding others, participating in conversation, or using language appropriate to the listener or to the situation

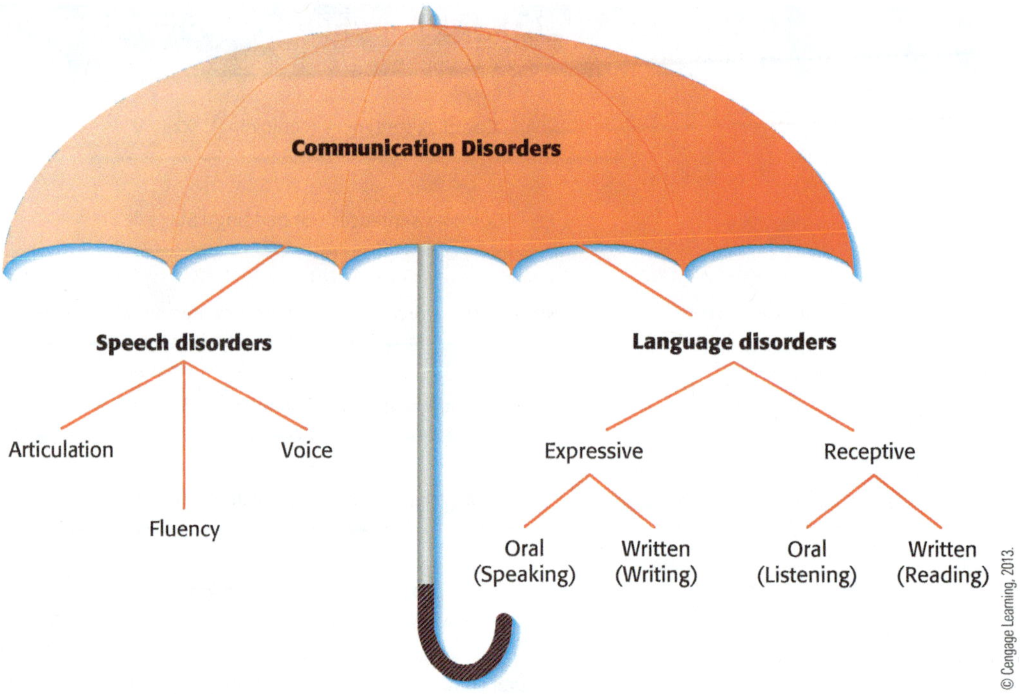

Communication Disorders

Speech disorders

Articulation

Voice

Fluency

Language disorders

Expressive

Receptive

Oral
(Speaking)

Written
(Writing)

Oral
(Listening)

Written
(Reading)

© Cengage Learning, 2013.

FIGURE 10.4

Relationship of communication, language, and speech disorders

(ASHA, 1997). Speech disorders include articulatory, fluency, and voice impairments. Figure 10.4 shows the relationship among communication disorders, language disorders, and speech disorders. Hearing loss, discussed in depth in the next chapter, also results in difficulties in acquiring and using language and speech.

Language Disorders

A language disorder is the impaired comprehension or use of spoken or written language.

Although most children acquire language through natural interactions with the people around them, some do not. Those children experience either language delay (slower development) or language disorders (Fahey, 2000a). The American Speech-Language-Hearing Association (ASHA), the national professional organization for speech-language pathologists and audiologists, defines **language disorder** as

> A language disorder is impaired comprehension and/or use of spoken, written and/or other symbol systems. The disorder may involve (1) the form of language (phonology, morphology, syntax), (2) the content of language (semantics), and/or (3) the function of language in communication (pragmatics) in any combination (American Speech-Language-Hearing Association, 1993).

A more straightforward definition from the same organization:

> When a person has trouble understanding others (**receptive language**), or sharing thoughts, ideas, and feelings completely (**expressive language**), then he or she has a language disorder. (Source: http://www.asha.org/ public/speech/disorders/)

Think about the five components of language described earlier—phonology, syntax, morphology, semantics, and pragmatics (look at Figure 10.2 again). The ASHA definition tells us that a language disorder can occur as a result of a problem with one or more of these components. Since they are interrelated, difficulties often occur in combination.

There has been considerable debate among professionals about how to classify children with language disorders (Kaderavek, 2011). Should a child receive the primary label of disability, such as learning disability, autism, or motor disabilities? Certainly, many children who qualify for special education services in those specific disability areas have significant problems with language, spoken and written. Or should professionals describe children by the specific area of language that they have difficulty with—children with syntactical difficulties, for example? These descriptions would cut across traditional disability areas, but many children do have problems with language that involve more than one specific area.

For this discussion, we refer to children whose *primary* difficulty is in learning and using language. (The language problems of children with other disabilities will be described in the chapters that focus on specific disabilities.) These children are sometimes referred to as those with **specific language impairment** (McCormick, Loeb, & Schiefelbusch, 2003). Their problems with learning and using language cannot be attributed to another disability—they have no other apparent problems. Later in their school careers, however, students with specific language impairment are much more likely than children without language impairments to have difficulties with reading and writing and, therefore, with school achievement—so they may end up with the label of *learning disability*. Table 10.4 describes some of the language problems associated with specific language impairment.

Remember, in real life children do not appear in neat little chapters as they do in this book. Their characteristics and needs are much more complex and challenging than the "categorical approach" we use here might suggest. Most current evidence supports the concept that students with language disorders follow the normal pattern of development, but more slowly and over a longer period of time.

A language disorder involves difficulty *using* spoken language—that is, expressive language—and sometimes, *understanding* other people's spoken language—receptive language. More than 50 percent of children with language disorders manifest significant problems with academic achievement over the

> Language disorders tend to involve more than one component of language.

Table 10.4 Language Difficulties Associated with Specific Language Impairment	
Language Dimension	**Difficulties**
Phonology	Failure to capitalize on regularities across words Slow development of phonological processes Unusual errors across sound categories
Morphology/syntax	Co-occurrence of more mature and less mature forms Fewer lexical categories per sentence than peers More grammatical errors than peers Slow development of grammatical morphemes Many pronoun errors
Semantics	Delayed acquisition of first words Slower rate of vocabulary acquisition Less diverse repertoire of verb types
Pragmatics	Intent not signaled through linguistic means Difficulty gaining access into conversations Less effective at negotiating disputes Less use of the naming function Difficulty tailoring the message to the listener Difficulty repairing communication breakdowns

Source: McCormick, Linda; Loeb, Diane Frome; Schiefelbusch, Richard L., *Supporting Children with Communication Difficulties in Inclusive Settings: School-Based Language Intervention*, 2nd edition, © 2003, po. 84, 242. Reprinted by permission of Pearson Education, Inc., Upper Saddle River, NJ.

A CLOSER LOOK   Recognizing Children with Language Impairment in the Classroom

The child may have some or all of the following characteristics:

- Seems to fail to understand and follow directions.
- Is unable to use language to meet daily living needs.
- Violates rules of social interaction, including politeness.
- Lacks ability to read signs or other symbols and to perform written tasks.
- Has problems using speech to communicate effectively.

- Demonstrates a lack of appropriate organization and sequence in verbal and written efforts.
- Does not remember significant information presented orally or in written form.
- May not recognize humor or indirect comments.
- Seems unable to interpret the emotions or predict the intentions of others.
- Responds inappropriately for the situation.

_____

Source: R. E. Owens (2008), *Language Disorders: A Functional Approach to Assessment and Intervention* (5th ed.), Upper Englewood Cliffs, NJ: Allyn & Bacon; adapted from N. Nelson, 1992.

course of their school careers; their language difficulties are connected to problems with reading and writing (Kaderavek, 2011).

The evidence suggests that, despite special education services, a substantial number of children will not catch up with their peers. In other words, a language disorder is usually an ongoing condition that persists into adulthood (Owens, Metz, & Haas, 2003).

● *The Link Between Language and Behavior*   If you were in a foreign country in which you did not know the language, or the alphabet, but needed food or shelter, what might you do? Some of us would use gestures, or attempt to act out our needs—we would change our behavior in order to communicate, and our actions would communicate for us. This is exactly how researchers believe children without a communication system behave. If they cannot ask for what they need, or express their preferences, or initiate interaction with others, they act in such a way to communicate. They cannot use gestures or signs that represent their needs—after all, gestures and signs are linguistic symbols too. So as the preschoolers sit down on the rug for "circle time," one boy pinches another on the leg (instead of saying, "Hi"). The little girl whose teacher is absent screams repeatedly (instead of saying, "Where's Mrs. Gonzalez?"). Sometimes, the function of the behavior is communication. Think about that the next time you see a very young child or a nonverbal student "act out."

We discussed the link between behavior and communication in Chapter 8, but it bears reiterating as we discuss students with language disorders. Communication is our way of controlling our environment. Without that means of control, students may behave inappropriately in an attempt to have an impact, and end up being considered "a behavior problem."

The link between communication and behavior has an important connection to intervention. The technique of **functional behavior analysis** has evolved as a means of designing interventions for students with communication and behavior problems based on that link. If a student behaves inappropriately, and we can determine the **communicative intent** of his or her behavior, perhaps we can substitute a more appropriate behavior—a picture card or another form of communication—for the undesirable one.

Speech Disorders

The most common reason that children are referred for help in schools is not language impairment, but speech problems—difficulty in the way words are said or letters are pronounced, rather than the message or the content of what is being said. Following are some of the speech disorders that you may encounter in classrooms and schools.

● *Articulation Disorders*   Children with speech disorders may have difficulties performing the neuromuscular movements of speech as well as problems in the underlying conceptual knowledge of the sound system and the rules for its use. Speech problems can be described by their primary characteristics: articulation, fluency, or voice. *Articulation* is the accurate and clear production of sounds within words. Educators would probably identify **articulation disorders,** which are problems in understanding and using the sound system, as the most common communication problem seen during the early elementary years. Articulation difficulties are not unusual in children having difficulties in learning to read. They may interfere with the establishment of letter-sound relationships in reading and spelling (McCormick & Loeb, 2003). It is important to realize, though, that what appears to be a disorder may just be a normal difference in a child's rate of mastering certain articulation processes, particularly when the child is under 5 years old.

Normally developing children simplify adult speech so that they may acquire it. For example, they often simplify the production of a multisyllabic word (such as *nana* for *banana*). Another common process is simplifying two consonants produced together (such as *pin* for *spin*). Other pronunciation errors include addition, omission, substitution, and distortion of phonemes. These processes are developmentally natural and are eventually discarded as the child becomes more skilled with the phonological system of the language.

Whether a child has an articulation disorder is determined by two factors: whether she is making articulation errors far longer than normal, and whether the errors themselves are unusual; that is, they are not seen in normally developing children at any age. If a child's speech characteristics are embarrassing her or lead to teasing from classmates, or if you are uncertain about whether a child has an articulation disorder, consulting with your school speech-language pathologist (SLP) will help you come to a decision about whether to take action.

● *Fluency Disorders*   **Fluency disorder** is a broad term that describes interruptions in the flow of speaking (ASHA, 1993a). The most familiar and the most prevalent fluency disorder is **stuttering.** The primary symptoms of stuttering are excessive sound, syllable, and word repetitions, and sound prolongations and pauses. A child who stutters may also display a visible or audible struggle when talking.

In the past, it was believed that stuttering was a learned behavior: Children were conditioned to stutter because of stress in their environment. Today that explanation has been largely abandoned, for two reasons. First, there is substantial evidence of genetic transmission (Guitar, 2006) and second, there is little empirical evidence to support environmental explanations of stuttering (Haynes, Moran, & Pindzola, 2012). Some children go on to develop more severe forms of stuttering and clearly need treatment, whereas the stuttering of others does not progress in severity and resolves with or without treatment. The problem is that we don't know which stutterers will recover on their own and which ones will not. Since stuttering treatment has a good success rate (Haynes, Moran, & Pindzola, 2012), it is a good idea to always refer a student who stutters to a speech-language pathologist for evaluation and possible treatment.

Because the onset of stuttering most typically occurs in the preschool to early elementary years, teachers need to know that referral to a speech-language

> The most common type of speech disorder is an articulation disorder.

 TeachSource VIDEO CASE

Can We Help Nonverbal Students Have a Voice?

Visit Chapter 10 on the CourseMate website and watch the video case entitled "Assistive Technology in the Inclusive Classroom: Best Practices." You will meet Jamie, a kindergartener with cerebral palsy who uses assistive technologies to help her learn the core curriculum. You'll see Jamie in action using a speech output device that gives her a voice, and hear her teacher and the inclusion facilitator share their insights about how assistive technologies enhance her learning. How might assistive technology help Jamie make friends with her classmates?

> Fluency disorders are interruptions in the flow of speaking, such as stuttering.

pathologist is essential for appropriate diagnosis and the development of an intervention plan. Two organizations provide support and resources for people who stutter, their families, and teachers. They are the Stuttering Foundation of America at **www.stutteringhelp.org** and the National Stuttering Association at **www.nsastutter.org.**

A vignette from Haynes, Moran, & Pindzola (2012) illustrates the avoidance behaviors that people who stutter sometimes use.

> Mario is moving through the school's cafeteria line. One of the day's selections is his favorite, spicy chicken tortilla soup. He wants to ask for some but has a feeling he will block on the word soup. He says to the cafeteria worker, "I'd like some chicken, urn, so to speak, uh, some chicken s-s-s-s—." The cafeteria worker hastily interrupts and says, "You want what?" Mario responds saying "A cup of—you know—that stuff with chicken, onions, celery . . ." "You mean chicken salad?" snaps the cafeteria worker while trying to hand it to Mario and continuing, "You have to keep the line moving." Mario, in frustration, ekes out, "Well, just give me some fingers!" Mario continues down the line thinking to himself how sick he is of eating chicken fingers! In this scenario Mario is using a variety of avoidance tactics to

Teaching Strategies & Accommodations

Help for the Child Who Stutters

Teachers should:

- Refer the child suspected of stuttering to the speech-language pathologist.
- Help all members of the class learn to take turns talking and listening. All children—especially those who stutter—find it much easier to talk when there are few interruptions and they have the listener's attention.
- Expect the same quality and quantity of work from the student who stutters as the one who doesn't.
- Speak with the student in an unhurried way, pausing frequently.
- Convey that you are listening to the content of the message, not how it was said.
- Have a one-on-one conversation with the student who stutters about needed accommodations in the classroom. Respect the student's needs but do not be enabling.
- Create relaxed communication environments for the child who stutters.
- Reduce the pressure to communicate.
- Slow down their rate of speech.

- Always keep in mind that each child is different and your caring, positive attitude will make a big difference.

Teachers should *not:*

- Assume that a child's stuttering will go away.
- Directly address the behaviors that the child uses to attempt to hide his or her stuttering.
- Make stuttering something to be ashamed of.
- Talk about stuttering just like any other matter.
- Interrupt or finish the child's sentences or talk for him or her.
- Assume a child is stuttering to gain attention.
- React with alarm to speech blocks or repetitions.
- Assume that a child who stutters has additional speech, language, or learning problems.

Sources: D. F. Williams (1999). The child who stutters: Guidelines for the educator. *Young Exceptional Children, 2* (3), 10–14; R. E. Cook, M. D. Klein, & A. Tessier (2008). *Adapting Early Childhood Curricula for Children in Inclusive Settings* (7th ed.). Upper Saddle River, New Jersey, Pearson Prentice Hall; and Stuttering Foundation of America, http://www.stutteringhelp.org (updated 7/1/11).

postpone . . . and/or start . . . saying the feared word soup. By describing the ingredients, Mario is using the technique of *circumlocution* to talk around the feared word. Finally, in disgust, he gives up and substitutes an easier word, ordering fingers. (p. 228)

● *Voice Disorders*   **Voice disorders** may result from difficulties in breathing, abnormalities in the structure or function of the larynx, and certain dysfunctions in the oral and nasal cavities. These disorders can affect the pitch, loudness, and quality of a voice, all of which can have important social and emotional ramifications for a child. Whenever you become concerned that a child's voice is very unusual or abnormal, it's important to consult with the school nurse to rule out the possibility of a medical problem, then with the speech-language pathologist for suggestions about treatment. A common cause of voice disorders in school-age children is nodules on the vocal folds caused by chronic vocal abuse (Derkay & Wold, 2010). Teachers should monitor symptoms such as breathiness, harshness, or hoarseness of the voice and discuss them with the school nurse or speech-language pathologist (SLP).

> Voice disorders can affect the pitch, loudness, or quality of a voice.

Dialects and Language Differences

Not all speech differences are disorders. Other kinds of pronunciation differences may be dialect-related. A **dialect** is "a variation of a symbol system used by a group of individuals that reflects and is determined by shared regional, social, or cultural/ethnic factors. A regional, social, or cultural/ethnic variation of a symbol system should *not* be considered a disorder of speech or language" (ASHA, 1993a, p. 41). For example, one of the more common dialects in the United States is African American English (AAE). AAE includes not only the spoken word, but also nonverbal factors such as body language, use of personal space, body movement, eye contact, narrative sequence, and modes of discourse (Terrell & Jackson, 2002). A dialect is *not* a communication disorder, but teachers need to be aware of how dialects are used in their students' communities to prevent misidentifying a language difference as a disorder. Teachers also need to be aware of dialects in order to recognize when a speech or language problem coexists with a dialect. Children's use of English will reflect the characteristics of their cultural and ethnic communities. Table 10.5 below describes some of those differences in the use of English. We believe, along with many in the scholarly community (for example, Craig & Washington, 2006), that schools must build understanding in their students about the relationships between the home dialect and Standard American English in a respectful context. Ideally, our students will become fluent "code-switchers" who are able to move back and forth between the dialect of their native community and Standard American English.

> A dialect is a regional, social, or cultural variation of a symbol system; it is not a speech disorder.

❓ Pause and Reflect

As you might have discerned from your reading in this chapter up to this point, communication is a tremendously complex human process, and communication disorders are varied and multifaceted. This is also one of the most jargon-laden topics we cover in this book, and no doubt you are struggling to comprehend some of the terminology if it is new to you. So let's make it more personal. Do you think you know someone with a communication disorder, or have you experienced one yourself? How do you think it feels to be unsure about such a basic human function as speech or language? ●

Table 10.5 Contrasting Cultural Conventions in the Use of English

	African American English	Asian Speakers of English	Standard American English	Hispanic English
Morphological and Syntactical Components				
Plural *s* marker	Nonobligatory use of marker *s* with numerical quantifier. *I see two dog playing. I need ten dollar. Look at the dogs.*	Omission of plural marker *s* or over-regulation. *I see two dog. I need ten dollar. I have two sheeps.*	Obligatory use of marker *s* with a few exceptions. *I see two dogs. I need ten dollars. I have two sheep.*	Nonobligatory use of marker *s*. *I see two dog playing. I have two sheep.*
Past tense	Nonobligatory use of *ed* marker. *Yesterday, I talk to her.*	Omission of *ed* marker or over-regulation. *I talk to her yesterday. I sawed her yesterday.*	Obligatory use of *ed* marker. *I talked to her yesterday.*	Nonobligatory use of marker *ed*. *I talk to her yesterday.*
Pragmatic Components				
Rules of conversation	Interruption is tolerated. The most assertive person has the floor.	Children are expected to be passive; are discouraged from interrupting teachers; are considered impolite if they talk during dinner.	Appropriate to interrupt in certain circumstances. One person has the floor until point is made.	Official or business conversations may be preceded by lengthy introductions.
Eye contact	Indirect eye contact during listening. Direct eye contact during speaking denotes attentiveness and respect.	May not maintain eye contact with authority figure but may make eye contact with strangers. May avert direct eye contact and giggle to express embarrassment.	Indirect eye contact during speaking. Direct eye contact during listening denotes attentiveness and respect.	Avoidance of direct eye contact is sometimes a sign of respect and attentiveness. Maintaining eye contact may be considered a challenge to authority.

Source: V. Ratner & L. Harris (1994). *Understanding Language Disorders.* Eau Claire, WI: Thinking Publications. Reprinted by permission of the author

Causes of Communication Disorders

Communication disorders can be caused by a range of factors.

A number of communication disorders have known causes. In some cases, they are associated with genetic disorders such as congenital hearing impairment, fragile-X syndrome, or cleft palate and other structural malformations.

Other communication disorders appear to be caused by a range, and sometimes a mix, of biological and environmental factors (Pennington & Bishop, 2009; Windsor, Reichle, & Mahowald, 2009). For example, maternal substance abuse affects fetal brain development and can result in delayed speech and language development. Severe traumatic brain injury, sometimes associated with child abuse, is also associated with communication disorders (Vu, Babikian, & Asarnow, 2011). Recently a gene locus for severe speech and language impairment was located in families with patterns of communication disorders, confirming the suspicions of many professionals that there is a genetic cause for some (but not all) communication disorders (Kaderavek, 2011; Marcus & Fisher, 2003). Still, in many cases the causes of children's speech and language disorders are not clear or are unknown. That is the case for the majority of children described in this chapter—particularly those with specific language impairment, or language difficulties not caused by any other disability or condition.

Hearing Loss

The normal processing of spoken language is through hearing. Children with hearing loss frequently have significant communication problems, so hearing loss is a cause of communication problems. Since IDEA treats children with hearing loss separately, we address the needs of children in this category in greater detail in Chapter 10.

Prevalence

The federal government uses the label "speech or language impairments" to describe the students we are discussing in this chapter. The *Twenty-Ninth Annual Report to Congress on the Implementation of the Individuals with Disabilities Education Act* (2010) documented that fully 46.4 percent of preschoolers (aged 3 to 5) receiving special education services were classified with speech-language impairments. By the time these children reach age 6, many are re-classified with other disability labels, but still 18.9 percent of children ages 6 through 21 receiving special education services were served in this category during 2005, making this the second largest group of students in special education programs. Only the category of specific learning disabilities is larger.

Recognizing Risk for Language Disorders

Teachers are often the first professionals to encounter children whose patterns of language development place them at risk for subsequent academic and social failure. Because you, as a future teacher, will have this unique "gatekeeping" role, it is important to know what patterns may indicate risk at different points in a child's school career. In the next sections, we discuss significant stages in language development and identifiable risk indicators.

● *Preschool Years*   Under IDEA, many states now provide programs for infants and toddlers who are at risk developmentally. If you are an early childhood education teacher, you will encounter very young children who appear to have significant delays in the development of language and communication. Some of these children may be late talkers (by definition, "late talker" refers to delayed onset of speech). Late talkers usually improve in vocabulary between age 2 and 3 and have normal language skills by age 5 or 6, but they may be more likely to have reading and spelling weaknesses at later ages (Rescorla, 2009). Others may have a **language delay**—delayed development in all areas of language. The child with language delay may have greater difficulties understanding what is being said, describing events, having conversations, and articulating sounds, and may be less likely to use meaningful gestures for communicating (ASHA, 2003; Owens, 2010). Discriminating between young children who are late talkers and those with language delay—which may be categorized as specific language impairment as the child gets older—is a complex process, usually requiring the expertise of a speech-language pathologist. Which category do you think the following little girl would fall into?

CASE STUDY

Darla is 2 and a half years old, and she has not yet started to use any recognizable words. She is usually bright-eyed and cheerful, but lately she has begun to become frustrated easily and have frequent tantrums. Her parents are frustrated too, since Darla does not follow their simple requests and commands ("Come here," or "Stand up," for example). Darla repeats sounds as she plays, and screams to get attention, but often her family cannot figure out what Darla wants. Her parents have come to their pediatrician for help.

It's true that there isn't enough information in this brief description for you to conclude much. But because Darla does not seem to understand what is said to her (in other words, she has poor receptive language), and is not pointing to what she wants (not using nonverbal forms of communication), it may be that she has a language delay. In any case, the safe path is for her pediatrician to refer Darla's parents for a communication evaluation.

As a teacher who may serve young children and their families, your understanding of risk for language delay is essential for effective early identification and intervention. As mentioned earlier, at a national level, 46.5 percent of preschoolers receiving special education services are categorized with a speech or language impairment, making it the most prevalent disability category for children aged 3 through 5 (U.S. Department of Education, 2010). It is a serious problem, and early childhood teachers can play a key role in obtaining help for young children.

● *Kindergarten and the Early School Years* The profile of a language disorder changes over time. As children reach school age, patterns of difficulty can emerge that often involve learning to read and write. At this point, children with language disorders are often "relabeled" as learning disabled, or even as having emotional

> Speech and language impairments are the most common reason for young children to be referred for special education services.

The happy connection between father and child— or caregiver and child—is the foundation of communication development.

or behavioral disorders (Kaderavek, 2011). Again, a teacher's awareness of who may now be at risk is vital to helping children remain in the general education setting whenever possible.

The American Speech-Language-Hearing Association describes school-age children with language disorders as follows:

> Children with communication disorders frequently do not perform at grade level. They may struggle with reading, have difficulty understanding and expressing language, misunderstand social cues, avoid attending school, show poor judgment, and have difficulty with tests.
>
> Difficulty in learning to listen, speak, read, or write can result from problems in language development. Problems can occur in the production, comprehension, and awareness of language sounds, syllables, words, sentences, and conversation. Individuals with reading and writing problems also may have trouble using language to communicate, think, and learn. (Source: http://www.asha.org/public/speech/development/schoolsFAQ.htm)

The issue of identification of language problems in kindergarten and the early school years is complicated when children enter school as English language learners. It takes an experienced teacher with knowledge of the child's home language—often in consultation with a speech-language specialist—to determine whether the child's language problem exists in both the native language and in English. Only if the difficulty exists in both languages is there reason for concern.

> School professionals must take great care before classifying a child learning English as having a communication disorder.

● *Phonological Awareness as a Risk Indicator* How does a teacher recognize risk for language and learning problems in these early school years? One important indicator is the child's ease in acquiring **phonological awareness,** or the ability to identify and manipulate phonemes, the sounds of language. This ability is critical to emerging literacy.

> Phonological awareness is the ability to recognize that words consist of sounds.

Phonological awareness is the child's explicit awareness that words consist of sounds, or phonemes (Snow, Burns, & Griffin, 1998). It is an aspect of **metalinguistic awareness**—the child's developing knowledge of his or her use of language, spoken and written. When we consciously analyze and compare the sound structure of words or the meaning of words and sentences in either oral or written language, we are using metalinguistic strategies for thinking critically about language. A strong connection exists between aspects of oral language development and the word-recognition skills necessary for learning to read (decode) and spell. In fact, in kindergarten, the best predictor of learning to read in first grade is a child's level of phonological awareness (Scarborough, 2001).

> Metalinguistic awareness is the ability to think about language.

Children who are less sensitive to the sound structure of their language may also have a less-well-developed vocabulary, because words consist of collections of phonemes. During the early school years, despite experience with reading, these same children may encounter persistent problems in learning new vocabulary words. Most likely, they will also have serious difficulties with phonics approaches that require breaking words into their phonemic parts (for example, "What sound does *dish* begin with?" or "How many sounds does *fish* have?") and blending the parts into a whole. Difficulty with phonemic segmentation and blending will also affect the ability to engage in more advanced manipulations of the phonological code, such as deleting, adding, or reversing phonemes, and in managing conventional spellings (Owens, 2008).

> Reading fluency may be jeopardized by difficulties with phonological awareness.

Research tells us that all students should have explicit instruction in phonological awareness to maximize success with word recognition in both reading and spelling (Snow, Burns, & Griffin, 1998). (For ideas, see Teaching Strategies and Accommodations, "Developing Phonological Awareness.") Some forms of

Teaching Strategies & Accommodations

Developing Phonological Awareness

- Beginning at the preschool level, teachers can integrate phonological awareness activities in meaningful ways by using children's literature that plays with the sounds in language, for example, through nursery rhymes and word games, and only then moving to judgments about sound similarities and differences (Phillips, Clancy-Menchetti, & Lonigan, 2008).
- A variety of writing experiences offers children rich opportunities to pay attention in a deliberate way to each letter in a word as they or the

teacher actually write words (Schickendanz & Casbergue, 2009).
- All children need to show the developmental evidence that they can consistently engage in these earlier phonological awareness activities before explicit instruction in phoneme segmentation and blending is introduced.
- Finally, following mastery of segmentation and blending, children should be introduced to letter-sound correspondences.

reading failure may be avoided if students are given explicit instruction in phonological awareness, and the instruction follows a developmental sequence.

? Pause and Reflect

The relationship between speaking, reading, writing, and listening is complex—most of us have strengths in one or another of those areas. Think about how life would be if one of those strengths was taken from you! What kind of accommodations would you need if you were not able to speak or communicate clearly?

Teaching Strategies and Accommodations

Every one of us who works in schools teaches communication skills. Some of us do it explicitly, as we teach reading or language arts; others model by using the vocabulary of our disciplines and good communication strategies. But the students described in this chapter need the opportunities to interact with school professionals who are prepared to focus on the development of communication skills through their knowledge of evidence-based practices. We will describe some of those practices in the following section.

Assessment

Before teaching comes assessment—the process we use to determine who qualifies for services, and what will be taught.

The speech-language pathologist identifies, assesses, and teaches students with communication disorders in collaboration with teachers.

● *Assessment for Identification of Communication Disorders* Identification of students who are at educational risk for a speech or language disorder often begins with a concerned teacher or parent. Once the teacher has voiced that concern to the speech-language pathologist (SLP), he or she provides the teacher with pre-referral criteria to guide their observation of the student in the general education classroom prior to the formal referral for a suspected speech or language disorder. For an example of a pre-referral form, see Figure 10.5.

The following behaviors may indicate that a child in your classroom has a language impairment that is in need of clinical intervention. Please check the appropriate items.

_____ Child mispronounces sounds and words.

_____ Child omits word endings, such as plural _–s_ and past-tense _–ed_.

_____ Child omits small unemphasized words, such as auxiliary verbs or prepositions.

_____ Child uses an immature vocabulary, overuses empty words, such as _one_ and _thing_, or seems to have difficulty recalling or finding the right word.

_____ Child has difficulty comprehending new words and concepts.

_____ Child's sentence structure seems immature or overreliant on forms, such as subject-verb-object. It's unoriginal, dull.

_____ Child's question and/or negative sentence style is immature.

_____ Child has difficulty with one of the following:

_____ Verb tensing	_____ Articles	_____ Auxiliary verbs
_____ Pronouns	_____ Irregular verbs	_____ Prepositions
_____ Word order	_____ Irregular plurals	_____ Conjunctions

_____ Child has difficulty relating sequential events.

_____ Child has difficulty following directions.

_____ Child's questions are often inaccurate or vague.

_____ Child's questions are often poorly formed.

_____ Child has difficulty answering questions.

_____ Child's comments are often off-topic or inappropriate for the conversation.

_____ There are long pauses between a remark and the child's reply or between successive remarks by the child. It's as if the child is searching for a response or is confused.

_____ Child appears to be attending to communication but remembers little of what is said.

_____ Child has difficulty using language socially for the following purposes:

_____ Request needs	_____ Pretend/imagine	_____ Protest
_____ Greet	_____ Request information	_____ Gain attention
_____ Respond/reply	_____ Share ideas, feelings	_____ Clarify
_____ Relate events	_____ Entertain	_____ Reason

_____ Child has difficulty interpreting the following:

| _____ Figurative language | _____ Humor | _____ Gestures |
| _____ Emotions | _____ Body language | |

_____ Child does not alter production for different audiences and locations.

_____ Child does not seem to consider the effect of language on the listener.

_____ Child often has verbal misunderstandings with others.

_____ Child has difficulty with reading and writing.

_____ Child's language skills seem to be much lower than other areas, such as mechanical, artistic, or social skills.

FIGURE 10.5

Sample teacher referral form for children with possible language impairment

Source: McCormick, Linda; Loeb, Diane Frome; Schiefelbusch, Richard L., _Supporting Children with Communication Difficulties in Inclusive Settings: School-Based Language Intervention,_ 2nd edition, © 2003, po. 84, 242. Reprinted by permission of Pearson Education, Inc., Upper Saddle River, NJ.

In most educational settings, the speech-language pathologist has primary responsibility for the identification, assessment, and treatment of students with communication disorders. When classroom teachers and speech-language pathologists work collaboratively, they are more likely to serve the best interests of children with speech and language problems. (For more information about a career in speech-language pathology, see A Closer Look, "Collaboration: Who Is the Speech-Language Pathologist?")

A CLOSER LOOK
Collaboration: Who Is the Speech-Language Pathologist?

Speech-language pathologists in the schools are members of the educational team. Their traditional role has been to be the "expert" specialist who serves students in special education with speech, language, or hearing problems. This service has typically been provided outside of the classroom in a pullout model of service delivery. Today, the speech-language pathologist's role is changing from one of outside expert to a true educational partner with both general and special education teachers. Because you are likely to work with these professionals, it's helpful to know about their background and training.

Speech-language pathologist is a professional title. Individuals holding this title must meet a number of academic and clinical requirements established by the American Speech-Language-Hearing Association (ASHA). This national organization is the professional, scientific, and credentialing body for more than 126,219 speech-language pathologists. Approximately 57 percent of speech-language pathologists work in schools.

The professional credential is the Certificate of Clinical Competence (CCC). To be eligible for the CCC in either speech-language pathology (CCC-SLP) or audiology (CCC-A), individuals must have a master's or doctoral degree from an academic institution with an educational program accredited by ASHA.

Source: Reprinted with permission from Information for AAC users. Available from the website of the American Speech-Language-Hearing Association: www.asha.org/public/speech/diorders/Infoaacusers.htm. All rights reserved.

Speech-language pathologists do not engage in medical or psychological diagnoses. However, they do have the professional and ethical responsibility to (1) determine what may have caused the onset and development of the problem; (2) interpret whether other causal factors, such as the language demands of the classroom, may contribute to the maintenance of a speech or language problem; and (3) clarify the problem for a student and the family and counsel them appropriately (Luterman, 2001). Identifying causes may not be possible given the many factors that can influence the changing profile of a language disorder. Moreover, knowing that an initial cause, such as a birth injury or fetal alcohol syndrome, is related to the communication problem is not always useful for planning meaningful intervention for individual students—it doesn't affect the child's treatment.

> Assessment should be an ongoing process.

Regardless of the emphasis given to causal factors in assessment, there is common agreement that assessment is not a one-time snapshot of a student at a particular point in time. It is a portrait that continuously evolves because it incorporates diagnostic information with new information obtained from the ongoing monitoring of progress. Teachers, families, and speech-language pathologists should work together to paint that ongoing portrait.

● *Assessment of Students from Language Minority Backgrounds* When a child comes from a non-English-speaking background, then the identification, assessment, and intervention for a language problem is complicated. As we described in Chapter 2, there is great concern among scholars and specialists that there is considerable misdiagnosis and overdiagnosis of such children (Artiles & Ortiz, 2002; Sullivan, 2011). In order to diminish the possibility of misidentification, a bilingual professional must conduct a careful assessment with a child from language minority background in order to determine whether a language problem exists in the child's native a language as well as in English. Only when the

> To be considered a delay or a disorder, a language problem must occur in the home language and the school language.

problem crosses both languages is it considered a language delay or disorder; otherwise, the child may simply be a nonfluent user of English. Professionals must take great care not to identify such children with a disability label. There is considerable evidence that this occurs with some frequency (Harry & Klingner, 2006; Ortiz & Yates, 2002).

Research makes the strongest possible case that a teacher must have good working knowledge of the language and communication system and its many normal developmental and cultural variations in order to know who should be referred (Adger, Snow, & Christian, 2002). A delicate balance exists between failing to refer a child who needs assessment and referring a child who may be wrongly classified as disabled. Before referring a student for special education services, a system of prevention and early intervention should be implemented (Garcia & Ortiz, 2006).

Caesar & Kohler (2007) surveyed speech-language pathologists about the kinds of assessments they use to determine whether children from non-English-speaking backgrounds had speech-language impairments. Most reported that they used the results of formal, standardized tests in English to make those determinations. The authors noted the history of bias in standardized assessment in English with non-English speakers, and urged that the field consider alternative assessments conducted in naturalistic settings to make decisions.

> Alternative assessment models include (a) descriptive approaches, including language sampling, interviewing, direct observations, and rating scales; (b) dynamic approaches, which incorporate an instructional component into the assessment process; and (c) curriculum-based language approaches, which are designed to assess language performance using both the context and content of the curriculum. (p. 191)

Caesar and Kohler review the requirements of IDEA for assessment of students from culturally and linguistically diverse backgrounds. According to IDEA, assessment must be provided in the child's home language whenever possible; not racially or culturally discriminatory; focused on assessing for presence of a disability, not English language skills; validated for the purposes for which it is used, and administered by trained professionals.

> IDEA further clarifies the process for determining eligibility and placement by stating that information regarding the child's performance should be gleaned from a "variety of sources, including parent input, teacher recommendations, social or cultural background and adaptive behavior" (Sec. 300.535). (Caesar & Kohler, 2007, p. 192)

As we have said throughout this book, the decision about whether a student is eligible for special education—and therefore acquires a disability label—is a critical one for a child's future. As part of the team of professionals making such a decision, as you may someday be, you must advocate for the use of sound assessment practices for children from culturally and linguistically diverse backgrounds.

● *Approaches to Assessment* The specific approaches used in traditional speech and language assessment may be determined by special education policies at state or local levels. However, speech-language pathologists generally use a combination of approaches, or tools, for information gathering, which can be classified as standardized (norm-referenced) or nonstandardized (descriptive) (Owens, 2010). Some of these assessment tools are very useful for teachers as well. Typically, a speech-language pathologist uses some or all of the following assessment tools (ASHA, 2004):

- *Parent/staff/student interviews.* Parents, teachers, and the student can provide rich information on the student's functioning across a variety of settings. Parents can help, particularly when the child is very young or has severe disabilities; teachers can provide information on classroom functioning and peer interactions, and sometimes the student can describe specific problems that he or she faces.

- *Student history.* A review of records, interviews, and observation help professionals to understand background information so they can draw as complete a picture as possible of the student's current status and needs.

- *Checklists and developmental scales.* These tools can help the teacher or speech-language pathologist describe specific types of communication behavior.

- *Curriculum-based assessment.* Using the student's performance in the curriculum (especially speaking, writing, and reading tasks) can assist the teacher and speech-language pathologist in determining the student's classroom communication performance and planning language interventions.

- *Dynamic assessment.* These procedures assess what the student is capable of doing with assistance and may help plan useful interventions (Austin, 2010; Peña & Bedore, 2009).

- *Portfolio assessment.* Defined as a collection of products, such as student work samples, language samples, dictations, writing samples, blog and journal entries, video/audio recordings, and transcriptions.

- *Observation/anecdotal records.* Observation and recording of communication behaviors by teacher, families, and the speech-language pathologist can be used to determine the *present level of educational performance* for the Individualized Education Program (IEP).

- *Standardized assessment information.* Standardized test results can be useful when a student's performance must be compared to that of his or her peers. ASHA says, "Although all areas of speech, language, and communication are interrelated, broad spectrum, norm-referenced tests may be used to measure such skills of language comprehension and production as syntax, semantics, morphology, phonology, pragmatics, discourse organization, and following directions" (ASHA, 2000, p. III-263).

Remember that standardized tests do not typically generate information that can be used to plan for the student in the classroom. Teachers and speech-language specialists must turn to other types of assessment to generate goals for teaching and learning. They have a professional obligation to be informed test consumers, though—that is, knowledgeable about the proven purposes and limitations of standardized tests.

● *Assessment for Teaching* The kind of assessments that help teachers plan instruction are the *descriptive* assessments referred to in the paragraphs above—particularly curriculum-based assessment and portfolio assessment, which build on naturally occurring events in the classroom.

Another useful assessment, one based on careful observation, is a **language sample.** Language sampling can provide a picture of the student's current level of communication in the classroom (and in other environments, if samples are collected outside the classroom). It's useful when teachers and SLPs can plan, implement, and evaluate the results of a language sample together. During the course of a day, or several days, the teacher and the SLP record 50 to 100 utterances of the target student. The utterances must be exactly what the student has said—it's easy to add the correct tense or make a singular a plural, since we tend to "hear" proper usage.

The language sample can provide the teacher and the SLP with useful information. How long is the student's average utterance? Does the student respond to questions appropriately? What is the nature of the student's vocabulary? Teachers are often surprised by the results of an objective sample, since we usually understand so much more than what the student actually says.

An interesting way to use a language sample is to take two samples—one from a target child with communication problems, and one from a typical child of the same age who communicates effectively. A comparison of the two can help the teacher see where the target child needs to go.

Ecological Assessment   **Ecological assessment** is based on the concept that the child's behavior (in this case, communication) is shaped by the environment in which she finds herself. An experience from Nancy Hunt's early classroom teaching years illustrates this point.

CASE STUDY

In my kindergarten classroom I taught a little girl named Nancy Lopez. She was hard of hearing and came from a Spanish-speaking home. She was extremely sweet and compliant, and she seemed to understand much of what went on in the English-only classroom, but she was very silent. Perplexed, I called her parents in for a conference, and her father came in to speak to me. He brought Nancy's brother with him, and the two children went out to play while the adults talked.

While Mr. Lopez and I were talking, we heard the children playing through an open window. I soon noticed that there was a lot of talking—in Spanish—going on between the brother and sister, and much of it was coming from my sweet and shy little student. Nancy was speaking in long, animated paragraphs as she and her brother laughed and played.

I was mortified. Mr. Lopez must have thought (correctly) that I was incredibly naïve. But the experience taught me an unforgettable series of lessons. Among them: It matters whom the child is speaking to; it matters where the child is communicating, and, most importantly, the willingness and ability to speak English may be totally unrelated to the child's willingness and ability to speak her native language. Nancy was operating more like an English language learner than a hard-of-hearing child; we soon placed her in the general education kindergarten where she did very well. I provided support to her general education teacher as he needed it.

In an ecological assessment, Nancy would have been assessed in the classroom, on the playground, during one-to-one interaction, and, if possible, at home. The assessor would have to be bilingual to do a complete evaluation.

Table 10.6 describes the differences between standardized assessment and ecological assessment. If you're interested in learning more about ecological assessment, see the resources at the end of this chapter. Ecological assessment represents an example of the movement away from formal standardized assessment toward more naturalistic, authentic measurement of the child's abilities. **Authentic assessments** are based on observations of children's performance

Table 10.6	Differences Between Ecological Assessment and Traditional Assessment	
	Ecological Assessment	**Traditional Assessment**
Reference	Compares child's performance to the demands and expectations of activities and tasks in the child's environments	Compares child's test performance with that of a sample of similar children who were administered the same test items
Focus	Child's ability to meet setting and task expectations and participate in activities and routines in natural settings	Language forms and structures described in the normal development research as representative of children at the child's age or stage of development
Procedures	Observes the child's behavior in daily activities and interviews with persons who know the child well	Elicits the child's responses to a set of standardized tasks thought to represent major skills/abilities in the area
Assessment context	Natural settings: Assessment team includes parents and peers	Contrived settings: Independent assessments by discipline representatives
Best use of results	To generate individualized goals and objectives and plan special instruction	To determine child's status relative to same-age peers; for diagnosis and determination of eligibility for special education services

Source: McCormick, Linda; Loeb, Diane Frome; Schiefelbusch, Richard L., *Supporting Children with Communication Difficulties in Inclusive Settings: School-Based Language Intervention,* 2nd edition, © 2003, po. 84, 242. Reprinted by permission of Pearson Education, Inc., Upper Saddle River, NJ.

in natural settings, and typically do not involve contrived tasks administered by unfamiliar people in strange settings (Hebbeler, 2009; Neisworth & Bagnato, 2005). Authentic assessments are more likely to generate functional outcomes—those which are a necessary and useful part of everyday life—that children can generalize and use.

For the speech-language specialist, the assessment process functions to determine whether a speech or language disorder exists, and, if present, its severity and variability. Eligibility for special education and service options depends on how this evaluation question is answered and whether a diagnostic category, or label, can be assigned, such as speech impairment or language disorder. Although these categories may be global and imprecise, they allow us to understand the commonalities that make up a particular disability and to design assessment and intervention approaches for students who share common symptoms.

For the teacher, the assessment should provide a focus for instruction and language use during classroom activities and routines. The great majority of children—those with disability labels as well as the hard-to-find "average" child and those identified as gifted—will benefit from a teacher focused on language assessment and language development (Adger, Snow, & Christian, 2002; Moats, 2009).

All students benefit when teachers focus on language development and expansion.

Placement and Service Options

The placement and service options for students with communication disorders are similar to those already discussed in previous chapters, with one exception: an emphasis on the pullout mode of service delivery. Students with speech impairments or language disorders are often removed from the general or special education classroom for one-to-one or small-group treatment. The majority of SLPs continue to use the pullout model to provide services to elementary-aged students (ASHA, 2008).

The thinking behind this service option for language intervention has had a practical basis. In a smaller group setting, the speech-language pathologist can

Individual interactions with students are opportunities to model and teach language.

control some of the many variables that affect a student's successful performance in the classroom. On another level, many children can be served, which gives the appearance of cost-effective services but in reality often results in caseloads exceeding 75 to 100 students per week.

The pullout model may not be "best practice" and has been criticized for several reasons (Cirrin et al., 2010; McCormick, 2003b). First, students' language learning may become increasingly isolated from the natural communication context of the classroom. Second, students tend to be stigmatized even further through their removal from the classroom and may suffer academically from missing important curricular content. Last, because speech-language pathologists were themselves isolated from the classroom and curriculum, teachers too often developed the unrealistic view that pulling students out was a way to "make them better and put them back" (Nelson, 1998). Also, when students leave the classroom, teachers lose the benefit of observing the speech-language pathologist at work, providing a model of language-building for interaction with students.

The "pullout" model used with students with communication disorders may not provide the most effective services.

In recent years, the trend has been toward integrated classroom-based services, in which language and communication instruction is provided within the context of daily activities *in the classroom.* When speech and language intervention is provided in the classroom, the general education or special education teacher can collaborate with the speech-language pathologist to provide the most effective intervention program for the child, in the natural setting in which the child will use the skills learned (see Teaching Strategies and Accommodations, "Advantages of Integrated Classroom-Based Speech and Language Intervention").

The speech-language pathologist can now provide services in a number of configurations and settings: using the collaborative consultation model to partner with the classroom teacher, in the community, in a "pullout" setting, or in a combination of those options (Giangreco, Prelock, & Turnbull, 2009).

Sometimes it's challenging for teachers and SLPs to find time to collaborate, or even talk together about implementing communication goals for their students. A recent survey of SLPs from 49 states found that the average "caseload"—the number of students the SLP is expected to provide service to—is 49. ASHA guidelines for school-based SLPs recommends a caseload no larger than 40. Sixty percent of the respondents considered their caseload "unmanageable" (Katz, Maag,

Teaching Strategies & Accommodations

Advantages of Integrated Classroom-Based Speech and Language Intervention

- The student gains and maintains access to "regular" educational opportunities and learning outcomes.

- Opportunities for team collaboration are maximized, and fragmentation (gaps, overlaps, and/or contradictions) in services is avoided.

- The input and methods of all team members are synthesized as they address a shared vision for the student's participation in social, educational, and vocational settings.

- Skills taught through integrated intervention are likely to generalize because they were learned and practiced in the integrated, natural environments where they need to be used.

- Students learn language in their natural environment, receive services that target all areas of language impairment, including reading and writing, and receive knowledge and skills from a range of expert professionals.

Sources: From L. McCormick, D. F. Loeb, & R. L. Schiefelbusch (2003), *Supporting Children with Communication Difficulties in Inclusive Settings: School-Based Language Intervention,* Boston: Allyn and Bacon. Copyright © 2003 by Pearson Education. Reprinted by permission of the publisher; and L. A. Katz, A. Maag, K.A. Fallon, K. Blenkarn, and M. K. Smith (2010). What makes a caseload (un)manageable? School-based speech-language pathologists speak. *Language, Speech, and Hearing Services in the Schools,* 41, 139–151.

Blenkorn, Fallon, & Smith, 2010). Interestingly, the authors of this study found that among SLPs with the largest caseloads, engaging in high levels of collaboration increased the likelihood of feeling that their caseload was not manageable.

> Level of collaboration was computed using responses from four survey questions that asked participants to indicate the frequency with which they (a) engaged in team teaching with a general education teacher in a general education classroom, (b) engaged in team teaching with a special educator in a resource or special education classroom, (c) provided services to students on their caseload in the general education classroom, and (d) provided services to mixed groups (i.e., students both on and not on their caseloads). (p. 145)

So the very practices that we advocate seem to lead to a sense of "umanageability" among the SLPs! Clearly something has to shift for these valued and frequently overworked school professionals.

Although integrated, in-classroom intervention may be desirable, in many school districts across the country, students are still being "pulled out" of the classroom for speech and language services (Katz et al., 2010). There are many obstacles to changes in practice, and support for this change has come slowly. Professionals in speech-language pathology are currently working to revamp their roles in inclusive school settings, with many suggesting that they become part of an in-classroom intervention team with shared responsibility for student success.

Cirrin and his colleagues (2010) reviewed the literature, looking for a research-based answer to the question of which service-delivery model (pullout, classroom, consultation) produces better learning outcomes for children, but the number of studies that addressed that question was very small, and no robust conclusions were warranted. In-classroom services had a slight advantage for improving vocabulary, but even these results should be interpreted with caution, given the small number of studies. The authors conclude that "for the time being, IEP teams must rely more on reason than research in making service delivery decisions for individual students" (p. 251). Teachers and speech-language pathologists must advocate for the practices they feel are most productive for their students and for themselves.

Strategies for Working with Students with Communication Learning Needs

Across the United States, but particularly in urban school districts, there is an increasingly large population of students who are English language learners. Because of our changing population, every teacher should focus on English language acquisition with his or her students. A focus on language potentially benefits *all* students, from the fifth-grader identified with a language disorder to the newly immigrated seventh-grader from Central America, to the academically gifted child of any age. Integrating the teaching of both social and academic language—through listening, speaking, writing, and reading—into daily routines and curriculum may strengthen school learning for every child. Knowledge of language and language development strategies is crucial for all teachers in today's schools so we can best develop our students' spoken and written language, and as the foundation for literacy instruction (Moats, 2009).

● *Integrating Language and Literacy Learning*   Focusing on language development in your classroom should lead to improvements in your students' literacy skills, since the two are so closely connected. Several principles of language and literacy learning guide the teacher's focus on classroom language learning:

1. All children naturally learn language through social interaction with adults and peers. Every time you converse with a student you are modeling language and communication skills.

2. Children learn best when they are guided by a "big picture" or theme and when they understand the reasons for learning.

3. Real learning is functional; it is also "messy" because active choice and risk-taking are required.

4. Real learning is challenging and involves cooperating with others.

5. All children are capable of learning; the guiding premise is that the learner's ability to be successful is always the focus of assessment and instruction.

For students with language disorders, these principles mean that the goal for instruction remains one of *enabling communicative competence.* Guided by these principles, the focus of instruction is twofold: to support the student's abilities through the teaching of active "learning-how-to-learn" strategies and to help the student develop more effective communication.

Supporting Classroom Discourse   The normal language routines of the classroom are referred to as **classroom discourse.** The most common pattern of classroom discourse is the pattern of *teacher initiation, student response,* and *teacher evaluation* (Falk-Ross, 2002). An example would be:

> TEACHER: Who remembers where we left off yesterday? JEFF: We had just finished the Bill of Rights. TEACHER: Good, Jeff, thank you.

Teachers use discourse strategies to communicate expectations for learning to students.

Instructional discourse strategies are the ways in which teachers communicate to students expectations for learning, how they are to learn, how they know they are learning, and, most important, the meaning of learning. So when the teacher gives directions such as, "We are going to work on this list of vocabulary words because they could be on the test you are taking next week. Look up the meanings of the words in the dictionary; when you finish, write a sentence for each word and read your sentences to your partner," he is using a classroom discourse routine.

Scaffolding is the guidance an adult or peer provides for students who cannot yet do a task alone.

Another way of thinking about these discourse strategies is to consider them as a scaffold, or support for learning. **Scaffolding** refers to supporting a child so that she or he can understand or use language that is more complex than she or he could understand or use independently. Scaffolding occurs when a teacher (or another child, or a parent) breaks down directions step by step, asks questions about the elements of a story, elaborates on the themes or vocabulary of a story, asks "thought" questions, or restates or summarizes concepts or themes. As the child is able to use the language independently, scaffolding is gradually withdrawn. Russian psychologist Lev Vygotsky described the process of supporting a child to the next level of learning—his "zone of proximal development" (Vygotsky, 1978). The process of teaching and moving the child toward a higher level of knowledge and understanding is scaffolding. The supports provided by an adult or another child are gradually internalized and become part of the child's knowledge.

Members of the Collaborative Team

A collaborative approach requires the willingness to cross disciplinary boundaries. Members of an educational team must be willing to maintain their existing roles, or expertise, and also to expand their roles, or even relinquish them, when appropriate, to meet students' needs. Classroom-based instruction and intervention mean that general and special education teachers and speech-language pathologists will work together in new ways to achieve the goals of an integrated curriculum. Typically, members of the team for a student with a communication disorder will be the classroom teacher, whether general or special education; the student's parents; an instructional assistant; and the speech-language specialist.

Teachers and speech-language pathologists should work together in collaborative teams.

Despite the speech-language pathologist's intensive training and expertise, it is important that the classroom teacher not be intimidated by this able professional colleague. Typically, teachers are experts themselves in classroom learning, curriculum, and management—areas in which the speech-language pathologist has little training. Each collaborative partner has important contributions to make (Bauer, Iyer, Boon, & Fore, 2010).

In fact, role expansion in a collaborative approach means that teachers, with the support of speech-language pathologists, can learn to incorporate communication goals and strategies for individual students into everyday classroom activities. Most important, effective role expansion depends on continuous planning and communication among all team members, as well as on changes in attitudes and expectations. Ehren (2000) makes specific suggestions for operationalizing shared responsibility in the classroom; see Teaching Strategies and Accommodations, "Sharing Responsibility for Student Success."

As schools shift toward more collaborative and integrated models of education, including inclusive models, we need to start with the basics: challenging our existing beliefs about how we work together, and what students are capable of when given appropriate support.

In working with students with communication disorders, as well as students with a range of other disabilities and all other students with language-learning

Teaching Strategies & Accommodations

Sharing Responsibility for Student Success

1. Promote the writing of Individualized Education Program (IEP) goals that teachers and speech-language pathologists (SLPs) work collaboratively to achieve, as opposed to goals that are identified only with the teacher or the SLP.

2. SLPs should be prepared to make suggestions for modifications at IEP meetings. What can the teacher do to adjust assessment and instructional activities to accommodate a student's language disorder so that the student can benefit from classroom instruction?

3. SLPs should make specific suggestions to teachers on how to modify lessons, tests, and assigned work, and consider demonstrating appropriate modifications for the teacher.

4. Teachers and SLPs should agree on progress assessment procedures and work together to assess progress based on specific progress criteria.

5. Broadcast successes to other faculty members and administration. Brag about each other's hard work and mutual accomplishments.

Source: B. J. Ehren (2000). Maintaining a therapeutic focus and sharing responsibility for student success: Keys to in-classroom speech-language services. *Language, Speech, and Hearing Services in Schools,* 31 (3), 225–226.

needs, it might be helpful to consider three levels of language intervention strategies. Intervention becomes more focused and intensive at each level. Here are some examples that can be used by classroom teachers at each level.

Level One   Best practices for typical language learners; enrichment for students who are learning language successfully.

- Give your students plenty of opportunities to talk, and listen carefully to what they say. Students need to talk as much or more than teachers. You might consider tape recording one of your lessons, then listening for who is doing the talking. Teachers should allow a wide variety of students an opportunity to talk, and not monopolize all the talking themselves.

- Provide a "wait time" when a student is called on, and try not to interrupt. Students from some cultures unfold their narratives more slowly than others (Reid, 2000).

- Expand and extend your students' utterances. Respond to students' talk not with correction, but with an enriched, correct pattern (McCormick, 2003b). For example:

STUDENT: This not lighting. Bulb broken.
TEACHER: Your bulb isn't lighting up? Let's look at your circuit.

- Provide plenty of contextual supports for new language learning as well as new concepts: pictures, graphic organizers, films, hands-on experiences, and so on. Visual aids help all students but are especially helpful for students who have difficulty with language.

- Have a place in your classroom where new vocabulary is recorded, and find opportunities to use new vocabulary in different contexts. Reward students for their use of new vocabulary as well.

- Through your dialogue with students, use *scaffolding* to move them to a higher level of speaking and understanding. Remember that scaffolding is "a process of enabling students to solve a problem, achieve a goal, or carry out a task that would be beyond their ability if they were not given help" (Reid, 2000, p. 28). Your goal is to improve students' levels of participation until they become independent.

Level Two   Procedures used with children who are not acquiring language at the same rate as their peers, or those who are learning English.

- Find the time for work on English language development every day.
- Preteach critical vocabulary prior to student reading (Gersten & Baker, 2000).
- Provide the students frequent opportunities to use oral language in the classroom. Don't let the more fluent students monopolize the discussion. Oral language use should include both conversation and discussion of academic content.

A CLOSER LOOK   Guidelines for English Language Development (ELD) Instruction

Guidelines Based on Relatively Strong Supporting Evidence from English Learner Research

1. Providing ELD instruction is better than not providing it.
2. ELD instruction should include interactive activities among students, but they must be carefully planned and carried out.

Guidelines Based on Hypotheses Emerging from Recent English Learner Research

3. A separate block of time should be devoted daily to ELD instruction.
4. ELD instruction should emphasize listening and speaking although it can incorporate reading and writing.
5. ELD instruction should explicitly teach elements of English (e.g., vocabulary, syntax, grammar, functions, and conventions).
6. ELD instruction should integrate meaning and communication to support explicit teaching of language.
7. ELD instruction should provide students with corrective feedback on form.
8. Use of English during ELD instruction should be maximized; the primary language should be used strategically.
9. Teachers should attend to communication and language-learning strategies and incorporate them into ELD instruction.
10. ELD instruction should emphasize academic language as well as conversational language.
11. ELD instruction should continue at least until students reach level 4 (early advanced) and possibly through level 5 (advanced).

Guidelines Applicable to ELD but Grounded in Non-English Learner Research

12. ELD instruction should be planned and delivered with specific language objectives in mind.
13. English learners should be carefully grouped by language proficiency for ELD instruction; for other portions of the school day they should be in mixed classrooms and not in classrooms segregated by language proficiency.
14. The likelihood of establishing and/or sustaining an effective ELD instructional program increases when schools and districts make it a priority.

Source: W. A. Saunders & C. Goldenberg (2010). Research to guide English language development instruction. In *Improving Education for English Learners: Research-Based Approaches.* Reprinted by permission from California Department of Education, CDE Press, 1430 N. Street, Suite 3207, Sacramento, CA 95814.

- Be aware of classroom discourse strategies and routines, and use them consciously to scaffold new vocabulary in a meaningful context.

- Focus on vocabulary building, but do not overwhelm students with new vocabulary—lists of seven or fewer words should be worked on over relatively long periods. Vocabulary should convey key concepts, be useful, relevant to the concepts being taught, and meaningful to the students (Gersten & Baker, 2000).

- Use more visuals as you teach. For students who are learning a new language, visuals such as semantic maps and story maps "help students visualize the abstractions of language" (Gersten & Baker, 2000, p. 463).

- Promote peer interactions, peer tutoring, and cooperative work groups. Students who are learning language, whether they are English language learners or students with disabilities, will benefit from peer models, prompts, and supports.

- Teach communication skills to replace challenging behaviors (McCormick, 2003b). Remember that your student may not have the appropriate language to communicate his or her needs and feelings, and engage in challenging behavior as a result. Try to discern the communicative intent—what does the student want to say? Then teach the student more acceptable ways of communicating that intent.

For more on what research tells us about research-based strategies for teaching English learners, see A Closer Look, "Guidelines for English Language Development (ELD) Instruction."

Level Three Interventions that are disability specific:

- Incorporate sign language and finger spelling for students with hearing loss. It often helps other students too. If you're not an expert, buy a book and learn with your students. Teach *all* your students signs so they will use them with one another and develop new vocabulary.

- Build in concept development for students who are visually impaired or those with intellectual disabilities. Concepts that sighted students learn through vision must be explicitly taught to students who are blind or have low vision, and sometimes restated for students with intellectual disabilities.

- Through your school speech-language pathologist, investigate augmentative communication systems for students who cannot or do not speak. Students with physical disabilities can use picture boards and computer systems with adaptations (see Chapter 13). Students with autism might use systems like the Picture Exchange Communication System (PECS) described in Chapter 9.

- Students with developmental delay or intellectual disabilities will benefit from exposure to short, direct sentences that contain functional vocabulary—words they need to function in everyday routines. Adding signs to those short sentences can be helpful too—it makes the message more redundant.

Developing useful communication skills can be challenging, but it is not impossible—even for students with the most significant communication disorders. As an incentive, remember that the work you do to promote language growth and expansion will benefit *all* your students. As the teacher, you are crucial to what may be the most important goal for your students—learning to communicate effectively and therefore connect with others.

ASSISTIVE TECHNOLOGY FOCUS

Introduction to Augmentative and Alternative Communication

Personal achievement in life is a function of the ability to communicate.

Augmentative and alternative communication (AAC) refers to ways (other than speech) that are used to send a message from one person to another. We all use augmentative communication techniques, such as facial expressions, gestures, and writing, as part of our daily lives. In difficult listening situations (noisy rooms, for example), we tend to augment our words with even more gestures and exaggerated facial expressions.

People with severe speech or language problems must rely quite heavily on these standard techniques as well as on special augmentative techniques that have been specifically developed for them. Some of these techniques involve the use of specialized gestures, sign language, or Morse code. Other techniques use communication aids, such as charts, bracelets, and language boards. On aids such as these, objects may be represented by pictures, drawings, letters, words, sentences, special symbols, or any combination thereof.

Electronic devices are available that can speak in response to entries on a keyboard or other methods of input. Input can come from any number of different switches that are controlled with motions as simple as a push of a button, a puff of air, or the wrinkle of an eyebrow. The possibilities increase virtually every day! *Augmentative communication users don't stop using speech!* When speech is used with standard and special augmentative communication, not only does communication increase, but so do social interactions, school performance, feelings of self-worth, and job opportunities.

The goal of AAC is the most effective communication possible and, in turn, the greatest potential for personal achievement.

A WORD OF CAUTION

Selecting the communication methods that are best for an individual is not as simple as getting a prescription for eyeglasses. But, language is also complex, and we learn to use it every day. Indeed, developing the best communication system for a person with a severe speech and language problem requires evaluation by many specialists, all of whom may not have offices in the same building or even in the same city. Communication boards may need to be made. Vocabulary to meet the needs of a wide range of communication situations must be selected. Equipment may need to be ordered and paid for. Health plans or other third-party payors may need to be contacted.

© Ellen B. Senisi

Learning to use an augmentative communication device can unlock the world of communication for a child, and change her life for the better.

And once all the parts of the communication plan are in place, the user must learn to operate each part of the system effectively and efficiently. Professionals need to help the user and his or her communication partners learn a variety of skills and strategies, which might include the meaning of certain hand shapes and how to make them; starting and stopping a piece of electronic equipment at a desired word or picture; ways to get a person's attention; ways to help a communication partner understand a message; and increasing the rate of communication. *Communication planning is a lifelong process.* And problems will come up that threaten the plan. Without effort by the user, professional help, ongoing practice, and support from friends, family, and colleagues, the promises of augmentative communication may not be realized. And even with all the parts in place, chances are that problems will arise. Continue to find out what can be done to solve these problems.

Users of AAC will tell you the effort is worth it and that selection of their AAC system was the single most important event in their lives.

Source: Reprinted with permission from Augmentative and Alternative Communication. Available from the website of the American Speech-Language-Hearing Association: www.asha.org/public/speech/disorders/aac.

SUMMARY

- Communication is the exchange of ideas. Language is one type of symbolic communication; its code expresses ideas or content. Language is functional, or pragmatic. A community of language users agrees on the appropriate ways to behave as speakers and listeners.

- Speech is one component of the total language system. It involves the physical actions needed to produce meaningful spoken words.

- Language develops very rapidly and in generally the same sequence in all children, although the ages at which children reach particular developmental milestones can vary significantly. Several theories have been proposed to explain the acquisition of language and communication. It is likely that social interaction with others in the language community plays a vital role in speech and language development. By 5 years of age, the basic system of oral communication has been acquired.

- Language disorders involve difficulties in the comprehension and expression of the meaning and content of language. Speech disorders include phonological, fluency, and voice impairments. *Communication disorders* is a more general term used to include difficulties with speech and hearing, as well as language and speech disorders.

- Identification and assessment of students with communication disorders are typically the tasks of the speech-language pathologist (SLP).

- Collaboration between the teacher and the SLP is crucial for student success, but challenging to implement.

- Placement options for students with communication disorders are increasingly focusing on inclusion in the integrated classroom. This has led to a shift in the philosophy, principles, and practices of educators.

- Instructional strategies focus on integrating language and literacy development and supporting the use of oral communication for a variety of functional purposes. Good language instruction benefits all students, not simply those who are behind in language learning.

KEY TERMS

communication (page 335)
language (page 336)
phonology (page 337)
phonemes (page 337)
morphology (page 337)
morphemes (page 337)
syntax (page 337)
semantics (page 337)
pragmatics (page 337)
discourse (page 337)
speech (page 337)
communication disorder (page 343)
language disorder (page 344)

receptive language (page 344)
expressive language (page 344)
specific language impairment
  (page 345)
functional behavior analysis (page 346)
communicative intent (page 346)
articulation disorders (page 347)
fluency disorder (page 347)
stuttering (page 347)
voice disorder (page 349)
dialect (page 349)
language delay (page 351)
phonological awareness (page 353)

USEFUL RESOURCES

- The website for the American Speech-Language-Hearing Association (ASHA) at **http://www.asha.org** offers information and resources to professionals in the field and others interested in speech and language.

- Visit the website of the National Institute on Deafness and Other Communication Disorders at **http://www.nidcd.nih.gov.** This arm of the National Institutes of Health (NIH) supports research on communication disorders and serves as a resource in the field. Click on "Health Info" for information for teachers and students.

- Two journals will be particularly interesting for those of you writing papers or working on projects in this area. They are *Language, Speech, and Hearing Services in the Schools,* published by ASHA, and the *Journal of Communicative Disorders,* published by the Division of Communication Disorders and Deafness of the Council for Exceptional Children.

- Visit the website of the Stuttering Foundation of America at **http://www. stuttersfa.org.** The Stuttering Foundation provides free online resources, services, and support to those who stutter and their families, as well as support for research into the causes of stuttering. They offer a very inexpensive video entitled *Stuttering: Straight Talk for Teachers.*

Resources on Normal Language Development

Earlier in the chapter we promised to provide you with further resources on normal language development. Here are two:

- Robert E. Owens (2008). *Language Development: An Introduction* (7th ed.). Boston: Allyn & Bacon.

- The American Speech-Language-Hearing Association (ASHA) website also covers this topic at **http://www.asha.org/public/speech/development.**

Resources on Ecological Assessment

L. McCormick, D. F. Loeb, & R. L. Schiefelbusch (2003). *Supporting Children with Communication Difficulties in Inclusive Settings: School-Based Language Intervention* (2nd ed.). Boston: Allyn & Bacon. Chapter 7, "Ecological Assessment and Planning," provides an excellent overview of the topic; the ten-step planning process will be very useful for teachers.

Resources on Augmentative Communication

- The website **http://www.augcominc.com** is a compendium of resources and links.

- *AAC: Augmentative and Alternative Communication* is a professional journal devoted to AAC issues.

Also:

- The IRIS Center's module on English language learners provides an overview of research-based teaching strategies that can be effectively used with this group. Find it at **http://iris.peabody.vanderbilt.edu/ell/chalcycle. htm/.**

PORTFOLIO ACTIVITIES

1. Talk to a school speech-language pathologist and take notes on your discussion.
   - Ask her to describe the students she sees: How many are there on her caseload? What speech and language needs do the students have?
   - Ask her about her training: Does she have both a graduate and under-graduate degree in communication disorders? How many hours did she work with children before obtaining certification?
   - Ask her about collaboration: Does she see children in their classrooms or in a pullout program? How does she find time to confer with their classroom teachers?
   - Write a description for your portfolio of the role of the speech-language pathologist on the collaborative team.

   CEC This activity will help students meet CEC Initial Content Standard 10: Collaboration.

2. Classrooms that include students with communication disorders should encourage multiple modes of communication. Students can express their ideas and feelings through painting, drawing, singing or the use of a musical instrument, creative writing, drama, e-mail—the possibilities are vast. Can you design a lesson or unit of lessons in which multiple modes of communication will be encouraged? At the preschool level? At the secondary level? You may include your lesson plan or unit plan in your portfolio.

   CEC This activity will help students meet CEC Initial Content Standard 6: Language.

    To access Portfolio Activities for this chapter and other useful study resources including an interactive eBook, related web links, quizzes, flashcards, and videos, visit the Education CourseMate website at CengageBrain.com.

CHAPTER 11

Children Who Are Deaf and Hard of Hearing

Learning Objectives

After reading this chapter, the reader will:

● Understand how we hear and the major types of hearing loss.

● Describe the relationship between hearing and language development.

● Understand Deaf culture and the Deaf community, and the role they play in the education of children who are deaf.

● Describe the communication options available for people who are deaf.

● Identify the supports that a student with hearing loss needs in the general education classroom.

I often tell my students how I got into the field of special education. I was in college, an English major, and a boy I had a crush on worked part-time at St. Mary's School for the Deaf. I decided to try to get a job there, too, so I could "run into him" accidentally. Well, I did get the job, and I never once saw him at work in the two years that I worked in the school. But serendipity was at work—I found out what I wanted to do professionally for the rest of my life.

The little boys I worked with were between 3 and 5 years old, and they lived at the school. (This was before the days of IDEA; parents who had no programs for their children in their communities were required to send their children to residential schools, often far from home.) Some spoke, some were silent, but they all used sign language as their preferred form of communication. The fascination I felt then with the possibility of teaching them more language has never left me. Do you remember the moment in the film *The Miracle Worker* when Annie Sullivan takes Helen Keller to the water pump, puts her hands under the water, and signs "water" into those hands? Helen's eyes light up. This is the moment she finally understands that water has a name, and that all things have a name. I wanted to see the eyes of those little boys light up as they learned to communicate.

Many of you share my interest in teaching language. It is at the heart of our instruction of English language learners, of instruction for children with many of the disabilities we discuss in this book, and of foreign language instruction. In fact, teaching the complexity and richness of language is important for every learner. Sign language, used by many deaf students, is a source of great fascination as well. Join me now in learning about the students who taught me to be a teacher—those who are deaf and hard of hearing.—Nancy Hunt

Terms and Definitions

Deafness is defined as a hearing loss "so severe that a child experiences difficulty in processing linguistic information through hearing, with or without amplification" (Northern & Downs, 2002, p. 341). People who are deaf usually rely primarily on their vision both for their understanding of the world and for communication. **Hard of hearing** is a term used to describe a hearing loss that, although serious, is less severe than deafness and usually permits the understanding of spoken language with the use of hearing aids. **Hearing impairment** is an umbrella term that refers to all degrees of hearing loss, from slight to profound. Since many individuals in the **Deaf community**—those adults bound together by their deafness, the use of American Sign Language (ASL), and their culture, values, and attitudes— dislike the term *impairment,* we will avoid it in this chapter and instead use the term **hearing loss** when referring to individuals who are deaf and hard of hearing. Table 11.1 defines some of the other terms that are important to this topic.

Deafness is a hearing loss that precludes the learning of language through hearing.

Hard of hearing describes a loss that is less severe than deafness.

Table 11.1 Table of Terms	
Residual hearing	The remaining hearing of a person with hearing loss that, with the help of a hearing aid, detects sounds within the environment and can be used to hear some sounds and learn speech
Congenital hearing loss	A loss that is present at birth
Acquired hearing loss	A loss that occurs after birth
Prelingual deafness	A hearing loss that occurs before the child develops spoken language
Postlingual deafness	A hearing loss that occurs after the child develops spoken language
Bilateral hearing loss	A hearing loss in both ears (although one ear may have more hearing than the other)
Unilateral hearing loss	Normal hearing in one ear and a hearing loss in the other

Please note that in keeping with today's conventions, throughout this chapter, the word *Deaf* is capitalized when it refers to Deafness as a cultural entity.

Causes of Hearing Loss

Before we discuss the causes of hearing loss, it will be helpful to have a basic understanding of how we hear. You will see that the agents that cause hearing loss damage different parts of the auditory mechanism, and can cause hearing problems that are temporary or permanent.

Hearing and Hearing Loss

The human auditory system, as shown in Figure 11.1, is complicated and extremely delicate. Sound energy creates vibration, and the vibration travels in sound waves through a passageway called the ear canal to the eardrum, or tympanic membrane, a thin layer of tissue between the outer and middle ear. The vibration of the eardrum sets off a chain of vibrations in the three small bones of the middle ear: the malleus, incus, and stapes. The sound is transmitted through the cochlea, a tiny, spiral-shaped structure in the inner ear. Finally, it reaches the brain via the auditory nerve, where it is interpreted as meaningful.

Because hearing depends on the transmission of sound waves across numerous tiny structures throughout the auditory mechanism, malfunctions or damage to any part of the system can result in temporary or permanent hearing loss.

Damage or obstruction in the external or middle ear that disrupts the efficient passage or conduction of sound through those chambers results in a **conductive hearing loss.** Most conductive losses can be successfully treated medically, but research has shown that recurrent conductive hearing losses in young children—even though temporary—can affect early language development. Most of the time, though, effects on language have disappeared by school age (McQuiston & Kloczko, 2011).

Damage to the cochlea or the auditory nerve in the inner ear is called a **sensorineural hearing loss.** A sensorineural loss is almost always permanent and irreversible (Hyde, 2011). Most students with hearing loss in our schools have a sensorineural hearing loss, although some of them have a **mixed hearing loss,** with both conductive and sensorineural components. Table 11.2 below is an overview of the two major kinds of hearing loss.

> Sound waves travel through the auditory canal to the eardrum, middle ear, cochlea, and via the auditory nerve to the brain.

> Conductive hearing loss can be temporary, but recurrent conductive loss can affect language development.

> Sensorineural hearing loss is permanent and irreversible.

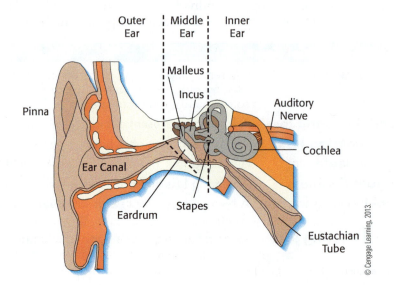

© Cengage Learning, 2013.

FIGURE 11.1

Structure of the ear

Table 11.2 Characteristics of the Two Major Kinds of Hearing Loss

	Conductive Hearing Loss	Sensorineural Hearing Loss
Duration	Usually temporary	Permanent
Location of the problem	Occurs as a result of a problem in the outer or middle ear	Occurs as a result of a problem in the inner ear or the auditory nerve
Treatment	Treatable by a physician with medication and/or surgery	Not routinely treatable*
Impact on hearing	Tends to be a mild or moderate hearing loss	Tends to be a severe or profound hearing loss
Impact on learning	Depends on the length of the problem; can vary from no impact at all to significantly affecting early language learning	Usually affects spoken language development
Educational services provided	Special education services not routinely provided for this short-term hearing loss	Special education provided when the hearing loss affects the student's educational performance

*Sometimes treated by a cochlear implant (see p. 408).
© Cengage Learning, 2013.

Hearing loss can range in severity from slight to profound. Children with losses described as mild and moderate are usually called hard of hearing; those with severe and profound losses are usually considered deaf. Even most deaf people, though, have some **residual hearing** (see Table 11.1) that can make a hearing aid helpful. Table 11.3 describes the effects of the varying degrees of hearing loss on children.

Knowledge of the cause of hearing loss in young children is important for several reasons. In the case of conductive losses, which are usually treatable, the cause dictates the treatment; in the case of sensorineural loss, which is permanent and often congenital, knowledge will help families gather information about the probability of hearing loss in any subsequent children and may help them master the feelings of stress related to their child's disability.

Conductive Hearing Loss

The most common cause of conductive hearing loss in children is middle ear infection, or **otitis media.** When, because of a cold or for some other reason, fluid gathers in the middle ear, it dampens or restricts the movement of the eardrum, and hearing loss may result. Middle ear infection, or simply the presence of fluid in the middle ear, can cause mild to moderate hearing loss in children, and it should always be brought to the attention of the child's pediatrician. *Chronic* otitis media (ear infection that lasts for twelve weeks or longer, or returns repeatedly), can have long-term effects on hearing, and may have subtle adverse effects over time on a child's achievement in school, long after the ear infection has disappeared, although results of follow-up of these children is mixed (Golz et al., 2005; Zumach, Gerrits, Chenault & Anteunis, 2010).

Children should be treated by a physician when warning signs of middle ear infection appear, and especially when they persist over time. Some of those signs are fever, redness of the ear, rubbing of the ear, or, in a young infant, rubbing of the head against a mattress or blanket; reports of pain or itching; and, in extreme cases, dripping from the ear. Sometimes middle ear infections are treated with antibiotics. Pediatricians are concerned with the development of resistance to antibiotics, however, and may encourage families to treat ear infections by other means (see the American Academy of Pediatrics parent website for more information). Ear infections should always be treated promptly in babies and young

Otitis media—middle ear infection—is the most common cause of conductive hearing loss in children.

Table 11.3 Degrees of Hearing Loss

Average Hearing Level	Description	Possible Condition	What Can Be Heard without Amplification	Handicapping Effects (If Not Treated in First Year of Life)	Probable Needs
0–15 dB*	Normal range		All speech sounds	None	None
15–25 dB	Slight hearing loss	Conductive hearing losses, some sensorineural hearing losses	Vowel sounds heard clearly; may miss unvoiced consonants sounds	Mild auditory dysfunction in language learning	Consideration of need for hearing aid; speech reading, auditory training, speech therapy, preferential seating
25–30 dB	Mild hearing loss	Conductive or sensorineural hearing loss	Only some speech sounds, the louder voiced sounds	Auditory learning dysfunction, mild language delay, mild speech problems	Hearing aid, speech reading, auditory training, speech therapy
30–50 dB	Moderate hearing loss	Conductive hearing loss from chronic middle ear disorders; sensorineural hearing losses	Almost no speech sounds at normal conversational level	Speech problems, language delay, learning difficulties	All of the above, plus consideration of other special education services
50–70 dB	Severe hearing loss	Sensorineural or mixed losses due to a combination of middle ear disease and sensorineural involvement	No speech sounds at normal conversational level	Severe speech problems, language delay, learning difficulties	All of the above; need for special education services
70+ dB	Profound hearing loss	Sensorineural or mixed losses due to a combination of middle ear disease and sensorineural involvement	No speech or other sounds	Severe speech problems, language delay, learning difficulties	All of the above; need for special education services

*dB stands for *decibels*, or units of loudness.

Source: Jerry L. Northern & Marion P. Downs (2002), *Hearing in Children*, 5th ed. Baltimore: Lippincott Williams & Wilkins. Reprinted by permission of the author.

children: Their long-term effects can be serious. You, as a professional working with young children and families, can play an important role in the prevention of conductive hearing loss by encouraging prompt medical treatment when an ear infection is suspected.

Sensorineural Hearing Loss

Conductive hearing loss can often be successfully treated in young children, and it is not usually the major cause of hearing loss that places school-age children in special education services. Children with sensorineural hearing loss, though, usually have a permanent condition that cannot be medically treated and that makes special education services necessary. Many cases are present at birth. With universal newborn hearing screening more children with congenital sensorineural hearing loss are being identified at birth or soon after, rather than as toddlers, when they are already behind typical children in language acquisition (Hyde, 2011). The number of newborns screened for hearing loss has increased from 46.5 percent in 1999 to 97 percent in 2007 (Centers for Disease Control, 2010). Of those screened, 1.6 percent did not pass; of those who did not pass, about 68 percent received a diagnosis within three months, although the majority of those were "false positives"; they did not have hearing loss. In the end, 1.4 of every 1000 infants screened was identified with hearing loss, and 68 percent of those infants began early intervention (Centers for Disease Control, 2009).

The early identification of hearing loss allows intervention to begin in the first months of life, before children have fallen behind much in their communication development. This is a long way from age of identification before newborn hearing screening, when confirmed diagnosis often did not come until children were 20 months of age (Kittrell & Arjmand, 1997). It has brought renewed hope to a field that has long advocated for early identification and intervention for children with hearing loss.

Knowledge of the cause of a child's sensorineural hearing loss is often important for families. Parents may want to know if a child's hearing loss is hereditary. A genetic counselor can help a family know whether or not that determination can be made (Hood & Keats, 2011). Also, many parents feel a strong desire to know the cause of their child's disability. In fact, Kathryn Meadow (1968) found that parents who knew the probable cause of their child's hearing loss were better able to cope with the complex feelings associated with the diagnosis. Summers, Behr, and Turnbull (1989) suggest that identifying the cause of disability may be a positive process of adaptation for families.

The major causes of sensorineural hearing loss in children change over time, depending on the occurrence of epidemics, the development of new drugs and medical treatments, and public health conditions. For example, most of the children who lost their hearing as a result of maternal exposure to rubella during the 1960s rubella epidemic have by now left special education services, and since the rubella vaccine was introduced in 1969, rubella has become a much less prominent cause of hearing loss. See A Closer Look, "Causes of Sensorineural Hearing Loss," for a list of the current most common causes of sensorineural hearing loss in children.

> Children with sensorineural hearing loss usually require special education services.

Students with Hearing Loss and Additional Disabilities

Roughly 40 percent of the children who are deaf and hard of hearing and enrolled in special education programs have been identified with a disability in addition to their hearing loss (Gallaudet Research Institute, 2008). Table 11.4 shows the numbers of children with hearing loss and additional disabilities. The most common are the cognitive-behavioral disabilities: intellectual disability, specific learning disabilities, and attention deficit disorders. Part of the explanation for this relationship comes from the linkage between the cause of hearing loss and the additional disability. Moores (2001) reminds us:

> One out of four of children with hearing loss has additional disabilities.

All of the major contemporary known causes of early childhood deafness may be related to other conditions to some extent. These include maternal rubella, prematurity, cytomegalovirus, mother-child blood incompatibility, and meningitis. Even in the case of inherited deafness, whether dominant, recessive, or sex-linked, the hearing loss may be only one manifestation of a syndrome that includes a wide range of conditions. (p. 118)

A CLOSER LOOK — Causes of Sensorineural Hearing Loss

1. **Heredity.** In a great number of cases (probably about 60 percent) hearing loss is caused by heredity, or genetic factors (Davis & Davis, 2011).

2. **Meningitis.** Meningitis is a bacterial or viral infection that causes inflammation of the coverings of the brain and spinal cord. If the infection reaches the inner ear, it can destroy the delicate organs within, resulting in deafness. Meningitis is the major cause of *acquired* deafness in children around the world (Davis & Davis, 2011). It may also be associated with other neurological disabilities.

3. **Prematurity.** Prematurity and the traumatic medical events frequently associated with premature birth and low birth weight are sometimes associated with hearing loss (see Chapter 3).

4. **Cytomegalovirus (CMV).** CMV (see Chapter 3) is the most common intrauterine infection of pregnancy (Davis & Davis, 2011). When a pregnant woman contracts CMV, she can pass it to her fetus, which can result in hearing loss as well as other disabilities. Some infants recover completely (Centers for Disease Control, 2010).

5. **Other causes.** There are many other, less common causes of childhood hearing loss, including mother-child blood incompatibility, or RH incompatibility, head trauma, prenatal infections, maternal illness, and toxins consumed by the mother during pregnancy (American Speech-Language Hearing Association, n.d.; Davis & Davis, 2011).

Although there are benefits to knowing the cause of sensorineural hearing loss, that information is frequently unavailable. In at least 25 percent of the reported cases of hearing loss, despite the best efforts of parents and counselors to determine the cause, it remains unknown (Centers for Disease Control, 2011).

There may also be social or environmental causes for a condition in addition to hearing loss: An impoverished communication system, late entry to school, an inappropriate school program, and a lack of consistent behavioral limits, for example, could combine to allow the development of an additional disability.

Hearing loss is also frequently associated with other conditions that may be considered a student's primary disability, such as Down syndrome, cerebral palsy, and cleft palate. In addition, children who are both deaf and blind constitute a small but unique group of students who often have intensive communication and mobility needs and are best served by a multidisciplinary group of professionals (Chen & Klein, 2008b, 2009). Family members can learn to interpret communication cues in infants with multiple disabilities that include both hearing and vision; these cues can serve as the foundation for a system of communication (Chen & Klein, 2007).

Prevalence

A small percentage of all the children in special education programs are deaf or hard of hearing.

In comparison to other groups of children served in special education programs, the number of children who are deaf and hard of hearing is small. Only 0.1 percent of the children served under IDEA in the school years between 1995 and 2004 were labeled as hearing impaired (U.S. Department of Education, 2009). In fact, a recent examination of 12 years of data from the National Health Survey (Boyle et al., 2011) found that reports of moderate to profound hearing loss in American children aged 3 to 17 dropped by 31 percent between 1997–2008.

Like visual impairment, in the U.S. hearing loss is a disability that primarily affects adults. As many as 29 million adult Americans have a hearing loss that affects their ability to hear spoken language (Agrawal, Platz, & Niparko, 2008).

Table 11.4 Additional Disabilities of Deaf Children

Specific Classifications	Percentage
No condition in addition to deafness	60.7
Visual impairment	3.8
Deaf-blindness	1.6
Developmental delay	4.8
Specific learning disability	8.3
Orthopedic impairment (includes cerebral palsy)	4.4
Attention Deficit Disorder (ADD/ADHD)	5.6
Traumatic brain injury	0.3
Mental retardation*	8.7
Emotional disturbance	2.0
Autism	1.6
Other health impairments	5.2
Other conditions	9.1

Note: Percentages may total more than 100 percent because some students have more than one classification.

*Author's note: We use the more contemporary term *intellectual disabilities* throughout this book.

Source: Gallaudet Research Institute (2008). *Regional and National Summary Report of Data from the 2007–08 Annual Survey of Deaf and Hard of Hearing Children and Youth.* Washington, DC: GRI, Gallaudet University.

Measurement of Hearing Loss

If you work with students with hearing loss, you will most likely come into contact with a number of other professionals who interact with the child and family. As you review your students' records, you will see their reports.

The **otologist** is a physician whose specialization is diseases of the ear. He or she may participate in the diagnosis of hearing loss and treat the child later for related problems. The otologist is also the specialist many children see for chronic middle ear infections.

The **audiologist** has special training in testing and measuring hearing. Professionally trained audiologists have the skills and equipment needed to evaluate the hearing of any child at any age with a high degree of accuracy. Many audiologists also participate in the process of rehabilitation, or treatment of the effects of hearing loss, and prescribe and evaluate the effectiveness of hearing aids.

The traditional hearing test given by an audiologist is called a pure-tone test. You have probably had a test like this yourself, since hearing screenings are common in schools. In a pure-tone test the individual, wearing headphones, is exposed to a series of tones or beeps measured in decibels (units of loudness). The tones vary in loudness, or intensity, from soft to loud, and in pitch, or frequency, from low to high. The **audiogram** is the chart on which the audiologist records the individual's responses to the tones. People with normal hearing generally respond to very soft sounds, whether they are high or low in frequency (pitch). Figure 11.2 explains an audiogram. Note that each ear is tested separately.

There are a couple of simple principles that make interpreting an audiogram easier. First, the farther down on the audiogram the responses are recorded, the less residual hearing a person has, or the louder the tones have to be before the person responds to them. Second, the most crucial sounds for a person to hear

> The audiologist is trained to test and measure hearing.

> The audiogram is the chart on which the audiologist records the individual's responses to sounds presented.

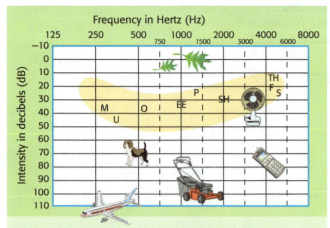

An audiogram is a picture of your hearing. The results of your hearing test are recorded on an audiogram. The audiogram above demonstrates different sounds and where they would be represented on an audiogram. The yellow, banana-shaped figure represents all the sounds that make up the human voice when speaking at normal conversational levels.

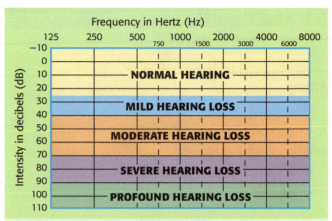

The softest sound you are able to hear at pitch is recorded on an audiogram. The softest sound that you are able to hear is called your threshold. Thresholds of 0–25 dB are considered normal (for adults). The audiogram above demonstrates the different degrees of hearing loss.

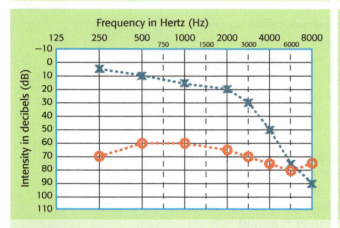

The audiogram above represents the hearing of an individual with normal hearing in low frequencies (pitch) sloping to a severe high frequency hearing loss in the left ear and a moderate to severe hearing loss in the right ear. The blue X's indicate the thresholds for the left ear and the red O's indicate the thresholds for the right ear.

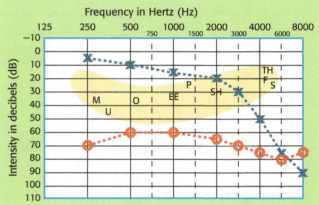

If we now superimpose the normal speech area on the audiogram, we can obtain some information regarding this individual's ability to hear speech. The listener is able to hear all the low and mid speech sounds, but is not able to hear the high pitch speech sounds (i.e., F, S, TH) in the left ear (blue X's). The listener is not able to hear any of the normal speech sounds in the right ear. This person would rely on the left ear for speech understanding and would probably experience difficulty hearing in noisy environments.

FIGURE 11.2

Understanding the Audiogram

Source: Allan S. Mehr (2003). Understanding your audiogram. In *Consumer Guides,* American Academy of Audiology, available at http://audiology.org/consumer/guides/uya.php. Reprinted by permission of the author.

are those that fall primarily between 500 and 3,000 Hertz, or cycles per second. Those are the "speech frequencies," the pitch range within which most speech sounds fall. Most professionals believe that it is more important for children with hearing loss to hear speech than any other sound. It is through amplification with hearing aids and the training of their residual hearing to respond to speech sounds that children with hearing loss can most efficiently learn to understand and express spoken language.

? Pause and Reflect

The preceding pages have provided you with some of the background information you will need to understand the implications of hearing loss in your students. Do you know an older person who might have a hearing loss? Would any of this background information help you to understand that person better? ●

Characteristics of Students with Hearing Loss

The impact of hearing loss on a person's ability to naturally acquire the spoken language of his or her community is often substantial. Those communication difficulties may adversely influence school achievement, social and emotional development, and interaction with others.

Language Development

Hearing loss has its most pervasive effect on the development of spoken language. It does not appear to affect cognitive or intellectual development, but it can have a significant impact on school achievement.

If you were to become deaf right now, your primary disability would be your inability to hear. Your relations with your family and friends might be strained by your inability to understand everything they say through lip reading. You would be particularly uncomfortable at parties and restaurants, where the noisy background would make it difficult for you to use your residual hearing to follow the conversation. Television and movies would be harder to follow, and listening to music would bring you less pleasure. Well, you might say, that's what deafness is all about, isn't it? Well, yes—for those of us who have already acquired language. For the prelingually deaf child, deafness is much more than that.

Kathryn Meadow (1980; 2005) said that for a child the primary disability of hearing loss is not the deprivation of sound, but the deprivation of *language.* Think about it. Young children with normal hearing learn how to talk by listening to the people around them use language meaningfully. They begin to understand and to say words. As they have more experiences listening and using language for different communicative purposes, and mature cognitively, their ability to communicate becomes much more sophisticated. But for the child who does not hear, or does not hear well, that listening experience does not occur, or occurs much less consistently. Unless sign language is used in the home, there are fewer occasions for practice in using language to communicate. Some children who are deaf, particularly those who have not been involved in early intervention programs, come to school at age 3 (and sometimes much later) without any speech or signing skills at all. So, although there are exceptions, many children who are deaf or hard of hearing start school with a language delay, and many of them never catch up to their hearing peers linguistically or academically while they are in school.

Genoval, for example, was an 8-year-old boy who was profoundly deaf. His family had recently moved from El Salvador to Los Angeles, and he had never been in school or had any help learning to communicate. The language of his home was Spanish, but his family reported that he used no recognizable Spanish words. The language of the school was English (presented orally and accompanied by an English-order sign language system), but on entering school, Genoval used no recognizable English vocabulary, either signed or spoken. This boy was very

Many children with hearing loss start school with a significant language delay.

Adults are not the only teachers of sign. Here preschooler Lennette helps her classmate Noah.

bright and sociable; he had developed his own gesture language, and through this pantomime could communicate simple needs and actions. But catching up to the other students who were deaf in his class presented a formidable challenge to Genoval and his teachers.

> The more residual hearing children have, the more likely they will speak the language of their home.

The first language of children who are deaf and hard of hearing depends to some extent on the language they are exposed to in the home. The more residual hearing a child has, the more likely it is that the child will learn to speak the home language. Children who have little usable residual hearing, however, may develop a relatively unique "first language" based on what they are exposed to— spoken words and formal signs, for example—and what they invent themselves— gestures and "home signs" that may be understood only by the child and family members. On the other hand, deaf children of deaf parents who use American Sign Language may begin school with communication abilities that are developmentally appropriate for their age—and continue to excel throughout their school careers (Meadow, 2005).

> Some children with hearing loss do not learn English until they begin school.

Many children with hearing loss begin learning *English* when they enter school. Research that has examined the acquisition of English literacy skills— speaking, reading, and writing—of children with hearing loss tells us that the English language of children who are deaf typically develops in the same order as that of hearing children, but at a considerably slower rate (Paul, 2008).

Cognitive and Intellectual Development

> Most people with hearing loss have normal cognitive and intellectual abilities.

People who are deaf and hard of hearing as a group have normal cognitive and intellectual abilities (Spencer, 2010). For many years, however, psychologists believed that the thinking and reasoning capacities of deaf people were "inferior" (Pintner & Patterson, 1917) or qualitatively different (Myklebust, 1964).

These earlier conclusions stemmed from the assessment process. People who are deaf or hard of hearing have, at times, been administered IQ tests that weigh verbal skills heavily; when they did not do well because of their limited understanding and use of English, they were judged to be cognitively below normal—sometimes intellectually disabled (Moores, 2001). Even when a relatively "fair" test is used, the person with hearing loss may not understand the test directions given by a psychologist who does not have the skills necessary for communicating with him or her. Like all assessment of students with disabilities, the assessment of students with hearing loss should take place in the language in which they are most expert, by a person who is also fluent in that language. Although psychologists and other test administrators have become more knowledgeable about testing people who are deaf and thus fewer abuses seem to occur today, great care should always be taken in interpreting test scores (Edwards & Crocker, 2008). As always, they are just one piece of the puzzle.

In the past, inadequate psychological assessment labeled individuals with hearing loss as socially and emotionally deficient.

School Achievement

Despite the normal cognitive and intellectual abilities of most children with hearing loss, their average school achievement has historically been significantly below that of their hearing peers (Mitchell & Karchmer, 2011).

Despite normal abilities, most children with hearing loss do not achieve at grade level.

Why this discrepancy between ability and achievement? It hinges on the lack of mastery of the English language among students who are deaf. If a person can't comprehend and use the language fluently, then he or she can't read it, since even basal reading materials incorporate sophisticated grammatical structures. Reading ability is crucial for success in nearly all academic areas.

Recent research on the academic achievement of students with hearing loss is encouraging (Antia, Jones, Reid, & Kreimeyer, 2009); results are more nuanced than they have been in the past, when so many research studies reported that the average deaf student graduated from high school with a third (or fourth) grade reading level. Antia and her colleagues followed almost 200 students included in general education classrooms for at least two hours a day, both deaf and hard of hearing, for five years. These authors collected a great deal of information, including achievement test results, measures of communicative competence, and teachers' perceptions of the students' academic performance. Over the five years, 63 to 79 percent of the students scored in the average or above-average range in math, 48 to 68 percent in reading, and 55 to 76 percent in language/writing. The students scored on average lower than their hearing peers, but 79 to 81 percent of the students made one or more year's progress annually (Antia et al., 2009). These results do reflect one important connection to earlier research, though: The students with hearing loss performed best in math, and worst in reading. Connect this back to our earlier description of the effects of hearing loss on language development. Math computation does not involve understanding language or decoding print, so it comes more easily to many students with hearing loss; reading involves both those skills, and is the most challenging of the academic areas (Trezek, Wang, & Paul, 2010).

Difficulties acquiring English often lead to poor reading skills for children who are deaf.

Similar results come from a look at the school performance of secondary students; although many students did well (average scores or above), more students scored below average on the Woodcock-Johnson III Tests of Achievement than did their hearing peers (Shaver et al., 2011). Figure 11.3 shows the results graphically.

More students with hearing loss scored below average on all the subtests; again the highest test scores were in math and the lowest in passage comprehension and science, both of which require a high-level understanding of written English.

Toscano, McGee, and Lepoutre (2002) found that deaf students who were highly successful in school tended to have the following experiences:

- Heavy parental involvement
- Extensive family communication
- Early exposure to and intensive experiences with reading and writing

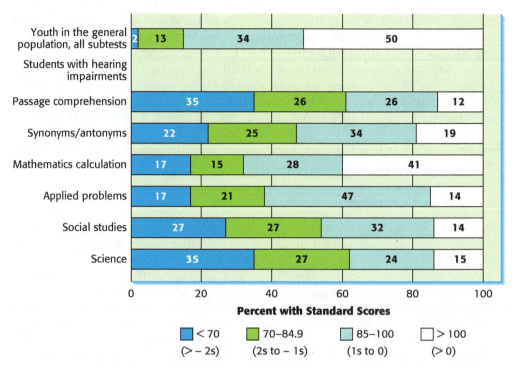

Youth in the general population, all subtests: 2, 13, 34, 50

Students with hearing impairments

	<70 (>−2s)	70–84.9 (2s to −1s)	85–100 (1s to 0)	>100 (>0)
Passage comprehension	35	26	26	12
Synonyms/antonyms	22	25	34	19
Mathematics calculation	17	15	28	41
Applied problems	17	21	47	14
Social studies	27	27	32	14
Science	35	27	24	15

Percent with Standard Scores

Note: Percentages are population estimates based on weighted samples that range from approximately 540 to 550 youth across variables. Percentages for subtests may not sum to 100 because of rounding. Youth in the general population refers to the Woodcock-Johnson norming sample. Scores are reported as standard scores, which have a mean of 100 and a standard deviation of 15, so the scores shown in white are above average.

Source: Woodcock-Johnson, Tests of Cognitive Ability: Standard and Supplemental Batteries, Norm Tables, 1989; U.S. Department of Education, Institute of Education Sciences, National Center for Special Education Research, National Longitudinal Transition Study-2 (NLTS2), student assessments, 2002 and 2004.

FIGURE 11.3

Performance of students with hearing impairments compared with youth in the general population on Woodcock-Johnson III subtests

Source: Shaver, D., Newman, L., Huang, T., Yu, J., Knokey, A. M., & SRI International (2011). *Facts from NLTS2: The secondary experiences and academic performance of students with hearing impairments.* Washington, DC: Institute of Education Sciences, U.S. Department of Education. http://www.nlts2.org/fact_sheets/2011_02.html

---

- An enjoyment of reading
- A relatively limited social life
- High parental and secondary school expectations
- Access to television viewing with captioning
- Positive self-image

Here's one student who speaks of the importance of ongoing and consistent communication:

> . . . For 8 years my parents went to sign classes, and kept going, and going, and going. They needed to keep up with me, since it was my first language, and I progressed very quickly. . . . I have a brother, younger. But he can sign also. . . . My aunt knows some sign. Here and there some of my other relatives know some sign. Even though I am the only deaf person in the family, they all made the effort to include me. I know that doesn't happen everywhere, that you are included at the dinner table. They always made me part of the family conversation. Always. (Toscano, McGee, & Lepoutre, 2002, p. 13)

Social and Emotional Development

Traditionally, psychologists and other professionals concerned with the social and emotional development of individuals who are deaf have concentrated on the differences in this group from the "norms" set by hearing subjects. From this approach has arisen what Donald Moores (2001) calls a "deviance model," which implies that there is something deficient in the psychological makeup of people who are deaf. Many of these conclusions have arisen because of the psychological assessment of students with hearing loss by examiners who are not trained in using sign language and who administer tests that are not appropriate, thereby obtaining an inaccurate picture of the person's true capabilities.

Contemporary perspectives on social development of individuals with hearing loss focus on the development of a healthy, whole, well-integrated person rather than concentrating on what is different or deficient. It assumes that all humans have similar basic needs, which must be met satisfactorily for healthy personal development—among them, the need to communicate with others. For people who are deaf, this need for basic human communication is not always met. Think about this example. Parents of young children who are deaf often feel they do not have the command of communication necessary to explain complicated events, such as a relative's death, a separation, a forthcoming move, or marital problems, and so do not fully communicate the meaning of these experiences to their child. As a result, the child's world may change drastically from one day to the next with no explanation, leaving him or her anxious, frightened, resentful, or confused. The frustration that can arise from unsatisfactory communication can spill over into the child's behavior, relationships, and motivation.

This is not to say that people who are deaf and hard of hearing, young and old, do not have problems like everyone else, only that those problems are not particular to hearing loss. Rather, they may arise from experiences within the family, school, and community where poor communication or no communication is the rule.

> Frustration over inadequate communication may result in behavior or emotional problems for children who are deaf.

In summary, the primary effect of deafness on the developing child is that it places the development of communication at risk. Because communication skills are so essential for school learning, when these skills are affected, school achievement is too. But cognitive and social development need not be delayed in children with hearing loss when they are provided with a means and reason to communicate from an early age.

Pause and Reflect

It takes some thought and experience to fully appreciate the effect of deafness on language learning, and therefore on literacy development and school achievement. Can you think of any similar learning challenges from your own experience? ●

Deafness and Culture

Our discussions so far in this chapter have centered on definitions and descriptions that place deafness in the context of *disability*—and that tend to measure people who are deaf by the yardstick of people who are hearing. We speak of deafness as hearing *loss* or hearing *impairment*—yet, as one deaf professional put it: "How would women like to be referred to as male-impaired, or whites like to be called black-impaired? I'm not impaired; I'm deaf!" Many professionals in the field of deafness, particularly those who are deaf themselves, have been urging

> The clinical perspective of deafness views it as a disability; many prefer that a cultural perspective be adopted.

FIRST PERSON

Claudia Gordon

Claudia L. Gordon is the first deaf African American female attorney in the United States. She embraces each of these descriptors—first, deaf, African American, female, attorney—so seamlessly that everyone who meets her is awed.

Born in Jamaica, Claudia became deaf when she was eight years old. Unable to get an education in her home country, she moved to the United States and enrolled at Lexington School for the Deaf in Jackson Heights, New York. After graduating from Lexington, she received a bachelor's degree in political science from Howard University and a Juris Doctor degree from the Washington College of Law at American University.

Claudia is a now Special Assistant to the Director of the Office of Federal Contract Compliance Programs (OFCCP) in the U.S. Department of Labor. At OFCCP, Claudia works on ensuring that contractors doing business with the Federal government do not discriminate.

Claudia Gordon delivering the opening keynote in American Sign Language at the 50th Biennial Conference of the National Association of the Deaf in Philadelphia, PA. http://www.whitehouse.gov/blog/2010/08/30/meet-women-administration-claudia-gordon

GROWING UP, WHO WERE YOUR ROLE MODELS?

My mother was my most influential role model. She was a woman of profound faith and perseverance up until the very day she lost her six-year battle with ovarian cancer in 2000. Growing up, I witnessed her hard work and sacrifices as she struggled to raise my two siblings and me, all on her own, deep in the rural countryside of Jamaica, W.I. A domestic servant with only an eighth-grade education, she literally scrubbed her way to America one garment at a time. When she immigrated to America— the South Bronx— she kept right on working to ensure that within a few years she would be reunited with her three children, whom she had left in the care of her eldest sister, my aunt Mildred Taylor. My mother taught me that we all control our own destiny and should never become victims of our circumstances. She taught me about the unbelievable power of faith and love.

HOW DID YOU BECOME INTERESTED IN WORKING FOR THE FEDERAL GOVERNMENT?

My interest in working for the Federal government was sparked while working as a Skadden Fellow and staff attorney at the National Association of the Deaf (NAD) Law and Advocacy Center from 2000 to 2002. The NAD operates on a shoestring budget and the law center staff fluctuates from two to four full-time attorneys working tirelessly to keep pace with incoming discrimination claims and requests for technical assistance from among the 36 million deaf and hard of hearing individuals in America. It was there that I confronted the truth that passing legislation is one thing but actual implementation with enforcement is another. I felt that a job with the Federal government would more effectively allow me to affect the actual enforcement of laws such as the Americans with Disabilities Act of 1990 and the Rehabilitation Act of 1973, thereby alleviating the blatant discrimination that people with disabilities continue to face.

WHAT INSPIRED YOU TO PURSUE YOUR FIELD OF INTEREST?

When I suddenly lost my ability to hear at the age of eight, I was taken out of school and kept at home to perform chores. Friends slowly disappeared and what was usually a cheerful hello was replaced by an awkward smile, curious stares and even outright ridicule. There were also those long road trips on the bumpy Jamaican roads to distant towns where healers would perform rituals in attempts to cure me. I thought I was the only deaf person in the world. I did not realize until years later that a woman who everyone in my town knew as "dummy," and who children my age would incessantly harass with stone throwing, was deaf. Looking back, I wish I knew her real name. What I do know is that the life of this woman—ostracized as "dummy"—almost became my own but for my mother's triumph in successfully bringing me to America by the time I was eleven years old.

By my junior year in high school, I made it known to all that I would go to law school and become an attorney. Many shrugged off my grand intention as wishful thinking. Some cited my deafness as an obstacle rendering it impractical if not impossible to pursue a law degree. Thanks to the values that were instilled in me during my formative years, I understood then that those voices of doubt neither dictated my worth nor my capacity. I want to contribute to a better society where there is more understanding and acceptance of people with disabilities and where the same opportunities are provided for all.

WHAT KEEPS YOU MOTIVATED?

I am motivated by knowing that although progress is being made towards inclusion and access, there is still a great deal more work to be done. Also, mentoring youth and young adults with disabilities keeps me motivated. I have an innate desire to give back. It is uplifting when you are able to empower another and help someone discover a sense of self-worth and confidence in his or her abilities.

When my service to the President is over and I have to face my family, my friends and my communities—as an African American, as a woman, and as a deaf person—what I hope to look back on is not a single moment, but rather a series of opportunities where I used my seat at the table and my voice in the decision-making process to improve the lives of those who seek to redeem the promise of America, the promise that brought my mother here all those years ago.

HOW DO YOU BALANCE WORK AND FAMILY LIFE?

To be honest, I don't. But I am blessed with supportive family and friends who know that the long hours I spend at work are spent doing something important. And I know they are proud, patient, and ready to welcome me home when this tour of duty, in service of our country, is done.

Sources: Background: Adapted from Gallaudet University, text from the awarding of the 2011 Amos Kendall Award. http://www. gallaudet.edu/documents/alumni/claudia_gordon_cit%5B1% 5D.pdf/. Interview: http://www.whitehouse.gov/blog/2010/08/30/ meet-women-administration-claudia-gordon/. Posted by Maude Baggetto on August 30, 2010.

teachers of deaf children to drop the clinical perspective, in which deafness is seen as a pathology, a deviance from the "normal" condition of hearing, a condition that must be "cured" or "fixed." These deaf professionals are exhorting the field to adopt the *cultural* perspective, which describes people who are deaf as members of a different culture—a culture with its own language, social institutions, class structure, history, attitudes, values, and literature—that must be studied, understood, and respected (Padden & Humphries, 2006).

Adoption of a cultural perspective on deafness demands knowledge of **Deaf culture,** which Crittenden (1993) defined as "the view of life manifested by the mores, beliefs, artistic expression, understandings, and language particular to Deaf people" (p. 218). Deaf culture is the mainstay of the **Deaf community,** that group of people who share common goals deriving from Deaf cultural influences and work together toward achieving these goals. Crittenden (1993) described the characteristics that members of the Deaf community share as follows:

> Deaf culture unites those in the Deaf community who share common goals.

- "Attitudinal deafness," the desire to associate with other deaf people with whom values and experiences are shared
- The use of American Sign Language (ASL), considered by members of the Deaf community to be their native language
- The similar life experiences of many people who are deaf in relation to family, schooling, and interaction with "the hearing world"
- The bond between deaf people, the friendships and relationships that grow out of those shared experiences

Members of the Deaf community may not be physically deaf (that is, they may be hearing people), but they must actively support the goals of the Deaf community and work together with people who are deaf to achieve them (Padden, 1980). Padden and Humphries's book *Deaf in America: Voices from a Culture* (1988) portrays members of the Deaf community. These authors, deaf themselves, write:

> In contrast to the long history of writings that treat [deaf people] as medical cases, or people with "disabilities," who "compensate" for their deafness by using sign language, we want to portray the lives they live, their art and performances, their everyday talk, their shared myths, and the lessons they teach one another. We have always felt that the attention given to the physical condition of not hearing has obscured far more interesting facets of Deaf people's lives. (p. 1)

Matthew Moore describes Deaf culture less formally:

> One possible definition of U.S. Deaf culture (and there must be many!) is a social, communal, and creative force of, by, and for Deaf people based on American Sign Language (ASL). It encompasses communication, social protocol, art, entertainment, recreation (e.g., sports, travel, and Deaf clubs), and worship. It's also an attitude, and, as such, can be a weapon of prejudice— "You're not one of us; you don't belong."
>
> Despite the mighty efforts of generations of oralists, deaf people still prefer to communicate and mingle with their own kind. That is the psychosocial basis of Deaf culture. Deaf people in the United States have staunchly resisted the unstinting attempts of oralists to eradicate the use of sign language and assimilate them into the hearing mainstream. The simple fact is that deaf people who attend the common residential schools for the deaf—no matter what mode of communication is forced on them in the

classroom—tend to seek out other deaf people and communicate in sign language. This is true, to some extent, in other countries, but the U.S. arguably has the most sophisticated and creative—and public—Deaf culture of any. (http://www.deafculture.com/definitions/)

Thomas Holcomb (1997) argued that it is important to offer deaf children opportunities to develop a Deaf identity from a young age, so that they see themselves as bicultural in a diverse world (see A Closer Look, "Deaf Culture and History"). McIlroy and Storbeck (2011), in a more contemporary ethnographic study, write that deaf identity "is not a static concept but a complex ongoing quest for belonging, a quest that is bound up with the acceptance of being deaf while 'finding one's voice' in a hearing-dominant society" (p. 494). David Stewart and Thomas Kluwin (2001, p. 119) describe how a teacher can integrate Deaf studies into the curriculum, and describe the basic premises of the study of deaf people:

> Studying Deaf culture helps students who are deaf develop their own identities.

- Deaf people are individuals first.
- The thoughts of a deaf person are shaped by a unique set of experiences that occur inside and outside of the classroom.
- A variety of information about deaf people is available from a variety of resources.
- There are diverse perspectives about deaf people that are related to their use of communication, interactions with deaf and hearing people, cultural affiliation with different ethnic groups, social patterns, use of technology, educational experiences, participation in the workforce, and more.
- Studying about deaf people is an opportunity for gaining knowledge about and appreciation for these perspectives.
- Deaf studies is a means for helping deaf students discover their own identity.

See Teaching Strategies & Accommodations, "Themes in the Curriculum for Students Who Are Deaf" for more specific curriculum ideas for Deaf students.

Teaching Strategies & Accommodations

Themes in the Curriculum for Students Who Are Deaf

David Stewart and Thomas Kluwin (2001) believe that, because of lack of experiences and adequate opportunities for communication in their home environments, the curriculum for deaf students must reflect these themes:

- *Creating authentic experiences.* Teachers must engineer experiences for students that are directly tied to the teaching content.
- *Integrating vocabulary development.* Teachers must make words visible—write them, finger spell them, provide pictures to illustrate them when possible—and teach them as part of broader concepts and in meaningful contexts.

- *Creating opportunities for self-expression.* Deaf students need opportunities to practice elaborate verbal skills, as well as opportunities for defining and refining ideas.
- *Providing deaf role models.* Deaf role models let deaf students know "this is what you need to do to succeed." Actress Marlee Matlin, former Miss America Heather Whitestone, percussionist Evelyn Glennie, former Gallaudet University President I. King Jordan, and this chapter's "First Person" Claudia Gordon are just a few who might be studied.

Teaching Strategies and Accommodations

Students with hearing loss need the benefit of an interdisciplinary team of professionals who will cooperatively plan and implement their educational program, whether it is an Individualized Family Service Plan (IFSP) for the child from birth to age 3, an Individualized Education Program (IEP) for the school-aged child, or an Individualized Transition Plan (ITP) for the high-school student. First we will discuss the implementation of programming for the youngest children.

Early Identification and Intervention

The early diagnosis of hearing loss is essential so that intervention can begin.

Because hearing loss affects language development so directly, and the years from birth to age 3 are so critical for language, the early diagnosis of hearing loss is essential so that work with the family and language intervention with the child with hearing loss can begin.

As we wrote above, the national trend to provide newborn hearing screenings has lowered the age at which children with hearing loss are identified and begin intervention. There is hope that, ultimately, earlier intervention will improve the long-term outcomes for children who are deaf or hard of hearing (Joint Committee on Infant Hearing, 2000). Meinzen-Derr, Wiley, and Choo (2011) found that children enrolled in early intervention before 6 months of age were more likely to have age-appropriate language skills when they began services than children enrolled at or after 6 months, and maintained age-appropriate skills over time.

Newborn hearing screenings may eventually improve long-term outcomes for deaf children.

An early intervention program can serve many purposes for the family of a newly diagnosed child with hearing loss. Parents often need support from professionals in dealing with their reactions to the diagnosis of hearing loss; they also need information about the effects of hearing loss on language development. Families must make the important decision about how they will teach their child to communicate—will it be signs or speech? If signs are chosen, will it be American Sign Language (ASL) or manually coded English?

The early intervention professional will help the family continue to communicate naturally to the child about everyday experiences, sometimes with the addition of sign language. She will help the family and the child understand how hearing aids are used and what they can and cannot do. Children with hearing loss do not automatically know where a sound comes from the first time they hear it with their hearing aids; they must be taught the association, for example, between the noise they hear and the airplane flying overhead. The child, the family, and the teacher must collaborate to maximize every communication opportunity during the child's everyday routines and waking hours.

Developing Communication Skills

Most educators of children who are deaf or hard of hearing agree that early diagnosis, amplification, and intervention are of paramount importance for their students, but there is no such unanimity on the topic of how these children should be taught to communicate. Should speech alone be emphasized, or signs be added? How much emphasis should there be on the use of residual hearing? Which sign language system should be used? What should be the role of the native language of the student, be it Spanish, Russian, or ASL, in school learning? Before we attempt to grapple with these thorny issues, take a look at Table 11.5, which provides an overview of communication methods.

Most teachers of students who are deaf or hard of hearing have as their ultimate goal that their students become fluent, competent users of English. There is also increasing emphasis placed on the acquisition of fluency in ASL. Although

Table 11.5 Approaches to Communication Used with Students with Hearing Loss

Type	Name of Approach	Description
Oral English approaches	Auditory-oral	These programs teach children to make maximum use of their residual hearing through amplification (hearing aids or cochlear implants), to augment their residual hearing with speech (lip) reading, and to speak. This approach excludes the use of sign language.
	Auditory-verbal	The auditory/verbal approach is similar to the auditory/oral approach, except it does not encourage speech reading.
Simultaneous communication approaches	Manually Coded English (MCE) Signing Exact English (SEE II) Signed English	Visual representations of English. MCE systems are typically used in educational settings with children rather than in social interactions among deaf adults.
	Rochester method	Use of fingerspelling along with speech.
	Cued speech	A visual communication system combining eight handshapes (cues) that represent different sounds of speech. These cues are used simultaneously with speaking to aid in lip reading.
	Pidgin Signed English (PSE)	Use of ASL signs in English word order.
Dual-language approach	Bilingual (American Sign Language and English)	Supports development of ASL as a first language. ASL is a visual/gestural language with vocabulary, grammar, idioms, and syntax different from English that utilizes signs and facial/body grammar. English skills are developed as a second language through reading, writing, and spoken language specific to each child's potential and needs.
Total communication		A philosophy (rather than a specific method) that incorporates any of the above approaches based on what each child needs at any given time.

Sources: Laurent Clerc National Deaf Education Center. Communication Choices with Deaf and Hard of Hearing Children. http://clerccenter.gallaudet.edu/supportservices/series/4010.html; Alexander Graham Bell Association for the Deaf and Hard of Hearing. Communication Options. http://nc.agbell.org/page.aspx?pid=739/.; Ellen Schneiderman, Ph.D., California State University–Northridge.)

the most intensive language teaching will take place in early intervention programs and in special schools and classes, the general education teacher who works with the deaf or hard-of-hearing student will also play a role in introducing and expanding English vocabulary, structures, and use. Because of this emphasis, teachers of students with hearing loss must focus on learning techniques related to language development, assessment, and teaching.

Traditionally, programs for students who are deaf and hard of hearing have differed in their approach to teaching communication skills. Some have emphasized the development of speech and auditory skills, while others have encouraged the growth of signs along with those skills. Let us take a closer look at these philosophies, the oral approach and the manual approach.

● *Oral Approaches* **Oral communication approaches** are built on the belief that children who are deaf and hard of hearing can learn to talk and that speech should be their primary method of expression. Also, they should understand the speech of others through a combination of speech reading (lip reading) and residual hearing. The overall goal of oralism is that children with hearing loss learn intelligible speech and age-appropriate language. There are

Oral approaches are based on the belief that children with hearing loss can learn to speak.

A CLOSER LOOK Speech and Hearing Checklist

This checklist will help you to detect any hearing or speech problems in your child at a very young age. *Even if a hearing loss was not detected during your child's infant screening,* it is important to continually monitor speech and language development in order to identify a potential later loss as soon as possible.

Early detection is crucial because undetected hearing loss has a direct effect on the development of speech and language in young children. It is through the sense of hearing that infants begin to naturally learn their native language. If your child can't hear sounds or differences in sounds, then understanding words and speaking will be difficult. No child is too young to be tested or to be helped if a hearing loss is suspected. The earlier a child with hearing loss is identified, the less effect the loss will have on his/her speech development, social growth, learning ability, and classroom performance.

If your child fails to respond as the checklist for the appropriate age level suggests, have your child's hearing tested immediately. Don't delay! If your child does have a hearing loss, early detection means early solutions to hearing and speech problems through the help of medical intervention, education, and amplification. The earlier a hearing loss is identified, the less effect the loss will have on your child's future.

Average Speech and Hearing Behavior for Your Child's Age Level

Birth to 3 Months
Startled by loud sounds
Soothed by caretakers' voices

3 to 6 Months
Reacts to the sound of your voice
Turns eyes and head in the direction of the source of sounds
Enjoys rattles and noisy toys

7 to 10 Months
Responds to his/her own name
Understands *mama, dada, no, bye-bye,* and other common words
Turns head toward familiar sounds, even when he/she cannot see what is happening:

- Dog barking or paper rustling
- Familiar footsteps
- Telephone
- Person's voice

11 to 15 Months
Imitates and matches sounds with own speech production (though frequently unintelligible), especially in response to human voices or loud noises
Locates or points to familiar objects when asked
Understands words by making appropriate responses or behavior:

- "Where's the dog?"
- "Find the truck."

15 to 18 Months
Identifies things in response to questions, such as parts of the body
Uses a few single words; while not complete or perfectly pronounced, the words should be clearly meaningful
Follows simple spoken directions

several different oral methods, but all high-quality oral programs share common goals:

- The earliest possible detection of hearing loss
- Amplification, either with hearing aids or the cochlear implant, and intervention
- Intensive parent involvement in the child's education
- The use of residual hearing
- The exclusive use of speech, without sign language, for communication

Teaching speech and auditory skills is theoretically part of the educational program for the majority of children with hearing loss. Teaching speech is one of

2 Years

Understands yes/no questions

Uses everyday words heard at home or at daycare/school

Enjoys being read to and shown pictures in books; points out pictures upon request

Interested in radio/television as shown by word or action

Puts words together to make simple sentences—although they are not complete or grammatically correct:

- "Juice all gone"
- "Go bye-bye car"

Follows simple commands without visual clues from the speaker:

- "Bring me that ball."
- "Get your book and give it to Daddy."

2½ Years

Says or sings short rhymes and songs; enjoys music

Vocabulary approximately 270 words

Investigates noises or tells others when interesting sounds are heard:

- Car door slamming
- Telephone ringing

3 Years

Understands and uses simple verbs, pronouns, and adjectives:

- Go, come, run, sing
- Me, you, him, her
- Big, green, sweet

Locates the source of a sound automatically

Often uses complete sentences

Vocabulary approximately 1,000 words

4 Years

Gives connected account of some recent experiences

Can carry out a sequence of two simple directions:

- "Find your shoe and bring it here."
- "Get the ball and throw it to the dog."

5 Years

Speech should be intelligible, although some sounds may still be mispronounced—such as the /s/ sound, particularly in blends with other consonants (e.g., *street, sleep, ask*). Neighbors and people outside the family can understand most of what your child says and her grammatical patterns should match theirs most of the time.

Child carries on conversations, although vocabulary may be limited

Pronouns should be used correctly:

- *I* instead of *me*
- *He* instead of *him*

Don't Delay!

If your child does not exhibit the average behavior for his/her age, get professional advice from your doctor, your hospital, or a local speech and hearing clinic. No child is too young to be tested or to be helped if a hearing loss is suspected. Keep in mind that clapping hands or making loud noises behind a child's back are never accurate tests for hearing loss!

Source: Speech and Hearing Checklist. Washinton, D.C.: The Alexander Graham Bell Association for the Deaf and Hard of Hearing (AG Bell), 2007. Reprinted with permission from AG Bell (www.agbell.org).

the teacher's most complicated and challenging responsibilities, and doing it well takes considerable training and skill.

The teaching of listening skills, sometimes called **auditory training,** requires that the child be fitted with effective, appropriate hearing aids—preferably one in each ear. It begins with developing the child's awareness of all the sounds in the environment—doorbells ringing, dogs barking, people calling the child's name. The most important goal of training residual hearing, however, is to assist the child in understanding spoken language, and thereby support the development of oral language and speech (Cole & Flexer, 2011).

Auditory training itself does not enable the child to hear new sounds or words; it simply helps the child make sense of what is heard and use his or her

> Teaching speech takes training and skill.

residual hearing as well as possible. Attention to listening skills is important for the regular class teacher as well as the specialist, since there are safety issues involved for the student as well as language-learning issues. For example, attention to environmental sounds will help the student stay safe while riding a bike or crossing the street.

The increase in the number of children with cochlear implants has coincided with the rising popularity of **auditory-verbal therapy** (Estabrooks, 2006), which focuses on early identification of hearing loss, amplification, and the development of speaking skills through listening. "Parents and caregivers actively participate in therapy. Through guidance, coaching, and demonstration, parents become the primary facilitators of their child's spoken language development" (A.G. Bell, 2011). Some researchers (e.g. Dornan, Hickson, Murdoch, & Houston, 2009) maintain that children with hearing loss in these programs can make the same language progress as typically developing children; these findings should probably be interpreted with some caution, given the small numbers of subjects in the studies.

● *Manual Approaches*   The use of **manual communication approaches** by and with people who are deaf has a long history. According to Baker and Cokely (1980), "Wherever there were deaf people who needed to communicate there have been signed languages that they and their ancestors have developed" (p. 48). The first to systematize a sign language for teaching purposes was the Abbé de l'Epée, a French monk who started the first school for deaf children in Paris in 1755 (Armstrong, 2011).

Manual communication approaches have two components—fingerspelling and signs.

Manual communication has two components: **fingerspelling,** in which words are spelled out letter by letter using a manual alphabet (see Figure 11.4), and **signs,** which are symbolic representations of words made with the hands. Teaching Strategies & Accommodations, "Fingerspelling: Critical for Literacy Development," describes its importance.

Teaching Strategies & Accommodations

Fingerspelling: Critical for Literacy Development

Fingerspelling—representing the letters of the alphabet on the fingers—may be a critical bridge for deaf and hard-of-hearing children in learning English. Children should be exposed to fingerspelling on a regular basis. This exposure begins with the child's identification as deaf or hard of hearing. Infants and toddlers should be immersed in fingerspelling. They may not immediately understand the letters, but the exposure will prepare them for acquisition of reading and literacy.

Experts emphasize the importance of practice. It is important to make transitions between the letters of words as smoothly as possible. For example, do not fingerspell *CAT* as *C* pause *A* pause *T* pause. Instead, hold the wrist steady and practice until able to move easily between the letters *C-A-T*.

Two techniques—the sandwich technique and the chaining technique—are useful in reading to deaf children. In the sandwich technique, signs are "sandwiched" between fingerspellings. Individuals fingerspell the word or the phrase that appears in the book, then sign the word or phrase, then fingerspell it again (Blumenthal-Kelly, 1995; Humphries & MacDougall, 1997). In the chaining technique, the process is elongated. Individuals point to the word in the book, fingerspell it, sign it, then point to the printed word again.

Source: David R. Schleper (2000). "Fingerspelling: Critical for Literacy Development," *Odyssey*, 1 (3). Washington, DC: Laurent Clerc National Deaf Education Center, Gallaudet University. © by Laurent Clerc National Deaf Education Center. Reprinted with permission.

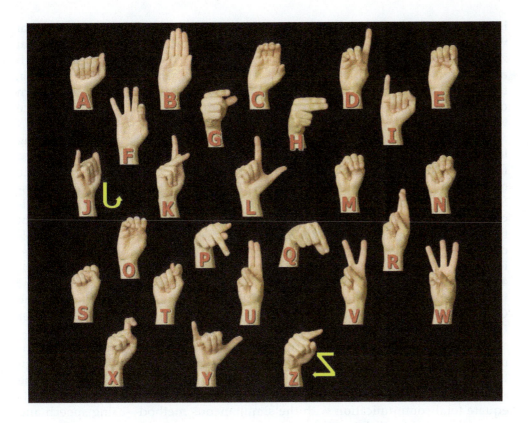

FIGURE 11.4

The manual alphabet

Source: Reprinted by permission of William Vicars.

The sign language considered by many deaf adults to be their "native language" is **American Sign Language (ASL).** ASL uses the same lexicon, or vocabulary, as English, but a different grammatical structure. Today, linguists consider ASL a legitimate language of its own, not simply a form of English (Stokoe, 1960). Because it does not correspond directly to English, and because there is no widely practiced method of writing in ASL, it has not traditionally been used as the primary language of instruction for children who are deaf. Instead, sign language systems that have been designed to represent English manually are generally used for educational purposes, since it is thought that their correspondence to reading and writing in English is closer. In these English-order systems, the intent is that every word and every inflection (for example, verb tense markers such as *-ed* and *-ing)* of English are signed.

> American Sign Language uses the same vocabulary as English but has a different grammatical structure.

● *Communication Controversies*   Since education of deaf children began in the sixteenth century, teachers have argued passionately about the best method of instruction. As Moores (2010) notes:

> These longstanding debates have not been resolved after two centuries, and represent different perceptions of deafness, the requirements for leading a full, rich life, and resultant educational and social goals (p. 17).

Advocates of the oral approach have maintained that teaching the child who is deaf to speak and to use residual hearing and speech reading to comprehend language provides the skills the individual needs to function both in the hearing world and in the community of deaf people. But teaching oral language and speech to a child who is profoundly deaf is an extremely difficult and laborious process.

The best results seem to occur when early diagnosis is combined with early amplification and early and consistent family involvement. Family involvement

> Children taught with the oral method do best when early diagnosis is combined with early amplification and family involvement.

is the key. Typically, a preschool-aged child who is deaf speaks only a handful of words. Therefore, the family's commitment to teaching the child to talk is crucial in an oral program, and parents must be willing to experience the slow growth of communication skills in their child. For children who are hard of hearing, the growth of oral skills proceeds significantly faster; they frequently can learn oral language in the general education classroom, with support from a resource teacher or a speech-language specialist.

However, for many children who are deaf—including those whose hearing loss is diagnosed after age 2, those with additional disabilities, or those whose families are unable to supply them with the complete support that they need—the oral approach is frequently not satisfactory. During the 1960s and 1970s, dissatisfaction with the oral approach grew, and school programs using total communication (English-order signs and speech) proliferated. By 2002, about 53 percent of the students included in the Annual Survey of Deaf and Hard of Hearing Children and Youth attended schools in which some form of sign was used (Gallaudet Research Institute, 2003); in the latest survey, that percentage was down to about 46.3 (Gallaudet Research Institute, 2008). Today, with the advent of the cochlear implant, interest in oral methods is reviving; about 52 percent of students in the Gallaudet survey went to schools in which speech alone was used. (See A Closer Look, "The Cochlear Implant Controversy.")

Total communication was designed to use any and all methods of communicating with students who are deaf—speech, fingerspelling, English-order sign language, American Sign Language—depending on the learning needs of the student at the moment (Garretson, 1976). In practice, however, most professionals equate total communication with the simultaneous method—using speech and manually coded English together.

Today, the controversies in the field revolve not so much around whether speech or sign should be used but on which form of sign should be used in the classroom. Proponents of viewing Deafness as a cultural difference rather than as a disability believe that American Sign Language should be the first language of all children who are deaf and that therefore it should be the first language taught in schools (Drasgow, 1998), advocating what has been called a **bilingual-bicultural approach**. These professionals, both deaf and hearing, use theories of first- and second-language acquisition of spoken language to support their

> Many in the Deaf community believe that ASL should be the first language of all children who are deaf.

Effective signed communication involves both the sign and facial expression, the punctuation of sign language.

© Ellen Senisi/The Image Works

argument that once fluency in the first language is acquired, second-language learning can and will follow (Drasgow, 1998). They propose teaching ASL first and then, when children have a solid ASL base, introducing English as a second language. Others object to this model, suggesting that because there is no widely accepted written form of ASL, reading and writing skills in English will be introduced too late. Also, because ASL is used without speech, young children may not be given the opportunity to develop speech skills through listening and observation. Donald Moores (2008) expressed regrets that the enthusiasm for the bilingual-bicultural approach has not been followed by rigorous research demonstrating its effectiveness, and called for studies to be conducted and published.

Only research, study, and the introduction of model programs will demonstrate whether teaching ASL as a first language in a bilingual program will ultimately succeed in improving the English literacy of children who are deaf, and in the process make them fluent ASL users who are comfortable in their own culture as well as in the "hearing world."

Researchers at the National Technical Institute for the Deaf, a college of the Rochester Institute of Technology, conducted a study of a group of deaf college students who were strong readers and writers (Toscano, McGee, & Lepoutre, 2002). The students used a variety of communication methods, including speech, sign language (ASL and manually coded English systems), cued speech, total communication, and fingerspelling; they had attended oral and sign language programs. These students described ongoing, committed involvement of parents in their schooling, particularly in the areas of reading and writing; their mothers were often the ones who taught them to read. Their families—not just their mothers, but fathers, siblings, and sometimes grandparents—went to great efforts to learn to communicate with them, and to ensure that the deaf children were included in all family conversations. The researchers concluded:

> While communication may or may not have been easy, students were unanimous in their perception of positive support within the family unit. The development of strong reading and writing skills, therefore, cannot be said to be the result of the consistent use of a single communication method. (Toscano, McGee, & Lepoutre, 2002, p. 14)

No matter what the communication method, then, the ongoing involvement and support of families in communication and academic achievement appear to be what made the difference for these students: "the mode of communication is less important than the quality of communication" (Toscano, McGee, & Lepoutre, 2002, p. 21). Unfortunately, about 71 percent of parents of children who use sign language do not use sign regularly at home (Gallaudet Research Institute, 2008).

As we mentioned earlier in the chapter, in addition to the study of communication and the content areas, many professionals advocate for the study of Deaf culture in the school curriculum. There is hope that an understanding of the history and heritage of people who are deaf will help students appreciate their cultural heritage. See Teaching Strategies & Accommodations, "Integrating Deaf Studies into the Curriculum," for additional information.

Today, the focus of the curriculum for most deaf students is in the area of literacy. The skills involved in learning to read and write and the application of those skills in life have not traditionally come easily to deaf students, and teachers and researchers are working to address the best ways for deaf students to acquire literacy skills.

Stewart and Kluwin apply their "themes" (in the Teaching Strategies box on page 400) to the teaching of literacy:

> The strategies that we described for teaching literacy are similar to those for teaching other subject matter to deaf students. Authentic activities must be incorporated into the learning experience, the students must be provided

Teachers and researchers alike are focusing on improving the literacy of deaf children.

A CLOSER LOOK   The Cochlear Implant

A cochlear implant—"one of the twentieth century's most consequential developments in communication" (Niparko, 2000, p. 1)—is an electronic device designed to provide sound information for adults and children who have sensorineural hearing loss in both ears and obtain limited benefit from hearing aids. In the last thirty years, the technology has evolved from a device with a single electrode (or channel) to systems that transmit more sound information through multiple electrodes (or channels). The cochlear implant has been approved for use with children since 1990. A small but growing number of children with deafness are currently using cochlear implants; the annual survey done by the Gallaudet Research Institute reported 13.7 percent of students in surveyed programs had cochlear implants, 15.4 of those students had a second cochlear implant (presumably in the other ear), and 92.4 percent of those implants were still in use (Gallaudet Research Institute, 2008). Because the implant is expensive and not routinely covered by medical insurance, some are concerned that it is only available to relatively affluent families.

Advocates such as Dr. Mary Jo Osberger, a researcher who has studied children with cochlear implants, assert that they can help children who do not benefit from hearing aids develop speech and language understanding and skills. She says that "no other sensory aid has had such a dramatic impact on improving the acquisition and use of spoken language by children with profound hearing impairments." Advocates argue that the earlier the children receive implants, the greater their chances of improvement.

Recent research suggests that the benefits of the cochlear implant vary greatly among individuals,

© Brian Mitchell/Corbis

but in general, children with cochlear implants surpass children who wear conventional hearing aids in speech perception, speech production, and speech intelligibility (Cheng & Niparko, 2000; Kirk, 2000). The best outcomes appear in children who receive their implants early in life, who undergo a period of intensive training after the implant, and who have had the implant for at least two years.

with opportunities to talk about what they are reading and writing, and modeling and guidance must be provided to help them overcome their lack of proficiency in the English language. (p. 109)

Assessment

Undertaking an educational assessment with a student who is deaf or hard of hearing is a difficult endeavor, because the typical student's English language competency is often significantly delayed for his or her age (Mitchell &

The Controversy

However, the implant has been called "cultural genocide" by many in the Deaf community who believe American Sign Language is the linguistic base for a separate culture. Their response is built on a legacy of failed attempts to teach deaf children oral communication—in their view, to be more like hearing children.

To many, the argument implies that deaf children belong to the Deaf community and not to their hearing parents, a view to which people like Donna Morere take exception. "There is a large segment within the community that identifies with Deaf culture and feels like hearing parents are not competent to make a decision like choosing a cochlear implant for their children," she says.

Morere is in a unique position to see both sides of the debate. As a psychology professor at Gallaudet University—the only liberal arts college for the deaf in the United States—she has taught at the heart of the Deaf culture movement. Morere has normal hearing, but when her son Thomas was diagnosed as profoundly deaf, she was suddenly faced not with the abstract arguments of ethicists and anthropologists, but with the hard reality that her child could not hear. Initially, Morere says, she was persuaded by some of her colleagues at Gallaudet who cautioned her against opting for a cochlear implant. Her eventual decision to go ahead with the procedure is one she now says she wished she'd made earlier. "When I saw what the CI could do, I really regretted the little over a year that he didn't have it," she says. "I'm so relieved when Thomas can ride his bicycle in the street with other kids and instead of having to run after him and drag him off the street when a car comes, I can yell 'Car!' and he will ride his bike off the street," Morere says. "If that was all the cochlear implant accomplished, that would have satisfied me, but it's gone way beyond that."

The National Association of the Deaf (NAD) is an education and advocacy group that has long worked on behalf of deaf individuals. In its position statement on cochlear implants, the NAD has provided a measured (but still passionate) view of the potential drawbacks and benefits of the implant. The paper's authors describe the importance of viewing people who are deaf according to a "wellness model," emphasizing the large number of deaf adults who live productive lives; they believe that "cochlear implants are not appropriate for all deaf and hard-of-hearing children and adults" (p. 2) and that they do not eliminate or "cure" deafness. The recommendations to parents are sound:

> Despite the pathological view of deafness held by many within the medical profession, parents would benefit by seeking out opportunities to meet and get to know successful deaf and hard-of-hearing children and adults who are fluent in sign language and English, both with and without implants. The NAD encourages parents and deaf adults to research other options besides implantation. If implantation is the object of choice, parents should obtain all information about the surgical procedure, surgical risks, postsurgical auditory and speech training requirements, and potential benefits and limitations so as to make informed decisions. (pp. 3–4)

Local branches of the NAD would be a good place for families to start looking for such models.

Sources: Adapted from M.J. Osberger & H. Lane (1993). The debate: Cochlear implants in children. *Hearing Health,* 9 (2), 19–22. The NAD Position Statement on Cochlear Implants is available at http://www.nad.org/issues/technology/assistive-listening/cochlear-implants/.)

Karchmer, 2011). As a result, each test, with directions and questions written (or spoken) in English, becomes a test not of its content but of the student's mastery of English. When a student does not do well on a test, it is often because he or she does not understand the language of the directions or the test items. Rephrasing or paraphrasing the language makes the test standardization invalid, so the results cannot be used comparatively (Salvia, Ysseldyke, & Bolt, 2009). Although it is possible to work around these complicating factors, it takes skill and considerable experience in communication to obtain valid educational assessment results with students with hearing loss, particularly those who are deaf.

Many tests are not reliable or valid for use with test takers who are deaf.

Teaching Strategies & Accommodations

Integrating Deaf Studies into the Curriculum

Grade Level	Content Area Topics	Deaf Culture Components
Kindergarten	Science/Social Studies: sound awareness and Deaf awareness	Basics for interacting with Deaf people
First grade	Social Studies: family life of the Deaf	Deafness and communication
Second grade	Social Studies: Deaf people in the community	Sensitivity activities, ASL as a language
Third grade	Sound, hearing measurement, and amplification	Deaf vs. hard of hearing, social interaction norms
Fourth grade	Reading: biography and history of Deaf people	Deaf history, Deaf identity, interview Deaf adult
Fifth grade	Health: hearing and deafness	Deaf community, organizations, and recreation
Sixth grade	Science: communication and assistive devices for the Deaf	Deafness and literature, Deaf values

Source: D. A. Stewart & T. N. Kluwin (2001). *Teaching Deaf and Hard of Hearing Students: Content, Strategies, and Curriculum,* p. 118. Boston: Allyn and Bacon. Copyright © 2001 by Pearson Education. Reprinted by permission of the publisher.

School Placement

Deaf and hard-of-hearing students can be found in every educational setting.

Although the majority of students with hearing loss spend all or part of their day in the general education classroom, students who are deaf and hard of hearing can be found in a wide variety of educational settings, from the general education classroom to the residential school. According to the Gallaudet Research Institute (2003), about 60 percent of the children with hearing loss were placed in the general education classroom (see Figure 11.5). According to the GAO report (2011), based on U.S. Department of Education numbers, just 8 percent attended special schools, 53 percent spent more than 80 percent of their day in general education, and 17 percent spent more than 40 percent of their day in general education.

Let us discuss the most frequent placements.

● *The General Education Classroom*   More and more deaf or hard-of-hearing students are included in the general education classroom. From that classroom base they may receive a variety of specialized services and supports. Their classroom amplification devices, whether they be personal hearing aids, cochlear implants, or classroom hearing aids connected to a teacher microphone, may be evaluated regularly by the school audiologist; they may receive direct services in speech, signs, or the development of auditory skills from the itinerant teacher with a specialization in hearing loss or from the speech-language therapist; perhaps they receive extra help with communication skills or academic subjects from the resource teacher, who is also a specialist in hearing loss. Students who participate in school programs with their hearing peers are likely to have more residual hearing than those who do not (Gallaudet Research Institute, 2002); they are also likely to have better communication skills.

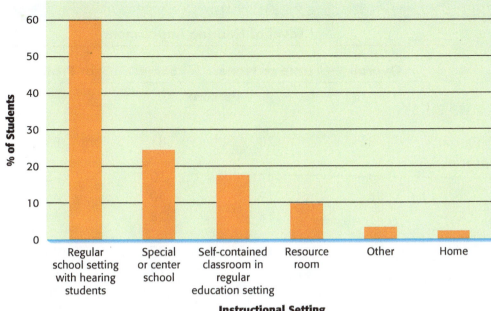

FIGURE 11.5

Educational settings for students with hearing impairments

Source: U. S. Department of Education, 2011

In the Shaver et al. (2011) study, the most common accommodations for secondary students in general education were more time on tests, additional time to complete assignments, having a test read to a student, slower paced instruction, and modified tests. Table 11.6 shows the learning supports used by those secondary students.

Some students with hearing loss will be integrated in the general education classroom with a sign language interpreter (see A Closer Look, "The Interpreter"); others will rely on their speech-reading skills and residual hearing to gain information in the classroom. Most integrated students will need preferential seating so they are close enough to the teacher or other speaker to speech read. Remember that in a noisy setting, students with hearing loss must rely heavily on vision to obtain information; often if they are not looking at the source of the sound, they are not "hearing" it or getting the information. Teaching Strategies & Accommodations,

A CLOSER LOOK   The Interpreter

Interpreters provide an essential service to both students and teachers in classrooms. Oral interpreters silently repeat, with clear but unexaggerated lip movements, the message of another speaker. Sign language interpreters translate the spoken message into signs and fingerspelling.

Leah Ilan is an interpreter in Los Angeles who has a busy career as both an oral and sign language interpreter. Leah believes that the most important factors in the relationship between the classroom teacher and the interpreter are communication and trust, and that the better the interpreter knows the teacher, the better work she does. Leah finds oral interpreting

somewhat more difficult than sign interpreting. She describes the job as "sounding out every single sound and making it visible—with the mouth, jaw, eyes, and facial expression. I use it all." Leah finds the need for concentration greater with oral interpreting, since the oral "consumer"—the person with hearing loss—relies on small parts of speech and word endings for comprehension. She hastens to add that sign interpreting is not easy; in fact, the preference now is that sign interpreters work in teams of two on long assignments. This allows sign interpreters periods of rest and avoids the appearance of hand and arm injuries such as carpal tunnel syndrome, which can limit or end their careers.

Table 11.6 Learning Supports

	Level of Hearing Impairment			
	Overall	Little or None	Some	Substantial or Profound
	Percent			
Students were provided				
At least one type of learning support	73	70	81	83
Monitoring of progress by special education teacher	43	44	50	35
Reader or interpreter	34	19	30	45
More frequent feedback	27	14	28	34
Learning strategies/study skills assistance	25	17	27	28
Tutoring by an adult	18	9	19	23
Self-advocacy training	17	11	13	24
Teacher aide, instructional assistant, or other personal aide	14	12	12	17
Peer tutor	12	10	14	12

Note: Percentages are population estimates based on weighted samples that range from approximately 460 to 480 youth across variables.

Source: U.S. Department of Education, Institute of Education Sciences, National Center for Special Education Research, National Longitudinal Transition Study-2 (NLTS2), Wave 1 student's school program survey, 2002.

"Communication Tips for Deaf and Hard-of-Hearing Children in the Classroom," outlines some approaches designed to eliminate classroom problems.

● *Special Classes*   A special class is composed of a group of students who are deaf and hard of hearing of similar age who are taught on an elementary, middle-school, or high-school campus by a specialist teacher of deaf and hard-of-hearing students. Some students with hearing loss attend special classes on public school campuses, because this placement provides a home base for integrating these students with their hearing peers.

Some students in the special class are integrated with their hearing peers for academic subjects, and others for subjects such as art, music, or physical education; still others may have contact with their hearing peers only at recess and lunch. The amount of time each student spends with hearing peers is specified on his or her Individualized Education Program (IEP). Although characteristics of the student are obviously of prime importance in the decision whether or not to integrate, the availability of willing and competent general education teachers to work with the students with hearing loss is often what makes or breaks the opportunity for the student.

The nature of residential schools has changed dramatically since 1975, when IDEA mandated education in the least restrictive environment.

● *Residential Schools*   The deinstitutionalization movement (see Chapter 1) has had an important influence on the education of children who are deaf. Thirty years ago, most children with hearing loss attended large residential schools, either as day students or as residents. These schools hold a special place in the heart of the Deaf community. Many people who were deaf had left their homes to live at residential schools when they were very young; they learned to communicate there, made their lifelong friends there, met their spouses there, and settled in the surrounding area. They were anxious that their own deaf children attend these schools too.

Teaching Strategies & Accommodations

Communication Tips for Deaf and Hard-of-Hearing Children in the Classroom

Classrooms often move at a fast pace. Making sure that the deaf or hard-of-hearing child has access to everything that is going on will be of the utmost importance. Here are some considerations that may help facilitate communication in the classroom. Many of these strategies, which make the classroom a more visual environment, will be helpful for all children in the classroom.

For all deaf or hard-of-hearing students

- The student should have a clear view of the faces of the teacher and the other students.
- Do not seat the student facing bright lights or windows where a glare or strong backlighting will make it difficult to see the faces of others.
- Remember that the best place for a deaf or hard-of-hearing student may change with the teaching situation. Make sure the student feels free to move about the room for ease of communication.

For students depending on spoken language communication

- When possible, seat the student close to the teacher's desk for the best listening and viewing advantage.
- Familiarize yourself with how to check a child's hearing aid.
- Do not exaggerate mouth movements or shout; this may cause distortion of the message through the hearing aid and greater difficulty for the student.
- If communication breakdowns occur, try repair strategies such as rephrasing the message, saying it at a slower pace, or writing the message when appropriate.

For students depending on visual communication

- Try to remove "visual noise" (visual interference) from communication situations (e.g., bottle on table, door open, paper in hand while signing, jewelry of signer, overhead projector in the way).
- When a sign language interpreter is being used in the classroom, make sure the interpreter has an opportunity to complete the message before moving on to the next point.

Facilitating classroom discussions

- When possible, have students sit in a circle.
- Remind students to speak one at a time.
- Point to the student who will speak next. Wait for the deaf or hard-of-hearing student to locate the speaker.

Methods that will help deaf or hard-of-hearing students

- DO use as many visual aids as possible. Use written instructions and summaries, and write key words and concepts on the blackboard. Utilize captioned films when possible.
- DO use attention-getting techniques when they are needed: Touch the student lightly on the shoulder, wave your hands, or flash the lights in the classroom.
- DO set up a buddy system to help deaf or hard-of-hearing students with taking notes, clarifying assignments, etc.
- DO ask questions and spend individual time with deaf or hard-of-hearing students periodically to make sure they are following the instructions.

Don'ts to keep in mind

- DON'T change the topic of conversation quickly without letting the deaf or hard-of-hearing students know that the topic has changed.
- DON'T talk with your back to the class, your face obstructed by a book, or with a pencil in your mouth.
- DON'T call attention to misunderstandings or speech errors in front of the class. If this becomes a problem, discuss it with the child's family or other support personnel who may be working with the child.

Source: Material developed by Debra Nussbaum, audiologist, Kendall Demonstration Elementary School, Laurent Clerc National Deaf Education Center, Gallaudet University, Support Services Handout, Series Number 4009. © by Laurent Clerc National Deaf Education Center. Reprinted with permission.

The concept of the "least restrictive environment" in IDEA has mandated a less segregated school setting for most children who are deaf, and the nature of residential schools has changed dramatically since the law was signed by President Gerald Ford in 1975, much to the dismay of many members of the Deaf community. Student enrollment has declined notably (Gallaudet Research Institute, 2008). Some of the schools have closed; many of them have become centers for students who are deaf with multiple disabilities; most have become day schools.

With a wider range of program options available in public schools, some professionals, often from outside the field of deafness, have seen very little justification for the removal of a child from his or her family in order to attend school. Nonetheless, many members of the Deaf community and professionals in the field of deafness continue to fight for the right to choose a residential school for a child who is deaf. The schools are sometimes seen as the birthplace of Deaf culture in this country, places where students who are deaf can develop their own positive identities rather than being forced to accept the values and norms of the hearing world.

> *Historically, residential schools have been the birthplace of Deaf culture in the United States.*

? Pause and Reflect

There are so many specific instructional issues for students with hearing loss that it's a wonder so many of them are integrated into general education. After your reading, do you feel any better prepared to tackle the challenge of teaching a student who is deaf or hard of hearing? Why or why not? •

Technological Advances

As you will learn in the section below, modern hearing aids are much more efficient and compact than their predecessors.

Hearing Aids

Hearing aids today are considerably more efficient than the hearing aids of old. They have been reduced in size, so they are more appealing cosmetically, and the majority of children are now fitted with behind-the-ear aids. More important, their capabilities have improved, and they can be designed to match each individual's hearing loss. Most children can benefit from wearing two hearing aids. New designs in hearing aids include those that have been miniaturized to the point that they fit completely in the ear. Although these tiny and lightweight in-the-ear hearing aids are just beginning to be recommended for young children or profoundly deaf users, they are prescribed more frequently for adolescents and adults, who often have great concerns about the visibility of their hearing aids.

> *Digital hearing aids can be customized for each person's hearing loss.*

In recent years, hearing aid technology has changed and improved dramatically. Most of today's hearing aids are digitally programmable or fully digital—they can be programmed by computer and customized to match an individual's hearing loss and characteristics of the environment. The traditional analog hearing aid amplifies all sounds to the same volume. That means that in the classroom, for example, the teacher's voice, children talking, and the sounds of the hallway outside would be heard at a similar volume. Digitally programmed hearing aids can improve the wearer's ability to hear in the presence of background noise, and can be set to work differently in different listening environments.

ASSISTIVE TECHNOLOGY FOCUS

Technology Can Eliminate Communication Barriers

Many of the advances in services and opportunities for people who are deaf have occurred in the area of technology. Improved hearing aids, cell phones, telecommunication devices and relay systems, and television captioning have made life more convenient and everyday experiences more accessible for many people with hearing loss.

For many years in telecommunications, the process of two people communicating over a distance was the same for everyone. You used a device called a telephone with a receiver for listening and a microphone for speaking. Your telephone was connected to a telephone line leading to a single telephone network, as was the telephone of the person you called. Communication took place exclusively by voice, without benefit of visual information, and was either inaccessible or "accessible with great difficulty" to individuals with hearing loss.

However, over the last fifteen years there has been a real paradigm shift in how people use telecommunications. Many of the new protocols such as social networking sites and text messaging are mainstream and popular, and afford individuals with hearing loss the benefit of visual information either as a supplement to or replacement for voice communication.

Individuals with hearing loss now have a variety of ways to accomplish their home and business telecommuting needs:

- Auditory systems that enhance the traditional voice phone, known as *assistive telephone technology*
- Auditory plus visual systems such as *Internet videoconferencing*
- *TTYs* and computers with TTY software
- *Email* and *instant messaging*
- The *Telecommunications Relay Service* (TRS), which provides a protocol for a hearing person with a voice telephone and a TTY user to communicate via a regular telephone line
- *Video relay service* that allows for sign language interpretation, rather than typing on a TTY, for relaying the speech of the hearing party

Source: Adapted from L. Kozma-Spytek, *Accessing the World of Telecommunications*, http://www.audiologyonline.com/articles/article_detail.asp?article_id=345/.

Not all children need digital hearing aids, and they are considerably more expensive than analog aids. Families must discuss the pros and cons of this expense with their audiologist before committing to digital hearing aids. It is likely that the appearance and the functioning of hearing aids will continue to improve through the refinement of digital-based technology.

Cochlear Implants

Physicians in large medical centers around the country have been surgically inserting **cochlear implants** in a growing number of profoundly deaf children with sensorineural hearing loss (See the A Closer Look box about Cochlear Implants earlier in this chapter.). A cochlear implant involves a major operation in which surgeons drill through the thick temporal bone (put your hand behind your ear to feel it) of the skull to implant an electrode array in the cochlea. There are both external and internal parts of the implant, which you can see in Figure 11.6. The surgery carries with it the risks attached to any major procedure which involves a general anesthetic. It is likely that the device will have to be replaced at least once during a person's lifetime. Figure 11.6 illustrates how the cochlear implant works when it is implanted.

It's important to note that the cochlear implant does not restore normal hearing. Unlike the hearing aid, the implant does not amplify sound; instead it bypasses

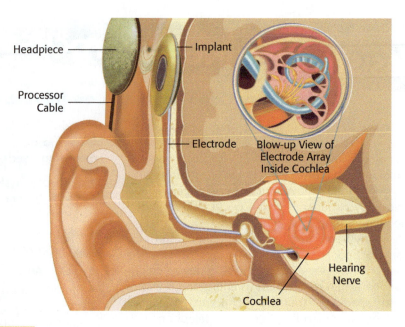

FIGURE 11.6

An illustration of a surgically implanted cochlear implant

Source: Reprinted by permission of Advanced Bionics.

damaged parts of the ear and directly stimulates the auditory nerve (National Institute on Deafness and Other Communication Disorders, 2011). It translates sound into electrical energy which is then (like natural sound waves) transmitted by the auditory nerve to the brain. A friend who is implanted in one ear describes the sound she hears as "mechanical," and quite different from the "natural" amplified sound she hears when wearing her hearing aid in her better ear.

It takes at least a year of intensive rehabilitation for the person who has been implanted to learn to recognize and use the sounds she/he hears.

Here is how the House Ear Institute in Los Angeles describes how the cochlear implant works:

> Regardless of manufacturer or model, all cochlear implants have the same basic features: a microphone picks up sound and converts it to an electrical signal, which is transmitted to a speech processor worn either behind the ear or on the body. The processor encodes the signal in a manner that is specific to the particular implant, and the encoded signal is relayed to a transmitting coil held in place on the side of the head, usually by means of a magnet. The signal is sent across the skin via a radio frequency to the receiver which has been surgically implanted under the skin above and behind the ear. The receiver decodes the signal and relays the information to electrodes that have been placed in the cochlea. The electrodes stimulate structures connecting to the auditory nerve and thus the system provides improved access to sound. (Source: House Research Institute, Los Angeles, CA. http://www.hei.org/care/services/devices/cochlear%20implants.html)

The cochlear implant has deepened schisms between "auditory/oral" deaf people and their teachers, audiologists, and physicians, and members of the Deaf community who consider themselves Deaf and not disabled. Reading the literature emanating from experts in each group makes it difficult to believe that they

This classroom at Gallaudet University is designed so that all students can see and be seen by the instructor.

are talking about the same thing. The Closer Look box on pages 398–399 provides more information on the controversies.

Despite the objections of the Deaf community, the number of children being implanted is increasing each year. These children are more likely to be included in general education, use speech as their preferred mode of communication, and have higher socioeconomic status (Yoshinaga-Itano, 2006).

Assistive Listening Devices

Although a hearing aid makes all sounds in the environment louder, assistive listening devices increase the loudness of a desired sound—the teacher's voice, the actors on a stage, or the voice on the telephone. There are different types of assistive listening devices for different settings: Some are used with hearing aids and cochlear implants, and some without. They can be used in classrooms, in theaters, at meetings—wherever they are needed. An audiologist can help a teacher or an individual determine which assistive listening device will be most helpful (American Speech-Language-Hearing Association, n.d.).

Telecommunication Devices

Telecommunication devices for the deaf (TDDs) are telephones with small screens that display the message of the sender. The system works like this: One person dials the number of a friend. The phone rings, and a light flashes in the home of the person receiving the call. When the receiver is picked up and placed in the cradle of the TDD, the two people can begin to type their communication into the TDD. The messages appear on paper, or, in the newest models, on a tiny screen on the TDD. Many agencies and businesses now routinely train their employees to use the TDD; they are used for business as well as social calls.

The primary advantage of TDDs today are that they allow deaf people to utilize the relay system authorized by the Americans with Disabilities Act; a hearing operator reads the TDD screen and speaks the message to someone without a TDD at the other end of the connection (used, for example, when a deaf person must make

Today most people with hearing loss use text-messaging and TDDs to comminucate over distances.

an appointment). Many people with hearing loss now prefer text messaging—real-time conversation via the cell phone screen—to TDDs. Even better are internet telephone services such as Skype, which enable live transmission of sign-language communication. Deaf people have enjoyed and utilized new technologies (Lartz, Stoner, & Stout, 2008) as quickly as they have been invented; by the time you read this, there is likely to be a new way to communicate that they will have adopted.

Captioning

Television captioning for viewers with hearing loss began as a system of open captioning in which captions that paralleled the verbal content of the television program appeared on the bottom of every viewer's screen. Today, though, a system called **closed captioning** exists. Viewers with hearing loss can buy a decoder that, when connected to their television set, allows them to receive broadcasts carrying a coded signal that the decoder makes visible. Since July 1, 1993, all TV sets thirteen inches or larger that are sold or built in the United States have been caption-chip-equipped, allowing viewers to select captioning of all available programs. Captioning is also available at selected movie theaters and live performance events. The Described and Captioned Media Center (visit its website), a joint effort of the U.S. Department of Education and the National Association of the Deaf, is a good place to start looking for captioned materials. As the population ages and hearing loss in the aging population becomes more common, there will likely be increased demand for these services.

> Closed captioning allows viewers with hearing loss to receive captions that parallel the verbal content of many TV programs.

> Captioning is also available in selected movie theaters and live performances.

SUMMARY

- Deafness is hearing loss that prevents the learning of language through hearing. Conductive hearing loss results from damage to the outer or middle ear and can usually be corrected. Sensorineural loss involves damage to the cochlea or auditory nerve and cannot be fully corrected.

- The most common cause of conductive hearing loss in children is chronic otitis media, or ear infection. Conductive hearing loss is treatable and usually temporary.

- The most common causes of sensorineural hearing loss are inherited genetic factors, rubella, meningitis, and premature birth. Sensorineural hearing loss is almost always permanent.

- Approximately 40 percent of children with hearing loss have additional disabilities.

- Hearing loss is measured by an audiologist using a series of tests, including pure-tone tests. The results of these tests are illustrated by an audiogram.

- Newborn Hearing Screening has lowered the age of identification of hearing loss, allowing for earlier intervention.

- Language is the most critical area affected by hearing loss.

- The cognitive abilities of students who are deaf and hard of hearing as a group are the same as those of hearing individuals. Despite this, students with hearing loss frequently underachieve in school because of the heavy emphasis on English language skills.

- The Deaf community views deafness as a culture rather than a deficit and urges that understanding of Deaf culture be integrated into the curriculum for students.

- Manual communication includes fingerspelling and signs. American Sign Language (ASL) is considered a language of its own and does not correspond directly to English. Total communication uses oral, auditory, and manual modes of communication and advocates adopting whatever system seems most appropriate for a child at a given time.

- Many students with hearing loss attend general education classes and use amplification devices, special services provided by an audiologist or itinerant teacher, or an oral or sign language interpreter.

- Greater numbers of young children with profound sensorineural deafness are receiving cochlear implants, which enable them to detect sounds more effectively, although not to "hear."

- Hearing aids and telecommunication devices have greatly improved in recent years, and technological advances continue to provide opportunities for people with hearing loss to communicate freely across long distances.

KEY TERMS

deafness (page 373)

hard of hearing (page 373)

hearing impairment (page 373)

Deaf community (page 373)

hearing loss (page 373)

congenital hearing loss (page 373)

acquired hearing loss (page 373)

prelingual deafness (page 373)

postlingual deafness (page 373)

bilateral hearing loss (page 373)

unilateral hearing loss (page 373)

conductive hearing loss (page 374)

sensorineural hearing loss (page 374)

mixed hearing loss (page 374)

residual hearing (page 375)

otitis media (page 375)

otologist (page 379)

audiologist (page 379)

audiogram (page 379)

Deaf culture (page 388)

oral communication approaches (page 391)

auditory training (page 393)

auditory-verbal therapy (page 396)

manual communication approaches (page 394)

fingerspelling (page 394)

signs (page 394)

American Sign Language (ASL) (page 395)

total communication (page 396)

bilingual-bicultural approach (page 396)

cochlear implants (page 405)

Telecommunication devices for the deaf (TDDs) (page 407)

closed captioning (page 408)

USEFUL RESOURCES

- *Hands & Voices* is a parent-driven, nonprofit organization dedicated to providing unbiased support to families with children who are deaf or hard of hearing (that is, no bias toward one form of communication). They provide support activities and information concerning deaf and hard-of-hearing issues to parents and professionals. Access their website at **http://www .handsandvoices.org.** In the *Products* section of Hands & Voices you can order the video *A is for Access: Creating Full & Effective Communication Access for Students Who Are Deaf or Hard of Hearing.*

- Marc Marschark has written a well-regarded book for families and teachers titled *Raising and Educating a Deaf Child: A Comprehensive Guide to the Choices, Controversies, and Decisions Faced by Parents and Educators,* (2nd ed.), 2009. It's available through Oxford University Press.

- The Alexander Graham Bell Association for the Deaf website has an excellent section for parents; look especially for *My Child Has a Hearing Loss*. It's an excellent introduction to hearing loss for teachers as well. There is also a good list of organizations and associations on the site, located at **http://nc.agbell.org/.**

- Gallaudet University Press (at **http://gupress.gallaudet.edu**) publishes a range of books of interest to deaf and hearing readers; many are about sign language. There is also an extensive collection of books for children that incorporate sign language.

- It's a Noisy Planet is a website developed by the National Institute on Deafness and other Communication Disorders (NIDCD) to help families and kids understand the causes of noise-induced hearing loss. Visit at **http://www.noisyplanet.nidcd.nih.gov/.**

- Raising Deaf Kids is another terrific website from NIDCD. Find it at **http://www.raisingdeafkids.org/.**

- *Handspeak* is a sign language dictionary online that contains video illustrations of over 3,000 signs (go to **http://www.handspeak.com**). Another excellent source for ASL vocabulary is the American Sign Language Browser at **http://www.commtechlab.msu.edu/sites/aslweb/.**

- Information on open-captioned movie locations is available through Captionfish at **http://www.captionfish.com/.** Live performance captioning is identified at c2 (the Caption Coalition) at **http://c2net.org.**

- The National Deaf Education Network and Clearinghouse (**http://www.gallaudet.edu/x17217.xml**) has a service call*ed Info to Go* that is an excellent source of additional information on deafness. *Info to Go* responds to a wide range of questions received from the general public, deaf and hard-of-hearing people, their families, and professionals who work with them.

- Read Carol Padden and Tom Humphries (1988). *Deaf in America: Voices from a Culture.* Cambridge, MA: Harvard University Press. This book, now a classic, focuses on the stories of people who are deaf and offers intriguing insights into those who share the culture of American Sign Language. Padden and Humphries' more recent book, *Inside Deaf Culture*, was published in 2005 by Harvard University Press.

- The field of Deaf studies has blossomed over the last thirty years. One example of a collection of writing on Deaf topics is *Open Your Eyes: Deaf Studies Talking*, edited by H-Dirkson L. Bauman. It was published by the University of Minnesota Press in 2008.

 PORTFOLIO ACTIVITIES

1. Explore Deaf culture and interact with deaf individuals:

- Contact an adult service agency to find a Deaf adult who would agree to being interviewed.

- Volunteer to be a note-taker for a deaf student.

- Volunteer at a nursing home for elderly people who are deaf.

 Write about your experiences in a journal that becomes part of your portfolio. This activity will help the student meet CEC Initial Content Standard 3: Individual Learning Differences.

2. How does your college or university provide support services to students with hearing loss? In particular, find out what types of career counseling are offered. How might these services be improved? With others in your class, create a list of services that could be used by students who are deaf.

 This activity will help the student meet CEC Initial Content Standards 3: Individual Learning Differences and 4: Instructional Strategies.

3. Devise a unit on deafness and Deaf culture to include in your curriculum. Its components might include the following:

- What is sound? How is it made?
- What are the parts of the ear? What causes deafness?
- How does a cochlear implant work?
- What are Deaf culture and the Deaf community?
- Invite a Deaf theater group to visit your classroom.
- Describe the types of manual languages and systems to transcribe them.
- What are the abilities, attitudes, and accomplishments of deaf artists?
- Who are some famous deaf people?
- Making communication work: What can deaf students tell their hearing friends so that they can improve their communication?
- Organize a Deaf Awareness Week at school.
- Explore jobs and higher education opportunities for deaf students.
- Offer sign classes by students with hearing loss for hearing students.
- Visit or host pen pal programs with students who are deaf in other programs, states, or countries.

(Material adapted from B. Luetke-Stahlman and J. Luckner (1991). *Effectively Educating Students with Hearing Impairments* (p. 352). New York: Longman. Copyright © 1991. Used by permission of the authors.)

 This activity will help the student meet CEC Initial Content Standards 3: Individual Learning Differences and 4: Instructional Strategies.

 To access Portfolio Activities for this chapter and other useful study resources including an interactive eBook, related web links, quizzes, flashcards, and videos, visit the Education CourseMate website at CengageBrain.com.

CHAPTER 12

Children Who Are Blind or Have Low Vision

Outline

Learning Objectives

After reading this chapter, the reader will:

- Understand and explain the definitions of blindness and low vision.

- Describe how we see, and the major causes of visual impairment in children.

- Discuss how a visual impairment affects a child's learning and development.

- Identify how education for students with visual impairments should be different from that of sighted students, and how it should be the same.

- Describe some teaching strategies, accommodations, and assistive technology supports that can be used with students with visual impairments.

People who are sighted develop a concept of what it is like to be blind from maneuvering in the dark or wearing a blindfold during childhood games. As a result of these experiences, most of us believe that we understand what it is like to be blind. We are probably wrong. In the first place, our experiences are based on the condition of total blindness. Contrary to popular stereotype, most people who are visually impaired respond to some visual stimuli, such as shadows, light and darkness, or moving objects. The majority of people with visual impairments can read print, either regular print or print that is magnified or enlarged; just 20.8 percent of students with visual impairments use Braille as their primary learning medium (American Printing House for the Blind, 2010).

Second, some of our manufactured early experiences of "blindness" may have been negative or frightening because we lacked the skills that successful people who are blind have acquired. Most people rely on vision for protection and information. So, during the course of our childhood games, we were usually tempted to peek or turn on the light for reassurance and confirmation. In contrast, people who are blind receive instruction in daily living skills and rely on their other senses to gain information about their world. Most people who are blind can move independently around their homes and travel in the community; they are productively employed and lead active lives. So our negative or fearful concepts of blindness probably do not reflect the real life of a person who is blind.

These common misconceptions about the ability of people who are visually impaired are important to remember when preparing to teach a child who is blind or visually impaired. We must look beyond our traditional view of blindness and our misconceptions and stereotypes to realize that, with specialized instruction, children with visual impairments are quite capable of succeeding in our classrooms.

Terms and Definitions

Like *hearing impairment,* we use **visual impairment** as an umbrella term that includes all levels of vision loss, from total blindness to uncorrectable visual limitations. The IDEA definition states that visual impairment, including blindness, is "an impairment in vision that, *even with correction,* adversely affects a child's educational performance. The term includes both partial sight (low vision) and blindness" (IDEA, Sec. 300.8, c-13).

It is helpful to think about the phrase *with correction* in this definition. Even with the best possible corrective lenses, these children have a vision problem that interferes with their learning at school. Many of us wear glasses or contact lenses that correct our vision, but we are not considered visually impaired if our vision is correctable.

In schools, we make a distinction between legal definitions and educational definitions. A person is considered **legally blind** when his or her **visual acuity,** or sharpness of vision, is 20/200 or worse in the better eye *with* correction, or when he or she has a visual field no greater than 20 degrees. (A person with 20/200 vision has to get as close as 20 feet to an object to see the same object that a person with typical vision can see from 200 feet.) If vision can be corrected through glasses or contact lenses to 20/200 or better, the person is not considered legally blind. The term *legal blindness* describes visual impairments that qualify a person for a variety of legal and social services. This definition is used to determine eligibility for governmental funding, tax deductions, rehabilitation, and other services. Although the legal definition is widely used, it is somewhat misleading, since many legally blind people have a good deal of useful vision. In fact, the majority of people who are legally blind read using large print!

> The term *visual impairment* covers all degrees of vision loss.

> Legal blindness refers to visual acuity of 20/200 or less in the better eye after correction, or a visual field of less than 20 degrees.

This photograph illustrates reduced visual acuity.

This is an example of a restricted visual field, or "tunnel vision."

Educational definitions of visual impairment are based on whether the student reads print or Braille.

For educators, actual measurements of visual acuity are less important than a description of how the student functions in school. **Educational definitions** are generally based on the way a student uses his or her vision in an educational setting. For educational purposes, students who learn primarily through touch or listening are considered **functionally blind** and those who gain most of their information through their vision (and read large print) may be designated as having **low vision** (Corn & Lusk, 2010). Table 12.1 lists the levels of visual impairment and their educational implications. These definitions rely less on visual acuity measurements and more on **functional vision**—"the ability to use vision in planning and performing

Table 12.1 Educational Implications of Visual Impairments

Levels of Visual Impairment	Educational Implications
Visual impairment	Often defined clinically as a visual acuity of 20/70 or worse in the better eye with best correction, or a total field loss of 140 degrees. Additional factors influencing visual impairment might be contrast sensitivity, light sensitivity, glare sensitivity, and light/dark adaptation.
Total blindness	An inability to see anything with either eye.
Functional blindness	Students use their senses of touch and hearing as their primary means of learning, but may have some sight useful for orientation and mobility. Common daily activities affected by vision loss are reading, safe pedestrian travel, self-care, cooking, and recreational activities.
Low vision	A term often used interchangeably with visual impairment. Refers to a loss of vision that may be severe enough to hinder an individual's ability to complete daily activities such as reading, cooking, or walking outside safely, while still retaining some degree of useable vision.
Blindness in one eye	Students with vision in only one eye may or may not be considered visually impaired, depending on the vision in the sighted eye; they may have difficulty with depth perception and may need special consideration in physical education or other classroom activities.

Source: Adapted from American Foundation for the Blind (2008), Key Definitions of Statistical Terms. http://www.afb.org/Section.asp?SectionID=15&DocumentID=1280

(*Note:* AFB=American Foundation for the Blind)

a task" (Corn & Erin, 2010). At times, students with exactly the same acuity will function very differently. In fact, professionals in the field of blindness and visual impairment often say that no two people see exactly alike (Augusto, 1996). Whereas one student might respond visually to educational tasks, the other might rely more on hearing or sense of touch, depending on his or her background, experience, type of visual impairment, and preference. The real test of how well a student sees is how she accomplishes daily activities while using her sight as well as her other senses. Figure 12.1 presents the definitions pictorially, and Figure 12.2 illustrates the reading medium of students classified as legally blind.

Functional vision refers to how well a person uses his or her remaining vision.

Pause and Reflect

You have read that use of the term *blind* does not necessarily mean that the person has *no* vision. How could you explain that idea to students in elementary school, so that they might have a more accurate picture of what their classmate with a visual impairment can see?

Causes of Visual Impairment

Before we discuss the causes of visual impairment in children, it will be helpful to have a basic understanding of how we see. You will see that the agents that cause visual impairment damage different parts of the eye, and the site of the damage often determines the nature of the vision loss.

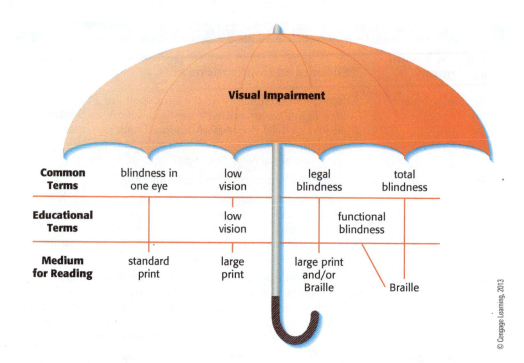

© Cengage Learning, 2013

The visual impairment umbrella

How We See

The eye is a small but extremely complex structure that contains an immense network of nerves, blood vessels, cells, and specialized tissues (Ward, 2000). For most people, this complicated structure works quite efficiently. Even if we need corrective lenses, most of us can see well. (Figure 12.3 shows the eye and its structures.) But impairments of vision can result from any interference with the passage of light as it travels from the outer surface of the eye, through the inner structures of the eye, and back through the visual pathways in the brain to the cortical brain centers.

When we look at an object, the light rays reflecting off it first pass through the outer membrane of the eye, the transparent, smooth **cornea,** through the **pupil** (the opening in the center of the eye), and through the **lens,** a transparent structure that lies between the iris and the tissue inside the eyeball, called the **vitreous humor.** The muscles in the **iris,** or colored part of the eye, expand or contract according to the amount of light available. The lens focuses the light rays so that they form clear images where they strike the **retina,** a layer of specialized cells at the back of the eye. The light rays activate the special cells on the retina; they then transmit signals of the images through the fibers of the **optic nerve,** which connects the eye to the brain, where they are interpreted. Damage to any of these

> Light rays pass through the cornea, pupil, and lens and are then projected onto the retina, which sends signals of the image by the optic nerve to the brain.

Reading medium of students who meet the definition of blindness

Source: Data from American Printing House for the Blind (2009). Distribution of Eligible Students Based on the Federal Quota Census of January 05, 2009 (Fiscal Year 2010). http://www.aph.org/fedquotpgm/dist10.html/.

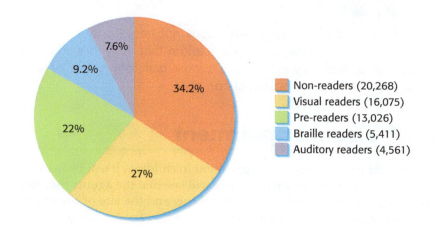

Non-readers (20,268)
Visual readers (16,075)
Pre-readers (13,026)
Braille readers (5,411)
Auditory readers (4,561)

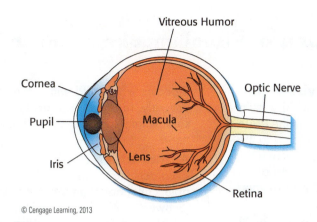

Vitreous Humor

Cornea

Optic Nerve

Pupil

Macula

Iris

Lens

Retina

© Cengage Learning, 2013

FIGURE 12.3

Structures of the eye

structures, or a breakdown in the processing of visual information, can result in visual impairment.

Marjorie Ward (2010) makes the point that while knowledge of the eye is important

> ... the major focus must remain on the human being, for whom low vision is only one characteristic. Keeping that perspective should help the reader appreciate the many physical, personal, and environmental factors that can influence the manner in which a person receives, interprets, and responds to visual information. (p. 112)

In the next section, we discuss some of the more common causes of visual impairment in children and their implications for learning.

Causes of Vision Loss

Most cases of visual impairment in school-age children are congenital in origin. Congenital conditions may be caused by heredity, maternal or fetal infection, or damage during fetal development or shortly after birth. Hereditary conditions that cause visual impairment include albinism, some forms of glaucoma, and retinitis pigmentosa. Other conditions, such as cataracts and underdevelopment or absence of parts of the eye structure, may be caused by damage during fetal development. Some conditions that cause visual impairment are stable, and others cause progressive vision loss (Schwartz, 2010). It is important for classroom teachers to understand the eye conditions of their students, since the specific condition may affect what we expect for the child's visual functioning in the classroom. See A Closer Look, "Causes of Visual Impairment in Children," for additional details.

Congenital conditions are those that are present at birth or shortly thereafter.

Most visual impairments in children are congenital.

Prevalence

According to the *Twenty-Eighth Annual Report to Congress* (U.S. Department of Education, 2009), students with visual impairments account for just 0.4 percent, or 26,130, of the total number of students aged 6 to 21 served under IDEA. As with many other disabilities, accurate counts are difficult because of differences in definition and classification. However, even when the highest estimates are used, visual impairments are still among the low-incidence (or least frequently occurring) disability conditions in children; about one in 1,000 school-age children has a visual impairment. Approximately ten percent of school-age children with visual impairment are blind, and the remainder have low vision (Council for Exceptional Children, 2011). Visual impairment is much more common among adults, especially those aged 65 and older.

A relatively large number of children who are visually impaired have additional disabilities as well—sometimes intellectual disabilities, learning disabilities, physical and health impairments, and other disabilities accompany visual

As many as 75 percent of students who are blind have additional disabilities as well.

A CLOSER LOOK   Causes of Visual Impairment in Children

- **Cortical visual impairment** (CVI) results from damage to the brain rather than to the eye. If the occipital lobes in the brain are damaged, the brain cannot receive the images from the eye. Causes of cortical visual impairment include inadequate blood and oxygen supply to the brain at or around the time of birth. About 75 percent of children with this condition have other disabilities as well, such as cerebral palsy and seizures (Schwartz, 2010). At present, CVI is the most common cause of visual impairment in children in developed countries.

- **Retinopathy of prematurity (ROP)** occurs most commonly in premature babies or even full-term babies suffering from respiratory distress syndrome (see Chapter 3) who require high levels of oxygen over an extended period of time for survival.

- In **optic nerve hypoplasia** and *optic nerve atrophy,* the optic nerve does not develop normally or degenerates, causing vision loss. This is an increasingly common cause of vision loss in children (Schwartz, 2010).

- **Albinism** is the congenital absence of pigmentation (including that of the eye), which can result in vision loss.

- **Glaucoma**, a leading cause of blindness in adults (Ward, 2000), also appears in children.

It occurs when fluid within the eye cannot drain properly, resulting in a gradual increase of pressure within the eye and damage to the optic nerve.

- A **cataract** is a clouding of the lens of the eye. Cataracts cause 5 to 15 percent of preventable childhood blindness throughout the world (Schwartz, 2010; World Health Organization, 2000). Children with cataracts will have difficulty seeing the board clearly and may need increased lighting or high-contrast educational materials.

- Diabetes can result in a condition known as **diabetic retinopathy**, another major cause of blindness in this country, but much more frequently occurring in adults.

There are many other less frequently occurring causes of visual impairment in children, including optic atrophy and congenital infection (Schwartz, 2010). Blindness is much more common in developing countries; the World Health Organization monitors its international incidence closely:

An estimated 1.4 million children under age 15 are blind. Yet approximately half of all childhood blindness can be avoided by early treatment of disease and correcting abnormalities at birth such as cataract and glaucoma. (World Health Organization, 2006).

impairment. Although the exact number is hard to come by, it may be as high as 75 percent of children with visual impairments (Silberman, 2000).

Pause and Reflect

There are many causes of visual impairments, and the causes affect what a person can see. Do you think you can change your own focus to what a student *can see*, rather than what he or she cannot? ●

Characteristics of Students Who Are Blind or Have Low Vision

Negative attitudes and stereotypes can deprive the student with visual impairment of important experiences and opportunities.

Society's lack of knowledge or negative attitudes toward visual impairment may indirectly affect the child by depriving her of opportunities or experiences important for development. As you will read in the upcoming case study about Brenda, it is a fairly common belief that people who are blind cannot accomplish certain tasks. Unfortunately, this attitude may deprive them of the opportunity to compete with people who are sighted.

Even when differences are caused directly by the visual impairment, the degree to which the person's development is affected depends on the severity and cause of the visual impairment and on whether the child has additional disabilities. Environmental factors, such as family background and the child's daily experience, are also significant. Kay Ferrell states that the factors which make a difference in how a child with visual impairments develops are *the opportunities to learn* and *the presence or absence of additional disabilities* (2000). As you read the following sections, think about the ways in which the areas of development are related to one another.

CASE STUDY

Brenda is 9 years old and is in the fourth grade. She was born prematurely and is blind because of retinopathy of prematurity. Brenda has above-average intelligence and is on grade level in every academic subject. In some subjects, she requires more time than the rest of the class to complete daily assignments. During the first and second grades, Brenda's general education teachers decided that she should not be required to do all of the work that the rest of the class was required to. When the rest of the class was assigned twenty addition problems, Brenda was told to complete only ten. By the time Brenda was in the third grade, she would complain that the assignments she was given were too hard, or that she couldn't complete them because she was blind. Brenda's third-grade teacher, Ms. Garcia, was concerned and contacted a vision specialist teacher and Brenda's parents. They all agreed that this attitude could lead to a decline in Brenda's self-esteem and confidence. At their meeting it was decided that Brenda would benefit from completing all class assignments.

Ms. Garcia re-examined the assignments she gave to her entire class realizing that if ten addition problems were enough for her to determine mastery for Brenda, they were enough for the other members of her class, as well. However, at this point in her education, it takes Brenda longer to complete the assignment than her classmates, regardless of the amount of material. Ms. Garcia, therefore, arranged her class schedule so that all students would have some time to complete assignments during school hours and could also take work home to complete.

It still takes Brenda more time to accomplish these assignments, but when she is finished she is confident that she can compete with the other students in her class. At the same time, she is learning strategies to help her complete her work more efficiently.

Language and Concept Development

Although communication through babbling and early sound production is generally the same for children who are blind and children who are sighted (Warren, 1984), developmental differences arise when children begin to associate meaning with words. In a classic study, Thomas Cutsforth (1932) researched the use of words and the understanding of their meaning by children who were totally blind from birth. He discovered that children who are blind often use words for which they could not have firsthand knowledge through other senses, such as when describing a blue sky. Cutsforth (1951) called this use of words without concrete knowledge of their meanings **verbalisms.**

Children who are blind may have other unusual language characteristics. For instance, they may ask frequent inappropriate or off-the-topic questions in order to maintain contact with partners or to respond to frightening or confusing situations (Fazzi & Klein, 2002). They may also engage in **echolalia,** the repetition of statements used by other people. Interventions should be responsive to the content of the child's utterance, but teachers should not reinforce language behaviors that would not be acceptable in a sighted child.

> Children with visual impairments may be prone to verbalisms; they may use words without firsthand knowledge of their meanings.

Children with visual impairments should have direct experience with complex concepts.

Those of us who are sighted may take for granted the role that vision plays in learning and development, but Kay Ferrell (2000) reminds us that vision provides an incentive for communication and helps children develop concepts. Teachers and families of children with visual impairments *must make all the features of concepts explicit.* For example, an apple is not just red (or green or yellow); it is white on the inside, and the seeds are brown. Teachers working with children who are blind should be aware that even though a child may use verbal expressions that indicate an understanding of a concept, she may not really have the deeper understanding that comes with actual personal experience. If a child writes or reads a story about a big gray elephant but has had no firsthand experience with an elephant or the color gray, she is writing and/or reading about something that she does not truly understand. Jane Erin (2010) provides examples:

> Teachers of students with visual impairments become skilled in interpreting ideas in a way that makes concepts immediate, concrete, and meaningful to their students. As a teacher, I was often overwhelmed by the variety of concepts that were needed for my young students to understand a natural or scientific phenomenon. One of my blind students could imitate cows and pigs, but he had no idea whether they had tails. Another could discuss the causes of the drop in gasoline prices, but she did not know how many wheels were on a car. Their concepts were based on what they heard others discuss as well as what they had personally touched or heard. (p.197)

The teacher may want to work more closely with the child on these concepts, providing rich and meaningful experiences (see Teaching Strategies & Accommodations, "Promoting Language Development").

By the way, this may also be true of children who are sighted; teachers can never assume that children's use of concepts in verbal or written communications indicates a clear understanding of those concepts. The challenge to educators, therefore, is to use Universal Design for Learning practices to provide *all* children with a wealth of opportunities that increase their experiences through all senses, thus increasing their understanding of the language they use.

Motor Development

The acquisition of motor skills may be delayed by lack of vision.

From infancy, motor development is stimulated by vision. An infant who sees a brightly colored object or her mother's face reaches out for it and thus begins the development of gross motor skills. Children who are blind have difficulty in this area. Children who are sighted learn how to move by watching the movement of others and imitating it. Then, they practice variations of this movement and observe their own movement, which gives them the feedback they need to change and modify their movements. Children who are blind, however, cannot observe others and imitate their movements. They are slow to begin to move in response to the sounds around them (Fazzi & Naimy, 2010).

Also, many children with visual impairments have fewer opportunities than their sighted peers to engage in motor activities. Teachers, parents, and caregivers may "overprotect" the child and inadvertently limit opportunities to explore; fathers (and mothers) may not engage in as much "rough and tumble" play as they would with their sighted children. This can also contribute to delays in motor development.

IDEA, as you have learned, provides that children with disabilities receive "related services" in order to fully benefit from schooling. Under this law, children who are blind may receive instruction in **orientation and mobility** (O&M), a set of skills involved in establishing one's location in the environment and moving safely through it (Weiner, Welsch, & Blasch, 2010). Early intervention with an O&M specialist can help very young children avoid or overcome sensorimotor delays

Teaching Strategies & Accommodations

Promoting Language Development

The following strategies will help professionals and family members support the development of verbal communication in young children who are visually impaired.

- *Make playful games out of vocal imitation and turn taking.* Repeating, rephrasing, and using pauses can encourage vocal turn taking and have positive effects on language development (Chen & Klein, 2008b).

- *Model appropriate ways to initiate and maintain social interactions.* Good social skills can be modeled and practiced during symbolic play routines (e.g., pretend kitchen and food preparation or talking on a play telephone).

- *Support the child's participation in a variety of everyday activities.* Hands-on experiences will support language development and provide topics of interest to talk about.

- *Provide extra information about things that are discussed.* Instead of merely labeling objects, events, and actions, *describe* the things that are of interest to the child. Also talk about and describe others' actions so that the child with a visual impairment does not become too self-involved in his or her own experiences or language use.

- *Avoid bombarding children with questions.* Since children with visual impairments often rely on imitation to learn language strategies and may also have a tendency to become overreliant on questioning, modeling an overuse of questions could be counterproductive.

- *Express your own feelings verbally and help put the child's feelings into words.* Children with visual impairments cannot easily read frowns, smiles, and expressions of others. Other people's feelings need to be explained, and the child should be taught to express his or her feelings appropriately.

- *Try to expand on the child's existing language.* The child's attempt to communicate can be used as the basis for further communication. For instance, if a child says "ba-ba," the father can respond with, "Yes, that is your bottle," and go on to describe it or its function.

- *Help children act out videos, stories, and songs to increase their understanding of embedded concepts* (Darrow, 2010). For example, preschool children commonly act out the events in the song "The Wheels on the Bus." Doing so helps children understand concepts such as windows going up and down.

Source: Reprinted with permission of the publisher from D. L. Fazzi and M.D. Klein, "Cognitive Focus: Developing cognition, concepts, and Language," in Rona L. Pogrund and Diane L. Fazzi, (Eds.), *Early Focus: Working with Young Children Who Are Blind or Visually Impaired and Their Families,* 2nd ed, pp. 152–153. Copyright © 2002 by AFB Press, American Foundation for the Blind. All rights reserved.

and develop fluid mobility skills (Rosen, 2010). When children who have visual impairments enter school, they should be able to move efficiently and safely through their environment with the support of the O&M specialist (Fazzi & Naimy, 2010).

Cognitive and Intellectual Development

Blindness affects cognitive development in young children in much the same way as it affects motor development, by restricting the range and variety of their experiences, limiting their ability to move around, and diminishing their control of the environment and their relationship to it (Lowenfeld, 1981).

With emerging research on newborns and infants, we are discovering more and more about the importance of vision in early learning. In early infancy the eyes are the child's primary avenue for exploring the world. The newborn uses vision to follow objects with her eyes, for example, and can stick out his tongue after watching someone else do it (Freidrich, 1983). The visual sense motivates the infant to interact with people and objects, guides that interaction, and verifies the success of the interaction. Vision thus stimulates motor activity and exploration, forming the basis for cognitive growth.

Blindness affects cognitive development by restricting the range and variety of a child's experiences.

Some research has suggested that there are critical periods for certain kinds of learning (Bailey et al., 2001). If infants who are visually impaired miss out on those critical periods for reaching, crawling, or walking, for example, it may be difficult for them to "catch up" and develop at a normal rate later in life. School-age children may continue to experience difficulties in their developmental progress. Thus, early intervention for infants with visual impairments is designed to use the child's intact senses to provide the kind of experiences that will promote cognitive growth (Fazzi & Klein, 2002).

> Children who are blind often encounter social difficulties because of how society perceives them and how they perceive themselves.

Social and Emotional Development

Most researchers agree that there is no unique psychology of blindness. The principles and issues related to the social and emotional development of people who are sighted are the same as those related to the social and emotional development

FIRST PERSON

Perspectives from a Blind Man: What Blindness Is, What It Isn't

My name is Daniel Kish. I am totally blind from birth, and the President of World Access for the Blind—a nonprofit organization using a modern, No-Limit approach to equalize opportunities for the success of blind people. I hold Master's degrees in developmental psychology (where I focused on children at risk) and special education. I am the first totally blind, nationally certified Orientation and Mobility Specialist, as this certification was withheld from blind people until very recently.

In my experience, what we call "kindness" or "compassion" has stood among the biggest threats to blind people. It is compassion with lack of understanding that has landed many blind people in institutions and kept us out of the mainstream "for our own protection" over the years. Compassion without understanding of human strength and respect for dignity and purpose becomes a dangerous and hurtful thing. I know. I and my students worldwide confront this reality every single day. Some have told me after losing their vision, "It isn't the blindness that most bothers me, it's the way I'm now treated."

Here Dan is working as an orientation and mobility specialist and is engaged in playful rough-housing with a student. The student likely has some degree of residual vision and is blindfolded to encourage use of his other senses.

They're not generally referring to people being cruel, callous, or insensitive, but rather too helpful, smothering, condescending, and often lacking recognition of personal potency.

Please understand, for many blind people, blindness isn't at all about being led around,

of people who are blind (Tuttle & Tuttle, 2000). However, children who are blind do encounter unique difficulties in social situations. Primarily, the difficulties arise because of the way that the child is perceived by society and the way that the child perceives himself (Sacks & Wolffe, 2006).

For example, the child who completes class assignments develops a clear sense of accomplishment. Children who are visually impaired, however, are often allowed to turn in incomplete work or partial assignments, as in the case of Brenda. As a result, such children may believe that they are not "smart enough" to complete the same work that other children in the class do. The perception of other students in the class—and of the teacher—may also be that the child with a visual impairment cannot accomplish as much as the rest of the class.

Teenagers with visual impairments engage in fewer activities with peers and spend more time after school alone than their sighted peers do. Students with low vision in particular tend to involve themselves in more "passive" activities than

relying on others' kindness, or craving the light of day. Blindness isn't about fear of the dark, vulnerability, or suffering. It is definitely not about what we can't do, or wish we could do. Blindness is about adaptation and resourcefulness, about effective, purposeful, dignified, self-directed living in the dark, about achievement through perseverance. Blindness is about the joy, freedom, and beauty of making our own choices by exercising our own sound judgments and capabilities. It is about the gratification of embracing the world and making the unknown known.

Blindness need not be a thing that we must regard as a condition of "suffering." The suffering part of it is ultimately a matter of personal choice as is true when faced with any challenge. While most blind people would probably rather see than not, at the same time many would not regard their circumstances as "suffering." We see and live blindness from a "gain" perspective, not a "loss" perspective. That is the only way we can find and own our power. I think the purpose of fighting blindness isn't so much to combat it as an affliction, but to bring a positive light to the situation of blindness. I call it the "new light." Blindness may be eradicated in a few instances, and good riddance to it, but more realistically and importantly, I submit that the afflictive nature of blindness can and should be addressed in positive, respectful ways without casting aspersions on the condition.

World Access for the Blind, for example, teaches blind people worldwide how to "see without sight," and how to approach life with a perspective of success and purpose, not loss. Our main message is "No-Limits," and we mean it. Our students learn to use sound and sonar imaging natural to humans, together with belief in their own capacity, to interact with their environment gracefully and energetically in astounding ways not previously imagined. Solo bicycling, competitive ball play, and wilderness survival without need for the eyes of others are just a few things that become readily possible, not to mention finding quality and enrichment in one's day-to-day life. The impact on self-worth and confidence is immeasurable in this positive light. But, for the capacity of blind people to be fully realized and accepted, with or without technology or special training, I submit that we must work with rather than against blindness in a positive way without disrespecting or dishonoring the condition. To do otherwise throws a pall over everything that we blind people strive for—to stand as equals with our sighted comrades, not because of their kindness towards us, but because of our own intrinsic capacity to achieve and to shine.

Source: http://www.worldaccessfortheblind.org

their sighted or blind peers—and they sleep more (Sacks & Wolffe, 2006). The lack of independent mobility that sometimes accompanies visual impairment seems to have serious implications for friendships and social life in high school. Our First Person, Daniel Kish, is committed to assisting people who are blind to engage in more vigorous activities.

School Achievement

With appropriate assistance and placement, a student who is visually impaired and has no additional disabilities should be able to participate actively in all aspects of school and compete with sighted peers in academic areas. If a student with visual impairment is having trouble achieving academic goals, the teacher and the vision specialist should work together to determine if he is receiving proper instruction and has the needed adapted materials. The sections later in this chapter on teaching strategies and technological aids will provide more information for this purpose.

Effects on the Family

The reaction of families to the fact that their infant or child is blind or has low vision depends on many factors. Most important, as we saw in Chapter 4, may be the degree of support available to the family through its informal network of relatives and friends and its formal network of agencies and professionals.

Several other characteristics of the family and the child may affect the parents' attitude toward their child's visual impairment (Ferrell, 1986):

1. *The severity of the handicap* may be an important issue, because many children with visual impairments also have additional disabilities. Parents of children whose visual impairment is severe or is complicated by other disabilities must respond to a variety of physical and developmental issues; in some cases they must also cope with anxiety about life-threatening medical procedures.

2. *The age of onset of the visual impairment.* The later the diagnosis of disability, the more difficult the news is for the parents; they have had more time for their hopes and expectations for their child to develop. On the other hand, the development of bonding, that crucial early parent-child tie that is so important to social and emotional development, may be affected when the infant is congenitally blind. Babies who have visual impairments are less likely to make eye contact with their mothers, which can reduce the amount of the "mutual gazing" that occurs between infants and mothers. In addition, these babies may smile less regularly and consistently at their parents. Smiling in infants is important to elicit social interactions with other people and serves as a means to include the infant in the social relationship (Warren, 1984).

3. *How the information or diagnosis concerning visual impairment was initially received.* Stotland (1984), the parent of a child who is blind, says, "Ask any five parents of visually impaired children how they first learned their child had vision problems and you will get five different horror stories. These stories will range from blatant misdiagnoses to inaccurate predictions of total blindness, to expressions of pity" (p. 69).

4. *Support from medical professionals and educators* is critical in the initial discovery of a child's visual impairment. Parents must feel comfortable asking questions and expressing concerns and emotions if they are to accept their child's visual impairment.

Parents' attitudes toward their child's visual impairment are affected by a range of factors.

A child with visual impairment creates a dynamic within the family that affects it in many ways long after the initial diagnosis. These effects might include changes in daily routines, social interactions, and parent involvement at school (J. B. Chase, as quoted in Wolffe, 2000). As we saw in Chapter 4, there are often high expectations on the part of school professionals for parental involvement with their child and with the school.

Families of children with visual impairments are often able to incorporate their child into the family routine, ensuring that the child feels she is a vital member of the family. In some cases, family members allow more time for the child to complete a particular task, such as clearing the dishes from the table. Family members can also use special adapted materials for more complicated tasks—for example, Braille labels on the washing machine and dryer. Participation in family routines helps children learn to complete tasks that they have started, to perform as independently as possible, to take responsibility for their actions, and to feel like a contributing family member.

Outside their daily routines, families often must deal with changes in their social relationships as an indirect result of their child's visual impairment. Parents, for example, may have difficulty coping with the attitudes and misconceptions of their friends. This anecdote from Deborah Barton (1984), the parent of a child who is blind, still rings true. She recalled, "When my child started walking and talking, my friends considered him a genius and thought of me as a saint. They misinterpreted what they saw, and I let them. They praised Jed for ordinary behavior ('he's walking,' 'he likes peanut butter,' 'he doesn't whine') and talked about me as if I was a cross between Madame Curie and the Flying Nun" (p. 67). Although at first this kind of acknowledgment might seem welcome, it is difficult for parents to endure misconceptions such as these over time because they indicate a lack of understanding of their child's needs and abilities.

Social interactions between the child who is visually impaired and children who are sighted may also require special attention and effort. Families of children with a visual impairment must be even more careful to provide social activities for that child outside of the family so that good social skills are established throughout the early years of a child's development. Unfortunately, some parents of sighted children may be reluctant to invite the child who is blind to participate in activities such as birthday parties or slumber parties because of their lack of understanding about blindness. Parents of children with visual impairments may need to initiate some of this social interaction and to educate the parents of their child's sighted peers. When inexperienced adults begin to learn about the abilities and needs of a child with visual impairment, they can model acceptance and understanding for their own children. See Teaching

> Parents of children who are visually impaired may be challenged by the attitudes and misconceptions of others.

© Peter Byron/PhotoEdit

This boy uses the long cane to assist his mobility—but having a couple of friends around helps too.

Teaching Strategies & Accommodations

Promoting Social Inclusion at Home and at School

- Encourage the child to explore the environment by providing many hands-on experiences. Take him or her on outings to various community sites (such as parks, playgrounds, and restaurants) and on shopping trips (to the grocery store, shopping mall, or video store), for example.

- Allow the child to be an active participant in each hands-on experience. For example, when grocery shopping, have the child choose a favorite snack or select a favorite fruit from the produce section.

- Provide opportunities for the child to participate in structured group activities that facilitate socialization, such as swimming lessons, gymnastics, story hour at the public library, and rhythm and music groups. Many of these activities can be done with a family member.

- Encourage the child to take risks and try new activities. Provide opportunities for the child to experience a variety of multisensory activities (such as tasting new foods and feeling a variety of textures; playing rough-and-tumble games; engaging in climbing activities; and playing in water, sand, and snow).

- Provide opportunities for the child to assume responsibility for classroom jobs or home chores on a consistent basis. Young children can be responsible for putting away their toys, putting their dirty clothes in a clothes hamper, helping to set the table for a family meal, clearing the table after eating a meal, or helping to take out the trash or recycle bins.

- Form partnerships with other parents and teachers and become involved in play groups and community groups (such as a church, Tiny Tots, dance classes, music lessons, ice skating, and skiing).

Source: S. Z. Sacks & S. K. Silberman (2000). Social skills. In A. J. Koenig & M. C. Holbrook (Eds.), *Foundations of Education*, Vol. II, (2nd ed., pp. 633–634). New York: American Foundation for the Blind.

Strategies & Accommodations, "Promoting Social Inclusion at Home and at School," for ideas that family members can use to promote social relationships.

School is another area in which family participation and adaptation are important. Parents or caregivers should participate in the IEP team, which gathers as much information as possible concerning the child's abilities and needs, including the degree to which the child uses remaining vision. The family plays a crucial role in providing the professionals with information on how the child uses his vision. Once decisions have been made regarding adaptive materials and curricular activities, parents become vital participants in their child's education. If, for example, a child is learning to travel independently with a cane, the parents can reinforce this skill by communicating closely with their child's teachers to monitor progress and to learn about the skill from them (Perla & O'Donnell, 2002). In doing so, they encourage independence for their child. If a child is learning Braille, parents can learn it too. Close communication between parents and teachers and direct involvement of parents in the education of the child are critical to educational success.

> Family participation in the child's education, especially on the IEP team, is crucial.

? Pause and Reflect

Though many adults with visual impairments become content and productive, there is no doubt that visual impairment significantly affects a child's development. How does what you have read so far fit in with your preconceptions of visual impairment, and how does it differ?

Teaching Strategies and Accommodations

Teaching students with visual impairments can be very much like teaching typical students, but often the additional content and accommodations that students need are unique and challenging. Understanding the following issues will help teachers and parents provide an appropriate education for children with vision loss.

Early Intervention

Professionals have long recognized the need for intervention programs for infants and their parents as soon as a visual impairment is diagnosed. For babies with congenital blindness, this diagnosis comes at birth or soon after; for babies with lesser degrees of visual impairment, the diagnosis may occur later in infancy. Children with a moderate degree of impairment may receive a diagnosis only after they encounter difficulty in completing school tasks.

Kay Ferrell (1986, 2011) has described several reasons for early intervention with infants who are visually impaired. First, as discussed earlier, vision is an important component of early cognitive development, and there may be particular periods of early development when optimal learning occurs. Early intervention may also prevent the development of secondary disabilities. Failure to develop language, ear-hand coordination, or attachment to a significant adult may form the foundation for disabilities in addition to visual impairment that will emerge later in the child's life, such as cognitive delay or behavioral and emotional problems.

Early intervention can take numerous forms. Teachers of young children with visual impairments will encourage parents to continue to talk to their baby, to "show" things to the baby by allowing her to touch and explore them, to teach the baby to listen for clues to what is happening around her, to play games that involve moving and identifying parts of the body, using the baby's hands to find her head, nose, ears, tummy, knees, and so on. Early intervention specialists can also help parents make the most of the learning opportunities that arise in the routines of daily life with their baby. This role is important, since parents sometimes alter their interactions with a child who is visually impaired. They may assume that a child who cannot see is less interested in his or her environment or does not need the stimulation of playing with household objects and toys or of playing baby games with parents.

Hatton, McWilliam, and Winton (2002) have described exemplary practices for early interventionists serving infants with visual impairments and their families:

- Establish reliable alliances (Turnbull, Erwin, Turnbull, Soodak, & Shogren, 2010) with families and other service providers based on family and child strengths, respect for diversity and culture, and collaboration.
- Collaborate with families and other professionals to complete the Individualized Family Services Plan (IFSP) process.
- Serve as an effective member of the early intervention team, help families and other team members understand medical information, and be familiar with service coordination responsibilities.
- Approach early intervention from a support, rather than provision of services, perspective.
- Make home visits that promote functional outcomes for both the child and family. (Remember that functional outcomes are those that will be useful in the child's life, or help the family care for the child.)

Infants who are visually impaired and have additional disabilities have especially intensive intervention needs, and their parents need a great deal of support (Chen & Klein, 2008a). Reading the cues of a baby who is blind and may be deaf or

Early intervention with infants with visual impairments may prevent the development of secondary disabilities.

Infants with visual impairment and additional disabilities need intensive intervention.

intellectually or physically disabled can be complex. How can a mother tell when the baby is pleased or sad? What are the baby's preferences? How do the family members and the baby build relationships? Effective intervention for these families requires an early intervention specialist who knows each disability area well and can build on the family strengths to foster communication and loving relationships (Chen & Klein, 2008a, 2009).

After a review of the literature to identify evidence-based instructional practices used with students with visual impairments, Kay Ferrell (2006) described her findings: "For students with visual impairments . . . best practices are more often than not based on tradition, superstition, anecdote, and common sense rather than science" (p. 42). In a field with such a small number of students, finding subjects and conducting empirical research is challenging, but Ferrell urges her colleagues to add to the small number of studies that validate practices.

Identification and Assessment

Assessment of students who are visually impaired is difficult, partly because of lack of standardized tests for this population.

Educational assessment for students who are visually impaired is especially difficult for three reasons: the lack of standardized assessment instruments, the need for adaptations of existing assessment instruments to meet the needs of students with visual impairments, and the need for a fair interpretation of test results. The lack of standardized assessment instruments is a direct result of the small number of students with visual impairments. It has been impossible to standardize tests on this population because of the great diversity of children with visual impairments caused by differences in age of onset and degree of visual impairment, and differences in educational experiences.

● *Identification in School*   Every state mandates vision screening in the schools to determine which students have visual problems that warrant further assessment. At least one in four school-age children have eye problems that need professional attention (Prevent Blindness America, 2011), and that number is considerably higher among children with other disabilities. (Part C of IDEA requires a vision and hearing screening for all children from birth to age 2 who are referred for the evaluation of a disability [34 CFR 303.322].) To learn more about the prevention of eye problems, visit the website of the non-profit organization Prevent Blindness.

The Snellen Chart is the most common visual screening test.

The most common visual screening test is one you have probably taken yourself, although you may not know the name of it—the **Snellen Chart.** The person being examined is positioned twenty feet from the chart, on which eight rows of letters ranging from large to small are printed, and is asked to read the letters with each eye (while the other eye is covered). If that individual has difficulty reading any of the letters on the chart, the school nurse or other person conducting the screening usually makes a referral for a more comprehensive evaluation of vision.

The Snellen Chart is used to screen for distance vision problems only. If you suspect that one of your students has a near vision problem (which would affect reading) or another kind of vision problem, then urge your school nurse to conduct or recommend a more complete visual evaluation for that student. (See A Closer Look, "Detection of Vision Problems.")

There are a number of ways to screen for visual impairments in very young children or those who do not know the letter names. The most common are the Snellen E Chart and Apple/House/Umbrella Screening. There are also a variety of means for evaluating the vision of students with severe disabilities that the experienced examiner will be able to use (Erin & Topor, 2010a). No student should be excluded from vision screening because he or she cannot provide traditional responses. Continuous observation of the student in the classroom and in other natural settings should accompany the screening, plus referral of identified

A CLOSER LOOK — Detection of Vision Problems

Teachers are often the first to detect vision problems in their students. This checklist will help you identify potential vision problems in your students.

If you observe the following behavior in the child:

- one eye drifts or aims in a different direction than the other (look carefully—this can be subtle). This is significant even if it only occurs when the child is tired or stressed.
- turns or tilts head to see
- head is frequently tilted to one side or one shoulder is noticeably higher
- squinting or closing of one eye
- excessive blinking or squinting
- poor visual/motor skills (often called "hand-eye coordination")
- problems moving in space, frequently bumps into things or drops things

While reading or doing close work the child:

- holds the book or object unusually close
- closes one eye or covers eye with hand
- twists or tilts head toward book or object so as to favor one eye
- frequently loses place and fatigues easily
- uses finger to read
- rubs eyes during or after short periods of reading

The child frequently complains of:

- only being able to read for short periods of time
- headaches or eyestrain
- nausea or dizziness
- motion sickness
- DOUBLE VISION!

Say no more. If the child reports seeing double, please refer the child to the school nurse immediately.

If you observe any of these problems in the child, talk to his or her caregivers and ask your school nurse for advice.

Source: Adapted from A Parent's Checklist, Optometrists Network. Retrieved from: http://www.children-special-needs.org/parenting/preschool/children_eye_exams.html.

---

students for further visual evaluation and follow-up to ensure that the recommendations have been carried out.

- *Functional Vision Assessment*   In addition to the medical evaluations just discussed, it is critical to test the functional vision of students with visual impairments—in other words, how well they use the vision that they do possess. If, for example, it is noted during a functional vision assessment that a student has difficulty moving and performing tasks in limited lighting, teachers will be more prepared to accommodate him in low-lighting situations.

In addition to medical evaluations of vision, it is important to assess a student's functional vision.

Functional vision assessments vary according to the type of information needed. Commercially produced functional vision assessments are available, but most are informal and may be a compilation of other assessments. Functional vision assessments are usually conducted by a vision specialist and an orientation and mobility specialist and may include the following (Erin & Topor, 2010a):

- Information on the student's visual disability and prognosis
- Current print functioning and classroom modifications for distance and near vision tasks
- Assessment of reading level and reading speed
- Informal assessments of visual field, color vision, eye preference, and light sensitivity

- Equipment adaptations for classes
- Travel skills

Functional vision assessments are individualized. By carefully considering the information provided by the assessment, teachers can make more informed decisions about educational programming.

 ● *Assessment for Teaching*   Students who are visually impaired must demonstrate knowledge through both informal classroom evaluations and formal standardized tests, just as their sighted peers do. Accommodations can be made in the way the test is presented (for example, in Braille or large print, or using a magnification device); in the way the student responds (marking responses on a large print answer sheet, using a computer or communication board); or in the setting, timing, and scheduling of the test (take the test alone, take more time, take more breaks—it generally takes longer to read material in Braille or in large print) (Allman, 2002). Most commercially produced achievement tests are available in Braille and large-print versions. A vision specialist will be able to obtain copies of these tests. Visit the Accessible Tests Department at the American Printing House for the Blind website for more information.

 Finally, interpretation of test results should take into consideration the modification of test items and the testing situation as well as whether any test items

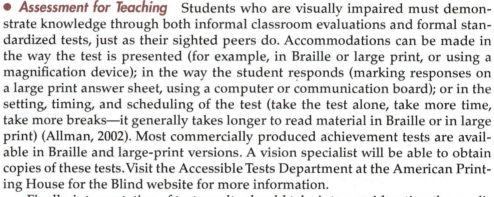

Teaching Strategies & Accommodations

Common Accommodations for People with Visual Impairments

In the classroom

While accommodations are usually identified for each student as an individual by the IEP Team, here are some of the more frequently used accommodations provided for students with visual impairments.

Materials

Raised-line or bold-line paper, templates, and/or writing guides
Soft lead pencils
Felt-tip pens (various widths; high-contrast colors)
Supplementary light source (e.g., desk lamp)
Braille writer; slate and stylus
Magnification device
Book stand
Cassette tape recorder/player
Sun visor or light shield to reduce glare
Large print reading materials (preprinted or produced using computer technology)
Physical education equipment with auditory signals (e.g., beep balls)

Safety considerations

Evaluate environment for potential hazard areas (e.g., stairs, playground structures, dimly lit areas)

Ensure that doors and storage areas are completely open or completely closed at all times
Ensure that student knows routines for fire drills and other emergency procedures

Instructional strategies

Have student sit closer to see board, videos, demonstrations, etc.
Give student copies of teacher notes
Read notes aloud while writing them on board
Provide all classroom materials in the student's preferred format (Braille, large print, audio materials)
Allow student to turn in taped rather than written responses
Enlarge books, worksheets, etc.
Provide opportunities for hands-on learning

During testing

Use large print tests in the font-size needed by the student
Oral administration of the test
Extended time
Use of manipulatives
Use of calculators
Extra/extended breaks

rely heavily on visual experiences for correct answers. The scores of students who are visually impaired should not be compared with standardized scores since standardized scores do not reflect modifications for these students. Vision specialists can assist in the interpretation of test results for individual students.

Students with visual impairments should also be assessed in the areas of the expanded core curriculum (the areas that support learning of the core curriculum), which you will read about below, and they will also require assistive technology assessments, which will determine the need for such equipment as screen readers, screen magnification, scanners, adaptive keyboards, portable note-takers, closed-circuit televisions, augmentative communication devices, Braille translation software, Braille embossers, and Braille writing equipment. Finally, students must be assessed to determine their learning medium: whether he or she should read using Braille, large print, or regular print, and which instructional materials and methods should be used (Koenig & Holbrook, 2010).

Curriculum

Students who are visually impaired require instruction not only in academic areas but also in skills needed to compensate for their loss of vision. These skills are critical to students' success in life after school and so are important parts of the curriculum. Instruction in most of these areas should begin during early

In the workplace

Most people who are visually impaired have low vision, and many of them can be accommodated by low-tech solutions, such as improved contrast, magnification, and lighting.

Examples of low-tech, low-cost accommodation

- Adjust lighting for alternative source and illumination type (natural, incandescent, halogen, fluorescent)

- Use large print in communications and documents; also use electronic and Braille communications

- Use large print, Braille labels, or tactile dots on equipment, tools, facilities, and documents

- Provide magnification devices (e.g., magnifying glasses)

- Use electronic text and voice mail communiqués instead of written notes

- Assign human readers to help with printed and handwritten materials that cannot be converted electronically

- Adjust work schedule to allow for mass transit rather than car use

- Provide for sharing or switching certain job tasks

Examples of high-tech accommodation

- Synthetic speech output to translate text to speech

- Screen-magnification programs that change font size and shape, enlarge icons, enhance mouse pointer, and change screen colors

- Devices such as closed-circuit television (CCTV) to enlarge printed documents

- Refreshable Braille systems that transcribe information from the computer screen into Braille text

- Portable notetakers: handheld devices that electronically receive, store, and retrieve data and are equipped with speech and/or refreshable Braille display output

Sources: Adapted from P. R. Cox and M. K. Dykes (2001), Effective classroom adaptations for students with visual impairments. *Teaching Exceptional Children* 33 (6), 68–74; A. Adkins, Education Specialist, TSBVI, Accommodations for visually impaired students on statewide assessments, Spring 2005, Retrieved from: http:// www.tsbvi.edu/seehear/spring05/accommodations.htm; and AFB CareerConnect, and AFB CareerConnect, retrieved from: http://www .afb.org/Section.asp?SectionID=7&TopicID=116&SubTopicID =65&DocumentID=2867.

Table 12.2 Curriculum for Students with Visual Impairments	
Existing Core Curriculum	**Expanded Core Curriculum**
English language arts	*All of the existing core curriculum, PLUS*
Other languages, to the extent possible	Compensatory or access skills
Mathematics	Orientation and mobility skills and concepts
Science	Social interaction skills
Health	Independent living skills
Physical education	Recreation and leisure skills
Social studies	Career education
History	Use of assistive technology
Economics	Sensory efficiency skills
Business education	Self-determination skills
Fine arts	
Vocational education	

© Cengage Learning, 2013

childhood, and spiral through elementary and high school. Phillip Hatlen (2000b) has described the necessary school program for students with visual impairments as the **expanded core curriculum**—the existing core curriculum plus the additional areas of learning needed by students who are visually impaired, including those with additional disabilities (see Table 12.2).

For Hatlen, the **compensatory academic and access skills** of the expanded core curriculum are the skills that students with visual impairments need to access the core curriculum. They include concept development, spatial understanding, study and organizational skills, and speaking and listening skills. Communication modes might include Braille, large print, print with the use of optical devices, regular print, tactile symbols, a calendar system, sign language, recorded materials, or combinations of these means. These skills might be taught by the teacher who is a visual impairment specialist, or by other specialists; some, like concept development, could be taught by the general education teacher.

Not every student who is blind or has low vision will need instruction in every component of the expanded core curriculum. Each student's needs must be determined individually through careful, comprehensive assessment. Let's take a closer look at the most common of these components.

● *Braille* Learning Braille is essential for students who are so severely visually impaired that they cannot read print. It is also recommended for students who are legally blind and those with visual impairments that are progressive (will worsen over time). **Braille** was devised by Louis Braille, a French musician and educator, in 1829. It is a code that uses raised dots instead of printed characters (letters). A unit in Braille is called a *cell.* Each cell consists of six dots, three dots high and two dots wide. The dots are numbered from 1 through 6, and the Braille alphabet is made of combinations of these six dots (see Figure 12.4). The Braille alphabet is only a small part of the literary Braille code, which also consists of contractions (or combinations of letters). Braille is produced on a Braillewriter or on a hand-held slate and stylus. A computer can also produce it with a Braille printer.

Learning to read Braille should begin long before a student enters school, just as learning to read print should (Koenig & Holbrook, 2002). Sighted children begin the reading process by recognizing symbols in the environment. For example, children at an early age might learn to associate a hamburger and French

The expanded core curriculum includes the specialized skill areas that students with visual impairments need in order to benefit from the core curriculum.

Some students who are blind read by using Braille, a tactile code of raised dots.

The six dots of the Braille cell are arranged and numbered thus:

1 ● ● 4
2 ● ● 5
3 ● ● 6

The capital sign, dot 6, placed before a letter makes it a capital. The number sign, dots 3, 4, 5, 6, placed before a character, makes it a figure and not a letter.

1 a	2 b	3 c	4 d	5 e	6 f	7 g	8 h	9 i	10 j
11 k	12 l	13 m	14 n	15 o	16 p	17 q	18 r	19 s	20 t
21 u	22 v	23 w	24 x	25 y	26 z	Capital sign	Number sign	Period	Comma

FIGURE 12.4

Braille alphabet and numerals

Source: Division for the Blind and Physically Handicapped, Library of Congress, Washington, DC 20542.

fries with the golden arches of McDonald's. Children who are sighted have experience watching adults read books, looking at picture books, and having books read to them long before they know how to read. They also build background experiences through observation and participation.

In contrast, children who are severely visually impaired will not have experiences equating symbols with their meanings unless they are given tactile symbols. Children who are blind cannot watch adults read books, so they gain knowledge about books only if they have the opportunity to explore Braille books prior to school. Parents who give children opportunities to become familiar with Braille and tactile symbols help them achieve readiness for Braille reading. Without these experiences, it becomes necessary for the teacher to begin the process of developing an understanding of symbols. Children with visual impairments also need to be provided with the experiences that are described in their school reading series—usually the games and routines of sighted children. All children need experiential background to fully understand what they read, but it is especially important to provide background experiences for children who are blind, for they may not have developed symbolic meanings for themselves (Koenig & Holbrook, 2000). Classroom teachers should request Braille copies of all classroom materials so that the student who reads Braille can be included in all activities.

● *Low-Vision Aids and Training* Many students who are visually impaired do not use Braille as their primary literacy medium; instead, they can learn to use large print or even regular print with magnification or low-vision aids. In other words, their primary source of information is still visual.

Professionals in visual impairment no longer believe that using vision can damage it. In fact, professionals who work with students who are visually impaired now realize that instruction can actually help children develop better use of their vision.

Instruction in the use of low vision touches on three areas: environmental adaptations, which may involve making changes in distance, size, contrast,

The majority of students who are visually impaired read large print.

Students with low vision get most of their information through their vision.

This brother and sister read side-by-side. She is normally sighted and reads print; he is blind and reads the Braille equivalent.

illumination, or time; enhancement of visual skills, such as attention, scanning, tracking, and reaching for objects, through integration of these skills into functional activities; and integration of vision into activities, or teaching skills within the actual activities where they are needed (Erin & Topor, 2010b). Teaching these skills is usually the responsibility of the teacher specialist in visual impairment.

> Students with visual impairments must learn to use their remaining vision well.

Some examples of low-vision aids are optical aids, such as a hand-held magnifying glass; closed-circuit television (CCTV) sets that enlarge printed material onto a screen; computer software that varies type size and type; computer hardware such as large monitor screens and screen magnifiers; large-print textbooks; and materials used to provide greater contrast in written and printed matter: yellow acetate, bold-line paper, and felt-tip markers (Zimmerman, 1996). Low-vision instruction is designed to help the student make the best possible use of the vision that he or she has.

● *Developing Listening Skills* Since students who are visually impaired receive a large percentage of information through their auditory sense, it is important to give them instruction and experience in using this sense to the fullest. Many people believe that people who are blind automatically have superior auditory skills, but this is not true.

> Students who are visually impaired develop acute listening skills through careful instruction.

Listening to recorded materials does not replace reading print or Braille as a means for developing literacy; however, it is important for students who are blind since it allows for efficient gathering of large amounts of materials over a short period of time. With instruction, a student can become more efficient in the use of listening for learning.

● *Orientation and Mobility* In addition to academic skills, students with visual impairment must develop skills to ensure that they can be independent adults, able to work and to move around in their environment with as little assistance as possible (Fazzi & Naimy, 2010). For this reason, instruction in orientation and mobility is a critical component of the curriculum for students who are blind (see A Closer Look, "Who Are the Professionals Interacting with the Student Who Is Visually Impaired?"). Orientation and mobility training is "teaching the concepts and skills necessary for students to travel safely and efficiently in

A CLOSER LOOK

Benefits of the Expanded Core Curriculum (ECC)

Pat, a 20-year-old man with low vision, graduated from high school last year. He began receiving services from a teacher of students with visual impairments as a toddler. Throughout his education, teachers of students with visual impairments worked with him three hours a week, three to five days a week, enlarging his reading materials, tutoring him in academics, and explaining his special needs to his classroom teachers and other students. Pat was on the A-B honor roll throughout school. His teacher of students with visual impairments saw that his materials were organized, helped him to study and complete assignments, and ensured that he was able to pass his end-of-course test and standardized examinations. Pat entered college but discovered that he was unable to keep up with his course work. His roommate became frustrated because Pat was unable to wash his laundry, keep track of his belongings, or find his way to a new location independently. Pat thought about getting a part-time job, but he did not know which jobs he could do or even how to go about applying for one. He had only one close friend, who attended a different college, and he did not know how to meet new people. At the end of the semester, he dropped out of school, moved home, and began collecting Social Security Disability Income.

Aaron, another 20-year-old young man with low vision, attended the same college as Pat. From the time he began receiving early intervention services as an infant, his family and teachers focused on helping Aaron to be independent upon graduation from high school. Throughout his educational career, his teacher of students with visual impairments and his O&M specialist identified and focused on skills that would prepare Aaron to thrive without the support of professionals. As a result of carefully planned instruction, by the time Aaron entered high school he was able to function independently in his classrooms, advocating for his needs when teachers forgot to make reasonable accommodations. He had a well-developed social network with whom he spent much of his free time. He traveled independently to meet his friends, go on dates, and get to his part-time job. His teacher of students with visual impairments and O&M instructor each worked with him one hour a week during his senior year of high school to provide instruction on the few skills that needed refining, such as independent living (for example, budgeting and shopping for food), career (for instance, identifying his career interests and the requirements for those careers), O&M (for example, how to orient to a new campus and community when going to college), and assistive technology. Aaron is thriving in his college community. He has joined two clubs and spends time with several new friends when he has a few moments free. He has received As and Bs in his courses and has even found time for a part-time job at a lawyer's office, since he hopes to become a lawyer himself. The resident adviser (RA) in his dorm has suggested that he consider becoming an RA next year, since he has adjusted so successfully to college life and is well liked by the other students in the dormitory.

As these two examples have demonstrated, success in school goes beyond ensuring that students are able to pass their courses and graduate from high school on time. Children and youths with visual impairments deserve the opportunity to have full, rich lives that include good educations, strong social lives, meaningful careers, and the ability to live and travel independently. The components of the ECC have long been recognized as critical for promoting the quality of life of students who are visually impaired, and recent research has supported the provision of instruction in these areas.

Source: From Sapp, W., & Hatlen, P. (2010). The Expanded Core Curriculum: Where We Have Been, where We Are Going, and How We Can Get There. Journal of Visual Impairment & Blindness (JVIB), 104 (6) 338–348. Copyright © 2010 by AFB Press, American Foundation for the Blind. All Rights Reserved.

their environmental settings" (Griffin-Shirley, Trusty, & Rickard, 2000, p. 530). Orientation and mobility specialists (again, refer to the Closer Look box for further information) should begin their work as soon as a child is identified with visual impairment—even in infancy! The skills needed to travel within the environment are rooted in the child's early experiences at home (Fazzi & Naimy, 2010).

Orientation and mobility consist of two equally important subparts: **orientation,** the ability to use one's senses to establish where one is in space and in

Orientation is the ability to use one's senses to establish one's relationship to objects and people; mobility is the ability to move about the environment.

A CLOSER LOOK — Who Are the Professionals Interacting with the Student Who Is Visually Impaired?

A number of professionals with different educational backgrounds and specialized skills will likely work with the student who is visually impaired, and you as the teacher will have the opportunity to collaborate with some of them to provide services to the student.

The *teacher of students with visual impairments* has advanced training in providing specialized skills—reading skills, including Braille and large print; concept development; daily living skills; and so on. The teacher may provide direct services to students on an itinerant basis or in a special day class, resource room, or residential school; or may consult with the general education teacher. The *orientation and mobility specialist* teaches the skills for safe and independent travel, from toddlerhood through adulthood, as well as the use of specialized travel devices. Orientation and mobility instructors help students learn to detect obstacles and eventually to cross streets alone; they will be required whenever a student needs to become familiar with a new setting, such as a new school. The *vocational rehabilitation counselor,* usually associated with a state or private agency, assists adolescents with visual impairments when making the transition from school to work by helping them and their families plan for post-high-school education and training, as well as job placement.

Source: Adapted from I. Torres and A.L. Corn (with D. McNear, J. Erin, C. Farrenkopf, and K.M. Haebner), "When You Have a Visually Impaired Student in Your Classroom a Guide for Teacher," New York: AFB Press, American Foundation for the Blind, 1190, 2002.

Teaching Strategies & Accommodations

Integrating Expanded Core Curriculum Activities into Academic Instruction

by Elizabeth Eagan, CTVI, Houston Independent School District

The Expanded Core Curriculum (ECC) includes skills that are not part of the core curriculum of reading, writing, mathematics, science, and social studies. Without this expanded core, a student with a visual impairment is not able to actively participate in the world. Without learning banking skills, for example a student may think money just magically appears to anyone out of a machine on a wall. These students must learn the process that leads up to the ATM giving you money.

For every subject taught in school there is a way to tie it into the ECC. For example, when looking at the Texas Essential Knowledge and Skills (TEKS) objectives for fourth grade:

§110.6. English Language Arts and Reading

(4.15) Writing/purposes: The student writes for a variety of audiences and purposes, and in a variety of forms. (F) The student is expected to choose the appropriate form for his/her own purpose for writing, including journals, letters, reviews, poems, narratives, and instructions (4-5).

The objective is clearly defined. Educators simply need to review the nine ECC areas individually and consider how one might incorporate them. Following is an example of how I have incorporated the nine ECC areas in this TEKS objective.

- Assistive Technology
  The student will utilize a computer or note-taking device to write reviews after reading books. The student writes the reviews as a newspaper critic, a book jacket review, an Amazon website review, etc.

- Compensatory
  The student will write poetry utilizing the different parts of speech and punctuation correctly. Students will utilize free verse, diamante poems, etc.

- Career Education/Transition
  Invite a journalist from the local paper to talk with the student about writing as a career path. Get with classroom teacher to arrange this activity for entire class or as a pull-out activity.

relation to other objects and people, and **mobility,** the ability to move about in one's environment. Skill in orientation and mobility is crucial for several reasons:

- Psychological reasons, including the development of a positive self-concept
- Physical and health reasons, including the development of fitness
- Social reasons, including the increase of opportunities for social interactions through independent travel
- Economic reasons, including the increase of employment opportunities and options

There are four generally accepted orientation and mobility systems: **human guide, cane travel, dog guide,** and **electronic travel aids.** The first three systems will be discussed in this section, and electronic travel aids in the section on assistive technology. People who are blind often use a combination of these systems, depending on the nature of the task they wish to accomplish.

Human Guide   In this system, the person who is blind can travel safely through the environment, including maneuvering around stairs and obstacles, by holding lightly onto the elbow of a sighted person and following the movement of that person as he or she walks. Even though these techniques are relatively safe and efficient, and human guides are often able to assist the person who is blind in the development of kinesthetic awareness (awareness of movement), the continuous use of a human guide may also lead to a level of dependence instead

A *human guide* can help a person who is blind travel safely but may also lead to a high level of dependence.

- Independent Living Skills

  The student will be assigned a pen pal with a similar visual disability at another campus or in another town. Letters will be exchanged via email or U.S. mail.

- Orientation and Mobility

  The student will keep a travel journal of different routes, contacts, and businesses visited throughout the school year. Collaborate with O&M instructor.

- Recreation and Leisure

  The student will start a diary of thoughts, poetry, or whatever the student wishes as a means to put his or her thoughts to paper. The student will be assured that only the pages the student wishes to share will be viewed.

- Self-determination

  The student will write a letter to a city councilman, state representative, senator, etc. of his or her choice, vocalizing a personal opinion of any type, ranging from issues such as accessibility to crime.

- Social Interaction Skills

  The student will create an address book or use a commercial one (APH's EZ Track Address Book), gathering phone numbers of friends, family, local business, and other persons of interest. Business cards should be included for future reference.

- Visual Efficiency Skills

  The student will edit a selected written passage for misspellings and punctuation errors. I have given the student a passage I have created, or one from another student, as well as working on editing his or her own work.

Begin work from the student's comfort level and gradually increase the complexity. Include the parents and classroom teachers as much as possible. One of my favorite activities is to have my students interview their parents on how they do a task. This gives the students an opportunity to see their parents as the expert and to learn from them.

Teaching the ECC is a joint effort by all on the educational team. Collaboration with the classroom teacher is vital in assisting the student to be a well-rounded individual on the road to independence.

Source: Adapted from http://www.tsbvi.edu/resources/3118-integrating-expanded-core-curriculum-activities-into-academic-instruction, Texas School for the Blind and Visually Impaired.

of the independence that is the goal of instruction in orientation and mobility (Fazzi & Naimy, 2010). It is also difficult to use human guide techniques—those used to optimally support and guide a person who is blind—properly, since few members of the general public are aware of them.

Cane Travel   One of the most common systems of orientation and mobility is the use of the long cane for independent travel. Students who are visually impaired and use a cane must learn a variety of techniques in order to travel efficiently and safely. The canes used today are generally made from aluminum and vary in length according to a person's height, stride, and the time it takes him or her to respond to information gathered by moving the cane (Weiner, Welsh, & Blasch, 2010). Instruction in the use of the cane is very specialized and should be provided individually. This instruction is very important, since in many cases the safety of the student depends on the use of proper techniques. Instruction is most commonly given by an orientation and mobility specialist. Orientation and mobility specialists must undergo hundreds of hours of training while blindfolded themselves in order to learn to teach independent travel skills to people who are visually impaired.

> With proper training, students who are visually impaired can use a cane to travel independently.

Dog Guides   The use of dog guides, though well publicized, is very limited. Only a small percentage of people with visual impairments use a dog guide for travel. Not everyone is suited to the strict relationship that a dog guide and its owner must maintain, and they are not typically used by children for that reason. Dog guides are trained to assist people who are blind in safe travel; however, it is the person who is blind who makes decisions regarding travel route and destination. The use of a dog guide does not negate the need for a person who is blind to have good independent orientation and mobility skills.

> Dog guides are used only by a small percentage of people with visual impairments and not usually by children.

● *Development of Independent Living Skills*   Another important element in the expanded core curriculum is the development of **independent living skills** for students with visual impairments. Independent living skills increase their ability to accomplish daily routines, such as selecting and caring for clothes, managing (including identifying) money, preparing food, shopping, and so on (Sticken & Kapperman, 2010).

Children who are sighted learn most daily living skills through observation and imitation or instruction from parents or family members. Children who are blind may not be able to observe daily living activities with enough detail to imitate, and their parents may be unaware of adapted techniques for instruction. It is usually the responsibility of the vision specialist to provide this instruction. Consider, for example, Roberto's predicament:

> One of the responsibilities of the vision specialist is to teach independent living skills.

CASE STUDY

The vision specialist was unaware until Roberto was in the eighth grade that he was unable to tie his shoes. After investigating, the teacher found out that Roberto's parents had attempted several times to teach him, but he had difficulty accomplishing the task as it was described to him and consequently took a very long time to tie his shoes. As in most families, the mornings were hectic, so, two minutes before Roberto's bus arrived each morning, his mother gave in and tied his shoes. The problem came in junior high school, when Roberto had to get dressed and undressed for gym class, and no one was there to tie his shoes. Had instruction in independent living skills been a priority in earlier grades, this difficulty (and embarrassment for Roberto) might have been avoided. The vision specialist immediately began intensive instruction in independent living skills with Roberto. She taught him not only how to tie his shoes but also how to fold the bills in his wallet so that he could tell the difference between a $5 bill and a $10 bill and how to make healthy after-school snacks. As a result, Roberto is more confident and more independent.

Table 12.3 Typical Independent Living Activities for Children with Visual Impairments

Preschool	Dressing
	Mealtime routines
	Toileting
	Use of eating utensils
Elementary years	Selection of clothes according to preference and weather
	Washing and caring for hair
	Household chores
	Handling small amounts of personal money
High school years	Grooming
	Self-care
	Organization of personal possessions
	Ordering and maintaining special devices and equipment
	Application of appropriate social skills

Source: From *Visual Handicaps and Learning*, Third Edition (p. 152–153), by N.C. Barraga and J.N. Erin, 1992, Austin, TX: PRO-ED. Copyright 1992 by PRO-ED, Inc. Reprinted by permission.

See Table 12.3 for examples of daily living skills that can be taught to children who are visually impaired.

Social Interaction Skills   Think about how much of what we have learned about interacting with others came through watching others—through vision. Posture, eye contact, facial expression, when to shake hands, when to touch and not to touch—for all these skills and more, we unconsciously imitate what we see. Without vision, these skills must be taught explicitly, so that people with visual impairments can be accepted by others and form friendships (Sacks, 2010). Teachers can help by quietly requesting that the student with a visual impairment conform to the social expectations of the situation: "Josh, shake hands with Mr. Hudson"; "Lupe, stand up straight." If this is done without embarrassment, it should lead to greater social acceptance in the long run.

Recreation and Leisure Skills   Many students with visual impairments may not know how many options there are for the use of leisure time (Weiner, Welsh, & Blasch, 2010). Learning about these options and acquiring the skills needed to perform them are part of the responsibility of the specialized teacher. Among the options that can be learned by people with visual impairments are cross-country and downhill skiing, bicycling, sailing and canoeing, running, skating, bowling, swimming, waterskiing, scuba diving, snorkeling, and martial arts—you name the activity, it can be adapted. For information on world-class mountain climber and author Erik Weihenmayer, who is blind, visit the National Foundation for the Blind's website.

Use of Assistive Technology   The technological adaptations for people with visual impairments are impressive, although not all students have access to them. We will discuss technology separately later in the chapter.

Career Education   Career education must start early for the child with visual impairment and must focus on developing knowledge of the range of possible careers and interest and skills in particular areas (Sapp & Hatlen, 2010). Since underemployment is a serious issue for adults with visual impairment, this is an essential part of the core curriculum (Goertz, Van Lierop, Houkes, & Nijhuis, 2010).

ASSISTIVE TECHNOLOGY FOCUS

AIM | Accessible Instructional Materials

At the beginning of the academic year, the teacher usually hands out the textbook to every child in the class. But what if you can't read or process printed material? When a child is blind, schools know it's foolishness to hand the child a book unless it's in Braille or in digital format. Much less obvious is that literally tens of thousands of children have disabilities that severely impair their ability to read printed text.

Quite fortunately, the 2004 amendments to IDEA have emphasized making instructional materials accessible to students with print disabilities, and a serious amount of effort has gone into setting up systems to make that happen. Take advantage of those systems, because students with disabilities will benefit enormously! To connect you with those systems, we've listed seminal resources below.

What IDEA requires

Heard of NIMAS? If not, read The National Dissemination Center for Children with Disabilities (NICHCY)'s training module on the subject. It'll tell you what IDEA requires and why it's such a fabulous step forward. http://www.nichcy.org/laws/idea/legacy/module1/

The National Center for Accessible Instructional Materials

Find just about everything AIM at http://aim.cast.org/ including:

- Clear explanations of accessible media
- Who's eligible for AIM
- Primary contacts in your state
- Educator's guide to accessible textbooks in the K-12 classroom
- Online decision-making tools to help IEP teams match AIM with student needs

Bookshare

Bookshare is free for all U.S. students with qualifying disabilities, thanks to an award from the U.S. Department of Education Office of Special Education Programs (OSEP). http://www.bookshare.org/

Recording for the blind and dyslexic

RFB&D is a national nonprofit with more than 62,000 accessible audiobook titles. http://www.rfbd.org/

Louis

The American Printing House for the Blind (APH) currently houses a database called the Louis Database of Accessible Materials for People Who Are Blind or Visually Impaired. Louis contains information about tens of thousands of titles of accessible materials, including Braille, large print, sound recordings, and computer files from over 170 agencies throughout the United States. Find Louis at http://www.aph.org

Source: NICHCY's eNews You Can Use, October 2010. Retrieved from: http://nichcy.org/newsletters/oct2010#special/.

Visual Efficiency The term *visual efficiency* refers to the best possible use of the remaining vision in the person who is blind or has low vision. The specialized teacher must assess functional vision, plan learning activities, and teach students to use their functional vision effectively (Sapp & Hatlen, 2010).

School Settings for Students Who Are Blind or Have Low Vision

Students with visual impairments can be found in every kind of educational setting. Each decision about *where* the child learns is made on the basis of the individual student's needs, by the IEP team. Here are some of the options, ranging from the least restrictive to residential schools.

• *Public School Programs* Public school programs are today the most frequently used service delivery model for students who are visually impaired. The major educational models used within public schools are consultative services, itinerant services, resource rooms, and self-contained classrooms.

Most children with visual impairments are now educated in public schools.

In the **consultant model,** the general education teacher and specialized teacher set up the needed classroom adaptations together, and the specialized teacher is available to the general education teacher for help as needed. This model might be appropriate for the student functioning at grade level or for the student with multiple disabilities that include visual impairment (Ferrari, 2009).

Itinerant services, in which a trained teacher travels from school to school within a specific area, providing direct or indirect services to students with visual impairments, are available for students enrolled in public schools who need additional one-to-one assistance.

In **resource room programs,** the student who is visually impaired is enrolled in the general education classroom, where he or she receives most instruction. **Self-contained classrooms** are classrooms within a public school in which only children with visual impairments are enrolled. The teacher of the class is certified in special education that focuses on the needs of students with visual impairments. Self-contained classrooms may be very useful in the education of very young children who are blind in order to prepare them for full, successful inclusion in general education classrooms.

● *Residential School Programs* Residential schools, in which students go to classes and live on campus, have traditionally offered comprehensive services, providing instruction in academic skills, daily living skills, and vocational skills.

Lewis and Allman (2000) see the following advantages for residential schools:

- All the adults are trained and knowledgeable about the complex educational needs of students with visual impairments.

- The students spend all day learning, rather than spending time waiting while sighted students are instructed visually.

- Students continue learning beyond the six-hour school day, since instruction occurs in dormitories and in community-based settings on weekends and after school.

- Goals related to the expanded core curriculum are infused into all activities by knowledgeable specialists.

- Students have the opportunity to interact with other students with visual impairments.

These advantages must be weighed against the drawbacks of being separated for long periods from family and community.

One of the most critical decisions to be made for children with visual impairments and their families is placement, or school setting—*where* they will go to school. It is difficult to obtain the "ideal" placement for the student who is blind or has low vision, since each student has such complex needs (Lewis & Allman, 2000). Following the initial placement decision, it is important that the appropriateness of the decision be re-evaluated frequently so that the child will receive not only the best possible instruction, taking into account the need for adaptive skills, but also the social interactions and experiences that will prepare the child for adult life in a competitive world.

Education for Students with Additional Disabilities

As we discussed earlier in the chapter, many students with visual impairment have additional disabilities such as deafness, emotional disturbance, intellectual disabilities, learning disabilities, and physical impairment. Regardless of additional disabilities, students with visual impairments should be encouraged to make use of their functional vision and also be taught adaptive techniques for independent living and vocational skills. In most cases, special education teachers who have students with multiple disabilities in their classroom will receive consultation services from the vision teacher in order to provide them with adaptive instruction.

Itinerant teachers travel from school to school to provide services to students with visual impairments.

Residential schools have played a major role in the education of children with visual impairments and today offer support for professionals in public schools.

▶❚❚ **TeachSource VIDEO CASE**

Can an Inclusive Setting Meet the Needs of a Student with Complex Needs?

Amy is a sixth grader in an inclusive middle school. She's a gifted literature student but has challenges with both hearing and visual impairments. Visit Chapter 12 on the CourseMate website and hear Christine Golliver, her teacher, describe the modifications and adaptations she has made to address Amy's needs in the classroom. How could Ms. Golliver's ideas be used to help Amy with her homework?

Students with visual impairment and other disabilities will also need specialized instruction.

In science lab, Jeremy is using his sense of touch to determine the type of animal bones found at a mountain site. This skill will be crucial for him in every aspect of his life.

Pause and Reflect

Is there a "best" setting for students with visual impairments? Can you think of an advantage and a disadvantage of each of the options we have described? •

Assistive Technology

Assistive technology allows people who are blind or have low vision to function independently.

Technological changes have had a significant effect on the educational and vocational outlook for students with visual impairments. Many assistive technology devices are now available to increase a student's ability to function independently in educational and employment settings, and, most important, to increase access to print. (See the Assistive Technology Focus feature on page 444.) Teachers have a role to play, though, in making this technology accessible and understandable to their students (Presley, 2010). Teachers need to provide effective instruction, to maximize time management, and to advocate for the purchase of equipment. There are four major categories of available technology:

1. *Devices to increase visual access to print* often start with video magnifiers, which are closed-circuit televisions (CCTV) that enlarge print size on a television screen. A student may use such devices to magnify all or some of his class work. The video magnifier should be in a place where the student has easy access and is still a part of the class. Some students may have access to a portable version with a small hand-held camera that is TV compatible. As soon as the student is introduced to the video magnifier, he or she will receive instruction from the vision specialist on its use and should, within a short

time, be able to use it independently. The student should then be allowed to use the video magnifier whenever he or she believes it will help accomplish the class work. Software that enlarges the size of print and images on the computer screen (for example, Zoom Text) is another essential for many low-vision computer users.

2. *Devices to increase auditory access to print,* including voice output devices for personal computers and devices that convert print to auditory output, are now widely available. For students who are unable to read the print on a computer screen, a voice output device with screen-reading software may allow them to use the computer to complete assignments. Headphones are available so that the student can use the device without disturbing other students.

3. *Devices to increase tactile access to print,* including Braille printers that can be attached to word processors for immediate access to print work and devices that convert print to a tactile output. In the past, students who were blind would complete assignments in Braille, but the classroom teacher who was unable to read Braille would have to wait for the vision specialist to transcribe the Braille into print before grading the assignment. With the introduction of devices that can convert print into Braille and Braille into print, students can print their assignments in both Braille and English.

   For the student, though, the most helpful tool may be the Braille note-taker (for example, Braille Lite). With these devices, students can take notes on a Braille keypad, and receive auditory output or download their notes to their computer.

4. *Devices to increase independent travel,* including electronic travel aids that are independent or provide supplementary information about the environment. There are a variety of devices, such as the laser cane, which use sonar and/or laser technology to aid in the detection of obstacles or drop-offs while traveling. The global positioning satellite (GPS) with speech and talking maps are increasingly being used as orientation aids (Fazzi & Naimy, 2010). Although these devices are not directly relevant to academic work, the classroom teacher should know as much as possible about any device the student is using, including how it works, when the student should use it, and how to reinforce the student's proper use of the device. An orientation and mobility specialist will be able to answer all these questions.

Using some of these adaptive devices, people with visual impairments can also use the Internet. Web accessibility is an increasingly important issue for people who are visually impaired (American Foundation for the Blind, 2011)

As you know, changes in technology occur so quickly that it can be difficult to keep up to date. Consult the Useful Resources section at the end of this chapter for some websites that can provide you with the most current information about assistive technology.

> Technology can improve access to print through visual, auditory, or tactile modalities.

? Pause and Reflect

The needs of students with visual impairments present us with a significant challenge. We know that, given the appropriate instruction and supports, they can become successful, productive adults, but providing the instruction and the supports takes considerable expertise and teamwork on the part of the student, the family, and the professionals working on the student's behalf. Do you think you could be part of that "support team"? ●

☀ ASSISTIVE TECHNOLOGY FOCUS

What Special Devices Will the Student with Visual Impairment Use?

Students who are visually impaired may use a variety of equipment, devices, and tools to assist them with various academic and everyday tasks. Some students may need only a few adaptive devices, while others need to use several in combination.

OPTICAL DEVICES

Eyeglasses with special prescriptions
Magnifiers
Telescopes

NONOPTICAL DEVICES

. . . to enhance VISUAL FUNCTIONING	. . . to enhance TACTILE FUNCTIONING	. . . to enhance AUDITORY FUNCTIONING
Book stands	Braille	Digital tape recorders
Wide felt-tipped pens and markers	Tactile graphics	Talking books, recorded books, and e-books
Acetate	Braillewriter	Talking calculators
Lamps	Slate and stylus	Voice organizers and recorders
Large-print books	Raised-line paper	Audible gym equipment (such as beeper balls, sound emitters)
Bold-line paper	Templates and writing guides	Additional auditory devices (talking watches, alarm clocks, thermometers, money identifiers, etc.)
Line markers and reading windows	Raised-line drawing boards and other tactile writing devices	
Sun visors and other shields	Raised marks	
Measurement tools	Braille labeler	
Additional tools (many other adaptations are readily available, like calculators with large displays and keys with large print, etc.)	Measurement tools with Braille and raised markings	
	Abacus	
	3-D models	
	Teacher-made materials	
	Additional tactile materials and tools	

ASSISTIVE TECHNOLOGY DEVICES

Video magnifiers
Braille translation software
Braille printer
Synthetic speech

Screen-enlargement software
Refreshable Braille displays
Audible and Braille note-takers
Electronic Braillewriter

Optical character recognition (OCR) with speech and scanner
Tactile graphics maker

© David Barber/PhotoEdit

The student who is blind can use this Braille note-taker to take notes using Braille. The notes can be read back via voice, through the speaker on top, or via Braille, using the "refreshable Braille" display at the bottom.

Source: Adapted and updated from S. Spungin (Ed.) (2002). *When You Have a Visually Impaired Student in Your Classroom: A Guide for Teachers.* New York: AFB Press.

SUMMARY

- Students with visual impairments make up a relatively small percentage of school-age children. This low-incidence population includes children who are blind, who have low vision, and who are visually impaired and have additional disabilities. Although legal blindness is required for some services, educational services are also offered to students with less severe visual impairments.

- The process of seeing involves the passage of light through the eye and interpretation of the image by the brain. Damage to any of the eye structures, the nerves connecting them to the brain, or the brain itself can result in visual impairment.

- Visual impairments may affect a child's development by limiting one source of sensory feedback from the environment. In language, children may use verbal expressions without understanding what they mean; in physical development, children may be less motivated to move and explore; in cognitive development, children may interact less with the environment, which may result in poorer concept development.

- Early intervention involves allowing the child to explore and touch and helping parents make the most of learning opportunities in daily life.

- Teachers are often the first to recognize milder visual impairments. The most common screening test is the Snellen Chart. Ideally, vision screening is the product of a team approach, with continuous observation in the classroom, referral for evaluation, and follow-up provided by appropriate professionals.

- A functional vision assessment is used to make decisions about the student's educational program. Interpretation of test results should take into account modifications to the test and items that rely heavily on visual experience. Teachers should know what the child's functional vision is like.

- The expanded core curriculum for students who are blind or have low vision includes instruction in the core academic areas and in specialized skill areas such as Braille and low-vision aids, development of listening skills, self-determination, and orientation and mobility.

- Placement options for students who have visual impairments were initially limited to residential schools; however, public schools now provide self-contained classrooms, as well as resource programs, itinerant services, and consultation services for students included in the general education classroom.

- Advances in assistive technology have resulted in increasing visual, auditory, and tactile access to print; new technology for mobility has also been developed.

KEY TERMS

visual impairment (page 413)
legally blind (page 413)
visual acuity (page 413)
educational definitions (page 414)
functionally blind (page 414)
low vision (page 414)
functional vision (page 414)
cornea (page 416)

pupil (page 416)
lens (page 416)
vitreous humor (page 416)
iris (page 416)
retina (page 416)
optic nerve (page 416)
cortical visual impairment
    (page 418)

retinopathy of prematurity (ROP)
(page 418)

optic nerve hypoplasia (page 418)

albinism (page 418)

glaucoma (page 418)

cataract (page 418)

diabetic retinopathy (page 418)

verbalisms (page 419)

echolalia (page 419)

orientation and mobility (page 420)

Snellen chart (page 428)

expanded core curriculum (page 432)

compensatory academic and access
skills (page 432)

Braille (page 432)

orientation (page 435)

mobility (page 437)

human guide (page 437)

cane travel (page 437)

dog guide (page 437)

electronic travel aids (page 437)

independent living skills
(page 438)

consultant model (page 441)

itinerant services (page 441)

resource room programs (page 441)

self-contained classrooms
(page 441)

USEFUL RESOURCES

- Susan Spungin (Ed.) (2002). *When You Have a Visually Impaired Child in Your Classroom: A Guide for Teachers.* New York: AFB Press. This small book is available at low cost from the American Foundation for the Blind (AFB). It is just about the most useful resource a teacher whose class includes a student with vision loss could have.

- The American Printing House for the Blind (APH) also publishes a book for teachers *Teaching the Student with a Visual Impairment: A Primer for the Classroom Teacher.* It is available through the APH website at **http://www.aph .org.** APH provides special media, tools, and material needed for education and daily life by people with visual impairments.

- The British Columbia Ministry of Education has an extensive website including practical information on disabilities for general education teachers. **http://www.bced.gov.bc.ca/specialed/visimpair/.**

- The Texas School for the Blind and Visually Impaired has extensive publications and online resources for working with kids with VI: **http://tsbvi.edu// resources/.**

- The Blind Children's Center in Los Angeles publishes a series of books, DVDs, and brochures that are useful, inexpensive, and reader-friendly on topics such as communicating and encouraging movement with the young child with visual impairments. They are written with parents in mind but are helpful for early intervention specialists and teachers too. Contact them at **http://www.blindchildrenscenter.org/pubs.html.**

- The Library of Congress National Library Service for the Blind and Physically Handicapped is a free lending library of Braille and recorded materials circulated to eligible borrowers through a network of cooperating libraries. Visit their website at **http://www.loc.gov/nls.**

- The APH currently houses a database called the *Louis Database of Accessible Materials for People Who Are Blind or Visually Impaired.* Louis contains information about more than 374,499 titles of accessible materials, including Braille, large print, sound recordings, and computer Braille files from agencies throughout the United States. You can access Louis several ways: through the Internet at **http://louis.aph.org/catalog** by phone (800) 223-1839, ext. 705, or by e-mail **resource@aph.org.**

- *AccessWorld: Technology and People Who Are Blind and Visually Impaired* is a bi-monthly journal from the AFB that covers a wide range of topics related to assistive technology and visual impairment. It is available online, in large print and Braille, or on tape or disk.
- Explore the activities of the United States Association of Blind Athletes at **http://www.usaba.org/** or search for their Facebook page.
- *Family Connect* is a website put together by the American Foundation for the Blind (AFB) for families of children with visual impairments. Find it at **http://www.familyconnect.org.**
- AFB offers an excellent video: *What Do You Do When You See a Blind Person:* **http://www.afb.org/store/.**
- The Braille Bug is a website for kids from the American Foundation for the Blind. It introduces basic Braille and has activities, riddles and games at **http://www.afb.org/braillebug/.** Your students should enjoy The Helen Keller Kids' Museum Online, available there too.

There are four excellent online modules at the IRIS Center site that address the needs of students with visual impairments and their teachers. Go to **http://iris .peabody.vanderbilt.edu/resources.html/.** Click on *Resources*, then in the left-hand column click on *Disability*, then in the middle column click on *Modules*. They are:

- Accommodations to the Physical Environment: Setting up a Classroom for Students with Visual Disabilities. The resources in this module offer helpful tips on setting up the physical aspects of your classroom and will introduce types of equipment used by students with visual disabilities.
- Instructional Accommodations: Making the Learning Environment Accessible to Students with Visual Disabilities. This module highlights tips for modifying lessons and ways to make lessons accessible for students with disabilities.
- Serving Students with Visual Impairments: The Importance of Collaboration. This module underscores the importance of the general education teacher's collaborating with professionals and other individuals knowledgeable about the needs of students with visual disabilities.

 PORTFOLIO ACTIVITIES

1. Now that you've read the chapter, have your assumptions about what it is like to have a visual impairment changed? Try a simulation exercise: Wear a blindfold during the first half of class. Concentrate on orientation and mobility, using listening skills, and memorizing spatial relationships. What were your impressions? What training would you need to live independently with a visual impairment? Write a short paper for your portfolio describing your experience.

  CEC This activity will help the student meet CEC Initial Content Standard 3: Individual Learning Differences.

2. What are the limitations of the simulation exercise you just experienced? Now that you've experienced the simulation, what are you going to do to improve the quality of life for people with visual impairments? What resources for training exist in your community for persons with VI? Write a one-page plan for your portfolio.

  CEC This activity will help the student meet CEC Initial Content Standard 1: Foundations.

3. Contact the Office for Students with Disabilities on your campus and ask if there is a need for readers for blind students. Some textbooks are not immediately available electronically in Braille, or in large print, so listening to a book on audiotape is the only way students have access to text material. Your journal describing your experiences as a reader could be included in your portfolio

 This activity will help the student meet CEC Initial Content Standard 4: Instructional Strategies.

4. Plan a social studies or science unit and modify it to meet the needs of students who are blind. Include this unit plan in your portfolio.

 This activity will help the student meet CEC Initial Content Standard 10: Collaboration.

To access Portfolio Activities for this chapter and other useful study resources including an interactive eBook, related web links, quizzes, flashcards, and videos, visit the Education CourseMate website at CengageBrain.com.

Children with Physical Disabilities and Health Impairments

Learning Objectives

After reading this chapter, the reader will:

- Describe the general differences between physical disabilities and health impairments.

- Discuss how knowing the cause and treatment of a student's condition can help you work effectively with the student.

- Identify how the age of onset and severity of a condition can affect a child's social and emotional development.

- Discuss the ways technology can facilitate communication and social interaction among all students in a classroom, including those with significant physical disabilities.

- Identify strategies that can be used to increase students' access to academic content in classrooms.

- Describe various strategies and agencies that facilitate the transition from school to adult life for individuals with physical and health challenges.

Children with physical disabilities and health impairments are a diverse group. This category includes students with a wide range of individual differences, abilities, and challenges. Because many people with physical disabilities and health impairments acquire their disabilities after infancy or have short life expectancies, they often face emotional stress, in addition to their primary disability.

Many individuals with physical disabilities or health impairments play a pivotal role in the ongoing fight for civil and human rights due to all people with disabilities. Their participation in this struggle has resulted not only in many legal and physical changes in the environment, but also in a long tradition of self-advocacy. The visibility of physical disabilities creates a common bond among individuals with disabilities and allows advocates to make powerful statements. That visibility, however, can also set up nonphysical barriers and other difficulties in interpersonal situations, particularly for young children with disabilities. For example, imagine having to explain many times a day why you have no hair, why your hands are in splints, or why you have to rest a few seconds between words. In this chapter, we will rely frequently on the voices of persons with physical disabilities and health impairments as they answer these types of questions to help you learn more about them as people—friends, relatives, and students.

Terms and Definitions

Probably more than any other disability, the presence of a physical disability makes us explore the meaning of such words as *disability, handicap,* and *severity.* This is because the degree of physical involvement and the degree to which the disability affects an individual's life are not necessarily correlated. You might consider paralysis from the neck down to be an extremely severe disability. Yet, the many persons with this condition who lead fulfilling lives may not view themselves as "handicapped" at all. Individuals with physical disabilities adjust, adapt, and contribute to the community. Their disabilities become handicaps only when society uses them as a reason to discriminate against and segregate people.

It is also helpful to recognize that not all children and adolescents with physical disabilities or health impairments receive special education services. Simply having a physical difference or a chronic illness does not mean you must be identified and provided with specialized services—you may not need or want them. In this chapter, we describe what these differences might be—whether special education services are required will depend on the needs and wants of each individual child and his or her family.

> Many people with physical disabilities view their physical condition as a challenge rather than a handicapping condition.

Physical Disabilities

Many people with physical disabilities prefer to use the term **physically challenged.** They view their physical conditions as a challenge to be faced rather than as a situation that disables or handicaps their existence. A pointed quote from an individual with a physical challenge reflects this spirit: "Living as a spinal cord-injured individual is really no different than living as an able-bodied individual, except that you're doing it on wheels. Some of the technical aspects of living on wheels are different" (Corbet, 1980, p. 54).

Physical disability refers to a condition that incapacitates the skeletal, muscular, and/or neurological systems of the body to some degree. Many individuals with physical disabilities have no concurrent mental disability. This is an important point for us to keep in mind. Later in the chapter we will discuss conditions of coexisting mental and physical disabilities.

The Individuals with Disabilities Education Act (IDEA) identifies students who experience physical disabilities as "orthopedically impaired":

> "Orthopedically impaired" means having a severe orthopedic impairment. The term includes impairments caused by a congenital anomaly (e.g., clubfoot, absence of some member, etc.), an impairment caused by disease (e.g., poliomyelitis, bone tuberculosis, etc.), and an impairment from any other cause (e.g., cerebral palsy, amputations, and fractures or burns which cause contractures). (Individuals with Disabilities Education Act, 1990, Sec. 300.6[6])

Health Impairment

The term **health impairment** also focuses on the physical condition of individuals. It includes conditions in which one or more of the body's systems are affected by diseases or conditions that are debilitating or life-threatening or that interfere with the student's ability to perform in a regular classroom setting. The definition of health impairment found in IDEA is as follows:

> "Other health impaired" (OHI) means having limited strength, vitality, or alertness, due to chronic or acute health problems such as heart condition, tuberculosis, rheumatic fever, nephritis, asthma, sickle cell anemia, hemophilia, epilepsy, lead poisoning, leukemia, or diabetes. (Amendments to the Individuals with Disabilities Education Act, 1990, Sec. 300.5[7])

Prevalence

Students with physical disabilities are one of the smaller groups of students served through IDEA. In 2008-2009 about 70,000 students ages 3 to 21 with physical disabilities (referred to as *orthopedically impaired* in the law) were served under IDEA. On the other hand, about 659,000 students were served as Other Health Impaired (OHI) (National Center for Educational Statistics, 2011). It is important to realize, as we look at those numbers, that the group of kids served as OHI includes not only the children with the health impairments we discuss here, but also many, many other children—such as children with ADHD and Asperger's syndrome—who receive this label in order to receive special education services.

Although listed as a separate category of special education, we will define and discuss traumatic brain injury later in this chapter, as many individuals with traumatic brain injury also have physical disabilities. According to the National Center for Educational Statistics (2011) about 26,000 children, ages 3–21 with traumatic brain injury received special education services in 2008-2009.

? **Pause and Reflect**

In Chapter 1 we talked about the nature of the following words that describe disabilities. Many individuals with physical disabilities clearly distinguish between the use of the terms challenge, disability, and handicap. Do you believe that these words can affect the way you or others perceive students with physical challenges? ●

Types of Physical Disabilities

In this section, we will look at the most prevalent types, causes, and treatments of physical disabilities in children. There are several reasons why you, as a prospective teacher, should know about particular disabilities. Understanding the cause may help you to know what to expect from a student, since certain causes lead to characteristic behavior. Understanding treatment requirements can also help you plan classroom time (for example, a student may need to miss class for dialysis) and become comfortable with helping the student with in-school treatment such as tube feeding. Once you know what to expect, you will be better able to plan instruction and to prepare the classroom from a physical perspective.

The abilities of students within each type of physical disability can vary widely. Resist stereotyping and base your expectations on the abilities and efforts of each individual student.

> Within each disability category, the individual range of ability varies greatly.

Neurological Conditions

A neurological condition is one that affects the nervous system—the brain, nerves, and spinal cord (Fraser, Hensinger, & Phelps, 1990). The muscles and bones are healthy, but the neurological messages sent to them are faulty or interrupted. Three of the neurological conditions are cerebral palsy, spina bifida, and seizure disorders.

> Cerebral palsy—caused by damage to the brain before birth or in infancy—results in disabilities in movement and posture.

● *Cerebral Palsy* **Cerebral palsy** is a condition involving disabilities in movement and posture that results from damage to the brain before or during birth, or in infancy. The muscles and the nerves connecting the muscles to the brain are normal; the problem lies in the "communication" process between the brain and the muscles. Events like cerebral hemorrhages (bleeding in the brain), anoxia (lack of oxygen at birth), and fetal strokes can cause neurological damage that results in some type of cerebral palsy. Other possible causes include abnormal brain development, insufficient circulation to the brain before or after birth, infection in/or beside the brain, or the indirect effects of the mother's immune

Between friends, the focus is on fun, not on disability.

system that may occur while she fights infection (Mayo Clinic, 2002). However, in many instances of cerebral palsy, no specific cause can be identified, and the condition is not considered to be preventable given our current level of knowledge (Hankins, 2003).

The area and severity of brain injury, the cause of the injury, and when it occurs determine the type of cerebral palsy that appears and the extent of its effect on the body. Prevalence figures suggest that about 8,000 infants and 1,500 preschool children are identified with cerebral palsy each year, and that about 176,000 individuals in the United States have cerebral palsy—data that appeared constant for years (Hankins, 2003; UCP, 2011). Recent research, however, suggests this might be changing, although there are no clear reasons why. Haastert et al. (2011) found that the incidence of cerebral palsy among a large sample of premature infants (a high-risk population) decreased from 6.5 percent to 2.2 percent between 1990 and 2005.

Some children are identified as having cerebral palsy at birth, whereas others are not definitively diagnosed until they are a year old or even older. Young children are often identified as having cerebral palsy because of delay in meeting the milestones of motor development, such as walking at twelve months, and the persistence of certain infant reflexes. Cerebral palsy also can be diagnosed in children up to age 6 who have brain damage due to external causes such as suffocation, near drowning, or encephalitis.

Cerebral palsy is often classified by type of motor dysfunction. The most common type of dysfunction is *spasticity,* or hypertonia. Spasticity involves a mild to severe exaggerated contraction of muscles when the muscle is stretched. It is present in about 70 to 80 percent of all cases of cerebral palsy and occurs when the area injured is on the surface of the brain or on the nerves leading from the surface to the interior of the brain (UCPA, 2011). Spasticity can involve the entire body or only some parts of the body.

Dyskenesia is a type of cerebral palsy characterized by involuntary extraneous motor activity, especially under stress. This type of cerebral palsy occurs in 10 to 20 percent of all cases and is caused by injury to the basal ganglia, the brain's motor switchboard (UCPA, 2001). The involuntary movements sometimes accompany the individual's attempts at voluntary movement. One type of movement *(athetosis)* involves a slow, writhing type of movement. The person may appear to be repeatedly and slowly stretching his or her arms or legs when simply trying to reach for a book. *Choreoathetosis* refers to quick, jerky movements that may accompany the athetoid movements. Movements also may be slow and rhythmic and involve the entire limb or trunk *(distonia).*

Ataxia, a third type of cerebral palsy, is much less common. It occurs in about 5 to 10 percent of all cases, when the injury has occurred in the cerebellum. Ataxia refers to a lurching walking gait. People with ataxia also experience difficulty maintaining their balance.

Some individuals with cerebral palsy have a mixture of types. For example, a student might have spastic quadriplegia and ataxia. As we have already mentioned, the range of severity and involvement can be great. Some individuals may only experience slight difficulty in muscle control—difficulty that may be undetectable by an observer. Others have almost no voluntary movement—they are not able to smile, move a hand, or turn their head intentionally.

Some children with cerebral palsy also experience learning disabilities, intellectual disabilities, ADHD, or other disabilities such as visual impairment and hearing loss. The coexistence of other types of disabilities depends on the extent and location of brain injury as well as on early interventions. Recent statistics suggest that approximately 65 percent of individuals with cerebral palsy experience one or more of these additional disabilities (UCPA, 2011).

Historically, the variability in the estimates of IQ ranges for children with cerebral palsy was largely due to difficulties in administering intelligence tests to individuals with severe physical disabilities. Because many children with severe cerebral palsy may have significant difficulties in both speech and motor abilities, even nonverbal IQ tests may be difficult to administer. The student may have difficulty articulating a response, and difficulty pointing to the correct answer. Parents, teachers, and psychologists must therefore attend closely to academic, task-oriented, and behavioral characteristics of students with cerebral palsy to get a clearer idea of each student's abilities. Characteristics such as maturity, determination and persistence, goal orientation, insight, and the use of one's intellect to cope with disability have been coupled with early academic success in students with severe cerebral palsy (Willard-Holt, 1998). Although typical standardized tests may be difficult to administer, students will find other ways of revealing their potential. Assistive technology has greatly improved our ability to administer tests to children with extensive physical disabilities, and will continue to do so. Clearly, identifying a truly efficient method of communication is the critical factor in both the assessment and instruction of students with cerebral palsy.

Medical interventions such as braces, surgery, and prescribed therapies can help a student with cerebral palsy. For example, physical and occupational therapies exercise, strengthen, and position muscles, bones, and joints. Prevention of serious and painful contractures, dislocations, and rigidity is critical for individuals with cerebral palsy. Physical and occupational therapies facilitate the development of normal reflexes and maximize the control a person can have over the environment.

Positioning is a critical intervention for persons with limited mobility, especially in helping them meet the demands of the classroom. For example, although a physically capable individual can change positions when uncomfortable or fatigued, a student in a wheelchair or one who wears braces may need assistance for minor repositioning. A student with cerebral palsy may need an adult, such as the teacher, to provide physical assistance related to positioning, feeding, and other everyday needs. In the classroom, use of a tape recorder or a "note buddy" for writing notes are simple accommodations that teachers commonly arrange. Assistive technology, another significant intervention for students with cerebral palsy, will be discussed later in the chapter. To learn more about cerebral palsy and to find resources for parents and teachers, please visit the United Cerebral Palsy Association website.

● Spina Bifida **Spina bifida,** or open spine, and *neural tube defects* (NTDs) are general terms used to describe the incomplete development of the brain, the spinal cord, or their protective coverings during prenatal development. An estimated 7 out of every 10,000 births is affected (SBAA, 2011). Spina bifida seems to occur more frequently in both the southeastern and southwestern sections of the United States, and children of Hispanic descent seem to be at higher risk than other children (SBAA, 2011). Spina bifida and other NTDs have been correlated with a lack of folic acid, a vitamin found in green vegetables and fresh fruit, in the diet early in the pregnancy. Studies have found that minimal intakes of folic acid before and during pregnancy significantly decrease the incidence of spina bifida and other NTDs, even in women who have had children with NTDs. Women of childbearing age should carefully evaluate their diets for proper amounts of folic acid or consult with a doctor about appropriate vitamin supplements.

Children with spina bifida have spines that did not properly close during development, so the spinal cord protrudes from the weak point. As a result, nerves that control the lower parts of the body are not properly connected to the brain. When the spinal cord protrudes outside of the body, surgery typically is done within twenty-four hours of birth, in order to protect the spinal cord and to reduce the probability of additional nerve damage. Spina bifida usually results in limited or even no muscle control of the affected area. The extent of the defect depends on the location of the spinal cord damage. If the damage is at the base of the spine, the weakness may be limited to the muscles of the ankles and feet and the child may

> In spina bifida, the spine does not close properly during fetal development, resulting in varying degrees of paralysis.

require only short leg braces for walking. A defect in the middle of the spine may result in paralysis below the waist, necessitating the use of a wheelchair. Bladder control problems and recurring kidney infections are also present (SBAA, 2011).

Hydrocephalus, a condition in which cerebrospinal fluid builds up in the skull and puts pressure on the brain, occurs in about 80 percent of cases of spina bifida. Untreated hydrocephalus may cause brain damage and intellectual disabilities. Since spina bifida and other NTDs can now be detected early in pregnancy, children with this disability are likely candidates for prenatal surgery. Shunts (artificial openings) can be inserted while the fetus is still in the uterus to minimize damage to the brain from excess spinal fluid. Although the paralysis itself cannot be corrected, shunt implants, physical therapy, and surgery can help minimize the effects of the disability (SBAA, 2011).

In hydrocephalus, cerebrospinal fluid builds in the skull, sometimes causing brain damage and intellectual disabilities.

● *Seizure Disorders*   Seizures occur when the normally ordered pattern of movement of electricity along the nerve pathways of the brain is disrupted by an unorganized burst of electric impulses. These bursts periodically disrupt the normal functioning of the brain. The sudden change in how the cells of the brain communicate with each other results in a seizure. Seizure disorders occur in about 3 percent of the population. A condition of the nervous system that makes us susceptible to seizures is known as **epilepsy;** the occurrence of seizures is the primary characteristic of epilepsy (Epilepsy Foundation, 2011). There are a number of possible causes, including any direct injury to the brain, conditions such as cerebral palsy, or scarring of the brain as a result of infections or illness such as meningitis or rubella. In some instances, there appears to be a genetic component or predisposition. In many instances of epilepsy, however, there is no identifiable cause. Not all seizures are epileptic in nature. For example, sometimes a young child with a high fever has an isolated seizure.

Epilepsy is a neurological condition characterized by recurrent seizures.

About three million individuals in the United States have epileptic seizures; 326,000 of those are children under the age of 15 (EPPA, 2011). Two types of seizures found frequently in children are grand mal seizures and petit mal seizures. **Grand mal seizures,** also called generalized tonic-clonic seizures, are experienced by about 60 percent of all individuals with seizure disorders. The seizures, which involve the whole body, usually last a few minutes and often result in a loss of consciousness. Most people experience a warning (called an *aura)* before the occurrence of a grand mal seizure. The aura may be characterized by unusual feelings or numbness. The seizure itself begins with a *tonic phase,* in which there is a stiffening of the body, often a loss of consciousness, heavy and irregular breathing, and drooling. In a few seconds, the seizure goes into the second or *clonic phase.* At this time, the muscles alternately clench and relax, in a jerking motion. Finally, the seizure is followed by a period of fatigue or disorientation. (See Teaching Strategies & Accommodations, "What to Do If Someone Has a Tonic-Clonic Seizure.")

Petit mal seizures, also called absence seizures, occur most frequently in children between the ages of 4 and 12. Petit mal seizures often disappear as the child grows older; however, one-third to one-half of children with a history of petit mal seizures are likely also to have or eventually develop grand mal seizures. Petit mal seizures are very brief—usually lasting between fifteen and thirty seconds. The episodes are sometimes difficult to recognize. The child will lose consciousness, but this is not accompanied by any observable physical changes. In other words, the child may appear to be just blinking his or her eyes or staring into space for a few seconds.

Medications are used extensively in the treatment of seizure disorders. In most cases, appropriate medication can prevent seizures; some adjustment in prescription may be necessary as the child gets older or if different types of seizures begin to occur. It is important for teachers to know when students are receiving medication for seizures because medication can affect school performance by causing changes in alertness and other school-related behaviors. A few children who experience a number of different kinds of seizures or who have extensive brain damage may have seizures that are difficult to keep under control. Another treatment for epilepsy, especially for people who do not benefit from medications, is electrical stimulation of the vagus nerve. An electrode implanted in the chest sends signals to the vagus nerve, which is located in the neck. Other possible treatment options include surgery and a ketogenic diet, which is a diet high in fats and low in carbohydrates (Epilepsy Foundation, 2011).

Up until very recently, surgery for epilepsy required extensive and traumatic brain surgery. Today, however, research trials are underway for a minimally invasive surgery that appears to have great results. In 2011, doctors at Texas Children's Hospital reported five successful surgeries using an MRI-guided laser ablation technique. Laser ablation surgery uses a laser to destroy the brain lesion responsible for seizures and requires only a small hole in the skull, so it is minimally invasive and requires only a few days recovery time. Although not an option for all types of lesions, the success of these surgeries is very promising (Brunton, 2011).

Musculoskeletal Conditions

In addition to physical disabilities caused by damage to the brain are conditions that directly affect muscles and bones. These musculoskeletal and neuromuscular conditions debilitate the muscles, bones, or joints to such a degree that they cause limitations in their functional use.

> In muscular dystrophy, the voluntary muscles of the body progressively weaken.

● *Muscular Dystrophy* **Muscular dystrophy (MD)** is a neuromuscular condition in which the voluntary muscles of the body are affected by progressive weakness. Although there are nine types of muscular dystrophy, the most common in school-age children is Duchenne muscular dystrophy. This genetically transmitted condition, which primarily affects boys, is usually diagnosed between the

Teaching Strategies & Accommodations

What to Do If Someone Has a Tonic-Clonic Seizure

Keep calm. Reassure the other children that the child will be fine in a minute.

Ease the child gently to the floor and clear the area of anything that could hurt him.

Put something flat and soft (like a folded jacket) under his head so it will not bang against the floor as his body jerks.

Turn him gently onto his side. This keeps his airway clear and allows any fluid in his mouth to drain harmlessly away.

Don't try to force his mouth open.
Don't try to hold on to his tongue.
Don't put anything in his mouth.
Don't restrain his movements.

When the jerking movements stop, let the child rest until full consciousness returns.

Breathing may have been shallow during the seizure and may even have stopped briefly.

This can give the child's lips or skin a bluish tinge, which corrects naturally as the seizure ends. In the unlikely event that breathing does not begin again, check the child's airway for any obstruction. It is rarely necessary to give artificial respiration.

Some children recover quickly after this type of seizure; others need more time. A short period of rest, depending on the child's alertness following the seizure, is usually advised. However, if the child is able to remain in the classroom afterward, he or she should be encouraged to do so.

_____

Source: Epilepsy Foundation of America (2011).

ages of 2 and 6. Neither the cause of Duchenne muscular dystrophy nor a specific treatment has yet been discovered, although many therapies, including drug and physical therapies, are available to lessen symptoms. The incidence is usually cited as 1 per 3,500 live male births (NCBI, 2003). Another type of muscular dystrophy you might see in boys is Becker muscular dystrophy. Although similar to Duchenne, onset can be between the ages of 2 and 16; symptoms are less severe, typically, and the course of the condition is less predictable (MDA, 2011).

Because muscular dystrophy is a progressive condition, the child becomes increasingly weak and less mobile with age. A young child with muscular dystrophy may have barely noticeable weakness; by the time the child reaches his teens, however, walking may no longer be possible. The muscle weakness usually begins in the shoulders and hips and then spreads to other areas, including the heart muscles and muscles that affect the lungs. Secondary effects of muscular dystrophy include scoliosis (curvature of the spine) and a gradual loss of cardiac and respiratory function. Respiratory disease is often a cause of death of individuals with muscular dystrophy, whose life expectancy is now in the early 20s (MDA, 2011).

Teachers of students with muscular dystrophy must develop individualized modifications in the curriculum, depending on the child's age and the condition's progress. It is important to be aware of the social and emotional effects that muscular dystrophy may have on the family and the child's understanding of his or her own mortality. See Figure 13.1 for an illustration of related concerns.

● *Juvenile Rheumatoid Arthritis* **Juvenile rheumatoid arthritis (JRA)** is a broad term used to describe a collection of autoimmune and inflammatory conditions in children. It affects the tissue lining of the joints, primarily the joints of the

> Juvenile rheumatoid arthritis affects the tissue lining of the joints, making them painful and stiff.

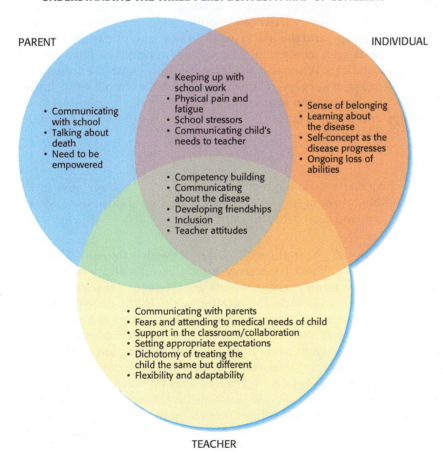

UNDERSTANDING THE THREE PERSPECTIVES: A MAP OF CONCERNS

PARENT

INDIVIDUAL

- Communicating with school
- Talking about death
- Need to be empowered

- Keeping up with school work
- Physical pain and fatigue
- School stressors
- Communicating child's needs to teacher

- Sense of belonging
- Learning about the disease
- Self-concept as the disease progresses
- Ongoing loss of abilities

- Competency building
- Communicating about the disease
- Developing friendships
- Inclusion
- Teacher attitudes

- Communicating with parents
- Fears and attending to medical needs of child
- Support in the classroom/collaboration
- Setting appropriate expectations
- Dichotomy of treating the child the same but different
- Flexibility and adaptability

TEACHER

FIGURE 13.1

Common and unique concerns for students with neuromuscular disabilities

Source: K. Strong & J. Sandoval (1999). Mainstreaming children with a neuromuscular disease: A map of concerns. *Exceptional Children*, 65, 358.

knees, ankles, elbows, hips, wrists, and feet, causing them to become painful and stiff. JRA is found in children between the ages of 3 and adolescence, affects twice as many girls as boys, and typically is diagnosed before age 16. It is estimated that approximately 294,000 children have JRA (Arthritis Foundation, 2011).

One complication of JRA is *iridocyclitis,* an inflammation of the eye that occurs without warning. If a student with JRA complains about bright lights or painful eyes, a teacher should help the student seek immediate medical attention. Some children with JRA may have difficulty holding pencils or typing on a keyboard; others may have difficulty walking, going up stairs, or participating in some physical education activities.

● *Congenital Malformations* A **congenital malformation** is an incomplete or improperly formed part of the skeletal or muscular system that is present at birth. Congenital malformations occur in 2 to 4 percent of all live births (Medline, 2003; Bacino, 2011). Often, there is no known cause for these malformations, although many of the risk factors discussed in Chapter 3 have been partially implicated. In some instances, there may be a genetic component. In other cases, birth defects have been associated with medications or drugs taken during pregnancy, with illness, such as rubella, and with infections experienced by the mother during pregnancy.

Congenital malformations can take many forms; a few of them have particular implications for physical movement. One example is a clubfoot, in which the foot is structured so that the forefoot and heel are turned in and down toward the body and the toes are turned down and away from the body. A clubfoot is sometimes hereditary, with an incidence of 2 per every 1,000 live births. Surgery, physical therapy, and the use of casts are treatment options for children with this condition. Other malformations that can affect mobility are congenital hip dislocations, discrepancies of leg length, shortened or missing limbs, and scoliosis, or curvature of the spine. In some instances, treatment options include surgery, braces, special shoes, physical therapy, and the use of artificial limbs, or prostheses.

Many students with congenital physical malformations have no other accompanying disabilities. When the condition interferes with the student's regular education—because of surgery-related absences, for example—the student may qualify for special education and related services, such as physical or occupational therapy and transportation.

Traumatic Injury

Traumatic injury is damage to the brain or body that occurs after birth.

Traumatic injury refers to damage inflicted to the brain or body after birth. There are many possible causes of traumatic injury, including child abuse and accidents, spinal cord injury, and closed-head injury.

● *Spinal Cord Injuries* Spinal cord injuries, in which the spinal cord is damaged or severed, occur most frequently in adolescents and young adults. Diving, automobile, and motorcycle accidents are frequent causes of this injury in young people. As in spina bifida, the location of the injury determines its effects. A lower-spine injury may result in limited use or paralysis of the legs. An injury higher up the spine or to the neck may result in more extensive involvement, including the arms, trunk, and neck. In some cases, respiration is greatly affected, and only facial muscles can be moved voluntarily.

Consider a student who falls from a tree or is involved in a car accident. The student recovers but must now use a wheelchair. The student has missed several months of school, his friends have moved on to the next grade, and he must adjust to a new perception of himself. A severe spinal cord injury may change how the student approaches all aspects of education. One very promising area for assisting students is technology. Technological advances have provided new opportunities for mobility of individuals with spinal cord injury. We will discuss these advances in more detail later in this chapter.

● *Traumatic Brain Injuries*   **Traumatic brain injury (TBI),** or acquired brain injury, became a separate diagnostic category in the Individuals with Disabilities Education Act (IDEA, 1990). Traumatic brain injury is defined as:

> an acquired injury to the brain caused by an external physical force, resulting in total or partial functional disability or psychosocial impairment, or both, that adversely affects a child's educational performance. The term applies to open and closed head injuries resulting in impairments in one or more areas, such as cognition; language; memory; attention; reasoning; abstract thinking; judgment; problem-solving; sensory, perceptual, and motor abilities; psychosocial behavior; physical functions; information processing; and speech. The term does not apply to brain injuries that are congenital or degenerative, or brain injuries induced by birth trauma. [Code of Federal Regulations, Title 34, Sec. 300.7(b)(12)]

Since the brain controls and processes how one acts, damage to the brain can cause serious disabilities. The student who survives an automobile accident but who suffers a moderate or severe brain injury may physically recover well, but changes in memory, problem solving, attention span, impulse control, and overall cognition are likely to persist. The student may look the same, but these changes in behavior have a significant impact on school, home, and friends.

Statistics suggest that over 1.4 million children each year receive head injuries, and over 165,000 of these children will require hospitalization. TBI is the most common cause of death and disability among children living in the United States. The leading causes of TBI for infants are falls and violent shaking by adults; the most common causes of TBI for adolescents and young adults are automobile and motorcycle accidents, and violent crimes (NICHCY, 2011). Most cases involve individuals between the ages of 15 and 24, but the number of younger children affected is almost as high. A small school district can anticipate having several children with traumatic brain injury; a large district can anticipate having over a hundred such students. Although the use of seat belts and bike and motorcycle helmets has reduced the rate of death and of severe brain injury, improvements in emergency medical services and technology have increased the number of students who become TBI survivors.

An individual who survives TBI will usually be in a coma for a period of time. The length of the coma is one of the predictors of how severe the injury is. A mild brain injury usually results in loss of consciousness for less than an hour without skull fracture. A moderate injury results in 1 to 24 hours of unconsciousness and may be complicated by swelling of the brain and skull fractures. These symptoms persist for some time. A severe injury results in loss of consciousness for more than 24 hours. Bruising of the brain tissue *(contusion)* or bleeding in the brain *(intracranial hematoma)* is usually present. These serious conditions can result in lifelong cognitive deficits and difficulty with learning new information. Some deficits will be apparent immediately, and some will appear only after a period of time (Witte, 1998). On average, children return to school between 3 and 24 months after a brain injury. Estimates of how many of these children receive special education services vary, but the general perception is that this population is underserved (Keyser-Marcus et al., 2002; Vu, Babikian, & Asarno, 2011). Children with TBI, especially those who have sustained moderate and severe injuries, may have significant, persistent deficits over time (Vu, Babikian, & Asarnow, 2011).

Traumatic brain injuries are caused by an external physical force and may result in functional disability or psychosocial impairment.

Brain injuries affect each individual differently.

Teaching Strategies & Accommodations

Teacher Guidelines for Students with TBI

Tips for teachers

- Find out as much as you can about the child's injury and his or her present needs. Find out more about TBI through the resources and organizations listed below. These can help you identify specific techniques and strategies to support the student educationally.

- Give the student more time to finish schoolwork and tests.

- Give directions one step at a time. For tasks with many steps, it helps to give the student written directions.

- Show the student how to perform new tasks. Give examples to go with new ideas and concepts.

- Have consistent routines. This helps the student know what to expect. If the routine is going to change, let the student know ahead of time.

- Check to make sure that the student has actually learned the new skill. Give the student lots of opportunities to practice the new skill.

- Show the student how to use an assignment book and a daily schedule. This helps the student get organized.

- Realize that the student may get tired quickly. Let the student rest as needed.

- Reduce distractions.

- Keep in touch with the student's parents. Share information about how the student is doing at home and at school.

- Be flexible about expectations. Be patient. Maximize the student's chances for success.

Source: National Dissemination Center for Children with Disabilities: http://nichcy.org/disability/specific/tbi#teachers, 2011

Teachers should be aware that the student returning to school with a traumatic brain injury will fatigue quickly for the first few months. Adjustment to schedules, reduction in the amount of reading and writing, memory helpers, and organizers are strategies that will help the student who survives brain injury become adjusted to school. Generally, the establishment of specific routines and highly structured learning environments is recommended for students returning to the classroom. Teachers must be flexible and must remember that each student with a traumatic brain injury will have different symptoms and may respond to different interventions.

? Pause and Reflect

When we hear the word disabilities, many of us picture first a person with a physical disability, perhaps someone in a wheelchair. Yet, many kids with physical disabilities don't need special education services at all. What do you think may be the most important services these students do need to succeed in class? •

Types of Health Impairments

Many conditions and diseases can significantly affect a child's health and the ability to function successfully in school. Most health impairments are chronic conditions; that is, they are always present or recur. Unfortunately, many of these conditions result in gradual deterioration of health and eventual death.

Students with health impairments typically receive their education in the regular classroom as long as their health allows. Some require home-based instruction for periods of time or support services when they must miss school for an extended time. Teachers will need to be sensitive to the obstacles to learning that can arise from the condition itself, the side effects of prescribed treatments, and the emotional challenges the student faces. Knowledge of the condition and the individual student's treatment regimen will help you plan and prepare appropriate educational programs.

Let's look at some conditions that can fall into the category of health impairment. In some cases, only some forms of the condition are severe enough to warrant special education or support services.

> Students with health impairments typically stay in the regular classroom for as long as possible.

Asthma

Asthma is a chronic obstructive lung condition characterized by an unusual reaction to a variety of stimuli that cause difficulty in breathing and coughing, wheezing, and shortness of breath. Estimates are that, in 2009, about 10 million children in the United States had some level of asthma, making it the most common chronic health impairment of young children (EPA, 2011). Any child has about a 1 in 400 or 500 chance of developing asthma, but this risk increases to 1 in 20 if a child has a parent or sibling with asthma. Many things can trigger an asthma attack. Some of the more common irritants are smoke, a cold or other infection, chalk dust, exercise, cold air, pollen, animal hair, emotional stress, and classroom pets. Asthma most frequently appears for the first time in children during their first five years.

Asthma can be managed. Special attention should be paid to the child's overall fitness. Allergens that cause the reactions can be removed or minimized wherever possible. Children can also receive *bronchodilators,* which are drugs that reverse the narrowing of the airways (Ranshaw et al., 2001). Because there may be side effects to any drug treatment, parents and teachers should learn the possible side effects of the particular medications a child is receiving.

Some forms of exercise are better tolerated than others by children with asthma. Running may result in narrowing of the airways and severe wheezing. Swimming is less likely to cause wheezing, but the child should be carefully watched, for obvious reasons. Overall participation in regular games and activities is encouraged, and many students have little or no difficulty participating in active sports.

Much attention has been given to the psychosocial effects of asthma. Loss of sleep is a frequent problem when attacks flare up at night, and it can be terrifying for a parent to watch a child fighting to breathe. Sometimes parents hesitate to discipline their child or to set limits for fear of triggering an asthmatic reaction. The child may also experience low self-esteem from a deformity in the chest cavity caused by the condition. In general, however, the prognosis for future health is good for these children.

As a teacher, you need to know the recommended physical activity levels for the student with asthma. Also, you should know the early warning signs of asthmatic episodes and what emergency procedures to take if a student has an asthma attack. Visit our Education Coursemate website at **CengageBrain.com** to view a sample of a detailed asthma care plan for teachers or caregivers of a child with asthma. This care plan can serve as a model for children with other health impairments or physical disabilities that require emergency action and special procedures.

Juvenile Diabetes

Juvenile diabetes is a disorder of the metabolism caused by little or no insulin being produced by the body, which results in difficulties in digesting and obtaining energy from food. It is estimated that **juvenile onset diabetes,** or **Type 1 diabetes,** affects over 1.5 million children, and the disorder's overall prevalence appears to be increasing at the rate of 6 percent a year.

Juvenile onset diabetes can appear at any point between birth and the age of 30; it cannot be cured, but it can be controlled by daily intake of insulin, by exercise, and by a special diet. Sometimes diabetes can also affect the eyes and the kidneys; unmanaged or severe diabetes may result in early blindness.

Even when children are receiving treatment for diabetes, teachers should be aware of two possible emergency conditions caused by insulin reactions. One condition, which results from low blood sugar and can cause unconsciousness and seizures, is called **hypoglycemia.** Symptoms include confusion, drowsiness, perspiration, a pale complexion, sudden hunger, lack of coordination, trembling, or the appearance of intoxication. Hypoglycemia is most likely to occur if the child has gone without eating for a while or has been exerting him- or herself physically. Although parents should be informed of the reaction, certain foods, such as sugar, can be given to the child immediately to mitigate the condition. A can of cake frosting is a good thing to keep on hand, since it not only contains sugar but is also easy to administer (JDRF, 2011)

Another condition, **hyperglycemia,** results from high blood sugar. Its symptoms include extreme thirst, lethargy, dry hot skin, heavy labored breathing, and eventual unconsciousness. Severe hyperglycemia can result in ketoacidosis, which may result in unconsciousness, coma, and death (JDRF, 2011). Students experiencing hyperglycemia will need to drink water, diet soda, or other sugarless fluids.

If you have a child with juvenile diabetes in your class, it is a good idea to have a complete list of symptoms and emergency actions handy. You will need to be flexible regarding certain aspects of your classroom management. For example, students with juvenile diabetes must have immediate bathroom privileges, immediate access to a nurse, and may need to eat at specific times during the day. Teachers should communicate regularly with parents regarding classroom activities, patterns of high and low blood sugar episodes, and any deviations from those patterns. The Juvenile Diabetes Research Foundation has developed a social network site that is child-friendly and provides an opportunity for children with Type 1 diabetes to share information with friends, teachers, and classmates.

Cystic Fibrosis

Cystic fibrosis is a progressive and usually fatal disorder characterized by lung damage, abnormal mucus production within the lungs, and difficulties in the absorption of protein and fat. Damage to the lungs results in inadequate amounts of oxygen being delivered to the body, which stresses the heart. Children with cystic fibrosis are susceptible to lung infections, pneumonia, and collapsed lungs.

The disorder is an inherited recessive gene disorder; that is, both parents must be carriers in order for the child to have the condition. Parents who both are carriers have a 25 percent chance per pregnancy of having a child with cystic fibrosis. Parents can be tested to determine if they are carriers, but the test is not accurate for many populations, and there are many possible genetic mutations involved. It is estimated that about one-third of the adult population are carriers of the gene (CFF, 2011). The test is most accurate for Caucasian populations of Northern European descent and Ashkenazi Jews, and most often recommended for parents with a known family history of cystic fibrosis (CFF, 2011). The condition occurs in approximately 30,000 Americans each year (CFF, 2011). Children with cystic fibrosis often die at a young age; the average lifespan is about 33.4 years. With early and continuous treatment, however, individuals with cystic fibrosis continue to live longer. In 1990, the gene carrying cystic fibrosis was identified; this is the crucial first step in finding a cure or treatment for this condition. This discovery led to the establishment of the first gene therapy centers. Although treatment is still in the earliest stages, it is apparent that a major breakthrough is at hand.

Treatment for cystic fibrosis is extremely vigorous and often painful, including physical therapy (in some cases daily) to loosen the mucus secretions in the lungs, drugs such as anti-inflammatories, and bronchodilators. Because of problems in digestion, children must have dietary supplements of vitamins and enzymes, as well as antibiotics to fight off frequent infections. Hospitalization may be required because of bouts with pneumonia, other serious lung conditions, or lung collapse.

Teachers must be aware of the reduced energy level characteristic of children with cystic fibrosis and must understand that they may miss school because of therapy or hospitalization. Particularly difficult aspects, of course, are the child's awareness of the course of the disease, the fact that it is often a very painful condition, and the prospect of early death.

Acquired Immune Deficiency Syndrome (AIDS)

Acquired immune deficiency syndrome (AIDS) is a condition that has had a great impact on health concerns in recent years, and its effect on children has been recognized for some time. AIDS is a disease caused by the human

Children with AIDS often face social isolation.

FIRST PERSON

My Midlife Crisis

JANUARY 2000

I am having a midlife crisis. Tomorrow I will be nineteen. It sounds melodramatic. But technically I should have had this crisis five years ago—my life expectancy according to average statistics is twenty-eight years.

However, most without cystic fibrosis (also known as CF) have a midlife crisis at age forty and some die at sixty-five, so I imagine it's okay for mine to be a little late. Had I been born ten years earlier, in 1971, I would've had my midlife crisis at age five. How does a kindergartner have a midlife crisis? Friends tell me not to worry, that I should be more optimistic. So, I sit in my dorm room each morning with Irish Breakfast tea in my Coffee Exchange mug, the sky blue carpet scattered with papers, books newly bought from the bookstore, and an unmade bed.

. . .

I'm a typical college student, if there is such a thing. Except that I won't be able to look back

on my life from an old age. The minute I begin to hypothesize about when and where and who—it upsets me. I often imagine scenarios in my head as I fall asleep—my lung collapses, they rush me to the hospital, I have to take a leave of absence from Brown, or I suddenly spike a high fever and I'm coughing up blood. . . . I could go on and on, but it even makes me queasy. I think about death every day. I wrote a poem about my funeral when I was seventeen.

Part of me wants to grow as old as I can, to live, but the other part is worried about living.

Laura Rothenberg

Laura Rothenberg, a young woman with cystic fibrosis wrote the autobiography *Breathing for a Living.* She died in 2003.

Source: L. Rothenberg (2003). *Breathing for a living.* (New York: Hyperion), 1–3.

immunodeficiency virus (HIV) that breaks down the body's immune system, destroying its ability to fight infections (AIDS Organization, 2003). When a child gets even the slightest cold or infection, the symptoms linger as the child weakens. AIDS is progressive, resulting in increasingly greater weakness and illness, particularly lung disease and pneumonia, which are frequently the immediate cause of death. Typical diseases of childhood, such as measles and mumps can also result in problems, as they will last longer and have more significant symptoms than with other children (AVERT, 2011).

AIDS is transmitted by the exchange of body fluids from an infected individual engaged in unprotected, high-risk behavior, such as unprotected sexual contact or sharing needles. AIDS also can be transmitted through blood transfusions, and passed from infected mothers to infants in utero and at birth. Because of increased screening of mothers, and HIV-positive mothers taking antiretroviral drugs, the occurrence of new pediatric AIDS cases *in the United States,* is decreasing. In 2008, there were 4,043 children living with AIDS in the United States. Data indicate that 13 new AIDS diagnoses were made in American children in 2009 compared to 896 new diagnoses in 1992 (Avert, 2011). Although much money and effort have been devoted to research on the virus that causes AIDS, no cure or vaccine is available yet. The cost of treatment has been drastically reduced in the United States, from about $20,000 per year to $50 per year in 2009.

AIDS is the only condition we have discussed that can be transmitted to others. So, in addition to the health maintenance procedures, hospitalization, and medication required for children with this condition, children often face the unwarranted prospect of social isolation. There have been many instances in which children with AIDS have been avoided or ostracized because of fear.

Although transmission of AIDS in the normal course of school activities has never been documented, many parents—and therefore their children—have an extreme fear of this condition and sometimes fight the presence of the child with AIDS in the regular classroom. When a teacher is aware of a student with AIDS, he or she must work to facilitate appropriate and normal social interaction and to educate other children in the classroom. Children with AIDS and their families have the most difficult task of not only dealing with a painful and probably fatal illness but also of fighting for love and acceptance from the people around them. Parent support is a critical factor in the continued effective treatment protocols for children with AIDS (AVERT, 2011).

Childhood Cancer

Although the prognosis for children with cancer is steadily improving, cancer continues to result in more fatalities among school-age children than any other disease (Beale, Baile, & Aaron, 2005). Current statistics suggest that approximately 35 percent of children affected with childhood cancer will not survive to adulthood (Childhood Cancer Foundation, 2003). The extent to which childhood cancer will affect a child's school performance depends on whether the child is undergoing active treatment such as chemotherapy, the immediate state of the disease, and the general prognosis for the child.

Attention Deficit / Hyperactivity Disorder (ADHD)

Although we have already discussed ADHD in some detail in Chapter 8, educational practice also places it in the category of Other Health Impaired. Because ADHD is a specific diagnosis but is not a separate category of special education, teachers and particularly parents seeking comprehensive services must find a category that will include their children. Many children may not meet the specific identification criteria of categories that commonly co-occur with ADHD, such as learning disabilities or behavioral disorders. The category of health impairments

Alex's Lemonade Stand: Fighting cancer one cup at a time and taking matters into her own hands

You may have heard of this little girl—Alexandra Scott—diagnosed with neuroblastoma as a toddler. Alex took charge of things and set up a lemonade stand to raise money for her treatment.

is defined in fairly general terms, and many school districts include some children with ADHD in this category. The use of this category to serve children with ADHD, not surprisingly, has resulted in great increases in the number of children served who are identified as Other Health Impaired. Remember, however, that despite the name of the category, the interventions used with students with ADHD will parallel those presented in Chapters 5 (learning disabilities) and 8 (behavior disorders).

Multiple Disabilities

This chapter focuses on individuals whose primary disability is a physical disability or health impairment. Some children born with other disabilities, including intellectual disabilities, hearing or visual impairments, and communication disorders, also experience physical disabilities or health impairments. For example, some children with Down syndrome experience congenital heart problems, and some children born with cerebral palsy have intellectual disabilities. The IDEA Amendments of 1990 (Sec. 300.6[5]) define multiple disabilities as "concomitant impairments (such as intellectual disabilities-blindness, intellectual disabilities-orthopedic impairments, etc.) the combination of which causes such severe educational problems that they cannot be accommodated in special education programs solely for one of the impairments. The term does not include deaf-blindness."

Children whose multiple disabilities include physical or health disabilities may need comprehensive treatment and educational programming. A child with both severe cerebral palsy and intellectual disabilities, for example, requires an effective avenue for communication, mobility instruction, physical and occupational therapy, and a program that facilitates maximum physical, social, and intellectual development.

? Pause and Reflect

Perhaps you are surprised to see that children with chronic diseases like cancer, or even asthma, may receive special education and related services. Remember, it is the extent to which the condition affects school performance that is the determining factor. How might you adjust your instruction for a child who has a severe and chronic illness? Where might you look to find resources or ideas? ●

Characteristics of Individuals with Physical Disabilities and Health Impairments

Many things contribute to the way a disability manifests in a child. The severity of the disability, the level of support a student requires, life expectancy, family support, and the resilience of the child all can affect the impact of a disability on an individual's life. In some instances, mobility or communication may be the areas in which a child feels the greatest effect; in others, the child's overall energy and motivation for making it through a day may be his or her most difficult task. The visibility of the disability may also play a major role, but not always in the way you might think. A mild disability or condition such as infrequent asthma attacks may affect the child a great deal if unwanted attention during an attack makes the child feel embarrassed. A child with a visible orthopedic disability may adjust well to challenges. It's important for you as a teacher to understand that each child is an individual with unique needs and abilities, rather than a collection of characteristics of a particular condition.

Cognitive Development

In most cases, a physical disability has no direct effect on intellectual disability.

In most instances, a physical disability or illness has no direct effect on intellectual growth or development. The presence of a physical disability, even a severe physical disability, does not mean that the individual's intellectual ability has been affected. Sometimes, however, both physical and cognitive disabilities occur. Cerebral palsy, for example, may include intellectual disabilities, and some children who experience extensive brain damage are affected in many areas of functioning, including intellectual ability. Some conditions result in the gradual deterioration of both physical and cognitive abilities. For example, Rett syndrome, a condition that affects 16,000 girls and women in the United States, will cause significant and progressively more severe deficits in motor skills, cognitive functioning, and communication abilities (Rett Syndrome Research Trust, 2011).

A health impairment can interfere directly with learning by affecting the speed of mental processing or the ability to focus for long periods of time. Children with asthma, muscular dystrophy, or other chronic or progressive conditions may require extensive therapy or stays in the hospital, which may interrupt their academic progress. A serious illness or condition also might greatly affect the child's stamina. As children tire more and more easily and lose energy, they may require school accommodations so that they can more readily handle academic work and attend to tasks.

Finally, cognitive development is closely dependent on communication abilities. This is particularly obvious in educational settings. Students with severe physical disabilities are most likely to succeed in academic subjects, particularly in regular classroom settings, if they are able to communicate visually, orally, or in writing. Students with physical disabilities who are able to speak and write may experience no exceptional difficulty with their academic tasks. We discuss communication further in the next section.

Communication and Language Development

Many of the physical disabilities we've discussed, such as cerebral palsy and muscular dystrophy, can affect a child's ability to communicate. The effects of a congenital disability, however, may be quite different from the effects of a condition with a gradual or sudden onset. If a child is born with a serious physical disability that affects speech, he or she may learn to communicate using various methods and materials at once—such as a communication board, maybe signs, scanning equipment, perhaps some speech. This will be difficult not only for the student, but also a challenge for others in the environment. On the other hand, most persons with progressive conditions, or those who experienced a sudden onset of a disability, have had a number of years during which they could communicate using more conventional means. Their intellectual abilities were probably tested using standard assessment instruments, and there was time to plan for the future and teach alternative communication systems to the student and to others in his or her home, school, and social environments.

Because many children born with severe physical disabilities are frequently unable to communicate clearly, their cognitive capabilities may remain hidden until they are old enough to use an alternative system, several of which we will describe later in the chapter. Throughout the years, people born with severe physical disabilities have faced extreme bias concerning their intellectual abilities, largely because of their inability to communicate with those around them. The assumption that severe physical disabilities were automatically associated with severe intellectual disabilities resulted in the placement of many individuals in institutional settings with very little, if any, attempt to engage in reciprocal social interaction or communication. As you might imagine, this was not only a deplorable condition in its own right, but extremely frustrating and painful for the people involved. Never make assumptions about what a child knows or understands based on his or her physical abilities.

One eloquent spokesperson, Ruth Sienkiewicz-Mercer, who lost bodily control and speech at age 5 due to encephalitis, describes her first communication breakthrough with her caretakers in a residential placement. Ruth was born at a time when placement at an institution was not unusual for someone, even a young child, with severe physical involvement. Although institutions are few and far between these days, some young people are still placed in nursing home settings to receive total care. Fortunately, those types of placements occur rarely, as home care and school services have been expanded. Ruth was not so lucky. At the time of the experience she talks about below, she had lived in the institution for three years without communicating with *any* of the adults present. Try to imagine what this must have been like—put yourself in her shoes:

> As she brought the next spoonful of food to my mouth, she noticed that I was doing something funny with my eyes, obviously in reaction to what she had just said. I kept looking up at the ceiling, but Wessie couldn't figure out why I was doing that. She put the spoon down and thought for a few seconds, then asked, "Ruthie, are you trying to tell me something?"
>
> With a broad grin on my face, I looked at her squarely. Then I raised my eyes up to the ceiling again with such exaggeration that I thought my eyes would pop up through the top of my head.
>
> Wessie knew she was on to something, but she wasn't sure just what. She pondered for a few more seconds ... then it clicked! A silent

TeachSource VIDEO CASE

How Might a Teacher Include a Student with a Physical Disability?

Marianne is an elementary school student with spina bifida. Visit Chapter 13 on the CourseMate website and watch the video case entitled "Including Students with Physical Disabilities: Best Practices." See how teacher Lisa Kelleher, in collaboration with her classroom aide, provides an optimal educational experience for Marianne. Lisa also offers advice to new teachers about working with children who have physical disabilities. How does Marianne interact with her classmates in ways that enrich the overall classroom environment?

People with severe physical disabilities find their intellectual abilities underestimated because they communicate differently.

conversation flashed between us as loud and clear as any spoken words. Even before she asked me a dozen times over, and before I exuberantly answered a dozen times with my eyes raised skyward, Wessie knew. And I knew that she knew.

I was raising my eyes to say yes.

We both started laughing. Then I started laughing really hard, and before I knew it I was crying so uncontrollably that I couldn't see because of the tears. They were tears of pure joy, the kind of tears a person sheds on being released from prison after serving three years of what she had feared would be a life sentence. (Sienkiewicz-Mercer & Kaplan, 1989, p. 110)

Social and Emotional Development

Children with physical disabilities and health impairments are faced with an incredible array of stressful emotions—both their own and the emotions of others. They must struggle with perceptions of themselves, the reactions of others, and the impact on their families.

Young people with physical disabilities or health impairments may experience difficulty making friends, or just meeting new children. Often, particularly for children without verbal communication skills, the beginnings of friendships are dependent on the children in the classroom or playground who are willing to make the first move. Anderson, Balandin, and Clendon (2011) interviewed children, ages 7 to 14 who were long-time friends of children with severe cerebral palsy—children who used electronic speech-generating devices instead of verbal speech. The children were asked about their friendships, what they talked about, and why they began friendships. Although all of the children had different responses, some common themes were that they wanted to make the other child happy or help him; the new friends filled their own needs for social and emotional companionship; and they like who the kids were—funny, nice—personal qualities that attract us to all of our friends. An important finding was that the friends were now advocates and sources of information for other peers around them.

Of course, not all children or adults are attracted to the idea of making friends with folks who are different from themselves. Sometimes, we avoid interacting with persons with physical disabilities not because we are insensitive or uncaring, but because we are confused about how to act. Sometimes, it's difficult to judge whether or not you should provide assistance to someone, and often we become aware that we are noticing the disability—and this makes us uncomfortable with ourselves. Unfortunately, these concerns may result in the appearance of indifference or actual avoidance of persons with physical disabilities. Regardless of our reasons, the result is the same—a lack of communication and interaction with someone simply because of his or her physical appearance. Some children with chronic health conditions actually develop high levels of prosocial behavior, perhaps because they learn to manage the concerns and fears of families and friends throughout their illness (Belete, 2010).

As you consider your reactions to persons with physical disabilities, past and future, remember our axiom of looking at the *person* first. We've alluded to the fact that sometimes our fear of acting patronizing or too helpful will insult or embarrass the individual with whom we are interacting. People with physical disabilities realize your apprehension (many may have experienced these feelings themselves if their disability is injury-related) and appreciate the fact that any meaningful social interaction must be reciprocal in nature.

Most of us are only too aware of the importance society places on appearance. As children get older, teasing someone who looks different is, unfortunately, fairly common. Unkind and humiliating situations are encountered. This happens, of course, to most children—but children with disabilities often get more than their share. The child with a disability must have the opportunity to cry, vent anger, and talk in order to learn to deal with these situations. A key factor in a child's ability to develop a positive self-image is the extent to which he or she can accept his or her physical differences. See A Closer Look, "Positive Exposure: The Spirit of Difference," to see a powerful and unique movement to develop the self-image of students with physical differences while developing empathy, advocacy, and knowledge in others.

> A key factor in a child's positive self-image is accepting his or her physical disability.

Another significant source of stress is the struggle for independence. For people with certain types of disabilities, such as seizure disorders or diabetes, it is very difficult to accept the fact that a certain level of dependence on others or on medications will be a continuing part of their lives. The protectiveness of parents and other family members, and the possible adjusted expectations of others, may make the process of growing up very difficult.

Some children with progressive illness or deteriorating conditions must face the inevitable fact of an early death. Clearly, family, friends, and other support services and people can help children as they try to face this possibility. Experts advise teachers and other adults to be gentle, yet direct, with children who want to discuss death. Often, because children find it difficult to discuss this emotional topic with their parents, they may need to confide in another trusted adult. Although many children display incredible courage and consideration of others in the face of their disabilities, it is only natural for a part of this process to include the inevitable questions of "why me?" and "what if . . . ?" Sometimes these questions are directed at the condition itself, and sometimes at the pain or discomfort involved. Research suggests that most children want to know the truth and that information helps them to shift their attention or focus to things happening in the near future—a trip with their family, a new movie, etc. (Beale, Baile, & Aaron, 2005).

Effects on the Family

The impact of a child's physical disability or health impairment on a family can vary as greatly as the types of disabilities. The effects on the family of a child with cerebral palsy will be very different from the effects on the family of a child with muscular dystrophy, cancer, an amputated leg, or epilepsy. Yet parents of children with special needs do share many common experiences, such as dealing with medical professionals, educators, community prejudices, and the joys of loving a child. There is no uniform reaction to disability. Some families appear able to accept the child for who he is and become strong while dealing with challenges and decisions that may overwhelm most of us. Other families seem frayed as the child with the disability siphons all their emotional and physical energies. Some families face a potentially lifelong commitment to the education of their child; others must face daily the agony of watching their child's physical abilities and health deteriorate. Children are often well aware of the impact of their disability on their families and may themselves feel a sense of guilt or responsibility for the ensuing emotional or financial strain. Sometimes, children will respond to this by avoiding discussion of their condition with their parents or by being careful of what they say or do. The child may focus on "taking care" of his or her parents. This unexpected interaction is illustrated in a touching passage from Frank Deford's book *Alex: The Life of a Child*, the story of his young daughter, who died of complications from cystic fibrosis.

> Practical issues faced by the family include decisions about treatment and placement.

> And so then Alex and I laughed. Unfortunately, at that point, late in her life, it was difficult for her to laugh without coughing and starting to choke. So she made sure she laughed gently, and I laughed extra hard, for both of us. Then she came over, sat in my lap, and this is what she said: "Oh, Daddy, wouldn't this have been great?"

A CLOSER LOOK   "Positive Exposure: The Spirit of Difference"

Positive Exposure is a foundation founded in 1997 by Rick Guidotti and Diane Mclean. The purpose of this foundation is to develop the self-confidence of young people with genetic differences and to be a source of information, through visual media to the public and to educational and medical persons. Positive Exposure accomplishes that task in many innovative ways, but the two primary vehicles for communication are pictures and voices:

...pictures, because Rick Guidotti is a former fashion photographer. His incredible pictures of the children and adolescents involved in his projects communicate the beauty of each person to the individual and to the world at large. See the gallery of pictures at the Positive Exposure website at: www.positiveexposure.org.

...voices, because children can tell their story better than anyone else. Through projects, such as the PEARLS Project, Positive Exposure incorporates blogs of young people with various health or physical conditions to encourage knowledge, advocacy, and empathy. In the PEARLS project, individuals are presented with pictures and blogs of the students and asked to respond creatively—to present their responses through the arts or to problem solve—how to make dance class more accessible, for example.

For a description of the Pearls Project in a Ridgewood, NJ, high school, a link to the *New York Times* article "Learning Empathy by Looking Beyond Disabilities" (June 21, 2011) is available at the Positive Exposure website. You can also see samples of the students' blogs at: www.positiveexposure.org/pearsproject.

That is what she said, exactly. She didn't say, "Hasn't this been great?" She said, "Oh, Daddy, wouldn't this have been great?" Alex meant her whole life, if only she hadn't been sick.

I just said, "Yes," and after we hugged each other, she left the room, because, I knew, she wanted to let me cry alone. Alex knew by then that, if I cried in front of her, I would worry about upsetting her, and she didn't want to burden me that way. She was the only one dying. (Deford, 1983, p. 9)

Because physical disabilities and deteriorating health are usually apparent to others, families also try to cope with the emotional pain faced by their children as they integrate into educational and social settings and deal with the countless questions about "what happened to you?" or "what's wrong with you?" Although it is important for families to encourage independence for their children, it is often difficult for them to let go of their desire to protect the child from more potentially painful situations. One of the greatest emotional challenges faced by families of children with physical or health disabilities is encouraging their children to experience life and take risks, just as they would with children without disabilities. Parents worry about the social and emotional well-being of their children, and report that their greatest concerns for their school-age children with physical disabilities are not the physical barriers they face, but rather the attitude barriers

courtesy of Kids in Motion Dance Group, College of Kinesiology, University of Saskatchewan

Children with physical disabilities can participate in a range of community based activities given the appropriate accommodations.

that can result in their child becoming isolated and having low self-esteem (Pivik, McComas, & LaFlamme, 2002).

Practical issues faced by the family include treatment decisions. Families must make constant decisions about the type or extent of therapy they will select for the child involved. In some instances, these decisions may be relatively simple (selecting a type of medication, choosing a particular kind of prosthesis). When the child has a severe illness or disability, however, these decisions can be very complex and include considerations of time allocated to the child and other family members; finances; emotional stress on the part of the parents, siblings, and involved child; and sometimes the actual physical abilities of the family caretakers. Certainly, one of the biggest decisions related to treatment is whether the child with severe physical involvement, particularly a child with multiple disabilities, should be at home or in a residential placement. These decisions are never easy, and each family's financial resources, personal obligations to siblings and spouse, and the simple physical and emotional strength of caregivers all figure into the decision. Although there may be some similarities in the ways families deal with the impact of a physical disability or health impairment, families are composed of individuals. The child with the disability and the other family members develop the pattern of interaction that works for them. Educators must be aware of the needs of individual families and the type of support services that might help them make informed decisions about the education and placement of their children.

Fortunately, the emphasis on parent services and training available through P.L. 99-457 enables greater education and support for parents of young children with physical disabilities and health impairments. Parents and families of older children who incur physical or health disabilities need immediate and continued information and assistance. Social, spiritual, and physical support are all important predictors of more successful family adaptations (Lin, 2000). Therapists stress the need to attend to the needs of all family members and to recognize the heterogeneity of family structures when assessing families (Alderfer et al., 2008).

Often, local, state, or national groups related to a specific disability area can be a great source of available services, information, and emotional support. The website of the Muscular Dystrophy Association compiled by individuals with disabilities is full of information for parents and others interested in making contributions.

Teaching Strategies & Accommodations

Recommendations for Parents of Children with Duchenne or Bender Muscular Dystrophy

"When a family member has DMD or BMD, all members of the family are affected by caregiving demands and emotional reactions. Many people find help and support from religious sources, families with similar experiences, self-help books or professional counseling. These experts usually suggest the following:

For the child:

Answer children's questions about the disease when they arise, with honesty and in language they understand.

Always view the child as an individual, with the disease only one aspect of his life.

Emphasize what the child can do and let him find ways to do things he wants. Children often find creative ways to participate in sports and other hobbies.

Treat him as you would any other child, providing discipline, responsibility, hope and love. Don't overprotect him, and do help him become independent.

Undertake normal family activities, including vacations.

For the family:

Respect each other's emotions and stress levels; be kind and patient.

Schedule regular breaks from caregiving responsibilities.

Deal with the disease one day at a time, one crisis at a time, one year at a time. Don't focus on future complications.

Give yourself credit for effort and the difficulty of your task.

Build a support team, and ask for help when you need it.

Get information from every available source, starting with MDA."

_____

Source: Muscular Dystrophy Association, http://www.mda.org, 2011.

Look at Teaching Strategies & Accommodations, "Recommendations for Parents of Children with Duchenne or Bender Muscular Dystrophy" on the previous page. As you read it, you will probably notice that the information would be applicable to all children and families dealing with a chronic health condition.

Pause and Reflect

The range of characteristics of individuals with physical disabilities and health impairments is arguably wider than in any other categories of special education. One of the greatest errors we've made, as a society is assuming that individuals with significant physical disabilities also have severe cognitive disabilities. How can this type of assumption affect expectations of individuals with physical disabilities? •

Teaching Strategies and Accommodations

In the past, the diverse educational needs of children with physical disabilities and health impairments often kept them away from public education. Today's teachers need to know, however, that in most cases, these children can be part of the regular class with accommodations and support.

Early Intervention

For many children with physical disabilities or health impairments, the first educational issues to arise are the appropriate and early diagnosis of the condition, and assessment of physical, cognitive, and language abilities. The diagnoses tend to be made by physicians rather than school personnel, and many diagnoses of conditions, such as spina bifida or cerebral palsy, are made long before the child reaches school age.

As with other disabilities, early intervention services—both medical and educational—significantly affect the well-being of these children. For some of them, early intervention can mean the difference between life and death. For others, early intervention can mean the difference between a mild disability and a severe and long-term disability. Early and consistent therapy can help children to maximize their physical skills and sometimes prevent the occurrence of muscular atrophy and skeletal deformities.

Early intervention services that focus on family-centered service delivery models may have positive effects on the family as well as the child. Family-centered services can help parents establish a support network, as well as provide them with knowledge about their child's disability and a sense of empowerment (Raina et al., 2005).

Educational Planning

Most physical disabilities and health impairments are diagnosed before schooling begins, but some conditions will not be identified until later in the child's life. As a teacher, you should be alert to gradual or sudden changes in children's physical abilities, energy level, and general behavior. For children who are out of school for extended periods of time for treatment or because they are recovering from a traumatic injury, reintegration into school will require careful planning with the family and entire educational team in order to identify appropriate supports, including peer education, that are acceptable to all (Georgiadi & Kourkoutas, 2010; Geva, Yosipof, & Eshel, 2009).

Regardless of the severity of any condition, it is your responsibility continually to assess and address the educational needs of the individual child. If you notice motor difficulties, a physical or occupational therapist may be called in to consult on the case or to provide assistance. See the accompanying Teaching

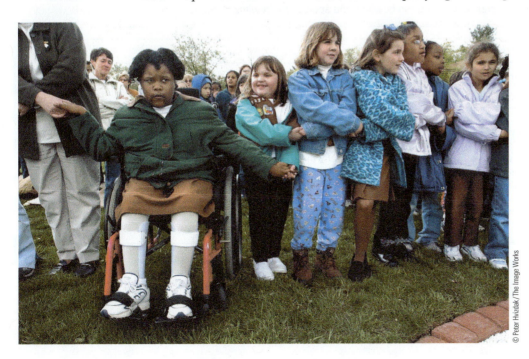

The Connecticut Trails Council of Girl Scouts Brownies of the Dunbar Hill Accelerated School have a traditional ceremonial Girl Scout "Closing Circle" as they sing "Make New Friends."

© Peter Hvizdak/The Image Works

Strategies box, "Some Considerations for Students with Mobility Impairments" for some general recommendations for interacting with students with physical disabilities or health impairments.

In the transdisciplinary model, professionals work together to ensure continuity for the child.

● *The Transdisciplinary Approach* Integrated, multidisciplinary planning is a requirement for appropriate education. IDEA requires that a multidisciplinary team evaluate each student in special education programs. On a multidisciplinary team, professionals work independently, or directly, with the child. Figure 13.2

Student Background

Name: George
Age: 14
Present Level of Performance: Walks independently with a slight scissor gait; able to perform reach, grasp, and release skills when accommodations are made for slight upper extremity hypertonicity; eye-hand coordination skills are good but George requires extra time to complete eye-hand coordination tasks; balance is generally good and protective extension is used when balance is challenged.
Annual Goal: Transition to community bowling alley

Role of the Physical Therapist (PT)

The PT will work with George to develop body mechanics of balance and posture needed to transfer weight while walking down the lane from the ball carriage to the foul line and maintaining balance during ball release and follow-through. To accomplish these goals, the PT also will work with George on strength and stability as well as joint mobility.

Role of the Occupational Therapist (OT)

The OT will work with George to develop arm and wrist strength to support the weight of a 9-lb bowling ball as he engages in the pendulum swing action. The OT will also assist George with developing the fine motor skills he needs to release the ball during return arm swing as well as reflex integration.

Role of the Therapeutic Recreation Specialist (TR)

The TR will help George learn about bowling equipment and selection, relevant interpersonal and social skills as it relates to bowling, self-initiated independent behavior in bowling, and appropriate bowling etiquette.

Role of the Adapted Physical Educator (APE)

The APE will provide instruction in the technique of bowling, including arm action, four-step approach, and ball release and follow-through. Skills will be taught in the gymnasium and will be taught in a whole-part-whole method.

Role of the General Physical Educator (PE)/Special Education Teacher

The general PE and/or special education teacher can facilitate the TR specialist's goals by providing opportunities for students to study and research the sport of bowling and practice appropriate interpersonal skills with classmates. Physical therapy goals can be addressed in the classroom by encouraging George to walk throughout the school and outside in the playground as much as possible, giving him opportunities to improve posture and balance. With training the general PE/special education teacher can look for the interaction of reflexes to facilitate and reduce its impact on George's fine motor skills.

FIGURE 13.2

Combining expertise in a sample IEP

Source: D. R. Shapiro & L. K. Sayers (2003). Who does what on the interdisciplinary team regarding physical education for students with disabilities. *Teaching Exceptional Children, 35*(6), 35.

illustrates the instructional roles of different team members, including physical therapists, occupational therapists, and special education teachers (Shapiro & Sayers, 2003). As you can see, the responsibilities of each participant are clearly defined. Today, however, most professionals recommend the **transdisciplinary model** of service delivery, particularly for young children, because it encourages integration of services, which helps not only with generalization but provides opportunities for everyone to know what the other is doing.

In the transdisciplinary, or indirect service, model service providers work as a team, sharing roles and, therefore, service delivery (Rapport, McWilliam, & Smith, 2004). King, Strachan, Tucker, Duwyn, Desserud, and Shillington (2009) identified three major components of transdisciplinary models.

1. Arena assessment—All of the professionals involved in the child's care assess the student simultaneously.

2. Ongoing team interaction—All of the professionals involved in a child's care share information and work collaboratively.

3. Role release—Each professional is willing to step outside of his or her role, or share role with other professionals.

In a transdisciplinary model, a student who needs physical therapy to learn to walk is helped by his or her regular teacher to complete mobility exercises several times a day. This does not mean that the physical therapist never sees the student. It does mean that the physical therapist works closely with the teacher to carry out therapeutic activities properly and sees the student directly as needed. In a multidisciplinary team, the student might be pulled out of the class and given physical therapy once a week for thirty minutes. The teacher and parents would have little idea of how to help the student learn and practice mobility the rest of the week.

A transdisciplinary team of professionals, in conjunction with the family and, when appropriate, the child, works together to assess educational needs in a variety of areas and to determine appropriate program goals. For example, the group would work together to determine what type of computer keyboard is most appropriate for a student with cerebral palsy who cannot use a regular keyboard.

The family's role on the transdisciplinary team is critical because family members are able to give insight into the child's abilities, motivation, emotional adjustment, and goals. Whenever special therapy, communication systems, or adaptive equipment is suggested, the willingness and ability of the family members to accept and use them or to participate must be assessed and evaluated.

Accessing Instruction

Today, most children with physical disabilities or health impairments spend most of their day in the general education classroom (NCES, 2011). In the past, children whose only disabilities were physical or health-related were placed in a variety of educational settings, ranging from a state hospital or institution to the regular classroom. Although there are still separate classes for children with "orthopedic handicaps," they are no longer the primary educational placement for children with physical disabilities. Instead, these classes provide a setting for initial instruction in skills such as mobility and language, which can then be used in regular class settings. Support or special education services are often provided in physical therapy, occupational therapy, speech or language therapy, counseling, and, in some instances, homebound instruction for periods of time.

● *Academic Access* Because placement options now focus on the general education classroom, general education teachers are largely responsible for educating students with physical or health impairments in their classrooms. In some instances, it is not necessary to make any specific instructional modifications for

When interventions are integrated into the classroom, teachers better understand how to help students learn useful skills.

Teaching Strategies & Accommodations

Some Considerations for Students with Mobility Impairments

Many students with mobility impairments lead lives similar to those without impairments. Dependency and helplessness are not characteristics of physical disability.

A physical disability is often separate from matters of cognition and general health; it does not imply that a student has other health problems or difficulty with intellectual functioning.

People adjust to disabilities in myriad ways; students should not be assumed to be brave and courageous on the basis of disability.

When talking with a wheelchair user, attempt to converse at eye level as opposed to standing and looking down. If a student has a communication impairment as well as a mobility impairment, take time to understand the person. Repeat what you understand, and when you don't understand, say so.

A student with a physical disability may or may not want assistance in a particular situation. Ask before giving assistance, and wait for a response. Listen to any instructions the student may give; by virtue of experience, the student likely knows the safest and most efficient way to accomplish the task at hand.

Be considerate of the extra time it might take a student with a disability to speak or act.

Allow the student to set the pace walking or talking.

A wheelchair should be viewed as a personal assistance device rather than something one is "confined to." It is also part of a student's personal space; do not lean on or touch the chair, and do not push the chair, unless asked.

Mobility impairments vary over a wide range, from temporary to permanent. Other conditions, such as respiratory conditions, affect coordination and endurance; these can also affect a student's ability to perform in class.

Physical access to a class is the first barrier a student with a mobility impairment may face, and this is not related only to the accessibility of a specific building or classroom. An unshoveled sidewalk, lack of reliable transportation, or mechanical problems with a wheelchair can easily cause a student to be late.

Common accommodations for students with mobility impairments include priority registration, notetakers, accessible classroom/location/furniture, alternative ways of completing assignments, lab or library assistants, assistive computer technology, exam modifications, and conveniently located parking.

Source: Used by permission of Disability Services.

the student; in other cases, you will need assistance from special education teachers or other members of the student's education team to learn the best ways to encourage and facilitate communication, class participation, class interaction, and physical movement or activity. See Teaching Strategies & Accommodations, "Specific Strategies for Integrating Students with Physical Disabilities or Health Impairments in the Classroom."

In fact, some of the responsibilities of general education teachers who work with children with physical disabilities and other health impairments can be quite challenging. Even special education teachers often feel unprepared to deal with situations such as working with terminally ill students and their families, or identifying appropriate forms of augmentative communication and assistive technology (Heller et al., 1999). Teachers often use children's literature on topics such as HIV/AIDS to educate both peers and themselves about specific conditions of children in their classrooms and to gain new perspectives on dealing with illness and disability (Prater & Sileo, 2001).

Sometimes, individuals with severe physical disabilities may have a paraprofessional, an aide, who travels with them to assist in educational and healthcare activities. The major role of the paraprofessional should be to promote the student's independence. It is important for the aide to step back whenever possible

Teaching Strategies & Accommodations

Continuum of Service Models

Direct service model

One-on-one therapy

The therapist treats the student in a separate therapy room or a segregated portion of the classroom.

Small group therapy

The therapist treats several students with similar needs at one time.

One-on-one therapy (inclusive)

The therapist works with the student during a classroom activity to facilitate his or her participation. Therapy can also occur during activities in the gymnasium, on the playground, or at a community site.

Small-group therapy (inclusive)

The therapist works with the student with special needs and a group of his or her classmates on an educationally appropriate activity. The activity also promotes the therapeutic goal for the student with special needs. For example, the therapist leads a craft project that facilitates the fine motor manipulation for all students, yet the project is modified to include and instruct the student with special needs.

Transdisciplinary indirect service model

Consultation

The therapist recommends and instructs educators, paraprofessionals, or caregivers to carry out therapeutic programs. This may include instruction modification, activity enhancement, environmental modification, adaptation of materials, routine or schedule alterations, or team member training.

Monitoring

The therapist maintains contact with the student to monitor his or her status. Effective monitoring consists of check-ups scheduled on a regular basis in the student's educational environment.

The restrictive models of treatment should be used only as a last resort. Therapy should be provided in an inclusive model that facilitates integration with peers. Special education services should be structured to support placement in the regular classroom.

Source: J. L. Szabo (2000). Maddie's story. *Teaching Exceptional Children, 33* (2), 49–53.

---

to allow full integration of the student and to encourage communication and other social interactions with peers. The specific responsibilities of paraprofessionals should be delineated in each child's IEP. Figure 13.3 illustrates one framework that can be used to clarify the role of the paraprofessional in the classroom (Muellor & Murphy, 2001).

Specify Class Activity	Identify need for paraeducator	Identify areas to increase socialization (utilize natural supports, peers)	Identify how independence will be encouraged	Total time needed for paraeducator support	Total anticipated time reduction in paraeducator support by annual review

FIGURE 13.3

Plan for paraeducator assistance

Source: P. H. Mueller & F. V. Murphy (2001). Determining when a student requires paraeducator support. *Teaching Exceptional Children, 33* (6), 25.

Teaching Strategies & Accommodations

Specific Strategies for Integrating Students with Physical Disabilities or Health Impairments in the Classroom

Place students with limited physical movement front and center in a traditional classroom setting to facilitate access to the teacher's presentation and material on the board. There are exceptions to this guideline; for example, a student with a traumatic brain injury might have a limited field of vision on one side and might follow the visual presentation of material more easily if seated at an angle.

If students gather around small tables or learning centers, make sure the tables are at an appropriate height for the student who is in a wheelchair. If the students gather in groups on the floor, try to use chairs instead so the child in a wheelchair is not sitting above and apart from the group. This is important for social integration as well as physical accessibility.

Use bookshelves, material drawers, pencil sharpeners, and cubbies that are the appropriate height and can be reached by a student in a wheelchair. If a student cannot physically reach and grasp, make sure he or she has a trustworthy assistant for retrieving and putting away materials.

Avoid the use of carpet squares or other floor materials, such as number lines, with raised sides or edges.

Classrooms with fixed furnishings, such as science labs, can be particularly problematic for the student in a wheelchair. Creating an accessible work area may require significant changes in the classroom construction so that the student will be truly integrated into the classroom setting.

If a student requires assistive technology for communication, establish clear signals for typical classroom activities such as hand raising and asking a question. These signals should be clearly recognized by all students in the classroom, as well as the teacher. Provide training to all the students in the classroom on how to communicate with the student using his or her specific assistive device. Always be careful to allow the student time to respond.

Become an expert at identifying and creating learning experiences that allow all students in the classroom to participate fully.

When a student is too sick to attend school, he or she may receive a homebound program, either in the student's home or at a hospital. This homebound program should always include plans for the student to reenter school as soon as possible. The teacher who visits the student at home or in the hospital coordinates with the student's regular teachers so that proper assignments, homework, tests, and other activities are completed.

Technology is quickly improving the quality of homebound programs. In some school districts, distance learning is now available, which permits the student to watch educational television programs along with classroom peers. For students with long-term homebound needs, telephones can be set up in the classroom that allow the student to listen to the teacher and respond to questions just like the other students. The homebound teacher makes sure the student has the necessary materials each week to follow along with the class. Fax machines and web access are also used to connect the homebound student to the regular classroom.

● *School Accessibility* With the passage of the Americans with Disabilities Act in 1990, all public facilities and buildings were required to be barrier-free by 1994. Your classroom, therefore, will probably be adapted to the needs of students with physical disabilities.

Sometimes, however, schools may not take into account accessibility to such items as play equipment, furniture, or educational equipment. One potential problem area is the surface of floors and walls. For example, carpeting, rugs, or uneven

Teachers should be sure that equipment and furniture are arranged for maximum accessibility.

floor surfaces can cause difficulties for students using wheelchairs or other types of assistance for walking. Pivik, McComas, and LaFlamme (2002) interviewed a number of students with physical disabilities, including those who used wheelchairs and walkers. The students were asked questions about the accessibility of their schools. Many of these students reported that they still experienced difficulty negotiating the physical school environment. Specific barriers identified by the students were as follows: entering school (because the ramps were located in the back of the school) heavy doors, narrow passageways, the height of lockers, types of locks, and inaccessible recreation equipment. Most of the students were also very worried about what would happen to them in case of fire.

Although some of these areas should be addressed by working in conjunction with the student's therapists, you, as a classroom teacher, can take some simple precautions yourself to ensure optimum accessibility. Widening aisles between desks and placing equipment such as computers, tape recorders, and bookshelves appropriately are some tasks that teachers can attend to in their classes. When planning field trips, it is always a good idea to call ahead and check to ensure that the visiting site has been adapted to accommodate students with disabilities. Although adapted school buses are quite common, some public buses still cannot be used by persons in wheelchairs. The student then needs to be lifted onto the bus and the wheelchair folded up and carried along. This may present difficulties, particularly with an older student, so advance planning will be necessary.

● *Physical Supports* As a teacher, you may be required to assist students with physical disabilities in the use of equipment for moving, eating, breathing, and other bodily functions. These aspects of care are called physical handling and health maintenance.

Physical handling involves moving the student from one place to another or adjusting his or her placement in a fixed setting. For example, you might need to move a student from a wheelchair to another setting such as a group activity on the floor. There are very specific professional guidelines for picking up and carrying students with physical disabilities. It is important that you not try to lift or move students until you have received the information necessary to do it appropriately. In some instances, more than one person is needed to move a child, and in others, a specially trained aide or nurse will assist or do the lifting.

Other aspects of physical handling include adjusting physical placement, or using physical props to allow greater range of motion. If students have a tendency to lean to one side or have difficulty reaching needed materials, you can make simple adjustments such as using pillows to prevent leaning, having armrests or trays attached to wheelchairs to allow the closer placement of manipulative materials, or providing wedge-shaped props that children can lie on to allow greater range of arm movement. Again, the physical and occupational therapists on each child's team can provide needed information and equipment.

Health maintenance involves assisting students in eating, drinking, and using the bathroom. A student with severe cerebral palsy, for example, might be unable to feed herself. Some students run the risk of choking when they eat or drink, so it is important that the person feeding the student be skilled in CPR. Often a nurse or trained aide will assist in this process, as they will when medically oriented processes such as catheterization are required. Because the courts consistently rule that the school is responsible for providing any and all medical care to students in school as long as it does not require a physician, children with very severe medical needs may be in your classroom (Katsiyannis & Yell, 2000). Students requiring medical technology for support, such as ventilators for breathing, and students with other conditions requiring constant health maintenance, such as gastrostomies and tracheostomies, may be placed in the general education class for instruction and require monitoring and maintenance procedures by nurses or other health care professionals.

Other health maintenance activities may include administration of medication, injections, and monitoring students for signs of distress such as diabetic shock. School nurses typically are responsible for the administration of any medical procedures, but as we mentioned previously, it is important for you to be aware of any particular signs or symptoms that signal a specific health problem. If you assist students with these activities, you must be taught correct procedures and be aware of potential risks. Federal guidelines and school district interpretations regulate who may or may not perform health care services. These guidelines should be reviewed by the teachers, administrators, and parents on the IEP team when decisions are being made about the delivery of these services in school.

Integrating Technology

Throughout this chapter, we have alluded to the importance of technology for many individuals with physical disabilities and health impairments. For individuals with physical disabilities, most of the technological assistance is either medical technology or assistive technology that is designed to help the individual perform life tasks. Augmentative/Alternative Communication (AAC) may be one of the first types of assistive technology provided for a young child who has no language due to motor involvement. For school-age students with disabilities, assistive technology may be considered special education or a related service. Teachers, parents, students, and other members of the evaluation team must evaluate the student's needs and indicate the need for appropriate assistive technology on the student's IEP. When selecting appropriate technology for a student, it is most important to look at the way the individual functions in his or her environment and to determine what specific pieces of equipment or training may help to support the student in various settings. This is particularly important when looking at communication needs (Bausch & Ault, 2008).

It is also important to keep in mind cultural issues related to the use of assistive technology. Parette (1999) suggests that areas of cultural sensitivity include (1) the family's desire for the degree of independence that assistive technology can provide, (2) the balance between providing technological assistance and what may be perceived as the stigma of drawing attention to an individual because of technology use, (3) the information a given family desires about the choices, costs, and goals of assistive technology, (4) the impact of assistive technology on family routines and demands, and (5) the experiences with assistive technology of the child and the family. Teachers must be sensitive to these issues as they work with families and students to identify appropriate assistive technology for students.

Socialization

Lau (2000) suggests that technology also can serve an important role as a focal activity for prompting social interaction among young children with physical disabilities and their peers. Table 13.1 provides a checklist for teachers to use to determine proper positioning at the computer for children with physical disabilities. Lau suggests that when an appropriate software program is used in a well-structured cooperative learning group, young children can learn social interaction skills. This type of instructional activity can be used to teach young children with or without physical disabilities skills such as turn taking, group decision-making, and helping.

In addition to using technology as an activity or platform through which social activity can be encouraged, technology increasingly is becoming a vehicle for social initiation. All of you reading this chapter use some form of electronic technology for social purposes—texts, email, social network sites such as Facebook or Myspace. All of these activities can be done from your couch, the local coffee shop, or from a wheelchair. Children and adolescents who previously did not have access to the most common social networks of their peers now can.

Table 13.1 Classroom Checklist for Proper Positioning at the Computer for Social Interaction

Criterion	Met	Not Met
1. Is the child's head at midline? (e.g., ears are directly over shoulders and face is facing forward)		
2. Is the child's pelvis at midline? (e.g., hips are in the back of the seat and are not tilted to one side)		
3. Is the child's trunk at midline? (e.g., trunk is not tilted to one side)		
4. Are the child's shoulders at midline? (e.g., shoulders are not hunched forward)		
5. Are the child's forearms supported? (e.g., elbows are flexed at 90 degrees and supported by the table, arm rest, or tray)		
6. Are the child's legs in a neutral position? (e.g., thighs are slightly apart; knees and ankles are bent at 90 degrees)		
7. Are the child's feet in a neutral position and supported? (e.g., feet are directly under the knees and facing forward; feet are supported by the floor or foot rest)		
8. Is the child seated at the same height as other children at the computer? (e.g., eye contact and verbal exchange can easily be achieved among children in the group)		
9. Is the computer monitor at the child's eye level? (e.g., the child can easily see the monitor without tilting his or her head)		
10. Is the computer table accessible to the child? (e.g., the child can easily reach the computer peripherals)		

Source: Lau, C. (2000). I learned how to take turns. *Teaching Exceptional Children,* 32 (4), 8.

Software is now available that can place symbol-based communication systems on computers that can be used by children with severe physical disabilities to send email—with or without accompanying voice activation. Once children learn to use the necessary software and how to send email messages, they use email to initiate and continue social interactions with school peers, friends, and family (Sundqvist & Ronnberg, 2010).

● *Instructional Accommodations* Instructional needs of students with physical disabilities and health impairments include both assessment and instruction. Assessment of students with complex physical involvement, particularly if they have no speech, can be difficult—it is an inexact science. Increasingly, technology is being used to help get accurate information about the skills and abilities of young children in important academic or preacademic areas. For example, Geytenbeek, Heim, Vermeulen, and Oostrom (2010) are evaluating an assessment system designed to determine the extent to which young children (ages 14 to 60 months) with severe motor disabilities and no verbal language understand spoken language. Because receptive language is the foundation for not only communication but literacy as well, learning what children can understand can assist families and teachers as they present and adapt information to the child. The ways in which young children with motor involvement and no verbal language learn literacy skills, and how the use of AAC and various touch and symbol systems affect written language learning, is a relatively new area of study designed to increase our understanding of how to provide effective instruction (Van Ballkom & Verhoeven, 2010).

An increasingly important area of technological interventions is the development of materials for use in the classroom. Technology allows children with physical disabilities to have access to materials they would not otherwise be able to enjoy or use. Beck (2002) describes the successful use of assistive technology in preschool classes to promote early literacy skills in young children. As you can imagine, a three- or four-year-old child with fine or gross motor disabilities might not be able to hold books, turn pages, or follow along with group literacy activities. Beck found that by creating electronic books, or e-books, preschool children were able to participate fully in classroom activities. The e-books she used were created using Intellipics (Intellitools, 2000). By activating a single switch, the pages of the text turned on the computer screen, story illustrations moved, and the text on the screen was read. Such e-books have three basic components: (1) hardware to serve as the reader of the program (e.g., computer, PDA); (2) software, the reader software program that displays the book; and (3) book files, the electronic data files that contain the content of the actual book (Cavanaugh, 2003). Teachers can use existing technology available online to create electronic books for their own classes. To learn more about creating e-books for your own classroom, see the Useful Resources list at the end of this chapter.

Examining the role assistive technology can play in a given student's educational program is part of the IEP team's educational plan. It is important, however, that these determinations are carefully made and that they are based on the individual abilities and needs of each child. Webb (2000) recommended the following steps for conducting an assistive technology assessment—this protocol would work well when looking at instructional technology:

I. Conduct an assistive technology environmental use assessment

List times and subjects in which student needs assistance to satisfactorily complete assignments.

List times student needs assistance to satisfactorily function in his or her school environment.

List adaptations currently in use (shortened assignment, notetakers, etc.).

List an assistive technology device currently used by student, what setting, and time used.

II. Conduct an assistive technology functional use assessment

Describe student's present level of functioning.

List characteristics of student.

What are the student's academic skills?

Does student have keyboarding skills and at what level?

What are the student's preferences for types of assistive technology?

What technology courses are available in the current curriculum?

What technology instructional services are available at the school site?

III. Match environmental use assessment with functional use assessment to identify appropriate assistive technology services.

(Webb, 2000, p. 51)

● *Mobility*   New designs in wheelchairs and controls for wheelchair movement have resulted in opportunities for independence for people who previously were dependent on others for even limited transportation. For example, individuals with very severe disabilities were unable to use conventionally designed wheelchairs to move because they had limited or no arm movement. A now-common mouth apparatus allows them to control wheelchair movement by blowing puffs of air through a tube.

Technology has also made it possible for people with physical disabilities to control some aspects of their home environment. Through the use of switches from a wheelchair panel or a voice-activated control device, it is possible to open doors, turn on lights from across the room, use keys to enter their homes, and operate alarm systems (Access Ingenuity, 2003; Bigge, 1991a). These devices provide an option for independent living that might not otherwise be available. Home accounting and banking software are examples of how technology has facilitated personal life-skills management for individuals with severe physical disabilities. When software is not available for printed materials, alternative format services can translate documents from print and electronic files into alternative, accessible formats (Access Ingenuity, 2003; Bigge, 1991b).

● *Communication*   The most critical factor in using technology to meet communication needs is to identify processes that meet the individual's needs, allow and

ASSISTIVE TECHNOLOGY FOCUS

Movement: Functional Electronic Stimulation (FES)

Muscles that are not used because of injury (typically a spinal cord injury) can be given electronically stimulated "exercise" to make them contract, thereby preventing muscle atrophy, contractions, and skeletal deformities. This process of systematically causing electrical muscle contractions is called **Functional Electrical Stimulation** (Peckman & Knutson, 2005). Research on Functional Electrical Stimulation (FES) has been conducted for over 40 years and is now the most frequently used intervention, other than occupational therapy or physical therapy, for increasing motor function in people with spinal cord injuries (Lynch & Popovic, 2008; Peckman & Knutson, 2005). Studies using electrical stimulation and feedback have restored and strengthened muscle function in paralyzed individuals and provided opportunities for some people to walk a few steps even though they may not feel the movement of their legs, or learn to use arms or other parts of their bodies. FES has obvious advantages—movement, developing or maintaining muscle strength, and improvements in circulation and lung function. There are also some risks, including broken bones; not all individuals with paralysis are candidates.

The following are some specific uses of FES, described by the Christopher and Dana Reeve Foundation: Paralysis Resource Center (2011).

- Therapeutic Exercise (e.g, bicycles)—for the purpose of recovering some function and muscle tone in legs
- Improve bladder and bowel control
- Increasing function of hands or arms
- Walking/ambulation
- Breathing support

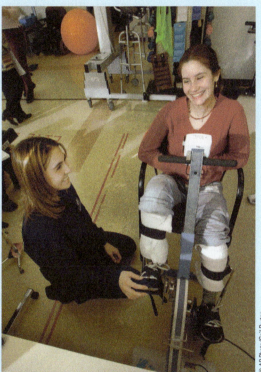

© AP Photo/Gail Burton

This student is receiving FES during therapeutic exercise with guidance from her physical therapist.

___

Want more information?

Christopher and Dana Reeve Foundation: http://www.christopherreeve.org/

International Functional Electrical Stimulation Society: http://www.ifess.org/

SpinalCord Injury Information Network: http://www.spinalcord.uab.edu

Cleveland FES Center: http://fescenter.org

FES Resource Guide: FES Resource Guide lists a variety of international programs that deal with FES research and delivery.

encourage intellectual and physical growth and development, and can be used by others in the environment. This last point is of the greatest importance. The latest high-tech system is useless if no one else takes the time to understand how it is used and to participate in the communication process. In this section we discuss some of the major developments in communication technology for people with physical disabilities. In addition to functionality, communication systems must be evaluated by examining research evidence for both effectiveness and efficiency of the tool or technique (Schlosser & Raghavendra, 2004).

Most advances in communication technology provide access to the symbols of written or oral language. The majority of these advances are associated with computer use. **Eye-gazing scanning systems** are a good example. As the individual scans a keyboard and focuses, a small and very sensitive camera detects the direction of the person's eyes and registers the letters, words, or phrases. A typed message or voice message can then be produced.

Augmentative/Alternative Communication (AAC) aids are used in addition to the individual's existing speech or vocalizations to encourage communication and participation (Lasker & Garrett, 2008). A person using an augmentative communication aid can directly select the desired message elements (such as words or pictures) from the display or can scan and then identify one of a series of potential message elements. In direct selection, the individual points to the desired message or message component using a finger, an adapted handpiece with a pointer attached, or a light beam attached to the head. In school settings, direct selection aids often take the form of alternative computer keyboards and overlays. These keyboards can look like an enlarged version of the typical keyboard, may contain numbers, pictures, or other symbols, and are designed to accommodate specific difficulties a person with limited motor control might encounter (such as difficulty pressing two keys at one time) (Intellitools, 2011).

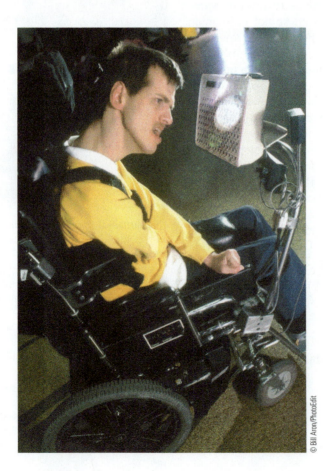

Technology provides many opportunities for communication and mobility to individuals with extensive physical challenges.

© Bill Aron/PhotoEdit

In scanning, message elements are presented one at a time on flashcards, transparent charts, or a computer screen. As the potential messages are presented, the individual indicates which message(s) he or she wants to choose by making a sound, flexing a muscle, or fixing a visual gaze for a few seconds. This process eliminates the need for great mobility. An adapted form of scanning is a multi-signal process, in which the individual:

Scans groups (for example, fifteen groups of four messages)

Selects a group (for example, group 9: I want to go see a movie. I want to see a television show. I want to turn the television off. Let's go to the video store.)

Scans the message elements in that group to select the appropriate message (I want to see a television show). This type of encoding allows the individual with limited movement and a large message vocabulary to cover a wide range of potential messages. Computers facilitate scanning because they can store and present many groups of messages quickly.

Another communication option available through advanced technology is synthesized and digitized speech. **Digitized speech** is the storage of words or phrases that can be recalled as needed; **synthesized speech** is the storage of speech sounds—a phonetic alphabet that can be put together to form any word using a sound-by-sound process similar to the spelling process. Synthesized speech allows greater variety of words and phrases but can be a much slower process. These devices can be designed in various sizes and can be portable or connected to a large computer screen. Digitized speech devices can be designed with customized keyboard overlays and can present language at various speeds (Breakthroughs, 1997). Recent research suggests that synthetic speech can do more than serve as augmentative communication. Blischak (1999) found that young children with severe speech difficulties who used synthetic speech during language training sessions significantly increased their production of natural speech, when compared to students who used graphic or pictorial representations of speech. This research suggests that children can actually improve their speech while using synthesized speech technology.

Technological advances clearly have opened many new avenues for individuals with severe difficulties in communication. Not all procedures need to have a high-tech component; many augmentative communication processes can be integrated in very simple ways. The role of technology is to expand these options, particularly for individuals with limited movement or advanced cognitive capabilities.

Pause and Reflect

Look around your college classroom or the classroom in which you teach. Can you identify ways you could adapt the physical or instructional environment to address the instruction, mobility, or communication needs of a student with severe physical disabilities? ●

Adult Life

Legislation has refined the legal requirements of accessibility for schools, public services, and places of employment. The **Americans with Disabilities Act (ADA) of 1990 (P.L. 101-336)** extends civil rights protection to individuals

Anthony Robles: NCAA Wrestling Champion , 2011: A young man of strength, talent, and determination

with disabilities in private-sector employment. In addition, the law requires that public services such as transportation make accommodations for individuals with disabilities. For example, transportation systems such as buses and railroads must include access for individuals with physical disabilities. Other public accommodations and facilities (stores, hotels, schools) must be accessible and must provide any supporting material necessary to allow individuals to use their services.

For young adults with physical disabilities, accessibility to colleges and universities is an important and logical extension of school programs. According to data from the National Longitudinal Transition Study-2 (Newman, Wagner, Cameto, Knokey, & Shaver, 2010), over 50 percent (54.2 percent and 55.8 percent, respectively) of students with physical disabilities and other health impairments/autism attended some type of postsecondary college program. The process can, however, be difficult and frustrating. Although colleges and universities provide a range of technological support for students with disabilities, research found that many schools provide limited resources, primarily because of the cost (Michaels, Prezant, & Jackson, 2002). For example, resources such as scanners and screen magnification devices were found at only three-fourths of campuses, and items such as recorded textbooks and adapted keyboards were only found at one-half of the campuses surveyed. Lehmann, Davies, and Laurin (2000) organized a summit of a number of college students with disabilities, including a number with physical disabilities and other health impairments. These students identified barriers to their successful transition to postsecondary programs. The students then listed specific suggestions for students and teachers at both the secondary and postsecondary levels. These suggestions are found in the accompanying Teaching Strategies & Accommodations, "Tips for Eliminating Barriers to Postsecondary Education."

Young adults with disabilities typically will establish and maintain contact with the **adult service agencies** that can provide guidance and assistance once the students have graduated from high school or college. Recent data shows that 58 percent of young adults with OI (Orthopedic Impairment) and a remarkable 71 percent of young adults with OHI/Autism are receiving paid employment four years after high-school graduation (Newman, Wagner, Cameto, Knokey, & Shaver, 2010). Adult service agencies can provide medical and psychological examinations and counseling, training and job placement, and financial assistance for adaptive equipment, prostheses, and basic living costs during training. Once

Teaching Strategies & Accommodations

Tips for Eliminating Barriers to Postsecondary Education

Ask students to conduct workshops that describe the nature of various disabilities to faculty and staff.

Provide staff development to postsecondary faculty regarding adaptations and accommodations they can implement.

Reward faculty who are willing to adapt instruction to address the learning needs of students.

Evaluate transportation availability to campus and on campus.

Inform students about the documentation requirements of the local postsecondary institution before their senior year in high school.

Identify potential financial resources for students entering into postsecondary settings.

Teach high-school students time and money management skills.

Tour the college campus with interested students during transition planning.

Provide summer classes addressing compensatory strategies on college campuses for high-school students interested in obtaining a postsecondary education.

Role-play with students ways of communicating to college faculty about students' disability and learning needs.

Encourage networking between college students via focus groups, student meetings, and informational workshops.

Source: J. P. Lehmann, T. G. Davies, & K. M. Laurin (2000). Listening to student voices about postsecondary education. *Teaching Exceptional Children, 32* (5), 63.

---

a person is determined to be eligible for vocational rehabilitation services, a vocational rehabilitation counselor will serve as case manager and outline specific employment goals and needed services in an Individual Plan of Employment (IPE) (Neubert & Moon, 2000). Although such services may be provided automatically for persons under the care of state-run facilities, individuals with disabilities who are living on their own will need to seek out and secure available services. Each state has a vocational rehabilitation department. Find a list of contacts for the vocational rehabilitation department in your state and a description of the services it provides for more information.

In addition to postsecondary education and employment opportunities, residential options are important considerations for individuals with physical disabilities and health impairments. Historically, many individuals with extensive physical disabilities, such as severe cerebral palsy, lived in institutional settings. Today, most of the individuals who in times past lived in segregated settings have moved directly and successfully into the community in group homes, or apartments. Some, however, continue to live in smaller segregated settings such as nursing homes. Many individuals with physical disabilities or health impairments live independently in homes within the community. Sometimes adaptive equipment is necessary or a personal attendant is required, so financial resources may be the factor that determines independent living for some people.

Important aspects of adult life include forming relationships, marrying, and perhaps having children. Of course, many individuals with physical disabilities and health impairments become parents. Often, they face challenges related to their personal mobility, in addition to accommodating the constant needs of a young child. The website of Parents with Disabilities On-Line offers a great site for parents, who also have physical disabilities, to find resources, share their stories, and learn about recent research and technology.

Individuals with physical disabilities and health impairments are increasingly participating fully and successfully in all aspects of adult life. Because many of us view a disability as an adverse condition, we may ascribe certain characteristics to the person with a disability who has been able to get a successful job and conduct a relatively normal existence. We speak frequently of the bravery of people who must deal with sensory impairments, debilitating illnesses, or physical conditions. Sometimes we wonder if we would be able to exhibit the same strength if we were in similar situations. There is no doubt that many people with disabilities are engaged in mighty struggles and exhibit courage and tenacity.

It is important for us to realize, however, that these struggles are often due to the physical and social barriers imposed by others—they are not a necessary consequence of disability. As in all historical battles for human and civil rights, ordinary people must become heroes in order to gain their rightful place in society. Although we admire the risks heroes take and the strength they show, it is unfortunate that we live in a society in which heroic acts are still necessary before basic rights and acceptance can be obtained.

Educating people about the challenges faced by individuals with physical disabilities has an important purpose—to facilitate change. Although it's been a long time coming, public awareness and technology are combining to create a much more accessible environment for persons facing physical challenges. Change in interpersonal areas—efforts at communication, comfortable social exchanges, and acceptance—cannot be legislated and must be instigated at an individual level.

We hope that by listening to our words as well as to the words of children and adults who have experienced disabilities, you have gained some insight into their strength, optimism, struggles, and educational needs. The past decade has resulted in great strides in medical management and technology, which have dramatically increased the options for individuals with physical disabilities and health impairments. We look forward to the doors that will be opened in the future through continued advances in science, social awareness, and knowledge. Visit our Education CourseMate website at **CengageBrain.com** to read articles written by Harriet McBryde Johnson, a lawyer and advocate in Charleston, SC, who also faced significant physical challenges.

> People with disabilities may struggle more with physical and social barriers imposed by others than with their own disabilities.

Pause and Reflect

Adults with physical disabilities are among the most vocal advocates for personal and civil rights. In what ways can you participate as an advocate, whether or not you have a physical disability, in your community or at the national level?

SUMMARY

- Physical disabilities and health impairments as currently defined by IDEA include a wide range of conditions. Physical disabilities can be grouped into neurological conditions, musculoskeletal conditions, and traumatic injuries. Health impairments include debilitating or life-threatening diseases or conditions such as cystic fibrosis and AIDS. Being familiar with what is known about the causes, prevalence, and treatment of these various conditions may help you to understand what to expect from the student, plan time for the student's treatment, and become comfortable with helping the student with in-school treatment.

- One of the most difficult aspects of physical disabilities and health impairments is the issue of mortality, since many conditions involve shortened life expectancy. Another issue is the continual need to educate others.

- Educational issues to be aware of include transdisciplinary planning, the importance of early intervention, and the use of technology to increase access for students in the regular class as well as to provide opportunities to students at home.

- New technologies for environmental control, health management, and communication have allowed people with physical disabilities and health impairments to participate more fully in many aspects of life. Legislation provides safeguards and regulations that facilitate the integration of individuals with physical disabilities and health impairments into the work force and the community.

KEY TERMS

physically challenged (page 450)

physical disability (page 450)

health impairment (page 451)

cerebral palsy (page 452)

spina bifida (page 454)

hydrocephalus (page 455)

epilepsy (page 455)

grand mal seizures (page 455)

petit mal seizures (page 455)

muscular dystrophy (MD) (page 456)

juvenile rheumatoid arthritis (JRA) (page 457)

congenital malformation (page 458)

traumatic brain injury (TBI) (page 459)

asthma (page 461)

juvenile onset diabetes (page 461)

type 1 diabetes (page 461)

hypoglycemia (page 462)

hyperglycemia (page 462)

cystic fibrosis (page 462)

acquired immune deficiency syndrome (AIDS) (page 463)

transdisciplinary model (page 475)

physical handling (page 479)

health maintenance (page 479)

Functional Electrical Stimulation (page 483)

eye-gazing scanning systems (page 484)

augmentative communication aid (page 484)

digitized speech (page 485)

synthesized speech (page 485)

Americans with Disabilities Act (ADA) of 1990 (P.L. 101-336) (page 485)

adult service agencies (page 486)

USEFUL RESOURCES

- Access the Disability Rights Civilian Defense Fund (DREDF) at **http:// www.dredf.org.** This website provides information to individuals with disabilities and their parents and advocates about legal rights and courses of political action.

- Contact World Communications, ACS Software, for software designed for students who use scanning techniques for communication: Freedom Writer Software, Academics with Scanning: Language Arts and Math. **http:// www.m-media.com/products/remotes/interlink/freedomwriter.**

- Visit the National Organization for Rare Disorders (NORD): **http:// rarediseases.org/.** NORD is a unique federation of voluntary health organizations dedicated to helping people with rare "orphan" diseases and assisting the organizations that serve them. NORD is committed to the identification, treatment, and cure of rare disorders through programs of education, advocacy, research, and service. Since its inception in 1983, NORD has served as the primary nongovernmental clearinghouse for information on over 5,000 rare disorders. NORD also provides referrals to additional sources of assistance and ongoing support.

● Contact the National Sports Center for the Disabled, P.O. Box 36, Winter Park, CO 80482, (303) 726-5514 (**http://www.nscd.org/**). It provides information and contacts for individuals with disabilities who wish to engage in a variety of sports, classes, and organized competitions. Alpine skiing, biking, kayaking, golf—if you want to do it, they have it.

● Access the Office of Disability Employment Policy at **http://www.dol.gov/ odep.** This office provides information in many areas related to the employment of individuals with disabilities, including laws, benefits, publications, federal programs, and special projects.

● Laura Rothenberg (2003). *Breathing for a Living.* This is the thoughtful autobiography of a young woman with cystic fibrosis who was a college student at the time of the book's writing. Rothenberg died in March 2003. In addition to her book, she created a video diary and radio diary "My So-Called Lungs" that aired on National Public Radio (NPR) and may be obtained through their archives **http://discover.npr.org.**

● For more information on e-books for individuals with physical disabilities, please visit **www.EbookExpress.com.**

 PORTFOLIO ACTIVITIES

1. Make an appointment with a physical therapist or occupational therapist who serves your school district. Discuss with him or her the types of activities typically provided to the students he or she serves. Accompany the therapist on a visit to a local school to observe individual service delivery and describe your observations.

> **CEC** This activity will help students meet CEC Content Standard 2: Development and Characteristics of Learners.

2. Visit the center for disability services at your college or university. Review the services and materials that are available for college students with physical disabilities. Talk to some of the students who provide services, or, if possible, with some of the college students who receive services. Based on your interviews, identify the services the college students find most helpful.

> **CEC** This activity will help students meet CEC Content Standard 3: Individual Learning Differences.

3. Create an annotated bibliography of children's literature on a variety of physical disabilities and health impairments. Create a series of learning objectives and lesson plans designed to integrate the literature into a curriculum.

> **CEC** This activity will help students meet CEC Content Standard 2: Development and Characteristics of Learners.

4. Identify a job in your community often held by high school students (working in a fast-food restaurant or music store). Observe and identify the specific skills that are required. Describe the adaptations that would be needed for a student who is in a wheelchair to hold that job.

CEC This activity will help students meet CEC Content Standard 5: Learning Environments and Social Interactions.

5. Invite an adult with a physical disability to visit your class and talk about work, living, social opportunities, challenges to acceptance, and achievement. Perhaps an adult with a disability is in your class and would also be interested in sharing his or her experiences. Describe your personal and professional reactions to the presentation.

CEC This activity will help students meet CEC Content Standard 5: Learning Environments and Social Interactions.

To access Portfolio Activities for this chapter and other useful study resources including an interactive eBook, related web links, quizzes, flashcards, and videos, visit the Education CourseMate website at CengageBrain.com.

Children Who Are Gifted and Talented

Learning Objectives

After reading this chapter, the reader will:

● Construct a definition of giftedness using his or her own words and reflecting his or her own values, as well as understand the federal definition of giftedness.

● Describe the traditional means of identifying gifted and talented students and identify contemporary strategies for identification.

● Describe historical and present-day theories of intelligence.

● Identify the major program models and curriculum adaptations recommended for students who are exceptionally able and/or talented.

Giftedness is not just a gift—much practice is required. (Plomin & Price, 2003, p. 114)

Each of us has something that we are very good at, and each of our students has an ability or potential that deserves nurturing. But who is *gifted*? Who is *talented*? And once we've decided, what should be done about it? What kinds of school programs, curricula, and teaching strategies are the ones that will nurture and develop our students' gifts and talents and keep them from becoming underachievers or dropouts? How can we provide students with meaningful incentives?

In order to develop gifts and talents, children need *opportunities.* Would you have developed your own talents without the opportunity to practice? Would J. K. Rowling have become a writer without the encouragement of family and teachers? Would Gustavo Dudamel have become a conductor without the music education of *El Sistema* in Venezuala? Would Colin Powell have become a leader without the opportunities to advance available in the military? Some families can provide many opportunities to their children—lessons, summer camp, traveling, meeting accomplished people. And some cannot. In either case, the school is the place where opportunities for all students should be found—opportunities to find their strengths and develop their talents. For many of today's accomplished adults, a teacher was the first person to identify their strengths. Perhaps you can be that teacher for the next generation of gifted and talented adults.

Terms and Definitions

Generally, it would be appropriate to begin a chapter on giftedness with a definition of that term. However, defining giftedness is not a straightforward task. Giftedness exists in a cultural and historical context—it is defined according to the values of the time and place. So instead of jumping directly to the federal definition, in this section you will read about the various concepts of giftedness that have evolved over the past hundred years or so. You will also read about some individuals who have devoted their lives to studying students with gifts and talents, as well as current ideas about intelligence and giftedness.

Definitions of giftedness are determined by the values and beliefs of a culture.

As you read, think about someone you know (or know of) whom *you* consider gifted or talented. What are the characteristics of that individual that distinguish him or her? In short, how would *you* define giftedness?

It's hard to find two "experts" who agree on a single definition of giftedness. For that matter, it is difficult to find two experts who agree on whether **giftedness** and **talent** are synonyms or merely related terms. Giftedness often refers to exceptional intelligence or academic ability, whereas talent is often used to indicate exceptional artistic or athletic ability, often considered innate. You will see as you read this chapter, however, that these distinctions are too simplistic in a time when new theories and research are challenging our traditional ideas about intelligence, giftedness, and talents.

Although the problem of defining giftedness has perplexed educators and psychologists for generations, everyone seems to agree on at least one thing: There is a universal fascination with people—especially children—who are intellectually very capable, or exhibit precocious talents.

Early Scholars and Their Ideas on Giftedness

From the time of the earliest scholars to today's most influential theorists, debate has centered on whether abilities and talents are born or made. This question continues to be of interest to teachers, who have a considerable stake in the belief that experiences can make a difference. In the 1800s, giftedness was often considered a personality flaw. Cesare Lombroso, a nineteenth-century physician,

For these gifted young musicians, the payoff for hours of practicing is the pleasure of making music with others.

proffered a popularly held view that genius was just a short step from insanity. Other nineteenth-century theorists believed that each individual had only so much brain power to expend and that if a person used up this intellect early in life, she or he could expect an adulthood filled with madness or imbecility. This "early ripe, early rot" theory, though scientifically groundless, was believed by many nineteenth-century scholars.

● *Galton*   When Sir Francis Galton began his study of eminent scientists (*English Men of Science,* 1890), he concluded that "genius" (the nineteenth-century term for *giftedness)* was a natural talent composed of three traits: intellectual capacity, zeal, and the power of working. However, Galton believed fully in the idea that geniuses were born, not made; he dismissed the role of environment in the development of talent.

> Nineteenth-century studies of "genius" discounted the influence of the environment.

● *Terman*   Using Galton's work as the cornerstone of his own, Lewis M. Terman became the "father" of gifted education in the United States. Beginning with the publication of his article "Genius and Stupidity" (1906) and continuing until his death in the 1960s, Terman left his mark on all psychological research with his longitudinal study of over 1,500 children determined to be gifted after scoring an IQ of 140 or above on the Stanford-Binet Intelligence Test. Today, the survivors of this original group of 1,500 "Termites" is still being studied (Kern, Friedman, Martin, Reynolds, Luong, 2009). The Terman legacy can be found in his five-volume series *Genetic Studies of Genius* (Terman et al., 1925, 1926, 1930, 1947, 1959).

> Terman's longitudinal study of 1,500 gifted children dispelled many misconceptions about giftedness.

Terman's work did much to dispel the above-mentioned myths of the eventual mental breakdown of individuals with gifts or talents, for his picture of highly able children was one of absolute mental health—of children who were immune from social and emotional crises. As his career progressed and his knowledge of gifted persons deepened, Terman realized how complex the phenomenon of giftedness was. Near the end of his career, Terman acknowledged the powerful influence of family, marriage, self-confidence, work habits, and mental health on the development of talent, for even among his 1,500 high-IQ subjects, vast discrepancies existed in their contributions to society (Delisle, 2000).

● *Hollingworth*   Leta S. Hollingworth, a contemporary of Terman at Columbia University, added another dimension to the understanding of people with gifts and talents. A psychologist by training, she had tested thousands of children with mental disabilities before becoming interested in extreme intelligence. Hollingworth, who began a public school program for gifted elementary students in New York City, is best remembered for her recognition of the vulnerability that she knew to be a characteristic of these very bright children.

Hollingworth's research and writing concentrated on the humanity of children with gifts and talents and on the idea that individual students had unique personalities in addition to their IQs. In effect, Hollingworth presented a middle ground: She identified specific social and emotional concerns that might affect the behavior of students with gifts and talents (Delisle, 2000).

Hollingworth identified social and emotional concerns that might affect students who are gifted and talented.

Current Definitions of Giftedness

A complete history of ideas about giftedness, talent, or intelligence cannot be written in these few pages. More thorough analysis of these topics is available elsewhere (Thurstone, 1924; Robinson & Clinkenbeard, 2008), and you may wish to consult such work once you have completed this book and this course. Now let us turn to the theorists who are influential today in the education of gifted children.

Contemporary views on the nature and scope of giftedness are still tied to concepts of that nebulous construct, **intelligence**. As you recall from Chapter 6, intelligence is thought of as the capacity to acquire, process, and use information. Terman's early work suggested that giftedness was limited to a select few who scored 140 or above on an IQ test. One important contributor to contemporary understanding, Paul Witty, moved the thinking in a different direction. Witty suggested that anyone "whose performance is consistently remarkable in any potentially valuable area" (1940, p. 516) should be considered gifted. He based this assertion less on statistical evidence and more on observation of the world around him. Thus, the poet whose words make you weep, the teacher who inspires you to learn, and the architect who causes you to look skyward in awe would be considered gifted, regardless of their IQ scores.

Taking this thought a few steps further, Joseph Renzulli (1978) elaborated on the idea that giftedness lies not so much in the traits you have as in the deeds you do. His conception of giftedness highlights the importance of combinations of **creativity** (the ability to generate original or imaginative ideas) and **task commitment** (the ability to stay focused on a task to its completion), in addition to above-average intellectual abilities, in the development of gifted behaviors (see Figure 14.1). Like Witty, Renzulli believed that IQ alone provides insufficient evidence of giftedness, and only after a student, an architect, or a poet creates a visible product can an analysis be made of that person's intellect. This product-based formula for giftedness fits right in with our own culture's emphasis on performance and educational accountability. For these reasons, Renzulli's concept of giftedness has enjoyed wide popularity among educators; his 1978 article describing his theory has become the most widely read article in the field (Renzulli, 2011) and has been cited as the starting point for broadened conceptions of giftedness.

According to Renzulli, giftedness includes creativity and task commitment as well as above-average intellectual ability.

Robert Sternberg and Howard Gardner, two psychologists whose work has revitalized the debate on intelligence, have proposed broader views of human capabilities. Gardner defines intelligence as "a biophysical potential" and giftedness as "a sign of early or precocious biophysical potential in the domains of a culture" (2000, pp. 78–79). Gardner is best known in education for his **theory of multiple intelligences** (1983, 2006; Von Károlyi, Ramos-Ford, & Gardner, 2003), which postulates that there are at least eight distinct intelligences (see Table 14.1 below). An abundance of talent in any of these areas constitutes giftedness, according to

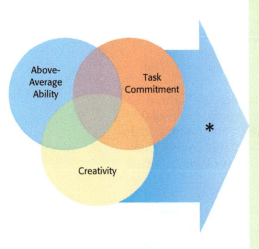

General Performance Areas		
Mathematics	Visual Arts	Physical Sciences
Philosophy	Social Sciences	Law
Religion	Language Arts	Music
Life Sciences		Movement Arts

Specific Performance Areas		
Cartooning	Demography	Electronic Music
Astronomy	Microphotography	Child Care
Public Opinion Polling	City Planning	Consumer Protection
Jewelry Design	Pollution Control	Cooking
Map Making	Poetry	Ornithology
Choreography	Fashion Design	Furniture Design
Biography	Weaving	Navigation
Film Making	Play Writing	Genealogy
Statistics	Advertising	Sculpture
Local History	Costume Design	Wildlife Management
Electronics	Meteorology	Set Design
Musical Composition	Puppetry	Agriculture
Landscape	Marketing	Research
Architecture	Game Design	Animal Learning
Chemistry	Journalism	Film Criticism
etc.	etc.	etc.

*This arrow should be read as "brought to bear upon. . ."

FIGURE 14.1

Graphic representation of renzulli's definition of giftedness

Source: COLANGELO, NICHOLAS; DAVIS, GARY A., *HANDBOOK OF GIFTED EDUCATION*, 3rd Edition, © 2003, pp. 76. Adapted by permission of Pearson Education, Inc., Upper Saddle River, NJ.

> For Gardner, great talent in any of eight different domains constitutes intelligence.

Gardner, and although people may be capable in several different intelligences, one does not have to excel in every area to be considered gifted. Gardner points out that the manifestation of intelligence depends on what is valued in a culture; if a person is good at something that is not valued in a culture, then that capacity would not be considered an intelligence (Gardner, 2000).

Robert J. Sternberg adds yet another tile to this mosaic with his **triarchic theory**, which includes three kinds of intellectual giftedness: analytic, creative, and practical (Sternberg, 1985, 1997, 2009b). Students who are analytically gifted are effective at analyzing, evaluating, and critiquing; those who are creatively gifted are skillful at discovering, creating, and inventing; and those who are practically gifted are good at implementing, utilizing, and applying (see Figure 14.2). In Sternberg's view, "the big question is not how many things a person is good at, but how well a person can exploit whatever he or she is good at and find ways around the things that he or she is not good at" (1991, p. 51). Sternberg now describes this combination as "successful intelligence" (Sternberg, 2003, 2009a). (For a look into the development of Sternberg's own intelligence, see A Closer Look "Robert J. Sternberg," on page 500.)

> Sternberg's triarchic theory describes analytic, creative, and practical giftedness.

One of Sternberg's current interests lies in the nature of *wisdom* as a form of giftedness (Sternberg, Jarvin, & Grigorenko, 2009, 2011). He asks that we think, for example, of four extremely gifted individuals of the twentieth century—Mahatma Gandhi, Mother Theresa, Dr. Martin Luther King, Jr., and Nelson Mandela. Would

Table 14.1 Gardner's Multiple Intelligences

Category	Core Operations	Example
Linguistic Mastery, sensitivity, desire to explore, and love of words and spoken and written language(s).	Comprehension and expression of written and oral language, syntax, semantics, pragmatics.	William Shakespeare, Toni Morrison
Logical-mathematical Confront, logically analyze, assess, and empirically investigate objects, abstractions, and problems, discern relations and underlying principles, carry out mathematical operations, handle long chains of reasoning.	Computation, deductive reasoning, inductive reasoning.	Paul Erdos, Isaac Newton
Musical Skill in producing, composing, performing, listening, discerning, and sensitivity to the components of music and sound.	Pitch, melody, rhythm, texture, timbre, musical, themes, harmony.	Charlie Parker, Wolfgang Amadeus Mozart
Spatial Accurately perceive, recognize, manipulate, modify and transform shape, form, and pattern.	Design, color, form, perspective, balance, contrast, match.	Leonardo da Vinci, Frank Lloyd Wright
Bodily-kinesthetic Orchestrate and control body motions and handle objects, skillfully, to perform tasks or fashion products.	Control and coordination, stamina, balance, locating self or objects in space.	Martha Graham, Tiger Woods
Interpersonal Be sensitive to, accurately assess, and understand others' actions, motivations, moods, feelings, and other mental states and act productively on the basis of that knowledge.	Ability to inspire, instruct, or lead others and respond to their actions, emotions, motivations, opinions, and situations.	Virginia Woolf, Dalai Lama
Intrapersonal Be sensitive to, accurately assess, understand and regulate oneself and act productively on the basis of one's actions, motivations, moods, feelings, and other mental states.	Knowledge and understanding of one's strengths and weaknesses, styles, emotions, motivations, self-orientation.	Mahatma Gandhi, Oprah Winfrey
Naturalist Expertise in recognition and classification of natural objects, i.e., flora & fauna, or artifacts, i.e., cars, coins, or stamps.	Noting the differences that are key to discriminating among several categories or species of objects in the natural world.	Charles Darwin, Jane Goodall
Existential* Capturing and pondering the fundamental questions of existence; an interest and concern with "ultimate" issues.	Capacity to raise big questions about one's place in the cosmos.	Soren Kierkegaard, Martin Luther King, Jr.

*Unconfirmed ninth intelligence.

Source: COLANGELO, NICHOLAS; DAVIS, GARY A., *HANDBOOK OF GIFTED EDUCATION*, 3rd Edition, © 2003, pp. 76. Adapted by permission of Pearson Education, Inc., Upper Saddle River, NJ.

their gifts have been identified through any kind of test, or with the definitions we identify in this chapter? Perhaps not. But they instigated change that led to great good in the world, the scope of which few others can claim. Sternberg argues that we need to start developing wisdom in children:

Sternberg identifies wisdom as a form of intelligence, and believes that schools should try to teach wisdom.

For example, students need to learn how to think dialogically, understanding points of view other than their own, and to think not only in terms of their own interests, but in terms of the interests of others and of the society, as well. . . . Unless students are specifically taught to focus upon the common good, rather than only upon the good of themselves and those close to them, they may simply never learn to think in such a fashion. (2000, p. 252)

The Teaching Strategies box later in this chapter, "Developing Wisdom in Children," on page 502, provides Sternberg's suggestions for this endeavor. These strategies would be particularly successful with teenagers.

FIRST PERSON

Danielle Evans

anielle Evans has a gift for words. Read these excerpts from a "self-interview" and see if you agree.

SELF-INTERVIEW, HUH? HOW OFTEN DO YOU TALK TO YOURSELF?

Kind of a lot, actually. I'm an only child who's never had any kind of a roommate, so I got used to getting away with it. Besides, it comes in handy on public transit. I apparently have one of those faces that says: Talk to me. Confess. Strangers sit next to me on buses and start telling their life stories. There's something overwhelming about being that approachable, and on days when I feel like I don't have enough to offer in return, which is most days, I ride the bus holding a book and wearing headphones, but sometimes that doesn't work. I rode into Chicago once with a teenage runaway who had told me all about her boyfriend troubles by the time we arrived, and out of Chicago once with a man who'd just gotten out of jail and needed to talk about it. I ran into a woman I'd never met before in a hotel lobby and she began telling me about the measures she was taking to escape an abusive marriage. A man on a bus in Missouri once sniffed me, and somehow got

from inquiring about my perfume as a potential gift for his wife to telling me about the problems in his marriage. Three bus drivers in three different states have proposed to me. Once, I was hungover and limping across an Iowa City parking lot because I'd twisted my ankle the night before, and a man came running over and said I looked like a writer and maybe I could help him, and handed me a cassette tape he said contained government secrets. On my second day in Paris, people came up to ask me for directions in several languages that I didn't speak. Years ago, in an Amtrak snack car, I sat with some guys who, apropos of nothing, asked me if I thought they'd be extradited from the state they were visiting in order to face drug charges in the state we'd just left. Last week I was standing at the bus stop with about ten people, and a woman walking by ignored all ten other people and stopped and stood in front of me and kept talking until I took my headphones out. She asked me if I was ready to have my palm read, and when I said no, gave me her address and told me she'd be there when I was ready. I'm hoping this is the beginning of a narrative arc that leads to me being told I have superpowers, preferably the zappy lightning bolt kind.

The National Association for Gifted Children's definition of giftedness endorses the idea that giftedness can exist in a number of different domains, and defines the term:

> Gifted individuals are those who demonstrate outstanding levels of aptitude (defined as an exceptional ability to reason and learn) or competence (documented performance or achievement in top 10 percent or rarer) in one or more domains. Domains include any structured area of activity with its own symbol system (e.g., mathematics, music, language) and/or set of sensorimotor skills (e.g., painting, dance, sports). (National Association for Gifted Children, 2008)

Anyway, since I am currently without zappy powers, I find talking to myself in public cuts down on the number of people who trust me enough to launch into personal conversations.

I DON'T LIKE YOUR SHOES.

They hurt. Grammy always said suffer for beauty. It applies to both footwear and writing.

YEAH, OK. REMIND ME OF THAT THE NEXT TIME YOU END UP CARRYING YOUR HEELS HOME FROM THE METRO. SPEAKING OF OUR GRANDMOTHER, I READ ON THE INTERNET SOMEWHERE THAT SHE TRIED TO DROWN YOU OR SOMETHING?

Sigh. No, you read on the internet that there's a story in my book where a black child has a white mother and a white grandmother who is not very kind to her, for reasons both race-related and not. Because I am also a black person with a white grandmother, some people seem to have assumed that story is true, in spite of the fact that my actual grandmother herself married a black man and had four black children, and has probably never been to Tallahassee unless it was when she was working as a traveling saleswoman, and has probably never been in a country club, unless it was when she was working as a bartender. Also, I did not burn down my high school and I did not lose my virginity the day that Tupac died. I write realism, but creation of a convincing illusion is my job. I don't understand why people think it's cool to be all wink wink nudge nudge aren't you really writing memoir? I don't go around asking people how often they get away with faking their way through their jobs, and pretend it's a compliment. Then again, I guess most people's jobs aren't to be liars.

SO YOUR BOOK IS ABOUT ADOLESCENCE?

No. There are eight stories and only two are about adolescence. The book is, I guess, substantially about the gulf between the people we discover we are and the people we imagined we'd be someday.

THE SORT OF GULF THAT MIGHT LEAD A PERSON TO FREQUENTLY TALK TO HERSELF?

Exactly. Danielle Evans is the winner of the 2011 PEN/Robert W. Bingham Prize. A graduate of Columbia University and the Iowa Writers' Workshop, her stories have appeared in The Paris Review, A Public Space, The Best American Short Stories 2008, and The Best American Short Stories 2010. Her collection of stories, *Before You Suffocate Your Own Fool Self*, is her first book. She teaches fiction writing at American University in Washington, D.C. daniellevaloreevans.com

Source: From The Nervous Breakdown. Reprinted by permission.

A CLOSER LOOK   Robert J. Sternberg

The Child is father of the Man. . . .
— *William Wordsworth*

Psychologist Robert Sternberg the creator of the triarchic theory of intelligence and past president of the American Psychological Association, is the author of over fifty books on a wide variety of topics—from intelligence and gifted children to wisdom, love, and hate, as well as countless professional journal articles. He must have been the epitome of the gifted child, correct? You'll be surprised. Let Sternberg tell his own story (2000, pp. 21–22):

As an elementary school student, Sternberg failed miserably on the IQ tests he had to take. He was incredibly test-anxious. Just the sight of the school psychologist coming into the classroom to give a group IQ test sent him into a wild panic attack. And by the time the psychologist said "Go!" to get the class started, he was in such a funk that he could hardly answer any of the test items. He still remembers being on the first couple of problems when he heard other students already turning the page as they sailed through the test. For him, the game of taking the test was all but over before it even started. And the outcome was always the same: He lost.

Sternberg was an ordinary student, convinced of his mediocrity,—"one more loser in the game of life"— until he reached Mrs. Alexa's fourth grade class:

. . . Mrs. Alexa did not know or did not care much about IQ test scores. She believed Sternberg could do much better than he was doing, and she expected more of him. In fact, she demanded more of him. And she got it. Why? Because he wanted to please her. . .

Mrs. Alexa did not seem particularly surprised, but her student was astonished when he actually exceeded her expectations. He became a straight-A student very quickly. For the first time, he saw himself as someone who could be an A student, and he was one thereafter. But at the time, it never occurred to him that he had become an A student *because* he was smart; on the contrary, he felt that he had become an A student *in spite* of his low intelligence, as witnessed by his low test scores.

In this painful memory of the little boy who was father to a brilliant man, it is not difficult to see the genesis of a psychologist who would widen our definition of intelligence. Read more of Sternberg's story, and explore his work, in *Teaching for Successful Intelligence*, cowritten with his colleague Elena Grigorenko. For more about Sternberg's work, visit our textbook website.

Source: R. J. Sternberg & E. Grigorenko (2000). *Teaching for Successful Intelligence* (pp. 21–22). Arlington Heights, IL: Skylight Training and Publishing, Inc.

Finally, the "official" definition of giftedness is the one in federal law, which states that gifted children are those

> . . .who give evidence of high performance capability in areas such as intellectual, creative, artistic, leadership capacity, or specific academic fields, and who require services or activities not ordinarily provided by the school in order to fully develop such capabilities. (P.L. 103-382, Title XIV, p. 388)

Federal law defines giftedness as evidence of high performance capability in intellectual, creative, artistic, leadership, and academic areas.

The federal definition specifies areas of giftedness; it allows for gifted traits and gifted behaviors; and it connects the definition with the need to provide special educational programs for children identified as gifted. Overall, it is a comprehensive definition that is now widely used in the United States.

Federal law does not *require* educational services for students identified as gifted, nor does it provide any funds for the implementation of gifted programs. Since its enactment, however, many individual states have incorporated the federal definition into state legislation; and, since 31 states have some kind of legal mandate to serve students identified as gifted or talented, this federal definition has encouraged a substantial increase in state-based

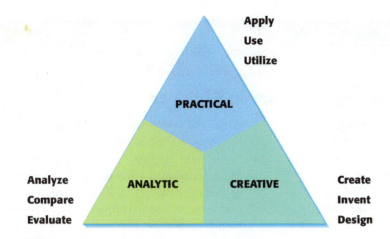

Sternberg's Triarchic Theory of Intelligence

According to Robert Sternberg, intelligence comprises analytic, creative, and practical abilities. In *analytical thinking,* we try to solve familiar problems by using strategies that manipulate the elements of a problem or the relationships among the elements (for example, comparing, analyzing). In *creative thinking,* we try to solve new kinds of problems that require us to think about the problem and its elements in a new way (for example, inventing, designing). In *practical thinking,* we try to solve problems that apply what we know to everyday contexts (for example, applying, using).

Source: From *In Search of the Human Mind* by Robert J. Sternberg, copyright © 1995 by Harcourt Brace & Company. Reproduced by permission of the author.

initiatives for serving students with gifts or talents (National Association for Gifted Children, 2011).

    It is doubtful that one definition of giftedness will ever be written that satisfies every theorist, educator, and parent. Nor is it likely that all gifted children will ever be identified for the special education they require. Still, it is important for you to realize that if you are unsure about "exactly" who is gifted, you share your lack of certainty with some of the world's experts on the theory and measurement of intelligence.

> Federal law does not require educational services for gifted students but encourages state initiatives for serving these students.

Criteria for Identification

If a child begins to read independently at the age of 3 or a 15-year-old graduates as high-school valedictorian, it is quite apparent that you are observing atypical behavior—not "abnormal" behavior, but behavior that appears in advance of its usual developmental onset.

    Advanced development is one of the most commonly applied criteria in the identification of students with gifts and talents. Historically, measurement of advanced development has been through standardized tests given by school psychologists or teachers.

    Individual IQ tests, like the WISC-IV or the Stanford-Binet (see Chapter 6), can be used to assess intellectual capacity. However, the extensive costs in terms of time and money needed to administer and score the tests have caused many school districts to forgo their use. Instead, standardized group intelligence tests are often used. When given as part of the annual battery of achievement tests administered to all students, these group tests provide a general assessment of how students compare intellectually with their classmates. Those students who score two or more standard deviations above the mean of the test (which generally results in an IQ of 130 to 135) are often classified as gifted (see Figure 14.3.)

Teaching Strategies & Accommodations

Developing Wisdom in Children

What we consider wisdom, argues Sternberg, is inextricably tied to our values, and we must begin by valuing wisdom itself and what it can contribute to society. Do we? Think of how older people are perceived in our culture to answer that question.

Here are Sternberg's own words (2000, pp. 257–258):

Wisdom is a form of giftedness that can be developed in a number of ways. Seven of these are particularly important:

- *First*, provide students with problems that require wise thinking.
- *Second*, help students think in terms of a common good in the solution of these problems.
- *Third*, help students learn how to balance their own interests, the interests of others, and the interests of institutions in the solution of these problems.
- *Fourth*, provide examples of wise thinking from the past and analyze them.
- *Fifth*, model wisdom for the students. Show them examples of wise thinking you have

done and perhaps not-so-wise thinking that has taught you lessons.

- *Sixth*, help students to think dialectically. . . . Most problems in the world do not have right or wrong answers, but better or worse ones, and what is seen as a good answer can vary with time and place.
- *Seventh*, show your students that you value wise information processing and solutions.

Finally, carry what you learn and encourage students to carry what they learn outside the classroom. The goal is not to teach another "subject" that will serve as the basis for an additional grade to appear on a report card. The goal is to change the way people think about and act in their own lives.

Source: Sternberg, Robert J., Gifted Child Quarterly, Wisdom as a Form of Giftedness, Vol 44, 9), pg. 9, © 2000 Sage Publications. Reprinted by permission of SAGE Publications.

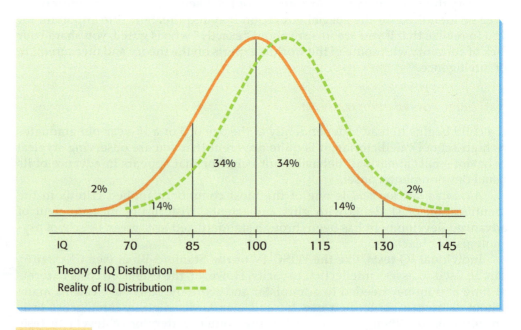

FIGURE 14.3

The Normal Curve and Average IQ Score Distribution

Source: From KIRK/GALLAGHER/COLEMAN/ANASTOSIOW. *Educating Exceptional Children*, 13E. © 2012 Wadsworth, a part of Cengage Learning, Inc. Reproduced by permission. www.cengage.com/permissions

Similarly, students who score at the 95th percentile or above on standardized achievement tests of reading, math, and other content areas are often identified as academically gifted.

Newman (2008) reminds us of something experienced teachers know well: Test scores are just one component of what makes a student successful. Tests do not measure motivation, creativity, family support, or other crucial influences on the student's performance.

The criteria for qualifying for special programs for gifted students varies; check with your local school district to determine the criteria in your area. In the Los Angeles Unified School District (LAUSD), for example, students can qualify for gifted programs in one of the following ways:

Major Categories of Identification of Giftedness in the Los Angeles Unified School District

Gifted/Talented students exhibit excellence or the capacity for excellence far beyond that of their chronological peers. Students whose abilities fall into one or more of the categories below may be considered for participation in the Gifted/Talented Programs.

Intellectual Ability: Students whose general intellectual development is markedly advanced in relation to their chronological peers. Students can only be tested one time.

High Achievement Ability—Grade 4 and above: Students who consistently function for two consecutive years at highly advanced levels in both English-Language Arts/reading/EL* (elementary), English/EL* (secondary), and mathematics.

Grade 2 only: Students who demonstrate high achievement on a nationally standardized, norm-referenced, group-administered measure of verbal and non-verbal school abilities.

Specific Academic Ability: Students who consistently function for three consecutive years at highly advanced levels in either English-Language Arts/reading/EL* (elementary), English/EL* (secondary), or mathematics. Students in Grades 9–12 may also be considered in either science or social science.

Creative Ability: Students who characteristically perceive significant similarities or differences within the environment, challenge assumptions, and produce unique alternative solutions.

Leadership Ability: Students who show confidence and knowledge; influence others effectively; have problem-solving and decision-making skills; express ideas in oral or written form clearly; show sense of purpose and direction.

Ability in the Performing or Visual Arts: Students who originate, perform, produce, or respond at exceptionally high levels in either dance, music (voice), drama, or in drawing or painting.

*English Learners (EL).

(*Source:* http://www.lausd.net/lausd/offices/GATE/intro-2.html#Intro2Pg1 CatsIden)

But qualification for the **highly gifted** programs comes through an IQ score alone—in this case, a score on an individually administered IQ test equivalent to 99.9 percent.

Underrepresentation of Students from Culturally and Linguistically Diverse Backgrounds

Achievement and IQ tests have been criticized as being too narrow in focus; they concentrate on analytic abilities (Sternberg, 2003), and the traditional areas of linguistic and logico-mathematical reasoning (Von Károlyi, Ramos-Ford, & Gardner, 2003). Many scholars have noted that using IQ tests as the primary means of identifying candidates for gifted programs inevitably leads to underrepresentation of children from culturally and linguistically diverse backgrounds as well as those with disabilities (Skiba et al., 2008). Any standardized test-based identification of giftedness leads to the under-identification of students who are American Indian/Alaskan Native, African American, and Hispanic (Donovan & Cross, 2002). Ensuring that gifted programs are inclusive of *all* children, regardless of race, home language, or disability, will involve developing more sensitive assessment procedures and changes in our reliance on tests and test scores.

> Some critics believe that standardized tests that determine giftedness leads to underrepresentation of children from minority groups.

Donna Ford (2006; Ford, Grantham, & Whiting, 2008) of Vanderbilt University has spent much of her career identifying and describing the reasons for the underrepresentation of culturally and linguistically diverse (CLD) students in gifted programs, with an emphasis on the African American male student (2010). She and her colleagues (2008) suggest that there are three primary reasons for the underrepresentation of CLD students in gifted programs: the use of traditional tests (especially IQ tests), the lack of teacher referral, and "deficit thinking"—

> *Deficit thinking* is negative, stereotypical, and prejudicial beliefs about CLD groups that result in discriminatory policies and behaviors or actions.
> Deficit thinking and resignation are reflected in the statement of two participants interviewed by Garcia and Guerra (2004) who believed that the success of some children is set early and it is irrevocable: "Some children are already so harmed by their lives that they cannot perform at the same level as other children," and "[if] those neurons don't start firing at 8 or 9 months, it's never going to happen. So, we've got some connections that weren't made and they can't be made up" (p. 160). (Ford, Grantham, Whiting, 2008, p. 292)

Deficit thinking can affect behavior and actions, including willingness to refer students into gifted programs, and may hinder a teacher's ability to see a student's strengths (Harry, 2008). We expect that the next generation of teachers and school professionals will avoid the behaviors that accompany deficit thinking.

Informal assessment by parents, teachers, peers, and community members who know the student can provide school personnel with non–test-based information about the range of a student's specific skills or talents. The yardsticks for measuring giftedness should be many and varied. The teacher's role in identifying and assessing giftedness and talent is discussed later in the chapter. For more information, visit the website of the Center for Gifted Education and Talent Development at the University of Connecticut.

Pause and Reflect

Conceptualizing giftedness is more complicated than you might have thought. What qualities do you think make someone gifted? Can you put your own definition of giftedness into writing? How is your definition influenced by your cultural experiences and values? ●

Factors Contributing to Giftedness

For as long as gifts and talents have been recognized and studied, the question of nature versus nurture has been pondered. Are individuals with gifts and talents endowed with a pool of superior genes, or is their environment responsible for the emergence of superior performance?

Hereditary and Biological Factors

Scientists and educators agree that genes are but one element in the complex development of human intelligence. Even geneticists disagree about the relative contributions of our genes to our abilities—estimates range from about 40 to 80 percent. Gage and Berliner (1998) saw the influences of heredity and environment on intelligence as about equal; Plomin and Price (2003) explained that "genes merely contribute to the odds that development will proceed in a certain direction . . . *genetic* does not mean innate" (p. 113). Today, in the "post-genomic era" (after the work of the Human Genome Project), scientists are studying the effects of environmental influence on gene expression (Gottlieb, 2009). The topic has not become any less complicated.

> It is likely that both genetics and environment play crucial roles in determining giftedness.

While innate ability appears essential, it may not emerge without an added dimension: hard work. Ericsson (2006; Ericsson, Krampe & Tesch-Romer, 1993) found that the highest achievers in ballet, violin, piano, chess, bridge, and athletics were those who engaged in the most "deliberate practice"—consistent effort designed to improve performance.

Environmental Factors

Abraham J. Tannenbaum writes: "Giftedness requires a social context that enables it to mature. These contexts are as broad as society itself and as restricted as the sociology of the classroom. Human potential needs nurturance, urgings, encouragement, and even pressures from a world that cares" (2003, p. 54). Good teachers and supportive families are part of that world that cares.

The role played by the family in the development of gifts and talents has been studied extensively, and virtually every study has shown the importance of nurturance. Benjamin Bloom (1985), in his study of Olympic athletes, musical prodigies, and others of exceptional achievement, points to the vital role played by the family (not just the parents) in channeling these remarkable talents and downplays the role of the school in the realization of noteworthy accomplishments. Sternberg (2003) reminds us that an individual's intelligence must be viewed within the context of the *opportunities* he or she has had—and people of higher socioeconomic status tend to have more opportunities than those of lower socioeconomic status.

> Family encouragement of the child's talents is of critical importance.

Sternberg (2007) reminds us that intelligence is conceived in different ways in different cultures, and cultural conceptions of intelligence are reflective of skills needed for successful adaptation to the environment.

> We therefore need to be hesitant in imposing one culture's view of intelligence across the board. The mental hardware may be the same across cultures. After all, in every culture, people have to recognize when they have problems, define what the problems are, solve the problems, and then evaluate how well they have solved them. But the content of the problems to be solved is different, and what is considered a good solution differs as well. If we recognize these facts, we may be more circumspect in passing judgments

on people from the diversity of cultures in the United States and around the world. (p. 152–153)

In short, the debate over the development of gifts and talents has grown far beyond the nature-nurture arguments of past generations. Today, the emphasis is on the practical: designing structure and strategies at home and at school that encourage these talents to blossom.

Prevalence

Considering the variety of definitions of giftedness, it is not surprising that the prevalence of gifts and talents in the population is also open to debate. For example, if you were to use the criterion of an IQ of 140 as the baseline for intellectual giftedness, you would exclude 99 percent of the population. (See Figure 14.3 again for a visual representation of this concept.) If, however, you were to use the federal definition of giftedness, 3 to 5 percent of the school-age population would qualify as having gifts or talents. Renzulli's concept of giftedness (1978, 2011) identifies a set of behaviors that can emerge in students who are above average (although not necessarily superior) in ability. Thus, he suggests a figure of 15 to 20 percent of the population as potentially gifted. The National Association of Gifted Children (2008) estimates that there are approximately 3 million academically gifted children in grades K–12 in the United States; that is approximately 6 percent of the student population.

> Estimates of the number of gifted students vary according to the definition used.

Pause and Reflect

Gifted performance seems to depend on a combination of innate ability and environmental factors such as opportunity and support. What are the opportunities you have had—or wish you had had—to develop your own areas of talent or interest? How do you plan to provide these opportunities to the students you teach? ●

Characteristics of Students Who Are Gifted and Talented

Students who are gifted and talented represent a cross-section of humanity: All races, cultures, sizes, and shapes are represented. Yet as different as these individual students seem at first glance, their intelligence has affected their cognitive and social-emotional development in similar ways. The following sections highlight some of these effects.

Cognitive Characteristics

Cognitive development is frequently accelerated in children with exceptional abilities, and although we may see this as a positive factor, it can cause problems in the classroom. For example, a child who learned to read independently at the age of 3 may have difficulty in a kindergarten class where he or she is expected to learn the alphabet. A junior-high student well versed in algebra may question the point of completing pages of long-division problems. A 10-year-old who perceives subtle distinctions in moral reasoning may be frustrated by age-mates who see only cut-and-dried, right-and-wrong solutions.

© TIZIANA FABI/AFP/Getty Images

This piano prodigy has benefited from the opportunity to learn, but is also motivated to practice.

Exceptionally gifted students may ponder questions deeply and consider many possible answers; they often pose complex philosophical questions themselves. If there is no special program available for students like these, problems and frustrations may occur for both the student and the teacher. In fact, these sophisticated cognitive characteristics may pose unique challenges even for the teacher who is committed to providing an enriched curriculum to gifted and talented students. See Table 14.2 for more on this topic.

Social and Emotional Characteristics

Very closely tied to the cognitive effects of giftedness and talents is the social and emotional impact of these talents on students' performance. While many students have the same social and emotional characteristics as other children their age, some students may feel "different," misunderstood, and socially isolated. They may benefit from the support of other gifted peers, as well as understanding families and teachers.

Some gifted students experience social isolation.

Nancy Robinson (2008) argues that there is no inherent social vulnerability in gifted students; in fact, as a group they may be more mature than their peers. Problems can arise, though, when there is a mismatch between the student's abilities and the school setting, and there are few peers with similar interests and abilities to become friends with.

Some people assume that gifted students must have plenty of friends of their own age in order to be socially "healthy." Schultz and Delisle (2003) believe that for gifted students, peers are not necessarily of the same age, but share the same abilities and interests—their commonalities may have nothing to do with age. Most would agree that relationships with peers of all ages can be appropriate for students who are gifted and talented.

The interplay between intellect and emotion is clear to people who work with students with talents and gifts. An intellectually able 6-year-old may cry uncontrollably when confronted with inequity or injustice, either on the schoolyard or while watching the evening news. A fastidious high-school junior may consider herself a failure if she receives a grade of B+ in advanced physics. Perfectionism is a scourge for many high-performing students, and a source of underachievement for others—impossibly high goals may provide an excuse for lack of effort

Table 14.2 Cognitive Characteristics of Gifted Students and Their Implications for Teaching

Differentiating Characteristics	Possible Problems	Teaching Strategies
Extraordinary quantity of information; unusual retentiveness	Boredom with regular curriculum; impatience with "waiting for the group."	Expose the student to new and challenging aesthetic, economic, political, social, and educational information about the culture and the environment.
Advanced comprehension	Poor interpersonal relationships with same-age peers; adults consider the child a "smart aleck."	Provide access to challenging curriculum and intellectual peers.
Unusually varied interests and curiosity	Difficulty conforming to group tasks; overextending energy levels, taking on too many projects at one time.	Expose student to varied subjects and concerns; allow student to pursue individual ideas as far as interest takes him or her.
High level of language development and verbal ability	Perception as a "show off" by same-age peers; domination of discussion; use of verbalism to avoid difficult thinking tasks.	Provide uses for increasingly difficult vocabulary and concepts; expect student to share ideas verbally in depth.
Unusual capacity for processing information	Resentment at being interrupted; perceived as too serious; dislike of routine and drill.	Expose student to ideas at many levels and in large variety.
Accelerated pace of thought processes	Frustration with inactivity and absence of progress.	Expose student to ideas at rates appropriate to individual pace of learning—often accelerated.
Comprehensive synthesis	Frustration with demand for deadlines and for completion of each level prior to starting new one.	Allow a longer incubation time for ideas.
Ability to generate original ideas and solutions	Difficulty with rigid conformity; may be penalized for not following directions; may deal with rejection by becoming rebellious.	Build skills in problem-solving and creative thinking; provide the opportunity to contribute to solutions of meaningful problems.

Source: Barbara Clark, *Growing Up Gifted: Developing the Potential of Children at Home and at School,* 7th ed., 2007. Reprinted by permission of Pearson Education Inc., Upper Saddle River, NJ.

(Rimm, 2003). It is your job, as a teacher, to understand that intellectually capable students, whatever their ages, must be appreciated for their strengths and their vulnerabilities; even though these young people are smart, they are not small adults—they still need support and guidance from the grown-ups in their lives.

Physical Characteristics

Early research by Terman (1925) showed students with high IQ test scores to be stronger, bigger, and healthier than their agemates. In fact, Terman's findings did much to dissolve the stereotype of the gifted student as a bespectacled weakling who carries a briefcase to school instead of a backpack. However, Terman's research included primarily children from advantaged backgrounds whose physical prowess was bolstered by nurturing and affluent home environments. Today, as gifted programs expand to embrace students from all cultures and socioeconomic backgrounds, we see an array of physical characteristics that defies any simple categorization. In effect, a gifted student has no certain look or appearance. Indeed, students with physical disabilities must not be overlooked in the identification of giftedness; they may have an impressive store of knowledge despite limited experiences, and use exceptional creativity in finding ways of communicating and accomplishing tasks (Fulk, Watts, & Bakken, 2011).

The gifted student cannot be identified by appearance.

? Pause and Reflect

Throughout this book, we have provided you with descriptions of the characteristics of students in each category. Remember that these lists of characteristics are general statements that are true of *many*—but not *all*—students in that group. Are there general statements made about a group that *you* identify with, perhaps based on your age or gender, that you have found untrue in your own experience? ●

Special Populations of Gifted Students

The following sections address some special populations of gifted students and the special needs these young people may have.

● *Gifted Adolescents*   Struggling for social acceptance, experiencing physical changes, and conducting inner searches for meaning in one's life are some of the benchmarks of adolescence. Gifted adolescents are as concerned about these issues as are their agemates, but there may be unique implications for them.

Schultz and Delisle (2003) point out that adolescence for gifted students involves special concerns in the social and emotional, educational, ethical and spiritual, and career and lifestyle domains. In the area of social and emotional issues, gifted females may struggle with decisions related to the often conflicting needs for social acceptance and the full expression of their talents (Kerr & Nicpon, 2003). In effect, gifted girls may feel they must suppress or disguise their abilities to be accepted by boys. Teachers should be aware of these potential issues and be prepared to provide appropriate support.

Educationally, adolescents with gifts and talents tend to question how best to further their intellectual development. For example, if they are admitted to college after their junior year in high school, do they stay in high school and not miss the senior prom and varsity football, or do they go on to college and seek social outlets there? Or, given the opportunity to pursue intellectual challenges independently, do they choose this route and forgo other options?

Career and lifestyle issues include a problem that many people see as a benefit: the ability to be successful in so many fields that selecting a career becomes problematic (Schultz & Delisle, 2003). The societal expectation that gifted students should become highly valued professionals (doctors, lawyers, professors) may intrude on an adolescent's personal choice if he or she wishes to enter a career such as artisan, laborer, or homemaker.

Secondary school teachers can help ward off some of these dilemmas by facilitating discussions among adolescents with similar talents, or through academic and curricular programs that address intellectual and emotional growth (Schultz & Delisle, 2003).

> Ethical and spiritual issues may be especially important to gifted students during adolescence.

● *Gay, Lesbian, Bisexual and Transgender Adolescents*   Gifted adolescents who may need special understanding and support are those who are gay, lesbian, bisexual, or trangender. Peterson and Rischar (2000) note that exceptional ability may contribute to a sense of "differentness" and may affect social relationships. When a gifted child is also gay, lesbian, bisexual or transgender (GLBT), that sense of differentness may intensify. A quest for perfection and a sexual identity that may not be approved of by the student's family and community can combine to form serious feelings of inadequacy in the adolescent who is gifted. Students who fall into these categories may be subject to overt acts of homophobia (Kerr & Nicpon, 2003), and at particular risk of depression and thoughts of suicide. Peterson and Rischar write:

All educators, particularly those involved in education for the gifted, need to be courageous in their support for GLB students, ensuring that their classrooms are physically and psychologically safe and intervening on behalf of students who are "out" or are bullied or teased when their behaviors fit popular GLB stereotypes. Even quiet acknowledgement that gayness is worthy of discussion, that some respected individuals in textbooks are/were GLB, that concerns about sexual orientation are common during childhood and adolescence, and that GLB individuals are probably present in all schools and classrooms may help to lessen the distress of those who believe that no one has ever felt as they do. (2000, p. 231)

The Gay Lesbian and Straight Education Network consists of parents, students, educators, and others working to end discrimination against GLBT students in schools. Visit their website for more information.

> Students who are gifted can become depressed and suicidal if their emerging sexual identity does not conform with societal expectations.

● *Gifted Girls* Until the impact of the women's movement began to be felt in American education in the 1970s and 1980s, little was done to identify and develop giftedness and talents in girls. Although it is now generally understood that it is illegal to discriminate on the basis of gender in any arena, unconscious biases may still prevent girls who are gifted and talented from being identified and from persevering through rigorous educational programs, particularly in middle and secondary school (Kerr & Nicpon, 2003). Girls may receive differential treatment in the classroom because of teacher attitudes that (as an example) stereotype girls as weaker than boys in math and science (Basow, 2010). Teachers may give less attention to girls, and respond to their questions and answers differently than to those of boys (Sadker & Zittleman, 2009). Gifted girls should be encouraged to take the most challenging coursework available, to engage in play activities that are physically challenging and occasionally competitive, and to speak out and defend their opinions in groups. Both girls and boys may need support from their families, counselors, and mentors if they deviate from the stereotyped gender roles of their communities (Kerr & Nicpon, 2003; Reis & Hébert, 2008;). For more information on gender equity, visit the website of educational researcher David Sadker.

> Gifted adolescent girls often feel they must suppress or disguise their abilities to be accepted.

Boys have need for special programs and supports as well. Boys are more likely to drop out of school, and are outnumbered by girls in most colleges and universities across the country.

> Gifted girls must be identified, supported, and challenged, particularly in the middle-school years.

● *Gifted Students with Disabilities* As early as 1942, Hollingworth saw the possibility that disabilities could coexist with giftedness. But only recently have the needs of these "twice exceptional" students been addressed.

June Maker (1977) was among the first to suggest that options should be provided in schools for highly able students who also had learning disabilities, sensory impairments, or physical disabilities. But she warned that her work was merely a beginning, serving to "identify issues and raise questions to a greater degree than it solves or answers them" (p. xi).

> Students in any special education category can also be gifted or talented.

Students who are gifted may also be on the autism spectrum, have emotional or behavioral disorders, physical handicaps or learning disabilities (Neihart, 2008); in fact, gifts and talents can occur in students in any special education category. Students with learning disabilities are a unique group. Sally Reis and her colleagues (Reis, Neu, & McGuire, 1997; Reis, McGuire, & Neu, 2000) conducted in-depth interviews with twelve young adults who were successful in college while receiving support services for their identified learning disabilities. All had been tested earlier in their schooling and were found to have high IQs. The researchers found that these students uniformly reported negative experiences in elementary and secondary school. Their learning disabilities tended to be identified

The development of future scientists depends on opportunities to experience the fun of scientific inquiry.

relatively late in their schooling, despite problems that had appeared early; they reported negative interactions with teachers, some of whom told the students they were lazy and could achieve if they worked harder; and they felt isolated from peers and unaccepted by them. But because these students developed compensation strategies, had parental support, and participated in a university learning disability program, they succeeded despite their early negative experiences (see Teaching Strategies & Accommodations, "Compensation Strategies Used by Gifted Students with Learning Disabilities," on page 513). Reis and her colleagues suggest that it was the combination of their high abilities and disabilities that set them up for problems in school, such as the late referrals to special education and poor relationships with teachers.

High-ability students with learning disabilities can succeed in college with the right supports.

These students had other advantages and a secret weapon:

> Each person in this study had a mother who devoted herself to using different strategies to help her child succeed. This assistance was given regardless of whether the mother worked outside of the home and regardless of how many other children were in the family. One may ask, therefore, what happens to children who do not have a similar source of support? (Reis, Neu, & McGuire, 1997, p. 477)

Table 14.3 describes some of the factors that may make it difficult to identify students with learning disabilities as gifted.

Students with disabilities who are gifted may show their abilities in unusual ways and may need unconventional assessment techniques because traditional assessments are not appropriate. According to Neihart (2008):

> There are many smart children in this country who are not considered gifted because their behaviors and achievement do not fit the stereotyped view of gifted children. Their superior ability can be recognized when adults realize that gifted children with learning or behavior problems do exist … (pp. 131–132).

In the end, underlying all approaches to locating and serving gifted children with disabilities is a need to change society's attitudes and perceptions. There remains a need for each of us to see that *capability* is more important than *disability*.

Table 14.3 Giftedness and Learning Disabilities

Common Attributes of Giftedness

- Motivation
- Problem-solving ability
- Well-developed memory
- Insight
- Imagination-creativity
- Advanced ability to deal with symbol systems

- Advanced interests
- Communication skills
- Inquiry
- Reasoning
- Sense of humor

Characteristics of Gifted Students with Learning Disabilities

Characteristics that hamper identification as gifted:

- Frustration with inability to master certain academic skills
- Learned helplessness
- General lack of motivation
- Disruptive classroom behavior
- Demonstration of poor listening and concentration skills
- Absence of social skills with some peers
- Deficiency in tasks emphasizing memory and perceptual abilities

- Lack of organizational skills
- Failure to complete assignments
- Supersensitivity
- Perfectionism
- Low self-esteem
- Unrealistic self-expectations

Characteristic strengths:

- Advanced vocabulary use
- High levels of creativity
- Specific aptitude (artistic, musical, or mechanical)
- Ability to think of divergent ideas and solutions
- Task commitment

- Exceptional analytic abilities
- Advanced problem-solving skills
- Wide variety of interests
- Good memory
- Spatial abilities

Sources: Adapted from M. M. Frasier & A. H. Passow (1994). *Towards a New Paradigm for Identifying Talent Potential.* Storrs, CT: University of Connecticut, the National Research Center on the Gifted and Talented. Also adapted from S. M. Reis, T. W. Neu, & J. M. McGuire (1995). *Talent in Two Places: Case Studies of High Ability Students with Learning Disabilities Who Have Achieved.* Storrs, CT: University of Connecticut, the National Research Center on the Gifted and Talented.

● *Underachieving Gifted Students*   Think of someone you knew in school who was always told by teachers, "You're a smart kid; I know you could do better if you wanted to." Usually, this type of student frustrates teachers and parents, for they see a lot of talent going to waste. The technical term applied to students whose aptitude is high but whose performance is low (or mediocre) is **gifted under-achiever**, but the less technical terms are the ones that sting—terms like *lazy, unmotivated,* or *disorganized.* Whatever you call these students, one thing is certain: When *you* get one in *your* classroom, you'll wish there was some magic elixir available that would cause this "underachievement" to disappear.

> Some gifted students do not achieve at the level of their potential.

What causes this disheartening underachievement? Hollingworth (1942) believed that students with an IQ of 140 spend half of each school day in activities that are unchallenging and monotonous, and the result is often a poor attitude toward school ("school is boring") or even misbehavior, as shown by the comment of this 12-year-old girl: "I learned I was gifted in third grade. I would finish my work early and disturb others because I had nothing to do" (Delisle, 1984, p. 11). Family, cultural, and peer issues may contribute to underachievement as well when education is not highly valued (Reis & McCoach, 2000). Boys may be somewhat more likely than girls to "disengage" from both leadership and academic activities in school (Kerr & Nicpon, 2003).

> Intellectually gifted students who dislike school may not develop their abilities.

Teaching Strategies & Accommodations

Compensation Strategies Used by Gifted Students with Learning Disabilities

Students with high-ability levels and learning disabilities found that the following strategies and supports helped them succeed in their college work:

Strategy	Components
Study and Performance Strategies	Notetaking
	Test-taking preparation
	Time management
	Monitoring daily, weekly, and monthly assignments and activities
	Using weekly and monthly organizers to maximize use of time; chunking assignments into workable parts
	Library skills
Cognitive/ Learning Strategies	Memory strategies such as mnemonics and rehearsal using flash cards
	Chunking information into smaller units for mastery
Compensation Supports	Word processing
	Use of computers
	Books on tape

These students also had other supports and strengths:

Parental Support

- Parents, particularly mothers, were energetic advocates for their children.
- The students in the university learning-disabilities program cited help with study skills, a network of support, and a consistent program director as important components of the program.

Self-Perceived Strength and Future Aspirations

- Students had a strong work ethic and the conviction that they could succeed.

Sources: S. M. Reis, T. W. Neu, & J. M. McGuire (1997). Case studies of high-ability students with learning disabilities who have achieved. *Exceptional Children 63*(4), 463–479, and S. M. Reis, J. M. McGuire, & T. W. Neu (2000). Compensation strategies used by high-ability students with learning disabilities who succeed in college. *Gifted Child Quarterly 44*(2), 123–134.

Methods of modifying school curriculum and structure for students with gifts and talents are discussed later in this chapter. What is important to note here is the intimate link between school achievement and school attitude; for if intellectually able students perceive school as drudgery, not stimulating, or irrelevant, it is unlikely that they will develop their talents fully.

Joanne Whitmore (1980) produced the definitive work on gifted underachievers, and her approach combines curricular changes (focusing on a child's strengths and interests), family involvement (parent conferences and "partnership" in rewarding even small improvements in performance), and self-concept education (based on the premise that students who feel good about themselves will choose to achieve).

Ford and Whiting (2008) have observed that students from culturally and linguistically diverse groups (especially African American males) are more likely to fall into this category.

However, there is one point on which all researchers agree: The earlier the problem of underachievement is detected and addressed, the more hopeful is the prognosis for positive change. The problem of underachieving behaviors will not be easy to solve, but if you look toward making the gifted child's school time relevant, interesting, and intellectually stimulating, chances are good that the student's response will be positive.

When underachievement is detected early, the prognosis for positive change is good.

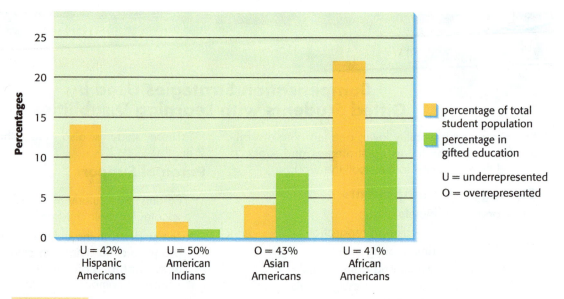

FIGURE 14.4

Representation of Students from Diverse Groups in Gifted Education Programs

Source: COLANGELO, NICHOLAS; DAVIS, GARY A., *HANDBOOK OF GIFTED EDUCATION*, 3rd Edition, © 2003, pp. 76. Adapted by permission of Pearson Education, Inc., Upper Saddle River, NJ.

> Using non-test-based indicators, children with gifts and talents can be found in every race, culture, and socioeconomic group.

● *Culturally Diverse Gifted Students* Gifts and talents exist in children of every race, culture, and socioeconomic group. However, school districts have often been criticized for not looking hard enough to find talents in children who may not represent the majority culture or its values. Indeed, African American students are overrepresented in all categories of special education except for one, gifted education, where they are significantly underrepresented (Ford, Grantham, & Whiting, 2008). Disproportionate representation occurs for children from other ethnic minority groups as well, particularly Latinos and American Indians (Ford & Whiting, 2008). Figure 14.4 depicts the over- and underrepresentation of gifted students from traditional minority groups in programs for gifted students. So, although every thinking person agrees that one's skin color and primary language are not intrinsic limitations to the expression of one's talents, many gifted programs are filled with students from the white, middle-class culture of our population.

Ford, Grantham, & Whiting (2008) describe some of the barriers to fair representation of culturally and linguistically different (CLD) children in gifted programs, and make some recommendations in Table 14.4.

Identifying gifted children from diverse cultural backgrounds has become a major goal of professionals involved in gifted child education (Clark, 2007). The National Research Council recently recommended that research be conducted on early identification and intervention of advanced performance in children from minority backgrounds (Donovan & Cross, 2002). Baldwin notes that this change will involve "accepting new paradigms." Among the new assumptions we must embrace, according to Baldwin (2002), are:

- Giftedness can be expressed through a variety of behaviors and the expression of giftedness in one dimension is just as important as giftedness expressed in another.

- Intelligence is a broad concept that goes beyond language and logic to encompass a wide range of human abilities.

- Carefully planned subjective assessment techniques can be used effectively along with objective measures.

Table 14.4 Underrepresentation Barriers and Recommendations

Barrier	Recommendation
Testing and assessment instruments that contain biases	Culturally sensitive measures that are reduced in cultural demand and linguistic demand
Policies and procedures that are both indefensible and have a disparate impact on CLD students	Policies and procedures examined for bias and negative impact, including teacher referrals, cut-off scores, weights assigned to items in matrices, and requirements associated with attendance, behavior, and GPA
Static definitions and theories of gifted that give little consideration to cultural differences and that ignore how students' backgrounds influence their opportunities to demonstrate skills and abilities	Culturally sensitive definitions and theories of gifted; definitions that recognize how differential opportunities result in poor outcomes for CLD students; definitions that recognize how differences can mask skills and abilities
Lack of teacher training in both gifted education and cultural diversity, which contributes to deficit thinking about CLD students	Substantive, ongoing preparation of teachers in gifted education, cultural diversity, linguistic diversity, and economic diversity

Source: Ford, D. Y., Grantham, T. C., & Whiting, G. W. (2008). Culturally and linguistically diverse students in gifted education: Recruitment and retention issues. *Exceptional Children, 74*(3), p. 299.

- Giftedness in any area can be a clue to the presence of potential giftedness in another.
- All cultures have individuals who exhibit behaviors that are indicative of giftedness.

The Los Angeles Unified School District's criteria for identification of students as gifted, which we described earlier in the chapter, are an example of the application of a new paradigm that extends considerably farther than the IQ test.

Once the students are identified as gifted or talented, the program itself must be tailored to suit the needs, interests, learning styles, and cultural values of its participants.

As the 21st century evolves and our world becomes even smaller through the wonders of travel and technology, program planners for gifted students, and *all* educators, must look for new ways to identify and foster the talents of each child. The challenge is great, but the individual and societal benefits, should we succeed, are even greater.

● *Highly Gifted Students*   Just as educators who work with students with developmental disabilities classify disabilities by level of severity—mild, severe, or profound, for example—gifted-child educators sometimes do the same thing regarding the label of gifted. Often, an IQ score is used to define a population that has come to be called the **highly gifted.** Terman and Merrill (1973) and Whitmore (1980) used an IQ score of 140 to classify a child as highly gifted. Hollingworth (1942), in an early and classic study, used an IQ of 180 as the point at which giftedness is manifest in an extreme form.

Gallagher (2000) believes that highly gifted students (who may constitute less than 1 percent of the total student population) need something different from other very capable students and suggests the following:

- These students should be the instructional responsibility of the specialist in gifted education rather than the general education teacher.

Highly gifted students make up less than 1 percent of the school-aged population.

- Highly gifted students need more individual attention, perhaps through tutoring, acceleration, or individualized studies and projects.

The problems and solutions involving highly gifted students are complex and varied, but the highly gifted child has been receiving increasing attention over the past years. Advocates for this population of students point out that even the best school program that includes opportunities for **academic enrichment** (broadening the experience base of the students without changing the instructional objectives) and acceleration may fall far short of meeting the needs of highly gifted children. **Radical acceleration** (for example, skipping several grades), early entrance to college (some preteen students have attended university full time), and homeschooling are some options that have been used effectively to meet the needs of this population. (See A Closer Look, "The EEPsters," on page 521.)

? Pause & Reflect

Engaging students in school work can be terrifically hard, and it can be especially frustrating for teachers when they know that their students have great potential. Have you ever had the experience of having a good teacher get you interested in something you didn't think you liked? Do you think you could do that for one of your own students? ●

Teaching Strategies and Accommodations

All students benefit from high expectations and good teaching, but sometimes those who are especially capable or talented become bored in school despite those factors. Next we will describe some of the strategies used to keep gifted students working at their potential while they are in school.

Early Intervention

Deciding when to identify a child as gifted or talented can be challenging.

Children are often not formally identified as gifted or talented until sometime during their school career, usually in third or fourth grade. Because of particular advanced behaviors, though, many gifted young children show signs of high potential before they enter the classroom, and the people who identify these talents are often the child's parents.

Disagreement exists regarding the appropriateness of early identification of gifts and talents. On the one hand, some educators believe that it is imperative to identify and challenge talents at the youngest age possible. Gottfried, Gottfried, and Guerin (2009) argue that such identification helps not only the child but also the child's caregivers, for if teachers, child-care workers, and parents are informed of a young child's strengths, they will be better able to provide academic and creative options that match those strengths. Joanne Whitmore (1980), in her classic study of underachieving gifted students, found that patterns of underachievement were developed during the primary school years, yet intervention seldom occurred until the intermediate grades. This unwillingness to address problems as they emerge means that much remediation will have to be done later, whereas preventive measures could have been less extreme yet equally effective.

On the other hand, critics of early identification of gifts and talents point to the "superbaby syndrome" as a problem that cannot be ignored. Parents who replace their gifted children's toys and free play with flash cards and classical concerts are, according to the critics, misguided in their attempts to challenge their children.

The label of "gifted" tells us little about a child's specific unique talents. As parents and teachers work together to match a child's needs with appropriate

ASSISTIVE TECHNOLOGY FOCUS

The Uses and Abuses of Technology with Gifted Children

Technology is an essential tool for research and creative efforts for students who are gifted and talented. Access to various kinds of software and to the Internet is vital for students who can learn independently, and the computer skills of these students grow quickly—often they teach *us* in this arena.

Michael Pyryt (2003) provides some examples of the advantages of technology use by gifted students:

- Technology use can provide *enrichment* through such programs as Odyssey of the Mind, a competition in which students respond to creative challenges, and the Center for Critical Thinking website. Technology-savvy teachers will find more such sites on the Internet for their students.

- Technology can also provide *content-area acceleration* for advanced students through distance-learning courses provided by universities.

- Technology can provide experiences that lead to *personal and social growth*. For example, email correspondence or social networking with other students all over the world—fostered and monitored by teachers—can broaden one's social milieu, reduce feelings of isolation, and create a worldwide community of students interested in a range of topics.

But Pyryt (2003) also describes the potential "dark side" of technology use by very capable students, and the steps teachers must take to avoid the misuse of technology:

- Teachers must teach ethics and integrity in the use of technology and absolutely insist on their practice. It's the most capable technology users who can also wreak the most havoc, both on the Internet and within computer networks.

- Teachers must manage "controlled curiosity" in Internet use so that students stay focused on their academic topic and do not use their Internet time on inappropriate or irrelevant exploration (and this is easier said than done, as many of you know).

- Teachers must demonstrate to students that the Internet has some limitations in terms of the breadth of information, and libraries and other compendiums of knowledge still play an important role.

- Finally, "educators need to remember that there is an affective dimension to giftedness that can be enhanced through positive human interaction" (Pyryt, 2003, p. 586). There's no substitute for the human face or a pat on the back!

In this age of technology, with the proliferation of information and widening access to our "global village," the sky's the limit for our very capable students. They may need our guidance, though, to use their knowledge wisely and well. For inspiration and ideas, see Parker (2010) and the work of Glynda Hull (2010; Hull & Kenney, 2009).

---

services, they must keep in mind that the child's individual physical, emotional, and intellectual needs must be considered in order to provide a healthy balance of rigor and fun.

Identification and Assessment: The Teacher's Role

It was once considered easy to identify gifted students. An individual intelligence test on which a student scored 130 or higher qualified him or her as intellectually gifted. A student who scored 126 was summarily excluded.

Today, as the validity of standardized intelligence test scores has become more suspect, especially for students from minority cultures, and as educators and parents have become more involved in the assessment of exceptional children, best practices call for multiple measures to be used to identify giftedness in students (Delisle, 2000; Pfeiffer & Blei, 2008). Most often, classroom teachers will be asked to supplement information about a child through the use of behavioral checklists. These checklists come in many varieties, but they generally require the teacher to rate a child on a scale of 1 to 4 (1 = seldom; 4 = always) on how often he or she observes behaviors such as these:

- Learns rapidly, easily, efficiently
- Prefers to work alone
- Has a vocabulary above that of classmates
- Displays curiosity and imagination
- Goes beyond the minimum required with assignments
- Follows through on tasks
- Is original in oral and written expression

Essentially, teachers are being asked to select children who "go to school well" and whom teachers love to have in their classes. Yet if teachers are asked to consider only positive student traits and behaviors, they may not identify some gifted children who could surely benefit from advanced instruction. Some researchers have cautioned against teacher referral as the method of identifying gifted students, for two reasons:

1. Teacher judgments may be influenced by low expectations for children from culturally and linguistically diverse learners (Ford & Whiting, 2008).

2. Teachers may not recognize characteristics of giftedness when exhibited in the nontraditional behaviors of minority children.

While some scholars cite these as reasons for underrepresentation of students from culturally and linguistically diverse backgrounds in programs for gifted students, Donovan and Cross (2002) remind us that research evidence on teacher bias is inconclusive. As we have emphasized, teachers must take care to look for manifestations of gifted behavior in all children.

Consider your own education. Were you ever in a class where you felt that your time was being wasted or your talents ignored? Perhaps it was a class that was repetitive to you, or one that provided few challenges or little outlet for creative expression. Whatever the reason for your dissatisfaction, do you recall how you acted in that class? It's unlikely that you led an animated discussion or that you were overly eager to answer the teacher's easy questions. In fact, if someone were to observe you in that class, he or she might find that you appeared bored, off-task, or looking for excitement in all the wrong places (like talking to your friends or passing notes). These would hardly seem to be behavioral indicators of giftedness but, in fact, they might be exactly that.

The point is this: When you, as a teacher, are asked to select children for gifted program services, remember that some indicators of giftedness in children are those very behaviors that teachers usually find distasteful—boredom, misbehavior, even incomplete assignments on easy tasks or worksheets. This is not to say that all gifted children display negative behaviors in class, but it is a reminder to you that some gifts are wrapped in packages (that is, "behaviors") that are not so pretty. Be aware of this possibility when you question why a seemingly bright child is responding negatively to a class assignment or lecture.

Renzulli and Reis (2003) described two kinds of giftedness: *Schoolhouse giftedness,* which can be identified through standardized tests as well as some of the techniques we have described, and *creative-productive giftedness,* which may result in "the development of original material and products that are purposefully designed to have an impact on one or more target audiences" (p. 185). Creativity and potential for innovation are much harder to recognize, but teachers should be open to ways in which those gifts might show themselves in children.

The identification of gifted children is a complex, ongoing process, and it sometimes appears that the main goal is not to locate talents in children but to find ways to exclude them from gifted program services. (In most states, very little

> Today there is a greater likelihood that multiple measures will be used to identify giftedness.

> Some indicators of giftedness are behaviors that teachers find irritating.

funding is available for gifted programs, and many states have cut funds for their programs drastically [Renzulli & Reis, 2008]. Often districts simply cannot afford to provide services to all the students who might be identified under a broad definition of giftedness.) However, with the insights that can be provided by using a variety of methods of identification of giftedness, and students' prior projects or portfolios as evidence of talent, we will do a better job of locating the variety of abilities that students display both inside and outside of school.

Placement Alternatives

The majority of students who are gifted and talented are served in the general education classroom—both those who have been identified and those who have not. Even though elementary and secondary classroom teachers can provide rich intellectual stimulation for gifted students, many school districts offer other options that take place outside of a regular classroom setting. Probably the most common service delivery model is **enrichment.** According to Barbara Clark (2007), "Enrichment can refer to adding disciplines or areas of learning not normally found in the regular curriculum, using more difficult or in-depth material to enhance the core curriculum, or enhancing the teaching strategies used to present instruction" (p. 264). Typically, students identified as gifted participate in pullout or afterschool enrichment activities. Clark believes that enrichment is the least desirable option for the gifted student, since it involves the least change in learning opportunities.

> Enrichment activities supplement the core curriculum for students identified as gifted.

Some school districts have special schools or self-contained classes for students who are gifted and talented. In other locales, a resource room model is preferred. Just as there are a variety of ways to serve students with gifts and talents within a classroom setting, there are multiple options for meeting the needs of these students in other settings. See Figure 14.5 for an overview of the models. Some of the more popular out-of-class methods are reviewed here.

● **Resource Rooms**   The most popular option at the elementary school level may be the resource room approach. Similar in design and structure to programs for children with disabilities, the gifted education resource room allows gifted students to work together. Often, cross-age grouping is used, and it is not unusual to see third-grade students working alongside fifth-grade students.

> The resource room is a part-time solution to the full-time challenge of educating gifted students.

Placement Options

The general education classroom	The general education classroom with resource room	Self-contained classes on general education campuses	Special schools
Possible teaching arrangements: • No special attention • Clustering gifted students together • Differentiated instruction by the general education teacher	Differentiated content for gifted students in the resource room	All content designed for gifted students	All content designed for gifted/talented students. Examples: • Magnet schools • State-sponsored residential schools • Visual and performing arts academies

© Cengage Learning 2013

FIGURE 14.5

Placement Options for Gifted and Talented Students

"Makeup work"—needing to complete worksheets and text assignments in addition to the work in the gifted program—can cause students stress and prompt them to question the benefits of their resource room participation. The conscientious classroom teacher, by testing to determine what the student already knows and using curriculum telescoping (see later in this chapter), can relieve many of these problems.

Another problem occurs when the classroom teacher relinquishes responsibility for educating gifted students by assuming that "they're getting all they need in the resource room." The resource room works best when its teachers communicate frequently with regular classroom teachers, and both work together to benefit gifted students.

● *Self-Contained and Homogeneously Grouped Classes*   Often the option of choice a generation ago, the self-contained gifted classroom is still used today, but less frequently. In this type of class, gifted students are identified and placed together for instruction. This placement limits participation to a select group of gifted children—enough to fill one classroom—while denying gifted program services to those students who may have talents only in particular areas.

● *Special Schools*   Some schools are exclusively designed for gifted/talented students. Magnet schools, for example, may be designed to place special emphasis on science, the arts, or some other content area and to attract students with interests or talents in that specific area.

State-sponsored residential schools, often called "governor's schools" because they are established by an individual state's legislature and governor, have continued to increase in popularity in recent years. Highly competitive, these schools seek nominations from across the state's high schools for unusually talented juniors and seniors who will spend up to two years in the residential setting. The first governor's schools focused almost exclusively on math and science, but now many states have incorporated the arts and humanities into their stringent curricula.

Some urban school districts have developed special high schools for talented students in the visual and performing arts. Students often go through competitive auditions in order to enter these schools. These special "academies" focus on making art—painting, dancing, instrumental and vocal music. Many well-known performers have come out of such settings to flourish in the entertainment business; other students go on to study their discipline in college.

● *Other Options*   Not all educational options for gifted students take place within the school building or, for that matter, within the school year. **Mentorships,** during which secondary students work with a community member to learn, firsthand, a specific skill, trade, or craft, are becoming increasingly common. Mentors can assume the interlocking roles of teacher, expert, guide, advisor, friend, and role model for the gifted/talented student (Clasen & Clasen, 2003). Research on the effectiveness of mentorships shows the very positive results of these community-school interactions, since participating students learn from the mentor's skill and expertise, receive valued and substantive praise and encouragement, and have as a role model a person who loves his or her field of study as much as the student does.

Summer and weekend programs are also offered for gifted students at many colleges and universities. Purdue University's Super Saturday Program, for example, serves children from preschool through high school with a variety of accelerated and enrichment classes each semester. The Purdue model has been replicated across the country.

State-sponsored residential schools for gifted and talented students have increased in popularity.

In mentorships, secondary students learn specific skills, trades, or crafts from community members.

A CLOSER LOOK   The EEPsters

The Early Entrance Program (EEP) at California State University, Los Angeles, provides highly gifted young people the opportunity to enter college as young as 11 years old. (The average entering age is currently 13.5 years.) These "EEPsters," as they are affectionately known on campus, typically earn their degrees in four to five years.

The Early Entrance Program admissions procedures look for students with the following qualifications:

- One who is not yet in the tenth grade unless accelerated by one or more grades, and is not yet over 16 years of age.
- One who consistently scores in the very top ranges on standardized ability and achievement tests.
- One who has a demonstrated ability to perform at an outstanding level in school.
- One whose educational needs will not be met in the school he/she is presently attending or would be attending.

The student likely to be admitted to the EEP is one who:

- Demonstrates a strong desire to attempt a challenging educational program.
- Possesses adequate maturity for self-motivation and appropriate behavior on a college campus, including appropriate verbal skills and critical-thinking abilities.
- Has the support of the parents to undertake a program of radical educational acceleration.
- Has a history of advanced intellectual and academic achievement.
- Performs at a level indicating a readiness for college-level work on the Washington Pre-College Test and University entrance exams for specific disciplines.

This kind of acceleration is unusual, and it is not for every bright student, but the program has had a good measure of success since its inception in 1982. Many EEP graduates have gone on to receive M.D., Ph.D., and law degrees at the country's most selective universities. Ryan Montgomery, an EEP graduate at 17, now works at the Jet Propulsion Lab on the Mars Rover team. Two physician graduates of the program recently married; Richard Maddox, Program Director, hailed it as "the first EEP wedding." He emphasized the importance of the support system available to the 100 students enrolled. "We create a high school within the university for them—they just take college classes, and experience little of the boring repetition of material they would have in a regular high school." So if you are sitting next to a young teenager in class—be respectful!

Summer programs can be either day programs or residential in nature, depending on the student's age. In Ohio, each of the thirteen state universities and several private colleges offer one- to three-week "summer institutes" that are financially supported by the state. Michigan and Iowa also offer extensive summer programs for gifted students.

In addition, early entrance to college or dual enrollment programs allow gifted secondary-school students to progress through high school and college at a more rapid pace. (See A Closer Look, "The EEPsters," for further discussion of this.) In high schools, students enrolled in advanced placement courses may earn up to a year's worth of transferable college credit by taking rigorous courses and advanced placement tests, generally in their junior and senior years. Also, many colleges have an "honors college" component, which offers rigorous and often accelerated courses to highly able students. Some colleges encourage full-time enrollment by students as young as 15. Simon's Rock in Great Barrington, Massachusetts (affiliated with Bard College), has been doing this for over twenty-five years, and Mary Baldwin College in Staunton, Virginia, has a similar program, called PEG (Program for the Exceptionally Gifted), which is open only to young women; these students generally attain both a high-school diploma and a college degree within five years.

You don't have to be gifted to succeed in a course in advanced placement calculus . . . but it helps!

Program Models

Acceleration and enrichment options for gifted students, as we have seen, have existed for generations. But only within the past fifteen years have organizational models been developed. These models structure the activities in which gifted children participate to provide a "skeleton" format for teachers and gifted program planners.

Schoolwide enrichment models help teachers differentiate the curriculum for all students.

● *School-Wide Models*   With so many interesting and innovative teaching strategies and models designed for students identified as gifted and talented, why not use them to benefit all children?

Renzulli's **Schoolwide Enrichment Model** was originally developed for gifted education, but it is now being used on a schoolwide basis to improve the creative productivity and academic achievement of *all* students (Renzulli & Reis, 2008). The model serves as a framework for organizational and curricular changes and rests on specific curriculum modification techniques, enrichment learning and teaching, and the recognition and development of student talents. See Figure 14.6 for a graphic description of this model. For more information, visit the website for National Research Center for the Gifted and Talented.

Curriculum Modifications in the General Education Classroom

Differentiated instruction can involve modifications in content, process, products, classroom environment, and teacher behavior.

Much of what is written about curriculum and instruction for highly able students is based on the belief that programming should be *differentiated* for gifted learners. You first read about differentiated instruction in Chapter 2; now we describe the original use of the concept with gifted learners. Differentiation is the adaptation of educational programs and teaching methods to meet the unique needs of gifted learners. Differentiation can involve modifications in *content,* by putting more depth in the curriculum; *process,* by using a variety of methods and

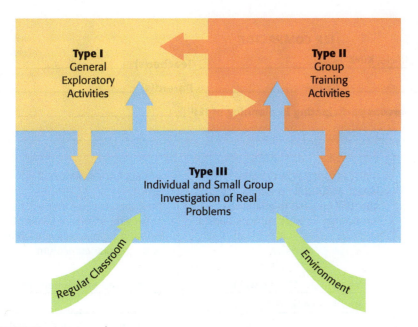

FIGURE 14.6

The Schoolwide Enrichment Model

Source: COLANGELO, NICHOLAS; DAVIS, GARY A., *HANDBOOK OF GIFTED EDUCATION,*
3rd Edition, © 2003, pp. 184–203. Adapted by permission of Pearson Education, Inc., Upper Saddle
River, NJ.

materials; *products, classroom environment,* and *teacher behavior* (Hall, Strangman, & Meyer, 2011).

Every classroom teacher has (or can develop) the skills to work with gifted students within a regular classroom structure. By adapting, modifying, and differentiating the basic curriculum through techniques such as curriculum telescoping and content acceleration, which we will describe next, teachers can determine when students have mastered particular skills, allowing them to move on to explore new ideas. Effective use of options such as independent study, cluster grouping, and cooperative learning can help satisfy students' individual learning interests. Finally, the appropriate use of higher-level thinking strategies and creative thinking skills can benefit *all* students, including those who are highly able. We'll discuss each of these methods in further detail.

● *Curriculum Telescoping* **Curriculum telescoping,** or compacting, involves an analysis of the specific subject matter (for example, spelling, math, language arts) to determine which parts of those subjects are inappropriate for gifted students because they have already mastered them. Return for a minute to your fourth-grade class. It's math time, and let's assume you are a strong math student. As the teacher hands out worksheets, you have a sinking sense of dèja vu, for you are confronted with fifty problems like these: 26 × 247; 69 × 189; 24 × 790; 126 ÷ 4; 4216 ÷ 57. You think to yourself, "Didn't I see these yesterday? And the day before too?" A conscientious math teacher would know that not all students in the class need extensive instruction in the basic math operations involved in these problems. In fact, a teacher who knew something about curriculum telescoping would probably not even require good math students like you to complete basic skill worksheets once you had mastered the concepts involved. What would be the point? If you already know how to multiply and divide large numbers, what possible benefit could there be to your completing more of these problems? There

Curriculum telescoping allows students to explore new concepts or subjects.

IEP COMPACTOR

Name _Wendy, Mike, Carol, Paul, Chris, Kurt_ **Age** _____ **Teacher(s)** _____

School _Smith_ _____ **Grade** _____ **Parent(s)** _____

Individual conference dates and persons participating in planning of IEP _____

_____

CURRICULUM AREAS TO BE CONSIDERED FOR COMPACTING: Describe basic material to be covered during this marking period and the assessment information or evidence that suggests the need for compacting.	PROCEDURES FOR COMPACTING BASIC MATERIAL: Describe activities that will be used to guarantee proficiency in basic curricular areas.	ACCELERATION AND/OR ENRICHMENT ACTIVITIES: Describe activities that will be used to provide advanced levels of learning experiences in each area of the regular curriculum.
Math: Houghton Mifflin Mathematics Level 6	Pre- and posttests will be used to check skill proficiency.	Selected enrichment masters
This group scored above 90% ile on CTBS math.	No assignment of math text examples or basic masters for skills already mastered.	Pre-algebra with Pizzaz and After-Math materials
	Students will be individually assigned student text pages and skill sheets as indicated by pretests.	Logic puzzles: mind benders, logic box
		Individual or small-group advanced-level independent study.

FIGURE 14.7

Individual Educational Programming Guide: The Compactor

Source: Alane J. Starko (1986). Meeting the needs of the gifted throughout the school day: Techniques for curriculum compacting. *Roeper Review, 9*(1), 27–33. http://www.informaworld.com

are dozens of more difficult concepts in math that you could probably work on instead of these basic skills.

That is the core of curriculum telescoping: determining what individual students already know and giving them the chance to explore concepts, subjects, or topics that better tap into their talents (Robinson, Shore, & Enersen, 2007). Teaching Strategies & Accommodations, "Steps in Curriculum Telescoping," will provide you with more information, and Figure 14.7 presents documentation for curriculum telescoping or "compacting."

● *Content Area Acceleration* Content area acceleration is another modification available to regular classroom teachers. Most often, educators equate *acceleration* with grade skipping. However, **content area acceleration** can occur within regular classes at virtually every grade level and within virtually every subject area. It happens every time a teacher allows students to "jump ahead" at a faster pace than most of their classmates. Thus, the first-grade teacher who provides literature to a child who has outgrown a basal reader is accelerating curriculum content for that child; so is the high school science teacher who works with a tenth-grader on physics experiments, even though physics is generally taken by

With content acceleration, students proceed at a faster pace than most of their classmates.

Teaching Strategies & Accommodations

Steps in Curriculum Telescoping

1. Provide evidence of students' mastery (left column of Figure 14.7).

2. Describe how students may have their basic curriculum modified (center column of Figure 14.7).

3. List options for enrichment activities that take advantage of students' talents (right column of Figure 14.7).

Source: A. J. Starko (1986). Meeting the needs of the gifted throughout the school day: Techniques for curriculum compacting. *Roeper Review, 9*(11), 27–33.

twelfth-graders. For more information about acceleration, see the National Association of Gifted Children's website.

When you accelerate a student's curriculum in a basic skill area, there is always the possibility that other teachers (especially those in subsequent grades) will disapprove of this strategy. Some may prefer that students pursue areas of study that do not infringe on the content they will teach. Others may believe that content acceleration complicates their role as teachers since not all students are taught the same thing at the same time.

The most important consideration, however, remains the student's learning needs, even if fulfilling those needs complicates scheduling or planning. If teachers lose sight of this basic principle, students may be deprived of instruction or content that matches their level of ability. In extreme cases, students may adopt a negative attitude toward school.

Content area acceleration can be a nonobtrusive way to modify the curriculum for gifted students, but like any other activity, it will take practice for you to perfect. See Teaching Strategies & Accommodations, "Guidelines for Modifying Curriculum," for some tips.

● *Independent Study and Self-Directed Learning*   Independent study is one of the more popular forms of classroom modification for gifted students. **Independent study** provides an opportunity for students to study deeply in an area of interest to them. Teachers have come to realize, however, that even highly able students need differentiated levels of support for directing their own learning.

> In independent study, students pursue topics on their own, under teacher supervision.

Like any strategy, independent study can be done improperly. Perhaps the most common mistake teachers make is to assume that since they're so smart, gifted students can succeed without any help. Teachers should introduce research skills such as library and computer information searching, hypothesis generation, and basic statistical analysis, which will give students tools for higher-level independent study. Unless a student selects a topic that is specific enough to be manageable, even a gifted student may wallow in a sea of confusion. As a teacher, you will need to provide appropriate direction as well as support for the independent work.

● *Cluster Grouping*   In **cluster grouping,** students who are identified as gifted at a given grade level are grouped together in the same classroom with a teacher who (ideally) has training in educating students who are gifted. The rest of the class is a diverse group of learners. The cluster arrangement allows the gifted learners to be grouped together for some activities and to be mixed with their age

> Cluster grouping allows gifted learners to be grouped for some activities and not others.

Teaching Strategies & Accommodations

Guidelines for Modifying Curriculum

1. Assess the student's skill level accurately, making sure he or she understands each of the concepts involved in any material that might be replaced or skipped over.

2. Talk with the student's teachers from the previous year and the teacher(s) who may be receiving this student the following year. Team planning can avoid many problems of miscommunication.

3. Remember that an option other than accelerating content is enriching it. So, if a student skilled in reading and language arts wants something more complex to do, consider activities such as playwriting, cartooning, interviewing, or designing posters for a schoolwide project. These projects increase the student's breadth and depth of understanding of a subject.

4. Speak with your school district's director of curriculum or assistant superintendent about materials, resources, and options about which you might be unaware.

peers for others. Cluster grouping appears to be an increasingly popular option (Reis & Renzulli, 2010; Winebrenner & Brulles, 2008).

● *Cooperative Learning*   **Cooperative learning** operates under the assumption that "all students are learners and teachers; all have an equal responsibility to explain to others and discuss with others. The pace of instruction is similar to what it would be in a traditional class, so high achievers are exposed to the same material they would have otherwise been taught" (Slavin, 1990, pp. 6–7). Under cooperative learning strategies, students are placed in mixed ability clusters of five or six, and they learn material by capitalizing on the strengths each member brings to the "team." Often, the same grades are awarded to all group members, which is meant to engender a team spirit in which everyone pulls his or her own weight.

Critics of cooperative learning contend that gifted students can be passive and disengaged in cooperative learning groups (Robinson, 2003). One opponent enumerates the objections:

> The disadvantages of cooperative learning for academically talented students are primarily those of limiting instruction to grade level materials, presented at the pace of a grade level group and evaluated primarily on basic skill measures. The corollary is that opportunities which can meet intellectual needs may be made unavailable to talented students because cooperative learning is assumed to be a substitute. (Robinson, 1990, p. 22)

Since there is no clear-cut agreement as to whether cooperative learning will benefit gifted students, the new teacher should approach this technique cautiously.

Teachers should be cautious in using cooperative learning with highly able students.

● *Creative and Higher-Level Thinking*   Creative and higher-level thinking processes are another area in which the curriculum can be modified. Consider the following two questions, either of which could appear on an elementary-level geography test:

1. What is the capital of Massachusetts?

2. Considering the geography of the state of Massachusetts, why might Boston have been chosen to be the state's capital?

The first question requires little thought, merely a good memory. Students need to know nothing about Boston other than that it is the state capital. The second question, though, requires analytical thought and some comprehension of the role that geography, location, and politics may have played in choosing the site for a state's capital.

Gifted students often think naturally—with little direction from parents or teachers—about these "bigger questions," the ones that require the use of more complex levels of thinking. When they are in a classroom setting where the majority of time is spent on activities or questions that have one right answer requiring only rote memorization to deliver, they often feel stifled intellectually. To compound this problem, classroom materials and texts usually emphasize the acquisition of low-level thinking skills (such as memorization) rather than the more sophisticated thinking patterns required to answer questions like the second one.

There are, however, methods and systems for incorporating higher-level thinking skills into your curriculum. Benjamin Bloom (1956) developed a taxonomy of educational objectives to distinguish among the various ways that questions and teaching strategies can be designed to promote varied levels of thinking. Figure 14.8 shows how to use this taxonomy in designing curriculum for gifted students.

Some problems, however, do not require analytical thinking as much as they require creative thinking. That is, rather than trying to find a *solution* to a problem, it is more important to first determine what the problem itself really is. **Brainstorming** is a basic, creative problem-solving technique. In brainstorming, there are no right or wrong answers, students cannot criticize each others' responses, and "piggybacking" an idea on someone else's is encouraged. Group brainstorming can be the first step in positive problem solving.

> Higher-level thinking skills should be incorporated into the curriculum for gifted students.

> In brainstorming, participants come up with many ideas on a specific subject.

● *Problem-Based Learning*   **Problem-based learning** is a method used in medical schools to focus on an "ill-structured problem" as a way for students to ask questions and hypothesize about how to clarify and solve the problem (Delisle, 2000). See Teaching Strategies & Accommodations, "Problem-Based Learning," on page 529.

Many of the methods used to teach gifted and talented students have a very limited evidence base in empirical research. Karen Rogers (2007) has summarized some basic "lessons" which have been validated by research that teachers should remember as they work with students. They are:

Lesson 1: Gifted and Talented Learners Need Daily Challenge in Their Specific Areas of Talent

Lesson 2: Opportunities Should Be Provided on a Regular Basis for Gifted Learners to Be Unique and to Work Independently in Their Areas of Passion and Talent

Lesson 3: Provide Various Forms of Subject-Based and Grade-Based Acceleration to Gifted Learners as Their Educational Needs Require

Lesson 4: Provide Opportunities for Gifted Learners to Socialize and to Learn with Like-Ability Peers

Lesson 5: For Specific Curriculum Areas, Instructional Delivery Must Be Differentiated in Pace, Amount of Review and Practice, and Organization of Content Presentation

(Rogers, 2007)

Evidence-based practices validated with typical students can certainly be expected to be successful with those identified as gifted and talented, but there is still a need to validate the particular practices (like the ones we have been describing) with students who are gifted and talented.

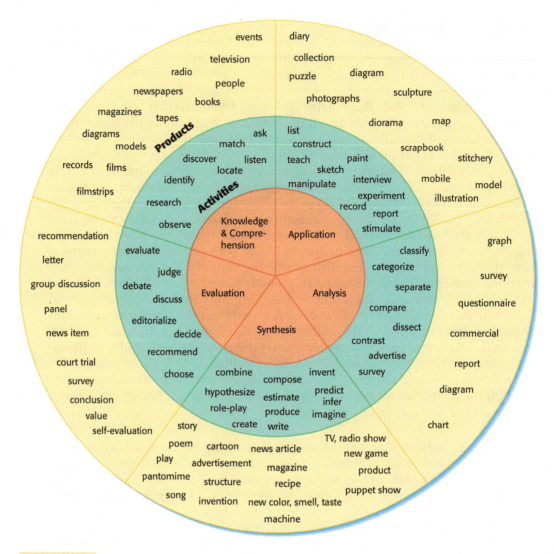

FIGURE 14.8

Cognitive Taxonomy Circle

The wheel was developed by Barry Ziff and a class of teachers of gifted students. They found it very useful in curriculum building.

Source: Barbara Clark, *Growing Up Gifted: Developing the Potential of Children at Home and at School,* *6th edition,* © 2002. Reprinted by permission of Pearson Education, Inc., Upper Saddle River, NJ.

Is Special Education for Gifted Students Necessary?

With many programs for gifted and talented learners being cut back or eliminated in difficult budget times (Renzulli & Reis, 2008; National Association for Gifted Children, 2011) some legislators are asking whether programs for these students are really necessary. The National Association for Gifted Children (2003) offers reasons for providing differentiated instruction to gifted learners:

- Gifted learners must be given stimulating educational experiences appropriate to their level of ability if they are to realize their potential.

- Each person has the right to learn and to be provided challenges for learning at the most appropriate level where growth proceeds most effectively.

- Only slightly over one-half of the possible gifted learners in the United States are reported to be receiving education appropriate to their needs.

Teaching Strategies & Accommodations

Problem-Based Learning (PBL)

What Is Problem-Based Learning?

Problem-based learning instruction is built on "ill-structured and complex problems" just like those encountered in real life. The problems require that students "search beyond the readily available information to solve the problem" which is offered to them (Torp & Sage, 1998). Students become inquirers and active learners, collaborating, creating, and using knowledge to construct solutions. Teachers facilitate, model, and coach students as they work together in small groups.

Why Is This Model Used?

Students learn best when they must "do" and when they are asked to think in authentic ways rather than abstractly. Use this model when you want students to apply, analyze, synthesize, and extend knowledge, and when you wish students to apply research skills.

What Are "Ill-Structured and Complex Problems" for PBL and What Are Some Examples?

Delisle (2000) explains:

> Unlike a thinking exercise that includes all necessary information or a traditional project that requires students to use information they already know, PBL problems should be designed so that students must perform research to gather the information needed for possible solutions. It should require students to think through information they already know and find additional information, interpreting preexisting knowledge in light of new data they discover. In addition, the problem should lead students to discover that there may be a number of solutions.

Here are two examples of problems used from elementary through middle school:

- Some students and our cafeteria staff have been complaining that the cafeteria is becoming so loud that it is hard to hear. We have been asked by our School Council to investigate this challenge and make a recommendation to them by next week. You will need to prepare a presentation for the council that includes the facts and conclusions we have reached.

- You are part of the Natural Science Museum Display team. You design all the display areas in the museum so that the people who come to the museum can easily see and learn from such displays. This week, the museum was given $50,000 to create an area of the museum for four wolves who cannot be released into the wild because they have lived all their lives in a zoo. The museum staff wants to construct an area that is as similar as possible to the natural habitat of the wolf and with a safe (for both wolves and the public) viewing area. The museum curator wants your team plans within two weeks so that preparations for construction can then be made. The curator would like you to present the background information your team used to develop its plans, as well as sketches or a model of what your team suggests.

Source: National Center for the Accelerated Schools Project, University of Connecticut Neag School of Education, 2131 Hillside Road, Unit 3224, Storrs, CT 06269-3224.

- Traditional education currently does not sufficiently value bright minds.
- When given the opportunity, gifted students can use their vast amount of knowledge to serve as a background for unlimited learning.
- Providing for our finest minds allows both individual and societal needs to be met.

A recent report from the Thomas B. Fordham Institute (Xiang, Dahlin, Cronin, Theaker, & Durant, 2011) identified students who were "high flyers" (that is, they were performing better than 90% of their peers on school achievement tests), and analyzed their success over time in reading and math. Nearly three in five maintained their "high flyer" status over time, but the remainder were "descenders"; their scores became lower. The authors do not offer an explanation for the lower scores of those students, but argue for additional focus on our highest-achieving students:

> No, these aren't the kids that the education-reform outlets fuss about . . . They don't tug at the heartstrings like the needy children in our most wretched school systems. (Some of them reside there, but most don't.) But they deserve attention, too: Eight, ten, twelve, seventeen years old, with little more than a coin toss determining whether they wind up their school careers simply "above average" or among the country's top achievers and brightest hopes for the future. (pp. 3–4)

Many believe that interest in high-achieving students has waned since the passage of the No Child Left Behind Act in 2001, and that our society will be the poorer for it (Reis & Renzulli, 2010).

Ellen Winner (2000) believes that in return for their special education, gifted children should be required to give back—a commitment to service should be built into their school experiences. The fulfillment of giftedness in adulthood is not just the optimal development of the self, according to Winner, but the use of ability and talents in service to others. Let's close this chapter with Winner's words:

> The moral value of service, of giving back to a society that has devoted extra resources to the gifted, ought to be considered as important as the value of self-actualization of the gifted. All children should be taught the value of service, and gifted children are no exception. (p. 167)

SUMMARY

- The concept of giftedness has changed greatly over time, as has our view of students who are gifted. Giftedness has been described in terms of creativity and task commitment, multiple intelligences, successful manipulation of the environment, and heightened sensitivity and understanding.

- Standardized test scores are one criterion for identifying giftedness, but they should be supplemented by other measures, as well as by informal observations by teachers and parents.

- A focus on using standardized test scores does not always allow culturally and linguistically diverse students to demonstrate their abilities.

- Although biological factors may play a role in giftedness, educators focus on environmental factors, especially family support, guidance, and encouragement that can contribute to the full expression of a student's gifts.

- The prevalence of giftedness varies because of differing definitions and criteria. Gifted females, students who are gifted and disabled, gifted underachievers, culturally diverse students, and the highly gifted are often underserved.

- Teachers usually play a central role in identifying gifted students through multiple measures, including observations of behavior (which might include negative as well as positive behaviors) as well as test scores and grades.

- The curriculum can be differentiated through telescoping, content area acceleration, independent study, cluster grouping, and cooperative learning. Modifications should be based on the student's needs and interests.

- Gifted students are usually served in the general education classroom and may be pulled out for resource room time. If self-contained classes are used, the students may be grouped according to their level or type of ability. Magnet schools are another setting in which students can receive a special emphasis on a specific type of ability.

- Many models for organizing gifted education have been proposed. These models help teachers plan curriculum modifications and activities to fulfill the needs of gifted students.

- Recently scholars have raised concerns that we are ignoring the needs of our highest-achieving students as we focus on those who are not succeeding.

KEY TERMS

giftedness (page 493)

talent (page 493)

intelligence (page 495)

creativity (page 495)

task commitment (page 495)

theory of multiple intelligences (page 495)

triarchic theory (page 496)

highly gifted (page 503)

gifted underachiever (page 512)

highly gifted (page 515)

academic enrichment (page 516)

Radical acceleration (page 516)

enrichment (page 519)

Mentorships (page 520)

Schoolwide Enrichment Model (page 522)

curriculum telescoping (page 523)

content area acceleration (page 524)

independent study (page 525)

cluster grouping (page 525)

cooperative learning (page 526)

brainstorming (page 527)

problem-based learning (page 527)

USEFUL RESOURCES

- Susan Winebrenner (2001). *Teaching Gifted Kids in the Regular Classroom* (2nd ed.). Minneapolis: Free Spirit Publishing. This book is an excellent source for teaching ideas.

- Families will enjoy James Delisle's book *Parenting Gifted Kids: Tips for Raising Happy and Successful Children*, published in 2006 by Prufrock Press.

- An influential national organization that advocates for gifted and talented students is the National Association for Gifted Children (NAGC), online at **http://www.nagc.org/.**

- *Parenting for High Potential* is a NAGC publication. This quarterly magazine is designed for parents who want to develop their children's gifts and talents, and help them develop their potential to the fullest. Each issue includes special features, expert advice columns, software and book reviews, ideas from parents, and a pullout children's section. NAGC has recently begun a publication for teachers called *Teaching for High Potential.*

- Carol Ann Tomlinson has written a series of books on differentiated instruction. All are published by the Association for Supervision and Curriculum Development (ASCD); visit **http://shop.ascd.org.**

- Prufrock Press has useful publications for teachers of gifted students. Among them are Jim Delisle and Barbara Lewis's *Survival Guide for Teachers of Gifted Kids* (2003).

PORTFOLIO ACTIVITIES

1. Select one or two books or articles about gifted students from the list in the Useful Resources section or the references that appear in this chapter. Compare the authors' perspectives with your own knowledge of and experiences with giftedness and talents. Make a chart contrasting the authors' views and your own, and place the chart in your portfolio.

   CEC This activity will help the student meet CEC Initial Content Standard 2: Development and Characteristics of Learners.

2. Investigate popular culture and media images:

   • How do films and television shows portray gifted children? How have those images changed? Are stereotypes evident?

   • Interview a gifted student, classmate, or other person and note how that person differs from media stereotypes. Why might these stereotypes exist?

   • Rent a film about a gifted person (some suggestions: *The Social Network, A Beautiful Mind, My Left Foot, Good Will Hunting*). Do you consider the portrait in the film realistic? Write a review of the movie based on your analysis. Place the review in your portfolio.

   CEC This activity will help the student meet CEC Initial Content Standard 3: Individual Learning Differences.

3. Identify an individual whom you consider gifted or talented. This person could be a public figure, a friend or family member, or a student you have known. Using the characteristics described in this chapter, write an analysis of how this person fits or does not fit the criteria for giftedness. Place the analysis in your portfolio.

   CEC This activity will help the student meet CEC Initial Content Standard 2: Development and Characteristics of Learners.

4. Survey attitudes in your class:

   • Find out what stereotypes or preconceptions students hold about gifted students.

   • Have the other students write about one area in which they feel they are gifted. Does this ability shape their view of themselves, or is it just one characteristic?

   • Compile the responses about individual areas of giftedness in a poster showing the range of gifts in the class.

   CEC This activity will help the student meet CEC Initial Content Standard 3: Individual Learning Differences, and CEC Initial Content Standard 9: Professional and Ethical Practice.

5. Using the information on curriculum modifications provided in this chapter and the recommended readings, develop some activities that would allow gifted students to enrich their learning in the general education classroom. Write up the activities as lesson plans and add them to your portfolio.

   CEC This activity will help the student meet CEC Initial Content Standard 7: Instructional Planning.

6. Where are gifted students in your school district served? Arrange to visit a local public school and see what combination of the general education classroom, resource room, and self-contained class instruction gifted students receive. If possible, observe students in each of these environments.

How do the settings vary? Write up your observations and add them to your portfolio.

 This activity will help the student meet CEC Initial Content Standard 5: Learning Environments and Social Interactions.

 To access Portfolio Activities for this chapter and other useful study resources including an interactive eBook, related web links, quizzes, flashcards, and videos, visit the Education CourseMate website at www.cengagebrain.com.

Glossary

AAMR Adaptive Behavior Scale one of the most widely used instruments for measuring adaptive behavior.

academic enrichment broadening the experience base of the students in an academic content area without changing the instructional objectives.

acceleration providing a more appropriate program for a gifted student by moving the student ahead in the curriculum; the most common example is grade skipping.

accommodation a change in timing, format, or response that helps a student overcome or work around his or her disability.

acquired hearing loss a hearing loss acquired at any time after birth.

acquired immune deficiency syndrome (AIDS) a viral disease that breaks down the body's immune system, destroying its ability to fight infections; AIDS is typically transmitted by the exchange of body fluids that can occur through sexual contact or sharing contaminated needles to inject intravenous drugs.

adaptive behaviors the age- and situation-specific social, maturational, self-help, and communicative acts that assist each individual in adapting to the demands of his or her environment.

adult service agencies agencies that provide medical and psychological examinations and counseling, training and job placement, and financial assistance for adaptive equipment, prostheses, and basic living costs during training to adults with disabilities.

age-appropriate behavior behavior considered normal for a particular age.

albinism a congenital lack of pigmentation that can cause vision loss.

alcohol-related neurodevelopmental disorder (ARND) a spectrum of learning and behavioral characteristics in a child caused by maternal alcohol ingestion during pregnancy.

American Sign Language (ASL) the sign language considered by many deaf adults to be their "native language"; it has the same vocabulary as English but a different grammatical structure.

Americans with Disabilities Act of 1990 (P.L. 101-336) a law that extends civil rights protection to individuals with disabilities in private-sector employment and requires that public accommodations and services like telecommunications and transportation provide barrier-free access to individuals with disabilities.

amniocentesis a prenatal testing technique that analyzes amniotic fluid to identify certain chromosomal and neural tube abnormalities.

anxiety-withdrawal behaviors, such as extreme sensitivity or depression, reflecting fear of performance and avoidance.

articulation disorders problems in understanding and using the sound system of speech; the most common communication problems of the elementary years.

Asperger's syndrome A syndrome in which individuals have social and behavioral deficits similar to those experienced by children with autism, but do not experience delays in language and cognition.

asthma a chronic obstructive lung condition characterized by an unusual reaction to a variety of stimuli that causes difficulty in breathing, coughing, wheezing, and shortness of breath.

at-risk infants and young children who have a higher likelihood of developing a disability because of biological or environmental factors like extreme prematurity, chronic poverty, or medical problems.

attention the ability to focus on information.

attentional deficits the inability to come to attention, to maintain attention, or to pay attention selectively.

attention deficit disorder (ADD) a condition determined by difficulty in focusing on information and in sustaining attention.

attention deficit/hyperactivity disorder (ADHD) a condition determined by difficulty in focusing on information, sustaining attention, and hyperactive behavior.

audiogram the chart on which the audiologist records an individual's responses to sounds during a hearing test.

audiologist the professional who tests and measures hearing.

auditory training enhancing the residual hearing of a student with hearing loss by teaching listening skills.

auditory-verbal therapy a means of providing intervention to students with hearing loss that focuses on early identification of hearing loss, amplification, and the development of speaking skills through listening.

augmentative communication aid a system designed to give individuals assistance in communication, such as a scanning system or communication board.

autism a severely incapacitating lifelong developmental disability characterized by certain types of behaviors and patterns of interaction and communication. Symptoms include disturbance in the rate of appearance of physical, social, and language skills; abnormal response to sensation; delayed or absent speech and language; and abnormal ways of relating to people, objects, and events. It usually appears during the first three years of life.

Autism Spectrum Disorders (ASD) a term used to refer to the range of syndromes and conditions that fall under the category of pervasive developmental disorder, including autism. Children with autism spectrum disorders may exhibit a few or many of the characteristics historically associated with autism to varying degrees of severity.

behavior disorder a term used by some states instead of "serious emotional disturbance" to classify children with behavior and emotional disorders.

behavior intervention plan (BIP) an empirically based individual program to address problem behavior that contains positive behavior support strategies designed to teach appropriate behavior.

behavior-rating scale an observation form that allows teachers, parents, and psychologists to rate patterns of behavior.

Bell, Alexander Graham nineteenth-century teacher of speech to deaf children; inventor of the telephone.

bilateral hearing loss hearing loss in both ears.

biological aging the physiological changes that occur over the lifespan.

biological risk the risk associated with damage to a child's developing systems before, during, or after birth.

Board of Education of Hendrick Hudson School District v. Rowley a 1982 Supreme Court decision that determined an "appropriate" education does not mean that a student must reach his or her maximum potential, but only that the student have access to educational opportunity.

Braille a tactile system of reading that uses raised dots to signify numbers and letters.

brainstorming a basic creative thinking technique used in problem solving; participants are asked to come up with as many ideas as possible relative to a certain topic—there are no right or wrong answers; responses cannot be criticized; piggybacking an idea onto someone else's is encouraged.

Brown v. Board of Education of Topeka, Kansas a 1954 Supreme Court ruling prohibiting the use of "separate but equal" schools for African American and white students.

cane travel using a long white cane to scan the environment while walking.

caregiver any person who takes care of or raises a child.

cataract a clouding of the lens of the eye.

cerebral palsy a neurological condition resulting from damage to the brain before or during birth or in infancy; it is characterized by disabilities in movement and posture.

chorionic villous sampling (CVS) a prenatal testing technique that analyzes cells from the chorion to determine whether certain genetic abnormalities are present.

civil rights movement the *1960s'* movement for social and political equality for African Americans; it provided a model for activists seeking similar rights for people with disabilities.

classroom discourse the verbal interactions of the classroom.

classroom discourse strategies ways in which teachers communicate their expectations for learning to students.

clinical judgment the use of knowledge and experience to make a decision about whether a disability is present.

closed captioning captions that parallel the verbal content of a television show; they are made visible through decoders built into all television sets manufactured after July 1, 1993, which allow viewers to select captioning of all available programs.

cluster grouping students who are identified as gifted at a given grade level are grouped together in the same classroom with a teacher who has training in educating students who are gifted. The rest of the class is a diverse group of learners.

cochlear implants tiny processors that are surgically implanted in the cochlea and serve to electrically stimulate the auditory nerve fibers and improve perception of sound.

code-emphasis approach an approach to reading instruction that focuses on teaching regular sound-symbol relationship in a structured and sequential way.

cognitive style the cognitive activity that takes place between the time a student recognizes the need to respond to something and actually does respond; cognitive styles are categorized along a continuum ranging from impulsive to reflective.

collaboration professionals working together with a shared purpose in a supportive, mutually beneficial relationship.

collaborative consultation teachers and other school professionals working together on an equal footing to solve students' problems.

communication the exchange of ideas, information, thoughts, and feelings.

communication disorders a language or speech disorder that adversely affects a child's educational performance.

communicative intent the intention or purpose of a behavior in communication with another.

community-based instruction working on a student's instructional goals in the community setting in which they would naturally be used.

compensatory academic skills skills needed to access the core curriculum.

conduct disorder individual disruptive, aggressive, noncompliant behaviors.

conductive hearing loss hearing loss resulting from damage or blockage to the outer or middle ear that disrupts the efficient passage or conduction of sound; most conductive losses can be treated medically.

congenital a condition present at birth.

congenital hearing loss a hearing loss present at birth.

congenital malformation a defect in a physical structure of the body that is present at birth.

consultation a means of providing specialized services in the general education classroom whereby the special education teacher observes students with disabilities and provides suggestions to the teacher about adapting instruction or materials to meet students' needs.

consultation model a special education resource teacher meets with classroom teachers to plan instructional adaptations for students and provide direct services in the classroom.

content area acceleration a curriculum modification for gifted students in a specific content area (for example math or language arts) that allows them to proceed at a faster pace than their classmates.

content standards descriptions of the knowledge and skills children should acquire in specific content areas, such as reading, arithmetic, and science. Each state develops content standards that reflect the curriculum goals for students at each grade level.

contingency intervention curriculum the immediate and distinct presentation of consequences in order to facilitate an understanding of the relationship between actions and their results; this curriculum is used to give infants with severe disabilities the opportunity to develop purposeful behavior and interact with the environment in a meaningful way.

cooperative learning a learning strategy that involves providing small groups of students of various skill levels with a task to complete so that each student makes a significant contribution.

cornea the transparent outer membrane of the eye.

cortical visual impairment vision loss resulting from damage to the brain rather than the eye.

creativity the ability to generate original or imaginative ideas.

cultural competence a respect for and knowledge of cultural differences and a willingness to accept that there are many ways of viewing the world.

cultural reciprocity a two-way process of information sharing and understanding between school professionals and families that can be truly reciprocal and lead to genuine mutual understanding and cooperation.

culture a way of perceiving, believing, evaluating, and behaving shared by a group of people.

curriculum-based assessment (CBA) a method of assessment based on materials in the child's curriculum rather than on an achievement test.

cytomegalovirus (CMV) a relatively common infection that, if contracted by a pregnant woman, can cause microcephaly, intellectual disabilities, neurological impairments, and hearing loss in the surviving infant.

Deaf community those adults bound together by their Deafness, the use of American Sign Language, and their culture, values, and attitudes.

Deaf culture the view of life manifested by the mores, beliefs, artistic expression, and language particular to Deaf people.

deafness a hearing loss that precludes the learning of language through hearing.

deinstitutionalization the movement away from housing people with intellectual disabilities in residential institutions and toward integrating them more fully into the community.

diabetic retinopathy a condition of the eye that can cause blindness; it occurs when the circulation problems associated with diabetes result in damage to the blood vessels of the retina.

diagnostic assessment the gathering of information about a child's developmental levels, usually through observation, interview, and formal testing, to determine whether the child has a disability.

dialect a variation of a spoken language used by a group of individuals that reflects and is determined by shared regional, social, or cultural/ethnic factors.

Diana v. Board of Education a 1970 California decision that children must be tested in their primary language when special education placement is being considered.

differentiation modifying the instructional content or process or the product of learning to meet the needs of learners with different levels of ability.

differentiated teaching teaching designed to meet the individual needs of students.

direct instruction the identification and instruction of specific academic skills and the use of teaching techniques that have been empirically demonstrated to be effective with students with learning difficulties.

disability a limitation, such as difficulty learning to read or inability to see.

discourse shared communication or conversation.

discrepancy the gap between a student's performance in school and his or her intellectual potential.

disproportionate representation the appearance of a group in larger or smaller numbers than would be expected by their percentage of the total population.

dog guide a trained dog used to identify obstacles to safe travel.

double deficit hypothesis the hypothesis that phonemic awareness and rapid naming difficulties are at the root of significant reading disabilities.

Down syndrome a condition caused by an extra 21st chromosome that results in intellectual disabilities and physical anomalies.

DSM-IV *The Diagnostic and Statistical Manual of Mental Disorders of the American Psychiatric Association,* fourth edition. A classification system for behavior and emotional disorders.

dual diagnosis a diagnosis of two or more coexisting conditions, for example intellectual disabilities and behavioral disorders.

due process hearing a procedure to resolve a conflict between school and family over the evaluation, program, or placement of a student with a disability.

duration the length of time a behavior lasts.

early intervention a comprehensive set of services provided to children from birth to 3 years, and their families, designed to minimize the effects of risk status or disability and provide support to the family.

echolalia the immediate or delayed repetition of someone else's utterance.

ecocultural theory seeks to explain family adaptations and activities through an understanding of the family's goals, dreams, and beliefs and the reality of the physical, material, and sociocultural environment in which they live.

educational definitions those definitions of vision loss focusing on academic functioning and reading medium.

electronic travel aids devices that use sonic waves to detect obstacles in the environment.

emotional disturbance a condition including one or more of the following characteristics over a long period of time and to a marked degree, which adversely affects educational performance: an inability to learn, an inability to build satisfactory interpersonal relationships, inappropriate types of behavior, a general mood of unhappiness or depression, and a tendency to develop fears associated with personal or school problems.

enclave a small group of individuals with disabilities who are placed in a work setting, usually within a large business or corporation, and receive on-the-job training from job coaches or social service agencies and from the business itself.

encoding processes processes used to organize information so it can be learned.

enrichment adding disciplines or areas of learning not normally found in the regular curriculum, using more difficult or in-depth material to enhance the core curriculum, or enhancing the teaching strategies used to present instruction.

environmental analysis *see* environmental inventory.

environmental inventory (environmental analysis) a technique used to identify skills for instruction; it involves a visit to the settings in which the student lives or works so a list can be made of the specific skills needed to be successful in that environment.

environmental risk risk factors related to the environment in which a child develops.

epilepsy a condition of the nervous system that results in seizures that disrupt the normal functioning of the brain.

ethnicity an individual's affiliation with a particular ethnic identity or group.

Eunice Kennedy Shriver advocate for people with intellectual disabilities and founder of Special Olympics. Sister of President John F. Kennedy and Rosemary Kennedy, who had an intellectual disability.

evidence-based practices in education, those instructional practices that have been proven effective in empirical studies.

exceptional the label used to describe the range of students who receive special education services in the school.

exclusion clause the sentence in the federal definition of learning disabilities that excludes from the definition learning problems that are primarily the result of visual, hearing, or motor handicaps, intellectual disabilities, emotional disturbance, or environmental, cultural, or economic disadvantage.

expanded core curriculum the existing core curriculum plus the additional areas of learning needed by students who are visually impaired.

expressive language a person's oral or signed communication.

extended family grandparents, aunts, uncles, cousins, and other relations who may or may not live with a child and parent(s).

externalizing behavior overtly expressed behavior directed toward others or the environment.

eye-gazing scanning system a system that allows an individual to select letters, words, and phrases from a display by simply focusing his or her eyes on the display; a small, sensitive camera detects the direction of the person's eyes and registers the selected elements so a typed message can be produced.

family two or more people who live together and are related by birth, marriage, or adoption.

family-centered practices a focus on the family as partner in determining what is best for a child.

family characteristics the traits such as size, socioeconomic status, cultural background, language, and geographic location that give each family its unique identity.

family configuration the adults present in a family.

family functions all the life tasks of the family necessary for meeting family needs, including economic, daily care, recreation, socialization, self-identity, affection, and educational/vocational functions.

family interaction the relationships among family members.

family life cycle the lifespan of a family, starting with marriage and evolving through the birth and growth of children.

family quality of life family members' sense of overall satisfaction with family life.

family size the number of children in a family.

family systems approach a framework for understanding the family as an interrelated social system with unique characteristics and needs.

fetal alcohol syndrome (FAS) a syndrome resulting from maternal alcohol intake during pregnancy; it is characterized by altered facial features, developmental delays in language and cognition, and behavior problems.

field independent student a student who does well on independent projects and on analytical tests.

field independent teacher a teacher who prefers to use the lecture approach, with limited interactions with students, and who encourages student achievement and competition among students.

field sensitive student a student who performs well in group work and cooperative learning situations.

field sensitive teacher a teacher who prefers to use interpersonal teaching methods, such as personal conversations.

fingerspelling spelling the manual alphabet with the fingers.

first trimester the first three months of pregnancy.

fluency disorder an interruption in the flow of speaking that significantly interferes with communication.

formal assessment using standardized tests to compare a student's performance with that of his or her peers.

formal supports individuals who provide services and supports to people with disabilities and their families as part of their professional role. Examples are teachers, rehabilitation counselors, and others.

fragile X syndrome an inherited disorder, caused by chromosomal abnormalities, that may result in intellectual disabilities, social, and communication deficits.

Framework of Support an outline of the supports necessary for a student with disabilities to meet the goals of access to the core curriculum and social integration in the general education classroom.

functional academics basic academic skills taught in the context of real-life activities; a curricular emphasis on academic skills that are meaningful and useful for daily living.

functional behavior assessment the planned observation and determination of the antecedents and consequences of a behavior.

functional communication verbal or nonverbal communication that is efficient, useful, understandable, and easy to use.

functional curriculum a curriculum that emphasizes preparation for life and includes only skills that will be useful to the student in home, community, school, or work environments.

functionally blind describes a person who uses his or her senses of touch or hearing as the primary means of learning.

functional vision how well a student uses whatever vision he or she may possess.

generalization *see* skill transfer.

genetic counseling the process of discussing with a trained counselor the likelihood that a child will inherit a genetic condition.

giftedness high performance capability in intellectual, creative, artistic, leadership, or academic areas.

gifted underachiever the term applied to students whose aptitude is high but whose performance is low.

glaucoma a disease of the eye that can lead to blindness if untreated; it occurs when fluid within the eye cannot drain properly, resulting in a gradual increase of pressure within the eye.

grand mal seizure an epileptic seizure that involves the whole body, usually lasts a few minutes, and often results in a loss of consciousness.

handicap the limitations imposed by the environment of a person with a disability or by people's attitudes toward disability.

hard of hearing a term that describes a hearing loss less severe than deafness that usually permits the understanding of oral speech through the use of hearing aids.

health impairment a term used to describe a condition in which one or more of the body's systems are affected by debilitating or life-threatening conditions or diseases.

health maintenance the assisting of or instruction of a student with a physical disability or health impairment in eating, drinking, or using the bathroom.

hearing impairment a term that refers to all degrees of hearing loss, from slight to profound.

hearing loss a term used to describe hearing problems.

highly gifted a term used to designate someone whose IQ score is in the 140+ range.

high-stakes testing or high-stakes assessment refers to testing that is used to make educational decisions. The term *high stakes* refers to the importance of the test result to the students taking the tests and to the teachers, schools, and educational agencies administering them.

home- or hospital-based instruction instruction provided by a special education teacher to students with chronic illness or other medical needs; it is usually temporary.

household one or more people, members of a family and others, who live under the same roof.

Howe, Samuel Gridley nineteenth-century educator and advocate for people with disabilities.

human guide a person, usually sighted, who accompanies someone with vision loss while walking.

human immunodeficiency virus (HIV) the virus that causes AIDS.

hydrocephalus a condition in which cerebrospinal fluid builds up in the skull and puts pressure on the brain; if untreated, it can cause brain damage and intellectual disabilities.

hyperglycemia a condition in which individuals with juvenile onset diabetes have high blood sugar, with potentially serious side effects including unconsciousness and coma.

hypoglycemia a condition in which individuals with juvenile onset diabetes have low blood sugar, with potentially serious side effects including unconsciousness and seizures.

hypoxia decreased availability of oxygen during pregnancy, labor, delivery, or after birth; it can result in death or brain damage.

immature behavior behavior that exhibits a low level of frustration tolerance and the inability to say and do socially appropriate things.

inclusion the provision of services to students with disabilities in the general education classroom.

independent living skills the skills and practices necessary for living everyday life on one's own.

independent study a curriculum modification for gifted students that allows them to explore topics of interest to them; the student does require teacher guidance to be sure a manageable topic is selected.

individual supported job model a form of supported employment in which a job coach provides on-site training and problem solving for a single individual; the goal is to gradually decrease the level of support until the individual is ready for independent competitive employment.

individualized education the concept that each student should have a program tailored to his or her unique learning needs.

individualized education program (IEP) the written plan for each student's individual education.

individualized family service plan (IFSP) a written account of the personal and social services needed to promote and support the child and family for the first three years of an exceptional child's life.

individualized transition plan the written plan designed to help prepare a student with a disability for life after schooling.

Individuals with Disabilities Education Act (IDEA) the name given in 1990 to the federal law formerly known as the Education for All Handicapped Children Act, Public Law 94-142, and its amendments.

informal assessment measures of student performance and progress in academic or behavioral tasks; focuses on individual growth and skill acquisition rather than on a comparison of one child's performance with that of others.

informal inventories a series of sequential passages or tasks, on different grade levels, used to assess the specific difficulties a student is having with reading, writing, or math skills.

inoculation vaccination against such infectious diseases as rubella, pertussis, measles, mumps, and polio.

institution a large, segregated, residential building used to house individuals with intellectual disabilities, mental illness, or physical disabilities.

instructional discourse strategies classroom interactions between teacher and students that are designed to teach.

intellectual disabilities a mild, moderate, or severe condition that is manifested in childhood and characterized by subaverage intellectual functioning and impairments in adaptive behavior.

intelligence the capacity to acquire, process, and use information.

intensity the strength or magnitude of a behavior.

interdisciplinary team a group of professionals from a variety of disciplines who work with a family to plan, coordinate, and deliver services.

intermediate-care facility (ICF) a community-based residential placement comprised of a number of individuals with disabilities living together in a supervised setting.

internalizing behavior self-directed behavior, such as withdrawal, avoidance, or compulsiveness.

iris the colored part of the eye.

Irving Independent School District v. Tatro a 1984 U.S. Supreme Court decision that schools must provide medical services that a nonphysician can perform if a child needs them to remain in school.

Itard, Jean-Marc-Gaspard early nineteenth-century French physician who attempted to teach the "wild boy of Aveyron" to talk.

itinerant services services provided by a specialized teacher who travels from school to school to work with students or to consult with teachers.

job coach a person trained in special education who trains people with disabilities on the job and works with onsite supervisors to help integrate the person into the employment setting.

joint attention two or more individuals attending to the same experiences, activities, or objects.

juvenile onset diabetes a metabolic disorder caused by an insufficient amount of insulin produced by the body, which results in difficulties in digesting and obtaining energy from food; it can appear at any point between birth and age 30.

juvenile rheumatoid arthritis a condition that affects the tissue lining of the joints.

Kennedy, John F. U.S. president with a strong personal interest in improving the quality of life for people with intellectual disabilities.

language the verbal means by which humans communicate.

language delay a delay in the acquisition of normal language milestones.

language disorders the impaired comprehension and/or use of spoken, written, and/or other symbol systems that may involve the form, content, or function of language.

language sample a written excerpt of a student's verbal communication over a specified period of time.

Larry P. v. Riles a 1979 California state court decision that IQ tests not be used in placing African American students in classes for students with intellectual disabilities.

learning disability a disorder in one or more of the basic psychological processes involved in understanding or using language. A student who has a learning disability does not achieve at the expected age and ability level in one or more academic areas and shows a severe discrepancy between achievement and intellectual ability.

learning style the way a student approaches learning.

Learning Strategies Curriculum a well-known curriculum developed at the University of Kansas Institute for Research in Learning Disabilities that focuses on strategy instruction.

least restrictive environment the setting that allows each child to be educated with his or her nondisabled peers to the maximum extent appropriate.

legal blindness a visual acuity of 20/200 or worse in the better eye after correction or a visual field of no greater than 20 degrees; this level of visual impairment qualifies a person for a variety of legal and social services.

lens the clear structure between the iris and the tissue inside the eyeball, which focuses light on the retina.

life-skills curriculum a course of study intended to provide the skills necessary to enable a student to live and work independently.

low birth weight a weight less than five and a half pounds at birth.

low vision a visual impairment in which there is enough remaining vision to use as the primary learning mode.

Macy, Anne Sullivan teacher and companion of Helen Keller.

manual communication approach an approach to teaching students who are deaf or hard of hearing that emphasizes the use of signs and sign language; its basic components are fingerspelling and signs.

mediation discussion between families and school districts over a point of disagreement, for the purpose of resolving the disagreement before a due process hearing can be held.

meningitis a serious illness that can cause brain damage and result in a range of disabling conditions such as hearing and vision loss and intellectual disabilities.

mentorship an arrangement whereby a student works with a community member to learn a specific skill, trade, or craft.

metacognition "thinking about thinking"; the ability to identify how one learns and to evaluate, monitor, and adapt the learning process.

metalinguistic awareness the ability to think about one's own communication and language.

Mills v. Washington, D.C., Board of Education a 1972 decision that required the District of Columbia to provide a free, appropriate public education for students with disabilities.

minority a numerical minority; it also suggests a subordinate position in society.

minority group a group that can be categorized by ethnicity, gender, language, religion, handicap, or socioeconomic status.

mixed hearing loss a hearing loss with both conductive and sensorineural components.

mobility the ability to move about in one's environment.

modification a change in the curricular content or standard from what is age-appropriate for a student to one that is better matched to his or her cognitive skills.

Montessori, Maria early twentieth-century Italian physician, teacher, and advocate for children with developmental disabilities; developed a method of teaching used with typically developing children today.

morphemes the smallest units of meaning in a language.

morphology the rules that govern how word meanings may be changed by adding prefixes, suffixes, and other forms that specifically indicate tense and number.

multiple intelligences Howard Gardner's theory that there are a number of distinct intelligences. An abundance of talent in any of these areas constitutes giftedness, according to Gardner.

muscular dystrophy a condition in which the voluntary muscles of the body are affected by progressive weakness.

natural environment one in which a child would spend time if he or she did not have special needs.

natural supports personal relationships that provide an improved, safer quality of life.

neonatal intensive care unit a specialized unit of the hospital for the care of high-risk newborns.

neonatology the study of high-risk newborns.

neurotoxins substances that adversely affect the developing central nervous system.

No Child Left Behind, or NCLB, is a phrase used to refer to a law, previously known as the Elementary and Secondary Education Act, which was reauthorized in 2002 and amended to call for greater accountability by local schools and state education agencies.

nondiscriminatory evaluation evaluation procedures conducted with fairness in the child's native language.

normalization a philosophy that assumes that people with disabilities should have education, socialization, and life experiences like those of their peers.

occupational hazards risks to health and life in the workplace.

optic nerve the nerve that connects the eye to the brain.

optic nerve hypoplasia faulty development or deteriorization of the optic nerve, resulting in vision loss.

oral communication approach an approach to teaching students who are deaf and hard of hearing that emphasizes the development of speech and listening skills through a combination of speech reading and use of residual hearing.

organization a cognitive skill that involves the ability to see and use similarities and differences and to categorize, arrange, and plan.

orientation the ability to use one's senses to establish where one is in space and in relation to other objects and people.

orientation and mobility the skills involved in being able to move around in the environment for a person with visual impairment.

otitis media middle ear infection; the most common cause of conductive hearing loss in children.

otologist a physician who specializes in diseases of the ear.

overrepresentation a representation in a specific group or class that is greater than would be expected based on actual population numbers.

parent-to-parent model a model for parent support that links experienced parents of children with disabilities to parents who are new to the programs and processes.

partial participation performing parts of a skill or activity that are in an individual's ability range.

partnerships individuals working as equals toward a shared goal.

Pennsylvania Association for Retarded Citizens (PARC) v. Commonwealth of Pennsylvania a 1972 state decision that required Pennsylvania to provide a free, appropriate public education for students with intellectual disabilities.

people-first language language that describes the person first, then the disability.

perception the ability to organize and interpret what one experiences through the senses.

perinatal period the period from the 22nd week of pregnancy to the seventh day of life.

perinatal stress traumatic events such as difficult or prolonged labor and delivery, hypoxia, low birth weight, or illness that occur during birth or the first days after birth.

pervasive developmental disorders a term given to a collection of developmental disabilities, including autism, Asperger's syndrome, and other disorders including autistic-like behavior.

petit mal seizure an epileptic seizure that occurs most frequently in children between the ages of 4 and 12; these seizures are very brief—usually only a few seconds—and although the child may lose consciousness, there may be no observable physical changes.

phoneme the smallest unit of speech.

phonological awareness the ability to recognize and manipulate the sounds contained in words.

phonology the rules for combining sounds in permissible ways to form words.

physical disability a condition that incapacitates to some degree the skeletal, muscular, and/or neurological systems of the body.

physical handling the moving of a student with a physical disability from place to place.

physically challenged the descriptive term preferred by many people with a physical disability; it describes their physical condition as a challenge to be faced rather than as a handicap.

polysubstance abuser someone who uses a combination of illegal drugs and alcohol.

positive behavior support preventive and positive interventions designed to create and maintain a supportive and successful environment.

postlingual deafness deafness that occurs after language is acquired.

postnatal period the period from the 28th day of life through the end of the first year.

postsecondary programs traditional or untraditional college or work opportunities designed to promote successful transition to adult life for individuals with disabilities.

pragmatic language the ability to use language effectively in different settings and for different purposes.

pragmatics the rules governing language use in differing situations.

predictive validity how accurately a test can predict academic performance.

prelingual deafness deafness that occurs before language is acquired.

premature a baby born before 37 weeks gestation.

prenatal care the care provided to an expectant mother during pregnancy by her physician, usually an obstetrician.

prenatal period the period from conception to birth.

prereferral intervention team a team of teachers and other professionals that works to keep children in the general education classroom instead of referring them to special education.

preterm *see* premature.

prevalence the number of students within a given special education category at a given time.

problem-based learning classroom learning based upon real-life problems.

profound intellectual disabilities cognitive ability characterized by an IQ of less than 20 and extreme deficits in adaptive behavior.

projective test an open-ended test that provides an opportunity for a child to express himself or herself and perhaps reveal evidence of behavioral or emotional trauma.

prompt a cue or guide that helps a student attend to or learn the appropriate material.

Public Law 94-142 a 1975 federal law (known now as the Individuals with Disabilities Education Act, or IDEA) that requires that every child between the ages of 3 and 21 with a disability be provided a free, appropriate public education in the least restrictive environment.

pullout program a service that involves the student leaving the classroom to receive specialized instruction.

pupil the opening in the center of the eye.

quality of life an index of adult performance, adjustment, and happiness.

radical acceleration skipping several grades or early entry to college.

rate how often a behavior occurs in a given time period.

reading comprehension the ability to understand the meaning of sentences and passages.

receptive language the language abilities involved in understanding and interpreting information.

related services those services, such as speech and language, adaptive physical education, and others, which the student with disabilities requires in order to benefit from schooling. Related services must be specified on the IEP.

relational meaning the meaning that goes beyond the individual meanings of words and links word meanings together into topics.

remedial instruction teaching the basic skill or content subject in which a student is having difficulty.

residential school a special school where students live during the school year.

residual hearing the remaining hearing most people with hearing loss possess.

resource room a service that involves students leaving the regular classroom for specialized instruction in academic areas of need.

respite care care given to a family member with a disability by a trained substitute caregiver.

response to intervention a tiered model of intervention in which students' progress is monitored and more intensive instruction is provided for those who are not making progress.

retina a layer of specialized cells at the back of the eye that are highly sensitive to light.

retinitis pigmentosa a hereditary condition of the eye characterized by degeneration of the retina caused by a deposit of pigment in the back of the eye; it is a progressive disease that results in tunnel vision.

retinopathy of prematurity damage to the eye that can cause vision loss in premature infants.

right to due process parents' right to a series of procedures designed to resolve a conflict between a school and family over the evaluation, placement, or program of a child with a disability.

risk factors biological and environmental conditions associated with the increased probability of developmental problems.

rubella also known as German measles; a highly contagious virus that can cause severe damage to the fetus if contracted by a mother in the first 16 weeks of pregnancy.

scaffolding the guidance an adult or peer provides through verbal communication as a way of doing for the student what the student cannot yet do alone.

school-based risk the risk that accompanies attendance in schools in which there is a higher degree of teacher turnover, fewer experienced teachers, larger class sizes, reduced educational resources, and fewer opportunities for quality instruction.

school-wide positive behavior support a tiered model of behavior intervention applied to all students in a school.

screening quick evaluation of large numbers of children for developmental and health problems.

Schoolwide Enrichment Model Joseph Renzulli's model for school change that is based on curriculum modifications and enrichment strategies used with gifted students.

Section 504 of the Rehabilitation Act of 1973 a law requiring that all facilities that receive federal funds be accessible to people with disabilities and prohibiting discrimination against people who are disabled.

Seguin, Edouard nineteenth-century teacher and advocate for children with intellectual disabilities.

self-determination active participation in decision making; having a voice in life decisions.

semantics the rules used to create and understand meaning in words and word combinations.

sensorineural hearing loss permanent hearing loss that usually results from damage to the cochlea or auditory nerve.

severe disabilities disabilities that require ongoing support in one or more major life activities, such as mobility, communication, self-care, and learning, in order to participate in integrated community settings and enjoy a quality of life available to people with fewer or no disabilities.

severe intellectual disabilities a level of cognitive ability characterized by an IQ of less than 40 and deficits in adaptive behavior.

sexually transmitted diseases (STDs) diseases spread through sexual intercourse.

sheltered employment contract work conducted in settings designed for individuals with disabilities—usually assembly-line workshops.

sheltered workshops large facilities for people with disabilities that provide simple contract work.

signs manual symbols for a word or concept.

skill transfer (generalization) the ability to apply a specific skill learned in one context to a different context.

Snellen Chart the most common visual screening test; it consists of eight rows of letters, each row smaller in size than the previous one; the person being tested is asked to read the letters with each eye while the other eye is covered. Each row represents the distance at which a person with normal vision can see the letters.

social integration inclusion, acceptance, and the development of friendships for students with disabilities.

socialized aggression aggressive and disruptive behaviors on the part of a group.

socioeconomic status a measure of a family's social and economic standing based on family income, education, and employment of the parents.

special class a class within an elementary or high school that groups children by exceptionality; a specialist teacher instructs these students together.

special education a set of services designed to meet the unique learning and developmental needs of exceptional students.

special school a school designed exclusively for students with exceptionalities.

specific language impairment primary difficulty in learning and using language that cannot be attributed to another disability.

speech the spoken component of the language system produced by complex, well-coordinated activity, from respiration to phonation to articulation.

speech disorders impairments of articulation, fluency, or voice.

speech-language pathologist the specialist concerned with the identification, assessment, and treatment of students with communication disorders.

spina bifida a midline defect of the skin, spinal column, and spinal cord that occurs during fetal development; it is characterized by varying degrees of paralysis.

Stanford-Binet a widely used standardized test of intelligence that places great emphasis on verbal judgments and reasoning.

stereotypic behaviors repetitive, non-harmful behaviors sometimes exhibited by people with severe intellectual disabilities and autism; examples include rocking, twirling of objects, and clapping of hands.

strategy instruction an approach to teaching students with learning disabilities that involves first breaking down the skills involved in a task or problem into a set of sequential steps and then preparing the steps so that students may read and later memorize them in order to perform the task correctly.

stuttering the habit of repeating a sound, syllable, or word while speaking, which significantly interferes with communication.

supported employment an employment setting in which a job coach trains a student at the job site, and a support system is established to help the student maintain the job and adjust to new job requirements over time.

syntax rules governing how words may be combined to form sentences.

synthesized speech the storage of words or phrases that can be recalled as needed, or the storage of speech sounds that can be put together to form words using a sound-by-sound process.

systematic progress monitoring ongoing assessment of student learning in a specific area such as reading, mathematics, or spelling.

talent a mental or physical aptitude or ability.

task analysis the process of breaking down a task or skill into its component parts.

task commitment the ability to stay focused on a task to its completion.

teacher assistance team a group of teachers and other professionals who work together to assist the general education teacher.

team teaching shared instruction of a lesson, a subject area, or an entire instructional program.

telecommunication devices for the deaf (TDDs) telephones with screens and keyboards that allow people who are deaf to communicate with others.

teratogen a substance that can cause birth defects.

thalidomide a drug prescribed to pregnant women in the 1950s that caused severe birth defects.

total communication the philosophy that advocates the use of whatever communication system is appropriate for a given child with a hearing loss at a given time.

toxic stress strong, frequent, and/or prolonged activation of the body's stress-response systems in the absence of the buffering protection of stable adult support. Examples of potential toxic stressors include extreme poverty, recurrent physical and/or emotional abuse, chronic neglect, severe maternal depression, parental substance abuse, and family violence.

transdisciplinary model an approach to assessment and planning in which professionals with differing specializations work together and share roles and responsibilities.

transition movement from one life period or event to another. In special education, the transition most frequently prepared for is that from school to work and adult life.

transition coordinator a person designated by the state, school district, or school to plan, coordinate, and supervise transition services.

transition programs programs designed to facilitate movement from school to work, from segregated to integrated settings, and from isolated living to community living and employment.

traumatic brain injury an acquired injury to the brain caused by an external physical force, resulting in total or partial functional disability or psychosocial impairment.

triarchic theory Robert Sternberg's theory that describes three kinds of intelligence: analytic, creative, and practical.

tutorial instruction helping the student in the specific subject in which he or she is having difficulty.

underrepresentation representation in a specific group or class that is less than would be expected based on actual numbers in the population.

unilateral hearing loss normal hearing in one ear and hearing loss in the other.

Universal Design for Learning (UDL) a philosophy and an approach to curriculum construction that emphasizes maximizing access of all individuals to all aspects of the curriculum.

verbalism the use of words without concrete knowledge of their meanings.

very low birth weight weight at birth of 3½ pounds or less.

Vineland Adaptive Behavior Scale one of the most widely used instruments for measuring adaptive behavior.

visual acuity sharpness of vision.

visual impairment a term that describes all levels of vision loss, from total blindness to uncorrectable visual limitations.

vitreous humor liquid-filled "eyeball."

vocational rehabilitation counselor person who assists adolescents and adults with disabilities in making the transition from school to work by helping them plan for post high school education and training, and job placement.

voice disorder any disorder resulting from difficulties in breathing, abnormalities of the larynx, or dysfunctions in the oral and nasal cavities that can affect the pitch, loudness, and/or quality of a voice.

Wechsler Intelligence Scale for Children, Third Edition (WISC-III) a test frequently used to predict academic achievement in school-age children.

word analysis the process of identifying written words; it involves the use of phonics, sight words, and context clues.

zero reject the principle that no child with a disability shall be refused an appropriate education by the schools.

References

A.G. Bell Association for the Deaf (2011). Auditory-verbal therapy. Retrieved from: http://agbell.org/NetCommunity/Page.aspx?pid=360/

Access Ingenuity (2003). http://www.accessingenuity.com/Disabilities/PhysicalDisability.htm/

Achenbach, T. M. (1991). Manual for the Child Behavior Checklist/4-18 and 1991 Profile. Burlington, VT: University of Vermont, Department of Psychiatry.

Achenbach, T., & Edelbrock, C. (1979). The child behavior profile II: Boys aged 12-16 and girls aged 6-11 and 12-16. *Journal of Consulting and Clinical Psychology, 47,* 223–233.

Adams, G. L. and Englemann, S. (1996). *Research on direct instruction: 25 years beyond Distar.* Seattle: Educational Achievement Systems.

Adelman, H.S. (1996). Appreciating the classification dilemma. In W. Stainback & S. Stainback (Eds.), *Controversial issues confronting special education: Divergent perspectives* (2nd ed.) (pp. 96–111). Boston: Allyn and Bacon.

Adger, C.T., Snow, C.E., & Christian, D. (Eds.) (2002). *What teachers need to know about language.* Washington, DC: ERIC Clearinghouse on Languages and Linguistics/Center for Applied Linguistics.

Agran, M., Wehmeyer, M., Cavin, M., & Palmer, S. (2010). Promoting active engagement in the general education curriculum for students with cognitive disabilities. *Education and Training in Autism and Developmental Disabilities, 45,* 163–174.

Agrawal, Y., Platz, E.A., & Niparko, J.K.(2008). Prevalence of hearing loss and differences by demographic characteristics among US adults. *Archives of Internal Medicine, 168*(14):1522–1530.

Ahearn, W.H., Clark, K.M., & MacDonald, R.P.F. (2007). Assessing and treating vocal stereotypy in children with autism. *Journal of Applied Behavior Analysis, 40,* 263–275.

AIDS Organization, 2003 www.aids.org/

Alberto, P.A., & Troutman, A.C. (2003). *Applied behavior analysis for teachers* (6th Ed.). Upper Saddle River, NJ: Merrill/Prentice Hall.

Aldefer, M.A., et al. (2008). Evidence-based assessment in pediatric psychology: Family measures. *Journal of Pediatric Psychology, 33,* 1046–1061.

Alessi, S.M., & Trollip, S.R. (2001). *Multimedia for learning: Methods and development* (3rd ed.). Boston: Allyn and Bacon.

Allinder, R.M., Dunse, L., Brunken, C.D., & Obermiller-Krolikowski, H.J. (2001).

Improving fluency in at-risk readers and students with learning disabilities. *Remedial and Special Education, 22,* 48–54.

Allman, C. (2002). *Guidelines for providing state assessments in alternate formats for students with visual impairments.* Austin, TX: Texas School for the Blind and Visually Impaired (Last revision: July 30, 2002). http://www. tsbvi.edu/Education/state-assess.htm

Allor, J.H., Champlin, T.M., Gifford, D.B., & Mathes, P.G. (2010). Methods for increasing the intensity of reading instruction for students with intellectual disabilities. *Education and Training in Autism and Developmental Disabilities, 45,* 500–511.

American Association for Mental Retardation (2002). Definition of mental retardation. Retrieved in September, 2003: www.aamr.org/Policies/faq_mental_retardation.shtml

American College of Obstetricians and Gynecologists (2008). Tobacco, alcohol, drugs, and pregnancy. Retrieved from http://www.acog.org/publications/patient_education/bp170.cfm/

American Foundation for the Blind (2008). Key definitions of statistical terms. Retrieved from: http://www.afb.org/Section.asp?SectionID=15&DocumentID=1280/

American Foundation for the Blind (2011). Web accessibility. Retrieved from http://www.afb.org/section.asp?SectionID=4&TopicID=167

American Printing House for the Blind (2009). Distribution of eligible students based on the federal quota census of January 05, 2009 (Fiscal Year 2010). Retrieved from: http://www.aph.org/fedquotpgm/dist10.html/

American Society for Reproductive Medicine (ASRM) (2003). *Age and Fertility: A Guide for Patients.* Birmingham, AL: ASRM.

American Society for Reproductive Medicine, 2009. http://www.asrm.org/

American Speech-Language-Hearing Association. (1993). *Definitions of Communication Disorders and Variations.* Retrieved from: www.asha.org/policy.doi:10.1044/policy.RP110103-00208

American Speech-Language-Hearing Association. (2007). *Scope of Practice in Speech-Language Pathology* [Scope of Practice]. Retrieved from: www.asha.org/policy. doi:10.1044/policy.SP2007-00283

American Speech-Language-Hearing Association. (2008). *2008 Schools Survey: Caseload characteristics.* Rockville, MD: Author.

American Speech-Language-Hearing Association. (2011). ASHA Counts for Year End 2010. Retrieved from: http://www.asha.org/research/memberdata/

American Speech-Language-Hearing Association. (n.d.) Causes of hearing loss in children. Retrieved from: http://www.asha.org/public/hearing/disorders/causes.htm#congenital.

Amish, P.L., Gesten, E.L., Smith, J.K., Clark, H.B., & Stark, C. (1988). Social problem-solving training for severely emotionally and behaviorally disturbed children. *Behavioral Disorders, 13,* 175–186.

Anderson, J.A., Kutash, K., & Duchnowski, A.J. (2001). A comparison of academic progress of students with EBD and LD. *Journal of Emotional and Behavioral Disorders, 9,* 106–121.

Anderson, K., Balandin, S., & Clendon, S. (2011). "He cares about me and I care about him." Children's experiences of friendship with peers who use ACC. *Augmentative and Alternative Communication, 27,* 77–90.

Ansell, S.E. (2004). Quality counts 2003: Put to the test. *Education Week, 23*(17), 75–76, 78–79.

Antia, S.D., Jones, P.B., Reid, S., & Kreimeyer, K.H. (2009). Academic status and progress of deaf and hard-of-hearing students in general education classrooms. *Journal of Deaf Studies and Deaf Education, 14* (3): 293–311.

Arick, J.R, Young, H.E., Falco, R.A., Loos, L.M., Krug, D.A., Gense, M.H., & Johnson, S.B. (2003). Designing an outcome study to monitor the progress of students with Autism Spectrum Disorders. *Focus on Autism and Other Developmental Disabilities, 18,* 75–87.

Arms, E., Bickett, J., & Graf, V. (2008). Gender bias and imbalance: girls in US special education programmes. *Gender and Education, 20,* (4), 349–359.

Armstrong, D.F. (2011). *Show of hands: A natural history of sign language.* Washington, DC: Gallaudet University Press.

Arnold, L., Christopher, J., & Huestiis, R. (1978). Megavitamins for minimal brain dysfunction: A placebo-controlled study. *Journal of the American Medical Association, 240,* 26–42.

Arthritis Foundation. www.arthritis.org: Retrieved July 7, 2011.

Artiles, A.J. &. Ortiz, A.A. (2002). *English language learners with special education needs: Identification, assessment, and instruction.* McHenry, IL: Center for Applied Linguistics/Delta Systems Co.

Artiles, A.J., Bal, A., & Thorius, K.A. (2010). Back to the future: A critique of Response to Intervention's social justice views. *Theory Into Practice, 49,* 250–257.

Artiles, A.J., Harry, B., Reschly, D.J., & Chinn, P.C. (2002). Over-identification of students of color in special education: A critical overview. *Multi-cultural Perspectives, 4,* 3–10.

Artiles, A.J., Kozleski, E.B., Trent, S.C., Osher, D., & Ortiz, A. (2010). Justifying and explaining disproportionality, 1968–2008: A critique of underlying views of culture. *Exceptional Children, 76,* 279–299.

Asaro-Saddler, K., & Saddler, B. (2010). Planning instruction and self-regulation training: Effects on writers with autism spectrum disorders. *Exceptional Children, 77,* 107–124.

ASHA (American Speech-Language-Hearing Association). (1993a). Definitions of communication disorders and variations. *ASHA, 35* (Suppl. 10), 40–41.

ASHA (American Speech-Language-Hearing Association). (2004). *Knowledge and skills needed by speech-language pathologists and audiologists to provide culturally and linguistically appropriate services.* Available from www.asha .org/policy

ASHA (American Speech-Language-Hearing Association). (1997). *Preventing speech and language disorders.* Rockville, MD: American Speech, Language, and Hearing Association.

ASHA (American Speech-Language-Hearing Association). (2008). *Roles and Responsibilities of Speech-Language Pathologists in Early Intervention: Guidelines.* Available at http://www.asha.org/ docs/html/GL2008-00293.html

Ashford, J., Smit, F., van Lier, P.A.C., Cuijpers, P., & Koot, H.M. (2008). Early risk indicators of internalizing problems in late childhood: A 9-year longitudinal study. *Journal of Child Psychology and Psychiatry, 49,* 774–780.

Atkins, T., & Bartuska, J. (2010). Considerations for the placement of youth with EBD in alternative education programs. *Beyond Behavior, 19*(2), 14–20.

Augusto, C. (1996). Foreword. In A.L. Corn & A.J. Koenig (Eds.), *Foundations of low vision: Clinical and functional perspectives* (p. v). New York: AFB Press.

Austin, L. (2010). Dynamic assessment: Whys and hows. *Perspectives on School-Based Issues, 11,* 80–87. doi:10.1044/ sbi11.3.80

Avert: Children, HIV, & AIDS. www .avert.org/children.htm: Retrieved July 14, 2011.

Avramdis E., & Norwich, B. (2002). Teachers' attitudes towards integration/inclusion: A review of the literature. *European Journal of Special Needs Education, 17,* 129–147. doi: 10.1080/08856250210129056.

Ayres, K.M., Lowrey, K.A., Douglas, K.H.. & Sievers, C. (2011). I can

identify Saturn, but I can't brush my teeth: What happens when the curricular focus for students with severe disabilities shifts. *Education and Training in Autism and Developmental Disabilities, 46,* 11–21.

Babyak, A.E., Koorland, M., & Mathes, P.G. (2000). The effects of story mapping instruction on the reading comprehension of students with behavioral disorders. *Behavioral Disorders, 25,* 239–258. *Disorders, 30,* 49–59.

Bacino, C.A. (2011). Approach to congenital malformations. Up to Date. www .uptodate.com: Retrieved July 11, 2011.

Bagnato, S.J., McKeating-Esterle, E., Fevola, A., Bortolamasi, P., & Neisworth, J.T. (2008). Valid use of clinical judgment (informed opinion) for early intervention eligibility: Evidence base and practice characteristics. *Infants and Young Children, 21*(4), 334–349.

Bailey, D.B., Bruer, J.T., Symons, F.J., Lichtman, J.W. (Eds.) (2001). *Critical thinking about critical periods.* Baltimore: Paul H. Brookes.

Baker, C., & Cokely, D. (1980). *American Sign Language: A teacher's resource on grammar and culture.* Silver Spring, MD: T.J. Publishers.

Baker, R.L., Mednick, B.R., & Hunt, N.A. (1987). Academic and social characteristics of low-birth-weight adolescents. *Social Biology, 34*(1–2), 94–109.

Baker, A.E.Z., Lane, A., Angley, M.T., & Young, R.L. (2007). The relationship between sensory processing patterns and behavioral responsiveness in Autistic Disorder: A pilot study. Journal of Autism and Developmental Disorders, 38, 867–875.

Baldwin, A.Y. (2002). Culturally diverse students who are gifted. *Exceptionality, 10*(2), 139–147.

Barclay, L. (2007). New guidelines recommend universal prenatal screening for Down syndrome. Medscape Medical News. Retrieved from: http://cme .medscape.com/viewarticle/550256/

Barclay, R.A. (1998). *Attention Deficit Hyperactivity Disorders: A handbook for diagnosis and treatment.* New York: Guilford Press.

Barraga, N.C., & Erin, J.N. (1992). *Visual handicaps and learning.* Austin, TX: Pro-Ed.

Barrett, S.B., Bradshaw, C.P., & Lewis-Palmer, T. (2008). Maryland statewide PBIS initiative: Systems, evaluation, and next steps. *Journal of Positive Behavior Interventions, 10,* 105–114. doi:10.1177/1098300707312541.

Barton, D.D. (1984). Uncharted course: Mothering the blind child. *Journal of Visual Impairment and Blindness, 78*(2), 66–69.

Basow, S.A. (2010). Gender in the classroom. In J.C. Chrisler & D.R. McCreary

(Eds.) *Handbook of Gender Research in Psychology, Vol. 1,* 277–295. doi: 10.1007/978-1-4419-1465-1_14.

Batshaw, M.L., & Rose, N.C. (1997). Birth defects, prenatal diagnosis, and prenatal therapy. In M.L. Batshaw (Ed.), *Children with disabilities* (pp. 35–52). Baltimore: Brookes.

Bauer, A.M., & Shea, T.M. (2002). *Parents and schools: Creating a special partnership for students with special needs.* Englewood Cliffs, NJ: Prentice-Hall.

Bauer, K.L., Iyer, S.N., Boon, R.T., & Fore, C. (2010). 20 ways for classroom teachers to collaborate with Speech–Language Pathologists. *Intervention in School and Clinic, 45* (5), 333–337. DOI: 10.1177/1053451208328833.

Baum, S.M., & Olenchak, F.R. (2002). The alphabet children: GT, ADHD, and more. *Exceptionality, 10*(2), 77–91.

Bausch, M.E., & Ault, M. (2008). Assistive Technology Implementation Plan: A tool for improving outcomes. *Teaching Exceptional Children, 41*(1), 6–14.

Bayat, M. (2011). Clarifying issues regarding the use of praise with young children. *Topics in Early Childhood Special Education, 31*(2) 121–128. doi: 10.1177/0271121410389339

Beale, E.A., Baile, W.F., & Aaron, J. (2005). Silence is not golden: Communicating with children dying from cancer. *Journal of Clinical Oncology, 23,* 3629–3631.

Beck, J. (2002). Emerging literacy through assistive technology. *Teaching Exceptional Children, 35*(2), 44–48.

Beck, A.R., Stoner, J.B., Bock, S.J., & Parton, T. (2008). Comparison of PECS and the use of a VOCA: A replication. *Education and Training in Developmental Disabilities, 2008, 43,* 198–216.

Becker, J.B., Berkley, K.J., Hampson, E., Herman, J.P., & Young, E. (Eds.) (2007). *Sex differences in the brain: From genes to behavior.* New York, Oxford University Press USA.

Beirne-Smith, M., Ittenbach, R.E., & Patton, J.R. (2002). *Mental retardation* (6th ed.). Upper Saddle River, NJ: Merrill/Prentice-Hall.

Belete, N. (2010). Parental perceptions of prosocial behavior in children with cancer. WireDSpace: WITS Institutional Repository on DSpace: http://hdl .handle.net. Retrieved July 16, 2011.

Bellinger, D.C. (2008). Neurological and behavioral consequences of childhood lead exposure. *PLoS Medicine, 5*(5), doi:10.1371/journal.pmed.0050115

Bellini, S., & Akulian, J. (2007). A meta-analysis of video-modeling and video self-modeling interventions for children and adolescents with autism spectrum disorders. *Exceptional Children, 73,* 264–287.

Bellini, S., Peters, J.K., Benner, L., & Hopf, A. (2007). A meta-analysis of school-based social skills interventions for children with autism spectrum disorders. *Remedial and Special Education, 28*, 153–162.

Berkeley, S., & Lindstrom, J.H. (2011). Technology for the struggling reader: Free and easily accessible, *Teaching Exceptional Children, 43*(4), 48–55.

Berkeley, S., Mastropieri, M.A., & Scruggs, T.E. (2011). Reading comprehension strategy instruction and attribution retraining for secondary students with learning and other mild disabilities. *Journal of Learning Disabilities, 44*, 18–32.

Berko, 1990

Berko, J. (1958). The child's learning of English morphology. *Word, 14*, 150–177.

Berkson, G. & Taylor, S.J. (2004). Intellectual and physical disabilities in prehistory and early civilization. *Mental Retardation, 42*(3), 195–208.

Berliner, D.C. (2002). Educational research: The hardest science of all. *Educational Researcher, 31*(8), 18–20.

Bernheimer, L.P., & Weisner, T.S. (2007). "Let me just tell you what I do all day…": The family story at the center of intervention research and practice. *Infants & Young Children, 20*(3), 192–201.

Bernheimer, L.P., & Keogh, B.K. (1995). Weaving assessment into the fabric of everyday life: An approach to family assessment. *Topics in early childhood special education, 15*(4), 415–433.

Bernheimer, L.P., Gallimore, R., & Weisner, T.S. (1990). Ecocultural theory as a context for the Individualized Family Service Plan. *Journal of Early Intervention, 14* (3), 219–233.

Berry, J.O., & Hardman, M.L. (1998). *Lifespan perspectives on the family and disability.* Boston: Allyn and Bacon.

Berry, M.R., Lindstrom, L., & Vovanoff, P. (2000). Improving graduation outcomes of students with disabilities: Predictive factors and student perspectives. *Exceptional Children, 66*, 509–529.

Bettleheim, B. (1967). *The empty fortress: Infantile autism and the birth of the self.* New York: Free Press.

Bickel, P.S. (2010). How long is a minute? The importance of a measured plan of response to crisis situations. *Teaching Exceptional Children, 42*, 18–22.

Bigge, J. (1991a). Self care. In J. Bigge, *Teaching individuals with physical and multiple disabilities* (3rd ed.) (pp. 379–398). New York: Merrill.

———. (1991b). Life management. In J. Bigge, *Teaching individuals with physical and multiple disabilities* (3rd ed.) (pp. 399–427). New York: Merrill.

Bigler, E.D. (1992). The neurobiology and neuropsychology of adult learning disorders. *Journal of Learning Disabilities, 25*, 488–506.

Blacher, J., & Baker, B. L. (2007). Positive impact of intellectual disability on families. *American Journal on Mental Retardation, 112*(5), 330–348.

Blachman, B.A. (1991a). Getting ready to read: Learning how to print maps of speech. In J.F. Kavanagh (Ed.), *The language continuum: From infancy to literacy* (pp. 41–62). Parkton, MD: York Press.

———. (1991b). Early intervention for children's reading problems: Clinical applications of the research in phonological awareness. *Topics in Language Disorders, 12*(1), 51–65.

Blischak, D.M. (1999). Increases in natural speech production following experience with synthetic speech. *Journal of Special Education Technology, 7*(2), 44–53.

Bloom, B. (Ed.). (1956). *Taxonomy of educational objectives, Handbook I: Cognitive domain.* New York: David McKay.

———. (1985). *Developing talent in young people.* New York: Ballantine.

Blumenthal-Kelly, A. (1995). Fingerspelling interaction: A set of deaf parents and their deaf daughter. In C. Lucas (Ed.). *Sociolinguistics in deaf communities* (pp. 62–73). Washington, DC: Gallaudet University.

Bondy, A., & Frost, L., (2001). *A picture's worth: PECS and other visual communication strategies in autism.* Bethesda, MD: Woodbine House.

Bono, K.E., Sheinberg, N, Scott, K.G., Claussen, A.H. (2007). Early intervention for children prenatally exposed to cocaine. *Infants and Young Children, 20*(1), 268–284.

Boris, N.W. (2009). Parental substance abuse. In C.H. Zeanah (Ed.), *Handbook of infant mental health* (3rd ed.), 171–179.

Borse, N.N., Gilchrist, J., Dellinger, A.M., Rudd, R.A., Ballesteros, M.F., & Sleet, D.A. (2008). *CDC Childhood Injury Report: Patterns of Unintentional Injuries among 0–19-Year-Olds in the United States, 2000–2006.* Atlanta, GA: Centers for Disease Control and Prevention, National Center for Injury Prevention and Control.

Bottge, B.A., Rueda, E., Serlin, R.C., Hung, Y., & Kwon, J.M. (2007). Shrinking achievement differences with anchored math problems: Challenges and possibilities. *Journal of Special Education, 41*, 31–49.

Bouck, E.C. (2009a). No Child Left Behind, the Individuals with Disabilities Education Act, and functional curricula: A conflict of interest? *Education and Training in Developmental Disabilities, 44*, 3–13.

Bouck, E.C. (2009b). Functional curriculum models for secondary students with mild mental impairment. *Education and Training in Developmental Disabilities, 44*, 435–443.

Boyd, B.A., & Correa, V.I. (2005). Developing a framework for reducing the cultural clash between African American parents and the special education system. *Multicultural Perspectives, 7*(2), 3–11.

Boyd, B.A, Odom. S.L., Humphreys, B.P., & Sam, A.M. (2010). Infants and toddlers with autism spectrum disorder: Early identification and early intervention. *Journal of Early Intervention, 32*, 75–98.

Boydell, C.B., & Stephens, C.B. (2006). Estimating the prevalence of early childhood serious emotional/behavioral disorders: Challenges and recommendations. *Public Health Reports, 121*(3), 303–310.

Boyle, C.A., Boulet, S., Schieve, L.A., Cohen, R.A., Blumberg, S.J., Yeargin-Allsopp, M., Visser, S., & Kogan, M.D. (2011). Trends in the prevalence of developmental disabilities in US children, 1997–2008. *Pediatrics*, May 23.

Boyle, J.R., & Weishaar, M. (2001). The effects of strategic notetaking on the recall and comprehension of lecture information for high school students with learning disabilities. *Learning Disabilities Research and Practice, 16*, 133–141.

Bradbury, J. (2002). Could treatment of neonatal RDS improve further? *Lancet, 360* (9330), 394.

Bradshaw, C.P., Mitchell, M.M, & Leaf, P.J. (2010). Results from a randomized controlled effectiveness trial in elementary schools. *Journal of Positive Behavior Interventions, 12*, 133–148.

Brady, N.C., & Halle, J.W. (1997). Functional analysis of communicative behaviors. *Focus on Autism and Other Developmental Disabilities, 12*, 95–104.

Brady, M.P., & Rosenberg, H. (2002). Job observation and behavior scale: A supported employment assessment instrument. *Education and Training in Mental Retardation and Developmental Disabilities, 37*, 427–433.

Branham, R.S., Collins, B.C., Schuster, J.W., & Kleinert, H. (1999). Teaching community skills to students with moderate disabilties: Comparing combined techniques of classroom simulation, videotape modeling, and community-based instruction. *Education and Training in Mental Retardation and Developmental Disabilities, 34*, 170–181.

Breakthroughs. (1997). Augmentative communication product catalog. Pittsburgh, PA: Sentient Systems Technology, Inc.

Brody, L.M., et al. (2003). Developmental trajectories of childhood disruptive behaviors and adolescent delinquency: A six-site, cross-national study. *Developmental Psychology, 39*, 222–245.

Brooke, V., Wehman, P., Inge, K., & Parent, W. (1995). Toward a customer-driven approach of supported employment. *Education and Training in Mental Retardation and Developmental Disabilities, 30*, 308–320.

Browder, D.M., & Minarovic, T.J. (2000). Utilizing sight words in self-instruction training for employees with moderate mental retardation in competitive jobs. *Education and Training in Mental Retardation and Developmental Disabilities, 35*, 78–89.

Brown, R.T., Amler, R.W., Freeman, W.S., Perrin, J.M., Stein, M.T., et al. (2005). Treatment of Attention-Deficit/Hyperactivity Disorder: Overview of the evidence. *Pediatrics, 115*, e749–e757.

Brownlie, E.B., Beitchman, J.H., Escobar, M., Young, A., Atkinson, A., Johnson, C., Wilson, B., & Douglas, L. (2004). Early language impairment and young adult delinquent and aggressive behavior. *Journal of Abnormal Child Psychology, 32*(4), 453–467.

Bruns, D.A. (2000). Leaving home at an early age: Parents' decisions about out-of-home placement for young children with complex medical needs. *Mental Retardation, 38*, 50–60.

Brunton, C. (2011, July 18). News Release: Texas Children's Hospital pioneers use of MRI-guided laser surgery for revolutionary new epilepsy treatment: Texas Children's Hospital. Retrieved from: http://www.texaschildrens.org/AllAbout/News/2011/epilepsy_treatment.aspx

Bryan, T. (1991). Social problems and learning disabilities. In B. Wong (Ed.), *Learning about learning disabilities* (pp. 196–231). San Diego: Academic Press.

Buck, G.H., Polloway, E.A., Smith-Thomas, A., & Cook, K.W. (2003). Prereferral intervention processes: A survey of state practices. *Exceptional Children, 69*(3), 349–360.

Buggey, T., Hoomes, G., Sherberger, M.E., & Williams, S. (2011). Facilitating social initiations of preschoolers with autism spectrum disorders using video self-monitoring. *Focus on Autism and Other Developmental Disabilities, 26*, 25–36.

Bullis, M., Yovanoff, P., Mueller, G., & Havel, E. (2002). Life on the "outs"—examination of the facility-to-community transition of incarcerated youth. *Exceptional Children, 69*, 7–22.

Burnstein, M., Stanger, C., Kamon, J., & Dumenci, L. (2006). Parent psychopathology, parenting, and child internalizing problems in substance-abusing families. *Psychology of Addictive Behaviors, 20*, 97–106.

Bursuck, W.D., & Damer, M. (2011). *Teaching reading to students who are at risk or have disabilities* (2nd ed.). Boston: Pearson.

Butler, A. (2007). *Preterm birth: Causes, consequences, and prevention*. R.

Behrman, (Ed.). Washington, D.C.: National Academies Press.

Butterfield, N., & Arthur, M. (1995). Shifting the focus: Emerging priorities in communication programming for students with a severe intellectual disability. *Education and Training in Mental Retardation and Developmental Disabilities, 31*, 41–50.

Buysse, V., Goldman, B.D., & Skinner, M.L. (2002). Setting effects on friendship formation among young children with and without disabilities. *Exceptional Children, 68*, 503–517.

Caesar, L.G., & Kohler, P.D. (2007). The state of school-based bilingual assessment: Actual practice versus recommended guidelines. *Language, Speech, and Hearing Services in the Schools, 38*, 190–200.

Campbell, J.M. (2003). Behavioral interventions for reducing problem behavior in persons with autism: A quantitative synthesis of single-subject research. *Research in Developmental Disabilities, 24*, 120–138.

Campbell, P.H., Bellamy, G.T., & Bishop, K.K. (1988). Statewide intervention systems: An overview of the new federal programs for infants and toddlers with handicaps. *Journal of Special Education, 22*, 25–40.

Canella, H.I., O'Reilly, M.F., & Lancioni, G.E. (2005). Choice and preference assessment research with people with severe to profound developmental disabilities: A review of the literature. *Research in Developmental Disabilities, 256*, 1–15.

Carlson, C.I. (1987). Social interaction goals and strategies of children with learning disabilities. *Journal of Learning Disabilities, 20*, 306–311.

Carlson, J.I., Luiselli, J.K., Slyman, A, & Markowski, A. (2008). Choice-making as intervention for public disrobing in children with developmental disabilities. *Journal of Positive Behavior Interventions, 10*, 86–90.

Carnine, D. (1991). Curricular interventions for teaching higher order thinking to all students: Introduction to the special series. *Journal of Learning Disabilities, 24*, 261–269.

Carnine, D.W., Silbert, J., Kameenui, E., Tarver, S.G., & Jungjohann, K. (2006). *Teaching struggling and at-risk readers: A direct instruction approach*. Pearson: Upper Saddle River, NJ.

Carnine, D.W., Silbert, J., Kameenui, E.J., & Tarver, S.G. (2010). *Direct instruction reading*, (5th ed.). Boston: Merrill.

Caro P., & Snell, M.E. (1989). Characteristics of teaching communication to people with moderate and severe disabilities. *Education and Training in Mental Retardation, 24*, 63–77.

Carter, E.W., Lane, K.L., Pierson, M.R., & Stang, K.K. (2008). Promoting self-determination for transition-age youth: Views of high school general and special educators. *Exceptional Children, 75*, 55–70.

Carter, E.W., Trainor, A.A., Ditchman, N., & Swedeen, B. (2009). Evaluation of a multicomponent intervention package to increase summer work experiences for transition-age youth with severe disabilities. *Research and Practice for Persons with Severe Disabilities, 34*(2), 1–12.

Cartledge, G., Kea, C.D., & Ida, D.J. (2000). Anticipating differences—celebrating strengths: Providing culturally competent services for students with serious emotional disturbance. *Teaching Exceptional Children, 32*(3), 30–37.

Catts, H.W. (1991). Facilitating phonological awareness: Role of speech-language pathologists. *Language, Speech, and Hearing Services in Schools, 22*, 196–203.

Cavanaugh, T. (2003). Ebooks and accommodations: Is this the future of print accommodations? *Teaching Exceptional Children, 35*(2), 56–61.

Cawley, J.F., Parmar, R.S., Yan, W.F., & Miller, J.H. (1996). Arithmetic computation abilities of students with learning disabilities: Implications for instruction. *Learning Disabilities Research and Practice, 1*, 230–237.

Center for Children's Health and the Environment (2002). Neurotoxins and the health of children. http://www.childrenvironment.org/factsheets/neurotoxins.htm

Center for Disease Control and Prevention (CDC), Attention Deficit/Hyperactivity Disorder (ADHD). http://www.cdc.gov/ncbddd/adhd/data.html: Retrieved, June 4, 2011.

Center for RTI in Early Childhood (2011). Retrieved from: http://www.crtiec.org/tiered_prevention_model/index.shtml

Centers for Disease Control and Prevention (2010). Cytomegalovirus (CMV) and Congenital CMV Infection. Retrieved from: http://www.cdc.gov/cmv/clinical/diagnosis-treatment.html/

Centers for Disease Control and Prevention (2011). Hearing loss in children: Facts. Retrieved from: http://www.cdc.gov/ncbddd/hearingloss/facts.html/

Centers for Disease Control and Prevention. (2010). Cytomegalovirus (CMV) disease: The congenital disease mothers don't know about. Retrieved from: http://www.cdc.gov/Features/dsCytomegalovirus/

Centers for Disease Control and Prevention. (2010). Lead. Retrieved from: http://www.cdc.gov/nceh/lead/

Centers for Disease Control and Prevention. (2010). Sexually transmitted diseases (STDs). Retrieved from: http://www.cdc.gov/std/

Centers for Disease Control and Prevention. (2010). What women can do. Retrieved from: http://www.cdc.gov/hiv/topics/perinatal/protection.htm#tested

Centers for Disease Control and Prevention. Autism spectrum disorders. Retrieved 7/11/11: www.cdc.gov/autism

Chambers, C.R., Hughes, C., & Carter, E.W. (2004). Parent and sibling perspectives on the transition to adulthood. *Education and Training in Developmental Disabilities, 39,* 79–94.

Chan, S., & Chen, D. (2011). Families with Asian Roots. In E.W. Lynch and M.J. Hanson (Eds.), *Developing cross-cultural competence* (4th ed.), pp. 234–311. Baltimore: Paul H. Brookes.

Chandler, L.K., Dahlquist, C.M., Repp, A.C., & Feltz, C. (1999). The effects of team-based functional assessment on the behavior of students in classroom settings. *Exceptional Children, 66,* 101–122.

Chapman, R.S., Streim, N.W., Crais, E.R., Salmon, D., Strand, C.A., & Negri, N.A. (1992). Child talk: Assumptions of a developmental process model for early language learning. In R.S. Chapman (Ed.), *Processes in language acquisition and disorders* (pp. 3–19). St. Louis: Mosby Year-Book.

Chard, D.J., Ketterlin-Geller, L.R., Baker, S.K., Doabler, C., & Apichatabutra, C. (2009). Repeated reading interventions for students with learning disabilities: Status of the evidence. *Exceptional Children, 75,* 263–281.

Chasson, G.S., Harris, G.E., & Neely, W.J. (2007). Cost comparison of early intensive behavioral intervention and special education for children with autism. *Journal of Child and Family Studies, 16,* 401–413.

Chau, M., Thampi, K., & Wight, V.R. (2010). Fact sheet: Basic facts about low-income children, 2009: Children under age 18. New York: National Center for Children in Poverty, Mailman School of Public Health, Columbia University.

Chen, D., & Klein, M.D. (2007). Promoting interactions with infants who have complex multiple disabilities: Development and field-testing of the PLAI curriculum. *Infants & Young Children, 20*(2):149–162. doi: 10.1097/01.IYC.0000264482.35570.32

Chen, D., & Klein, M.D. (2008a). Home-visit early intervention practices with families and their infants who have multiple disabilities. In C.A. Peterson, L. Fox, & P.M. Blasco (Eds.), *Young Exceptional Children Monograph (10): Early intervention for infants and toddlers and their families,* pp. 60–74. Missoula, MT: Division of Early Childhood.

Chen, D., & Klein, M.D. (2008b). Online professional development for early interventionists: Learning a systematic approach to promote caregiver interactions with infants who have multiple disabilities. *Infants & Young Children, 21*(2), 120–133. doi: 10.1097/01.IYC.0000314483.62205.34

Chen, D., & Klein, M.D. (2009). Interdisciplinary perspectives in early intervention: professional development in multiple disabilities through distance education. *Infants & Young Children, 22*(2), 146–158. doi: 10.1097/IYC.0b013e3181a030e0

Chen, X.K., Wen, S.W., Fleming, N., Demissie, K., Rhoads, G.G., & Walker, M. (2007). Teenage pregnancy and adverse birth outcomes: A large population-based retrospective cohort study. *International Journal of Epidemiology 36*(2), 368–373. doi: 10.1093/ije/dyl284

Cheng, A.K., & Niparko, J.K. (2000). Analyzing the effects of early implantation and results with different causes of deafness: Meta-analysis of the pediatric cochlear implant literature. In J.K. Niparko, K.I. Kirk, N.K. Mellon, A.M. Robbins, D.L. Tucci, & B.S. Wilson (Eds.), *Cochlear implants: Principles and practices* (pp. 259–265). Philadelphia: Lippincott Williams & Wilkins.

Chez, M.G., Buchanan, C.P., Bagan, B.T., Hammer, M.S., McCarthy, K.S., Ovrutskaya, I., Nowinski, C.V., & Cohen, Z.S. (2000). Secretin and autism: A two-part clinical investigation. *Journal of Autism and Developmental Disorders, 30,* 87–94.

Childhood Cancer Foundation (2003). http://www.candlelighters.org/

Cho, S.J., Singer, G.H.S., & Brenner, M. (2000). Adaptation and accommodation to young children with disabilities: A comparison of Korean and Korean American parents. *Topics in Early Childhood Special Education, 20*(4), 236–249.

Cicchetti, D.V., Sparrow, S.S., & Balla, D.A. (2005). Vineland Adaptive Behavior Scales, (2nd ed.). New York: Pearson.

Cihak, D.F., Kessler, K., & Alberto, P.A. (2008). Use of a handheld prompting system to transition independently through vocational tasks for students with moderate and severe intellectual disabilities. *Education and Training in Developmental Disabilities, 43,* 102–110.

Cirrin, F.M., Schooling, T.L., Nelson, N.W., Diehl, S.F., Flynn, P.F., Staskowski, M., Adamczyk, D.F. (2010). Evidence-based systematic review: Effects of different service delivery models on communication outcomes for elementary school-age children. *Language, Speech, and Hearing Services in the Schools, Language, Speech, 41,* 233–264.

Civil Rights Project, 2002 http://www.uchastings.edu/racism-race/docs/The_Civil_Rights_Project_at_Harvard_University.pdf

Clark, B. (2007). *Growing up gifted* (7th ed.). Upper Saddle River, NJ: Pearson Prentice Hall.

Clark, G.M., & Patton, J.R. (1997). *Transition planning inventory: Administration and resource guide.* Austin, TX: Pro-Ed.

Clasen, D.R., & Clasen, R.E. (2003). Mentoring the gifted and talented. In N. Colangelo and G.A. Davis (Eds.), *Handbook of gifted education* (3rd ed.) (pp. 254–267). Boston: Allyn and Bacon.

Clement-Heist, K., Siegel, S., & Gaylord-Ross, R. (1992). Simulated and *in-situ* vocational social skills training for youths with learning disabilities. *Exceptional Children, 58,* 336–345.

Cole, E.B., & Flexer, C. (2011). *Children with hearing loss: Developing listening and talking birth to six* (2nd ed.). San Diego, CA: Plural Publishing.

Committee on Disability Issues in Psychology (2003). *Guidelines for non-handicapping language in APA journals.* http://www.apastyle.org/manual/related/nonhandicapping-language.aspx/

Conners, C.K. (2008). *Conners,* (3rd ed.). Toronto, Ontario: Multi-Health Systems.

Cook, B.G. (2001). A comparison of teachers' attitudes toward their included students with mild and severe disabilities. *Journal of Special Education, 34,* 203–213.

Cook, B.G., & Semmel, M.I. (1999). Peer acceptance of included students with disabilities as a function of severity of disability and classroom composition. *Journal of Special Education, 33,* 50–61.

Cook, R., Klein, M.D., & Tessier, A. (2008). *Adapting early childhood curricula for children in inclusive settings* (7th ed.). Englewood Cliffs, NJ: Merrill/Prentice-Hall.

Copeland, S.R., McCall, J., Williams, C.R., Guth, C., Carter, E.W., Fowler, S.E., Presley, J.A., & Hughes, C. (2002). High school peer buddies: A win-win situation. *Teaching Exceptional Children, 35,* 16–21.

Corbet, E.B. (1980). Elmer Bartels. *Options: Spinal cord injury and the future* (pp. 145–147). Denver: Hirschfield Press.

Corn, A.L. & Erin, J.N. (Eds.), *Foundations of low vision: Clinical and functional perspectives* (2nd ed.). New York, NY: AFB Press.

Corn, A.L., & Lusk, K.E. (2010). Perspectives on low vision. In A.L. Corn & J.N. Erin (Eds.), *Foundations of low vision: Clinical and functional perspectives* (2nd ed.), pp. 3–34. New York, NY: AFB Press.

Cott, A. (1972). Megavitamins: The orthomolecular approach to behavioral disorders and learning disabilities. *Academic Therapy, 7,* 245–257.

———. (2001). Improving family involvement in special education. *Research Connections in Special Education, 9.* Reston, VA: Council for Exceptional Children.

Council for Exceptional Children (2001). Improving family involvement in special education. *Research Connections in Special Education, 9.* Reston, VA: Council for Exceptional Children.

Council for Exceptional Children (2011). Blindness and visual impairment. Retrieved from: http://www.cec.sped.org/AM/Template.cfm?Section=Blindness_Visual_Impairments&Template=/TaggedPage/TaggedPageDisplay.cfm&TPLID=37&ContentID=5625/

Council of State Governments Justice Center (2011). *Breaking schools' rules: A statewide study of how school discipline relates to students' success and juvenile justice involvement.* New York: Author. Available at http://justicecenter.csg.org/resources/juveniles#rpt/

Coutinho, M.J., & Oswald, D.P. (2006). *Disproportionate representation of culturally and linguistically diverse students in special education: Measuring the problem.* Tempe, Arizona: National Center for Culturally Responsive Educational Systems, Arizona State University.

Coutinho, M.J., Oswald, D.P., & King, M. (2001). *Differences in the special education identification rates for boys and girls: Trends and issues.* Richmond, VA: Project PROGRESS, Virginia Commonwealth University.

Couvillon, M., Peterson, R.L., Ryan, J.B., Scheuermann, B., & Stegall, J. (2010). A review of crisis intervention training programs for schools. *Teaching Exceptional Children, 42,* 6–17.

Craig, H.K., & Washington, J.A. (2006). *Malik goes to school: Examining the language skills of African-American students from preschool-5th grade.* Mahwah, NJ: Erlbaum.

Craig, S. et al. (2000). Promoting cultural competence through teacher assistance teams. *Teaching Exceptional Children, 32*(7), 6–12.

Crittenden, J.B. (1993). The culture and identity of deafness. In P.V. Paul & D.W. Jackson, *Toward a psychology of deafness.* Boston: Allyn and Bacon.

Cullinan, D. (2002). *Students with emotional and behavior disorders: An introduction for teachers and other helping professionals.* Upper Saddle River, NJ: Merrill/Prentice Hall.

Cutsforth, T.D. (1932). The unreality of words to the blind. *Teachers Forum, 4,* 86–89.

———. (1951). *The blind in school and society.* New York: American Foundation for the Blind.

Cystic Fibrosis Foundation (CFF). www.cff.org: Retrieved July 14, 2011.

Darrow, A.A. (2010). Early childhood special music education. *General Music Today, 24*(2) 28–30. doi: 1048371310385329

Data Accountability Center (2009). Individuals with Disabilities Act (IDEA) Data. Data Tables for OSEP State Reported Data. https://www.ideadata.org/arc_toc11.asp#partbCC.

Davidovitch, M., Glick, L., Holtzman, G., Tirosh, E., & Safir, M.P. (2000). Developmental regression in autism: Maternal perception. *Journal of Autism and Developmental Disorders, 30,* 113–119.

Davidson, P.W., & Myers, G.J. (2007). Environmental toxins. In M.L. Batshaw, L. Pellegrino, & N.J. Roizen (Eds.). *Children with disabilities* (6th ed.). Baltimore: Paul H. Brookes.

Davis, A., & Davis, K.A.S. (2011). Descriptive epidemiology of childhood hearing impairment. In R. Seewald and A.M. Tharpe (Eds.), *Comprehensive Handbook of Pediatric Audiology,* pp. 85–112. San Diego: Plural Publishing.

Dawson, G., & Osterling, J. (1997). Early intervention in autism. In M.J. Guralnick (Ed.), *The effectivenesss of early intervention.* Baltimore: Paul H. Brookes.

De La Paz, S., Owen, B., Harris, K.R., & Graham, S. (2000). Riding Elvis' motorcycle: Using self-regulated strategy development to PLAN and WRITE for a state writing exam. *Learning Disabilities Research and Practice, 15,* 101–109.

Deford, F. (1983). *Alex: The life of a child.* New York: Viking Press.

DeFries, J.C., Gillis, J.J., & Wadsworth, S.J. (1993). Genes and genders: A twin study of reading disability. In A.M. Galaburda (Ed.), *Dyslexia and development: Neurological aspects of extra-ordinary brains* (pp. 187–204). Cambridge, MA: Harvard University Press.

Delgado, C.E.F. (2009). Fourth grade outcomes of children with a preschool history of developmental disability. *Education and Training in Developmental Disabilities, 44,* 573–579.

Delisle, J.R. (1984). *Gifted children speak out.* New York: Walker.

———. (2000). *Once upon a mind: The stories and scholars of gifted child education.* Fort Worth: Harcourt Brace College Publishers.

Delisle, J.R., & Lewis, B.A. (2003). *The survival guide for teachers of gifted kids: How to plan, manage, and evaluate programs for gifted youth K–12.* Minneapolis, MN: Free Spirit.

DeNavas-Walt, C, Proctor, B.D.& Smith, J.C. (2011). Income, poverty, and health insurance coverage in the United States: 2010. U.S. Census Bureau, *Current Population Reports, 60–239.* U.S. Government Printing Office, Washington, DC.

Denning, C.B., Chamberlain, J.A., & Polloway, E.A. (2000). Guidelines for mental retardation: Focus on definition and classification practices. *Education and Training in Mental Retardation and Developmental Disabilities, 35,* 226–232.

Dennis, R.E. et al. (1993). Quality of life as a context for planning and evaluation of services for people with disabilities. *Exceptional Children, 59,* 499–512.

Deno, S.L. (1985). Curriculum-based measurement: The emerging alternative. *Exceptional Children, 49,* 36–45.

Derkay, C.S., & aWold, S.M. (2010). Hoarseness in children. *Pediatric Otolaryngology for the Clinician,* Part 4, 181–186, doi: 10.1007/1078-1-60327-127-1_23

Deshler, D.D., Warner, M.M., Schumaker, J.B., & Alley, G.R. (1983). Learning strategies intervention model: Key components and current status. In J.D. McKinney & L. Feagans (Eds.), *Current topics in learning disabilities.* Norwood, NJ: Ablex.

Devlieger, P.J., & Trach, J.S. (1999). Mediation as a transition process: The impact on postschool employment outcomes. *Exceptional Children, 65,* 507–523.

Diagnostic and Statistical Manual of Mental Disorders (4th ed., TR) (2000). Washington, DC: American Psychiatric Association.

Dieker, L.A. (2001). What are the characteristics of "effective" middle and high school co-taught teams? *Preventing School Failure, 46,* 14–25.

Dieker, L.A., & Murawski, W.W. (2003). Coteaching at the secondary level: Unique issues, current trends, and suggestions for success. *The High School Journal, 86,* 1–13.

Dingle, M., & Hunt, N. (2001). *Home literacy practices of Latino parents of first graders.* Paper presented at the American Educational Research Association Annual Meeting, Seattle.

DiSalvo, C.A., & Oswald, D.P. (2002). Peer-mediated interventions to increase the social interaction of children with autism: Consideration of peer expectancies. *Focus on Autism and Other Developmental Disabilities, 17,* 198–207.

Division for Learning Disabilities. (2007). *Thinking about response to intervention and learning disabilities: A teacher's guide.* Arlington, VA: Author.

Donahue, M., Cole, D., & Hartas, D. (1994). Links between langage disorders and emotional/behavioral disorders. *Education and Treatment of Children, 17,* 244–255.

Donovan, M.S., & Cross, C.T. (2002). *Minority students in special and gifted education.* Washington, DC: National Academy Press.

Dornan, D., Hickson, L., Murdoch, B., & Houston, T. (2009). Speech and language outcomes for children with hearing loss in auditory-verbal therapy programs: A review of the evidence. *Communicative Disorders Review, 2*(3), 155–170.

Dorris, M. (1989). *The broken cord: A family's ongoing struggle with fetal alcohol syndrome.* New York: HarperCollins.

Downing, J.E. (2005). Inclusive education for high school students with intellectual disabilities: Supporting communication. *Augmentative and Alternative Communication, 21,* 132–148.

Downing, J.E. (2011). Teaching communication skills. In M.E. Snell and F. Brown (pp 461–491). *Instruction of students with severe disabilities* (7th ed.). Boston: Pearson.

Drasgow, E. (1998). American sign language as a pathway to linguistic competence. *Exceptional Children, 64*(3).

Drew, C.J., Logan, D.R., & Hardman, M. (1992). Mental retardation: A life cycle approach (5th ed.) (pp. 233–341). New York: MacMillan.

Dubowitz, H., & Bennet, S. (2007). Physical abuse and neglect of children. *The Lancet, 369* (9576), 1891–1899.

Duncan, G.J., & Magnuson, K. (2011). The long reach of early childhood poverty. *Pathways,* Winter, 22–27. Palo Alto: Stanford University.

Dunlap, G., & Childs, K.E. (1996). Intervention research in emotional and behavioral disorders: An analysis of studies from 1980–1993. *Behavioral Disorders, 21,* 125–136.

Dunn, L.M. (1968). Special education for the mildly retarded: Is much of it justifiable? *Exceptional Children, 35,* 5–22.

Dunst, C.J. (2002). Family-centered practices: Birth through high school. *Journal of Special Education, 36,* 139–147.

Dunst, C.J. (2007). Early intervention for infants and toddlers with developmental disabilities. In S.L. Odom, R.H. Horner, M.E. Snell, & J. Blacher (Eds.) *Handbook of Developmental Disabilities,* pp. 161–180. New York: Guilford Press.

Dunst, C.J., Trivette, C.M., & Hamby, D.W. (2007). Meta-analysis of family-centered helpgiving practices research. *Developmental Disabilities Research Reviews, 13,* 370–378.

Durand, V.M., & Carr, E.G. (1985). Self-injurious behavior: Motivating conditions and guidelines for treatment. *School Psychology Review, 14,* 171–176.

Dyke, P., Mulroy, S., & Leonard, H. (2009). Siblings of children with disabilities: Challenges and opportunities. *Acta Paediatrica, 98*(1), 23–24.

Easter Seals (2010). *Living with disabilities study.* Chicago, IL: Author. Retrieved from: http://www.easterseals.com/site/PageServer?pagename=ntl_living_with_disabilities_study_home&s_src=LWDstudy&s_subsrc=bannerad/

Eddy, J.M., Reid, J.B., & Fetrow, R.A. (2000). An elementary school-based prevention program targeting modifiable antecedents of youth delinquency and violence: Linking the Interests of Families and Teachers (LIFT). *Journal of Emotional and Behavioral Disorders, 8,* 165–176.

Edelson, M.G. (2006). Are the majority of children with autism mentally retarded? A systematic evaluation of the data. *Focus on Autism and Other Developmental Disabilities, 21,* 66–83.

Educating Children with Autism. (2001). Committee on Educational Interventions for Children with Autism, Washington, DC: National Research Council.

Edwards, L., & Crocker, S. (Eds.). (2008). *Psychological processes in deaf children with complex needs: An evidence-based practical guide.* London: Jessica Kingsley Publishers.

Ehren, B.J. (2000). Maintaining a therapeutic focus and sharing responsibility for student success: Keys to in-classroom speech-language services. *Language, Speech, and Hearing Services in Schools, 31*(3), 219–229.

Ehri, L.C. (1989). Movement into word reading and spelling. In J.M. Mason (Ed.), *Reading and writing connections* (pp. 65–81). Boston: Allyn and Bacon.

Elbaum, B. (2002). The self-concept of students with learning disabilities: A meta-analysis of comparisons across different placements. *Learning Disabilities Research and Practice, 17,* 216–226.

Ellerd, D.A., Morgan, R.L., & Salzberg, C.L. (2002). Comparison of two approaches for identifying job preferences among persons with disabilities using video CD-ROM. *Education and Training in Mental Retardation and Developmental Disabilities, 37,* 300–309.

Emerson, E. (2007). Poverty and people with intellectual disabilities. *Mental Retardation and Developmental Disabilities Research Reviews, 13,* 107–113.

Englemann, S. et al. (2002). *Reading mastery plus.* Columbus, OH: SRA/MacMillan-McGraw-Hill.

Englemann, S., & Bruner, E. (1995). *Reading mastery II, fast cycle,* (Rainbow Edition). Columbus, OH: SRA/MacMillan-McGraw-Hill.

Englemann, S., & Hanner, S. (1982). *Reading Mastery, Level III: A direct instruction program.* Chicago: Science Research Associates.

Englemann, S., Carnine, L., & Steely, D.G. (1991). Making connections in mathematics. *Journal of Learning Disabilities, 24,* 292–303.

Englemann, S., et al. (1999). *Decoding Strategies: SRA Corrective Reading.* Chicago: SRA/McGraw-Hill.

Ennis, R.H. (1985). A logical basis for measuring critical thinking skills. *Educational Leadership, 43*(2), 44–48.

EPA, 2011 http://www.epa.gov/

Epilepsy Foundation (EPPA). www.epilepsyfoundation.org: Retrieved, July 6, 2011.

Epstein, M.H. et al. (1989). Mild retardation: Student characteristics and services. *Education and Training in Mental Retardation, 24,* 7–16.

Epstein, M.H., & Cullinan, D. (2010). *Scales for assessing emotional disturbance* (2nd Ed.). Austin TX: Pro-Ed.

Ericsson, K.A. (2006). The influence of experience and deliberate practice on the development of superior expert performance. In K.A. Anderson, N. Charness, R.R. Hoffman, & P.J. Feltovich (Eds.), *The Cambridge handbook of expertise and expert performance, 683–704.* Cambridge, UK: Cambridge University Press.

Ericsson, K.A., Krampe, R., & Tesch-Romer, C. (1993). The role of deliberate practice in the acquisition of expert performance. *Psychological Review, 199,* 363–406.

Erin, J.N., & Topor, I. (2010a). Functional vision assessment of children with low vision, including those with multiple disabilities. In A.L. Corn & J.N. Erin (Eds.), *Foundations of low vision: Clinical and functional perspectives* (2nd ed.), 339–397. New York, NY: AFB Press.

Erin, J.N., & Topor, I. (2010b). Instruction in visual techniques for students with low vision, including those with multiple disabilities. In A.L. Corn & J.N. Erin (Eds.), *Foundations of low vision: Clinical and functional perspectives* (2nd ed.), 398–441. New York, NY: AFB Press.

Estabrooks, W. (2006). *Auditory-verbal therapy and practice.* Washington, DC: Alexander Graham Bell Association for the Deaf and Hard of Hearing.

Estell, D.B., Jones, M.H., Pearl, R., VanAcker, R., Farmer, T.W., & Rodkin, P.C. (2008). Peer groups, popularity, and social preference: Trajectories of social functioning among students with and without learning disabilities. *Journal of Learning Disabilities, 41,* 5–14.

Evans, G.W. (2006). Child development and the physical environment. *Annual Review of Psychology, 57,* 423–51 doi: 10.1146/annurev.psych.57.102904.190057

Executive Committee of the Council for Children with Behavior Disorders, (1990). White paper on best assessment practices for students with behavioral disorders: Accommodation to cultural diversity and individual differences. *Behavioral Disorders, 14,* 263–278.

Fahey, K.R. (2000). Language problems exhibited in classrooms. In K.R. Fahey & D.K. Reid (Eds.). *Language development, differences, and disorders* (pp. 247–296). Austin, TX: Pro-Ed.

Falk, G.D., Dunlap, G., & Kern, L. (1996). An analysis of self-evaluation and videotape feedback for improving the peer interactions of students with externalizing and internalizing behavior problems. *Behavioral Disorders, 21,* 261–276.

Falk-Ross (2002). *Classroom-based language and literacy intervention: A programs and case studies approach.* Boston: Allyn and Bacon.

Falvey, M.A. (2005). *Believe in my child with special needs!* Baltimore, MD: Paul H. Brookes.

Farrall, J., & Lyon, K. (2011). An overview of assistive technology for students with severe disabilities. www.spectronicsinoz.com. Retrieved on 4/14/11.

Fazzi, D.L. & Naimy, B. (2010) Teaching orientation and mobility to school-age children. In W.R. Wiener, R.L. Welsch, & B.B. Blasch (Eds.), *Foundations of Orientation and Mobility*, Vol. 1, (3rd ed.) pp. 208–262. New York: AFB Press.

Fazzi, D.L., & Klein, M.D. (2002). Cognitive focus: Developing cognition, concepts, and language. In R.L Pogrund & D.L. Fazzi, (Eds.). *Early focus: Working with young children who are blind or visually impaired and their families* (2nd ed.). New York: AFB Press.

Federal Register. (1992). Washington, DC: U.S. Government Printing Office, September 29.

Feelings Game (2002). Do2learn (http://www.dotolearn.com/games/learningames.htm).

Feingold, B.F. (1975). Hyperkinesis and learning disabilities linked to artificial food flavors and colors. *American Journal of Nursing, 75,* 797–803.

Felce, D., & Emerson, E. (2001). Living with support in a home in the community: Predictors of behavioral development and household and community activity. *Mental Retardation and Developmental Disabilities Research Reviews, 7*(2), 75–83.

Felko, K.S., Schuster, J.W., Harley, D.A., & Collins, B.C. (1999). Using simultaneous prompting to teach a chained vocational task to young adults with severe intellectual disabilities. *Education and Training in Mental Retardation and Developmental Disabilities, 34,* 318–329.

Ferguson, D.L. (1987). *Curriculum decision making for students with severe handicaps: Policy and practice.* New York: Teachers College Press.

Ferrell, K.A. (1986). Infancy and early childhood. In G.T. Scholl (Ed.), *Foundations of education for blind and visually handicapped children and youth: Theory and practice.* New York: American Foundation for the Blind.

———. (2000). Growth and development of young children. In M.C. Holbrook and A.J. Koenig (Eds.), *Foundations of Education: Vol.1* (2nd ed., pp. 111–134). New York: American Foundation for the Blind.

Ferrell, K.A. (2006). Evidence-based practices for students with visual disabilities. *Communication Disorders Quarterly, 28*(1), 42–48. doi: 10.1177/15257401060280010701

Ferrell, K.A. (2011). *Reach out and teach: Helping your child who is visually impaired learn and grow* (2nd ed.). New York: AFB Press.

Ferreri, A.J. (2009). Including Matthew: Assessment-guided differentiated literacy instruction. *Teaching Exceptional Children Plus, 5*(3) Article 3. Retrieved from: http://escholarship.bc.edu/education/tecplus/vol5/iss3/art3

Ferri, B.A., & Connor, D.J. (2006). *Reading resistance: Discourses of exclusion in desegregation and inclusion debates.* New York: Peter Lang.

Fidler, D.J., Hodapp, R.M., & Dykens, E.M. (2002). Behavioral phenotypes and special education: Parent report of educational issues for children with Down Syndrome, Prader-Willi Syndrome, and Williams Syndrome. *Journal of Special Education, 36,* 80–88.

Firman, K.B., Beare, P., & Lloyd, R. (2002). Enhancing self-management in students with mental retardation: Extrinsic versus intrinsic procedures. *Education and Training in Mental Retardation and Developmental Disabilities, 37,* 163–171.

Fishbaugh, M.S.E. (2000). *The collaboration guide for early career educators.* Baltimore: Paul C. Brookes.

Fitzsimmons M.K. (1998). Beginning reading and phonological awareness for students with learning disabilities. ERIC EC Digest E565. Reston, VA: ERIC Clearinghouse for Special and Gifted Education, Council for Exceptional Children.

Fletcher, D., Boon, R.T., & Cihak, D.F. (2010). Effects of the TOUCHMATH program compared to a number line strategy to teach addition facts to middle school students with moderate intellectual disabilities. *Education and Training in Autism and Developmental Disabilities, 45,* 449–458.

Flory, K., Milich, R., Lynam, D.R., Leukefeld, C., & Clayton, R. (2003). Relation between childhood disruptive behavior disorders and substance use and dependence symptoms in young adulthood: Individuals with symptoms of attention-deficit / hyperactivity disorder are uniquely at risk. *Psychology of Addictive Behaviors, 17,* 151–158.

Foorman, B. (2007). Primary prevention in classroom reading instruction. *Teaching Exceptional Children, 39*(5), pp. 24–31.

Foorman, B.R., Francis, D.J., Fletcher, J.M., Schatschneider, C., & Mehta, P. (1998). The role of instruction in learning to read: Preventing reading failure in at-risk children. *Journal of Educational Psychology, 90,* 37–55.

Ford, A., Schnorr, R., Meyer, L., Davern, L., Black, J., & Dempsey, P. (1989). General community functioning. In A. Ford, R. Schnorr, L. Meyer, L. Davern, J. Black, & P. Dempsey (Eds.), *The Syracuse community-referenced curriculum guide for students with moderate and severe disabilities* (pp. 77–88). Baltimore: Paul H. Brookes.

Ford, D.Y. (2010). *Reversing underachievement among gifted Black students* (2nd ed.). Austin, TX: Prufrock Press.

Ford, D.Y., & Whiting, G.W. (2008). Recruiting and retaining underrepresented gifted students. In S.I. Pfeiffer (Ed.), *Handbook of giftedness in children* (293–308). New York: Springer.

Ford, D.Y., Grantham, T.C., & Whiting, G.W. (2008). Culturally and linguistically diverse students in gifted education: Recruitment and retention issues. *Exceptional Children, 74*(3), 289–306.

Fowler, M. (1995). *Maybe you know my kid.* New York: Carol Publishing Group.

Frank, A.R., & Sitlington, P.L. (2000). Young adults with mental disabilities: Does transition planning make a difference? *Education and Training in Mental Retardation and Developmental Disabilities, 35,* 119–134.

Fraser, B., Hensinger, R.N., & Phelps, J. (1990). *Physical management of multiple handicaps.* Baltimore: Paul H. Brookes.

Frasier, M.M., & Passow, A.H. (1994). *Towards a new paradigm for identifying talent potential.* Storrs, CT: University of Connecticut, the National Research Center on the Gifted and Talented.

Freeman, B.J., & VanDyke, M. (2006). Invited commentary "Are the majority of children with Autism mentally retarded?" *Focus on Autism and Other Developmental Disabilities, 21,* 86–88.

Freeman, B.J., Cronin, P., & Candela, P. (2002). Asperger Syndrome or Autistic Disorder? The Diagnostic dilemma. *Focus on Autism and Other Developmental Disabilities, 17,* 145–151.

Freidrich, O. (1983). What do babies know? *Time,* Aug. 15, pp. 70–76.

Frey, K.S., Hirschstein, M.K., & Guzzo, B.A. (2000). Second step: Preventing aggression by promoting social competence. *Journal of Emotional and Behavioral Disorders, 8,* 102–112.

Frick, P.J., & White, S.F. (2008). Research review: The importance of callous-unemotional traits for developmental models of aggressive and antisocial behavior. *Journal of Child Psychology and Psychiatry, 49,* 359–375.

Friend, A.C., Summers, J.A., & Turnbull, A.P. (2009). Impacts of family support in early childhood intervention research. *Education and Training in Developmental Disabilities. 44,* 453–470.

Friend, M., & Cook, L. (2009). *Interactions: Collaboration skills for school professionals* (6th ed.). Upper Saddle River, NJ: Prentice-Hall.

Fuchs, D., Fuchs, L., & Burish, P. (2000). Peer-Assisted Learning Strategies: An evidence-based practice to promote reading achievement. *Learning Disabilities Research and Practice, 15,* 85–91.

Fuchs, D., Fuchs, L.S., Mathes, P.G., & Simmons, D.C. (1997). Peer-assisted learning strategies: Making classrooms more responsive to diversity. *American Educational Research Journal, 34*, 174–206.

Fuchs, L.S., & Fuchs, D. (2007). A model for implementing responsiveness to intervention. *Teaching Exceptional Children, 39*(5), pp. 14–23.

Fuchs, L.S., & Fuchs, D. (n.d.) What is scientifically-based research on progress monitoring? Student Progress Monitoring, National Center on Student Progress Monitoring. http://www.studentprogress.org/weblibrary.asp/

Fuchs, L.S., & Fuchs, D. (2009). Creating opportunities for intensive intervention for students with learning disabilities. *Teaching Exceptional Children, 42*(2), 60–62.

Fuchs, L.S., Fuchs, D., & Speece, D.L. (2002). Treatment validity as a unifying construct for identifying learning disabilities. *Learning Disability Quarterly, 25*, 33–45.

Fuchs, L.S., Fuchs, D., Powell, S.R., Seethaler, P.M., Cirino, P.T., & Fletcher, J.M. (2008). Intensive intervention for students with mathematics disabilities: Seven principles of effective practice. *Learning Disability Quarterly, 31*, 79–92.

Fueyo, V. (1997). Below the tip of the iceberg: Teaching language-minority students. *Teaching Exceptional Children, 30*(1), 61–65.

Fujiura, G.T., & Yamaki, K. (2000). Trends in demography of childhood poverty and disability. *Exceptional Children, 66*(2), 187–199.

Fulk, B.M., Watts, E., & Bakken, J.P. (2011). The history of physical and health impairments. In A.F. Rotatori, F.E. Obiakor, J.P. Bakken (Eds.) *History of Special Education (Advances in Special Education, Volume 21)*, 269–288. Bingley, United Kingdom: Emerald Group Publishing Limited.

Furlong, M., & Morrison, G. (2000). The school in school violence: Definitions and facts. *Journal of Emotional and Behavioral Disorders, 8*, 71–82.

Gage, N.L., & Berliner, D. (1998). *Educational psychology* (6th ed.). Boston: Houghton Mifflin Co.

Gajira, M., & Salvia, J. (1992). The effects of summarization instruction on text comprehension of students with learning disabilities. *Exceptional Children, 58*, 508–516.

Gallagher, J.J. (2000). Unthinkable thoughts: Education of gifted students. *Gifted Child Quarterly, 45*, 5–12.

Gallaudet Research Institute (November 2008). *Regional and National Summary Report of Data from the 2007-08 Annual Survey of Deaf and Hard-of-Hearing Children and Youth.* Washington, DC: GRI, Gallaudet University.

Ganz, J.B., Earles-Vollrath, T.L., & Cook, K.E. (2011). Video-modeling: A visually based intervention for children with autism spectrum disorder. *Teaching Exceptional Children, 43*(6), 8–19.

Garbarino, J. (1990). The human ecology of early risk. In S.J. Meisels & J.P. Shonkoff (Eds.), *Handbook of early childhood intervention.* Cambridge: Cambridge University Press.

Garcia, S.B., & Guerra, P.L. (2004). Deconstructing deficit thinking: Working with educators to create more equitable learning environments. *Education and Urban Society, 36*, 150–168.

Garcia, S.B., & Ortiz, A.A. (2006). Preventing disproportionate representation: Culturally and linguistically responsive prereferral interventions. *Teaching Exceptional Children, 38*(4), 64–68.

Gardill, M.C., & Jitendra, A.K. (1999). Advanced story map instruction: Effects on the reading comprehension of students with learning disabilities. *Journal of Special Education, 33*, 2–17, 28.

Gardner, (2000). The giftedness matrix: A developmental perspective. In R.C. Friedman & B.M. Shore (Eds.), *Talents unfolding: Cognition and development*, pp. 77–88. Washington DC: American Psychological Association.

Gardner, H. (1983). *Frames of mind.* New York: Basic Books.

Gardner, H. (2006). *Multiple intelligences: New horizons.* New York, NY: Basic Books.

Gardner, J.E., & Edyburn, D.L. (2000). Integrating technology to support effective instruction. In J.D. Linsey (Ed.). *Technology and exceptional individuals* (3rd ed.). Austin, TX: Pro-Ed.

Garretson, M.D. (1976). Total communication. *Volta Review, 78*(4), 107–112.

Gathercole, S.E., Alloway, T.P., Willis, C., & Adams, A. (2006). Working memory in children with reading disabilities. *Journal of Experimental Child Psychology, 93*, 265–281.

Georgiadi, M., & Kourkoutas, E.E. (2010). Supporting pupils with cancer on their return to school: A case study report of a reintegration program. *Procedia Social and Behavioral Sciences, 5*, 1278–1282.

Gerber, P.J., & Reiff, H.B. (1994). *Learning Disabilities in adulthood: Persisting problems and evolving issues.* Boston: Andover Medical Publishers.

Gerber, P.J., Ginsberg, R., & Reiff, H.B. (1992). Identifying alterable patterns in employment success for highly successful adults with learning disabilities. *Journal of Learning Disabilities, 25*, 475–487.

Gersten, R., & Baker, S. (2000).What we know about effective instructional practices for English-language learners. *Exceptional Children, 66*(4), 454–470.

Gersten, R., & Woodward. J. (1994). The language minority student and special education: Issues, trends, and paradoxes. *Exceptional Children, 60*, 310–322.

Geva, R., Yosipof, R., Eshel, R., Leitner, Y., Valevski, A.F., & Harel, S. (2009). Readiness and adjustment to school for children with intrauterine growth restriction (IUGR): An extreme test paradigm. *Exceptional Children, 75*, 211–230.

Geytenbeek, J.J.M., Heim, M.M.J., Vermeulen, R.J., & Oostrom, K.J. (2010). Assessing comprehension of spoken language in nonspeaking children with cerebral palsy: Application of a newly developed computer-based instrument. *Augmentative and Alternative Communication, 26*, 97–107.

Giangreco, M.F., Prelock, P.A., & Turnbull, H.R. (2009). An issue hiding in plain sight: When are speech-language pathologists special educators rather than related-service providers? *Language, Speech, and Hearing Services in Schools, 41*, 531–538.

Gilbert, R., Widom, C.S., Browne, K., Fergusson, D., Webb, E., & Janson, S. (2009). Burden and consequences of child maltreatment in high-income countries. *The Lancet, 373* (9657), 68–81.

Goertz, Y.H.H., Van Lierop, B.A.G., Houkes, I., & Nijhuis, F.J.N. (2010). Factors related to the employment of visually impaired persons: A systematic literature review. *Journal of Visual Impairment & Blindness, 104*(7), 404–18.

Golz, A., Netzer, A., Westerman, S.T., Westerman, L.M., Gilbert, D.A., Joachims, H.Z., & Goldenberg, D. (2005). Reading performance in children with otitis media. *Otolaryngology Head & Neck Surgery, 132*(3) 495–499.

Goode, T.W., Jones, W., & Jackson, V. (2011). Families with African American roots. In E.W. Lynch & M.J. Hanson (Eds.), *Developing cross-cultural competence: A guide for working with children and their families* (4th ed.), pp. 140–181. Baltimore, MD: Paul H. Brookes.

Goodenough, N. (1987). Multi-culturalism as the normal human experience. In E.M. Eddy & W.L. Partridge (Eds.), *Applied anthropology in America* (2nd ed.). New York: Columbia University Press.

Goodwin, J. (2011). US Rates of Autism, ADHD continue to rise: Report. HealthDay: http://www.healthday.com/ Retrieved, June 4, 2011.

Gottfried, A.W., Gottfried, A.E., & Guerin, D.W. (2009). Issues in early prediction and identification of intellectual giftedness. In F.D. Horowitz, R.F. Subotnik, & D.J. Matthews (Eds.), *The development of giftedness and talent across the life span.* Washington, DC: American Psychological Association.

Gottlieb, G. (2009). Normally occurring environmental and behavioral influences on gene activity: From central dogma to probabilistic epigenesist. In K.E. Hood, C.T. Halpern, G. Greenberg, & R.M. Lerner (Eds.), *Handbook of Developmental Science, Behavior, and Genetics*, 13–38. Malden, MA: Wiley-Blackwell.

Graham, E.M., & Morgan, M.A. (1997). Growth before birth. In M.L. Batshaw (Ed.), *Children with disabilities* (4th ed.) (pp. 53–69). Baltimore: Paul H. Brookes.

Graham, S., & Harris, K.R. (2005). Students with learning disabilities and the process of writing: A meta-analysis of SRSD studies. In H.L. Swanson, S. Graham, & K.R. Harris (Eds.), *Handbook of learning disabilities*, (323–350). New York: Guilford Press.

Graham, S., Harris, K. R., & Olinghouse, N. (2007). Addressing executive function problems in writing: An example from the self-regulated strategy development model. In L. Meltzer (Ed.), *Executive function in education*, (216–236). New York: Guilford.

Grantham-McGregor, S., Cheung, Y.B., Cueto, S., Glewwe, P., Richter, L., Strupp, B., and the International Child Development Steering Group (2007). Developmental potential in the first 5 years for children in developing countries. *The Lancet, 369*, (9555), 60–70.

Gray, C. (2003). The Gray Center Retrieved 7/14/03 from (http://www .thegraycenter.org./sample_social_ stories.htm).

Green, C.W., & Reid, D.H. (1999). Reducing indices of unhappiness among individuals with profound multiple disabilities during therapeutic exercise routines. *Journal of Applied Behavior Analysis, 32*, 137–147.

Green, L. (2002). P.A. Parents try to save ill daughter. *San Jose Mercury News.* Retrieved from Sophia's Garden Foundation (www.sophiasgarden.org/ in_the_news.html), 2003.

Greene, G. (2011). *Transition planning for culturally and linguistically diverse youth.* Baltimore, MD: Paul H. Brookes.

Greenwood, C.R., Delquadri, J.C., & Hall, R.V. (1989). Longitudinal effects of classwide peer tutoring. *Journal of Educational Psychology, 81*, 371–383.

Gresham, F. (2001). Responsiveness to intervention: An alternative approach to the identification of learning disabilities. Paper presented at the Learning Disabilities Summit. Retrieved online at http://www.air.org/ldsummit//

Gresham, F.M., & MacMillan, D.L. (1997). Autistic recovery? An analysis and critique of the empirical evidence on the Early Intervention Project. *Behavioral Disorders, 22*, 185–201.

Griffin, D.K., Rosenberg, H., Cheyney, W., & Greenburg, B. (1996). A comparison of self-esteem and job satisfaction of adults with mild mental retardation in sheltered workshops and supported employment. *Education and Training in Mental Retardation and Developmental Disabilities, 31*, 142–150.

Griffin, M.M., McMillan, E.D., & Hodapp. R.M. (2010). Family perspectives on post-secondary education for students with intellectual disabilities. *Education and Training in Autism and Developmental Disabilities, 45*, 339–346.

Griffin-Shirley, N., Trusty, S., & Rickard, R. (2000). Orientation and mobility. In A.J. Koenig and M.C. Holbrook (Eds.), *Foundations of Education: Vol. II* (2nd ed., pp. 529–568). New York: American Foundation for the Blind.

Griffith, P.L., & Olson, M.W. (1992). Phonemic awareness helps beginning readers to break the code. *The Reading Teacher, 45*, 516–523.

Grigal, M., Neubert, M., & Moon, M.S. (2002). Postsecondary options for students with significant disabilities. *Teaching Exceptional Children, 35*(2), 68–73.

Griswold, D.E., Barnhill, G.P., Myles, B.S., Hagiwara, T., & Simpson, R.L. (2002). Asperger Syndrome and academic achievement. *Focus on Autism and Other Developmental Disabilities, 17*, 94–102.

Grullon, E., Cheas, L., & Canino, G. (2011) Psychological and school functioning of Latino siblings of children with intellectual disability. *Journal of Child Psychology and Psychiatry, 52*(6), pp. 696–703.

Guitar, B. (2006). *Stuttering: An integrated approach to its nature and treatment* (3rd ed.). Baltimore: Lippincott Williams & Wilkins.

Gunn, B., Biglan, A., Smolkowski, K., & Ary, D. (2000). The efficacy of supplemental instruction in decoding skills for Hispanic and non-Hispanic students in early elementary school. *Journal of Special Education, 34*, 90–103.

Guralnick, M.J. (1997). *The effectiveness of early intervention.* Baltimore: Paul H. Brookes.

Haager, D., Klingner, J., & Vaughn, S. (2007). *Evidence-based reading practices for response to intervention.* Baltimore: Paul H. Brookes.

Haastert, J., et al. (2011). Decreasing incidence and severity of cerebral palsy in prematurely born infants. *Journal of Pediatrics, 159*, 86–91.

Hagerman, R.J., Rivera, S.M., & Hagerman, P.J. (2008). The fragile-X family of disorders: A model for autism and targeted treatments. *Current Pediatric Reviews, 4*, 40–52.

Hall, T., Strangman, N., & Meyer, A. (2011). Differentiated instruction and implications for UDL implementation. National Center for Accessing the General Curriculum. Retrieved from: http://www.cast.org/publications/ ncac/ncac_diffinstruc.html

Hallmayer, J., Cleveland, S., Torres, A., Phillips, J., Cohen, B., Torigoe, T., Miller, J., Fedele, A., Collins, J., Smith, K., Lotspeich, L., Croen, L.A., Ozonoff, S., Lajonchere, C., Grether, J.K., & Risch, N. (2011, July 4). Genetic heritability and shared environmental factors among twin pairs with autism. *Arch Gen Psychiatry.* doi:10.1001/ archgenpsychiatry.2011.76

Halpern, A.S. (1993). Quality of life as a conceptual framework for evaluating transition outcomes. *Exceptional Children, 59*, 486–498.

Halvorsen, A.T., Doering, K., Farron-Davis, P., Usilton, R., & Sailor, W. (1989). The role of parents and family members in planning severely disabled students' transitions from school. In G.H.S. Singer and L.K. Irwin (Eds.), *Support for caregiving families* (pp. 253–268). Baltimore: Paul H. Brookes.

Hammond, D.L., Whatley, A.D., Ayres, K.M., & Gast, D.L. (2010). Effectiveness of video modeling to teach iPod use to students with moderate intellectual disabilities. *Education and Training in Autism and Developmental Disabilities, 45*, 525–538.

Hankins, C.S. (2003). Temporal and demographic trends in cerebral palsy fact and fiction. *American Journal of Obstetrics and Gynecology, 188*, 628–633.

Hanline, M.F., & Halvorsen, A. (1989). Parent perceptions of the integration transition process: Overcoming artificial barriers. *Exceptional Children, 55*, 487–492.

Hans, S.L. (1999). Demographic and psychosocial characteristics of substance-abusing pregnant women. *Clinics in Perinatology, 26*(1), 55–74.

Hans, S.L., & Thullen, M.J. (2009). The relational context of adolescent motherhood. In C.H. Zeanah (Ed.), *Handbook of infant mental health* (3rd ed.), 214–229.

Hanson, M.J. (1998). Ethnic, cultural, and language diversity in intervention settings. In E.W. Lynch & M.J. Hanson (Eds.), *Developing cross-cultural competence* (2nd ed.) (pp. 3–22). Baltimore: Paul H. Brookes.

Hanson, M.J. (2011). Diversity in service settings. In E.W. Lynch & M.J. Hanson (Eds.), *Developing cross-cultural competence: A guide for working with children and their families* (4th ed.), pp. 2–19. Baltimore, MD: Paul H. Brookes.

Hardin, Mereoiu, Hung, & Roach-Scott, 2009.

Harmon, C., Kasa-Hendrickson, C., & Neal, L.I. (2009). Promoting cultural competencies for teachers of students with significant disabilities. *Research and Practice for Persons with Severe Disabilities, 34*(3–4), 137–144.

Harris, C.A., Miller, S.P., & Mercer, C.D. (1995). Teaching initial multiplication skills to students with disabilities in general education classrooms. *Learning Disabilities Research and Practice, 10,* 180–195.

Harris, K.R., Friedlander, B.D., Saddler, B., Frizzelle, R., & Graham, S. (2005). Self-monitoring of attention versus self-monitoring of academic performance: Effects among students with ADHD in the general education classroom. *Journal of Special Education, 39,* 143–157.

Harris, S.L., & Handleman, J.S. (2000). Age and IQ at intake as predictors of placement for young children with autism: A four- to six-year follow-up. *Journal of Autism and Developmental Disorders, 30,* 137–142.

Harry, B. (1992a). Making sense of disability: Low-income, Puerto Rican parents' theories of the problem. *Exceptional Children, 59*(1), 27–40.

———. (1992b). Restructuring the participation of African-American parents in special education. *Exceptional Children, 59*(2), 123–131.

Harry, B. (2008). Collaboration with culturally and linguistically diverse families: Ideal versus reality. *Exceptional Children, 74*(3), 372–388.

Harry, B., & Klingner, J. (2006). *Why are so many minority students in special education?* New York: Teachers College Press.

Harry, B., & Klingner, J. (2007). Discarding the deficit model. *Educational Leadership, 64*(5), 16–21.

Harry, B., & Klingner, J.K. (2006). *Why are so many minority students in special education? Understanding race and disability in schools.* New York: Teachers College Press.

Harry, B., Allen, A., & McLaughlin, M. (1995). Communication versus compliance: African-American parents' involvement in special education. *Exceptional Children, 64*(4), 364–377.

Harry, B., Kalyanpur, M., and Day, M. (1999). *Building cultural reciprocity with families: Case studies in special education.* Baltimore: Paul H. Brookes.

Harry, B., Rueda, R., & Kalyanpour, M. (1999). Cultural reciprocity in sociocultural perspective: Adapting the normalization principle for family collaboration. *Exceptional Children, 66*(1), 123–136.

Hartman, R., & Stage, S.A. (2000). The relationship between social information processing and in-school suspension for students with behavioral disorders. *Behavioral Disorders, 25,* 183–195.

Harvey, H.M., & Sall, N. (1999). Profiles of the expressive communication skills of children and adolescents with severe cognitive disabilities. *Education and Training in Mental Retardation and Developmental Disabilities, 34,* 77–89.

Hasazi, S., Furney, K., & DeStefano, L. (1999). School and agency implementation of the IDEA transition mandates: Perspectives from nine sites. *Exceptional Children, 65*(4), 555–567.

Hatlen, P. (2000). The core curriculum for blind and visually impaired students, including those with additional disabilities. In A.J. Koenig and M.C. Holbrook (Eds.), *Foundations of Education: Volume II* (2nd ed., pp. 779–784). New York: American Foundation for the Blind.

Hatton, D.D., McWilliam, R.A., & Winton, P.J. (2002). Infants and toddlers with visual impairments: Suggestions for early interventionists. ERIC EC Digest E636. Reston, VA: The ERIC Clearinghouse on Disabilities and Gifted Education, Council for Exceptional Children.

Hauser-Cram, P., Warfied, M.E., Shonkoff, J.P., & Krauss, M.W. (2001). The development of children with disabilities and the adaptations of their parents: Theoretical implications and empirical evidence. *Monographs of the Society for Research in Child Development, 66,* 3.

Hayden, M., Gersten, R., & Carnine, D. (1992). Using coputer networking to increase active teaching in general education math classes containing students with mild disabilities. *Journal of Special Education Technology, 11,* 167–177.

Hayes et al. (1997). Ten-year survival of Down syndrome births. *International Journal of Epidemiology, 26,* 822–829.

Haynes, W.O., Moran, M.J., & Pindzola, R.H. (1990). *Communication disorders in the classroom.* Dubuque, IA: Kendall/Hunt Publishing.

Haynes, W.O., Moran, M.J., & Pindzola, R.H. (2012). *Communication disorders in educational and medical settings.* Sudbury, MA: Jones & Bartlett Learning.

Health Indicators (2011). http://www.childstats.gov/americaschildren/health5.asp

Hebbeler, K. (2009). Accountability for services for young children with disabilities and the assessment of meaningful outcomes: The role of the speech-language pathologist. *Language, Speech, and Hearing Services in the Schools, 40,* 446–456.

Heflin, L.J. & Alaimo, D.F. (2007). Students with autism spectrum disorders: Effective instructional practices. Upper Saddle, NY: Pearson.

Heflin, L.J., & Simpson, R.L. (1998). Interventions for children and youth with autism: Prudent choices in a world of exaggerated claims and empty promises. Part I: Intervention and treatment option review. *Focus on Autism and Other Developmental Disabilities, 13,* 194–211.

Heller, K.W., Fredrick, L.D., Dykes, M.K., Best, S., & Cohen, E.T. (1999). A national perspective of competencies for teachers of individuals with physical and health disabilities. *Exceptional Children, 65,* 219–234.

Heller, T., & Kaiser, A. (2008). Research related to siblings of individuals with disabilities. In T. Heller, A. Kaiser, D. Meyer, T. Fish, J. Kramer, & D. Dufresne (Eds.), *The sibling leadership network: Recommendations for research, advocacy, and supports relating to siblings of people with developmental disabilities.* Chicago, IL: Rehabilitation Research and Training Center on Aging with Developmental Disabilities, University of Illinois at Chicago. Retrieved from: http://www.siblingleadership.org/research/research-related-to-siblings-of-individuals-with-disabilities/

Hibbard and Desch (2007). Maltreatment of children with disabilities. *Pediatrics, 119*(5), 1018–1025 (doi: 10.1542/peds.2007-0565).

Hitchcock, C., Meyer, A., Rose, D., & Jackson, R. (2002). Providing new access to the general curriculum: Universal design for learning. *Teaching Exceptional Children, 35*(2), 8–17.

Hitchings, W.E., Luzzo, D.A., Ristow, R., Horvath, M., Retish, P., & Tanners, A. (2001). The career development needs of college students with learning disabilities: In their own words. *Learning Disabilities Research and Practice, 16,* 8–17.

Hobbs, N. (1975). *The futures of children: Categories, labels, and their consequences.* Nashville: Vanderbilt Institute for Policy Studies.

Hodapp, R.M., & Fidler, D.J. (1999). Special education and genetics: Connections for the 21st century. *Journal of Special Education, 33,* 130–137.

Holcomb, T.K. (1997). Social assimilation of deaf high school students: The role of school environment. In I. Parasnis (Ed.), *Cultural and language diversity and the Deaf experience.* Cambridge, UK: Cambridge University Press.

Hollingsworth, M., & Woodward, J. (1993). Integrated learning: Explicit strategies and their role in problem-solving instruction for students with learning disabilities. *Exceptional Children, 59,* 444–455.

Hollingworth, L.A. (1942). *Children above 180 I.Q. Stanford-Binet: Origin and development.* Yonkers-on-Hudson, NY: World Book Company.

Hood, L.J., & Keats, B.J.B. (2011). Genetics of childhood hearing loss. In R. Seewald and A.M. Tharpe (Eds.), *Comprehensive Handbook of Pediatric Audiology,* pp. 113–124. San Diego: Plural Publishing.

Horn, C. (Winter, 2003). High-stakes testing and students: Stopping or perpetuating a cycle of failure? *Theory into Practice,* 1–15.

Horne, P.E., & Timmons, V. (2009). Making it work: teachers' perspectives on inclusion. *International Journal of Inclusive Education, 13*(3), 273–286 (doi: 10.1080/13603110701433964)

Horner, R.H., Carr, E.G., Halle, J., Mcgee, G., Odom, S., & Wolery, M. (2005). The use of single-subject research to identify evidence-based practice in special education. *Exceptional Children, 71*, 165–179.

Hourcade, J., Parette, P., & Anderson, H. (2003). Accountability in collaboration: A framework for evaluation. *Education and Training in Developmental Disabilities, 38*, 398–404.

Hu, W. (June 21, 2011). Learning Empathy by Looking Beyond Disabilities. *The New York Times,* p. A18.

Hughes, C., Copeland, S.R., Agran, M., Wehmeyer, M.L., Rodi, M.S., & Presley, J.A. (2002). Using self-monitoring to improve performance in general education high school classes. *Education and Training in Mental Retardation and Developmental Disabilities, 37*, 262–272.

Hughes, C.A., Ruhl, K.L., Schumaker, J.B., & Deshler, D.D. (2002). Effects of instruction in an assignment completion strategy on the homework performance of students with learning disabilities in general education classes. *Learning Disabilities Research and Practice, 17*, 1–18.

Hull, G.A. (2010). Literate arts in a global world: Reframing social networking as cosmopolitan practice. *Journal of Adolescent & Adult Literacy 54*(2), 85–97. doi:10.1598.

Hull, G.A. and Kenney, N. L. (2009), Hopeful children, hybrid spaces: Learning with media after school. In K. Drotner, H.S. Jensen, & K.C. Schrøder (Eds.) *Informal learning and digital media*, 70–101. Newcastle, England: Cambridge Scholars.

Hume, K., & Odom, S. (2007). Effects of an individual work system on the independent functioning of students with autism. *Journal of Autism and Developmental Disorders, 37*, 1166–1180.

Humphries, T., & MacDougall, F. (1997). *Adding links to the chain: Discourse strategies in American Sign Language teaching.* Unpublished manuscript. Teacher Education Program, University of California, San Diego.

Hunt, N.A. (1982). *The relationship of medical, social, and familial variables with school-related performance of adolescents born at low weight.* Doctoral dissertation, University of Southern California.

Hurlbutt, K., & Chalmers, L. (2002). Adults with Autism speak out: Perceptions of their life experiences. *Focus on Autism and Other Developmental Disabilities, 17*(2), 103–111.

Hwang, B., & Hughes, C. (2000). The effects of social interactive training on early social communicative skills of children with autism. *Journal of Autism and Developmental Disorders, 30,* 331–343.

Hyde, M. (2011). Principles and methods of population hearing screening in EHDI. In R. Seewald and A.M. Tharpe (Eds.), *Comprehensive Handbook of Pediatric Audiology,* pp. 283–338. San Diego: Plural Publishing.

Iacono, T.A., & Miller, J.F. (1989). Can microcomputers be used to teach communication skills to students with mental retardation? *Education and Training in Mental Retardation, 24,* 32–44.

IDEA (1975). Section 300.8 http://idea.ed.gov/explore/view/p/,root,regs,300,A,300%252E8/

IDEA Sec. 300.8 (13). Child with a disability: Visual impairment. Retrieved from http://idea.ed.gov/explore/view/p/,root,regs,300,A,300%252E8

Idol, L. (2006). Toward inclusion of special education students in general education. *Remedial and Special Education, 27*(2), 77–94.

Individuals with Disabilities Education Act Amendments of 1997. (1997). P.L. 105–17, 105th Cong., 1st sess.

Individuals with Disabilities Education Act of 1990, 20 U.S.C. § 1400 et seq.

Ingersoll, B., & Schreibman, L. (2006). Teaching reciprocal imitation skills to young children with autism using a naturalistic behavioral approach: Effects on language, pretend play and joint attention. *Journal of Autism and Developmental Disorders, 36,* 487–505.

Ingram, K., Lewis-Palmer, T., & Sugai, G. (2005). Function-based intervention planning: Comparing the effectiveness of FBA function-based and non-function-based intervention plans. *Journal of Positive Behavior Interventions, 7,* 224–236.

Intellitools, 2000 http://www.intellitools.com/default.html

Intellitools, 2011 http://www.intellitools.com/default.html

Iovannone, R., Dunlap, G., Huber, H., & Kincaid, D. (2003). Effective educational practice for students with autism spectrum disorders. *Focus on Autism and Other Developmental Disorders, 18,* 150–165.

Irvin, M.J., Farmer, T.W., Weiss, M.P., Meece, J.L., Byun, S., McConnell, R.M., & Petrin, R.A. (2011). Perceptions of school and aspirations of rural students with learning disabilities and their nondisabled peers. *Learning Disabilities Research and Practice, 26,* 2–14.

Isaacs, J.S. (2007). Nutrition and children with disabilities. In M.L. Batshaw, L. Pellegrino, & N.J. Roizen (Eds.). *Children with disabilities* (6th ed.). Baltimore: Paul H. Brookes.

Ishii-Jordan, S.R. (2000). Behavioral interventions used with diverse students. *Behavioral Disorders, 25,* 299–309.

Ismail, S., Buckley, S., Budacki, R., Jabbar, A., & Gallicano, G.I. (2010). Screening, diagnosing, and prevention of fetal alcohol syndrome: Is this syndrome treatable? *Developmental Neuroscience, 32*(2), 91–100.

Jantz, K.M. (2011). Support groups for adults with Asperger Syndrome. *Focus on Autism and Other Developmental Disabilities, 26,* 119–128.

Jimenez Gonzalez, J.E., & Garcia Espinel, A.I. (2002). Strategy choice in solving arithmetic word problems: Are there differences between students with learning disabilities, poor performance, and typical achievement students? *Learning Disability Quarterly, 25,* 113–122.

Jiménez, R.T., & Gersten, R. (1999). Lessons and dilemmas derived from the literacy instruction of two Latina/o teachers. *American Educational Research Journal, 36,* 265–301.

Jitendra, A., Edwards, L., Sacks, G., & Jacobson, L. (2004). What research says about vocabulary instruction for students with learning disabilities. *Council for Exceptional Children, 70,* 299–322.

Joe, J.R., & Malach, R.S. (2011). Families with American Indian roots. In E.W. Lynch & M.J. Hanson (Eds.), *Developing cross-cultural competence: A guide for working with children and their families* (4th ed.), pp. 110–134. Baltimore, MD: Paul H. Brookes.

Johnson, E.S., Humphrey, M., Mellard, D.F., Woods, K., & Swanson, H.L. (2010). Cognitive processing deficits and students with specific learning disabilities: A selective meta-analysis of the literature. *Learning Disability Quarterly, 33,* 3–18.

Johnson, H.M. (2003). Unspeakable conversations. *New York Times,* February 16, section 6, p. 5.

Jonson-Reid, M., Drake, B., Kim, J., Porterfield, S., & Han, L. (2004). A prospective analysis of the relationship between reported child maltreatment and special education eligibility among poor children. *Child Maltreatment, 9*(4), pp. 382–394.

Jung, L.A. (2010). Identifying families' supports and other resources. In R.A. McWilliam (Ed.), *Working with Families of Young Children with Special Needs.* New York: Guilford Press.

Justice, L.M., Kaderavek, J.N., Fan, X., Sofka, A., & Hunt, A. (January 2009). Accelerating preschoolers' early literacy development through classroom-based teacher-child storybook reading and explicit print referencing. *Language, Speech, and Hearing Services in Schools, 40,* 67–85.

Juventation: Juvenile Diabetes Research Foundation (JDRF): juventation.org: Retrieved, July 13, 2011.

Kaderavek, J.N. (2011). *Language disorders in children: Fundamental concepts of assessment and intervention.* Boston: Allyn & Bacon.

Kalyanpur, M., and Harry, B. (1999). *Culture in special education: Building reciprocal family-professional relationships.* Baltimore: Paul H. Brookes.

Kalyanpur, M., Harry, B., & Skrtic, T. (2000). Equity and advocacy expectations of culturally diverse families' participation in special education. *International Journal of Disability, Development, and Education, 47*(2), 119–136.

Kamps, D., Abbott, M., Greenwood, C., Wills, H., Veerkamp, M., & Kaufman, J. (2008). Effects of small-group reading instruction and curriculum differences for students most at risk in kindergarten. *Journal of Learning Disabilities, 41,* 101–114.

Kamps, D., Kravits, T., Rauch, J., Kamps, J.L., & Chung, N. (2000). A prevention program for students with or at risk for ED: Moderating effects of variation in treatment and classroom structure. *Journal of Emotional and Behavioral Disorders, 8,* 141–154.

Kamps, D., Royer, J., Dugan, E., Kravits, T., Gonzalez-Lopez, A., Garcia, J., Carnazzo, K., Morrison, L., & Kane, L.G. (2002). Peer training to facilitate social interaction for elementary students with autism and their peers. *Exceptional Children, 68,* 173–187.

Kanner, L. (1943). Inborn disturbances of affective contact. *Nervous Child, 2,* 217–250.

Kasari, C., Paparella, T., Freeman, S., & Jahromi, L.B. (2008). Language outcome in autism: Randomized comparison of joint attention and play interventions. *Journal of Consulting and Clinical Psychology, 76,* 1125–1137.

Katsiyannis, A., & Yell, M.L. (2000). The Supreme Court and school health services: *Cedar Rapids v. Garret F. Exceptional Children, 66,* 317–326.

Katsiyannis, A., Yell, M.L., & Bradley, R. (2001). Reflections on the 25th anniversary of the Individuals with Disabilities Education Act. *Remedial & Special Education, 22*(6), 324–335.

Katz, L.A., Maag, A., Fallon, K.A., Blenkarn, K., & Smith, M.K. (2010). What makes a caseload (un)manageable? School-based speech-language pathologists speak. *Language, Speech, and Hearing Services in the Schools, 41,* 139–151.

Kauffman, J.M. (2001). *Characteristics of emotional and behavioral disorders of children and youth* (7th ed.). Upper Saddle River, NJ: Merrill/Prentice Hall.

Kavale, K.A., & Forness, S.R. (1983). Hyperactivity and diet treatment: A meta-analysis of the Feingold hypothesis. *Journal of Learning Disabilities, 16,* 324–330.

———. (1996). Social skill deficits and learning disabilities: A meta-analysis. *Journal of Learning Disabilities, 29,* 226–237.

Kavale, K.A., & Forness, S.R. (2000). What definitions of learning disability say and don't say: A critical analysis. *Journal of Learning Disabilities, 33,* 239–256.

Keen, D., Brannigan, K.L., & Cuskelly, M. (2007). Toilet training for children with autism: The effects of video-modeling. *Journal of Developmental and Physical Disabilities, 19,* 291–303.

Keller, B. (2004). Rigor disputed in standards for teachers. *Education Week, 23*(18), 1,14.

Kelly, J. F., & Barnard, K. E. (2000). Assessment of parent-child interaction: Implications for early intervention. In J. P. Shonkoff & S. J. Meisels (Eds.), *Handbook of early intervention* (pp. 258–288). New York: Cambridge University Press.

Kennedy, C.H. (2004). Students with severe disabilities. In C.H. Kennedy and E.M. Horn (Eds.), *Including students with severe disabilities* (pp. 1–16). Boston: Pearson.

Keogh, B.K., Gallimore, R., & Weisner, T. (1997). A sociocultural perspective on learning and learning disabilities. *Learning Disabilities Research and Practice, 12,* 107–113.

Kern, M.L., Friedman, H.S., Martin, L.R., Reynolds, C.A., & Luong, G. (2009). Conscientiousness, career success, and longevity: A lifespan analysis. *Annals of Behavioral Medicine, 37*(2), 154–163. Published online 2009 May 20. doi: 10.1007/s12160-009-9095-6

Kerr, B.A., & Nicpon, M.F. (2003). Gender and giftedness. In N. Colangelo and G.A. Davis (Eds.), *Handbook of gifted education* (3rd ed.) (pp. 493–505). Boston: Allyn and Bacon.

Keyser-Marcus, L., Briel, L., Sherron-Targett, P., Yasuda, S., Johnson, S., & Wehman, P. (2002). Enhancing the schooling of students with traumatic brain injury. *Teaching Exceptional Children, 34*(4), 62–67.

Kids Count Data Brief/Annie E. Casey Foundation (2009). Preventing low birthweight. Retrieved from: datacenter.kidscount.org/databook/2009/IndicatorBriefs/

KidsHealth, 2011 http://kidshealth.org/kid/grow/school_stuff/bullies.html#

KidsSource (2000). http://www.kidsource.com/NICHCY/brain.html

KidTools, 2011 The Curators of the University of Missouri, a public corporation. All Rights Reserved.

Kiernan, W. E., & Stark, J.A. (1986). *Pathways to employment for adults with developmental disabilities.* Baltimore: Paul H. Brookes.

Kinder, D., & Bursuck, W. (1991). The search for a unified social studies

curriculum: Does history really repeat itself? *Journal of Learning Disabilities, 24,* 270–275.

King, G., Strachan, D., Tucker, M., Duwyn, B., Desserud, S., & Shillington, M. (2009). The application of a transdisciplinary model for early intervention services. *Infants and Young Children, 22,* 211–223.

Kirk, K.I. (2000). Challenges in clinical investigations of cochlear implant outcomes. In J.K. Niparko, K.I. Kirk, N.K. Mellon, A.M. Robbins, D.L. Tucci, & B.S. Wilson, (Eds.), *Cochlear implants: Principles and practices* (pp. 225–255). Philadelphia: Lippincott Williams & Wilkins.

Kittrell, A., & Arjmand, E. (1997). The age of diagnosis of sensorineural hearing impairment in children. *International Journal of Pediatric Otorhinolaryngology, 40,* 97–106.

Klein, M.D., & Chen, D. (2001). *Working with children from culturally diverse backgrounds.* Albany, NY: Delmar.

Klingner, J.K, & Harry, B. (2006). The special education referral and decision-making process for English Language Learners: Child study team meetings and placement conferences. *Teachers College Record, 108*(11), 2247–2281.

Klingner, J.K., Ahwee, S., Pilonieta, P., Menendez, R. (2003). Barriers and facilitators in scaling up research-based practices. *Exceptional Children, 69*(4), 411–429.

Klingner, J.K., Artiles, A.J., & Barltell, L.M. (2006). English language learners who struggle with reading: Language acquisition of LD. *Journal of Learning Disabilities, 39,* 108–128.

Knapczyk, D.R. (1988). Reducing aggressive behaviors in special and regular class settings by training alternative social responses. *Behavioral Disorders, 14,* 27–39.

Knoblauch, B., & McLane, K. (1999). An overview of the Individuals with Disabilities Education Act Amendments of 1997 (P.L. 105–17): Update 1999. ERIC EC Digest E576. Reston, VA: ERIC Clearinghouse on Disabilities and Gifted Education, Council for Exceptional Children.

Koegel, R.L., Koegel, L.K., Frea, W.D., & Smith, A.E. (1995). Emerging interventions for children with autism: Longitudinal and lifestyle implications. In R.L. Koegel & L.K. Koegel (Eds.), *Teaching children with autism: Strategies for initiating positive interactions and improving learning opportunities* (pp. 1–16). Baltimore: Paul H. Brookes.

Koenig, A.J., & Holbrook, M.C. (2010). Selection and assessment of learning and literacy media for children and youths with low vision. In A.L. Corn & J.N. Erin (Eds.), *Foundations of low vision: Clinical and functional perspectives* (2nd ed.), 442–483. New York: AFB Press.

Koenig, A.J., & Holbrook, M.C. (2000). Planning instruction in unique skills. In A.J. Koenig and M.C. Holbrook (Eds.), *Foundations of Education: Vol. II* (2nd ed., pp. 196–224). New York: American Foundation for the Blind.

———. (2002). Literacy focus: Developing skills and motivation for reading and writing. In R.L. Pogrund & D.L. Fazzi, (Eds.). *Early focus: Working with young children who are blind or visually impaired and their families* (2nd ed.), New York: AFB Press.

Kohler-Evans, P. A. (2006). Co-teaching: How to make this marriage work in front of the kids. *Education, 127*, 260–264.

Kolb, S.M., & Hanley-Maxwell, C. (2003). Critical social skills for adolescents with high incidence disabilities: Parental perspectives. *Exceptional Children, 69*, 163–179.

Kolominsky, Y., Igumnov, S., & Drozdovitch, V. (1999). The psychological development of children from Belarus exposed in the prenatal period to radiation from the Chernobyl atomic power plant. *Journal of Child Psychology and Psychiatry and Allied Disciplines, 40*(2), 299.

Kopp, C.B. (1983). Risk factors in development. In M. Haith & J. Campos (Eds.), *Infancy and the biology of development* (Vol. II). In P. Mussen (Ed.), *Manual of child psychology.* New York: Wiley.

Kostewicz, D.E., Ruhl, K.L., & Kubina, R.M. (2008). Creating classroom rules for students with emotional and behavioral disorders: A decision-making guide. *Beyond Behavior, 17*(3), 14–21.

Kraijer, D. (2000). Review of adaptive behavior studies in mentally retarded persons with autism/pervasive developmental disorder. *Journal of Autism and Developmental Disorders, 30*, 39–47.

Krauss, M.W., (1990). New precedent in family policy: Individualized family service plan. *Exceptional Children, 56*(5), 388–395.

Kuhse, H., & Singer, P. (1985). *Should the baby live? The problem of handicapped infants.* New York: Oxford University Press.

Kutscher, M.L. (2003). Autism spectrum disorders: Sorting it out. Retrieved from http://www.pediatricneurology .com/autism.htm on November 23, 2003.

Lackaye, T.D., & Margalit, M. (2006). Comparisons of achievement, effort, and self-perceptions among students with learning disabilities and their peers from different achievement groups. *Journal of Learning Disabilities, 39*, 432–446.

Lagomarcino, T.R., & Rusch, F.R. (1989). Utilizing self-management procedures to teach independent performance. *Education and Training in Mental Retardation, 24*, 297–323.

Lam, K.S.L., Aman, M.G., & Arnold, L.E. (2006). Neurochemical correlates of autistic disorder: A review of the literature. *Research in Developmental Disabilities, 27*, 254–289.

Lam., K.S.L., & Aman, M.G. (2007). The Repetitive Behavior Scale—Revised: Independent validation in individuals with austism spectrum disorders. *Journal of Autism and Developmental Disorders, 37*, 855–866.

Lancioni, G.E., O'Reilly, M.F., Singh, N.N., Sigafoos, J., Olivia, D., & Severini, L. (2008). Enabling two persons with multiple disabilities to access environmental stimuli and ask for social contact through microswitches and a VOCA. *Research in Developmental Disabilities, 29*, 21–28.

Landrigan, P.J., Schechter, C.B., Lipton, J.M., Fahs M.C., & Schwartz, J. (2002). Environmental pollutants and disease in American children: Estimates of morbidity, mortality, and costs for lead poisoning, asthma, cancer, and developmental disabilities. *Environmental Health Perspectives, 110*(7), pp. 721–728

Lane, K.L. (2007). Identifying and supporting students at risk for emotional and behavioral disorders within Multi-level Models: Data-driven approaches to conducting secondary interventions with an academic emphasis. *Education and Treatment of Children, 30*, 135–164.

Lane, K.L., & Carter, E.W. (2006). Supporting transition-age youth with and at risk for emotional and behavioral disorders at the secondary level: A need for further inquiry. *Journal of Emotional and Behavioral Disorders, 14*(2), 66–70,

Lane, K.L., Barton-Arwood, S.M., Nelson, J.R., & Wehby, J. (2008). Academic performance of students with emotional and behavioral disorders served in a self-contained setting. *Journal of Behavioral Education, 17*, 43–62.

Lane, K.L., Graham, S., Harris, K.R., Little, M.A., Sandmel, K., & Brindle, M. (2010). The effects of self-regulated strategy development for second-grade students with writing and behavioral difficulties. *Journal of Special Education, 44*, 107–128.

Lane, K.L., Harris, K.R., Graham, S., Weisenbach, J.L., Brindle, M., & Morphy, P. (2008). The effects of self-regulated strategy development on the writing performance of second-grade students with behavioral and writing difficulties. *Journal of Special Education, 41*, 234–253.

Lane, K.L., Kalberg, J.R., & Menzies, H.M. (2009). *Developing schoolwide programs to prevent and manage problem behaviors: A step-by-step approach.* New York: The Guilford Press.

Lane, K.L., Menzies, H.M., Bruhn, A.L. & Crnobori, M. (2011). *Managing challenging behaviors in schools: Research-based strategies that work.* New York: Guilford Press.

Langone, J., & Mechling, L. (2000). The effects of a computer-based instructional program with video anchors on the use of photographs for prompting augmentative communication. *Education and Training in Mental Retardation and Developmental Disabilities, 35*, 90–105.

Lardieri, L.A., Blacher, J., & Swanson, H.L. (2000). Sibling relationships and parent stress in families of children with and without learning disabilities. *Learning Disability Quarterly, 23*(2), 105–116.

Lartz, M.N., Stoner, J.B., & Stout, L. (2008). Perspectives of assistive technology from Deaf students at a hearing university. *Assistive Technology Outcomes and Benefits, 5*(1), 72–91.

Lasker, J.P., & Garrett, K.L. (June 17, 2008). Aphasia and AAC: Enhancing communication across health care settings. The ASHA Leader: http://www .asha.org/leader.aspx: Retrieved July 20, 2011.

Lau, C. (2000). I learned how to take turns. *Teaching Exceptional Children, 32*(4), 8–13.

Laureate Learning (2003). Retrieved 7/11/03 from http://www.laureate learning.com/images/tvlg.gif

Lee, L.C., Harrington, R.A., Chang, J.J., & Connors, S.L. (2008). Increased risk of injury in children with developmental disabilities. *Research in Developmental Disabilities, 29*(3), 247–255.

Lee, S., Simpson, R.L., & Shogren, K.A. (2007). Effects and implications of self-management for students with autism. *Focus on Autism and Other Developmental Disabilities, 22*, 2–13.

Leekam, S.R., Nieto, C., Libby, S.J., Wing, L., & Gould, J. (2007). Describing the sensory abnormalities of children and adults with autism. *Journal of Autism and Developmental Disorders, 37*, 894–910.

Leffert, J.S., Siperstein, G.N., & Millikan, E. (2000). Understanding social adaption in children with mental retardation: A social-cognitive perspective. *Exceptional Children, 66*, 530–545.

LeGrice, B., & Blampied, N.M. (1994). Training pupils with intellectual disability to operate educational technology using video prompting. *Education and Training in Mental Retardation and Developmental Disabilities, 31*, 27–40.

Lehmann, J.P., & Baker, C. (1995). Mothers' expectations for their adolescent children: A comparison between families with disabled adolescents and those with non-labeled adolescents. *Education and Training in Mental Retardation and Developmental Disabilities, 31*, 27–40.

Lehmann, J.P., Davies, T.G., & Laurin, K.M. (2000). Listening to student voices about postsecondary education. *Teaching Exceptional Children, 32*(5), 60–65.

Lerman, P., Apgar, D.H., & Jordan, T. (2005). Longitudinal changes in adaptive behaviors of movers and stayers: Findings from a controlled research design. *Mental Retardation, 43,* 25–42.

Lerner, J. (1993). Young children with disabilities. *Learning disabilities: Theories, diagnosis, and teaching strategies* (6th ed.) (pp. 245–271). Boston: Houghton-Mifflin.

Levendoski, L.S., & Cartledge, G. (2000). Self-monitoring for elementary school children with serious emotional disturbances: Classroom applications for increased academic responding. *Behavioral Disorders, 25,* 211–224.

Levene, M.I., & Chervenak, F.A. (Eds.) (2009). *Fetal and neonatal neurology and neurosurgery* (4th ed.). Philadelphia: Churchill Livingstone Elsevier.

Lewis, B.A. (1992). Pedigree analysis of children with phonology disorders. *Journal of Learning Disabilities, 25,* 586–597.

Lewis, S., & Allman, C.B. (2000). Educational programming. In M.C. Holbrook and A.J. Koenig (Eds.), *Foundations of Education: Vol.1* (2nd ed., pp. 218–259). New York: American Foundation for the Blind.

———. (2000). *Seeing eye-to-eye: An administrator's guide to students with low vision.* New York: AFB Press.

Lidsky, T.I., & Schneider, J.S. (2003). Lead neurotoxicity in children: Basic mechanisms and clinical correlates. *Brain 126*(1), 5–19. doi: 10.1093/brain/awg014 Retrieved from: http://brain.oxfordjournals.org/content/126/1/5.full

Light, J., & Drager, K. (2007). ACC technologies for young children with complex communication needs: State of the science and future research directions. *Augmentative and Alternative Communication, 23,* 204–216.

Lim, L., Browder, D.M., & Bambara, L. (2001). Effect of sampling opportunities on preference development for adults with severe disabilities. *Education and Training in Mental Retardation and Developmental Disabilities, 36,* 188–195.

Lin, S.L. (2000). Coping and adaptation in families of children with cerebral palsy. *Exceptional Children, 66,* 201–218.

Loftus, S.M., Coyne, M.D., McCoach, D.B., Zipoli, R. . . . Pullen, P.C. (2010). Effects of supplemental vocabulary intervention on the word knowledge of kindergarten students at risk for language and literacy difficulties. *Learning Disability Research and Practice, 25,* 124–136.

Lonigan, C.J., Schatschneider, C., & Westberg, L. (2008). Identification of children's skills and abilities linked to later outcomes in reading, writing, and spelling. In *Developing early literacy: Report of the National Early Literacy Panel* (55–106). Jessup, MD: National Institute for Literacy.

Lopez-Reyna, N.A. (1996). The importance of meaningful contexts in bilingual special education: Moving to whole language. *Learning Disabilities Research and Practice, 11,* 120–131.

Los Angeles Unified School District (2006). *Language census report, 2005–06* (Publication No. 313). Los Angeles, CA: Author. Retrieved from: http://search.lausd.k12.ca.us/cgi-bin/fccgi.exe

Lowenfeld, B. (1981). *On blindness and blind people.* New York: American Foundation for the Blind.

Luckasson, R., Borthwick-Duffy, S., Buntinx, W.H.E., Coulter, D.L., Craig, E.M., Reeve, A. et al. (2002). *Mental Retardation: Definition, classification, and systems of supports* (10th ed.). Washington, DC: American Association on Mental Retardation.

Luetke-Stahlman, B., & Luckner, J. (1991). *Effectively educating students with hearing impairments.* New York: Longman.

Luterman, D.M. (2001). *Counseling persons with communication disorders and their families.* Austin, TX: Pro-Ed.

Lynch, C.L., & Popovic, M.R. (2008). Functional Electrical Stimulation. *Control Systems, IEEE, 28*(2), 40–50.

Lynch, E.W. (2011). Developing cross-cultural competence. In E.W. Lynch & M.J. Hanson (Eds.), *Developing cross-cultural competence: A guide for working with children and their families* (4th ed.), pp. 41–75. Baltimore, MD: Paul H. Brookes.

Lynch, E.W., & Hanson, M.J. (Eds.). (2004) *Developing cross-cultural competence* (3rd ed.). Baltimore: Paul H. Brookes.

Mabbott, D.J., & Bisanz, J. (2008). Computational skills, working memory, and conceptual knowledge in older children with mathematics learning disabilities. *Journal of Learning Disabilities, 41,* 15–28.

Maccini, P., & Hughes, C.A. (2000). Effects of a problem-solving strategy on the introductory algebra performance of secondary students with learning disabilities. *Learning Disabilities Research and Practice, 15,* 10–21.

MacMillan, D.L., Semmel, M.I., & Gerber, M.M. (1994). The social context of Dunn: Then and now. *Journal of Special Education, 27,* 466–480.

Magiera, K., Smith, C., Zigmond, N., & Gebauer, K. (2005). Benefits of co-teaching in secondary mathematics classes. *Teaching Exceptional Children, 37*(3), 20–24.

Maker, C.J. (1977). *Providing programs for the gifted handicapped.* Reston, VA: Council for Exceptional Children.

Malone, L.D., & Mastropieri, M.A. (1992). Reading comprehension instruction: Summarization and self-monitoring training for students with learning disabilities. *Exceptional Children, 58,* 270–279.

Mank, D., Cioffi, A., & Yovanoff, P. (1998). Employment outcomes for people with severe disabilities: Opportunities for improvement. *Mental Retardation, 36,* 205–216.

March of Dimes (2008). Alcohol and drugs. Retrieved from: http://www.marchofdimes.com/professionals/14332_1171.asp

March of Dimes (2009). Fact sheet: Teenage pregnancy. Retrieved from: http://www.marchofdimes.com/professionals/14332_1159.asp

March of Dimes (2011). Prematurity Campaign. Retrieved from: http://www.marchofdimes.com/mission/prematurity.html/

Marcus, GF., & Fisher, S.E. (2003). FOXP2 in focus: What can genes tell us about speech and language? *Trends in Cognitive Sciences, 7*(6), 257–262.

Marshall, K.J., Brown, W.H., Conroy, M.A., & Knopf, H. (2011). Early intervention and prevention of disabilities: Preschoolers. In D.P. Hallahan and J.M. Kauffman (Eds.), *Handbook of Special Education* (703–715). New York: Routledge.

Mastropieri, M.A., & Scruggs, T.E. (1991). *Teaching students ways to remember: Strategies for learning mnemonically.* Cambridge, MA: Brookline Books.

———. (2000). *The inclusive classroom: Strategies for effective instruction.* Columbus, OH: Merrill.

Mastropieri, M.A., Scruggs, T.E., & Graetz, J.E. (2003). Reading comprehension instruction for secondary students: Challenges for struggling students and teachers. *Learning Disability Quarterly, 26,* 103–116.

Mastropieri, M.A., Scruggs, T.E., Graetz, J., Norland, J., Gardizi, W., & McDuffie, K. (2005). Case studies in co-teaching in the content areas: Successes, failures and challenges. *Intervention in School and Clinic, 40,* 260–270

Mathes, P.G., Grek, M.L., Howard, J.K., Babyak, A.E., & Allen, S.H. (1999). Peer-Assisted Learning Strategies for first-grade readers: A tool for preventing early reading failure. *Learning Disabilities Research and Practice, 14,* 50–60.

Matson, J.K. & Mulick, J.A. (1991). *Handbook of mental retardation* (2nd ed.) Boston: Allyn and Bacon.

Maurice, C. (1993). *Let me hear your voice: A family's triumph over autism.* New York: Fawcett Columbine.

Mayo Clinic. 2002. www.mayoclinic.com/

McCleskey, J., & Waldron, N.L. (2011). Educational programs for elementary students with learning disabilities:

Can they be both effective and inclusive? *Learning Disabilities Research and Practice, 26*, 48–57.

McCormick, L. (2003a). Introduction to language acquisition. In L. McCormick, D.F. Loeb, & R.L Schiefelbusch, *Supporting children with communication difficulties in inclusive settings* (2nd ed.). Boston: Allyn and Bacon.

———. (2003b). Language intervention in the inclusive preschool. In McCormick, L., Loeb, D.F., & Schiefelbusch, R.L. *Supporting children with communication difficulties in inclusive settings* (2nd ed.). Boston: Allyn and Bacon.

McCormick, L., & Loeb, D.F. (2003). Characteristics of students with language and communication difficulties. In L. McCormick, D.F. Loeb, & R.L Schiefelbusch. (2003). *Supporting children with communication difficulties in inclusive settings* (2nd ed.) (pp. 71–112). Boston: Allyn and Bacon.

McCormick, L., Loeb, D.F., & Schiefelbusch, R.L. (2003). *Supporting children with communication difficulties in inclusive settings* (2nd ed.). Boston: Allyn and Bacon.

McDonald, H. (2002). Perinatal care at the threshold of viability. *Pediatrics, 110*(5), 1024–1027.

McDonnell, J.J., Hardman, M.L., & McDonnell, A.P. (2003). *An introduction to persons with moderate and severe disabilities: Educational and social issues* (2nd ed.). Boston: Allyn and Bacon.

McIlroy, G., & Storbeck, C.(2011). Development of Deaf identity: An ethnographic study. *Journal of Deaf Studies and Deaf Education, 16*(4), 494–511.

McIntosh, K., Campbell, A.L., Carter, D.R., & Dickey, C.R. (2009). Differential effects of a tier two behavior intervention based on function of problem behavior. *Journal of Positive Behavior Interventions, 11*, 82–93. doi:10.1177/1098300708319127.

McIntosh, K., Horner, R.H., Chard, D.J., Dickey, C.R., & Braun, D.H. (2008). Reading skills and function of problem behavior in typical school settings. *Journal of Special Education, 42*, 131–147.

McKinley, L.A., & Stormont, M.A. (2008). The school supports checklist: Identifying barriers for children with ADHD. *Teaching Exceptional Children, 41*, 14–19.

McKinney, J.D., Hocutt, A.M., Giambo, D.A., & Schumm, J.S. (2000). *Research on a teacher-implemented phonological awareness intervention for Hispanic kindergarten children.* Paper presented at the Council for Exceptional Children Convention, Vancouver, BC.

McLloyd, V.C. (1998). Socioeconomic disadvantage and child development. *American Psychologist, 53*(2), 185–204.

McMaster, K., Fuchs, D., & Fuchs, L. (2006). Research on peer-assisted learning strategies: The promise and limitations of peer-mediated instruction. *Reading & Writing Quarterly, 22,* 5–25.

McNamara, J.K., & Willoughby, T. (2010). A longitudinal study of risk-taking behavior in adolescents with learning disabilities. *Learning Disabilities Research and Practice, 25*, 11–24.

McQuiston S., & Kloczko, N. (2011). Speech and language development: Monitoring process and problems. *Pediatrics in Review, 32*, 230–239.

McWilliam, R.A. & Scott, S. (2001). A support approach to early intervention: A three-part framework. *Infants and Young Children, 13*(4), 55–66.

McWilliam, R.A. (2010). *Routines-based early intervention: Supporting young children and their families.* Baltimore: Paul H. Brookes.

Meadan, H., & Mason, L. (2007). Reading instruction for a student with emotional disturbance: Facilitating understanding of expository text. *Beyond Behavior, 16*(2), 18–26.

Meadan, H., Halle, J.W., & Ebata, A.T. (2010). Families with children who have autism spectrum disorders: Stress and support. *Exceptional Children, 77*, 7–36.

Meadan, H., Ostrosky, M.M., Triplett, B., Michna, A., & Fetting, A. (2011). Using visual supports with young children with autism spectrum disorder. *Teaching Exceptional Children, 43*(6), 28–37.

Meadow, K. (1968). Parental responses to the medical ambiguities of deafness. *Journal of Health and Social Behavior, 9*, 299–309.

Meadow, K.P. (2005). Early manual communication in relation to the deaf child's intellectual, social, and communicative functioning. *Journal of Deaf Studies and Deaf Education, 10*(4), 321–329.

Meadow-Orlans, K.P. (1980). *Deafness and child development.* Berkeley: University of California Press.

Mechling, L., & O'Brien, E. (2010). Computer-based video instruction to teach students with intellectual disabilities to use public bus transportation. *Education and Training in Autism and Developmental Disabilities, 45*, 230–241.

Mechling, L.C., & Bishop, V.A. (2011). Assessment of computer-based preferences of students with profound mental disabilities. *Journal of Special Education, 45*, 15–27.

Mechling, L.C., Gast, D.L., & Fields, E.A. (2008). Evaluation of a portable DVD player and system of least prompts to self-prompt cooking task completion by young adults with moderate intellectual disabilities. *Journal of Special Education, 42*, 179–190.

Mechling, L.C., Gast, D.L., & Seid, N.H. (2010). Evaluation of a personal digital assistant as a self-prompting device for increasing multi-step task completion by students with moderate intellectual disabilities. *Education in Autism and Developmental Disabilities, 45*, 422–439.

Medline Plus (2003). *Down syndrome.* Retrieved from http://search.nlm. nih .gov/medlineplus/, September, 2003.

Medline Plus (2011). http//www.nlm.nih .gov/medlineplus/bullying.html

Meinzen-Derr, J., Wiley S., & Choo, D. I. (2011). Impact of early intervention on expressive and receptive language development among young children with permanent hearing loss. *American Annals of the Deaf, 155*(5), 580–591.

Mercer, C., Mercer, A., & Pullen, P. (2010). *Teaching students with learning problems* (8th ed.). Boston: Pearson.

Mercer, C.D., & Mercer, A.R. (1993a). Assessing and teaching handwriting and written expression skills. *Teaching students with learning problems* (4th ed.) (pp. 533–581). New York: Merrill.

———. (1993b). Teaching math skills. In *Teaching students with learning problems* (4th ed.) (pp. 273–342). New York: Merrill.

Mercer, J. (1973). *Labeling the mentally retarded.* Berkeley: University of California Press.

Merrill, E.C. (1990). Attentional resource allocation and mental retardation. In N.W. Bray (Ed.), *International review of research in mental retardation, Vol. 16,* 51–88. San Diego, CA: Academic Press.

Mesibov, G.B. (1994). A comprehensive program for serving people with autism and the families: The TEACCH model. In J.L. Matson (Ed.), *Autism in children and adults: Etiology, assessment, and intervention* (pp. 85–97). Belmont, CA: Brooks/Cole.

Meyer, A., & Rose, D.H. (2006). Preface. In D.H. Rose & A. Meyer (Eds.), *A practical reader in universal design for learning*, pp.vii-xi. Cambridge, MA: Harvard Education Press.

Michaels, C.A. & Ferrara, D.L. (2006). Promoting post-school success for all: The role of collaboration in person-centered transition planning. *Journal of Educational and Psychological Consultation, 16*(4), 287–313.

Michaels, C.A., Prezant, F.P., & Jackson, K. (2002). Assistive and instructional technology for college students with disabilities: A national snapshot of postsecondary service providers. *Journal of Special Education Technology, 17*(1), 5–14.

Miller, B., Messias, E., Miettunen, J., Alarääiäsanen, A., Järvelin, M., Koponen, H., Räsänen, P., Isohanni, M., & Kilpatrick, B. Meta-analysis of paternal age and schizophrenia risk in male versus female offspring. *Schizophrenia Bulletin Advance Access,* first published online February 25, 2010. doi: 10.1093/schbul/sbq011

Millward, C., Powell, S., Messer, D., & Jordan, R. (2000). Recall for self and other in autism: Children's memory for events experienced by themselves and their peers. *Journal of Autism and Developmental Disorders, 30*, 15–28.

Minarovic, T.J., & Bambara, L.M. (2007). Teaching employees with intellectual disabilities to manage changing work routines using varied sight-word checklist. *Research and Practice for Persons with Severe Disabilities, 32*, 31–42.

Minskoff, E., & Allsopp, D. (2003). *Academic success strategies for adolescents with learning disabilities and ADHD*. Baltimore: Brookes.

Mitchell, R.E. & Karchmer, M. (2011). Demographic and achievement characteristics of deaf and hard-of-hearing students. In M. Marschark & P.E. Spencer (Eds.), *The Oxford Handbook of Deaf Studies, Language, and Education* (Vol.1, 2nd ed. 18–31). New York: Oxford University Press.

Mithaug, D.K. (2002). "Yes" means success: Teaching children with multiple disabilities to self-regulate during independent work. *Teaching Exceptional Children, 35*, 22–27.

Moats, L.C. (2009). Still wanted: Teachers with knowledge of language. *Journal of Learning Disabilities, 42*(5), 387–391.

Modell, S.J., & Cox, T.A. (1999). Let's get fit! Fitness activities for children with severe/profound disabilities. *Teaching Exceptional Children, 31*(3), 24–29.

Modell, S.J., & Valdez, L.A. (2002). Beyond bowling: Transition planning for students with disabilities. *Teaching Exceptional Children, 34*, 46–53.

Montague, M., Warger, C., & Morgan, T.H. (2000). Solve it! Strategy instruction to improve mathematical problem-solving. *Learning Disabilities Research and Practice, 15*, 110–116.

Moon, S., Simonsen, M.L., & Neubert, D.A. (2011). Perceptions of supported employment providers: What students with developmental disabilities, families, and educators need to know for transition planning. *Education and Training in Autism and Developmental Disabilities, 46*, 94–105.

Moores, D.F. (2001). *Educating the deaf: Psychology, principles, and practices* (5th ed.). Boston: Houghton Mifflin.

Moores, D. (2008). Research on bi-bi instruction. *American Annals of the Deaf, 153*(1), 3–4.

Moores, D.F. (2010). The history of language and communication issues in deaf education. In M. Marschark & P.E. Spencer (Eds.), *The Oxford handbook of deaf studies, language, and education* (Vol. 2, 17–30). New York, NY: Oxford University Press.

Moore, M.S., & Levitan, L. (2003). *For hearing people only: Answers to some of the most commonly asked questions about the deaf community, its culture, and the "Deaf Reality"* (3rd ed.). Rochester, NY: MSM Productions Ltd.

Moreno, G., & Wong-Lo, M. (2011). Practical considerations for working with Latino and Asian American students and families. *Multicultural Learning and Teaching, 6*(1), doi: 10.2202/2161-2412.1074. Retrieved from: http://www.bepress.com/mlt/vol6/iss1/4

Morgan, P.L., Farkas, G., Tufis, P.A., & Sperling, R.A. (2008). Are reading and behavior problems at-risk factors for each other? *Journal of Learning Disabilities, 41*, 417–436.

Morgan, R.L., & Horrocks, E.L. (2011). Correspondence between video-based preference assessment and subsequent community job performance. *Education and Training in Autism and Developmental Disabilities, 46*, 52–61.

Morgan, R.L., Gerity, B.P., & Ellerd, D.A., (2000). Using video and CD-ROM technology in a job preference inventory for youth with severe disabilities. *Journal of Special Education Technology, 15*(3), 25–33.

Morrissey, K.L., Bohanon, H., & Fenning, P. (2010). Positive Behavior Support: Teaching and acknowledging expected behaviors in an urban high school. *Teaching Exceptional Children, 42*, 26–35.

Morse, T.E., & Schuster, J.W. (2000). Teaching elementary students with moderate intellectual disabilities how to shop for groceries. *Exceptional Children, 66*, 273–288.

Morton, K. (1985). Identifying the enemy: A parent's complaint. In H.R. Turnbull & A.P. Turnbull. *Parents speak out: Then and now* (pp. 143–147). Columbus, OH: Merrill.

Mortweet, S.L. (1999). Classwide peer tutoring: Teaching students with mild mental retardation in inclusive classrooms. *Exceptional Children, 65*, 524–536.

Mueller, P.H., & Murphy, F.V. (2001). Determining when a student requires paraeducator support. *Teaching Exceptional Children, 33*, 22–27.

Mueller, P.H., & Murphy, F.V. (2001). Determining when a student requires paraeducator support. *Teaching Exceptional Children, 33*, 22–27.

Mull, C., Sitlington, P.L., & Alper, S. (2001). Postsecondary education for students with learning disabilities: A synthesis of the literature. *Exceptional Children, 68*, 97–118.

Murawski, W.W. (2006). Student outcomes in co-taught secondary English classes: How can we improve? *Reading & Writing Quarterly, 22*(3), 227–247.

Murawski, W.W., & Dieker, L. (2008). 50 ways to keep your co-teacher. *Teaching Exceptional Children*, Mar.–Apr., 41.

Murawski, W.W., & Swanson, H.L. (2001). A meta-analysis of co-teaching research: Where are the data? *Remedial and Special Education 22*(5) 258–267.

Murray, C., Goldstein, D.E., Nourse, S., & Edgar, E. (2000). The postsecondary school attendance and completion rates of high school graduates with learning disabilities. *Learning Disabilities Research and Practice, 15*, 119–127.

Murray, D.S., Creaghead, N.A., Manning-Courtney, P., Shear, P.K., Bean, J., & Prendville, J. (2008). The relationship between joint attention and language in children with autism spectrum disorders. *Focus on Autism and Other Developmental Disabilities, 23*, 5–14.

Muscott, H.S., Mann, W.L., & LeBurn, M.R. (2008). Positive behavioral interventions and supports in New Hampshire: Effects of large-scale implementation of school-wide positive behavior support on student discipline and academic achievement. *Journal of Positive Behavior Interventions, 10*, 190–205. doi:10.1177/1098300708316258.

Muscular Dystrophy Association (MDA). www.mda.org. Retrieved July 12, 2011.

Myer, J.A., & Minshew, N.J. (2002). An update on neurocognitive profiles in Asperger Syndrome and higher functioning autism. *Focus on Autism and Other Developmental Disabilities, 17*, 152–160.

Myklebust, H. (1964). *The psychology of deafness* (2nd ed.). New York: Grune & Stratton.

Nair, P., Black, M.M., Schuler, M., Keane, V., Snow, L. & Rigney, B.A. (1997). Risk factors for disruption in primary caregiving among infants of substance abusing women. *Child Abuse & Neglect, 21*(11), 1039–1051.

National Association for Gifted Children (2008). *Redefining giftedness for a new century: Shifting the paradigm*. http://www.nagc.org/index2.aspx?id=6404

National Association for Gifted Children (2011). *State of the nation in gifted education: A lack of commitment to talent development*. Washington, DC: Author.

National Association for Gifted Children (retrieved November 24, 2003). *Parent information*. http://www.nagc. org/ParentInfo/index.html/

National Center for Biotechnology Information (NCBI) (2003). http://www.ncbi.nim.nih.gov/

National Center for Culturally Responsive Education Systems (NCCRESt). (2005). *Cultural considerations and challenges in Response-to-Intervention models: An NCCRESt position statement.*

National Center for Education Statistics (1999). Inclusion of students with disabilities in the least restrictive environment. Section 2: *The Condition of Education*. http://nces.ed.gov/pubs99/condition99/pdf/section2.pdf

National Center for Education Statistics (2010, September). Statistics of Public

Elementary and Secondary School Systems, 1977 and 1980.

National Center for Educational Statistics (2010, April). Common Core of Data (CCD). State Nonfiscal Survey of Public Elementary/Secondary Education, 1990–91 through 2008–09.

National Center for Learning Disabilities (2003). *High stakes assessments and students with learning disabilities.* Retrieved from http:www.ld.org/advocacy/high_stakes.cfm, January 4, 2004.

National Center on Education Statistics (2011). Table 2. Public school student membership and percentage distribution of public school student membership, by race/ethnicity and state or jurisdiction: School year 2009–10. http://nces.ed.gov/pubs2011/snf200910/tables/table_02.asp?referrer=report

National Center on Learning Disabilities (2011). Assessment/Annual Testing. Retrieved from: http://www.ncld.org/on-capitol-hill/policy-agenda/policy-recommendations/assessment

National Crime Prevention Council, 2011 http://www.ncpc.org/cyberbullying

National Diabetes Information Clearing House. http://diabetes.niddk.nih.gov: Retrieved July 15, 2011.

National Dissemination Center for Children with Disabilities (2010). *Supports, modifications, and accommodations for students.* Retrieved from: http://nichcy.org/schoolage/accommodations#part1

National Dissemination Center for Children with Disabilities (2010). *Writing the IFSP for your child.* Retrieved from: http://nichcy.org/babies/ifsp/

National Dissemination Center for Children with Disabilities (2010). *Deafness and hearing loss.* NICHCY Disability Fact Sheet 3. http://nichcy.org/disability/specific/hearingloss

National Dissemination Center for Children with Disabilities (NICHCY): Traumatic Brain Injury: www.nichcy.org/disability/specific/tbi: Retrieved July 12, 2011.

National Down Syndrome Society website (2003). Information retrieved from http://www.ndss.org/, September, 2003.

National Fragile X Foundation (2011, July 13). Retrieved from: http://www.fragilex.org/html/autism_and_fragile_x_syndrome.htm

National Organization for Rare Disorders (2011). Rubella. Retrieved from: http://www.rarediseases.org/search/rdbdetail_abstract.html?disname=Rubella

National Reading Panel (2000). *Teaching children to read: An evidence-based assessment of the scientific research literature on reading and its implications for reading instruction* (NIH Publication No.

00-4769). Washington, DC: U.S. Government Printing Office.

National Resource Center on ADHD (2011). http://www.help4adhd.org/

National Scientific Council on the Developing Child (2005). *Excessive stress disrupts the architecture of the developing brain: Working paper no. 3.* Retrieved from: www.developingchild.harvard.edu/

National Scientific Council on the Developing Child (2007). *The science of early childhood development.* Cambridge, MA: Center on the Developing Child, Harvard University. Retrieved from http://developingchild.harvard.edu/index.php/resources/reports_and_working_papers/science_of_early_childhood_development/

National Scientific Council on the Developing Child (2004). *Young children develop in an environment of relationships.* Working paper no. 1. Retrieved from: http://www.developingchild.net

NDSS—retrieved March 1, 2011 http://www.ndss.org/

Needleman, H.L., & Reiss, J.A. (1996). Bone lead levels and delinquent behavior. *JAMA: Journal of the American Medical Association, 275*(5), 363–368.

Needleman, H.L., Gunnoe, C., Leviton, A., Peresie, H., Maher, C., Barret, P. (1979). Deficits in psychological and classroom performance of children with elevated dentine lead levels. *New England Journal of Medicine, 300,* 689–695.

Needleman, H.L., Schell, A., Bellinger, D., Leviton, A., & Allred, E.N. (1991). The long-term effects of exposure to low doses of lead in childhood. An 11-year follow-up report. *New England Journal of Medicine, 322*(2), pp. 83–88.

Neel, R.S., Meadows, N., Levine, P., & Edgar, E.B. (1988). What happens after special education: A statewide follow-up study of secondary students who have behavioral disorders. *Behavioral Disorders, 1,* 209–216.

Neihart, M. (2008). Identifying and providing services to twice-exceptional children. In S.I. Pfeiffer (Ed.), *Handbook of giftedness in children,* 115–137. New York: Springer.

Neisworth, J., & Bagnato, S.J. (2005). DEC recommended practices: Assessment. In S. Sandall, M. L. Hemmeter, M. McLean, & B. J. Smith (Eds.), *DEC recommended practices: A comprehensive guide for practical application in early intervention/early childhood special education* (45–69). Missoula, MT: Division of Early Childhood.

Nelson, J.A.P., Caldarella, P., Young, K.R., & Webb, N. (2008). Using peer praise notes to increase the social involvement of withdrawn adolescents. *Teaching Exceptional Children, 41,* 6–13.

Nelson, N.W. (1998). *Childhood language disorders in context: Infancy through*

adolescence (2nd ed.). Boston: Allyn and Bacon.

Neubert, D.A., & Moon, M.S. (2000). How a transition profile helps students prepare for life in the community. *Teaching Exceptional Children, 33*(2), 20–25.

Neubert, D.A., Tilson, G.P., & Ianacome, R.N. (1989). Postsecondary transition needs and employment patterns of individuals with mild disabilities. *Exceptional Children, 55,* 494–500.

Newborn Screening Task Force (2000). Newborn screening: A blue print for the future. *Exceptional Parent, 30*(10), 69–73.

Newcomer, P.L., & Barenbaum, E.M. (1991). The written composing ability of children with learning disabilities. A review of the literature from 1980–1990. *Journal of Learning Disabilities, 24,* 578–593.

Newman, L., Wagner, M., Cameto, R., Knokey, A.-M., & Shaver, D. (2010). *Comparisons across time of the outcomes of youth with disabilities up to 4 years after high school: A report of findings from the National Longitudinal Transition Study (NLTS) and the National Longitudinal Transition Study-2 (NLTS2).* (NCSER 2010-3008). Menlo Park, CA: SRI International.

Newman, T. (2008). Assessment of giftedness in school-age children using measures of intelligence or cognitive abilities. In S.I. Pfeiffer (Ed.), *Handbook of giftedness in children* (pp. 161–176). New York: Springer.

Nguyen, R.H.N., & Wilcox, A.J. (2005). Terms in reproductive and perinatal epidemiology: 2. Perinatal terms. *Journal of Epidemiology and Community Health, 59,* 1019–1021. Retrieved from: www.ncbi.nlm.nih.gov/pmc/articles/PMC1732966/pdf/v059p01019.pdf

NICHCY (2002). http://nichcy.org/

NICHCY: National Dissemination Center for Children with Disabilities: http://nichcy.org/disability/specific/intellectual#freq; Retrieved March 1, 2011.

Nickopoulos, C.K., & Keenan, M. (2007). Using video-modeling to teach complex social sequences to children with autism. *Journal of Autism and Developmental Disorders, 37,* 678–693.

Nietupski, J.A., & Hamre-Nietupski, S.M. (1987). An ecological approach to curriculum development. In L. Goetz, D. Guess, & K. Stremel-Campbell (Eds.), *Innovative program design for individuals with dual sensory impairments.* Baltimore: Paul H. Brookes.

———. (2003). Retrieved November, 2003 from http://www.nimh:nih.gov/publicat/autism.cfm#aut 6

Nihira, K., Leland, H., & Lambert, N. (1993). *Adaptive Behavior Scales-Residential and Community Edition, Second Edition: Examiner's manual.* Austin, TX: Pro-Ed.

NIMH (2011) National Institute for Mental Health http://www.nimh.nih.gov/index.shtml

Niparko, J.K. (2000). Introduction. In J.K. Niparko, K.I. Kirk, N.K. Mellon, A.M. Robbins, D.L. Tucci, & B.S. Wilson, (Eds.), *Cochlear implants: Principles and practices* (pp. 1–6). Philadelphia: Lippincott Williams & Wilkins.

Nissenbaum, M.S., Tollefson, N., & Reese, R.M. (2002). The interpretative conference: Sharing a diagnosis of autism with families. *Focus on Autism and Other Developmental Disabilities, 17,* 30–43.

No Child Left Behind (2002). Reauthorization of the Elementary and Secondary Education Act. Washington, DC: U.S. Department of Education.

Noonan, M.J., & Kilgo, J.L. (1987). Transition services for early age individuals with severe mental retardation. In R.N. Ianacone & R.A. Stodden (Eds.), *Transition issues and directions* (pp. 25–37). Reston, VA: Council for Exceptional Children.

Northern, J.L., & Downs, M.P. (2002). *Hearing in children* (5th ed.). Philadelphia: Lippincott Williams & Wilkins.

O'Brien, L., Lucas, N.H., Felt, B.T., Hoban, T.F, Ruzicka, D.I. et al., (2011). Aggressive behavior, bullying, snoring, and sleepiness in schoolchildren. *Sleep Medicine,* doi:10.1016/j.sleep.2010.11.012.

O'Connor, R.E., Bocian, K., Beebe-Frankenberger, M., & Linklater, D.L. (2010). Responsiveness of students with language difficulties to early intervention in reading. *Journal of Special Education, 43,* 220–235.

O'Shea, D.J., O'Shea, L.J., Algozzine, R., & Hammitte, D.J. (2001). *Families and teachers of individuals with disabilities.* Boston: Allyn and Bacon.

Odom, S. (2009).The tie that binds: Evidence-based practice, implementation science, and outcomes for children. *Topics in Early Childhood Special Education, 29*(1), 53–61. doi: 10.1177/0271121408329171

Odom, S.L., Brantlinger, E., Gersten, R. Horner, R.H., Thompson, B., Harris, K.H. (2005). Research in special education: Scientific methods and evidence-based practices. *Exceptional Children, 71*(2), 137–148.

Offit, P.A. (2008). *Autism's false prophets: Bad science, risky medicine, and the risk for a cure.* New York: Columbia University Press.

Ogilvie, C.R. (2011). Step by step: Social skills instruction for students with autism spectrum disorder using video models and peer mentors. *Teaching Exceptional Children, 43*(6), 20–27.

Olive, M.L., De la Cruz, B., Davis, T.N., Chan, J.M., Lang, R.B., O'Reilly, M.F., & Dickson, S.M. (2007). The effects of enhanced milieu teaching and a voice output communication aid on the requesting of three children with autism. *Journal of Autism and Developmental Disorders, 37,* 1505–1513.

Oller, D.K., & Eilers, R.E. (1982). Similarity of babbling in Spanish- and English-learning babies. *Journal of Child Language, 9,* 565–577.

Oller, D.K., Weiman, L.A., Doyle, W.J., & Ross, C. (1976). Infant babbling and speech. *Journal of Child Language, 3,* 1–11.

Olson, L. (2004). Enveloping expectations. Quality counts in 2004: Count me in: Special education in an era of standards. *Education Week, XXIII*(17), 8.

Omer, S.B., Salmon, D.A., Orenstein, W.A., deHart, M.P., & Halsey, N. (2009). Vaccine refusal, mandatory immunization, and the risks of vaccine-preventable diseases. *New England Journal of Medicine, 360,* 1981–1988.

Orosco, M.J. (2010). A sociocultural examination of Response to Intervention with Latino English-language learners. *Theory into Practice, 49,* 265–272.

Ortiz, A.A. & Yates, J.R. (2002). Considerations in the assessment of English language learners referred to special education. In A.J. Artiles & A.A. Ortiz, *English language learners with special education needs: Identification, assessment, and instruction* (pp. 65–86). McHenry, IL: Center for Applied Linguistics/Delta Systems Co.

Osberger, M.J., & Lane, H. (1993). The debate: Cochlear implants in children. *Hearing Health, 9*(2), 19–22.

Osborn, A. (1963). *Applied imagination.* New York: Scribners.

Ostrosky, M.M., Drasgow, E., & Halle, J.W. (1999). How can I help you get what you want? *Teaching Exceptional Children, 31*(4), 5–61.

Owen, L., & Dreker, L.A. (2003). How to spell success for secondary students labeled EBD: How students define effective teachers. *Beyond Behavior, 12*(2), 21.

Owen, R.L., & Fuchs, L.S. (2002). Mathematical problem-solving strategy instruction for third-grade students with learning disabilities. *Remedial and Special Education, 23,* 268–278.

Owen-DeSchryver, J.S., Carr, E.G., Cale, S.I., & Blakely-Smith, A. (2008). Promoting social interactions between students with autism spectrum disorders and their peers in inclusive school settings. *Focus on Autism and Other Developmental Disabilities, 23,* 15–28.

Owens, J. (2005). The ADHD and sleep conundrum: A review. *Journal of Developmental and Behavioral Pediatrics, 26,* 312–322.

Owens, R.E. (2008). *Language development: An introduction* (7th ed.). Boston: Allyn & Bacon.

Owens, R.E. (2010). *Language Disorders: A Functional Approach to Assessment and Intervention* (5th ed.). Boston: Allyn & Bacon.

Owens, R.E., Metz, D.E., & Haas, A. (2003). *Introduction to communication disorders: A life span perspective* (2nd ed.). Boston: Allyn and Bacon.

Ozgen, H., Hellemann, G.S., Stellato, R.K., Lahuis, B., van Daalen, E., Staal, W.G., Rozendal, M., Hennekam, R.C., Beemer, F.A., & van Engeland, H. (2011). Morphological features in children with autism spectrum disorders: A matched case-control study. *Journal of Autism and Developmental Disorders, 41,* 23–31.

Padden, C. & Humphries, T. (1988). *Deaf in America: Voices from a culture.* Cambridge, MA: Harvard University Press.

Padden, C. (1980). The deaf community and the culture of deaf people. In C. Baker & D. Cokely (Eds.), *Sign language and the deaf community: Essays in honor of William C. Stokoe* (pp. 89–103). Silver Spring, MD: National Association for the Deaf.

Padden, C.A., & Humphries, T.L. (2006). *Inside Deaf culture.* Cambridge, MA: Harvard University Press.

Parakeshwar, N., & Pargament, K.I. (2001). Religious coping in families of children with autism. *Focus on Autism and Other Developmental Disabilities, 16*(4), 14, 247.

Paralysis Resource Center (2011) http://www.christopherreeve.org/site/c.mtKZKgMWKwG/b.4451921/k.24E/Reeve_Foundations_Paralysis_Resource_Center.htm

Parette, P. (1999). Transition and assistive technology planning with families across cultures. *Career Development for Exceptional Individuals, 22,* 213–231.

Parette, P., & McMahan, G.A.(2002). What should we expect of assistive technology? Being sensitive to family goals. *Teaching Exceptional Children, 35*(1), 56–61.

Parish, S.L., Rose, R.A., Grinstein-Weiss, M., Richman, E.L., & Andrews, M.E. (2008). Material hardship in U.S. families raising children with disabilities. *Exceptional Children, 75*(1), 71–92.

Park, C.C. (1998). Exiting nirvana. *The American Scholar, 67*(2), 28–43.

Park, J., Turnbull, A.P., & Turnbull, H.R. (2002). Impacts of poverty on quality of life in families of children with disabilities. *Exceptional Children, 68*(2), 151–170.

Park, J.H., Alber-Morgan, S.R., & Fleming, C. (2011). Collaborating with parents to implement behavioral interventions for children with challenging behaviors. *Teaching Exceptional Children, 43,* 22–30.

Parker, J.K. (2010). *Teaching tech-savvy kids: Bringing digital media into the classroom, grades 5-12.* Thousand Oaks, CA: Corwin Press.

Patterson, D. (1987). The causes of Down syndrome. *Scientific American, 257*(2), 52–57.

Paul, P. V. (2008). *Language and deafness* (4th ed.). Sudbury, MA: Jones & Bartlett.

Paul, P.V. (2009). *Language and deafness* (4th ed.). Sudbury, MA: Jones & Bartlett.

Paulson, D., & Nicolle, C. (2004). Making Internet accessible for people with cognitive and communication impairment. *Universal Access in the Information Society, 3*, 48–56.

Pearls Project: www.positiveexposure.org Retrieved July 16, 2011.

Peckman, P.H., & Knutson, J.S. (2005). Functional electrical stimulation for neuromuscular applications. *Annual Review of Biomedical Engineering, 7*, 327–360.

PECS (Picture Exchange Communication System). http://pyramidproducts.com

Peeters, M., Cillessen, A.H.N., & Scholte, R.H.J. (2010). Clueless or powerful? Identifying subtypes of bullies in adolescence. *Journal of Youth Adolescence, 39*, 1041–1052.

Pena, E., Iglesias, A. & Lidz, C.S. (2001). Reducing test bias by dynamic assessment of children's word-learning ability. *American Journal of Speech-Language Pathology, 10*, 138–154.

Peña, E.D., & Bedore, L.M. (2009). Bilingualism in child language disorders. In R.G. Schwartz (Ed.), *Handbook of child language disorders*, (281–307). New York: Psychology Press.

Pennington, D.F., & Bishop, D.V.M. (2009). Relations among speech, language, and reading disorders. *Annual Review of Psychology, 60*, 283–306. doi: 10.1146/annurev.psych.60.110707.163548

Perla, F., & O'Donnell, B. (2002). Reaching out: Encouraging family involvement in orientation and mobility. *RE:view, 34*(3), 103–109.

Perren, S., & Alsaker, F.D. (2006). Social behavior and peer relationships of victims, bully-victims, and bullies in kindergarten. *Journal of Child Psychology and Psychiatry, 47*, 45–57.

Peterson, J., & Rischar, H. (2000). Gifted and gay: A study of the adolescent experience. *Gifted Child Quarterly, 44*, 231–246.

Peushel, S.M. (1991). Ethical considerations relating to prenatal diagnosis of fetuses with Down syndrome. *Mental Retardation, 29*, 185–190.

Pfeiffer, S.I., & Blei, S. (2008). Gifted education beyond the IQ test: Rating scales and other assessment procedures. In S.I. Pfeiffer (Ed.), *Handbook of giftedness in children* (pp. 177–198). New York: Springer.

Phillips, B.M., Clancy-Menchetti, J., & Lonigan, C.J. (2008). Successful phonological awareness instruction with preschool children. *Topics in Early Childhood Special Education, 28*(1), 3–17.

Picture Literacy Project at the University of Kansas (2003) Picture Reading Literacy Project. http://busboy.sped.ukans.edu.

Pignotti, M.S., & Donzelli, G. (2008). Perinatal care at the threshold of viability: An international comparison of practical guidelines for the treatment of extremely preterm births. *Pediatrics, 121*(1), 193–8.

Pintner, R., & Patterson, D. (1917). A comparison of deaf and hearing children in visual memory span for digits. *Journal of Experimental Psychology, 2*(2), 76–88.

Pivik, J., McComas, J., & LaFlamme, M. (2002). Barriers and facilitators to inclusive education. *Exceptional Children, 69*, 97–107.

Plomin, R., & Price, T.S. (2003). The relationship between genetics and intelligence. In N. Colangelo and G.A. Davis (Eds.), *Handbook of gifted education* (3rd ed.) (pp. 113–123). Boston: Allyn and Bacon.

Pogrund, R.L., & Fazzi, D.L. (Eds.) (2002). *Early focus: Working with young children who are blind or visually impaired and their families* (2nd ed.). New York: AFB Press.

Pollastri, A.R., Cardemil, E.V., & O'Donnell, E.H. (2010). Self-esteem in pure bullies and bully victims: A longitudinal analysis. *Journal of Interpersonal Violence, 25*, 1489–1502.

Polloway, E.A., & Patton, J.R. (1997). *Strategies for teaching learners with special needs* (5th ed.). Upper Saddle River, NJ: Merrill/Prentice Hall.

Polloway, E.A., Smith, J.D., Patton, J.R., & Smith, T.E.C. (1996). Historic changes in mental retardation and developmental disabilities. *Education and Training in Mental Retardation and Developmental Disabilities, 31*, 3–12.

Porter, A., McMaken, J., Hwang, J., & Yang, R. (2011). Common core standards: The new U.S. intended curriculum. *Educational Researcher, 40*(3), 103–116. doi: 10.3102/0013189X11405038

PositiveExposure: www.positiveexposure.org/about.html. Retrieved July 16, 2011.

Powell, S.R., Fuchs, L.S., & Fuchs, D. (2010). Embedding number-combinations practice within word-problem tutoring. *Intervention in School and Clinic 46*, 31–37.

Prater, L.P. (2002). African-American families: Equal partners in general and special education. In F.E. Obiakur & B.A. Ford (Eds.), *Creating successful learning environments for African-American learners with exceptionalities*. Thousand Oaks, CA: Corwin Press.

Prater, M.A., & Sileo, N.M. (2001). Using juvenile literature about HIV/AIDS: Ideas and precautions for the classroom. *Teaching Exceptional Children, 33*(6), 34–45.

Preciado, J.A., Horner, R.H., & Baker, S.K. (2009). Using a function-based approach to decrease problem behaviors and increase academic engagement for Latino English language learners. *Journal of Special Education, 42*, 227–240.

Presley, I. (2010). The impact of assistive technology: Assessment and instruction for children and youths with low vision. In A.L. Corn & J.N. Erin (Eds.), *Foundations of low vision: Clinical and functional perspectives* (2nd ed.), 589–654. New York: AFB Press.

Presley, J.A., & Hughes, C. (2000). Peers as teachers of anger management to high school students with behavioral disorders. *Behavioral Disorders, 25*, 114–130.

Prevent Blindness America (2011). Children's vision screening. Retrieved from: http://www.preventblindness.org/childrens-vision-screening/

Proly, J. L., Rivers, J., & Schwartz, J. (2009). Text comprehension: Graphic organizers to the rescue. *Perspectives on School-Based Issues, 10*, 82–89.

Pruher, L.W. (1994). Tips for working with a consultant. *RE:view, 25*(4), 174.

Pyryt, M.C. (2003). Technology and the gifted. In N. Colangelo and G.A. Davis (Eds.), *Handbook of gifted education* (3rd ed.) (pp. 584–589). Boston: Allyn and Bacon.

Quay, H.C., & Peterson, D.R. (1983). Behavior Problem Checklist: Revised. Coral Gables, FL: University of Miami.

Raina, P., et al. (2005). The health and well-being of caregivers of children with cerebral palsy. *Pediatrics, 115*, e626–e636.

Rais-Bahrami, K., & Short, B.L. (2007). Premature and small-for-dates infants. In M.L. Batshaw, L. Pellegrino, & N.J. Roizen (Eds.), *Children with Disabilities*, (6th ed.). Baltimore: Paul H. Brookes.

Ranshaw, H.S., Woodcock, J.M., Bagley, C.J., McClure, B.J., Heraus, T.R., & Lopez, A.F. (2001). New approaches in the treatment of asthma. *Immunology and Cell Biology, 79*, 154–162.

Rapport, M.K., McWilliam, R.A., & Smith, B.J. (2004). Practices across disciplines in early intervention: The research base. *Infants and Young Children, 17*, 32–44.

Raskind, M.H., Goldberg, R.J., Higgins, E.L., & Herman, K.L. (1999). Patterns of change and predictors of success in individuals with learning disabilities: Results from a twenty-year longitudinal study. *Learning Disabilities Research and Practice, 14*, 35–49.

Raths, L.E., Wassermann, S., Jonas, A., & Rothstein, A. (1986). *Teaching for thinking*. New York: Teachers College Press.

Ratner, V., & Harris, L. (1994). *Understanding language disorders: The impact on learning*. Eau Claire, WI: Thinking Publications.

Ravitch, D. (2003). *The language police: How pressure groups restrict what students learn.* New York: Alfred A. Knopf.

Rea, P.J., McLaughlin, V.L., & Walther-Thomas, C. (2002). Outcomes for students with learning disabilities in inclusive and pullout programs. *Exceptional Children, 68*(2), 203–222.

Rea, P.J., & Connell, J. (2005, Sept.). Minding the fine points of co-teaching. *Education Digest 7*(1), 29–35.

Reichard, A. (1995). The value of prenatal testing. *Exceptional Parent, 25*(8), 29–31.

Reichenberg, A., Gross, R., Weiser, M., Bresnahan, M., Silverman, J., Harlap, S., Rabinowitz, J., Shulman, C., Malaspina, D., Lubin, G., Knobler, H.Y., Davidson, M., & Susser, E. (2006). Advancing paternal age and autism. *Archives of General Psychiatry, 63,* 1026–1032.

Reichman, N.E. (2005). Low birth weight and school readiness. *The Future of Children, 15*(1), 91–116. Retrieved from: www.futureofchildren.org.

Reid, D.H., Everson, J.M., & Green, C.W. (1999). A systematic evaluation of preferences identified through person-centered planning for people with profound multiple disabilities. *Journal of Applied Behavior Analysis, 32,* 467–477.

Reid, D.K. (2000). Discourse in classrooms. In K.R. Fahey & D.K. Reid (Eds.). *Language development, differences, and disorders* (pp. 31–38). Austin, TX: Pro-Ed.

———. (2000). Ebonics and Hispanic, Asian, and Native American dialects of English. In K.R. Fahey & D.K. Reid (Eds.), *Language development, differences, and disorders* (pp. 219–244). Austin, TX: Pro-Ed.

Reid, R., Riccio, C.A., Kessler, R.H., DuPaul, G.J., Anastopoulos, A.D., Rogers-Adkinson, D., & Noll, M.B. (2000). Gender and ethnic differences in ADHD as assessed by behavior ratings. *Journal of Emotional and Behavioral Disorders, 8,* 38–48.

Reis, S.M. & Renzulli, J.M. (2010). Is there still a need for gifted education? An examination of current research. *Learning and Individual Differences, 20*(4), 308–317.

Reis, S.M., & Hébert, T.P. (2008). Gender and giftedness. In S.I. Pfeiffer (Ed.), *Handbook of giftedness in children* (pp. 271–291). New York: Springer.

Reis, S.M., & McCoach, D.B. (2000). The underachievement of gifted students: What do we know and where do we go? *Gifted Child Quarterly, 44*(3), 152–170.

Reis, S.M., McGuire, J.M., & Neu, T.W. (2000). Compensation strategies used by high-ability students with learning disabilities who succeed in college. *Gifted Child Quarterly, 44*(2), 123–134.

Reis, S.M., Neu, T.W., & McGuire, J.M. (1995). *Talent in two places: Case studies of high ability students with learning*

disabilities who have achieved. Storrs, CT: University of Connecticut, the National Research Center on the Gifted and Talented.

———. (1997). Case studies of high-ability students with learning disabilities who have achieved. *Exceptional Children, 63*(4), 463–479.

Renner, P., Klinger, L.G., & Klinger, M.R. (2000). Implicit and explicit memory in autism: Is autism an amnesic disorder? *Journal of Autism and Developmental Disorders, 30,* 3–14.

Renzulli, J.S. (1978). What makes giftedness? *Phi Delta Kappan, 60,* 180–184.

Renzulli, J.S. (2011). More changes needed to expand gifted identification and support. *Phi Delta Kappan, (92)*8, 61.

Renzulli, J.S., & Reis, S.M. (2003). The Schoolwide Enrichment Model: Developing creative and productive giftedness. In N. Colangelo and G.A. Davis (Eds.), *Handbook of gifted education* (3rd ed.) (pp. 184–203). Boston: Allyn and Bacon.

Renzulli, J.S., & Reis, S.M. (2008). *Enriching curriculum for all students* (2nd ed.). Thousand Oaks, CA: Corwin Press.

Rescorla, L. (2009). Age 17 language and reading outcomes in late-talking toddlers: Support for a dimensional perspective on language delay. *Journal of Speech, Language, and Hearing Research 52,* 16–30. doi:10.1044/1092-4388(2008/07-0171)

Rett Syndrome Research Trust: http://www.rsrt.org/about-Rett/prevelance-of-Rett-and-related-disorders.html Retrieved July 20, 2011.

Rimland, B. (1964). *Infantile autism: The syndrome and its implication for a neural theory of behavior.* Englewood Cliffs, NJ: Prentice-Hall.

Rimm, S.B. (2003). Underachievement: A national epidemic. In N. Colangelo and G.A. Davis (Eds.), *Handbook of gifted education* (3rd ed.) (pp. 424–443). Boston: Allyn and Bacon.

Risdal, D., & Singer, G.H.S. (2004). Marital adjustment in parents of children with disabilities: A historical review and meta-analysis. *Research and Practice for Persons with Severe Disabilities, 29*(2), pp. 95–103.

Rivers, J.W., & Stoneman, Z. (2003). Sibling relationships when a child has autism: Marital stress and support coping. *Journal of Autism and Developmental Disorders, 33*(4), 383–394.

Roberts, C.D., Stough, L.M., & Parrish, L.H. (2002). The role of genetic counseling in the elective termination of pregnancies involving fetuses with disabilities. *Journal of Special Education, 36,* 48–55.

Robins, D., Fein, D., Barton, M. (1999). *The Modified Checklist for Autism in Toddlers (M-CHAT).* Storrs, CT: University of Connecticut.

Robinson, A. (1990). Cooperation or exploitation? The argument against cooperative learning for talented students. *Journal for the Education of the Gifted, 14*(1), 9–27.

———. (2003). Cooperative learning and high ability students. In N. Colangelo and G.A. Davis (Eds.), *Handbook of gifted education* (3rd ed.) (pp. 282–292). Boston: Allyn and Bacon.

Robinson, A., & Clinkenbeard, P.R. (2008). History of giftedness: Perspectives from the past presage modern scholarship. In S.I. Pfeiffer (Ed.), *Handbook of giftedness in children* (pp. 13–31). New York: Springer.

Robinson, A., Shore, B.M., & Enersen, D.L. (2007). *Best practices in gifted education: An evidence-based guide.* Waco, TX: Prufrock Press.

Robinson, N. (2008). The social world of gifted children and youth. In S.I. Pfeiffer (Ed.), *Handbook of giftedness in children* (pp. 33–51). New York: Springer.

Rogers, K. B. (2007). Lessons learned about educating the gifted and talented: A synthesis of the research on educational practice. *Gifted Child Quarterly; 51*(382). doi: 10.1177/0016986207306324

Rosen, L.A., Gabardi, L., Miller, C.D., & Miller, L. (1990). Home-based treatment of disruptive junior high school students: An analysis of the differential effects of positive and negative consequences. *Behavioral Disorders, 15,* 227–232.

Rosen, S. (2010). Kinesiology and sensory functioning for students with vision loss. In W.R. Wiener, R.L. Welsch, & B.B. Blasch (Eds.), *Foundations of Orientation and Mobility,* Vol. 1, (3rd ed.) 169–171. New York: AFB Press.

Rosenshine, B., & Stevens, R. (1986). Teaching functions. In M.C. Wittrock (Ed.), *Handbook of research on teaching* (3rd ed.) (pp. 376–391). New York: Macmillan.

Rothenberg, L. (2003). *Breathing for a living.* New York: Hyperion.

Russell, M., Hoffmann, T., & Higgins, J. (2009). NimbleTools: A universally designed test delivery system. *Teaching Exceptional Children, 42*(2), 6–20.

Ryan, J.B., Pierce, C.D., & Mooney, P. (2008). Evidence-based teaching strategies for students with EBD. *Beyond Behavior, 17*(3), 22–29.

Rylance, B.J. (1998). Predictors of post–high school employment for youth identified as severely emotionally disturbed. *Journal of Special Education, 32,* 184–192.

Sacks, S.Z. (2010). Psychological and social implications of low vision. In A. L. Corn & J. Erin (Eds.), *Foundations of low vision: Clinical and functional perspectives* (2nd ed., pp. 67–96). New York: AFB Press.

Sacks, S.Z., & Silberman, R.K. (2000). Social skills. In A.J. Koenig and M.C. Holbrook (Eds.), *Foundations of Education: Vol. II* (2nd ed.), (pp. 616–652). New York: American Foundation for the Blind.

Sacks, S.Z., & Wolffe, K.E. (Eds.) (2006). *Teaching social skills to students with visual impairments: From theory to practice.* New York: AFB Press.

Sadker, D., & Zittleman, K.R. (2009). *Still failing at fairness: How gender bias cheats girls and boys in school and what we can do about it.* New York, NY: Simon & Schuster.

Sadker, M., & Sadker, D. (1994). *Failing at fairness: How America's schools cheat girls.* New York: Charles Scribner's Sons.

Saenz, L.M., Fuchs, L.S., & Fuchs, D. (2005). Peer-assisted learning strategies for English language learners with learning disabilities. *Exceptional Children, 71*(3), 231–247.

Safran, J.S. (2002). Supporting students with Asperger's Syndrome in general education. *Teaching Exceptional Children, 34*(5), 60–66.

Saha, S., Barnett, A.G., Foldi, C., Burnel, T.H., Eyles, D.W., Buka, S.L., & McGrath, J.J. (2009). Advanced paternal age is associated with impaired neurocognitive outcomes during infancy and childhood. *PLoS Medicine, 6*(3): e1000040. doi:10.1371/journal.pmed.1000040.

Salvia, J., Ysseldyke, J., & Bolt, S. (2009). *Assessment in special and inclusive education* (11th ed.). Stamford, CT: Cengage.

Sameroff, A.J.(2010). A unified theory of development: A dialectic integration of nature and nurture. *Child Development, 81*(1), pages 6–22.

Sandberg*, K. & Reschly, A.L. (2010). Curriculum-Based Measurement and English Learners: A review of the literature. *Remedial & Special Education. OnlineFirst.* DOI: 10.1177/0741932510361260

Sandberg, K.L., & Reschly, A.L. (2010). English Learners: Challenges in assessment and the promise of Curriculum-Based Measurement. *Remedial and Special Education, 32*, 144–154.

Sandmel, K.N., Brindle, M., Harris, K.R., Lane, K.L., Graham, S., Nackel, J., Mathias, R., & Little, A. (2009). Making it work: Differentiating tier two self-regulated strategies development in writing in tandem with schoolwide positive behavioral support. *Teaching Exceptional Children, 42*, 22–33.

Sapp W., & Hatlen, P. (2010). The Expanded Core Curriculum: Where we have been, where we are going, and how we can get there. *Journal of Visual Impairment & Blindness, (104)*6, 338–348.

Sartorius, G.A., & Nieschlag, E. (2010). Paternal age and reproduction. *Human Reproduction Update 16*(1), 65–79. Epub. Review. PMID: 19696093

Scanlon, D., & Mellard, D.F. (2002). Academic participation profiles of school-age dropouts with and without disabilities. *Exceptional Children, 68,* 239–257.

Scarborough, H. (2001). Connecting early language and literacy to later reading (dis)abilities: Evidence, theory, and practice. In S.B. Neumann & D.K. Dickinson (Eds.), *Handbook of early literacy research.* New York: Guilford Press.

Schickendanz, J.A., & Casbergue, R.M.(2009). *Writing in preschool: Learning to orchestrate meaning and marks.* Newark, DE: International Reading Association.

Schleper, David R. (2000). Fingerspelling: Critical for literacy development. *Odyssey,* Summer, p. 10.

Schlosser, R.W., & Raghavendra, P. (2004). Evidence-based practice in augmentative and alternative communication. *Augmentative and Alternative Communication, 20,* 1–21.

Schonberg, R.L., & Tifft, C.J. (2007). Birth defects and prenatal diagnosis. In M.L. Batshaw, L. Pellegrino, & N.J. Roizen (Eds.). *Children with disabilities* (6th ed.). Baltimore: Paul H. Brookes.

Schroeder, S.R. (2000). Mental retardation and developmental disabilities influenced by environmental neurotoxic insults. *Environmental health perspectives, 108* (Suppl 3), 395–399.

Schultz, R.A., & Delisle, J.R. (2003). Gifted adolescents. In N. Colangelo and G.A. Davis (Eds.), *Handbook of gifted education* (3rd ed.) (pp. 483–492). Boston: Allyn and Bacon.

Schumaker, J.B., & Hazel, J.S. (1984). Social skills assessment and training for the learning disabled: What's on second? Part I. *Journal of Learning Disabilities, 17,* 422–431.

Schwartz, T. (2010). Causes of visual impairment: Pathology and its implications. In A.L. Corn & J.N. Erin (Eds.), *Foundations of low vision: Clinical and functional perspectives* (2nd ed.), 137–191. New York: AFB Press.

Scorgie, K., Wilgosh, L., & McDonald, L. (1999). Transforming partnerships: Parents' life management issues when a child has mental retardation. *Education and Training in Mental Retardation and Developmental Disabilities, 34,* 395–405.

Scott, J., Clark, C, & Brady, M. (2000). *Student with autism: Characteristics and instructional programming.* San Diego, CA: Singular.

Scott, T.M., Liaupsin, C.J., Nelson, C.M., & Jolivette, K. (2003). Ensuring student success through team-based functional behavioral assessment. *Teaching Exceptional Children, 35*(5), 16–21.

Scruggs, T., Mastropieri, M., & McDuffie, K. (2007). Co-teaching in inclusive classrooms: A metasynthesis of qualitative research. *Exceptional Children, 73*(4), 392–416.

Scruggs, T.E., & Mastropieri, M.A. (1996). Teacher perceptions of mainstreaming/inclusion, 1958–1995: A research synthesis. *Exceptional Children, 63*(1), 59–74.

Scruggs, T.E., & Mastropieri, M.A. (2001). Mnemonic interventions for students with behavior disorders. *Beyond Behavior, 10*(1), 13–17.

Scudder, R.R., & Tremain, D.H. (1992). Repair behaviors of students with and without mental retardation. *Mental Retardation, 30,* 277–282.

Secada, W., Fennema, E., & Adajian, L.B. (1995). *New directions for equity in mathematics education.* New York: Cambridge University Press.

Seligman, M., & Darling, R.B. (2007). *Ordinary families, special children* (3rd ed.). New York: Guilford Press.

Seo, Y., Abbott, R.D., & Hawkins, J.D. (2008). Outcome states of students with learning disabilities at ages 21–24. *Journal of Learning Disabilities, 41,* 300–314.

Serna, L., Nielsen, E., Lambros, K., & Forness, S. (2000). Primary prevention with children at risk for emotional or behavioral disorders: Data on a universal intervention for Head Start Classrooms. *Behavioral Disorders, 26,* 70–84.

Severson, H.H., Walker, H.M., Hope-Dolittle, J., Kratochwill, T.R., & Gresham, F.M. (2007). Proactive, early screening to detect behaviorally at-risk students: Issues, approaches, emerging innovations, and professional practices. *Journal of School Psychology, 45,* 193–223.

Shah, N. (2011). Alternate-test rules ripe for revision in next ESEA. *Education Week,* Retrieved from: http://www.edweek.org/ew/articles/2011/03/09/23testing.h30.html?qs=alternate+assessment

Shalev, R.S., Manor, O., Kerem, B., Ayali, M., Badichi, N., Friedlander, Y., & Gross-Tsur, V. (2001). Developmental dyscalculia is a familial learning disability. *Journal of Learning Disabilities, 34,* 59–65.

Shapiro, D.R., & Sayers, L.K. (2003). Who does what on the interdisciplinary team? *Teaching Exceptional Children, 35*(6), 32–38.

Shaver, D., Newman, L., Huang, T., Yu, J., Knokey, A.M., & SRI International (2011). *Facts from NLTS2: The secondary experiences and academic performance of students with hearing impairments.* Washington, DC: Institute of Education Sciences, U.S. Department of Education. Retrieved from: http://www.nlts2.org/fact_sheets/2011_02.html

Shaywitz, S.E., & Shaywitz, B.A. (2001). The neurobiology of reading and dyslexia. *Focus on Basics, 5,* Issue A. Retrieved online at: http://ncsall.gse.harvard.edu/fob/2001/Shaywitz.html

Shaywitz, S.E., & Shaywitz, B.A. (2008). Paying attention to reading: The neurobiology of reading and dyslexia. *Development and Psychopathology, 20,* 1329–1349.

Shifter, L. (2011). High school graduation of students with disabilities: How long does it take? *Exceptional Children, 77,* 409–422.

Shin, H.B., & Kominski, R.A. (2010). *Language use in the United States: 2007.* Washington, DC: U.S. Census Bureau, Department of Commerce.

Shonkoff, J.P. (2010). Building a new biodevelopmental framework to guide the future of early childhood policy. *Child Development, 81*(1), 357–367.

Siegel-Causey, E., McMorris, C., McGowen, S., & Sands-Buss, S. (1998). In Junior High you take Earth Science: Including a student with severe disabilities into an academic class. *Teaching Exceptional Children, 31*(1), 66–72.

Sienkiewicz-Mercer, R., & Kaplan, S.B. (1989). *I raise my eyes to say yes.* Boston: Houghton Mifflin.

Sigafoos, J. (2000). Communication development and aberrant behavior in children with developmental disabilities. *Education and Training in Mental Retardation and Developmental Disabilities, 35,* 168–176.

Silberman, R.K. (2000). Children and youths with visual impairments and other disabilities. In M.C. Holbrook and A.J. Koenig (Eds.), *Foundations of Education: Vol.1* (2nd ed., pp. 173–196). New York: American Foundation for the Blind.

Silberman, R.K. (2000). Children and youths with visual impairments and other disabilities. In M.C. Holbrook and A.J. Koenig (Eds.), *Foundations of Education: Vol.1* (2nd ed., pp. 173–196). New York: American Foundation for the Blind.

Simmons, D., Coyne, M.D., Hagan-Burke, S., Kwok, O., Simmons, L., Johnson, C., Zou, Y., Taylor, A.B., McAlenney, A.L., Ruby, M., & Crevecoeur, Y.C. (2011). Effects of supplemental reading interventions in authentic contexts: A comparison of kindergartners' response. *Exceptional Children, 77,* 207–228.

Simmons, D.C., Kameenui, E.J., Horn, B., Coyne, M.D., Stoolmiller, M., Santoro, L.E., Smith, S.B., Beck, C.T., & Kaufman, N.K. (2007). Attributes of effective and efficient kindergarten reading intervention: An examination of instructional time and design specificity. *Journal of Learning Disabilities, 40,* 331–347.

Simon, C.S. (1991). Functional flexibility: Developing communicative competence in speaker and listener roles. In C.S. Simon (Ed.). Communication skills and classroom success: Assessment and therapy methodologies for language-learning disabled students. Eau Claire, WI: Thinking Publications.

Simonoff, E., Pickles, A., Charman, T., Chandler, S., Loucas, T., & Baird, G. (2008). Psychiatric disorders in children with autism spectrum disorders: Prevalence, co-morbidity, and associated factors in a population-derived sample. *Child and Adolescent Psychiatry, 47,* 921–929.

Simonsen, B., Fairbanks, S., Briesch, A., Myers, D., & Sugai, G. (2008). Evidence-based practices in classroom management: Considerations for research to practice. *Education and Treatment of Children, 31,* 351–380.

Simos, P.G., Fletcher, J.M., Sarkari, S., Billingsley-Marshall, R., Denton, C.A., & Papanicolaou, A.C. (2007). Intensive instruction affects brain magnetic activity associated with oral word reading in children with persistent reading disabilities. *Journal of Learning Disabilities, 40,* 37–48.

Simpson, R.L. (2005). Evidence-based practices and students with autism spectrum disorders. *Focus on Autism and Other Developmental Disabilities, 20,* 140–149.

Simpson, R.L., & Souris, L.A. (1988). Reciprocity in the pupil-teacher interactions of autistic and mildly handicapped preschool children. *Behavioral Disorders, 13,* 159–168.

Singer, L.T., Arendt, R., Minnes, S., Farkas, K., Salvator, A., Kirchner, H.L., & Kliegman, R. (2002). Cognitive and motor outcomes of cocaine-exposed infants. *JAMA, 287*(15), 1952–1960.

Singer, P. (1996). *Rethinking life and death: The collapse of our traditional ethics* (2nd ed.). New York: St. Martin's Press.

Singleton, D.K., Schuster, J.W., Morse, T.E., & Collins, B.C. (1999). A comparison of antecedent prompt and test and simultaneous prompting procedures in teaching grocery words to adolescents with mental retardation. *Education and Training in Mental Retardation and Developmental Disabilities, 34,* 182–199.

Siperstein, G.N., Leffert, J.S., & Widaman, K. (1996). Social behavior and the social acceptance and rejection of children with mental retardation. *Education and Training in Mental Retardation and Developmental Disabilities, 31,* 271–281.

Skiba, R.J., Horner, R.H., Chung, C.G., Rausch, M.K., May, S.L., & Tobin, T. (2011). Race is not neutral: A national investigation of African American and Latino disproportionality in school discipline. *School Psychology Review, 40,* 85–107.

Skiba, R., Simmons, A.B., Ritter, S., Gibb, A.C., Rausch, M.K., Cuadaob, J., & Chung, C. (2008). Achieving equity in special education: History, status, and current challenges. *Exceptional Children, 74,* 264–288.

Skiba, R.J. (2008). *Changing the data, changing our minds: Disproportionality and improving schools.* Presented at the OSEP Project Directors' Conference, Washington, D.C.

Skiba, R.J., Simmons, A.B., Ritter, S., Gibb, A.C., Rausch, M.K., Cuadrado, J., & Chung, C.G. (2008). Achieving equity in special education: History, status, and current challenges. *Exceptional Children, 74*(3), 264–288

Skinner, D. et al. (1999). Narrating self and disabilities Latino mothers' construction of identities vis-à-vis their child with special needs. *Exceptional Children, 65,* 481–495.

Slavin, R.E. (1990). Ability grouping, cooperative learning and the gifted. *Journal for the Education of the Gifted, 14*(1), 3–8.

Smedley, A. (2007). *Race in North America: Origin and evolution of a world* view (3rd ed.). Boulder, CO: Westview Press.

Smith, J.D. (1989). On the right of children with mental retardation to life-sustaining medical care and treatment: A position statement. *Education and Training in Mental Retardation, 24,* 3–6.

Smith, L.E., Hong, J., Seltzer, M.M., Greenberg, J.S., Almeida, D.M., Bishop, S.L. (2010). Daily experiences among mothers of adolescents and adults with Autism Spectrum Disorder. *Journal of Autism and Developmental Disorders.* DOI 10.1007/s10803-009-0844-y.

Smith, T., & Lovaas, O.L. (1997). The UCLA young autism project: A reply to Gresham and MacMillan. *Behavioral Disorders, 22,* 202–218.

Smith, T.E.C., Finn, D.M., & Dowdy, C.A. (1993). *Teaching students with mild disabilities.* Orlando, FL: Harcourt Brace Jovanovich.

Smokowski, P.R., & Kopasz, K.H. (2005). Bullying in school: An overview of types, effects, family characteristics, and intervention strategies. *Children and Schools, 27,* 101–110.

Snell, M.E. (1988). Curriculum and methodology for individuals with severe disabilities. *Education and Training in Mental Retardation, 23,* 302–314.

Snell, M.E., & Brown, F. (2000). *Instruction of students with severe disabilities* (5th ed.). Columbus, OH: Merrill.

Snell, M.E., & Drake, G.P. (1994). Replacing cascades with supported education. *Journal of Special Education, 27,* 393–409.

Snell, M.E., & Janney, R.E. (2000). Teachers' problem-solving about children with moderate and severe disabilities in elementary classrooms. *Exceptional Children, 66,* 472–490.

Snider, V.E. (1997). Transfer of decoding skills to a literature basal. *Learning Disabilities Research and Practice, 12,* 54–62.

Snow, C.E., Burns, M.S., & Griffin, P. (Eds.). (1998). *Preventing reading difficulties in young children.* Washington, DC: National Academy Press.

Solomon, G., Allen, N.J., & Resta, P. (Eds.) (2003). *Toward digital equity: Bridging the divide in education.* Boston: Allyn and Bacon

Son, S-H., Sigafoos, J., O'Reilly, M., & Lancioni, G.E. (2006). Comparing two types of augmentative and alternative communication systems for children with autism. *Developmental Neurorehabilitation, 9*, 389–395.

Sonnier-York, C., & Stanford, P. (2002). Learning to cooperate: A teacher's perspective. *Teaching Exceptional Children, 34*, 40–45.

Spencer, K.C., & Sands, D.J. (1999). Prediction of student participation in transition-related actions. *Education and Training in Mental Retardation and Developmental Disabilities, 34*, 473–484.

Spencer, P.E. (2010). Play and theory of mind: Indicators and engines of early cognitive growth. In. In M. Marschark & P.E. Spencer (Eds.), *The Oxford Handbook of Deaf Studies, Language, and Education* (Vol.1, 2nd ed.), pp. 407–424. New York: Oxford University Press.

Spencer, S.A. (2005). An interview with Dr. Lynne Cook and Dr. June Downing: The practicalities of collaboration in special education service delivery. *Intervention in School and Clinic, 40*, 296–300.

Spencer, T.D., Peterson, D.B., & Gillam, S.L. (2008). Picture Exchange Communication System (PECS) or Sign Language: An evidence-based decision-making example. *Teaching Exceptional Children, 41*(2), 40–49.

Spencer, V.G., Simpson, C.G., & Lynch, S.A. (2008). Using social stories to increase positive behaviors for children with autism spectrum disorders. *Intervention in School and Clinic, 44*, 58–61.

Spina Bifida Association (SBAA): www.spinabifidaassociation.org: Retrieved July 15, 2011.

Sprague, J., & Walker, H. (2000). Early identification and intervention for youth with antisocial and violent behavior. *Exceptional Children, 66*, 367–379.

Spungin, S. (Ed.) (2002). *When you have a blind or visually impaired child in your classroom: A guide for teachers.* New York: AFB Press.

Sternberg, R.J. & Grigorenko, E.L. (2000). *Teaching for successful intelligence.* Arlington Heights, IL: Skylight Training and Publishing Inc.

Stafford, A., Alberto, P.A., Fredrick, L.D., Heflin, L.J., & Heller, K.W. (2002). Preference variability and the instruction of choice making with students with severe intellectual disabilities. *Education and Training in Mental Retardation and Mental Disabilities, 37*, 70–88.

Stainback, G.H., Stainback, W.C., & Stainback, S.B. (1988). Superintendents' attitudes toward integration. *Education and Training in Mental Retardation, 23*, 92–96.

Stainback, S., Stainback, W., & Ayres, B. (1996). Schools as inclusive communities. In W. Stainback & S. Stainback (Eds.), *Controversial issues confronting special education: Divergent perspectives* (2nd ed.) (pp. 31–43). Boston: Allyn and Bacon.

Stecker, P.M., & Fuchs, L.S. (2000). Effecting superior achievement using curriculum-based measurement: The importance of individual progress monitoring. *Learning Disabilities Research and Practice, 15*, 128–134.

Stecker, P.M., Fuchs, L.S., & Fuchs, D. (2005). Using curriculum-based measurement to improve student achievement: Review of research. *Psychology in the Schools, 42*(8), 795–819.

Steere, D.E., & Cavaiuolo, D. (2002). Connecting outcomes, goals, and objectives in transition planning. *Teaching Exceptional Children, 34*(6), 54–59.

Stein, M., & Davis, C.A. (2000). Direct instruction as a positive behavioral support. *Beyond Behavior, 10*, 7–12.

Stephenson, J.R., & Dowrick, M. (2000). Parent priorities in communication intervention for young students with severe disabilities. *Education and Training in Mental Retardation and Developmental Disabilities, 35*, 25–35.

Sterling, L., Dawson, G., Estes, A., & Greenson, J. (2008). Characteristics associated with presence of depressive symptoms in adults with autism spectrum disorder. *Journal of Autism and Developmental Disorders, 38*, 1011–1018.

Sternberg, R.J. (2007). Who are the bright children? The cultural context of being and acting intelligent. *Educational Researcher, 36*(3), pp. 148–155.

Sternberg, R.J. (1985). *Beyond IQ: A triarchic theory of human intelligence.* New York, NY: Cambridge University Press.

Sternberg, R.J. (1991). Giftedness according to the triarchic theory of human intelligence. In N. Colangelo & G.A. Davis (Eds.), *Handbook of gifted education* (pp. 45–54). Boston: Allyn and Bacon.

———. (2003). Giftedness according to the theory of successful intelligence. In N. Colangelo and G.A. Davis (Eds.), *Handbook of gifted education* (3rd ed.) (pp. 88–99). Boston: Allyn and Bacon.

Sternberg, R.J. (1997). What does it mean to be smart? *Educational Leadership, 54*(6), 16–20.

Sternberg, R.J. (2009a) The theory of successful intelligence. In J.C. Kaufman & E.L. Grigorenko (Eds.), *The Essential Sternberg: Essays on Intelligence, Psychology, and Education,* 71–100. New York: Springer.

Sternberg, R.J. (2009b) Toward a triarchic theory of human intelligence. In J.C. Kaufman & E.L. Grigorenko (Eds.). *The Essential Sternberg: Essays on Intelligence, Psychology, and Education,* 33–70. New York: Springer.

Sternberg, R.J., Jarvin, L., & Grigorenko, E.L. (2009). *Teaching for wisdom, intelligence, creativity, and success.* Thousand Oaks, CA: Corwin Press.

Sternberg, R.J., Jarvin, L., & Grigorenko, E.L. (2011). *Explorations in giftedness.* New York: Cambridge University Press.

Stewart, D.A., & Kluwin, T.N. (2001). *Teaching deaf and hard of hearing students: Content, strategies, and curriculum.* Boston: Allyn and Bacon.

Sticken, J., & Kapperman, G. (2010). Integration of visual skills for independent living. In M.C. Holbrook and A.J. Koenig (Eds.), *Foundations of Education: Vol.1* (2nd ed., pp. 97–110). New York: American Foundation for the Blind.

Stiegler, L.N., & Davis, R. (2010). Understanding sound sensitivity in individuals with autism spectrum disorders. *Focus on Autism and Other Developmental Disabilities, 25*, 67–75.

Stokoe, W. (1960). Sign language structure: An outline of the visual communication system of the American deaf. *Studies in Linguistics Occasional Papers No. 8.* Washington, DC: Gallaudet College Press.

Stone, W.L., Coonrod, E.E., Turner, L.M., & Pozdol, S.L. (2004). Psychometric properties of the STAT for Early Autism Screening. *Journal of Autism and Developmental Disorders, 34*, 691–701.

Stoneman, Z. (2005). Siblings of children with disabilities: Research Themes. *Mental Retardation, 43*, 339–350.

Stoneman, Z. et al. (1988). Childcare responsibilities, peer relations, and sibling conflict: Older siblings of mentally retarded children. American Journal of *Mental Retardation, 93*, 174–183.

Stop Bullying, 2011 http://www.stopbullying.gov/

Storey, K., & Provost, O. (1996). The effect of communication skills instruction on the integration of workers with severe disabilities in supported employment settings. *Education and Training in Mental Retardation and Developmental Disabilities, 31*, 123–141.

Stotland, J. (1984). Relationships of parents to professionals: A challenge to professionals. *Journal of Visual Impairment and Blindness, 78*(2), pp. 69–74.

Strauss, et al. (1999). Causes of excessive mortality in cerebral palsy. *Developmental Medicine and Child Neurology, 9*, 580–585.

Stromer, R., Kimball, J.W., Kinney, E.M., & Tayor, B.A. (2006). Activity schedules, computer technology, and teaching children with autism spectrum disorders. *Focus on Autism and Other Developmental Disabilities, 21*, 14–24.

Strong, K., & Sandoval, J. (1999). Mainstreaming children with a neuromuscular disease: A map of concerns. *Exceptional Children, 65,* 353–366.

Strunk, J.A. (2010). Respite care for families of special needs children: A systematic review. *Journal of Developmental and Physical Disabilities, 22*(6), 615–630.

Sullivan, A.L. (2011). Disproportionality in special education: Identification and placement of English language learners. *Exceptional Children, 7*(3), 317–334.

Sullivan, C.A.C., Vitello, S.J., & Foster, W. (1988). Adaptive behavior of adults with mental retardation in a group home: An intensive case study. *Education and Training in Mental Retardation, 23,* 76–81.

Sulzer-Azaroff, B., Hoffman, A.D., Horton, C.B., Bondy, A., & Frost, L. (2009). The Picture Exchange Communication System (PECS): What do the data say? *Focus on Autism and Other Developmental Disabilities, 24,* 89–103.

Summers, J.A., Behr, S.K., & Turnbull, A.P. (1989). Positive adaptation and coping strengths of families who have children with disabilities. In G.H.S. Singer & L.K. Irvin (Eds.), *Support for caregiving families* (pp. 27–40). Baltimore: Paul H. Brookes.

Sundqvist, A., & Ronnberg, J. (2010). A qualitative analysis of email interactions of children who use augmentative and alternative communication. *Augmentative and Alternative Communication, 26,* 255–266.

Sutherland, K.S., Lewis-Palmer, T., Stichter, J., & Morgan, P.L. (2008). Examining the influence of teacher behavior and classroom context on the behavioral and academic outcomes for students with emotional or behavioral disorders. *Journal of Special Education, 41,* 223–233.

Sutherland, K.S., Wehby, J.H., & Yoder, P.J. (2002). Examination of the relationship between teacher praise and opportunities for students with EBD to respond to academic requests. *Journal of Emotional and Behavior Disorders, 10,* 1–19.

Swanson, H.L., Cochran, K.F., & Ewers, C.A. (1990). Can learning disabilities be determined from working memory performance? *Journal of Learning Disabilities, 23,* 59–67.

Swanson, H.L. (1993). Principles and procedures in strategy use. In L.J. Meltzer (Ed.), *Strategy assessment and instruction for students with learning disabilities* (pp. 61–92). Austin, TX: Pro-Ed.

———. (1999). Instructional components that predict treatment outcomes for students with learning disabilities: Support for a combined strategy and direct instruction model. *Learning Disabilities Research and Practice, 14*(3) 129–140.

Swanson, H.L., Cochran, K.F., & Ewers, C.A. (1990). Can learning disabilities be determined from working memory performance? *Journal of Learning Disabilities, 23,* 59–67.

Systematic Screening for Behavior Disorders—SSBD (1992).

Szabo, J.L. (2000). Maddie's story: Inclusion through physical and occupational therapy. *Teaching Exceptional Children, 33*(2), 12–18.

Tannenbaum, A.J. (2003). Nature and nurture of giftedness. In N. Colangelo and G.A. Davis (Eds.), *Handbook of gifted education* (3rd ed.) (pp. 45–59). Boston: Allyn and Bacon.

TASH (The Association for Individuals with Severe Handicaps). (2000). TASH Resolutions and Policy Statement. http:www.TASH.org. Retrieved June 2003.

Taylor, B.A., & McDonough, K.A. (1996). Selecting teaching programs. In C. Maurice, G. Green, & S.C. Luce (Eds.), *Behavioral intervention for young children with autism: A manual for parents and professionals* (pp. 63–177). Austin, TX: Pro-Ed.

Taylor, S.J., Lakin, K.C., & Hill, B.K. (1989). Permanency planning for children and youth: Out-of-home placement decisions. *Exceptional Children, 55,* 541–549.

Taylor, S.J., Racino, J.A., & Walker, P.M. (1992). Inclusive community living. In W. Stainback & S. Stainback (Eds.) *Controversial issues confronting special education: Divergent perspectives* (pp. 299–312). Boston: Allyn and Bacon.

Tellus 2. (2002). Voice Output Communication Aids, Techcess Ltd.

Temple, E., Deutsch, G.K., Poldrack, R.A., Miller, S.L., Tallal, P., Merzenich, M.M., & Gabrieli, J.D.E. (2003). Neural deficits in children with dyslexia ameliorated by behavioral remediation: Evidence from functional MRI. PNAS Online, February 25, 2003 (http://www.pnas.org/cgi/content/abstract/)

Terman, L.M., & Merrill, M.A. (1973). *Stanford-Binet Intelligence Scale-Third Revision Form L-M.* Boston: Houghton Mifflin.

Terman, L.M., et al. *Genetic studies of genius. I. The mental and physical traits of a thousand gifted children,* 1925; II: *The early mental traits of three hundred geniuses,* 1926; III: *The promise of youth,* 1930; IV: *The gifted child grows up,* 1947; V: *The gifted group at mid-life,* 1959. Stanford, CA: Stanford University Press.

Terpstra, J.E., Higgins, K., & Pierce, T. (2002). Can I play? Classroom-based interventions for teaching play skills to children with autism. *Focus on Autism and Other Developmental Disabilities, 17,* 119–126.

Terrell, S.L., & Jackson, R.S. (2002). African Americans in the Americas. In D.E. Battle (Ed.), *Communication disorders in multicultural populations* (3rd ed.). Boston: Butterworth Heinemann.

Test, D.W., Richter, S., Knight, V., & Spooner, F. (2011). A comprehensive review and meta-analysis of the social stories literature. *Focus on Autism and Other Developmental Disabilities, 26,* 49–62.

Tharp, R.G., Estrada, P., Dalton, S.S., & Yamauchi, L.A. (2000). *Teaching transformed: Achieving excellence, fairness, inclusion, and harmony.* Boulder, CO: Westview.

Tharpe, A.M., Bess, F.H., Sladen, D.P., Schissel, H., Couch, S., & Schery. T. (2006). Auditory characteristics of children with autism. *Ear and Hearing, 27,* 430–441.

Thurstone, L.L. (1924). *The nature of intelligence.* London: Kegan Paul, Trench, Trubner.

Till, C., Koren, G., & Rovet, G.F. (2008). Workplace standards for exposure to toxicants during pregnancy. *Revue Canadienne de Santé Publique, 99*(6), 472–474.

Timmons, J.C., Whitney-Thomas, J., Mcintyre, J.P., Butterworth, J., & Allen, D. (2004). Managing service delivery systems and the role of parents during their children's transitions. *Journal of Rehabilitation, 70*(2), 19–26.

Tomlinson, C. (1999). *The differentiated classroom: Responding to the needs of all learners.* Alexandria, VA: Association for Supervision and Curriculum Development.

Torgeson, J.K. (2000). Individual differences in response to early interventions in reading: The lingering problem of treatment resisters. *Learning Disabilities Research and Practice, 15,* 55–64.

Torp, L. & Sage, S. (1998). *Problems as possibilities: Problem-based learning for K-12 education.* Alexandria, VA: Association for Supervision and Curriculum Development.

Torppa, C.B. (2009). Autism, Asperger's Syndrome, and nonverbal learning disorder: When does your child need professional help? Fact Sheet, Family and Consumer Sciences, Columbus OH: Ohio State University.

Torres, I., & Corn, A.L. (1990). *When you have a visually handicapped child in your classroom: Suggestions for teachers.* (2nd ed.). New York: American Foundation for the Blind.

Toscano, R.M., McKee, B., & Lepoutre, D. (2002). Success with academic English: Reflections of deaf college students. *American Annals of the Deaf, 147*(1), 5–23.

Treiman, R. (1993). *Beginning to spell.* New York: Oxford University Press.

Trezek, B.J., Wang, Y., & Paul, P.V. (2010). *Reading and deafness: Theory, research, and practice.* Clifton Park, NY: Delmar/Cengage Learning.

Troia, G. (2011). How might pragmatic language skills affect the written expression of students with language learning disabilities? *Topics in Language Disorders, 31*, 40–53.

Tryon, P., Mayes, S.D., Rhodes, R.L., & Waldo, M. (2006). Can Asperger's disorder be differentiated from autism using DSM IV criteria? *Focus on Autism and Developmental Disabilities, 21*, 2–6.

Turnbull, A., & Turnbull, H. (1990). *Families, professionals, and exceptionality: A special partnership* (2nd edition). New York: Merrill.

Turnbull, A., Turnbull, R., Erwin, E.J., Soodak, L.C., & Shogren, K.A. (2011). *Families, professionals, and exceptionality: Positive outcomes through partnerships and trust* (6th ed.). Upper Saddle River, NJ: Pearson.

Turnbull, A.P., & Turnbull, H.R. (2001). *Families, professionals, and exceptionality: Collaborating for empowerment* (4th ed.). Upper Saddle River, NJ: Merrill/Prentice-Hall.

Turnbull, A.P., & Ruef, M. (1997). Family perspectives on inclusive lifestyle issues for people with problem behavior. *Exceptional Children, 63*, 211–227.

Tuttle, D.W., & Tuttle, N.R. (2000). Psychosocial needs of children and youths. In M.C. Holbrook and A.J. Koenig (Eds.), *Foundations of Education: Vol.1* (2nd ed., pp. 161–172). New York: American Foundation for the Blind.

Twenge, Campbell, & Foster (2003). Parenthood and marital satisfaction: A meta-analytic review. *Journal of Marriage and the Family, 65*(3), pp. 574–583.

U.S. Census Bureau (2010). Current Population Survey (CPS)—Definitions and Explanations. Last Revised: May 10, 2010 at 12:08:41 PM. http://www.census.gov/population/www/cps/cpsdef.html/

U.S. Department of Education (2006). Raising achievement: Alternate assessments for students with disabilities. http://www2.ed.gov/policy/elsec/guid/raising/alt-assess-long.html/

U.S. Department of Education, National Center for Education Statistics (2011). *Digest of Education Statistics, 2010* (NCES 2011-015), Table 45.

U.S. Department of Education, Office of Special Education and Rehabilitative Services, Office of Special Education Programs (2010). *29th annual report to Congress on the implementation of the Individuals with Disabilities Education Act, 2007*, vol. 1, Washington, D.C., 2010.

U.S. Department of Education, Office of Special Education and Rehabilitative Services (2010). *Thirty-five years of progress in educating children with disabilities through IDEA*, Washington, D.C.

U.S. Department of Education, Office of Special Education and Rehabilitative Services (March 1, 2003). *History of the IDEA.* http://www.ed.gov/policy/speced/leg/idea/history.html/

U.S. Department of Education, Office of Special Education Programs, Data Analysis System (DANS). http://www.ideadata.org/

U.S. Department of Education, Office of Special Education Programs (2010, September 13). Annual report to Congress on the implementation of the Individuals with Disabilities Education Act, selected years, 1979 through 2006. Retrieved from Individuals with Disabilities Education Act (IDEA) database: http://www.ideadata.org/PartBdata.asp

U.S. Department of Education. (1977, December 29). Education of handicapped children. Assistance of the states: Procedures for evaluating specific learning disabilities. *Federal Register, Part III.* Washington, DC: U.S. Department of Health, Education and Welfare.

U.S. Department of Education. (1995). www.ed.gov. IDEA/amend95.backgrnd.html

U.S. Department of Education. (2006). *28th annual report to Congress on the implementation of the Individuals with Disabilities Education Act* (Vol. 1). http://www2.ed.gov/about/reports/annual/osep/2006/parts-b-c/index.html/

UCPA. (2011) United Cerebral Palsy: www.ucp.org/

United Nations Convention on the Rights of Persons with Disabilities (2006). http://www.un.org/disabilities/convention/conventionfull.shtml

United States Environmental Protection Agency. Human Disease and Condition: Cfpub.epa.gov/eroe/: Retrieved July, 12, 2011.

United States General Accounting Office (2011). Deaf and hard-of-hearing children: Federal support for developing language and literacy. Washington, DC: USGAO.

Utley, C.A., Delquadri, J.C., Obiakor, F.E., & Mims, V.A. (2000). General and special educators' perceptions of teaching strategies for multicultural students. *Teacher Education and Special Education, 23*, 34–50.

Van Balkom, H., & Verhoeven, L. (2010). Literacy learning in users of AAC: A neurocognitive perspective. *Augmentative and Alternative Communication, 26*, 149–157.

VanDerHeyden, A.M., Witt, C., & Gilbertson, D. (2007). A multi-year evaluation of the effects of a Response to Intervention model on the identification of children for special education. *Journal of School Psychology, 45*, 225–256.

Vaughn, S. (1991). Social skills enhancement in students with learning disabilities. In B. Wong (Ed.), *Learning about learning disabilities* (pp. 409–440). San Diego: Academic Press.

Vaughn, S., Chard, D.J., Bryant, D.P., Coleman, M., Tyler, B.J.,

Linan-Thompson, S., & Kouzekanani, K. (2000). Fluency and comprehension interventions for third-grade students. *Remedial and Special Education, 21*, 325–340.

Vaughn, S., Levy, S., Coleman, M., & Bos, C.S. (2002). Reading instruction for students with LD and EBD: A synthesis of observation studies. *Journal of Special Education, 36*, 2–11.

Vaughn, S., Schumm, J., & Arguelles, M.E. (1997). The ABCDEs of co-teaching. *Teaching Exceptional Children, 30*(2), 4–10.

Vintzileos, A.M., Ananth, C.V., Smulian, J.C., Scorza, W.E., Knuppel R.A. (2002). The impact of prenatal care on neonatal deaths in the presence and absence of antenatal high-risk conditions. *American Journal of Obstetrics and Gynecology, 186*(5), 1011–1016.

Visser, S.N., Dalielson, M.L., Perou, R., & Blumberg, S.J. (2010). Increasing prevalence of parent-reported Attention-Deficit/Hyperactivity Disorder among children, United States, 2003 and 2007. *Morbidity and Mortality Weekly Report/CDCP, 59*(44), 1439–1443.

Von Károlyi, C., Ramos-Ford, V., & Gardner, H. (2003). Multiple intelligences: A perspective on giftedness. In N. Colangelo and G.A. Davis (Eds.), *Handbook of gifted education* (3rd ed.) (pp. 100–112). Boston: Allyn and Bacon.

Vu, J.A., Babikian, T., & Asarnow, R.F. (2011). Academic and language outcomes of children after traumatic brain injury: A meta-analysis. *Exceptional Children, 77*(3), 263–281.

Vukovic, R.K., & Siegel, L.S. (2010). Academic and cognitive characteristics of persistent mathematics difficulty from first through fourth grade. *Learning Disabilities Research and Practice, 25*, 25–38.

Vygotsky, L. (1978). *Mind in society: The development of higher psychological processes.* Cambridge, MA: Harvard University Press.

Wagner, M., Newman, L., Cameto, R., & Levine, P. (2005). Changes over time in the early postschool outcomes of youth with disabilities. A report of findings from the National Longitudinal Transition Study (NLTS) and the National Longitudinal Transition Study-2 (NLTS2). Menlo Park, CA: SRI International

Wagner, M., Newman, L., Cameto, R., Levine, P., & Garza, N. (2006). An overview of findings from Wave 2 of the National Longitudinal Transition Study-2 (NLTS2). NCSER 2006-3004. Menlo Park, CA: SRI International.

Walker, A.R., Uphold, N.M., Richter, S., & Test, D.W. (2010). Review of the literature on community-based instruction across grade levels. *Education and Training in Autism and Developmental Disabilities, 45*, 242–267.

Walker, B., Cheney, D., Stage, S., Blum, C. (2005). Schoolwide screening and positive behavior supports: Identifying and supporting students at risk for school failure. *Journal of Positive Behavior Interventions, 7*(4), 194–204.

Walker, H.M., & Severson, H.H. (1992). *Systematic screening for behavior disorders.* Longmont, CO: Sopris West.

Walker, H.M., Colvin, G., & Ramsey, E. (1995). *Antisocial behavior in school: Strategies and best practices.* New York: Brooks/Cole.

Wallace, G., & McLoughlin, J.A. (1988). *Learning disabilities: Concepts and characteristics* (3rd ed.). Columbus, OH: Merrill.

Ward, M.E. (2000). The visual system. In M.C. Holbrook and A.J. Koenig (Eds.), *Foundations of Education: Vol.1* (2nd ed.) (pp. 77–110). New York: American Foundation for the Blind.

Ward, M.E. (2010). Anatomy and physiology of the eye. In A.L. Corn & J.N. Erin (Eds.), *Foundations of low vision: Clinical and functional perspectives* (2nd ed.), 111–136. New York: AFB Press.

Warren, D.H. (1984). *Blindness and early childhood development* (2nd ed.). New York: American Foundation for the Blind.

Warren, J.S., Bohanon-Edmonson, H.M., Turnbull, A.P., Sailor, W., Wickham, D., Griggs, P., & Beech, S.E. (2006). School-wide positive behavior support: Addressing behavior problems that impede student learning. *Educational Psychology Review, 18,* 187–198. doi:10.1007/s10648-006-9008-1.

Washburn-Moses, L. (2011). An investigation of alternative schools in one state: Implications for students with disabilities. *Journal of Special Education, 44,* 247–255.

Watlawick, J., Beavin, J., & Jackson, D. (1967). *The pragmatics of communication.* New York: Norton.

Webb, B.J. (2000). Planning and organizing assistive technology resources in your school. *Teaching Exceptional Children, 32*(4), 50–55.

Webb, B.J. (2000). Planning and organizing assistive technology resources in your school. *Teaching Exceptional Children, 43*(4), 51.

Webb-Johnson, G. (2003). Behaving while black: A hazardous reality for African American learners? *Beyond Behavior, 12*(3), 3–7.

Wedemeyer, N.V. & Grotevant, H.D. (1982). Mapping the family system: A technique for teaching family systems theory concepts. *Family Relations, 82,* 185–193.

Wehman, P. et al. (1987). Transition services for adolescent age individuals with severe mental retardation. In R.N. Ianacone & R.A. Stodden (Eds.), *Transitin issues and directions* (pp. 49–76). Reston, VA: Council for Exceptional Children.

Wehman, P., & Kregel, J. (Eds.). (2004). *Functional curriculum for elementary, middle, and secondary students with special needs* (2nd ed.). Austin, TX: Pro-Ed.

Wehman, P., & Targett, P. (2002). Supported employment: The challenges of new staff recruitment, selection, and retention. *Education and Training in Mental Retardation and Developmental Disabilities, 37,* 434–446.

Wehman, P., West, M., & Krege, J. (1999). Supported employment program development and research needs: Looking ahead to year 2000. *Education and Training in Mental Retardation and Developmental Disabilities, 17,* 3–19.

Wehmeyer, M.L., & Kelchner, K. (1994). Interpersonal cognitive problem-solving skills of individuals with mental retardation. *Education and Training in Mental Retardation and Developmental Disabilities, 29,* 265–278.

Wehmeyer, M.L., Agran, M., Hughes, C., Martin, J., Mithaug, D.E., & Palmer, S. (2007). *Promoting self-determination in students with intellectual and developmental disabilities.* New York: Guilford Press.

Weiner, W.R., Welsch, R.L., & Blasch, B.B. (2010) Teaching orientation and mobility to older adults. In W.R. Wiener, R.L. Welsch, & B.B. Blasch (Eds.), *Foundations of Orientation and Mobility,* Vol. 2, (3rd ed.) pp. 286–312. New York: AFB Press.

Wenzel, C., & Rowley, L. (2010). Teaching social skills and academic strategies to college students with Asperger's syndrome. *Teaching Exceptional Children, 42*(5), 44–50.

Werner, E.E., Smith, R.S. (1982). *Vulnerable, but invincible: A longitudinal study of resilient children and youth.* New York: McGraw-Hill.

West, E., Leon-Guerrero, R., & Stevens, D. (2007). Establishing codes of acceptable schoolwide behavior in a multicultural society. *Beyond Behavior, 16*(2), 32–38.

Westling, D.L., & Fox, L. (2000). *Teaching students with severe disabilities.* Upper Saddle River, NJ: Merrill/Prentice Hall.

Wetherby, A.M., & Prizant, B. (2002). *Communication and Symbolic Behavior Scales: Developmental Profiles* (CSBS DP). New York: Brookes.

Whalen, C., Franke, L., & Lara-Brady, L. (2011). Teaching social skills using video modeling interventions. *Perspectives on School-Based Issues, 12,* 41–48.

What Color? (2002). Do2learn. http://www.dotolearn.com/games/learninggames.htm.

Whitmore, J.R. (1980). *Giftedness, conflict and underachievement.* Boston: Allyn and Bacon.

Whitney-Thomas, J., & Hanley-Maxwell, C. (1996). Packing the parachute: Parents' experiences as their children prepare to leave high school. *Exceptional Children, 63*(1), 75–87.

Wilens, T.E., Martelon, M., Joshi, G., Bateman, N., Fried, R., Petty, M.A., & Biederman, J. (2011). Does ADHD predict substance-use disorders? A 10-year follow-up study of young adults with ADHD. *Journal of the American Academy of Child and Adolescent Psychiatry, 50,* 543–553.

Will, M.C. (1984). *OSERS programming for the transition of youth with disabilities: Bridges from school to working life.* Washington, DC: Office of Special Education and Rehabilitative Services, U.S. Department of Education.

Willard-Holt, C. (1998). Academic and personality characteristics of gifted students with cerebral palsy: A multiple case study. *Exceptional Children, 65,* 37–50.

Williams, D.L., Goldstein, G., & Minshew, N.J. (2006). The profile of memory function in children with autism. *Neuropsychology, 20,* 21–29.

Williams, P.M., & Fletcher, S. (2010). Health effects of prenatal radiation exposure. *American Family Physician, 82*(5), 488493. Retrieved from: http://www.ncb.nlm.nih.gov/pubmed/20822083.

Windsor, J., Reichle, J., & Mahowald, M.C. (2009). Communication disorders. In C.H. Zeanah, Jr. (Ed.), *Handbook of infant mental health* (3rd ed.), 318–331. New York: Guilford Press.

Winebrenner, S. (2001). *Teaching gifted kids in the regular classroom* (2nd ed.). Minneapolis: Free Spirit Publishing.

Winebrenner, S., & Brulles, D. (2008).*The Cluster Grouping Handbook: A School-wide Model.* Minneapolis, MN: Free Spirit.

Winner, E. (2000). Giftedness: Current theory and research. *Current Directions in Psychological Science, 9*(5), 153–156.

Winner, E. (2000). The origins and ends of giftedness. *American Psychologist, 55*(1), 159–169.

Winterman, K.G., & Sapona, R.H. (2002). Everyone's included: Supporting young children with autism spectrum disorders in a responsive classroom learning environment. *Teaching Exceptional Children, 35*(1), 30–35.

Witte, R. (1998). Meet Bob, a student with traumatic brain injury. *Teaching Exceptional Children, 30*(1), 56–60.

Witty, P.A. (1940). Some considerations in the education of gifted children. *Educational Administration and Supervision, 26,* 512–521.

Wolery, M. (2011). Intervention research: The importance of fidelity measurement. *Topics in Early Childhood Special Education,* published online 25 May 2011. DOI: 10.1177/0271121411408621

Wolfensberger, W. (1972). *The principle of normalization in human services.* Toronto: National Institute on Mental Retardation.

Wolfensberger, W. (1977). The principle of normalization. In B. Blatt, D. Biklen & R. Bogden (Eds.), *An alternative textbook in special education* (pp. 305–327). Denver: Love.

———. (1983). Social role valorization: A proposed new term for the principle of normalization. *Mental Retardation, 21,* 234–239.

Wolffe, K.E. (2000). Growth and development in middle childhood and adolescence. In M.C. Holbrook and A.J. Koenig (Eds.), *Foundations of Education: Vol.1* (2nd ed., pp. 135–160). New York: American Foundation for the Blind.

Wong, B.Y.L. (1991). The relevance of metacognition to learning disabilities. In B.Y.L. Wong (Ed.), *Learning about learning disabilities* (pp. 232–261). San Diego: Academic Press.

Wood, F.B., & Grigorenko, E.L. (2001). Emerging issues in the genetics of dyslexia: A methodological preview. *Journal of Learning Disabilities, 34,* 503–511.

Woodward, J., Baxter, J., & Robinson, R. (1999). Rules and reasons: Decimal instruction for academically low achieving students. *Learning Disabilities Research and Practice, 14,* 15–24.

World Health Association (2011). *World report on disability.* Geneva, Switzerland: Author.

World Health Organization (2006). Blindness and visual impairment. Retrieved from: http://www.who.int/features/factfiles/vision/09_en.html

World Health Organization, International Agency for the Prevention of Blindness (2000). *Preventing blindness in children.* Report of WHO/IAPB scientific meeting. Geneva, Switzerland: World Health Organization.

Wunsch, M.J., Conlon, C.J., & Scheidt, P.C. (2002). Substance abuse: A preventable threat to development. In M.L. Batshaw (Ed.), *Children with disabilities* (5th ed.), 107–122. Baltimore: Paul H. Brookes.

Xiang, Y., Dahlin, M., Cronin, J., Theaker, R., & Durant S. (2011). *Do high-flyers maintain their altitude? Performance trends of top students.* Washington, DC: Thomas B. Fordham Institute. http://www.edexcellence.net/publications-issues/publications/high-flyers.html

Yell, M. (2011). *The law and special education* (3rd ed.). Upper Saddle River, NJ: Prentice Hall.

Yell, M.L., & Drasgow, E. (2000). Litigating a free appropriate public education: The Lovaas hearings and cases. *Journal of Special Education, 33,* 205–214.

Yell, M.L., & Shriner, J.G. (1997). The IDEA amendments of 1997: Implications for special and general education teachers, administrators, and teacher trainers. *Focus on Exceptional Children, 30*(1), 1–19.

Yoshinaga-Itano, C. (2006). Early identification, communication modality, and the development of speech and spoken language skills: Patterns and considerations. In P.E. Spencer & M. Marschark (Eds.), *Advances in the spoken language development of deaf and hard-of-hearing children.* New York: Oxford University Press, pp 298–327.

Yu, D.C.T., Spevack, S., Hiebert, R., Martin, T.L., Goodman, R., Martin, T.G., Harapiak, S., & Martin, G.L. (2002). Happiness indices among persons with profound and severe disabilities during leisure and work activities: A comparison. *Education and Training in Mental Retardation and Developmental Disabilities, 37,* 421–426.

Zeaman, D., & House, B.J. (1963). The role of attention in retardate discrimination of learning. In N.R. Ellis (Ed.), *Handbook of mental deficiency.* New York: McGraw-Hill.

———. (1979). A review of attention theory. In N.R. Ellis (Ed.), *Handbook of mental deficiency: Psychological theory and research.* (2nd ed.). Hillsdale, NJ: Erlbaum.

Zetlin, A.G., & Weinberg, L.A. (2004). Understanding the plight of foster youth and improving their educational opportunities. *Child Abuse and Neglect, 28*(9), 917–23.

Zhang, D., Landmark, L., Grenwelge, C., & Montoya, L. (2010). Culturally diverse parents' perspectives on self-determination. *Education and Training in Autism and Developmental Disabilities, 45,* 175–186.

Zimmerman, G.J. (1996). Optics and low vision devices. In A.L. Corn & A.J. Koenig, (Eds.), *Foundations of low vision: Clinical and functional perspectives* (pp. 115–142). New York: AFB Press.

Zirkel, P. (2009). Section 504: Student eligibility update. *Clearing House, 82*(5), 209–211.

Zuckoff, M. (2003). Choosing Naia: A family's journey. Boston: Beacon Press.

Zumach, A., Gerrits, E., Chenault, M. & Anteunis, L. (2010). Long-term effects of early-life otitis media on language development. *Journal of Speech, Language, and Hearing Research, 53,* 34–43.

Zuniga, M.E. (2011). Families with Latino roots. In E.W. Lynch & M.J. Hanson (Eds.), *Developing cross-cultural competence: A guide for working with children and their families* (4th ed.), pp. 190–229. Baltimore, MD: Paul H. Brookes.

Name Index

Subject Index

Tables, figures and display material are indicated by t, f, and d respectively. Authors are in a separate index, but names that are subjects are included here.